Volume XVII

Associate Editors

HIGHER EDUCATION:

Handbook of Theory and Research

Volume XVII

Edited by

John C. Smart

University of Memphis

Senior Associate Editor

William G. Tierney

University of Southern California

Published under the sponsorship of
The Association for Institutional Research (AIR)
and
The Association for the Study of Higher Education (ASHE)

KLUWER ACADEMIC PUBLISHERS

DORDRECHT / BOSTON / LONDON

Library of Congress Card Number 86-642109

ISBN 0-87586-136-9 (HB)
ISBN 0-87586-137-7 (PB)
ISSN 0882-4126

Published by Kluwer Academic Publishers,
P.O. Box 17, 3300 AZ Dordrecht, The Netherlands.

Sold and distributed in North, Central and South America
by Kluwer Academic Publishers,
101 Philip Drive, Norwell, MA 02061, U.S.A.

In all other countries, sold and distributed
by Kluwer Academic Publishers,
P.O. Box 322, 3300 AH Dordrecht, The Netherlands.

Formerly published by Agathon Press

Printed on acid-free paper

Printed in the Netherlands

TABLE OF CONTENTS

CONTRIBUTORS

JOAN S. STARK is Dean Emerita and Professor Emerita of education at the University of Michigan. She has been Director of the federally-funded National Center for Research to Improve Postsecondary Education (NCRIPTAL), Editor of the *Review of Higher Education*, and President of the Association for the Study of Higher Education (ASHE). She has conducted extensive research and published widely on issues related to college curriculum and curriculum leadership in higher education, and has received three awards from ASHE.

PAUL R. PINTRICH is Professor of Education and Psychology and Chair of the Combined Program in Education and Psychology at The University of Michigan, Ann Arbor. His research focuses on the development of motivation and self-regulated learning in adolescence and how the classroom context shapes the trajectory of motivation and self-regulation development. He has published over 100 articles and book chapters and he is co-author or co-editor of 8 books including a graduate level text on motivation, entitled *Motivation in Education: Theory, Research and Applications.*

AKANE ZUSHO is a doctoral candidate in the Combined Program in Educational Psychology at the University of Michigan, Ann Arbor. Her research focuses on the interplay between culture, conceptions of the self, and achievement motivation as well as the relation of culture and achievement motivation to self-regulated learning.

DEBORAH FAYE CARTER is an Assistant Professor of Higher Education in the Educational Leadership and Policy Studies department of the School of Education at Indiana University. Her research focuses on access and equity issues for students of color, college students' sense of belonging, and nontraditional student outcomes. Her book, *A Dream Deferred? Examining the Degree Aspirations of African American and White College Students,* was published by Garland Press in 2001.

STEPHEN L. DESJARDINS is Assistant Professor of Higher Education in the Planning, Policy, and Leadership Studies division, College of Education, at The University of Iowa. His research interests include strategic enrollment management issues, the study of student departure from college, and the economics of higher education. His work in these areas has been published in *Economics of Education Review, Research in Higher Education, Journal of Student Financial Aid, and the AIR Professional File.*

DONALD E. HELLER is an Associate Professor and Senior Research Associate in the Center for the Study of Higher Education at Pennsylvania State University. He teaches and conducts research on issues relating to higher education economics, public policy, and finance, as well as technology in higher education. He is the editor of the book *The States and Public Higher Education Policy: Affordability, Access, and Accountability* (Johns Hopkins University Press, 2001).

CORINNA A. ETHINGTON is Professor of Educational Research and Program Coordinator for Educational Research at the University of Memphis, where she teaches statistics and research methods. Her research interests include the college student experience and the broad domain of gender differences at all educational levels, with a decided focus on performance, persistence, and achievement in mathematics and scientific fields. Her recent work includes the book (coauthored with John C. Smart and Kenneth A. Feldman) *Academic Disciplines: Holland's Theory and the Study of College Students and Faculty.*

SCOTT L. THOMAS is Associate Professor of Higher Education in the Institute of Higher Education at the University of Georgia. His current research is on issues of access and stratification in higher education, with a focus on economic outcomes and indebtedness related to college quality and choice of major. His writings have examined topics in the areas of the sociology of education, labor economics, and student persistence. His methodological work includes a recent book (coauthored with Ronald Heck), *An Introduction to Multilevel Modeling Techniques*, published by Erlbaum and Associates.

GARY R. PIKE (PhD, Ohio State University, 1985) is Assistant Vice Chancellor for Student Affairs and Director of Student Life Studies at the University of Missouri-Columbia. His research interests include the assessment of college-student learning and development, as well as the influence of students' in-class and out-of-class experiences on their learning and development.

KEVIN J. DOUGHERTY is Associate Professor of Higher Education, Department of Organization and Leadership, and Senior Research Associate at the Community College Research Center, Teachers College, Columbia University. Dougherty has published widely on the community college and the educational excellence reform movement of the last twenty years. His research interests include the impact of federal, state, and private performance accountability systems (including performance funding) on community colleges, and the new role of community colleges in such workforce preparation and economic development activities as contract training, small business development, and local economic planning.

JAMES SOTO ANTONY is Assistant Professor of Educational Leadership & Policy and Assistant Professor of Multicultural Education at the University of Washington. Professor Antony's research interests lie in the social psychology of higher education, focused in two areas: (1) examining college student socialization and its impact on aspirations and attainment; and (2) examining the social and psychological determinants of ambition, role satisfaction, and career success among college students and faculty members.

ÅSE GORNITZKA is a research associate at the Norwegian Institute for Studies in Research and Higher Education (NIFU) in Oslo. Her dissertation in political science focuses on the organization of science and utilization of research in public policy making. Her current research is on comparative higher education policy in Europe and institutional change processes in higher education. Her recent work on these issues has been published in Higher Education and Higher Education Policy.

SVEIN KYVIK is a senior research associate at the Norwegian Institute for Studies in Research and Higher Education (NIFU) in Oslo. He has worked at NIFU since 1978, conducting research in the fields of sociology of science and higher education. He is a political scientist and a sociologist by training. His PhD dissertation was entitled *Productivity in Academia: Scientific Publishing at Norwegian Universities*. He has published widely in higher education journals such as *Higher Education*, *European Journal of Education*, and *Comparative Education*, as well as in journals devoted to science studies, like *Scientometrics*, *Science and Public Policy*, *Science Communication*, and *Science, Technology & Human Values*. He has recently been responsible for the evaluation of the Norwegian doctoral training system.

BJØRN STENSAKER is a research associate at the Norwegian Institute for Studies in Research and Higher Education (NIFU) in Oslo. He has worked with NIFU since 1993, mainly conducting research in the areas of quality assessment, national evaluation systems and higher education organization and management. He has published widely in relation to questions regarding design and effects of quality assurance and improvement systems in higher education. He is a member of the Executive Board of EAIR (European Association of Institutional Research) and is also a member of the International Advisory Board for the journal *Quality in Higher Education*. He is a political scientist by training.

JUDITH M. GAPPA is Professor of Educational Administration at Purdue University. Her scholarly interests include faculty careers and employment, equity, and general management issues within higher education. Her book, *The Invisible Faculty*, co-authored with David Leslie of Florida State University, is about part-time and temporary faculty. She was a Senior Associate with the American Association for Higher Education on the project, "New Pathways: Faculty Careers and Employment in the 21st Century," from 1995-1997.

1. AN UNPLANNED JOURNEY INTO HIGHER EDUCATION

Joan S. Stark
University of Michigan

The editor, John Smart, has invited me to describe how I entered higher education as a field of study, highlighting major individuals and developments that shaped my career. In addition, he asked that I give my perspectives on how the field of higher education has evolved during my career and offer suggestions to current scholars about possible future developments. I am honored to have this opportunity and especially pleased to be the first woman to write an autobiographical essay in this series. As I collected my thoughts, I was struck first by how unplanned my career development has been; second, by how vastly different my story is from those of my esteemed male colleagues who have written articles in this series; and third, by the fact that I am the first writer in the group whose advanced degree was in higher education rather than in a traditional discipline.

BALANCING GENDER, AMBITION, AND OPPORTUNITY IN THE 1950S

I certainly never aimed to be a higher education professor or researcher. Looking back, however, I suppose there were some predictors, such as my involvement in student government at Syracuse University. In fact, the positive interactions of Syracuse administrators with student leaders in the 1950s strongly influenced me. Over the years, I have observed that many individuals study higher education because of such influences during their undergraduate years. Other than this exposure to the roles of campus administrators, my career development was for the most part accidental. In the 1950s, what a young woman should *not* aspire to was much more important than what she *should* aspire to. Reflecting on what brought me to the field of higher education has

J.C. Smart and W.G. Tierney (eds.), Higher Education: Handbook of Theory and Research, 1–53.

caused me to realize how important gender used to be and how the context for women's career development has changed over the years. My male colleagues' careers were often influenced by issues related to military service but, apparently, seldom by gender or family demands; my story is quite different from that.

My school teacher parents had high expectations and, in their view, high ambitions for me. My father encouraged me to study the sciences (definitely not the impractical arts or literature!) and believed that a teaching certificate was good insurance for a young woman. After spending three college summers as an analytical chemist at Eastman Kodak, a job with minimal human contact, I accepted more readily the idea that I should be a public school science teacher. My father was also convinced that I should begin teaching immediately after graduating from Syracuse, so that my master's degree study would be more meaningful. Thus, I was pleased when, in my senior year in 1956-57, the chemistry department at Syracuse invited me to be a teaching assistant in general chemistry, replacing a graduate student who left.

For a brief period that year, I wondered aloud why I was not applying to medical school like most of my classmates. Despite my father's scientific interests, he was quite certain that medical school would be wasted on me since, like most young women, I would surely marry and have children rather than practice. My mother thought nursing or dental hygiene much more fitting than medicine or dentistry. Of course, had I strongly desired to become a doctor, I could have prevailed. Or, had I been convinced that the life of a research chemist was desirable, I might have accepted a casual invitation to follow one of my professors to his laboratory at a new university. Instead, I obtained a fellowship for full-time master's study in science education at Teachers College, Columbia University. When my father became severely ill just after my college graduation, I abandoned that path and under the duress of financial uncertainty fell back on his original plan. I got a job teaching physics at a high school close enough to New York City to let me start my graduate work at Columbia, part time.

My mother felt that when I was married I would be "settled," i.e., out of moral danger, during times when increasing freedom involved "temptations" for young women. Protecting me from such hazards, she thought, would then be my husband's responsibility. I became "settled" when I met Bill Stark, a merchant marine captain who was studying mathematics education at Teachers College, and married him during the spring of my first year of teaching. I went on maternity leave in May of the second year and the first of our four children was born in July. It caused quite a stir that I was allowed to teach for eight months of my pregnancy, since the school district's rules in 1959 dictated that a pregnant teacher must leave before the condition was "visible." Because the school very much wanted students to pass the New York State Regents examinations and because substitute physics teachers were hard to find, I was allowed to continue despite several parents who complained that their daughters should not view a pregnant teacher. Times certainly have changed. My three daughters have had the right to remain at their jobs until the day they gave birth, if they wanted to.

Finances were tight during our son's and first daughter's infancies. Because a kindly mother of six was willing to baby-sit, I taught as a substitute in several Long Island high schools while continuing my graduate studies. I enjoyed the academically-oriented schools, especially when students perceived I could offer them something in science and math classes. It was miserable at some other high schools, especially when I was called upon to teach physical education or even wood shop. Meanwhile, at Teacher's College, I changed my specialization from science education to educational administration and became certified as a high school principal in New York State. Somehow, I was convinced that when I finally returned to teaching full time, I could do more to improve schools as an administrator.

A turning point in my life occurred when a Columbia professor asked me to edit a paper he was preparing for a conference. His confidence and appreciation led me to write to several publishers proposing that I might do hourly freelance work on science and mathematics textbooks. I explained that I wanted to spend more time with my children but I also needed work. I was in luck. The early 1960s was a period of extensive curriculum revision in math and science and my skills fit a niche. For about nine years I worked at home on emerging programs in physics and chemistry and the "new math." As I gave birth to our third child, I progressed from editing copy and preparing indexes to writing answer books and teachers' manuals. Yes, I was a ghost writer for authors who didn't want to bother to develop materials for teachers. I learned to add and multiply in bases two, three, and four as quickly as I could in base ten!

After far too many years, I realized that I could ask to be listed as a coauthor or otherwise acknowledged in some of these materials. Having publications with my name on them helped me to bridge the employment gap that so many women experienced in the 1960s and 1970s when they tried to reenter the job market after a period of child-raising.

Doctoral Study, 1967-71

The first publication with my name on it and our fourth child appeared at about the same time. Almost simultaneously, Bill's community college needed a adjunct chemistry instructor on short notice for an evening class. I was offered the position for one semester — as a special exception to the anti-nepotism laws then in effect. I ended up teaching several semesters and this opportunity, more than anything else, led directly to my ensuing career in higher education.

It was the late 1960s, and collective bargaining was just beginning in the

New York state community colleges. Our institution experienced the first New York strike — with considerable detriment to the academic program and to the morale of both faculty and administrators. Observing these effects, I became convinced that community college administration could stand some improvement. One day, Bill, who was also studying for a doctorate in math education at the State University of New York at Albany, returned home to inform me that he had registered me for a class in community college administration. I protested that the scheduled class time conflicted with the PTA bowling league; but Bill thought I'd enjoy it and convinced me to try. Actually, the class was terrible, but the idea of being back in the university grabbed me fast. In 1967, ten years and four children after college graduation, I enrolled in Albany's doctoral program in educational administration, specializing in higher education. Despite the 110-mile round trip three to four days a week, I never again wondered if I might be better off bowling. Doctoral study was the right intellectual step to supplement my activities with Girl Scouts, Boy Scouts, PTA, and school board elections which had been filling my leisure time after caring for the children, teaching in the evenings, tutoring science and mathematics students, and doing free-lance editing. And the timing was perfect: only two of the children were still in diapers!

As I recall, only two other women students were in the educational administration doctoral program at Albany when I began. One was a mature public school administrator and the other was a young woman who has since pursued an administrative career in several universities. The department chair frequently teased us that we "dressed up" the place but probably would never complete the program. (My methods for handling such comments are amusing stories for another time and place.) Since I now had my sights on administration of colleges, not high schools, much of the departmental coursework, targeted at public schools, was not exciting. What did excite me were the elective cognate courses in the social sciences. I took several courses in social psychology, some of them with Walter Balk, a professor whose classes I enjoyed and who later served on my dissertation committee.

As a project for Dr. Balk's course, I conducted my first systematic social science research project, a study of conformity among neighborhood children of various ages. (As an incentive to participate, I gave each child a half-dozen tulip bulbs and our neighborhood bloomed colorfully the following spring.) For a sociology class project, I observed both the trustee meetings and the initial administrative meetings that accompanied the planning and opening of nearby Schenectady Community College. And most importantly, I linked up with the professor who became my advisor, Paul Bulger (deceased, 2000), a former provost at Teachers College and former president of State University College at Buffalo. Dr. Bulger actively cultivated my administrative leanings. I also encountered (more briefly) another professor, Joseph Bosco, who challenged me to become a researcher rather than an administrator. Both became my mentors.

Professor Bulger was an exceptionally supportive teacher. He shared with us his recent career experiences as a college president and his wisdom about administrative style and current issues. These were challenging times for college administrators. The 1972 Higher Education Act was on the drawing board (debates still raged about whether federal control would follow federal aid to institutions and/or students); the *Chronicle of Higher Education* had just begun publishing to keep us informed about such issues; New York and New Jersey were planning to serve adult learners with Empire State and Thomas Edison Colleges; CLEP exams were beginning to help adults enter college with advanced credit; and the National Center for Higher Education Management Systems (NCHEMS) had just been funded by the federal government.

Dr. Bulger had definite and traditional opinions about NCHEMS. He advised me to keep my eye on this dangerous movement that would attempt to quantify everything in higher education and change it dramatically for the worse. He felt considerably more positive about the American Association for Higher Education (AAHE) and saw to it that I was assigned as a recorder for a major session. The convener of the session, E. K. Fretwell, Jr., a long-time family and professional friend of Dr. Bulger's, totally surprised me by asking me to summarize the session for the group. I not only learned quickly how to think on my feet but I suppose it could be said that I also gained visibility from being linked to the "old boys' network" at this early point in my career. I regret that AAHE abandoned the practice of using graduate students as session recorders. It didn't cost anything, and it encouraged a great deal of student involvement. At AAHE in Chicago, Dr. Bulger also introduced me to the Association of Professors of Higher Education (APHE) (later to become the Association for the Study of Higher Education or ASHE), a Sunday afternoon informal meeting of the professors of higher education. My recollection is that students were allowed in for a very small portion of the discussions and that two other women were present, Mary Corcoran of the University of Minnesota and possibly Esther Lloyd-Jones or Ruth Eckert.

The Albany doctoral program required all students to serve a semester-long paid internship in a responsible administrative position, a requirement that most people met through their existing employment as principals or assistant superintendents. Since the higher education track was new, internship positions had not been developed. I canvassed nearby colleges and the SUNY central offices, but no one seemed willing to pay an inexperienced mother of four who wanted to work part time. Dr. Bulger solved the problem by convincing a local gentleman of means that I was the hope of the future and obtaining a grant for me. He then negotiated my appointment as departmental assistant assigned to develop a curriculum for the emerging higher education program. I shared his modest office, subject only to the requirement that my desk be neat and bare at the end of the workday, a habit I still try to maintain. In addition, I was to write a thank-you note and progress report to my benefactor once every couple months. I also occasionally answered Dr. Bulger's phone, which enabled me to meet some key people in Washington and Albany. The die was cast. I immersed myself in the limited higher education literature then available (1968), envisioning a career that was just emerging: professor of higher education.

Dr. Bulger was an administrator *par excellence*, but not a researcher. A quite different mentor, Dr. Joseph Bosco, instilled in me the necessary and complementary vision of a research career. The impetus came from a professor who taught the basic educational research course. He suggested that I pursue an advanced independent study with Dr. Bosco, instead of taking his class. (I tended to be a bit of an activist in those days, so I've always wondered if the professor had covert reasons for wanting me elsewhere.)

At the time, I was aiming toward a very ambitious dissertation, reviewing and synthesizing the burgeoning number of doctoral dissertations about community college administration. Upon reading my proposal, Dr. Bosco asked what conceptual scheme I planned to use to classify the hundreds of studies. I said that I planned to make my own, to which he replied something like: "And who the hell are you? Only a doctoral student whose opinion isn't worth a penny." He handed me a thick black book, Fred Kerlinger's *Foundations of Behavioral Research*. "Go away and memorize it," he instructed. "Then come back and we'll talk about what you've learned and your proposed project." "By the way," he added, "You might also look for a credible typology or conceptual scheme that would let you classify the studies with some validity and reliability." Of course I did not (indeed, could not) memorize the book, but I must have come close. Years later as Dean of Education at Michigan, I was privileged to nominate Fred Kerlinger for the UM distinguished alumni award, and I was still able to discuss that book with him in detail at dinner.

My thesis, needless to say, bit the dust in favor of a simpler, more controlled study based in social psychology. Dr. Bulger's confidence that I could make a mark in the world and the research skills that Dr. Bosco and Dr. Balk helped me acquire convinced me that I would have time for more comprehensive projects later, when I was a professor of higher education.

The route to this goal, however, still seemed somewhat circuitous and potentially lengthy. The few existing higher education programs primarily trained administrators, not researchers. Good administrators were surely needed, since it was 1970 and students were on the rampage about a number of causes. I recall once walking from the education building to the president's office at Albany by stepping carefully over the bodies of protesting students. It seemed to me that, in such times especially, a credible professor and higher education researcher needed substantial administrative experience. And I had essentially none.

TRYING MY ADMINISTRATIVE WINGS, 1970-74

Then came a call from Dean Rhoda Dorsey at Goucher College in Towson, Maryland. She was interested in hiring an assistant dean of the college to oversee the student advising program, run the experimental January term program, staff various committees, and generally do anything else the faculty wanted done. A historian, she hoped to balance her office by adding someone with a science background. She also thought that I might fill a gap by teaching occasionally in science or math education. I traveled to Towson and quickly fell in love with the college and the people. After some negotiation for a delayed starting date so I could finish collecting dissertation data in New York State, I moved my two dogs and four children (then ranging in age from 3 to 10) to Maryland in January 1970, leaving Bill behind to continue his work and studies. I hoped to analyze my dissertation data and write the thesis after beginning the new job. What I remember best about my first official day on the job is the ice storm that delayed the start of the public school day by several hours. I could take the 3-year old to nursery school, but my kindergartner would be on her own. I quickly taught her to recognize how the clock should look when it was time to stop coloring at the kitchen table and walk to school. She made it without mishap!

At Goucher, as at Albany, I gained from strong mentorship. Dean Dorsey helped me to understand the reasons for her administrative decisions and respected my observations and views. At Goucher I learned to enjoy doing research to provide information for program improvement. The college had no institutional research office, but I gradually built some of those responsibilities into the office of assistant dean. Dean Dorsey not only supported my efforts but also allowed me the time and funds to attend both the annual forum of the Association for Institutional Research (a group that continues to be important in my professional career) and the 4-1-4 conference, later the Association for Innovation in Higher Education.

Then a women's college, Goucher had a typically high attrition rate, and I often talked with students transferring out (frequently to coeducational institutions). Thus, my first research study was on reasons for withdrawal. The study was unique for its type since it included a control group of sorts. In addition to surveying students who had left by the junior year, I asked students who remained enrolled as juniors whether they had ever considered withdrawing, why, and what had influenced them to stay. The results were interesting and helpful because the same college characteristics that caused some students to leave caused others to remain. Thus, if a college makes substantial program changes to retain those who may leave, it risks alienating those who would have stayed. (Since then, I have not seen another attrition study done in this way.) I could now envision that my publication portfolio might turn from teachers' manuals in science and math instruction to research in higher education.

At Goucher I finished my dissertation and also conducted studies of the impact of the 4-1-4 academic calendar. Many liberal arts colleges were experimenting with calendar variations that freed students to explore new ideas or learn more effectively. Some, like Colorado College for Women (later briefly called Temple Buell College) tried a calendar of several one-month periods in which students studied a single subject intensively. A few colleges tried four courses in two main terms followed by a single one-month term at the year's end, called a 4-4-1 pattern. But most, like Goucher, adopted a 4-1-4 pattern — two four-month terms separated by January as a non-traditional, one-month term. I was charged with helping the faculty to develop non-traditional but academically sound and effective courses, shepherding these courses through a special curriculum committee, and making necessary arrangements for their implementation. Implementation frequently involved interesting tasks. Since several Goucher professors accompanied students on study groups abroad, I contracted for the travel arrangements, assisted with communication when students needed emergency appendectomies in Moscow, and, from time to time, heard the complaints of parents.

Some of the professors had quite a good time with this unusual one-month study period. For example, two Goucher chemistry professors were featured in national magazines describing their "nuts and bolts" course to teach young women the principles of car operation and repair. Another professor sponsored a wine-making course, as applied chemistry, but we had to get special licenses to produce potable alcohol. Of course not all the faculty were wild about the January term idea. I remember fondly a lengthy and quite humorous (but also bitter) poem I received from two philosophy professors about the process of thinking up "jazzy" titles to cater to student whims.

Representatives of colleges sponsoring these one-month study programs met to share experiences and advice, ranging from educational theory to the mundane details of registering and billing students three times a year and filling empty dormitories vacated by students on trips abroad or internships. The forum for these discussions was the 4-1-4 Conference, initiated primarily by Clark Bouwman and Edward Stevens of Florida Presbyterian College (now Eckerd College). The 4-1-4 Conference created non-traditional conference formats congruent with its non-traditional mission. One year, a substantial part of the conference was a simulated faculty meeting for a fictional institution. Within a few years, the group was attracting middle-level administrators and faculty from small colleges who were trying to "think out of the box," as we might say today. At the instructional level, innovative faculty members were experimenting with competency-based education and with the Keller Plan, which allowed students to move through a course at their own pace. At the institutional level, some colleges were experimenting with contract learning, eliminating grades, and abolishing senior comprehensive examinations in favor of integrative senior seminars. To broaden the organization's purpose and membership beyond calendar innovations, we changed the name to the Association for Innovation. Here I met Jack Lindquist, Bill Bergquist, and many others involved in various curricular experiments of the early 1970s. I served a term as this association's president in 1974 and have fond memories of my professional acquaintances of that period, but when I moved out of the small college arena, I lost track of the group, which dissolved soon after.[1]

The major conclusion of my studies about calendar innovations was that programs to improve learning don't always result in a financially viable college. In fact, students at Goucher soon learned that, by combining January term and summer school credits, they could graduate in fewer than four years. The resulting financial shortfall led first to adjusting, and then to abandoning the 4-1-4 calendar (Stark, 1972, 1973).

In the Association for Innovation, I met Barry Morstain from the University of Delaware, who had developed two interesting instruments called the Student Orientation Scales and the Faculty Orientation Scales. These scales measured the views of students and faculty members about the purposes, processes, and power relationships of collegiate education. Barry was anxious to work with college administrators to validate the scales and assess their correlation with other variables, so we formed a partnership for a time. Because I had just convened a special interest group of small colleges within the Association for Institutional Research, one of our projects involved studying faculty attitudes at several diverse small colleges where I knew willing collaborators. At Goucher I had already learned informally about the strong (and sometimes intransigent) views of faculty in different disciplines about educational purpose and process. Our study allowed us to document, at several supposedly homogeneous liberal arts colleges, a clear distinction between faculty members who saw the purpose of education as the pursuit of ideas and those who saw it as career preparation (Stark & Morstain, 1978).

At the time, these two purposes were hotly debated in small colleges struggling for continued viability. Independent colleges faced financial and enrollment pressure not only to introduce career-oriented programs but also to admit

[1] I didn't lose contact with small independent colleges entirely, since I also served as a trustee of Kalamazoo College (1979 to 1985).

older, non-traditional students. In general, the 1970s saw loosening requirements, meant both to satisfy student demands and to increase their responsibility for learning. Later, of course, educators and the public decided student freedom of choice had gone too far. Beginning about 1985 colleges began to tighten and consolidate requirements once more, especially in response to calls for assessing and documenting what students had learned.

Working with the Student Orientation Scales, I also found a relationship between early withdrawal at Goucher and the extent of the discrepancy between student and faculty beliefs about educational purpose, process, and student/faculty power relationships (Stark, 1975). Most Goucher students believed strongly that they should have an active voice in planning their education. Most faculty members were less likely to agree with this strong spirit of self-determination; consequently, Goucher had quite a structured academic program. Despite being like their peers in most other respects, I found that students who transferred out were considerably less likely to desire faculty control over their course of study than those who remained. This finding was consistent with other research reporting that college withdrawal is a function of the match between students' needs, interests, and abilities and the characteristics of the academic setting (Feldman & Newcomb, 1969).

These early studies formed a basis for my continuing interest in disciplinary differences and faculty views of educational purposes and processes. Although I didn't realize it then, the studies and my administrative duties also planted the seeds for my interest in curriculum development. At small colleges, curricular reform typically is discussed at the institutional level and proposed changes need endorsement from most, if not all, of the faculty. But the differing disciplinary cultures make consensus difficult, and attempts to reach consensus may further polarize groups of faculty. The process itself may so compromise the new proposals that no group is particularly satisfied with the result. These scenarios play out repeatedly in curriculum committees with deliberations yielding little fruit. Consequently, a crucial first step to curriculum change is helping faculty groups to understand and respect the reasons for their differing views. It allows them to identify common ground on which to build.

Looking back, I realize that these early studies undoubtedly laid the foundation for studies of professional preparation programs that my colleagues and I did 15 years later. They also convinced me that systematic institutional research not only helps a particular college make effective curriculum adjustments but also provides techniques that other colleges can readily adapt. When weeding out my files, I have never been able to throw away my copies of the Faculty Orientation Scales. I still have visions of doing more studies with them.

The studies involving several colleges were fun to do, although they generally occupied my weekends and evenings rather than my administrative working day. Such research became easier and more exciting as computer technology advanced. The computer director at Goucher ran my statistics on her treasured 8K machine that occupied an entire room. The maximum possible correlation matrix was about 6 by 6 variables. But it certainly was an advance over my hand calculator.

Technology didn't always seem so helpful, however. About this time, Goucher joined with neighboring Johns Hopkins University in an experimental project, a resource prediction model called RRPM 1.6, sponsored by NCHEMS. After time-consuming data input at our end, the NCHEMS computer program calculated an "induced course load matrix" that would show changes in resource needs in one department based on enrollment changes in other departments. For example, based on past patterns, the program could tell us the number of new student places needed in history courses if the English department were to admit additional literature majors. Two amusing things stand out in my memory of this project. First, while the matrices were apparently useful at Johns Hopkins or other large colleges, the system could not calculate Goucher's need for student places nearly as fast as our registrar who already knew by memory the names and numbers of all courses and which students elected them each year. While the activity wasn't dangerous, as Dr. Bulger had predicted, in those days of slow computers it did not improve on the efficiency of the experienced human mind.

Second, in the early days of computers, every variable and relationship was spelled out in great detail to facilitate correct programming in APL, FORTRAN, or COBOL. One corner of my office groaned under a tall stack of paper supplied by NCHEMS. The only words printed on each sheet in large letters were a variable name and value: 1 = Yes or 2 = No. Some liberal arts faculty members had a lot of fun with such absurdity, and the experience with this project may have hardened the resistance of some to providing academic credit for computer-related courses. Clearly, in their minds, the requisite skills were mechanical, not intellectual!

I believed then, and still believe, that administrative experiences, like mine on the firing line at Goucher, are essential preparation for a professor of higher education. No empirical data or course work can substitute for working with faculty members and students every day. In fact, until I encountered a roadblock in the liberal arts college setting, I expected to spend many more years in administrative positions at colleges like Goucher. When Dean Dorsey became president, she appointed a senior faculty member in history as interim dean. In promoting me to associate dean and placing me in charge of most of the operational work of the office, Dean Dorsey candidly informed me that no one with a doctoral degree in education could become academic dean in this type of liberal arts college regardless of demonstrated professional qualifications. Later I watched as a faculty committee reviewed the applications for dean, tossing those from people with education degrees aside after the briefest of examinations. The names of some of these applicants were well-known to me, as they would be to you. Finally, Goucher selected a man with a PhD in chemistry from outside the institution to be the dean. I had discovered a discipline prejudice as deep as gender prejudice.

AS A DEPARTMENT CHAIRPERSON AND EMERGING SCHOLAR, 1974-78

Despite no hope of advancement, I kept the dean's office running at Goucher, but when I heard that my alma mater, Syracuse University, was seeking a chair for its higher education department, I threw my hat in the ring. Much to my surprise, I was hired. The department consisted of four full-time faculty members (including me) and several adjuncts, mostly volunteers who held various administrative positions around the university. Sadly, in the summer preceding my fall 1974 arrival, the core faculty lost George Stern in a boating accident. I had looked forward to working with him.

Another full-time faculty member was assistant professor, Jim Heffernan, who was exploring the brand new Perry scheme of intellectual development and working with emergent external degree programs throughout New York state. Our third was John Honey, a former vice-president of the university who held a joint appointment with the Maxwell School of Citizenship. Jack was working on policy issues with his Maxwell students such as Aims McGuiness and Terry Hartle. Among the part-timers who made up this jerry-built department was Bob Diamond, an assistant vice chancellor who ran the Center for Instructional Development (CID). Bob was leading the redesign of large courses in the university and laying the foundation for his later books on curriculum design. Another part timer, Ed Kelly, was in great demand as an evaluator and conference designer. Two recent doctoral graduates in higher education, Ernest Pascarella and Patrick Terenzini, had each volunteered to teach courses while employed in other parts of the university. They also had permission to survey all incoming Syracuse freshmen and follow their development longitudinally. Obviously, the whole turned out to be much greater than the sum of the parts. What a team!

During my interview, someone at Syracuse probably asked me about my research agenda. If so, I remember neither the question nor my answer. Clearly, I needed such an agenda to maintain credibility as chair of this very active tribe. In order that I might get started, the School of Education assigned me no teaching duties during the first semester. Rather, Dean David Krathwohl suggested that I "sit in and oversee" the research design course that Ernie Pascarella was teaching for the first time. I did sit in, but more as a student than as an observer. I learned as much in that course about research design (and how it might be taught) as I had from memorizing Kerlinger's book. During that term I also readied myself for studies of my own by making the transition to a large university computer on which the first version of SPSS was up and running. I don't remember much about my administrative challenges as department chair. My sense is that overseeing normal operation and curriculum development in a small department was not taxing after my more extensive responsibilities at Goucher. I do remember that we were a happy, congenial group, doing our best to recruit top students and enhance their intellectual growth.

My concern for and interest in students motivated one of my few ventures into public policy studies. My experiences at Goucher had made me passionate about students' rights to accurate information for making educational decisions, especially about which college to attend. Naturally, I was interested when I heard that Congress might include "student consumer information" provisions in the higher education amendments of 1976. Although the primary target was unscrupulous proprietary schools that bilked students of federal financial aid without supplying the educational services promised, lobbyists for these profit-making schools were making sure that any new rules applied to colleges and universities as well. Legislators were proposing to apply Federal Trade Commission rules on misleading advertising to higher education.

After attending several conferences in Washington, I found that my concern for honesty with students was equaled by my conviction that higher education must not come under the control of the FTC or similar regulatory bodies. The criteria being proposed for honest advertising would penalize colleges if students did not get jobs "in the area for which they were trained." Among the most renowned individuals I knew, few could say (nor could I) that they were in a career for which they were trained as undergraduates. Clearly, such information would force colleges to gather essentially useless but very expensive information.

I decided that this misguided consumer protectionism needed alternative policy proposals. The key questions, as I saw them, were "How can students get better information for their academic decision-making?" and "Who is responsible for seeing that students' interests are protected?" I solicited the help of some equally concerned professional acquaintances and very knowledgeable doctoral students to analyze these questions. We wrote a book (part jointly authored, part contributed) to inform the higher education community and to urge them to take responsibility. Several early chapters were published as a Jossey-Bass *New Directions for Higher Education* volume under the misleading title "Promoting Consumer Protection for Students" (Stark, 1976). (Note that all New Directions issues must begin with a gerund, to imply action!).

The complete book, entitled *The Many Faces of Educational Consumerism* (Stark and Associates, 1977), suggested that the government's attempt to protect educational consumers was neither as logical nor as innocent as it sounded. The book traced the history of the student consumer protection initiative, analyzed the proposed regulations, and discussed the importance of local initiatives designed to ensure fair practice for students and institutional improvement, rather than to protect government funds. The book made its way into libraries, then faded rapidly into obscurity. Now, over twenty years later, I get occasional calls from graduate students who are concerned about improving information, but few of them know about the work done in the 1970s. Usually, I send them a book from the stack in my cellar for their historical enlightenment, with a reminder of the parallels between the consumer protection movement of the 1970s and the assessment movement of the 1990s. In both cases, advocates used the threat of government requirements to stir colleges and universities to independent action.

I opposed what Washington bureaucrats were proposing because I thought that educators should answer these questions and because I opposed additional federal control over colleges and universities. But intellectually, I was especially intrigued about what information students actually need to know in choosing colleges and what information they are prepared to recognize and use. Others were interested as well. A relatively new federal agency, the Fund for the Improvement of Postsecondary Education (FIPSE), solicited applications for a national project called Better Information for Student Choice. Those selected to participate were to experiment with the usefulness and feasibility of giving new and more directly honest information to prospective students.

Our Syracuse department received FIPSE funding as a "resource agency"; and, assisted by graduate students, I launched our research and action agenda. We worked with nine diverse colleges and universities in our area to develop comparable brochures for an experimental study. Our immediate research agenda was to see if we could influence prospective college students to view as important certain information about selected academic policies and career planning services that educators felt were especially important. Our longer-range political agenda was to develop proposals more useful than those being proposed, for example, statistics about how many students got particular jobs soon after graduation. To test the hypothesis that reading information about key services offered by the sample colleges would "raise the students' consciousness" of these services as factors in college choice, we supplied the materials under varying circumstances and in varying orders to randomly selected college-bound high school juniors. We were not very successful: students' pre-formed "images" of colleges were not much influenced by printed information.

Other projects also had inconclusive results. Better Information for Student Choice showed, by and large, the triumph of realism over idealism. The FIPSE participants tried to portray attrition rates more accurately, state clearly the bases of financial aid packages, list in catalogs only courses actually offered, and, as a simple illustration of honesty, include photos of snow as well as sun in recruiting materials. Critics — both on participating campuses and at other institutions — essentially said, "It's okay if you want to be honest and suffer drastic admissions declines, but not us." So, while we developed many models of good information and produced several reports published by AAHE, the National Association of Admissions Counselors, and the National Association of Financial Aid Administrators, other institutions did not rush to adopt the ideas. In fact, most colleges probably simply made their glossy recruitment materials glossier.

As a result, I measure the success of Better Information for Student Choice by the people I met whose friendships and associations have now spanned nearly 25 years. Bob Pace, who was then laying the groundwork for the College Student Experience Questionnaire, was UCLA's representative. Elaine El-Khawas, a young staff member at the American Council on Education, most ably drafted the task force national report. Ted Marchese, then director of institutional research at Barat College, not only developed new and more honest recruiting information but also got the national media to feature what Barat was doing. As a supplementary activity, Ted and I collaborated on an interesting project. He gathered data on Barat's student satisfaction surveys, financial aid records, attrition figures, etc. Then two Syracuse graduate students and I spent a long weekend in the Barat library doing an "audit" to certify that Barat's publicity materials fairly represented that data. Ted and I co-authored an article in the Journal of Higher Education describing our audit philosophy and process (Stark & Marchese, 1978). Interestingly, others have also proposed auditing college publicity material, but no one ever seems to have read our article.

FIPSE provided me with funding for a second three-year period to continue the work as "Project CHOICE" (Center for Helping Others Improve Choice in Education). Since the project was more than graduate students and I could handle alone, I hired Pat Terenzini as assistant director. Project CHOICE developed a slide-tape show and accompanying manuals that college units such as student affairs, academic affairs or admissions might use to review the arguments for better information and to stimulate discussion about needed local action. Hundreds of institutions borrowed these materials and, in follow-up surveys, reported some impact. CHOICE project staff also held workshops in cooperation with colleges in many regions.

What I learned from directing these two projects has been useful in other research and action projects over the years. First, I learned how to work with collegiate institutions — how to approach them, present a credible research project, gain their cooperation, and provide feedback. These coordinating tasks are absolutely essential for research with groups of human beings in organizational settings. Second, I learned how to marshal the talents of students and colleagues to apply for project funding and to carry out the funded tasks. I have continued throughout my career to work with small groups of doctoral students and colleagues in ways that I believe have facilitated student growth and dissertation completion. Typically I have been senior author of the first papers in a research project, but the students displace me as they mature and contribute their ideas and drafts. Third, I learned how to write and deliver speeches about policy issues. During this period I was asked to speak at numerous national and state conferences. I eagerly and fearlessly argued the case for better information without direct government intervention, often dragging my slide show through snow, wind, and rain. (Later, I'll say more about how I learned *not* to make speeches.) Fourth, I learned that research in education arises from the interaction of the interests of researchers, funders, and policy makers. Fifth, I developed a distaste for research about public policy issues generally, but strengthened my interest in higher education's self-improvement efforts, including accreditation and other forms of institutional and program evaluation.

THE DEANSHIP: NEW ADMINISTRATIVE CHALLENGES, 1978-1983

When Project CHOICE was concluding the first of its three years, my professorial career took a significant detour and my personal life changed dramatically. I was appointed dean of the School of Education at the University of Michigan. On the same day that I was in Michigan settling the final details of the offer, my husband died suddenly of a heart attack, in a hotel in Baltimore where he was attending a maritime seminar. I received this totally unexpected news when I landed in Syracuse that evening. At this point, my son, aged 17, was in graduate school at MIT; my oldest daughter, aged 16, was a college freshman; and the two younger daughters were in high school and elementary school respectively. Under the pressure of necessity we regrouped, purchased a house in Ann Arbor with the help of friends who inspected it for us, and sold two houses we owned in Syracuse. At age 40, I was a single parent in an unfamiliar state, faced with a job which no woman had held before and which I soon discovered could easily consume more than 24 hours a day.

I had accepted the challenge of trying to reorient a school of education that had grown flaccid and outmoded. Project Choice moved with me but its de facto directors for its remaining years were two recent Syracuse graduates — Dave Chapman, now a professor at the University of Minnesota, and John Griffith, now President of Presbyterian College. For five years I found very little time to be involved in specific research projects. The research agenda I had mapped out on better information for student choice produced several fine papers but I was seldom a co-author. My job now was primarily to foster research rather than to do it myself. Instead, I wrote an obligatory quarterly commentary column for the UM School of Education alumni newsletter and gave numerous high school and community college commencement addresses around the state. I was proud to have a faculty appointment in Michigan's well-known Center for the Study of Higher Education, but this association also remained underdeveloped during my deanship, partly because I felt I should be neutral about all the school's programs, and partly because I had no time.

The School of Education at Michigan employed about 135 faculty members and a large number of support staff. It included the Department of Physical Education, which was organizationally somewhat separate and whose budget did not fall under the dean's purview. It also included a Program in Speech and Hearing Sciences, whose faculty had reluctantly moved that year from the Medical School to education. The School of Education was also in charge of two children's camps, which presented interesting fiscal and legal liabilities, and staffed a Speech and Hearing Clinic that still belonged to the Medical School. The core of the school was twelve other programs, some of them consisting of only a few faculty who had splintered off from the mainstream programs over the years.

In the late 1970s, the School of Education faced several problems. Teachers were being laid off, the teachers' unions in Michigan opposed the placement of student teachers, and the number of master's degree students was falling rapidly. Nearly all of the faculty were teaching three courses per semester; many were also teaching off-campus evening extension courses for overload pay. Faculty members were serving on far too many committees but frowned on the idea of committee restructuring. Relatively few faculty were doing funded or unfunded research although the support staff included many persons who had stayed on when previous soft-money projects ended.

Two decades of unselective doctoral admissions had created an enormous backlog of candidates, many of whose dissertations were being poorly supervised. The budget of approximately $11 million dollars for the fiscal year just beginning was considerably short of meeting the existing obligations, and the university administration had just announced across-the-board budget taxes for priority reallocation. Deans at Michigan have a great deal of control over their budgets, once allocated. But, in the short run, I found little or no way to control obligations previously made. And finally, although it had not come up in interviews for the job, I now discovered that I was supposed to raise funds from philanthropic sources to meet shortfalls — all this at a time when alumni and the public perceived no need for new educators. Clearly, I faced a different set of administrative challenges from those I had experienced at Goucher and Syracuse.

Because all my previous administrative experience had been in private institutions, I was startled by proprietary interests at a public university. Even before I started packing, in Syracuse, many special interest groups in Michigan were urging me to fund their projects or submit to special demands. Over time, I received calls from state legislators and university regents demanding that I overrule a faculty committee to admit a particular friend or constituent, pass a student who had failed a doctoral examination, or supply a detailed time schedule for a faculty member whose research was viewed as politically incorrect. Legislators who claimed to be requesting "what the research says" often really wanted only research that agreed with bills they had already proposed. And of course, the tensions between education deans and athletic coaches over academic standards are legendary. I continued to feel that it was ethically correct to resist all unreasonable demands, but I learned that I was expected to be very flexible, especially in the case of non-admissible athletes. Sometimes I was simply overruled. The range of political realities never failed to astound me, even after I stopped being surprised.

I found, too, that deans in a large university may view themselves as competitors for a finite pool of funds rather than as collaborators for the educational welfare of the whole. Whether the apparent isolation I felt was gender-related (only two of Michigan's 19 deans were female at that time) or whether the central administration's style set a competitive tone, I'm not sure. But I have decided that a group of public university deans needs no rehearsals to star in *Survivor*, the television show that captured the American public in summer 2000.

I believed that the education faculty could improve research productivity and the quality of student work by reorganizing into larger units and receiving increased incentives, recognition, and opportunities. I proceeded, as was my custom, to pursue such goals through participatory means. The faculty and its executive committee deliberated with me, and the entire faculty held retreats, sometimes off-campus on weekends. To provide more research time, we decreased the teaching obligation from three 2-credit courses to two 3-credit courses per semester; phased out some extension classes for which there was little demand (unhappily reducing overload pay for some faculty); streamlined committees; substantially tightened standards and procedures for promotion, tenure, and salary increases; and, without public fanfare, eliminated two programs of questionable quality as faculty retirements and flexible appointments permitted.

As an administrator, I had very little time for my own projects. Despite this hectic administrative schedule, with the able assistance of Ann Austin (then a doctoral student and my graduate assistant), I managed to complete some studies concerning careers of our alumni/ae. Like my institutional research at Goucher, these studies were primarily designed to aid the School of Education's future planning. But we managed to set the studies in the context of similar investigations and publish some of the results.

When I had been dean just over two years and the faculty had begun to consolidate into five units that they found meaningful, we discovered that our time for self-initiated change had run out. While we were making substantial progress in developing a new climate of scholarly inquiry and intellectual vitality for the school, the university administration decided to deal with a sudden state-wide budget crisis by implementing a "smaller but better" program. Three colleges and many other units and institutes perceived as having quality problems became targets for review, with the announced intention of reducing their budgets up to 100%. Education was among them.

These budget reviews at Michigan involved a harmful process of public criticism that kept the schools, deans and faculties in humiliating financial, organizational, and intellectual chaos for about two years and failed to provide any immediate solution to the budget crisis. It should have been a fertile ground for researchers who study higher education administration, yet no one has ever done a careful case study, and the full story will probably never be told. Some of my Michigan colleagues who do such case studies at other institutions understandably do not wish to be viewed as churls at home. Part of the story appeared in *Ed School* by Geraldine Clifford and James Guthrie of UC-Berkeley; they attempted to compare review processes in three schools of education during that era. Unfortunately, the authors used *The Ann Arbor News* as a primary source, failing to interview key participants. They could not have known that a News reporter who wrote an article from the School of Education's perspective was immediately reassigned and that thereafter only releases from the vice president's office appeared in the paper.

During the ensuing 15 years, I have tried several times to summarize what I knew and had experienced, but the emotional stress at each attempt convinced me that I could never view those years as a dispassionate scholar. Finally, after all the administrators involved in the process had moved to other institutions, I gave my substantial archive of materials on the topic to the UM Bentley Historical Library, where it is available to future scholars. My only official account appears in the School of Education's celebratory booklet published April 13, 1997 for its 75th anniversary.

As the review process ground to its conclusion, I decided that, regardless of the outcome, I should not remain in the dean's role. The faculty and I had attempted to provide administrators and the public with a correct understanding of the school's role and with accurate assessment data. Numerous alumni and colleagues from all levels of education throughout the country had written and spoken in our behalf. But because the process itself had cast me as the administration's adversary, I felt that I was not the person either to reduce the size of the school or to build back its sacrificed prestige and morale. Thus, late in the summer of 1982, before the final outcome was announced, I told President Harold Shapiro that I planned to step aside at the end of my five-year term in summer 1983.

Other agendas and plans entered into my decision as well, namely the opportunity to resume my scholarly research and active participation as a professor of higher education. I had just been elected vice-president and program chair of the Association for the Study of Higher Education (ASHE), with the presidency to follow in the next year. The National Institute of Education (later OERI) in Washington had begun to discuss mission statements for funding several national educational research centers, one or two of which might focus on higher education. I discussed with President Shapiro and Provost Billy Frye my willingness to take research leadership in developing a grant proposal to sustain the good work of the Center for the Study of Higher Education, whose future was never in doubt during the review. Finally, on a more personal note, with the required permission of the president and provost, I had married a School of Education colleague, Professor Malcolm A. Lowther, in the winter of 1981. We had research as well as social agendas we wished to pursue together.

At the end of the lengthy review, the School of Education was cut by 40% but predictions of its demise were premature. Indeed, just when the final decision was being made, the timely release of the national report, *A Nation at Risk* (1983), made it politically unthinkable for the university to abandon education training. By executive decision, physical education became a separate unit, apparently with additional budget resources, and my successor, former associate dean Carl Berger, worked collaboratively and successfully for five years with a succession of provosts to downsize the rest of the school through buyouts and early retirements. Only then was another dean recruited from outside and charged with rebuilding the school. The story had an eventual positive outcome.

Following my five years as a dean at Michigan I never again considered an administrative position. In the 1950s when I was a young college graduate, women administrators were rare, but by the mid-1970s women were actively being sought for administrative posts to fill affirmative action goals. I had hardly arrived at Michigan when consulting groups wanted to enter my name in various presidential searches. I declined these opportunities and I continued to decline them after my deanship. By this time I had learned that I disliked fundraising; and, after giving many speeches on behalf of the School of Education, I had also developed an aversion to all public speaking that did not concern my research. Finally, I had learned that my niche in higher education was as a scholar and teacher; I wasn't planning any more detours.

This feeling of certainty has helped me to be an astute observer of those who take the administrative route. I am convinced that the rush to affirmative action has caused many women and minorities to move upward in administrative ranks before they are seasoned in positions that fully prepare them for the challenges they will meet. I advise my students headed for administrative positions to dally a bit at each administrative level until they have the job well enough in hand to recapture some leisure time without guilt feelings. I also suggest that, if they are committed to employee participation and faculty ownership of decisions as an administrative style, they had best make sure that their superiors value that style as well. The administrative practices espoused in the textbooks that higher education scholars study are effective only if the organizational context supports them.

RESUMING RESEARCH, 1983-1991

Upon returning to the faculty, I received a sabbatical and an administrative leave for 1983-84. During this year Mal and I, with the help of doctoral student Bonnie Hagerty (now associate professor of nursing at Michigan), developed an agenda for a comparative study of professions education. Its basic idea evolved from two sources: the tensions I had observed at liberal arts colleges between the liberal arts and career-oriented fields, and the sharp pecking order among professional fields that I had observed during Michigan's budget reviews. The prestigious, traditional professions (medicine, law, and dentistry) and younger entrepreneurial professions with high potential for grant funding (business, pharmacy, and engineering) had higher status than the helping and artistic professions (education, nursing, social work, environmental science, art). Even the seats that deans took at meetings tended to reflect this hierarchy.

Specifically, faculty members from the traditional professions who had served on the budget review committees at Michigan had exhibited, in my view, astounding arrogance in assuming that only their own pedagogical traditions were valid. For example, one law professor insisted that education must adopt the large lecture groups and interrogative spirit that characterize classes in law. Large classes were cheaper, he reasoned, and did not require the individual attention to students found in many smaller school of education classes. Thus, for Mal and me, one motivation for studying education in the professions was to try to educate provosts who are responsible for educational quality and accountability — and faculty members who serve on review committees — about the legitimate diversity of disciplinary cultures on campuses. Because professional preparation programs vary so greatly on such dimensions as educational goals, expected outcomes, teaching methods, student time commitments, and relations with practitioners, it is not easy for administrators to develop a working knowledge of each of them. We also hoped that our comparisons would be useful to professional school leaders seeking ways to collaborate with colleagues in other fields, and to admissions officers providing prospective students with information about various professions.

About this same time, however, some national reports were calling for the reduction or elimination of career-focused education in colleges and a return to the liberal arts for all students through a mandated and expanded core curriculum. National advocates for this position included William Bennett and Lynn Cheney, successive directors of the National Institute for the Humanities (Bennett, 1984; Cheney, 1989). To me, this position seemed simplistic in a country where more than half of undergraduates are enrolled in programs leading to careers and many students lack the financial means to prolong their college years beyond the baccalaureate. The arguments also seemed illogical since they made, without exploration or documentation, the *a priori* assumptions that (1) all undergraduate career education is "narrow" and excessively specialized, and (2) studying great writers and thinkers automatically produces critical thinking. We hoped that our studies might produce a more realistic alternative proposal that could strengthen both general education and career education.

Studying Undergraduate Professional Education

Mal, Bonnie, and I first developed a conceptual framework that might guide studies focused on understanding both the similarities and differences among pre-service professional education programs (Stark, Lowther, Hagerty, & Orczyk, 1986).[2]

In this framework we attempted to capture the various influences, processes, outcomes, and relationships that should be part of any systematic analysis of professional programs. We then constructed and conducted a national survey of faculty in ten professional fields to establish comparative profiles of their educational goals, processes, and influences. We also conducted interviews with many of these faculty members and did a close comparative reading of the educational journal literature for each field (Stark, Lowther, & Hagerty, 1986).

In trying to understand and compare the different fields, we quickly learned why so few scholars do comparative studies and read about education outside of their own field. As we had speculated in our framework, each field exhibited a unique "professional preparation environment" that must be considered in understanding its educational processes and outcomes. This environment is determined by influences within the program itself, and from its relationships within the university and with such external groups as the professional practice community, accrediting agencies, and society. The professional preparation environment is least dependent upon university influences, includ-

[2] Over the years, I have found that every research project benefits from the development of a guiding conceptual framework before the research questions are phrased and the data collection is designed. The best frameworks are as context-free as one can make them. Constant revision of the framework as new information is discovered is also essential.

ing the size and type of institution in which the program is situated (Stark, Lowther, & Hagerty, 1987).[3]

One of our most important findings was that, beyond the goals of acquiring and melding the theoretical knowledge base and skills that graduates need for the specific professional practice (conceptual, technical, and integrative competence), all the professional fields espoused similar objectives. In varying degrees, they all expected students to acquire communication skills, contextual understanding, aesthetic sensibility, the ability to adapt, the ability to lead, a scholarly concern for improvement, motivation for continued learning, professional identity, and a sense of professional ethics.

Some subgroups within the professional programs emerged, however, allowing us to group programs by educational ideologies. The programs differed primarily by the extent to which faculty within a field exhibited consensus on goals and the extent to which these goals included professional socialization of students. For example, nursing, social work, and education faculty felt it was important to teach professional ethics while business and engineering, for example, agreed neither on what professional ethics are appropriate nor whether they should be taught.

We also noticed that many of the outcomes that professional programs expected from their students were very similar to the goals being advocated for the liberal arts. The primary distinction was that, in one case, students would use their acquired skills and knowledge in professional situations, and, in the other case, in general life situations (Stark, Lowther, & Hagerty, 1987). Contrary to common belief, faculty in the professional fields do strive to maintain, and even to initiate, curricular breadth that is relevant to most developing professionals, but they also struggle with the amount of technical knowledge their students must learn in a limited timeframe and they are discontented with liberal arts colleagues' perceived detachment about real-world issues that professionals will face. The time seemed ripe to explore avenues for collaboration between liberal arts and professional program faculty members, particularly in courses that convey to students the importance of the social context in which the professions are practiced, the anticipated effect of technology on professional practice, and the need for broader interpersonal communication skills.

Based on our preliminary identification of goals common to both liberal arts and professional program faculty members, we received a two-year grant from FIPSE to launch the Professional Preparation Network. We selected pairs of faculty members from sixteen different campuses — an undergraduate profes-

[3] Our studies confirmed the perceived pecking order in the professions in universities; the professions that saw themselves as least valued on campuses and in society were often female-dominated (nursing, education, social work, library science, and journalism). Thus, it was difficult to separate the social stratification issue from gender issues.

sional program faculty member and a liberal arts colleague — and brought them together with a knowledgeable advisory board of leaders in the various professional fields. The entire group, the PPP Network, met with us in Ann Arbor several times over two years and engaged in active (and sometimes emotional) discussions of the common goals of liberal and professional education. On returning to their own campus, the pair of faculty members continued to explore their mutual goals for students and tested the possibilities of engaging their home departments in a collaboration. Several of the on-campus discussions began by using the Professional Liberal Undergraduate Self Study (PLUSS), a self-study instrument which guides groups of faculty members through the process of examining their common goals and activities.

The PPP Network was probably the most exciting thing Mal and I did in our professional careers. The activities of the network members clearly demonstrated that faculty could talk across disciplinary lines, could work through animosities caused by initial disagreements, and could carry enthusiasm for the project back to their campuses. Although parallel discussions took place on all the represented campuses, only modest changes and new alliances evolved. But powerful ideas eventually emerged for ways of integrating liberal and professional education and they gave concreteness to similar proposals that others were making at about the same time. (See for example, Boyer, 1987).

With the assistance of a writing team, we drafted a task force report called "Strengthening the Ties That Bind: Integrating Liberal and Professional Education" (1988). We released this report at an AAHE National Conference and sent it to presidents and provosts at all colleges and universities. The report, also featured in the *Chronicle of Higher Education*, called for a "ceasefire" between advocates of liberal and professional study. It urged intensive discussion, expansion, and refinement of the educational goals that inextricably bind the two. It encouraged educators to confront issues that hinder such discussion and suggested strategies and tasks for campus leaders, faculty members, and other concerned groups who want to improve curricular integration. The report gave examples of how the network members themselves had conducted these discussions and pointed out the typical pitfalls.

Our primary thesis was that education for life and for a career are related, not conflicting goals. Most students enter college with multiple purposes that include both liberal education and career objectives. To the extent that higher education can blend these goals to benefit students, institutions will succeed in their missions. The challenge is to integrate liberal and professional study in such a way that the students become "educated professionals," developing the values, attitudes, and skills necessary to make complex judgments appropriately in practice settings. The PPP group urged educators to reject sequential and separate programs of liberal and professional education and to recognize that joint problem solving among faculty, rather than unilateral decision-making, can productively integrate liberal and professional education.

Two network members edited a practical volume featuring articles by several of the faculty partnerships (Armour & Fuhrmann, 1989). Based on the network discussions, Bonnie Hagerty and I also produced the "Collaboration-Integration Matrix," which helps groups of faculty decide what method of collaboration would be best to achieve a specific educational outcome. Many colleges that were not involved in the PPP Network have experimented with integrating liberal and professional education by using these materials.

As I reflect on the ideas included in "Strengthening the Ties That Bind," I'm still proud of this report. I believe that it is a powerful policy statement with far more potential impact than most of the technical empirical articles I have written. In the twelve years that have passed since the PPP group concluded its work, accreditors and administrators have begun to take more seriously their obligation to assess whether students are achieving the desired outcomes. But they continue to disclaim a potentially powerful leadership role in helping faculty develop collaborative, integrative educational processes. In fact, the conviction that administrative leadership must set the stage for faculty to do their best work in curriculum development continues to be a foundation for my scholarly work.

Launching a National Research Center

The mid-1980s were extremely busy years, since the FIPSE grant supporting the PPP Network was not the only major research and action initiative in which I was engaged. As anticipated, the National Institute of Education announced a competition for national research centers, including two for postsecondary education, one to study teaching and learning issues and one to study governance and organization issues. I called Bill McKeachie, professor of psychology and former director of the Center for Research on Learning and Teaching (CRLT) at Michigan to ask if he would join with me in applying for the teaching and learning grant. With Bill's help and agreement to be associate director, I gathered twelve key researchers who worked in five teams. We developed a proposal that survived an extensive site visit, a changeover in Washington political power, the subsequent transition from NIE to OERI, and a last-minute attempt by the newly politicized funding agency to shape our research as a means to coerce colleges to adopt assessment measures.

Consistent with my earlier feelings about consumer protection, I steadfastly resisted any activity or language that would cause colleges to view this research center as a federal enforcement agency or as a group with a set political agenda. I felt that our task was to conduct research and disseminate it widely, allowing the colleges to use it for their own improvement. Consequently, we gave the research center the complex name of the National Center for Research to Improve Postsecondary Teaching and Learning (NCRIPTAL). Simpler versions all seemed to leave out the "research" and include only the "improve," suggesting a willingness to intervene directly in colleges and universities. On a more humorous note, many of the simpler acronyms that we composed had double meanings. (Try it, you'll see!) Bill McKeachie finally declared that we should have something unpronounceable so that no one could attribute an unintended meaning. At that we surely succeeded.

The NCRIPTAL project (1986-1991) included a heavy commitment from the University of Michigan to pay the faculty researchers' salaries. This commitment came from the UM Provost Billy E. Frye, School of Education Dean Carl Berger, CSHPE Director Marvin Peterson, and Director of CRLT, Donald Brown. This extensive salary support stretched our $4.9 million grant a long way and made NCRIPTAL more effective than it might have been; but it certainly kept us busy. During each of the five twelve-month years, the faculty researchers continued to teach as usual during the academic terms and to receive their research salaries in the four summer months.[4]

Of course, all of the work was spread over twelve months (and weekends and holidays) in a seamless way that made the faculty very productive and often very tired. We were able to engage many doctoral students in our work teams — for pay, for credit, and just as volunteers and observers — and we made them full partners in the research and publications. For this, some professional colleagues curse us, since NCRIPTAL articles and reports often had as many as seven authors.

The NCRIPTAL research teams studied five aspects of the learning environment: teaching and learning within classrooms, curriculum development, faculty issues, administrative support for teaching and learning, and the emerging use of technology. The programs varied in their scope of work and their visibility to scholars, faculty, and administrators. Paul Pintrich and Bill McKeachie developed the Motivated Strategies for Learning instrument, which remains in demand and continues to be updated. Marvin Peterson and Kim Cameron conducted influential studies of administrative support for academic practices. Bob Blackburn and Janet Lawrence made considerable strides in understanding faculty motivations in research and teaching and summarized their work in book form. Perhaps most visible was the NCRIPTAL-EDUCOM project, cleverly de-

[4] Once I left the deanship and returned to the faculty I usually taught two graduate courses each term as well as directing doctoral theses and independent studies. Over the years I taught primarily curriculum, evaluation, research design, personnel administration, and philosophy of academic leadership courses.

vised by Bob Kozma and Jerry Johnston. This national competition, which encouraged faculty members to develop and submit instructional software, helped Bob and Jerry to develop the first available criteria for judging such software.

I mention a few of the challenges of running a national research center like NCRIPTAL because we managed to turn them, I think, into productive strategies for enhancing our research and its potential for change. First, each federally-sponsored center was required to produce quarterly reports documenting its efforts and various other extensive documents (I counted a total of twenty quarterly reports, five annual reports and four applications for renewal over the five year period.) Each report was about 200 pages long, accompanied by drafts of articles in progress, surveys under development and other archival documents. The research teams found the report-writing irritating, but the process helped us to continually renew and refocus the research agenda, to document the reasons for methodological changes, and to educate graduate students new to the teams. In addition, the detailed research plans helped us recruit campuses to join various projects and formed the backbone of later papers. (These uses were fortuitous since I doubt that many of the reports were read in Washington.)

A second challenge was the tension between research and dissemination. Our project officers at OERI were always urging us to disseminate more quickly and more broadly. Trying to cope with these demands caused us to produce many interim products — from literature reviews to research plans to newsletter columns — which were useful to others outside our immediate group. While we felt we were researchers first and disseminators second, we did manage to make our complex name, NCRIPTAL, well-known in higher education circles. This name-recognition generated a demand for our research when it was completed.

A third challenge was the tension between maintaining our research schedules on new projects and providing timely feedback to institutions on completed ones. In nearly all our projects we collaborated with groups of institutions and took seriously the responsibility to give feedback to administrators and groups of faculty. This commitment of providing feedback often caused delays and readjustment in projects, but there is truly no other way, outside of the psychology lab, to do research on education. One cannot use institutions, students, and faculty as research subjects and then simply forget about them.

Fourth, we were often evaluated. A national advisory board met annually to give advice on our various projects and on future agendas. A team of formative evaluators annually examined our operation and products, surveyed constituents who had received our materials, and reported to the national advisory board. While we welcomed evaluation, some of our advisors failed to appreciate the lengthy time lines we needed to set up some research projects and pushed for faster results. Others wanted us to study very current topics — without realizing that we were funded for research programs submitted to OERI more than a year in advance. But the entire evaluation process kept us aware of how our efforts looked to the higher education community generally and often helped us adjust our plans.

Exploring Course Planning

As director, I was responsible for the overall effort of NCRIPTAL, but Mal and I also led the research team on Curriculum Influences and Impacts. My interest in curriculum issues had been growing since I returned to the faculty from the deanship. Prior to that time, based on my training and original interests, I had considered myself chiefly interested in organizational studies. However, my years as an administrator caused me to question the utility of organizational theory and left me with little enthusiasm for teaching about it. It was just as well, too, since my colleague Marvin Peterson was competently in charge of that segment of our teaching and research program. So I focused my interest on collegiate curriculum and evaluation issues, filling a gap in our program and learning a great deal from Mal, who taught these topics at the secondary school and adult education levels. Perhaps the first public expression of my interest in curriculum issues was my ASHE presidential address in March 1985, entitled "The Capricious Curriculum." Don't look for it among the presidential speeches in the *Review of Higher Education*, since I never submitted it for publication. My ideas were in the formative stages and the way they developed was very much influenced by the research at NCRIPTAL.

Our NCRIPTAL curriculum research team conducted a multi-phase study of course planning among college faculty members teaching introductory courses. This project lasted over three years and consisted of an extensive literature review on issues related to course and program planning, onsite interviews of selected faculty at eight colleges, and a national survey of course planning practices. At the time, NIE had just published the report, "Involvement in Learning" (1984), which stated that colleges should require more general education courses, clarify expectations, and encourage students to become more involved in learning. Another report (Association of American Colleges, 1985) maintained that the specific courses students take are not as important for curricular coherence as the experiences of students within those courses. Despite this emphasis on college and university courses, we found that no one in the United States had studied course planning in higher education as a faculty activity. In addition to curriculum reform at the college and program levels, coherence within individual courses, where the structure for much academic learning is established is also important. Theories about how students learn reinforced the important link between understanding academic course planning and improving student learning.

Thus, our studies of course planning linked with the work on classroom processes being done by Bill McKeachie and Paul Pintrich's team of researchers. Our team was particularly interested in how faculty members view their course structure and how they communicate that structure to students. Based on my earlier studies of disciplinary differences, we were also interested in knowing what influences faculty course planning — so we simply asked faculty about it.

We began by conducting in-depth interviews with 89 faculty members at diverse colleges who were teaching the types of general education courses so strongly criticized in the national reports. Based on these interviews, we developed a tentative "contextual filters model of course design" (Stark, Lowther, Ryan, & Genthon, 1988). We followed the earlier work of Toombs (1977-78), who suggested that faculty educational decisions are affected by (a) content influences such as discipline characteristics and (b) context factors such as college goals, program goals, student characteristics, faculty characteristics, and local internal and external influences.

Our more detailed model posits that faculty members' views of their academic fields, their own backgrounds, and their assumptions about educational purpose interact to form "discipline-grounded" perspectives that are the initial basis for course planning. It is not possible to completely separate influences of the discipline, graduate school socialization, and the characteristics of individuals attracted to certain disciplines. However, we were confident that there are "usual patterns" of course planning associated with specific academic fields and that the beliefs underlying them are very enduring. Characteristics of the specific instructional setting (including students' characteristics) serve as "contextual filters" that modify faculty members' views in varying degrees.

Next, we refined the contextual filters model by surveying a nationally representative set of faculty teaching introductory courses. We were able to estimate the relative strength of content and context influences for faculty planning courses in different disciplines and in different types of institutions. Definitely, a faculty member's background, disciplinary view, and related beliefs about the purpose of education combine to provide the single strongest influence on course planning. Most contextual influences are considerably weaker, although faculty members are greatly concerned with students' preparation and ability. With these results, we were actually able to correctly classify faculty in several disciplines based solely on their answers to survey questions about their planning assumptions and processes (Stark, Lowther, Bentley, & Martens, 1990). We also learned that, although they differ in their demographic characteristics and have less teaching experience, part-time faculty plan their courses in similar ways and attend to influences like the full-time faculty in the same discipline. In addition, a faculty member will plan an introductory course and an advanced course in the same field in a similar way.

Our findings about course planning have specific implications for faculty development. Clearly, faculty will most often resonate to new information about curriculum and teaching when it is appropriate to their own field or to closely related disciplines. Instructional development specialists need to design programs with this fact in mind. Second, faculty members may desire to gear their course planning to the students, but they often have little information about the students' interests and preparation. In noting this lack of knowledge, we compared the teacher with a surgeon who finds out the patient's diagnosis only as she or he begins surgery. Especially in the computer age, colleges could easily remedy this deficit and give each professor a useful class profile to improve planning.

Because they translated our research into practice, two of our most useful products were a booklet that applied the contextual filters model to syllabus construction and a course-design pamphlet, ostensibly meant for graduate teaching assistants but helpful to faculty members as well. Ten years later, we still receive requests for these two booklets.

For our studies of course planning, we adopted the useful view that curriculum is an academic plan that can be constructed at the unit, the course, the program, or the college level. We adapted this idea from many sources, especially from research on K-12 curriculum. But before Mal and I developed it (Stark & Lowther, 1988), no one had defined curriculum for higher education in this multi-faceted way. This is not to say that the typical college faculty member now knows or accepts our definition (as opposed to curriculum being a set of units or courses, or the content of a specific discipline, for example). However, other researchers are now working with this more systematic definition which also became the heuristic for the curriculum course I taught in CSHPE and a book I subsequently wrote (Stark & Lattuca,1997).

Students' Goals Are Important Too

We were well aware that an academic plan may be quite coherent— that is, logically consistent — in the view of its faculty creator(s), but neither intelligible nor useful to students. The degree to which the academic plan is useful to students depends on whether it meets their educational expectations, suits their abilities, and encourages them to relate it to their earlier learning and experiences. In other words, student goals, the quality of student effort (Pace, 1983), and student characteristics are three factors that influence whether students learn what their teacher's plan intends them to learn.

Because we recognized the importance of students' "fitting" the curriculum, our NCRIPTAL team also studied student goals for specific courses. After reviewing the literature on student goals and laying out a conceptual framework and rationale (Stark, Shaw, & Lowther, 1989), we constructed and pilot tested the Student Goals Exploration (SGE). We designed this inventory to help teachers engage their students in discussion about the relationship of course goals to their own goals. (A faculty version allows the teacher to assess his/her own goals for the course and compare them with the class profile.) It also measures changes in students' goals over time within a major or general education program. One important finding as we pilot tested the SGE was that students hold quite different goals for different courses in which they are enrolled. Thus, broad college goals (e. g., to make money, to develop a meaningful philosophy of life) form a contextual backdrop for students' course goals but are insufficient to explain what influences their performance in specific classes.

Although the SGE instrument is complete and validated (Stark, Bentley, Lowther, & Shaw, 1991), I believe that this work is still incomplete and I'm pleased that several doctoral students at other universities are working with the SGE. Educational success may depend on how well educators link the classroom goals they set for their students with the goals that students set for themselves. In my view, a deficit of current assessment procedures that follow Astin's input-environment-output strategy is the failure to statistically adjust outcome measures based on student goals. When attempting to account for outcomes, including a student's goals as an input measure seems just as important as entering test scores or demographic variables. In fact, I recall a striking illustration from my earlier studies of information for student consumers: government officials intended to judge community colleges on student degree completion measures even though many students came for a course or two and never intended to complete a degree. These students successfully achieved their goals, but the bureaucrats deemed them failures.

Moving On

All in all, I judged NCRIPTAL to be a success in the research it produced, the visibility it gained among both researchers and practitioners, and the experiences it brought to us and our graduate students. As NCRIPTAL entered its fifth year, a new competition for the national centers was scheduled. For this competition, the agenda that OERI had tried to impose upon us five years earlier—namely, advocacy of and experimentation with, assessment of learning in colleges— became more prominent in the request for proposals. Anticipating that this emphasis would lead to a stronger hand with colleges than I felt appropriate, I decided that the grant-directing phase of my scholarly life had lasted long enough.

After directing two major grants within five hectic years, I desired more leisure time to contemplate and write about what I had learned. Janet Lawrence ably led our five research teams in submitting a new proposal, but we were not successful in this competition. In summer 1991, NCRIPTAL turned over the reins and the federal funding to the National Center for Teaching, Learning, and Assessment (NCTLA), centered at Penn State. (Penn State has since finished its five years of work, and the succeeding center, National Center for Postsecondary Improvement [NCPI], now is headquartered at Stanford with components at Michigan and elsewhere.) Although nearly all NCRIPTAL materials are available on ERIC microfiche, we continued to circulate our materials for an additional five or six years. Many of them are still in demand. To cite an extreme case, in summer of 2001, I received a coupon from a college faculty member asking to be put on the NCRIPTAL mailing list. The coupon was clipped from our first general mailing sent in 1986!! I conclude that it can take more than ten years for new information from educational research to reach faculty and administrators in colleges and universities.

LIFE AFTER NCRIPTAL: 1991 TO 2001

My professional life between 1991 and 2001 has included the editorship of the *Review of Higher Education*, several interesting consulting and service projects that built on previous research, studies of disciplinary differences in course and program goals, publication of a book about the college curriculum, and an investigation of the curriculum leadership of department chairpersons. Although I have learned new things, I believe it has been a period of consolidation and summary, a pattern that may (and should) characterize professorial life after a lengthy period of grant-supported activity.

Editing

Just before NCRIPTAL ended in 1991, the Association for the Study of Higher Education sought a new editor for the *Review of Higher Education*. After soliciting financial support from the dean and program chair, I applied for this volunteer position and was selected. Linda Stiles, who had been my executive secretary when I was dean as well as the administrative manager for NCRIPTAL, became The Review's very competent managing editor. Although many people helped in various roles, I was especially assisted in my work as editor by John Creswell, associate editor, and David Leslie, review essay editor— especially faithful associates throughout the five years. I sought this position because journal editors hold critical positions in any academic field and I believe that qualified scholars have an obligation to serve. In supervising the peer review of about

100 manuscripts a year and the revision and publication of about 30% of them, I was privileged to help nurture numerous emerging scholars as they submitted their first articles.

My goal was to try to ensure that the ASHE journal represented all points of view and all research methods. With the concurrence of the editorial advisory board, I maintained the journal entirely on spontaneous submissions. I believe that fully juried journals are superior to those that sponsor special issues that happen to interest the editor. In fact, as an editor, I learned that my own expertise is insufficient to choose special topics on behalf of the scholarly community.

Service and Consulting: Putting Research to Work

Shortly before NCRIPTAL ended, I received two invitations to participate in exciting projects. One was to join the Accounting Education Change Commission (AECC), a five-year effort to change the curriculum and teaching practices in accounting. This commission was funded by the Big Eight (later Big Six) accounting firms which have considerable influence on accounting education. Traditional accounting education relies on students memorizing and applying rules. The objective of the new curriculum was to develop students' abilities to find information and make judgments. Through a proposal competition, the commission granted funds to accounting departments willing to achieve these new educational goals by using more active methods of teaching and placing more emphasis on such general professional objectives as good communication and critical thinking skills.

I served with pride for five years (1989-1994) as a nonpaid member of the AECC, which met in cities all over the country. Our growth was mutual. Accounting educators asked me about curricular and pedagogical matters and appreciated the advice I gave them. In turn, I read and commented on about 75 lengthy proposals and learned a great deal about how this well-organized professional field operates. Frequently I was struck by the similarity of the discussions in accounting, nursing, education, and engineering especially on questions of professional identity, accreditation, and relations with practicing professionals.

The AECC truly made an impact on accounting education. In reflecting about why its efforts were more successful in effecting change than, for example, FIPSE's projects on student choice or the PPP network, I have noted that the AECC was able to award grants directly to departments and hold them accountable. But other reasons are embedded in the AECC's very good practices. In a luncheon talk to the American Accounting Association, I summarized these curriculum leadership practices as the six Cs: achieving credibility for the change effort, using a constructive emphasis in the call to change, providing an exciting challenge to professors, maintaining open communication throughout the project, being willing to consult, and celebrating the work of the participating universities.

The second exciting opportunity was to work as a formative evaluator with Philadelphia College of Textiles and Science, an institution actively engaged, with support from FIPSE, in integrating liberal and professional study. Formative evaluators work with the faculty and administration to help shape and guide a change project in ways that a one-time speaker or workshop leader never can. At PCT&S, I met with the committee in charge of the project, attended and participated in faculty workshops, interviewed faculty members as they developed new courses, and gave the project leaders advice on readings and activities that might help. For me, it was a truly pleasant association and a very profitable, informal way to research how best to implement curriculum change. For example, I made this important observation: an academic vice-president who wants to foster successful curriculum change needs to participate fully in every seminar, workshop, meeting, and faculty retreat, as Richard Nigro at PCT&S did.

Exploring Connected Learning and Discipline Differences

Curricular coherence is a theme that has interested me throughout my career. In the mid-980s, I wrote some short essays, attempting to define this term that had been used so freely and with varying meanings in several national reports.[5]

Faculty members and policy makers all believe they know, or can sense, what coherence is; but when focused conversations begin, faculty members from different fields rarely agree. They disagree because they typically open their discussions by attempting to specify the content they consider to be necessary for coherence. In the 1980s, the term "connected learning" emerged as an occasional synonym for coherence. But based on disciplinary differences and the tension between liberal and professional study, reasonable people also disagreed about what learnings are to be connected.

My long-standing interest in the potential relationship among curricular coherence, connected learning, and disciplinary differences reemerged when the Association of American Colleges (AAC, now AAC&U) published *The Challenge of Connecting Learning* (1991a) and *Reports from the Fields* (1991b) as part of its reform efforts. AAC challenged twelve learned societies to develop plans that would increase the capacity of the major field for (a) achieving curricular coherence, (b) developing critical perspective in students, (c) connecting learning with

[5] Specifically, I attempted to distinguish coherence as a "logically consistent plan for learning," from other more value-laden terms such as "integrity," "integration," and "rigor."

other fields and with students' lives, and (d) including underrepresented students. Lisa Lattuca, a new graduate student, was also interested in these questions. So together we conducted content analyses of *Reports from the Fields* to explore how the various fields expressed their separate disciplinary visions of a coherent curriculum. In one study, we analyzed the reports for their direct answers to the challenges mentioned above (Lattuca & Stark, 1994). We found that structured fields like the sciences could agree on what constituted a coherent curriculum, while the humanities and social sciences could not. The faculty in humanities and social sciences, on the other hand, understood quite well what they meant by "critical perspective," while the science faculty had difficulty with this concept. Connected learning for the sciences meant links among scientific principles and concepts. For those who view knowledge as contextual, it meant connections to social problems and students' lives.

In a second study, we analyzed the unsolicited or "discretionary" comments, that is, the expressed curricular concerns or opinions of the task forces that were not direct answers to the AAC charge. We coded the comments, grouped them into themes, then compared the themes with the contextual filters model based on the previous studies Mal Lowther and I had done on course planning. We found that the three parts of the contextual filters model (content, context, and form) provided a good organizing framework for the unsolicited themes in the AAC report. Furthermore, within each of these three broad dimensions, we again found substantial differences among the traditional three types of disciplines (Lattuca & Stark, 1995). This work reinforced in two ways the research I had been pursuing for several years. First, the contextual filters model captured curriculum planning at the program level as well as the course level. Second, I was now firmly convinced that, since different disciplines place different values on specific educational purposes and student outcomes, clear consensus among them must be consciously cultivated. It won't just happen because a national commission calls for improving general education or a curriculum committee holds a meeting.

To seek further evidence of the need for conscious effort, three other students helped us examine some unanalyzed data from the NCRIPTAL survey of course planning. We examined open-ended responses from general education faculty about their course goals and readily classified them into the following broad categories: general skill development, knowledge acquisition, effective thinking, intellectual development, personal development, and future preparation. Then, using faculty words as the data source, we looked for varied themes within each of these broad categories.

Of particular interest are the various themes we identified as different types of effective thinking and intellectual development (Eljamal, Sharp, Stark, Arnold, & Lowther, 1998; Eljamal, Stark, Arnold, & Sharp, 1999). Intellectual development, the broader of these two goals, focused on helping students understand relationships. Yet we could identify several subgoals: relationships between academic fields, relationships between the discipline and students' lives, appreciation for the discipline's contribution to humanity, broadening horizons, tolerance of ambiguous ideas, and intellectual curiosity. Faculty teaching general education courses in nine fields placed different emphases on these various subgoals and used different words to describe them.¨ Similarly, we identified eight types of thinking goals that various fields emphasized differently. For example, mathematics professors use the term "problem solving", while social science professors say "logical reasoning" and humanities professors say "critical thinking." The differences are not superficial; they encompass different shades of meaning. We concluded that the umbrella term "effective thinking" was the best choice to express the common goal of higher-order thinking in college since "critical thinking" may not be equally useful in all fields. But we also discovered that the various effective thinking goals are not isolated in faculty members' minds or goals. We found multiple, sometimes indistinct, connections and various layers of discourse as faculty considered their goals for student learning. Consequently, we likened our analysis of the effective thinking categories to navigating the World Wide Web.

Clearly, evidence that faculty "connect learning" in different ways adds substantially to the growing literature on discipline differences. But we also extrapolated some practical suggestions from our work. We are convinced that faculty who engage in cross-disciplinary curriculum development would benefit from a better understanding of how their colleagues think about educational purposes and processes. Surely the testy debates that sometimes divert curriculum committees from their task resemble cultural misunderstandings. Progress might be smoother if faculty engaged in an early "multicultural exercise" to share and learn to respect each other's perspectives.

Our results also have implications for faculty groups that are attempting to foster and assess higher-order thinking in general education courses and programs. Given the diverse goals and interpretations we uncovered, a good assessment program requires multiple measures to determine whether students have acquired effective thinking skills. Finally, we found an implication for students: general education distribution requirements may be more logical than meets the eye, since each discipline obviously has something quite different to contribute to students' intellectual development. What may be lacking is guidance to help students synthesize and integrate these general education perspectives. The question of how students achieve "coherence" and "connect learning" is an important one that we have not addressed.

Pulling It All Together

From 1992 to 1996, my primary intellectual activity was writing *Shaping the College Curriculum* (1997). I began this book because my students in a graduate course, The Postsecondary Curriculum, had to consult literally hundreds of sources to understand what I wanted them to learn.[6]

So I began to write down, more systematically, important points to emphasize in each class and to record appropriate activities for helping students understand these points. Lisa Lattuca, a diligent and fastidious researcher during our content analysis of disciplinary differences, was also a star pupil in the curriculum course. She just naturally became the second author of *Shaping the College Curriculum.* We wrote what we believe is the most comprehensive treatment of the college curriculum, incorporating a nascent curriculum theory for higher education. We intended that it be useful to faculty members, graduate assistants, and researchers as well as students in a curriculum course.

The book's strength, in our view, is its organizing framework that defines the eight elements to consider when developing an academic plan: purpose, content, sequence, learners, instructional resources, instructional processes, evaluation, and adjustment. These eight elements are the major variables that typically surface when people discuss how to plan, implement, evaluate, or improve teaching and learning. This definition provides a suitable umbrella for the many disparate teaching and learning literatures. (From this perspective, teaching does not subsume curriculum planning; rather, it is the implementation of the plan.) The definition is also attractive because its built-in feedback mechanism (evaluation and adjustment) encourages interactive change and improvement. Nothing in the framework prescribes a specific content to be taught, a specific teaching approach, or a specific type of assessment. However, groups of faculty members in a particular setting, by defining curriculum as an academic plan, can make concrete not only their specific educational goals and the content to be taught, but also those aspects of learning that they believe are important, such as active learning, teaching culturally diverse classes, or setting clear expectations for students.

I found writing this book to be a very fulfilling experience. For most of my life I had been writing journal articles that adhered closely to accepted standards of data collection, analysis, and presentation. At last, I had a chance to write about some things that I believed I understood without focusing on methodological concerns. I believe that the major contribution of most of my research has been to provide grounded frameworks (not prescriptive models) that faculty

[6] Consolidating material is, of course, one of the primary motivations of many faculty members who write books that can be used as texts. Another is to organize the material in the way that the professor finds most meaningful.

and administrators can use to stimulate their creative thinking about curriculum planning at the course, program, and college-wide level. In the book, I tried to present frameworks in a way that would suggest ideas to faculty members rather than challenge their competence or autonomy as curriculum designers.[7]

A notable exception is the chapter on administering academic plans. My students tested the first draft with several administrators and learned that they preferred more definitive guidance. Thus, that one chapter contains checklists of steps administrators might take.

Among researchers, the academic plan framework has been popular as a heuristic, and it is guiding both dissertations and analyses of existing curricula. Administrators have used the book for faculty workshops, and it gets substantial use as a text in higher education programs. Based on a typical diffusion time over ten years, I anticipate that faculty members will become conversant with the idea of the curriculum as an academic plan by about 2010!

The Final Project?

A former dean at Syracuse whom I knew when I was an undergraduate was a single woman in her late fifties. She always joked that she hadn't realized that the last man who asked for her hand in marriage would be the last. (It turned out he wasn't, since she found her soul-mate after age 60!) In the same sense, the project we call CLUE (Curriculum Leadership for Undergraduate Education) seems to be my last research project, but one never knows. This project picked up a temporarily abandoned research thread from NCRIPTAL. During NCRIPTAL, Mal and I and several graduate students had completed an exploratory study of program-level curriculum planning and published a slightly modified version of the contextual filters model suited to this collaborative activity. This single study confirmed earlier research that external catalysts were important in bringing about curriculum change (Hefferlin, 1969). But we also found that leadership at the department and institutional level was crucial (Stark, Lowther, Sharp, & Arnold, 1997). That is, the leadership for design of coherent programmatic plans must come from within academic departments.

Unfortunately, department chairpersons and faculty members are not always willing to take the lead for programmatic changes, nor do they necessarily have the expertise in curriculum planning and teaching to do so. In *Shaping the College Curriculum*, I wrote about departmental leadership based on my own experience and the accumulated wisdom of others (Lucas, 1994, Tucker, 1992). At

[7] One thing I've discovered about working with faculty members is that they frequently like to give input. It is helpful to label products "draft" or "preliminary" so faculty can feel they are helping to shape research. It is also helpful to provide many open-ended questions on questionnaires so they can comment freely. They will do so anyway.

the time, I was struck with how little actual research I could find to support that wisdom. Just what do academic departments that regularly examine their curriculum look like? What type of leaders do they have? What contextual factors influence the success of the planning processes they initiate? Can we find models of effective planning to help faculty improve how they make academic plans in their group settings? Fortunately for me, a new doctoral student, Charlotte Briggs, was also interested in these questions, and I acquired yet another close colleague in my research.

We first developed a literature-based conceptual framework which has as its central concepts an individual's acceptance of a leadership role, his or her leader behaviors, and the expertise he or she possesses to be a curriculum leader. This individual may be the department chair or another faculty member. Of course the leader is influenced by context — specifically the cultures of the discipline, department, and institution — and by current catalysts for curriculum change. Based on this framework, we set out to study context, roles, curriculum planning processes, and curriculum decisions in departments that are especially attentive to regular self-appraisal and curriculum development for undergraduate programs. We identified such departments in many disciplines and institutional types by seeking nominations from randomly selected provosts, and we have learned about the departments in two ways — by surveying the chairs of nominated departments (with a gratifying 76% return) and by interviewing selected chairpersons and some very active faculty members.[8]

We are still analyzing a large volume of information. So far, we have learned that academic department chairs whose departments have a reputation for effectiveness in curriculum planning carry out a wide variety of leadership activities that foster teamwork, engage their faculty groups in discussion, and actively gather information from the external environment. However, especially in large, complex departments, leadership is exercised not only by the chair but by various committee leaders and course coordinators. Chairs and other leaders in effective departments keep curriculum planning and decision-making on the front burner through a great variety of major and minor, direct and symbolic, approaches. Chairs and other leaders are also managers to ensure that the program plans are implemented. Furthermore, they do so without having very clear signals from their deans about what is expected from them regarding curriculum leadership.

As the chairs and other faculty leaders told us about their roles as curriculum leaders, two problems stood out. First, despite recent state and institutional requirements, very few departments are actually assessing student outcomes or regularly collecting any other information. Those who do gather data seldom use

[8] In its second year, data collection for CLUE was partially supported by a small grant from the Spencer Foundation.

it for curriculum planning. The department chairs know they need new skills to carry out these tasks, and they are apprehensive because they don't know where to get the expertise. Second, we found that even chairs of effective departments seldom deliberately develop and improve their own curriculum planning skills or those of faculty members with whom they work. They are rarely involved with others on their own campuses or in professional organizations to enhance these skills. Clearly these two deficiencies, even in purportedly exemplary departments, suggest some practical remedies on campuses.

Like my previous studies, Project CLUE seeks to develop models of good practice for faculty to consider rather than to offer prescriptions. To this end, we found it necessary for research purposes to judge how strongly each department in our study reflects continuous curriculum planning practices. Based on the interviews and relevant literature, we developed four criteria for identifying a "continuous planning department" and five measures for assessing each criterion (Briggs, Stark, & Rowland-Poplawski, 2000). We believe that these criteria will provide another useful framework for departmental self-study.

COMMENTS ON CHANGING TIMES

Over the past few decades, debates about various research paradigms have made it clear that what researchers see depends upon their perspectives. I hardly need say, therefore, that my particular interests in academic and organizational issues and in research design have defined the changes I find worth noting during my career in higher education.[9]

My view has been that academic planning, including teaching as the implementation of curriculum design, is the heart of the educational enterprise. As such, academic planning is an arena worthy of intensive research that may suggest strategies for continuous improvement. It is also worth teaching about, so that future generations of faculty and administrators can play a strong role in educational leadership.

Teaching and Learning Take Center Stage

A fortunate aspect of my career is that my area of interest has moved from the periphery in higher education research to center stage. Ideas that circulated in the mid-1980s, during the "era of curriculum reform," often expressed quite contradictory views about what should be taught and learned in college. One could not agree with all of these disparate views, but the discussions they provoked did revitalize interest in teaching and learning. Among the catalysts for

[9] Of course there are many more trends that others have traced. See, for example, Hendley, 2000, Dezure, 2000, Levine, 2000.

this unprecedented interest in improving college teaching are new conceptions of learning (including the social construction of knowledge) — new active pedagogical approaches such collaborative learning, and learning communities — and new ways of assessing learning, such as classroom research. Faculty members are grappling with an increasingly diverse student body, incorporating new technology, and promoting community service. Institutions are coping more actively than ever before with the need to train graduate students for teaching, to provide development opportunities for current faculty, and to adjust the balance of teaching and research.

I can personally compare the substantial improvements in the years between 1985 and 2000 with the 1970-1985 period, when many innovations were tried and several experimental colleges were founded (only a few of which survived with their original plans). In the 1970s, student discontent was a potent force for change, so colleges concentrated on eliminating irritants by loosening the calendar and reducing requirements. In the 1990s, government initiatives, public opinion, and technology have converged to encourage a broader reconsideration of educational purpose and process. I have the sense that today's changes are sounder and more enduring because they less often tinker with such structures as calendars and grading systems and more often build on research about how students learn and how faculty change. Colleges today clearly are receptive to curriculum experimentation that holds promise for improving student learning outcomes.

Governmental and Institutional Relations

Another substantial change I have observed involves the entrance of the federal government directly into the affairs of higher education and the reactions of colleges to this intervention. At Teachers College, Columbia, in the late 1950s we debated the question "Will federal control follow federal aid?" By 1975, the answer was clearly yes. The debate repeated itself at the state level in the early Seventies. New York and Maryland (where I resided then) both started supplying funds to independent colleges, based on numbers of graduates. I recall that only a few months after the first state check arrived at Goucher College, we received notice that the state would inventory our facilities to determine why the campus was so spacious!

The intensifying relationships between higher education institutions and state and federal governments have required colleges and universities to expand administrative staff several times during the last forty years. Among the causes for increased administrative personnel are financial aid regulations, employment rules, student privacy provisions, crime reporting requirements, health and safety systems, and grants that require detailed accounting. Nor are such relationships optional today. Research universities as we know them could not exist without the significant funding they have come to expect from various federal agencies. Only one or two small colleges have tried, with varying success, to teach and organize without the constraints of federal largesse.

However, colleges are learning, I believe, to turn regulations to their own advantage. The assessment of student learning is an interesting example of colleges and universities creatively interpreting government regulations. Much of the original initiative for assessing learning was based on the view that colleges should be held accountable. Many colleges deeply involved with assessment have successfully redirected these initiatives to focus on improvement-guided assessment. In other words, when a government initiative is well-intentioned but misguided or poorly executed, colleges frequently step in to improve the idea.

Government regulations about affirmative action are another case in point. Colleges are no longer following affirmative action rules as originally conceived, but are creatively administering the regulations. In the early 1980s, when I was a dean, the university had affirmative action watchdogs who required hiring officials to close a search at the end of an application period, and then to consider on an equal basis only those who had formally applied. A great deal of paperwork documented the supposed fairness of this process, which was certainly an advance over the anti-nepotism rules that affected me in the 1960s. Today, colleges have accepted affirmative searches as the correct thing to do. They actively recruit for women and minorities but these searches have again moved behind the scenes. Now the operative mode is to leave the search open for a lengthy period while you persuade the under-represented person you have already selected to apply. This new recruitment mode, which I have been assured is not limited to my own institution, resembles the "old boy" network, but it is more inclusive. Colleges still seek to find the very best candidate but with a broader view of who that might be. The result is quite positive. For example, more than half of the administrators at the vice-president and dean level at the University of Michigan are now women. That conference table where I felt somewhat isolated as one of only two women deans has a quite different look and feel today.

Because of the trend toward increased government funding and regulation, higher education scholars now frequently discuss the extent to which their research agendas should be shaped by public policy issues. For the type of research I do, the question of influencing state or federal policy is less salient than it is for my colleagues who study finance or student retention. In contrast to those concerned with influencing government policies, the nexus of research and educational policy of greatest interest to me is at the institutional level where academic programs are developed and implemented. I see three ways in which higher education scholars can and do produce research that is policy relevant at the institutional level: (a) research on enacted policies or operating programs, (b) research on proposed policies or programs, and (c) research on future or potential policies or programs that are still in someone's imagination.

First, when we do research on operating programs, we are doing evaluative research to help policy makers determine whether the programs are meeting their goals. Here, the existing policy clearly shapes the research, and the decision makers are very likely to listen immediately. Examples are the consulting work I did with Philadelphia College of Textiles and Science and with the Accounting Education Commission. In each of these cases, while I learned a great deal about the actual processes of curriculum change, my primary role was to help policy makers who were eager to improve their decisions.

Second, when we focus on proposed policies or programs, we are trying to bring research knowledge to bear on someone's idea of what might be appropriate or expedient to do in the future. Our research results may or may not be used (or usable) to facilitate a good decision. This was the case with both Project CHOICE and the Professional Preparation Network. Although we explored and made strong cases for providing better information and for integrating liberal and professional study, not all institutions listened and used the ideas we developed.

Third, when we research ideas that have not yet been translated into proposals or that may result in policies not yet imagined, we conduct pure or basic research. In such cases the researcher is seeking truth, hoping to add to the accumulation of information about an issue of interest. The accumulated knowledge may or may not eventually inform policies or programs that cannot be foreseen. In this instance, the researcher's primary obligation is to follow acceptable research standards in the search for new knowledge and to make the research findings widely available. Examples from my own work are the development of the contextual filters model for course planning, the definition of curriculum as an academic plan with eight decision elements, the elucidation of disciplinary differences, and a typology of professional programs to guide further research (Stark, 1998). For the moment, no one may care about this research, a possibility that, to me, does not lessen the value of the research.

Erosion of the Tenure System

Numerous critics writing in a muckraking mode about faculty roles have joined with various reform commissions to criticize higher education. Some of these critics blame the faculty tenure system for nearly all identifiable ills. Over the last ten years, a substantial erosion of the tenure system has been fueled in part by these critiques, in part by the recognition that adjunct faculty already outnumber tenure-track faculty in many colleges, and in part by national discussions promoted by AAHE about alternatives to tenure. On the one hand, a few institutions are openly examining the arguments for and against tenure, and some are deciding to abolish it. On the other hand, many prestigious institutions, including my own, are quietly and covertly eroding tenure by hiring large numbers of "clinical" and "practice" faculty rather than regular professors.

Those engaged in this slow and stealthy process of destroying tenure obviously are not well versed in the events of the early 1900s and the dangers they are inflicting on creative research and teaching. They will be long gone, of course, when that history repeats itself. Given current trends, I am convinced that, at some point in the future, professors will once again find that they must defend themselves against arbitrary and capricious dismissal because of unpopular views. They will also find, no doubt, that many subjects with small enrollments, including many of the liberal arts fields, will disappear from the scene as contract employees are not rehired. When these events occur, faculty unions may or may not be ready or able to protect academic freedom as effectively as tenure. Although tenure is surely abused in a minority of cases, I hope administrators can learn to deal with the abuses forthrightly, rather than evade or weaken tenure by making short-term appointments. But as the demise of tenure approaches, I cannot be optimistic about the future of the higher education enterprise.

Growth of Technology

Over the course of my career, technology growth has been perhaps the greatest influence on the operation of higher education and research about it. I distinctly recall Dr. Bulger dictating personally to a secretary who took shorthand. As an administrator, I gained a bit more efficiency by dictating on tiny tapes that I could use at any hour of the day or night. But even with dictation, completing a manuscript involved much retyping, which fostered thinking about production mechanics rather than about the substance of what one was writing. Now, with computers, we produce a manuscript without even knowing how to spell, send it to an assistant for tidying up, and instantly forward it to colleagues for their input. Perhaps we now run even greater risks of not thinking enough about the substance before sending our first thoughts far and wide.

The computer has also revolutionized data collection and analysis. For my dissertation, I bought a $500 hand calculator that could take square roots; today the same calculator costs less than $10. Next we moved to punching cards and programming the computer with complex syntax statements to produce our calculations. Now we can collect our survey data or schedule our interviews on the Internet, do complex statistical analysis on the desktop computer by merely pointing and clicking, and import the tables and graphs produced directly into a written report.

This technology releases us from menial tasks, but an inverse relationship may exist between ease of analysis and careful thought. Too many statistical reports show evidence that researchers do not understand the operations they are performing. Recently, I have been working with qualitative data analysis programs like QSR Nudist Vivo. With these tools, the memory of the computer combines with the interpretation of the researcher to analyze masses of material in short order but, especially in this interpretative kind of research, no one has found a way to avoid the limitations of too little thought.

Other important and more positive results of technological advance have been the increased communication between students and faculty by e-mail and the use of the World Wide Web as an instructional device in almost every field.[10]

The influence of technology does not stop with new instructional processes. From our CLUE data, doctoral student Jean Rowland-Poplawski is extracting examples that show how technology is fundamentally transforming curriculum planning, including altering the purposes of courses and programs.

Emergence of the Formal Study of Higher Education

Doctoral programs in higher education had just begun when I started my career. I had the unusual good fortune of helping to shape one such program in its early stages and then to teach in two others. I believe these programs have an important role to play in the future of higher education. Graduates are in increasing demand as administrators in many colleges, universities and policy agencies. At last, many administrators with traditional disciplinary credentials have begun to read higher education research and to ask for advice from higher education programs.

By no means, however, has the prejudice against academic administrators with credentials in education (which I experienced early in my career) disappeared entirely. [11]

Despite the increasing awareness of higher education research, some faculty members still believe that only those with doctoral degrees in fields like history or philosophy are equipped to guard the values of a college. In other words, "colleges are not businesses and do not need managers." I believe the oft-heard debate about whether higher education is or is not a business is nonproductive. Like any other modern organization, a college has some aspects that

[10]Automated registration at some institutions has almost totally eliminated meetings between students and their advisors.

[11]Yet most colleges now avail themselves more freely of research literature and concepts from education than heretofore — to cite a familiar example, Goucher College, where I began by conducting some small institutional research studies, now has a director of institutional research.

need to be conducted like a business and other aspects that need to be organized in ways unique to its key purposes. The executive officer in charge of business affairs needs to remember the primary purpose of the university, and the executive officer in charge of academic programs needs to know that good management can further this goal as well. This fact carries a message for higher education programs: well-designed higher education programs should be producing graduates who are not models of either extreme.

By a well-designed higher education program, I mean that the curriculum should be comprehensive rather than narrowly specialized. At Michigan we have been fond of saying that we prepare scholar-administrators. By this we mean that our graduates who move into administrative positions should be prepared to examine issues analytically, inclined to sponsor inquiry when appropriate, and be open-minded to research results regardless of whether they contradict or reinforce traditional wisdom. At the same time, our graduates who move into positions as researchers and scholars of higher education should have sufficient experience in faculty and administrative roles that they understand the enterprise they are studying. They should be sufficiently flexible to move back into administration occasionally, to learn from the changing times. To foster this flexibility and reciprocity, I believe that doctoral students should have two internships, one in administration and one in research.

In addition, the course of study should be designed so that the graduate will be neither strictly a business manager nor an academic with no management skills. The doctoral program should include an in-depth study of the history of higher education. It should include a study of factors affecting the cognitive development of both traditional and non-traditional college students of all ages. It should include curriculum theory and development, organizational and administrative theory, financial management, personnel management, and sufficient attention to legal issues to know when an attorney should be consulted. Above all, it should include study in the techniques of educational evaluation and assessment which are too often neglected.

In addition, doctoral study in higher education should build on research expertise that includes a wide variety of both quantitative and qualitative methods. And finally, since the experiences that led me to research came from social psychology rather than education, I believe that students should study at the master's level in a cognate field relevant to their interests and build on this disciplinary foundation in their thesis work. Beyond this, students should have specialized course work in the area of higher education of greatest interest to them. For example, someone who intends a government career should study public policy issues, based on a solid background in political science and economics. But the total program must be much broader than a single student's interests.

Professional Growth and Associations

The Association for the Study of Higher Education (ASHE) has been my professional home base throughout the years. It is the place where I try out new ideas and argue with my colleagues, and it is the group whose respect I seek. ASHE and I grew up together professionally. Over the years, the annual conference has changed a great deal. When I was a graduate student, a few professors met informally on a Sunday afternoon before AAHE. Now an organization of over one thousand members with a respected scholarly journal, ASHE has a full-fledged conference of its own and has changed positively in many other ways. It has become more diverse in its membership and fosters a wide variety of research methods and growth opportunities for doctoral students; but there are negative changes, too. Over time, I think the association members have lost the talent of conducting dialogue that is analytical and critical, yet friendly and supportive. As a result, the delivery, without comment, of papers that are methodologically poor or logically inconsistent provides a negative role model for young scholars. We need to relearn the techniques of constructive, scholarly criticism so that we can use them effectively in public as well as in private.

I continue to attend and present papers at ASHE and the Association for Institutional Research (AIR) regularly. I used to attend several other conferences each year, but some are far too large for colleagueship, and some have become zealots for particular causes or specific innovations. At some conferences, presentations seem to be merely "show and tell" for campus or individual public relations. Unfortunately, these conferences have a great deal of potential to influence higher education leaders, faculty and the public. Yet the causes and innovations they tout, when not based in solid research, may not always be in the best interest of the enterprise. In general, all "scholar-administrators" ought to attend at least one annual conference where research is the primary agenda.

Dreams for the Future

Since I was trained to express views well grounded in data, I feel quite uncomfortable with predictions. In any case, I believe it is more productive to dream than to predict. Failed predictions are likely to be disappointments but fulfilled dreams may bring joy. Consequently, I will share some of my dreams for higher education by the end of the first quarter of the 21st century.

Improved Curriculum Planning and Evaluation

I dream that distance learning will provide a strong impetus for improved curriculum planning. Planning an on-line course will require more advance preparation than some faculty have found necessary in the privacy of their classrooms. In addition, distance learning courses are likely to be team efforts, involving not only the discipline expert but persons who specialize in learning strategies, assessment strategies, and technological delivery. Instructional designers have been advocating this team approach for years. Now it seems closer to fruition.

I dream that both departmental faculty leaders and faculty members who coordinate general education programs will cultivate the skills needed to exercise strong curriculum leadership. Fulfillment of such a dream will require that deans and vice presidents take the role of the department chair seriously and provide appropriate professional development and guidance.

A crucial but unanswered question is this: does the design of a college course or program affect student learning? If so, how? I believe that current knowledge from qualitative and survey research forms a strong base for a return to experimental design to help answer this question. I dream that controlled experiments will accompany intensive qualitative study of classrooms to test various curriculum designs and pedagogical approaches.

Most research on student achievement focuses on outcome measures at the institutional level, even though students' educational growth may more likely happen at the program and department level (Pascarella, 1985). Assessment at the program level is important to help students judge their own progress, to help students understand why they are learning certain concepts and skills, to help faculty members understand students' development, to help faculty members improve the academic program, and to help faculty members respond to changing times. Assessment really has three types: (a) describing what students can do, (b) describing how students have changed, and (c) attributing how students have changed to an educational program. The third type requires knowledge of students' beginning and ending capabilities to control for related skills and knowledge they already possessed. I dream that every academic department will employ one faculty member, trained in assessment skills, to conduct attributional studies of that department's educational efforts. This person will also assist colleagues in conducting classroom assessments.

To carry out effective assessment, faculty must grapple with the hard question of defining educational quality. Considerations for gathering evidence of quality include such questions as: (a) What are the characteristics of the person, program, unit, or institution about which judgments of quality are to be made? (b) What signifies the attainment of specified goals and objectives? (c) What is the standard or reference point to be used for comparison, and (d) What are the appropriate data collection and analytical procedures, given the nature of the evidence? I dream that faculty will find answers to such questions in their department and program units.

Professional Development for Faculty and Graduate Students

College teaching is a profession yet, unlike other prestigious fields such as law and medicine, it requires no specific training to be admitted to practice. I dream that by 2025 all colleges and universities will hire only doctoral graduates who have studied educational and disciplinary research in curriculum planning, learning theory, teaching strategies, and professional ethics and who have completed a successful teaching internship. I dream that journals in all disciplines and associations will have pedagogical sections on the "scholarship of teaching" (Boyer, 1990) that are avidly read by aspiring college teachers and senior faculty members alike. And, of course, I hope that the creativity of these faculty members will be protected by tenure. Increased professionalism (not professionalization!) of college teachers can do much to offset criticisms leading to the gradual demise of tenure that I described earlier.

Better Synthesis and Translation of Research

In my experience, higher education professionals will eventually use good basic research if it is synthesized and disseminated. Examples include the many positive uses of that information resulting from Ernest Pascarella and Patrick Terenzini's synthesis of the literature on how college affects students (1991), and Tom Angelo and Pat Cross's work on classroom assessment (1993).

Everyone develops positive role models during his or her career. I have come to admire colleagues who have important things to say and can say them in a simple and straightforward way that is appealing to faculty and administrators as well as researchers. Bob Pace, Bill McKeachie and Pat Cross are outstanding examples. Such people are effective translators between the research community and those who use research. Some colleagues constantly urge higher education researchers to mold their research into forms that will be directly useful to policy makers. I think it unlikely that most researchers can do this well; most of us were too thoroughly trained to highlight research limitations rather than to present unequivocal results and implications. Therefore, I think it is important to cultivate and support good synthesizers and translators who can carry the word effectively. I dream that in 2025, the scholar who synthesizes research in ways that make it useful to faculty members and administrators will get as much acclaim as the researchers. I expect that some of these scholars will be future graduates of higher education programs.

Eliminate Dichotomies

Perhaps because of the way academics are trained as critical scholars, we seem to have more than our share of dichotomies and polarizations. Most of these are false dichotomies, I believe, and with a bit of effort could be converted to positive influences. I think here of the unnecessary polarization between those who do qualitative and quantitative research, when the real issue is which method or combination of methods will answer the questions. I think also of the tension that sometimes exists between those who administer and those who teach, when the real issue is how to work together to provide the best possible education for students. I think of the tension between the sciences and non-sciences that typically accompanies curriculum discussions, when the real issue is to provide students with a balance of knowledge and perspectives. And, of course, I think of the continued polarization between liberal and professional study, when the real issue is how to integrate what students learn to help them be successful at both their lives and their professions. I dream that all such unnecessary dichotomies will be converted to productive interactions.

CONCLUDING THOUGHT

In my years as a higher education scholar and administrator, I have tried to contribute energy, enthusiasm, efficiency, and curiosity, and to mentor students and younger scholars. In return, my career has given back challenge, autonomy, and positive feedback from my doctoral students and from peers whose views I value. What more could one ask from a career that was never planned in the first place?

References

Angelo, T. A., & Cross, K. P. (1993). *Classroom Assessment Techniques: A Handbook for Faculty.* San Francisco: Jossey-Bass.

Armour, R. A., & Fuhrmann, B. S. (Eds.) (1989). *Integrating Liberal Learning and Professional Education. New Directions for Teaching and Learning*, No. 40. San Francisco: Jossey-Bass.

Association of American Colleges (1985). *Integrity in the College Curriculum: A Report to the Academic Community*. Washington, DC: The Association.

Association of American Colleges, Project on Liberal Learning, Study-in-Depth, and the Arts and Sciences Major. (1991a). *The Challenge of Connecting Learning.* Washington, DC: The Association.

Association of American Colleges, Project on Liberal Learning, Study-in-Depth, and the Arts and Sciences Major. (1991b). *Reports from the Fields.* Washington, DC: The Association.

Bennett, W. (1984). *To Reclaim a Legacy: A Report on the Humanities in Higher Education.* Washington, DC: National Endowment for the Humanities.

Boyer, E. L. (1987). *College: The undergraduate experience in America.* Princeton, NJ: Carnegie Foundation for the Advancement of Teaching.

Boyer, E. L. (1990). *Scholarship Reconsidered: Priorities of the Professoriate.* Princeton, NJ: Carnegie Foundation for the Advancement of Teaching.

Briggs, C. L., Stark, J. S., & Rowland-Poplawski, J. (2000, November). *How do we know a continuous planning department when we see one?* Paper presented at the annual meeting of the Association for the Study of Higher Education, Sacramento, CA.

Cheney, L. V. (1989) *50 Hours: A Core Curriculum for College Students.* Washington, DC: National Endowment for the Humanities.

Clifford, G. J., & Guthrie, J. (1988). *Ed School: A Brief for Professional Education.* Chicago: University of Chicago Press.

Dezure, D (2000, September). Three Decades of Lessons on Teaching and Learning. *AAHE Bulletin*, 53(1): 3-5.

Eljamal, M., Sharp, S., Stark, J. S., Arnold, G., & Lowther, M. .A. (1998). Listening for disciplinary differences in faculty goals for effective teaching. *Journal of General Education*, 47(2): 117-148.

Eljamal, M., Stark, J. S., Arnold, G., & Sharp, S. (1999). *Intellectual development: A complex teaching goal. Studies in Higher Education*, 24(1): 7-25.

Feldman, K. A., & Newcomb, T. R. (1970). *The Impact of College on Students.* San Francisco: Jossey-Bass.

Hefferlin, JB L. (1969). *Dynamics of Academic Reform.* San Francisco: Jossey-Bass.

Hendley, V. (2000, March,). 30 years of higher education. *AAHE Bulletin.* 52 (7): 3-8

Lattuca, L. R., & Stark, J. S. (1995). Modifying the major: Discretionary thoughts from ten disciplines. *The Review of Higher Education*, 18(3): 315-343.

Lattuca, L. R., & Stark, J. S. (1994). Will disciplinary perspectives impede curriculum reform? *Journal of Higher Education*, 65(4): 401-426.

Levine, A. E. (2000, October, 27). The future of colleges: 9 inevitable changes. *The Chroni-*

cle of Higher Education.

Lucas, A. F. (1994). *Strengthening Departmental Leadership.* San Francisco: Jossey-Bass.

National Commission on Excellence. (1983). *A Nation at Risk: The Imperative for Education Reform.* Washington, DC: US Department of Education.

National Institute of Education. (1984). *Involvement in Learning: Realizing the Potential of American Higher Education.* Report of the NIE Study Group on the Condition of Excellence in American Higher Education. Washington, DC: U.S. Government Printing Office.

Pace, C. R. (1983). *Measuring the Quality of College Student Experiences.* Los Angeles: University of California, Higher Education Research Institute.

Pascarella, E. T. (1985). College environmental influences on learning and cognitive development: A critical review and synthesis. In J. C. Smart (Ed.), *Higher Education: Handbook of Theory and Research* Vol. I. New York: Agathon.

Pascarella, E. T., & Terenzini, P. T. (1991). *How College Affects Students.* San Francisco: Jossey-Bass.

Stark, J. S. (1972). The 4-1-4 bandwagon. *Journal of Higher Education*, 43(5): 381-390.

Stark, J. S. (1973). The three-year B.A: Who will choose it? Who will benefit? *Journal of Higher Education*, 44(9): 703-715.

Stark, J. S. (1975). The relation of disparity in student and faculty educational attitudes to early student transfer from college. *Research in Higher Education*, 3(4): 329-344.

Stark, J. S. (1976). Promoting consumer protection for students. *New Directions for Higher Education*, No. 13. San Francisco: Jossey-Bass.

Stark, J .S. (1998). Classifying professional preparation programs. *Journal of Higher Education*, 69(4), 353-383.

Stark, J. S., and Associates (1977), *The Many Faces of Educational Consumerism.* Lexington, MA: D.C. Heath.

Stark, J. S., Bentley, R. J., Lowther, M. A., & Shaw, K. M. (1991). The student goals exploration: Reliability and concurrent validity. *Educational and Psychological Measurement*, 51:413-422.

Stark, J. S., & Lattuca, L. R. (1997). *Shaping the College Curriculum.* Needham Heights, MA: Allyn & Bacon.

Stark, J. S., & Lowther, M. A. (1988). Perspectives on course and program planning. In J. S. Stark, and L. A. Mets (Eds.). Improving Teaching and Learning through Research. *New Directions for Institutional Research*, No. 57. San Francisco: Jossey-Bass.

Stark, J. S., & Lowther, M. A. (1988). *Strengthening the Ties That Bind: Integrating Undergraduate Liberal and Professional Study.* Ann Arbor: The University of Michigan. Center for the Study of Higher Education.

Stark, J. S., Lowther, M. A. & Hagerty, B. M. K. (1986). Responsive Professional Education: Balancing Outcomes and Opportunities. (*ASHE-ERIC Higher Education Research Reports No. 3.*) Washington, DC: The George Washington University and the Association for the Study of Higher Education.

Stark, J. S., Lowther, M. A. & Hagerty, B. M. K. (1987). Faculty perceptions of professional preparation environments: Testing a conceptual framework. *Journal of Higher*

Education, 58(5): 530-541.

Stark, J. S., Lowther, M. A., Bentley, R. J., & Martens, G. G. (1990). Disciplinary differences in course planning. *The Review of Higher Education*, 13(2): 141-165.

Stark, J. S., Lowther, M. A., Hagerty, B. M. K., & Orczyk, C. (1986). A conceptual framework for the study of pre-service professional preparation programs in colleges and universities. *Journal of Higher Education*, 57 3): 231-258.

Stark, J. S., Lowther, M. A., Ryan, M. P., & Genthon, M. (1988). Faculty reflect on course planning. *Research in Higher Education*, 29(3): 219-240.

Stark, J. S., & Marchese, T. J. (1978). Auditing college publications for prospective students. *Journal of Higher Education*, 49(1): 82-92.

Stark, J. S., & Morstain, B. R. (1978). Educational orientations of faculty in liberal arts colleges: An analysis of disciplinary differences. *Journal of Higher Education*, 49(5): 420-437.

Stark, J. S., Shaw, K. M., & Lowther, M. A. (1989). Students Goals for College and Courses: A Missing Link in Assessing and Improving Teaching and Learning. (*ASHE-ERIC Higher Education Reports*, No. 6.) Washington, DC: The George Washington University and Association for the Study of Higher Education.

Toombs, W. (1977-78). The application of design-based curriculum analysis to general education. *The Review of Higher Education*, 1: 18-29.

Tucker, A. (1992). *Chairing the Academic Department: Leadership among Peers.* (3rd ed.). Phoenix: Oryx.

2. Student Motivation and Self-Regulated Learning in the College Classroom

Paul R. Pintrich and **Akane Zusho**
The University of Michigan

College student motivation is a persistent and persuasive problem for faculty and staff at all levels of postsecondary education. Faculty at community colleges, comprehensive universities, small liberal arts colleges, and private and public research universities all bemoan the lack of student motivation. The questions that college faculty and staff raise include: why don't the students seem to care about their work, why don't they seem more interested in the disciplinary content of the courses, why do they only care about their grades but not learning, why don't they try very hard, why don't they study very much, why do they procrastinate and try to study for an exam at the last minute, or try to write a paper the day before it is due, why can't they be more organized and plan their work better, and why don't they learn or perform very well. All of these issues can be partially explained by a motivation and self-regulation perspective on student learning in the college classroom. Of course, there are other models of college student cognition and learning that are relevant, but in this chapter we will focus on motivational and self-regulatory constructs. The purpose of this chapter is to provide an overview of current research on college student motivation and self-regulated learning that should provide some insights into these general problems.

Given the scope and page limitations of this chapter, we cannot review all the different theoretical models and all the research literature on the topic. In fact, we do not think a review of all the different theories and models is that helpful at this point in the development of our understanding of college student motivation and self-regulation. Accordingly, we organize our chapter around some general constructs that cut across different theoretical models; we hope that the model will then provide a conceptual framework that is useful for higher education researchers, college faculty, and college administrators and staff. In addition, we will propose some first-order principles or generalizations

J.C. Smart and W.G. Tierney (eds.), Higher Education: Handbook of Theory and Research, 55–128.

about motivation and learning based on empirical studies from our research program at Michigan as well as other studies. These generalizations should be useful in guiding future research as well as practice. The model explicitly focuses on college student motivation and self-regulation regarding academic learning, not motivation for non-academic activities (e.g., relationships, friendships, athletics, careers). Finally, the model is best applied to the college classroom or course level, not college in general, as there are other models that attempt to explain how college attendance influences a host of student outcomes including motivation and learning (see Pascarella and Terenzini, 1991).

This focus on the college classroom level has both theoretical and practical value. First, most of the current research on student motivation and self-regulation at the college and precollegiate levels has been at the classroom level and therefore is very relevant for developing a model of academic motivation and learning. More importantly, most academic student learning is situated in a college classroom or course context that includes not just the time spent in the actual classroom itself, but also the time spent outside formal class time working on the specific course tasks and assignments. Finally, a classroom level focus is the most meaningful and pragmatic for college instructors and our own teaching. We cannot change or easily influence factors outside our classroom (such as the institutional and community norms and structures, the attitudes and beliefs of the students' friends and roommates, or the students' family background and beliefs), but we can change and control what we do in our own classrooms. Of course, we are always operating under constraints in our classrooms, such as class size, time, and curriculum demands; nevertheless, we still have more control over our own classrooms than other aspects of the college environment. Accordingly, we have focused this chapter on the college classroom context and students' motivational beliefs and self-regulation in relation to various classroom and course features.

Before we discuss our general model, a description of two students who show differing patterns of motivation and self-regulation may help to ground the model in the realities of college student learning. Both Mike and Lyndsay were good students in high school, but both are having some difficulties in college. Mike studies in the same way for all his classes, even though they differ greatly in terms of their requirements (papers, exams, lab reports) and the nature of instruction (discussion, lectures, small group work). He doesn't think much about his goals for different classes, he just wants to get good grades such as an A or a B in all his courses. He studies by reading the course material over and over and when he studies for an exam, he concentrates on memorizing important terms and ideas. He finds some of his classes interesting, but others are fairly boring to him. He spends much more time on those classes where he likes the content, and as the term progresses, he finds it harder and harder to do the work in the boring classes. It always seems that when he sets aside time to work on those classes, his roommates ask him to go out with them; and he usually goes, instead of studying. He tends to wait until the week of an exam or the week a paper is due to start working on it and often feels rushed and realizes that he did not do his best work. In some of his classes his grades are fine, but in others he is getting C's or lower. When he thinks about why he does not do well in those classes, he thinks that he lacks the ability to do well in those classes — and they are boring anyway. He rarely asks other students or the instructors for help. He just keeps on working and studying the way he did in high school, since it worked for him then — although he does worry about his ability to succeed in college, since it is much harder than high school. Mike is not a terrible student. He does try to do his work and he does study, just as most college students do, but he is not as successful as he could be if he were more self-regulating.

Lyndsay approaches the same courses differently. She, too, wants to get good grades; but she also wants to learn and understand the material. She knows she will be able to use the course material in other classes and in her career, so she focuses not just on grades but on understanding. In addition, she thinks about how the courses are different and realizes that different tasks like exams and papers require different approaches to studying and learning. In some classes, where the exams test for recall, she does spend some time memorizing the important terms. However, in all her classes, when she reads the material, she tries to paraphrase it, write summaries, or make outlines of the text. This helps her see the connections between the lectures and the readings. Also, when she is studying, she gives herself mini-quizzes on the material and these self-tests help her to monitor her understanding. When she finds that she can't get 100% of the questions correct on her own quizzes, she goes back over the material and figures out what she did not understand. She also tries to keep a regular study schedule and plans her work by the week and month, so that she is not starting a paper the week it is due. Of course, when an exam is coming up or a paper is due, she concentrates on that course, but she usually feels prepared since she is not doing the work at the last minute. Of course, she finds some of the course material boring, but she makes sure she spends more time on those courses since she knows it is harder for her to concentrate on that material. She often studies with her friends. They work together, and then go out for a pizza after several hours of studying. She thinks of these pizza breaks as a reward for her studying. She also incorporates her friends into her study routine, which helps her regulate her studying and keep focused on her task, rather than having her friends be a distraction that takes her away from school work as in Mike's case. In the long run, Lyndsay will be much more successful than Mike. She may struggle with the transition to college, as do most college students, but she is using all her cognitive and motivational resources to try to become more self-regulating and a better student.

Our general model can capture some of the important differences between Mike's and Lyndsay's approaches to learning. We will first describe the general model and the components and then we will discuss the relations among the different components of the model. We will refer to the examples of Lyndsay and Mike throughout the chapter, to help the reader understand the different aspects of the model in concrete terms.

Figure 1 displays the model of student academic motivation and self-regulation in the college classroom that serves to organize this chapter. There are five major components in the model. First, there are student personal characteristics such as age, gender, and ethnicity (labeled A, in Figure 1) which are related to student motivation, self-regulation, and outcomes. There also are contextual factors (B) that include various features of the classroom environment (e.g., the different tasks that Mike and Lyndsay confront in their courses). These two factors are assumed to influence the operation of the motivational (C) and self-regulatory processes (D), the next two main components in the model. The motivational processes (C) reflect the internal thoughts and emotions that students have about themselves in relation to the context and their perceptions of that context. Both Mike and Lyndsay have goals for their learning. They think about how boring the courses are, they worry about doing well, and they wonder if they have the capabilities to succeed. Self-regulatory processes (D) include the internal strategies and processes that students can use to monitor, control, and regulate themselves. Both Mike and Lyndsay use a number of different strategies for studying and learning. The fifth factor in the model includes various student outcomes such as choice, effort, persistence, and actual achievement (E). Lyndsay and Mike make different choices about how to use their time and have different outcomes in terms of effort, persistence, and achievement.

It is important to note that although the general model is presented in a linear format with the direction of influence described as flowing from the classroom context and personal characteristics to motivation and self-regulatory processes to outcomes, this is only for ease of presentation in this chapter. Given that the model reflects a social cognitive perspective, it is assumed that all the relations between components in the model are reciprocal (Pintrich, 2000c; Zimmerman, 2000). College students' actual behavior and outcomes provide feedback to them that influences their motivation and self-regulation (dotted line flowing from box E to boxes C and D). For example, it has been shown in numerous studies that students' level of achievement (and the grades they receive) will influence their beliefs about their competence as well as their motivation in general (Bandura, 1986; Pintrich and Schunk, 1996; Weiner, 1986).

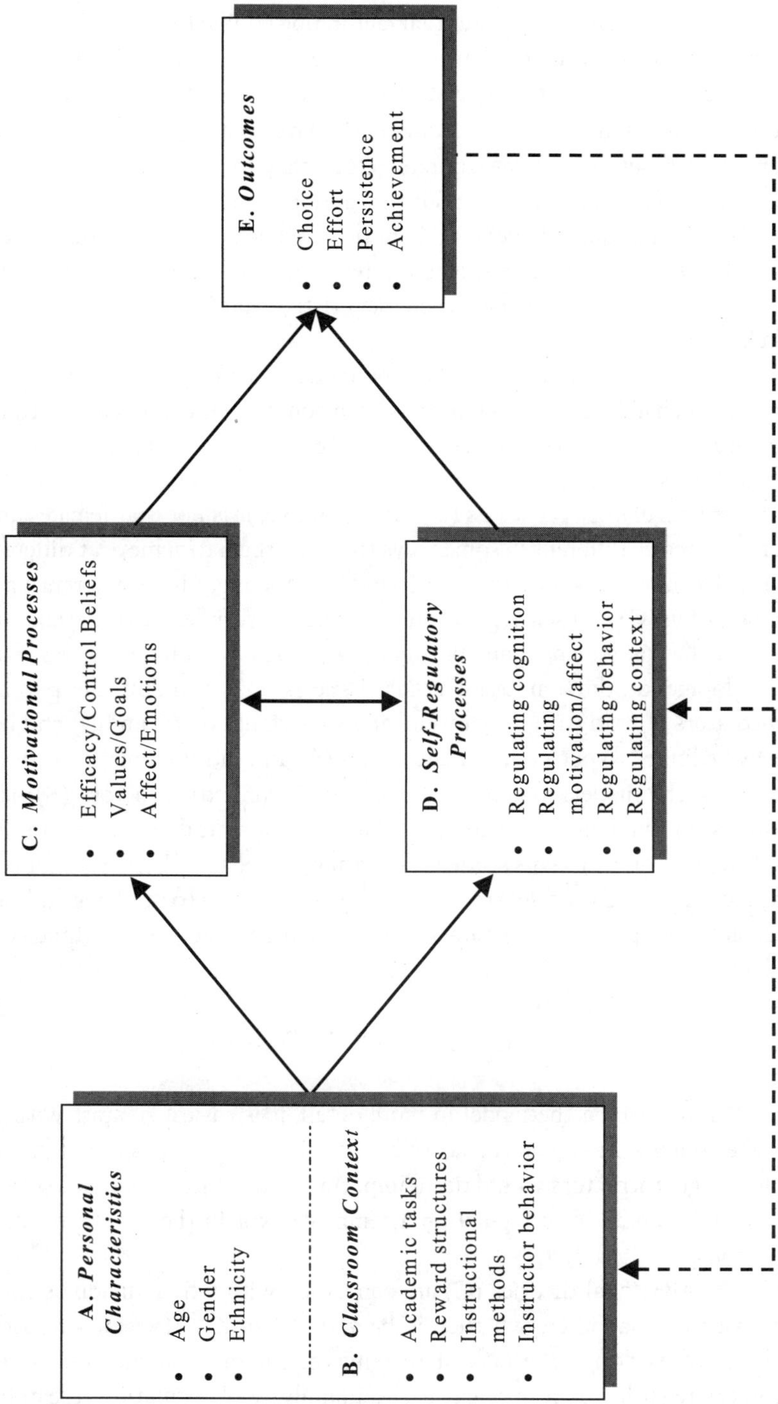

Figure 1.
A General Model for Student Motivation and Self-Regulated Learning in the College Classroom

In the same fashion, college student behavior in the class will influence the instructor's behavior (a contextual factor, dotted line from box E to B). For example, students who are actively engaged in class discussion may influence the instructor's choice of teaching strategies (e.g., a move away from lecture to more discussion). Finally, college students do have some *a priori* motivational beliefs about themselves and the course, before they even come to the first several classes, which can influence their perceptions of the college classroom context and their subsequent beliefs and behavior. Accordingly, the model represents an attempt to describe a dynamic and interacting system of the major components of classroom context, personal characteristics, motivation, self-regulation, and behavior.

It also should be noted that the model does not have a direct path from personal characteristics (A) or classroom contextual factors (B) to student outcomes (E). This reflects our assumption that the effects of personal and contextual factors on student outcomes (E) are mediated through the motivational (C) and self-regulatory processes (D). For example, it is not that females and males are inherently different in some ways that lead them to achieve at different levels (E). The model assumes that males and females might have different patterns of motivation (C) and self-regulation (D) which in turn lead to different outcomes. The same argument can be made for ethnic differences or even age-developmental differences. The key issue is understanding the psychological mediators of motivation, cognition, and self-regulation (C and D) and how they may be linked to personal characteristics (A) and the outcomes (E). In the same manner, the models assumes that classroom contextual factors (B) have their effects on outcomes (E) through their effects on student motivation (C) and self-regulation (D). This student mediating model also offers hope for educators as motivation (C) and self-regulation (D) are assumed to be changeable and malleable, whereas student characteristics (A) like gender and ethnicity are not changeable.

STUDENT OUTCOMES (E)

In describing the model in more detail, it is easiest to start with the outcome component (E) on the far right side of Figure 1. These are behaviors that all college instructors would deem important. In addition, psychological models of motivation and self-regulation attempt to explain the development of these outcomes.

Motivational theories (C) are concerned with why individuals choose one activity over another, whether it be the day-to-day decisions regarding the choice of working on a task or relaxing, or the more momentous and serious choices regarding career, marriage, and family. Self-regulation research (D) focuses on the different strategies that can be used to approach these goals or choices. In the achievement context of a college classroom, choice behaviors include students' choosing to work on the course material and study instead of watching television or talking with friends or roommates. Mike often chooses to go out with his friends instead of studying, while Lyndsay incorporates her friends into her studying patterns, thereby satisfying both the social goal of being with peers as well as the academic goal of studying. In addition, many faculty members would take as evidence of motivated behavior students' choice to take another course in their discipline, a choice to major in the discipline, or even to go on to graduate school in the discipline. In fact, many faculty members state explicitly that these latter types of choice behavior are some of the most important outcomes of their introductory classes. These choice behaviors are good exemplars of motivated behavior.

A second aspect of motivated behavior that psychological research has examined is the students' level of activity or involvement in a task. We would assume that students are motivated when they put forth a great deal of effort for our courses, from not falling asleep to more active engagement in the course. Behavioral indicators of this involvement could include taking detailed notes, asking good questions in class, being willing to take risks in class in terms of stating ideas or opinions, coming after class to office hours to discuss in more detail the ideas presented in class, discussing the ideas from the course with classmates or friends outside of class time, spending a reasonable amount of time studying and preparing for class or exams, spending more time on our course than on other activities, and seeking out additional or new information from the library or other sources that goes beyond what is presented in class. Lyndsay clearly spends more time and effort on her school work than Mike.

Besides these behavioral indicators, there are more covert or unobservable aspects of engagement which include cognitive engagement and processing, such as thinking deeply about the material, using various cognitive strategies to learn the material in a more disciplined and thoughtful manner, seeking to understand the material (not just memorize it), and integrating the new material with previously-held conceptions of the content. Lyndsay tries to use these deeper strategies, while Mike seems to rely mainly on memorization. All of these cognitive processes are crucial for deeper understanding and learning. Some of these cognitive processes will be discussed in more detail in the section on self-regulatory processes (D), but not all of them. A detailed discussion of all the various aspects of cognition that play a role in student learning is beyond the scope of this chapter. Nevertheless, it is important to note that it is not enough for students to be engaged in the course only behaviorally; they also must be cognitively engaged in order for true learning and understanding to occur.

The third general aspect of motivated behavior that has been examined in most motivational theories is persistence. If individuals persist at a task, even in the face of difficulty, boredom, or fatigue, we usually say they are motivated to do that task. Persistence is easily observable in general, although college faculty might not normally have access to the situations where the issue of persistence most readily arises for students. In precollegiate classrooms, teachers do have more opportunities to observe students actually working on course tasks during class time. It is common for teachers in precollegiate classrooms to comment on the students' willingness to persist and try hard on the class work. In contrast, college faculty often do not have the chance to see how the students work and study for their class.

However, casual observations of undergraduates studying in the library or conversations with students about their workload quickly reveal that the issue of persistence is an important one for most college students. For example, persistence is important when students confront a difficult task, whether it is working through calculus problems, balancing equations in chemistry, understanding conservative and Marxist economic theories, or applying deconstructionist theory to the interpretation of a novel; most college students will confront some tasks that are difficult for them, given their prior knowledge and skills. Students' willingness to persist in the face of these individually-defined difficult tasks is a good exemplar of motivated behavior. In addition, given their prior interests and selected majors, students may see some course material as boring or unimportant to them. Again, being able to persist at these tasks is an important feature of motivated behavior, which Lyndsay exhibits in contrast to Mike. Finally, students often have many competing demands on their time (i.e., school work, employment, social activities) and are often tired due to being involved in so many activities. In the face of this potential overexertion and fatigue, students who overcome their lassitude and continue to persist at their school work would be considered motivated.

Finally, the last outcome is student academic performance or achievement. This can be indexed by grades in the course or overall GPA. For most faculty, performance involves what the students have learned in the course including their understanding of new ideas, new theories, and new models as well as new skills (i.e., writing) or ways of thinking (i.e., critical thinking, scientific thinking, mathematical thinking). Of course, a key issue is how to assess these understandings and skills. Faculty assume that the assignments, exams, papers, and other tasks and activities that students engage in during the course should reflect these desired outcomes. However, it often is difficult, albeit not impossible, to assess these outcomes using standard multiple choice format examinations. Accordingly, there may be a need for diversity in assessment procedures in order to measure learning and understanding. In any event, student performance and achievement on all the different types of course assessments are partially a function of motivational and self-regulatory processes. Of course, they also are influenced heavily by the students cognition and prior knowledge, but we will focus on the role of motivation (C) and self-regulation (D) in this chapter. We turn now to a discussion of self-regulatory processes.

THE ROLE OF SELF-REGULATORY PROCESSES (D)

There are many different models of motivation and self-regulated learning that propose different constructs and mechanisms, but they do share some basic assumptions about learning and regulation. One common assumption might be called the active, constructive assumption, which follows from a general cognitive perspective. That is, all the models view learners as active, constructive participants in the learning process. Learners are assumed to actively construct their own meanings, goals, and strategies from the information available in the "external" environment as well as information in their own minds (the "internal" environment). College students are not just passive recipients of information from professors, parents, or other adults, but rather active, constructive meaning-makers as they go about learning. Accordingly, giving the "perfect" lecture does not necessarily mean that the students in the course will understand the material in the expected manner. The students will create their own meaning from this lecture, and part of their meaning will perhaps reflect the appropriate disciplinary knowledge, but other parts may be based on the students' own prior knowledge and misconceptions that they had when they came to the lecture hall.

A second, related assumption is the potential for control assumption. All the models assume that learners can potentially monitor, control, and regulate certain aspects of their own cognition, motivation, and behavior as well as some features of their environments. This assumption does not mean that college students will or can monitor and control their cognition, motivation, or behavior at all times or in all contexts, only that some monitoring, control, and regulation is possible. All of the models recognize that there are biological, developmental, contextual, and individual difference constraints that can impede or interfere with individual efforts at regulation.

In addition, it is clear that college students can most readily control or regulate their own personal goals for learning and understanding. There are obviously higher-order goals or standards that are defined externally by the college course (e.g., in an English course students need to write a certain way to get a good grade), or by the university (e.g., a certain GPA is what it takes to get on the Dean's List), or by society at large (e.g., the standards and requirements to become a medical doctor). These goals and standards are not readily controllable by the individual college student, but rather represent aspects of the context to which the students have to respond and adapt as they attempt to regulate their own behavior. Accordingly, to some extent, some aspects of the external environment do control or guide an individual college students' regulatory behavior. The important issue for the model discussed in this chapter is how individual college students respond to these external demands or goal stresses

A third general assumption that is made in these models of self-regulated learning — as in all general models of regulation stretching back to Miller, Galanter, and Pribram (1960) — is the goal, criterion, or standard assumption. All models of regulation assume that there is some type of criterion or standard (also called goals, reference value) against which comparisons are made in order to assess whether the process should continue as is or if some type of change is necessary. The common sense example is the thermostat operation for the heating and cooling of a house. Once a desired temperature is set (the goal, criterion, standard), the thermostat monitors the temperature of the house (monitoring process) and then turns on or off the heating or air conditioning units (control and regulation processes) in order to reach and maintain the standard. In a parallel manner, the general example for learning assumes that individuals can set personal standards or goals to strive for in their learning, monitor their progress towards these goals, and then adapt and regulate their cognition, motivation, and behavior in order to reach their goals. Mike and Lyndsay both have goals of getting good grades and they both do study. However, Lyndsay also has a goal of learning and understanding, which leads her to engage the material in a deeper manner.

A fourth general assumption of most of the models of motivation and self-regulated learning is that motivational beliefs and self-regulatory activities are mediators between personal and contextual characteristics and actual achievement or performance. That is, it is not just individuals' cultural, demographic, or personality characteristics that influence achievement and learning directly, nor just the contextual characteristics of the classroom environment that shape achievement (see Figure 1), but the individuals' motivation and self-regulation of their cognition, motivation, and behavior that mediate the relations between the person, context, and eventual achievement. Given this assumption, we do not include a direct path from personal characteristics (A) and classroom context (B) to outcomes (E) in Figure 1. Most models of self-regulation assume that self-regulatory activities (D) are directly linked to outcomes (E) such as achievement and performance, although much of the research examines self-regulatory activities as outcomes in their own right.

Given these assumptions, a general working definition of self-regulated learning is that it is an active, constructive process whereby learners set goals for their learning and then attempt to monitor, regulate, and control their cognition, motivation, and behavior, guided and constrained by their goals and the contextual features in the environment. These self-regulatory activities can mediate the relations between individuals and the context and their overall achievement. This definition is similar to other models of self-regulated learning (e.g., Butler and Winne, 1995; Zimmerman, 1989, 1998a, b; 2000). Although this definition is relatively simple, the remainder of this section outlines in more detail the various processes and areas of regulation and their application to learning and achievement in the academic domain, which reveals the complexity and diversity of the processes of self-regulated learning.

Phases of Self-Regulation

Figure 2 displays a simple four-phase model of self-regulated learning. The four phases are processes that many models of regulation and self-regulation share (e.g., Zimmerman, 1998a, b; 2000) and reflect goal-setting, monitoring, control and regulation, and self-reflection processes. These phases are suggested as a heuristic to organize our thinking and research on self-regulated learning.

Of course, not all academic learning follows these phases, as there are many occasions for students to learn academic material in more tacit or implicit or unintentional ways, without self-regulating their learning in such an explicit manner as suggested in the model. There are many cases where students study, learn, and think without much intentional or explicit goal-setting, monitoring, or attempt to control their cognition and learning. In fact, in some cases, it is important for college students to have automatized certain types of cognitive processing (e.g., basic reading skills). If students are spending most of their cognitive resources on decoding and understanding the words in a textbook, there are fewer cognitive resources left over for deeper thinking about the text material. The distinctions between consciousness and intentional, controlled or self-regulated learning in contrast to more unconscious, automatic processing or learning are still being debated in the research and represent important directions for future research. Nevertheless, there are occasions when students can bring their cognition and learning under conscious, explicit, and intentional control and the model in this chapter helps outlines the various processes involved when students do attempt to regulate their own learning.

Phase 1 involves planning and goal-setting as well as activation of perceptions and knowledge of the task and context and the self in relation to the task. For example, as Lyndsay begins a study session, she might ask herself questions such as, "what are my goals for the next three hours, what do I want to focus on as I read this course material, what do I already know about this topic?". The first two questions help frame Lyndsay's goals for her study session. These goals can then serve as the criteria she uses to help regulate her behavior. As she approaches the goals, she can note that she is making progress towards them and

Figure 2
Four Phase Model of Self-Regulated Learning

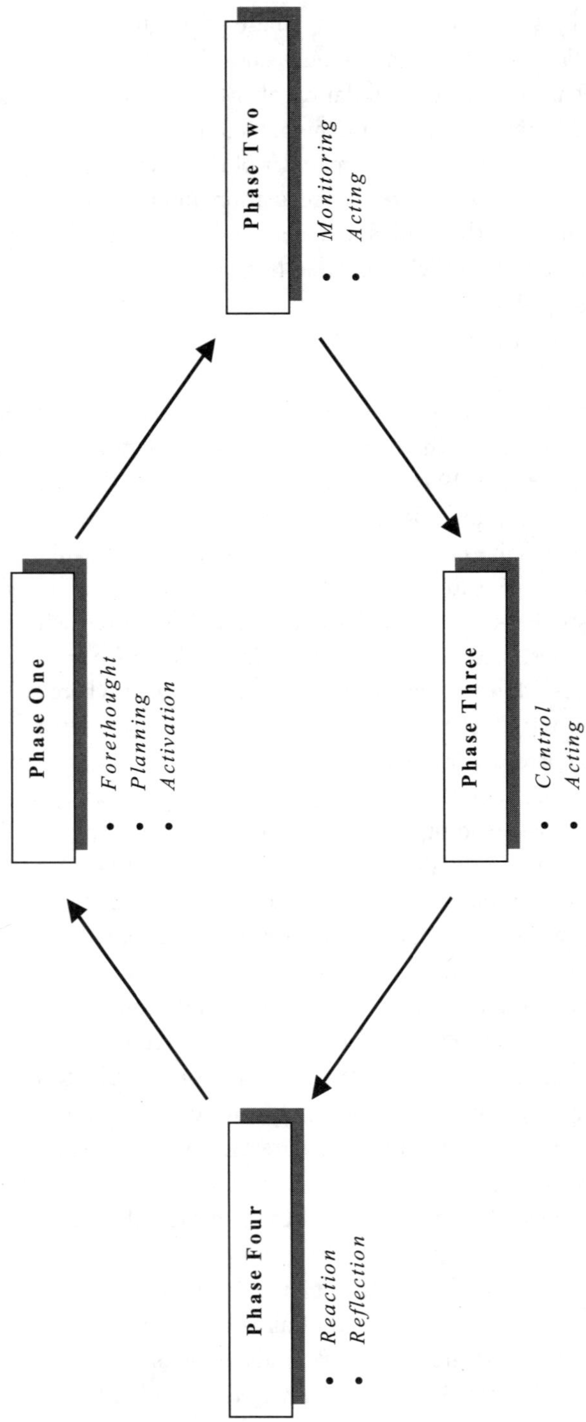

continue doing what she is doing. On the other hand, if she notes that she has not been focusing on what she set as her goals, she can adjust or change her studying to help her refocus her learning (as Lyndsay does when she goes back over material she does not understand). The last question involves the activation of prior knowledge. Prior knowledge has a huge effect on new learning, and thinking about what one already knows and how it relates to what he or she will study is a good regulatory strategy.

As the student actually starts to engage in the task, she is obviously doing certain activities and engaging in various cognitive processes (attending, comparing, analyzing, thinking, etc.). However, Phase 2 also concerns various monitoring processes that represent metacognitive awareness of different aspects of the self and task or context. For example, as she reads her textbook, Lyndsay might begin to think that she does not understand all that she is reading. This type of awareness is called metacognitive because it is "above" or about cognition. The student is basically monitoring her reading comprehension to see if she is understanding what she is reading. This type of metacognitive monitoring of learning is a very important self-regulatory process. Self-regulation depends heavily on students' monitoring what they are doing and thinking and then adjusting their behavior and cognition accordingly. The little self-quizzes that Lyndsay gives herself reflects this type of active monitoring of comprehension and understanding.

Phase 3 involves efforts to control and regulate different aspects of the self or task and context. As the student performs the task but also monitors her learning, she may come to realize that she is not understanding as much of the text as she had hoped (as Lyndsay comes to realize). One outcome of this metacognitive monitoring from Phase 2 is a decision to go back and repair her comprehension, for example, by rereading the whole text, by going back over certain parts of the text, by drawing a diagram of some of the relations between the ideas, or by taking notes on parts of the text. All of these strategies are designed to help the student regulate or control her reading comprehension, to bring her closer to the goals that she set for herself at the beginning of the task. These control and regulation processes can take place anytime during the task and help to change the behavior or cognition to make it more adaptive in terms of obtaining the goal for the task.

Finally, Phase 4 represents various kinds of reactions and reflections on the self and the task or context after the task is completed. This type of reaction often has to do with the types of attributions a student makes regarding the causes of his or her success or failure. For example, if a student thinks he was successful on a test, he can attribute it to his own high ability or effort, or he can attribute it to other factors such as good luck, the ease of the test, or another's help (such as the instructor) and many other factors. In the same way, if a student fails an exam, he can attribute it to the lack of ability (as did Mike in our earlier example) or effort on his part, bad luck, the difficulty of the task, lack of help from others, and countless other factors. The type and the nature of attribution the student makes has profound implications for future attempts at the task, future expectancies for the task, and general motivation and achievement (Pintrich and Schunk, 1996; Weiner, 1986). In general, if students attribute success to stable causes (such as high ability), they will expect to succeed in the future. In the same manner, students who attribute failure to unstable causes (such as lack of effort) will at least believe they can change the outcome in the future (Weiner, 1986). In research on college students, Perry and his colleagues (Perry, 1991; Perry and Dickens, 1988; Perry and Magnusson, 1989; Perry and Penner, 1990) have shown that students who believe they have some control over their own behavior achieve better than those who don't think they have much control. These types of reactions feed into the previous phases, especially Phase 1, and become part of the knowledge that individuals bring with them to the next task.

The four phases represent a general time-ordered sequence that individuals would go through as they perform a task, but there is no strong assumption that the phases are hierarchically or linearly structured such that earlier phases must always occur before later phases. In most models of self-regulated learning, the processes of monitoring, control, and reaction can be ongoing simultaneously and dynamically as the individual progresses through the task, with the goals and plans being changed or updated based on the feedback from theseprocesses. In fact, Pintrich, Wolters, and Baxter (2000) suggest that much of the empirical work on monitoring (Phase 2) and control/regulation (Phase 3) shows little separation of these processes in terms of people's experiences as revealed by data from self-report questionnaires or think-aloud protocols. These four phases of self-regulation can be applied to four general areas of self-regulation. Table 1 show how the four phases can be applied to four areas of self-regulation.

AREAS OF SELF-REGULATION

The four columns in Table 1 represent different areas for regulation that an individual learner can attempt to monitor, control, and regulate. The first three columns of cognition, motivation/affect, and behavior reflect the traditional tripartite division of different areas of psychological functioning (Snow, Corno, and Jackson, 1996). As Snow et al (1996) note, the boundaries between these areas may be fuzzy, but there is utility in discussing them separately, particularly since much of traditional psychological research has focused on the different areas in isolation from the others.

These first three areas in the columns in Table 1 represent aspects of the

Table 1
Phases and Areas for Self-regulated Learning

	Areas for Regulation			
Phases	Cognition	Motivation/Affect	Behavior	Context
1) Forethought, Planning, and Activation	1) Target goal setting 2) Prior content knowledge activation 3) Metacognitive knowledge activation	1) Goal orientation adoption 2) Efficacy judgments 3) Ease of learning judgments (EOLs), Perceptions of task difficulty 4) Task value activation 5) Interest activation	1) Time and effort planning 2) Planning for self-observations of behavior	1) Perceptions of task 2) Perceptions of context
2) Monitoring	1) Metacognitive awareness and monitoring of cognition (JOLs)	1) Awareness and monitoring of motivation and affect	1) Awareness and monitoring of effort, time use, need for help	1) Monitoring changing task and context conditions
3) Control	1) Selection and adaptation of cognitive strategies for learning, thinking	1) Selection and adaptation of strategies for managing motivation and affect	1) Increase/decrease effort 2) Persist, give up 3) Help-seeking behavior	1) Change or re-negotiate task 2) Change or leave context
4) Reaction and Reflection	1) Cognitive judgments 2) Attributions	1) Affective reactions 2) Attributions	1) Choice behavior	1) Evaluation of task 2) Evaluation of context

individual's own cognition, motivation/affect, and behavior that he or she can attempt to control and regulate. These attempts to control or regulate are "self-regulated" in that the individual is focused on trying to control or regulate his or her own cognition, motivation, and behavior. Of course, other individuals in the environment (such as instructors, peers, or parents) can try to "other" regulate an individual's cognition, motivation, or behavior as well, by directing or guiding the individual in terms of what, how, and when to do a task. More generally, other task and contextual features (e.g., task characteristics, feedback systems, evaluation structures) can facilitate or constrain an individual's attempts to self-regulate his or her learning.

The cognitive column in Table 1 concerns the different cognitive strategies that individuals may use to learn and perform a task as well as the metacognitive strategies individuals may use to control and regulate their cognition. Mike and Lyndsay both used a number of different cognitive and metacognitive strategies when they studied for their courses. In addition, both content knowledge and strategic knowledge are included in the cognitive column. The motivation and affect column (second column in Table 1) concerns the activation and control of various motivational beliefs that individuals may have about themselves in relation to the task, such as self-efficacy beliefs, goal orientation, and values for the task. In addition, interest or liking of the task would be included in this column as well as positive and negative affective reactions to the self or task. Finally, any strategies that individuals may use to control and regulate their motivation and affect would be included in this column. The behavior column (third column in Table 1) reflects the general effort the individual may exert on the task as well as persistence, help-seeking, and choice behaviors.

The fourth column in Table 1, context, represents various aspects of the task environment or general classroom or cultural context where the learning is taking place. Individuals do try to monitor and control their environment to some extent, and in fact, in some models of intelligence (e.g., Sternberg, 1985), attempts to selectively control and change the context are seen as very adaptable. In the same manner, in this model, it is assumed that individual attempts to monitor and control the environment is an important aspect of self-regulated learning. This area of contextual features is omitted from some models of self-regulation, as it reflects context, not the self or aspects of the individual, and in those models attempts to control the context are not considered part of self-regulation (see Boekaerts, Pintrich and Zeidner, 2000 for other models of self-regulation).

This general description of the rows and columns of Table 1 provides an overview of how the different phases of regulation relate to different areas for regulation. The next section describes in more detail the cells in the Table, organized by column.

REGULATION OF COGNITION

Table 1 displays the four general phases of self-regulation that can occur; within the first column for cognition, there are four cells going down the cognitive column that represent how these different phases may be applied to various aspects of cognition. Each of these four cells is discussed separately for rhetorical and logical reasons, including ease of presentation — although, as noted above, the phases may overlap or occur simultaneously with multiple interactions among the different processes and components. There is no strong assumption of a simple linear, static process with separable non-interacting components.

Cognitive planning and activation. At the intersection of the row for Phase 1 and the column for cognition in Table 1, there are three general types of planning or activation, 1) target goal setting, 2) activation of relevant prior content knowledge, and 3) activation of metacognitive knowledge. Target goal setting involves the setting of task-specific goals which can be used to guide cognition in general and monitoring in particular (Harackiewicz, Barron, and Elliot, 1998; Pintrich, et al., 2000; Pressley and Afflerbach, 1995; Schunk, 1994; Zimmerman, 1989; Zimmerman and Martinez-Pons, 1986, 1988). As noted above, the goal acts as a criterion against which to assess, monitor, and guide cognition, just as the temperature setting of a thermostat guides the operation of the thermostat and heating/cooling system. Of course, goal-setting is most often assumed to occur before starting a task, but goal-setting can actually occur at any point during performance. Learners may begin a task by setting specific goals for learning, goals for time use, and goals for eventual performance, but all of these can be adjusted and changed at any time during task performance as a function of monitoring, control, and reflection processes. Lyndsay set goals of both getting good grades and of understanding, while Mike only set a general goal of getting good grades.

The second aspect of forethought and planning involves the activation of relevant prior content knowledge. At some level, this process of activation of prior knowledge can and does happen automatically and without conscious thought. That is, as college students approach a task in a particular domain, for example, mathematics, some aspects of their knowledge about mathematics will be activated automatically and quickly without conscious control. This type of process would not be considered self-regulatory and involves general cognitive processing, as it is not under the explicit control of the learner. At the same time, college students who are more self-regulating can actively search their memory for relevant prior knowledge before they actually begin performing the task (Alexander, Schallert, and Hare, 1991; Flavell, 1979; Pintrich et al., 2000).

The third entry in the upper left-most cell in Table 1, the activation of metacognitive knowledge, includes the activation of knowledge about cognitive tasks and cognitive strategies and seems to be useful for learning (Pintrich et al, 2000; Schneider and Pressley, 1997). Again, as with prior content knowledge, this activation can be rather automatic, stimulated by individual, task, or contextual features or it can be more controlled and conscious. Metacognitive task knowledge includes knowledge about how task variations can influence cognition. For example, if more information is provided in a question or a test, then it will generally be more easily solved than when little information is provided. Most students come to understand this general idea and it becomes part of their metacognitive knowledge about task features. Other examples include knowing that some tasks, or the goals for the task, are more or less difficult, such as trying to remember the gist of a story versus remembering the story verbatim (Flavell, 1979).

Knowledge of strategy variables includes all the knowledge individuals can acquire about various procedures and strategies for cognition including memorizing, thinking, reasoning, problem solving, planning, studying, reading, writing, etc.. This is the area that has seen the most research and is probably the most familiar category of metacognitive knowledge. Knowledge that rehearsal strategies can help in recalling a telephone number, or that organizational and elaboration strategies can help in the memory and comprehension of text information, are examples of strategy knowledge.

Metacognitive knowledge has been broken down further into declarative, procedural, and conditional metacognitive knowledge (Alexander et al., 1991; Paris, Lipson, and Wixson, 1983; Schraw and Moshman, 1995). Declarative knowledge of cognition is the knowledge of the "what" of cognition and includes knowledge of the different cognitive strategies (such as rehearsal or elaboration) that can be used for learning. Procedural knowledge includes knowing how to perform and use the various cognitive strategies. It may not be enough to know that there are elaboration strategies like summarizing and paraphrasing; it is important to know how to use these strategies effectively. Finally, conditional knowledge includes knowing when and why to use the various cognitive strategies. For example, elaboration strategies may be appropriate in some contexts for some types of tasks (learning from text); other strategies such as rehearsal may be more appropriate for different tasks or different goals (trying to remember a telephone number). This type of conditional knowledge is important for the flexible and adaptive use of various cognitive strategies. It seems that Lyndsay has much more conditional knowledge than Mike and tries to adjust her strategy use to fit the different demands of the courses and tasks.

This is much more reflective of a self-regulating learner and helps her perform better than Mike.

Cognitive monitoring. The second cell down the cognitive column in Table 1 includes metacognitive monitoring processes. Cognitive monitoring involves the awareness and monitoring of various aspects of cognition and is an important component of what is classically labeled metacognition (Brown, Bransford, Campione, and Ferrara, 1983; Flavell, 1979; Koriat and Goldsmith, 1996; Pintrich, et al, 2000; Schneider and Pressley, 1997). In contrast to metacognitive knowledge (discussed in the previous section), which is more static and "statable" (individuals can tell whether they know it or not), metacognitive judgments and monitoring are more dynamic and process-oriented and reflect metacognitive awareness and ongoing metacognitive activities individuals may engage in as they perform a task.

One type of metacognitive judgment or monitoring activity involves judgments of learning (JOLs) and comprehension monitoring (Nelson and Narens, 1990; Pintrich et al., 2000). These judgments may manifest themselves in a number of activities, such as individuals becoming aware that they do not understand something they just read or heard, or becoming aware that they are reading too quickly or slowly given the text and their goals. Judgments of learning also would be made as students actively monitor their reading comprehension by asking themselves questions. Lyndsay does seem to make these judgments by using self-quizzes, while Mike seem to just plow on in his studying, without much metacognitive awareness. Judgments of learning also could be made when students try to decide whether they are ready to take a test on the material they have just read and studied or in a memory experiment as they try to judge whether they have learned the target words (Nelson and Narens, 1990). Pressley and Afflerbach (1995) provide a detailed listing of monitoring activities that individuals can engage in while reading. In the classroom context, besides reading comprehension or memory judgments, JOLs could involve students making judgments of their comprehension of a lecture as the instructor is delivering it or checking whether they could recall the lecture information for a test at a later point in time.

Cognitive control and regulation. Cognitive control and regulation includes the types of cognitive and metacognitive activities that individuals engage in to adapt and change their cognition. In most models of metacognition and self-regulated learning, control and regulation activities are assumed to be dependent on, or at least strongly related to, metacognitive monitoring activities, although metacognitive control and monitoring are conceived as separate processes (Butler and Winne, 1995; Nelson and Narens, 1990; Pintrich et al, 2000; Zimmerman, 1989, 1994). That is, it is assumed that attempts to control, regulate, and change cognition should be related to cognitive monitoring activities that provide information about the relative discrepancy between a goal and current progress towards that goal. For example, if a student is reading a textbook with the goal of understanding (not just finishing the reading assignment), then as the student monitors his or her comprehension, this monitoring process can provide the student with information about the need to change reading strategies. Lyndsay does this by going back over the material she does not understand, based on her answers to her self-quizzes.

One of the central aspects of the control and regulation of cognition is the actual selection and use of various cognitive strategies for memory, learning, reasoning, problem solving, and thinking. Numerous studies have shown that the selection of appropriate cognitive strategies can have a positive influence on learning and performance. An important aspect of selection is adapting or selecting strategies that fit the task requirements or course requirements. To use a tool metaphor, there are different cognitive tools for different cognitive tasks and the important issue is selecting when to use what cognitive tool or strategy for what type of academic task. These cognitive strategies range from the simple memory strategies very young children through adults use to help them remember (Schneider and Pressley, 1997) to sophisticated strategies that individuals have for reading (Pressley and Afflerbach, 1995), mathematics (Schoenfeld, 1992), writing (Bereiter and Scardamalia, 1987), problem solving, and reasoning (see Baron, 1994; Nisbett, 1993). Although the use of various strategies is probably deemed more "cognitive" than metacognitive, the decision to use them is an aspect of metacognitive control and regulation as is the decision to stop using them or to switch from one strategy type to another.

In research on self-regulated learning, the various cognitive and learning strategies that individuals use to help them understand and learn the material would be placed in this cell. For example, many researchers have investigated the various rehearsal, elaboration, and organizational strategies that learners can use to control their cognition and learning (cf., Pintrich and De Groot, 1990; Pintrich, Marx and Boyle, 1993; Pressley and Afflerbach, 1995; Schneider and Pressley, 1997; Weinstein and Mayer, 1986; Zimmerman and Martinez-Pons, 1986). These strategies include using imagery to help encode information on a memory task, as well as imagery to help visualize correct implementation of a strategy (e.g., visualization in sports activities as well as academic ones, cf., Zimmerman, 1998a). The use of mnemonics would be included in this cell, as well as various strategies like paraphrasing, summarizing, outlining, networking, constructing tree diagrams, and note-taking (see Weinstein and Mayer, 1986). Mike seems to rely on basic rehearsal and memorizing strategies, which can be helpful when the exams test for simple recall of information. However, he may have more difficulty when he is required to synthesize or analyze information, as in essay exams or in papers. Lyndsay, in contrast, uses a number of different strategies for summarizing and organizing the information and this seems to help her learn in a more meaningful manner as well as lead to better performance.

Cognitive reaction and reflection. The processes of reaction and reflection involve learners' judgments and evaluations of their performance on the task as well as their attributions for performance. As Zimmerman (1998b) has pointed out, good self-regulators evaluate their performance in comparison to learners who avoid self-evaluation or are not aware of the importance of self-evaluation in terms of the goals set for the task. In addition, it appears that good self-regulators are more likely to make adaptive attributions for their performance (Zimmerman, 1998b). Adaptive attributions are generally seen as making attributions to low effort or poor strategy use, not to a lack of general ability (e.g., "I did poorly because I'm stupid or dumb") in the face of failure (Weiner, 1986; Zimmerman and Kitsantas, 1997). These adaptive attributions have been linked to deeper cognitive processing and better learning and achievement (Pintrich and Schrauben, 1992) as well as a host of adaptive motivational beliefs and behaviors such as positive affect, positive efficacy and expectancy judgments, persistence, and effort (Weiner, 1986).

In the case of our two students, Lyndsay makes a much more adaptive attribution for her doing poorly in some courses. She attributes it to her lack of expertise in studying and seeks help from her professors and more successful peers to learn how to study more adaptively. Lyndsay knows that one can improve or change how to study and this attribution leads her to expect to do better in the future as well as search for ways to actually improve her studying. Mike, in contrast, attributes his poor performance to his lack of ability; he begins to doubt his ability to do well and does not expect to do as well in the future. Given that he thinks it is a question of general ability, and most people think that general ability is not changeable, he is not motivated to try new ways of learning or studying.

Regulation of Motivation and Affect

Just as learners can regulate their cognition, they can regulate their motivation and affect (the second column in Table 1 and the four cells down the second column). However, less research has been done on how students can regulate their motivation and affect than on regulation of cognition, including all the research on metacognition and academic learning by cognitive and educational psychologists. The area of motivational regulation has been discussed more by personality, motivational, and social psychologists (e.g., Kuhl, 1984; 1985), not educational psychologists (see Boekaerts, 1993; Corno, 1989; 1993; Garcia, McCann, Turner, and Roska, 1998 for exceptions), but this trend is changing as research on learning and self-regulation recognizes the importance of motivation in general and attempts to regulate motivation in the classroom (Wolters, 1998).

Regulation of motivation and affect would include attempts to regulate the various motivational beliefs that have been discussed in the achievement motivation literature (see Pintrich and Schunk, 1996; Wolters, 1998), such as goal orientation (purposes for doing task), self-efficacy (judgments of competence to perform a task), task value beliefs (beliefs about the importance, utility, and relevance of the task) and personal interest in the task (liking the content area or domain). Kuhl (1984, 1985) as well as Corno (1989, 1993) discuss, under the label of volitional control, various strategies that individuals might use to control their motivation. In their more global construct of volitional control they also include strategies for emotion control, as does Boekaerts (1993), which includes coping strategies for adapting to negative affect and emotions such as anxiety and fear.

Motivational planning and activation. In terms of the phases in Table 1, planning and activation of motivation (first cell in the second column in Table 1) would involve judgments of efficacy as well as the activation of various motivational beliefs about value and interest. In terms of self-efficacy judgments, Bandura (1997) and Schunk (1989, 1991, 1994) have shown that individuals' judgments of their capabilities to perform a task have consequences for affect, effort, persistence, performance, and learning. Of course, once a learner begins a task, self-efficacy judgments can be adjusted based on actual performance and feedback as well as the individual's attempts to actively regulate or change his efficacy judgments (Bandura, 1997).

In the cognitive research on memory, individuals can make determinations as to the difficulty level of the task, such as how hard it will be to remember or learn the material, or, in the Nelson and Narens (1990) framework, what they call ease of learning judgments (EOL). These EOL judgments draw on both metacognitive knowledge of the task and metacognitive knowledge of the self in terms of past performance on the task. In the classroom context, students might make these EOL judgments as the instructor introduces a lesson or assigns a worksheet, project, or paper. These EOL judgments are similar to self-efficacy judgments, although the emphasis is on the task rather than the self. In this sense, EOL judgments and self-efficacy judgments reflect the task difficulty perceptions and self-competence perceptions from expectancy-value models (e.g., Eccles, 1983).

Along with judgments of competence, learners also have perceptions of the value and interest the task or content area has for them. In expectancy-value models (Eccles, 1983; Wigfield, 1994; Wigfield and Eccles, 1992), task value beliefs include perceptions of the relevance, utility, and importance of the task. If students believe that the task is relevant or important for their future goals or generally useful for them (e.g., "Chemistry is important because I want to be a doctor"; "Math is useful because I need it to be a smart consumer"), then they are more likely to be engaged in the task as well as to choose to engage in the task in the future (Wigfield, 1994; Wigfield and Eccles, 1992). Lyndsay believes that what she is learning in different courses may be useful for her in her future career, even if she doesn't like all of the content. In terms of a model of self-regulated learning, it seems likely that these beliefs can be activated early on, either consciously or automatically and unconsciously, as the student approaches or is introduced to the task by instructors or others. In addition, in the current model of self-regulated learning, it is assumed that students can attempt to regulate or control these value beliefs (e.g., Wolters, 1998).

Besides value beliefs, learners also have perceptions of their personal interest in the task or in the content domain of the task (e.g., liking and positive affect towards math, history, science, etc.). Both Mike and Lyndsay find some of their courses boring or uninteresting, so they would have less personal interest in these courses. The research on personal interest suggests that it is a stable and enduring characteristic of an individual, but that the level of interest can be activated and may vary according to situational and contextual features, which are collectively labeled the psychological state of interest (Krapp, Hidi, and Renninger, 1992; Schiefele, 1991). Most importantly, this work suggests that interest is course- or domain-specific or even topic-specific, so it is important to keep in mind that interest and value can vary by course. Students are not interested in courses generally, at a very global level, but the different courses and even topics within a course will activate different interest beliefs. In addition, this research has shown that interest is related to increased learning, persistence, and effort. Mike shows much less persistence and effort in those courses that he finds less interesting — a common pattern for many college students. Although the research on interest has been pursued both from an expectancy-value framework (Wigfield, 1994; Wigfield and Eccles, 1992) and through intrinsic motivation or needs-based models (see Deci and Ryan, 1985; Renninger, Hidi, and Krapp, 1992), it seems clear that interest can be activated by task and contextual features and that learners also can try to control and regulate it (Sansone, Weir, Harpster, and Morgan, 1992; Wolters, 1998).

Finally, just as interest can be a positive anticipatory affect, learners also can anticipate other more negative affects such as anxiety or fear. This may also include the activation of implicit motives such as the need for achievement or the need for power (Pintrich & Schunk, 1996). These implicit motives can also generate affect that the college student has to cope with in dealing with different tasks. In the academic learning domain, test anxiety would be the most common form of anxiety and the most researched in terms of its links with learning, performance, and achievement (Hembree 1988; Hill and Wigfield, 1984; Wigfield and Eccles, 1989; Zeidner, 1998). Students who anticipate being anxious on tests and who worry about doing poorly even before they begin the test can set in motion a downward spiral of maladaptive cognitions, emotions, and behaviors that lead them to do poorly on the exam (Bandura, 1997; Zeidner, 1998). In this way, these anticipatory affects such as anxiety or fear can influence the subsequent learning process and certainly set up conditions that require active and adaptive self-regulation of cognition, motivation, and behavior.

Motivational monitoring. In terms of monitoring motivation and affect (the second cell in the second column in Table 1), there has not been as much research on how individuals explicitly monitor their motivation and affect as there has been on metacognitive monitoring, but it is implied in the research on how students can control and regulate their motivation and affect. That is, as in the cognitive research, it can be assumed that in order for individuals to try to control their efficacy, value, interest, or anxiety, they would have to be aware of these beliefs and affects, and monitor them at some level. In fact, paralleling the cognitive strategy intervention research (Pressley and Woloshyn, 1995), research on interventions to improve motivation often focus on helping students become aware of their own motivation so they can adapt it to the task and contextual demands. For example, research on self-efficacy focuses first on having individuals become aware of their own efficacy levels and self-doubts and then on changing their efficacy judgments to make them more realistic and adaptive (Bandura, 1997). Research on attributional retraining usually attempts to help individuals become aware of their maladaptive attributional patterns and then change them (Foersterling, 1985; Peterson, Maier, and Seligman, 1993). In the test anxiety research, besides attempts to change the environmental conditions that increase anxiety, there are a host of suggested coping strategies that individuals can adopt that include monitoring both the emotionality (negative affect) and cognitive (negative self-thoughts and doubts) components of anxiety (Hill and Wigfield, 1984; Tryon, 1980; Zeidner, 1998). In all these cases, the monitoring of motivation and affect is an important prelude to attempts to control and regulate motivation and affect.

Motivational control and regulation. The third cell in the second column in Table 1 represents attempts to control motivation. There are many different strategies that individuals can use to control their motivation and affect — not as many, perhaps, as have been discussed by cognitive researchers investigating strategies to control cognition, but still a fair number. Kuhl (1984, 1985), Corno (1989, 1993), and Boekaerts (1993; Boekaerts and Niemivirta, 2000) all have discussed various strategies for motivation and emotion control, including how to cope with negative emotions.

These strategies include attempts to control self-efficacy through the use of positive self-talk (e.g., "I know I can do this task"; see Bandura, 1997). Students also can attempt to increase their extrinsic motivation for the task by promising themselves extrinsic rewards or making certain appealing activities (taking a nap, watching TV, talking with friends, etc.) contingent on completing an academic task (Wolters, 1998; called self-consequenting in Zimmerman and Martinez-Pons, 1986; and incentive escalation in Kuhl, 1984). Lyndsay does this when she goes out with friends after a study session. Wolters (1998) found that college students would intentionally try to evoke extrinsic goals such as getting good grades to help them maintain their motivation. Students also can try to increase their intrinsic motivation for a task by trying to make it more interesting (e.g., "make it into a game", Sansone, et al., 1992; Wolters, 1998) or to maintain a more mastery-oriented focus on learning (Wolters, 1998). Finally, Wolters (1998) also found that students would try to increase the task value of an academic task by attempting to make it more relevant or useful to them or their careers, experiences, or lives. In all these cases, students are attempting to change or control their motivation in order to complete a task that might be boring or difficult. Lyndsay seems much more successful at attempting to control her motivation than Mike, especially in the case of boring courses.

In other cases, students may use a self-affirmation strategy whereby they decrease the value of a task in order to protect their self-worth, especially if they have done poorly on the task (Garcia and Pintrich, 1994). For example, students who fail on an academic task might try to affirm their self-worth by saying it doesn't matter to them, that school is not that important compared to other aspects of their lives that they value more. Steele (1988, 1997) has suggested that self-affirmation and dis-identification with school (devaluing of school in comparison to other domains) might help explain the discrepancy between African American students' achievement and their self-esteem.

In addition, there are strategies students can use to try to control their emotions that might differ from those that they use to control their efficacy or value (Boekaerts, 1993; Boekaerts and Niemivirta, 2000; Corno, 1989, 1993; Kuhl, 1984, 1985; Wolters, 1998). Self-talk strategies to control negative affect and anxiety (e.g., "don't worry about grades now", "don't think about that last question, move on to the next question") have been noted by anxiety researchers (Hill and Wigfield, 1984; Zeidner, 1998). Students also may invoke negative affects such as shame or guilt to motivate them to persist at a task (Corno, 1989; Wolters, 1998). Defensive pessimism is another motivational strategy that students can use to actually harness negative affect and anxiety about doing poorly in order to motivate them to increase their effort and perform better (Garcia and Pintrich, 1994; Norem and Cantor, 1986). Self-handicapping, in contrast to defensive pessimism, involves the decrease of effort (little or no studying) or procrastination (only cramming for an exam, writing a paper at the very end of the deadline) in order to protect self-worth by attributing the likely poor outcome to low effort, not to low ability (Baumeister and Scher, 1988; Berglas, 1985; Garcia and Pintrich, 1994; Midgley, Arunkumar, and Urdan, 1996).

Motivational reaction and reflection. The last cell in the second column in Table 1 concerns reaction and reflections about motivation. After the students have completed a task, they may have emotional reactions to the outcome (e.g., happiness at success, dismay at failure) as well as reflecting on the reasons for the outcome, that is, making attributions for the outcome (Weiner, 1986). According to attribution theory, the types of attributions that students make for their success and failure can lead to the experience of more complicated emotions like pride, anger, shame, and guilt (Weiner, 1986; 1995). As students reflect on the reasons for their performance, both the quality of the attributions and the quality of the emotions experienced are important outcomes of the self-regulation process. Individuals can actively control the types of attributions they make in order to protect their self-worth and motivation for future tasks. Many of the common attributional biases identified by social psychologists (Fiske and Taylor, 1991) may be used rather automatically (e.g., the fundamental attribution error, the actor-observer bias), but they could also be more intentional strategies used to protect self-worth (e.g., the self-serving or hedonic bias; the self-centered bias, see Fiske and Taylor, 1991; Pintrich and Schunk, 1996). Mike begins to have doubts about his ability and does not seem as hopeful as Lyndsay, who takes a more active approach to her poor performances.

In fact, much of the attributional retraining literature is focused on helping individuals change their attributions or attributional style in order to develop more adaptive cognitive, motivational, affective, and behavioral reactions to life events (Peterson, et al, 1993; Foersterling, 1985). Finally, these reflections and reactions can lead to changes in the future levels of self-efficacy, expectancy for future success, and value and interest (Pintrich and Schunk, 1996; Weiner, 1986; 1995). In this sense, these potential changes in efficacy, value, and interest from phase four flow back into phase one and become the "entry" level motivational beliefs that students bring with them to new tasks.

REGULATION OF BEHAVIOR

Regulation of behavior is an aspect of self-regulation that involves individuals attempts to control their own overt behavior (the third column in Table 1). Since this does not explicitly involve attempts to control and regulate the personal self, some models of regulation would not include it as an aspect of "self" regulation but would just label it behavioral control. In contrast, the framework in Table 1 follows the triadic model of social cognition (Bandura, 1986; Zimmerman, 1989) where behavior is an aspect of the person, albeit not the internal "self" that is represented by cognition, motivation, and affect. Nevertheless, individuals can observe their own behavior, monitor it, and attempt to control and regulate it and as such these activities can be considered self-regulatory for the individual.

Behavioral planning and activation. The first cell in the third column of Table 1 includes behavioral planning. Models of intentions, intentional planning, and planned behavior (e.g., Ajzen, 1988; 1991; Gollwitzer, 1996) have shown that the formation of intentions is linked to subsequent behavior in a number of different domains. In the academic learning domain, time and effort planning or management would be the kind of activities that could be placed in this cell in Table 1. Time management involves the making of schedules for studying and allocating time for different activities, which is a classic aspect of most learning and study skills courses (see Hofer, Yu, and Pintrich, 1998; McKeachie, Pintrich, and Lin, 1985; Pintrich, McKeachie, and Lin, 1987; Simpson, Hynd, Nist, and Burrell, 1997). Zimmerman and Martinez-Pons (1986) have shown that self-regulating learners and high achievers do engage in time management activities. In addition, Zimmerman (1998a) has discussed the fact that not only students but expert writers, musicians, and athletes also engage in time management activities. As part of time management, students also may make decisions and form intentions about how they will allocate their effort and the intensity of their work. For example, students might plan to study regularly one or two hours a night during the semester, but during midterms or finals intend to increase their effort and time spent studying. Lyndsay is a much more planned time and study manager than Mike, who seems to study when he has time, but also is susceptible to distractions such as friends pulling him away from his studies.

Zimmerman (1998a, 2000) also has discussed how individuals can observe their own behavior through various methods and then use this information to control and regulate their behavior. For example, writers can record how many pages of text they produce in a day and record this information over weeks, months, and years (Zimmerman, 1998b). In order to enact these self-observational methods, some planning must be involved in order to organize the behavioral record-keeping. Many learning strategy programs also suggest some form of behavioral observation and record-keeping in terms of studying in order to provide useful information for future attempts to change learning and study habits. Again, the implementation of these self-observational methods requires some planning and the intention to actual implement them during learning activities.

Behavioral monitoring. In Phase 2 (the second cell in the third column in Table 1), students can monitor their time management and effort levels and attempt to adjust their effort to fit the task. For example, in Phase 1, students may plan to spend only two hours reading two textbook chapters for the course, but once they begin reading, they might realize that the task is more difficult than they foresaw and that it will take either more time or more concentrated effort to understand each chapter. They might also realize that although they set aside two hours for reading the chapters in the library, they spent one hour of that time talking with friends who were studying with them. Of course, this type of monitoring should lead to an attempt to control or regulate their effort (e.g., set aside more time, don't study with friends; the next cell in Table 1). This type of monitoring behavior is often helped by formal procedures for self-observation (e.g., keeping logs of study time, diaries of activities, record-keeping, etc.) or self-experimentation (Zimmerman, 1998a, 2000). All of these activities will help students become aware of and monitor their own behavior, thus gaining information that they can use to actually control or regulate their behavior. Lyndsay seems much more aware of her studying behavior and monitors it much better than Mike does.

Behavioral control and regulation. Strategies for actual behavioral control and regulation are important aspects of self-regulated learning (cell 3 in the third column in Table 1). As noted in the previous section, students may regulate the time and effort they expend studying two textbook chapters based on their monitoring of their behavior and the difficulty of the task. If the task is harder than they originally thought, they may increase their effort, depending on their goals, or they may decrease effort if the task is perceived as too difficult. Another aspect of behavioral control includes general persistence, which is also a classic measure used in achievement motivation studies as an indicator of motivation. Students may exhort themselves to persist through self-talk ("keep trying, you'll get it") or they may give up if the task is too difficult, again depending on their goals and monitoring activities. Mike seems much more likely to give up and not put forth as much effort , compared to Lyndsay.

The motivational strategies mentioned earlier, such as defensive pessimism and self-handicapping, included attempts to control anxiety and self-worth but also had direct implications for an increase in effort (defensive pessimism) or decrease in effort (self-handicapping). As such, these strategies are also relevant to behavioral control efforts. One aspect of self-handicapping is procrastination, which is certainly behavioral in nature — putting off studying for an exam or writing a paper until the last minute. Of course, since effort and persistence are two of the most common indicators of motivation, most of the motivational strategies mentioned in the earlier section will have direct implications for the behaviors of effort and persistence. Mike does tend to procrastinate and begin studying or writing papers close to their due dates, while Lyndsay takes a much more planned and regulated approach to her work by pacing her work and trying to prepare before the due dates.

Another behavioral strategy that can be very helpful for learning is help-seeking. It appears that good students and good self-regulators know when, why, and from whom to seek help (Karabenick and Sharma, 1994; Nelson Le-

Gall, 1981; 1985; Newman, 1991, 1994, 1998a, b; Ryan and Pintrich, 1997). Lyndsay is a very good help-seeker and seeks out professors and other students who are doing well to help her improve her studying. Mike, in contrast, doesn't seek help and it is not clear that he is aware that he should ask for help. Help-seeking is listed here as a behavioral strategy because it involves the person's own behavior, but it also involves contextual control because it necessarily involves the procurement of help from others in the environment and as such is also a social interaction (Ryan and Pintrich, 1997). Help-seeking can be a dependent strategy for students who are seeking the correct answer without much work or who wish to complete the task quickly without much understanding or learning. In terms of this goal of learning and understanding, dependent help-seeking would be a generally maladaptive strategy, in contrast to adaptive help-seeking where the individual is focused on learning and is only seeking help in order to overcome a particularly difficult aspect of the task.

Behavioral reaction and reflection. Reflection is a more cognitive process (cell four in the third column in Table 1) and so there may be no "behavioral" reflection per se, but just as with forethought, the cognitions an individual has about behavior can be classified in this cell. For example, reflections on actual behavior in terms of effort expended or time spent on task can be important aspects of self-regulated learning. Just as students can make judgments or reflect on their cognitive processing or motivation, they can make judgments about their behaviors. They may decide that procrastinating in studying for an exam may not be the most adaptive behavior for academic achievement. In the future, they may decide to make a different choice in terms of their effort and time management. Certainly, in terms of reaction, the main behavior is choice. Students can decide not only to change their future time and effort management efforts, but they also may make choices about what classes to take in the future (at least, for high school and college students), or more broadly, what general course of study they will follow. This kind of choice behavior results in the selection of different contexts and leads us into the last column in Table 1.

It is important to note that while persistence is usually considered a good example of motivated behavior, more recent research on self-regulation and self-regulated learning (e.g., Zimmerman, 2000; Zimmerman and Schunk, 1989) suggests that students also have to be able to regulate their own behavior in order to be successful. In the case of persistence, "blind and willful" persistence on a difficult task that goes on too long without the student seeking help from others may not be the most adaptive coping strategy. If the student gives up too easily on a difficult task, that is not representative of adaptive or motivated behavior — but neither is the continual putting forth of more effort, when the student does not have the knowledge or skills to eventually succeed. Accordingly, help-seeking behavior can be an important self-regulatory strategy when the task is beyond the students' level of competence (Karabenick and Knapp, 1991). In the same way, just trying harder on a "boring" task may not be the most helpful strategy. There are strategies available to regulate motivation and reactions to the task to make it more interesting (e.g., Sansone, et al, 1992). Accordingly, the research on these strategies for self-regulation of effort and persistence suggests that it is not just overall persistence that is important, but persistence that is adapted to the nature of the task (e.g., difficulty, interestingness) and coordinated with the individual's own capabilities (e.g., knowledge and cognitive skills, motivation, and fatigue levels).

REGULATION OF CONTEXT

As noted above, regulation of context (last column on the right-hand side of Table 1) includes the individual's attempts to monitor, control, and regulate the context as an important aspect of self-regulated learning because the focus is on the personal self or individual who is engaged in these activities. Given that it is the active, personal self who is attempting to monitor, control, and regulate the context, it seems important to include these activities in a model of self-regulated learning.

Contextual planning and activation. The first cell in the last column of Table I includes college students' perceptions of the task and context. In a college classroom context, these perceptions may be about the nature of the tasks in terms of the norms for completing the task (e.g., the format to be used, the procedures to be used to do the task such as whether working with others is permitted or is considered cheating, etc.) as well as general knowledge about the types of tasks and classroom practices for grading in the course (Blumenfeld, Mergendoller, and Swarthout, 1987; Doyle, 1983).

In addition, perceptions of the college classroom norms and classroom climate are important aspects of college students' knowledge activation of contextual information. For example, when college students enter a classroom, they may activate knowledge about general norms or perceive certain norms (talking is not allowed, working with others is cheating, the faculty member always has the correct answer, students are not allowed much autonomy or control, etc.) which can influence their approach to the classroom and their general learning. Other aspects of the college classroom climate such as instructor warmth and enthusiasm as well as equity and fairness for all students (e.g., no bias on basis of gender or ethnicity) can be important perceptions or beliefs that are activated when students come into a classroom (Pintrich and Schunk, 1996). Of course, these perceptions can be veridical and actually represent the classroom dynamics, but there is also the possibility that the students can misperceive the classroom context because they are activating stereotypes without reflecting on the actual nature of the classroom. For example, there may be occasions when females accurately perceive a male math faculty member to be biased against females in math, but there also can be cases where this is a more stereotypical perception that is not reflected in the instructor's behavior. In any case, these perceptions, veridical or not, offer opportunities for monitoring and regulation of the context.

Contextual monitoring. Just as students can and should monitor their cognition, motivation, and behavior, they also can and should monitor the task and contextual features of the classroom (cell 2 in the last column in Table 1). In classrooms, just as in work and social situations, individuals are not free to do as they please; they are involved in a social system with various opportunities and constraints operating that shape and influence their behavior. If students are unaware of the opportunities and constraints that are operating, then they will be less likely to be able to function well in the classroom. Awareness and monitoring of the classroom rules, grading practices, task requirements, reward structures and general instructor behavior are all important for students to do well in the classroom. For example, students need to be aware of the different grading practices and how different tasks will be evaluated and scored for grades. For example, if they are not aware that "original" thinking is important in a paper (as opposed to summarizing other material from books or journal articles), then they will be less likely to adjust their behavior to be in line with these requirements. In college classrooms, entering freshmen often have difficulty in their first courses because they are not monitoring or adjusting their perceptions of the course requirements to the levels expected by the faculty. Many college learning strategy or study skills courses attempt to help students become aware of these differences and adjust their strategy use and behavior accordingly (Hofer et al., 1998; Simpson, et al., 1997). Mike seems to rely on a memorization-only strategy, which may not be what is required in some of his courses. He is having difficulty in understanding some of the new contextual norms. Lyndsay also might be having some difficulties in figuring out these norms, but she seeks out the professor and other students to help her determine how to do better in her courses.

Contextual control and regulation. Of course, as with cognition, motivation, and behavior, contextual monitoring processes are intimately linked to efforts to control and regulate the tasks and context (third cell in the last column in Table 1). In comparison to control and regulation of cognition, motivation, and behavior, control of the tasks or context may be more difficult because they are not always under direct control of the individual learner. However, even models of general intelligence (e.g., the contextual sub-theory, see Sternberg, 1985), often include attempts to shape, adapt, or control the environment as one aspect of intelligent behavior. Models of volitional control usually include a term labeled environmental control, which refers to attempts to control or structure the environment in ways that will facilitate goals and task completion (Corno, 1989; 1993; Kuhl, 1984, 1985). In terms of self-regulated learning, most models include strategies to shape or control or structure the learning environment as important strategies for self-regulation (Zimmerman, 1998a).

In the traditional classroom context, the instructor controls most of the aspects of the tasks and context and therefore there may be little opportunity for students to engage in contextual control and regulation. However, students often may attempt to negotiate the task requirements "downward" ("Can we write 10 pages instead of 20?", "Can we use our books and notes on the exam?", etc.) to make them simpler and easier for them to perform (Doyle, 1983). This kind of task negotiation has probably been experienced by all instructors from elementary through graduate school faculty and does represent one attempt by students to control and regulate the task and contextual environment even in classrooms with high levels of instructor control.

In postsecondary settings, students have much more freedom to structure their environment in terms of their learning. Much of the learning that goes on takes place outside the college lecture hall or classroom, and students have to be able to control and regulate their study environment. Monitoring of their study environment for distractions (music, TV, talkative friends or peers) and then attempts to control or regulate their study environment to make them more conducive for studying (removing distractions, having an organized and specific place for studying) can facilitate learning; this seems to be an important part of self-regulated learning (Hofer et al, 1998; Zimmerman, 1998a). Zimmerman (1998a) also discusses how writers, athletes, and musicians attempt to exert contextual control over their environment by structuring it in ways that facilitate their learning and performance. Lyndsay does attempt to control some aspects of her context by studying with her friends, thereby making them less likely to ask her to go out to socialize and take her away from her studies. Mike tends to be controlled by the environment, rather than controlling it, as he lets his friends talk him out of studying in order to go out with them.

Contextual reaction and reflection. Finally, in terms of contextual reaction and reflection (the last cell in the last column in Table 1), students can make general evaluations of the task or classroom environment. These evaluations can be made on the basis of general enjoyment and comfort as well as more cognitive criteria regarding learning and achievement. In some of the more student-centered classrooms, there is time set aside for occasional reflection on what is working in the classroom and what is not working in terms of both student and faculty reactions (Brown, 1997). As with cognition and motivation, these evaluations can feed back into Phase 1 components when the student approaches a new task.

In summary, this four phase by four areas for regulation in Table 1 represents a general framework for conceptualizing self-regulated learning in the academic domain. It provides a taxonomy of the different processes and components that can be involved in self-regulated learning. The format of the taxonomy also allows for the integration of much of the research on self-regulated learning that has spawned a diversity of terms and constructs, but organizes it in such a manner that the similarities and differences can be seen easily. As researchers traverse the different areas of self-regulated learning, the taxonomy allows them to locate their own efforts within this topography as well as to spy under-explored territories in need of further investigation and examination. The next section of this chapter turns to how different motivational beliefs (C in Figure 1) are linked to these self-regulatory processes (D in Figure 1) and to actual achievement (E in Figure 1).

THE ROLE OF MOTIVATIONAL BELIEFS (C)

The second process component in the model in Figure 1 is students' motivational beliefs (C). Although there are many models of motivation that may be relevant to student learning (see Heckhausen, 1991; Weiner, 1992, for reviews of different motivational theories), a general expectancy-value model serves as a useful framework for analyzing the research on motivational components (Pintrich, 1988a, b, 1989, 1994; Pintrich and Schunk, 1996). Three general components seem to be important in these different models: a) beliefs about one's ability or skill to perform the task (expectancy components), b) beliefs about the importance and value of the task (value components), and c)feelings about the self, or emotional reactions to the task (affective components). These three general components are assumed to interact with one another and, in turn, to influence the outcomes (E) in Figure 1 as well as the self-regulatory processes (D) outlined in the previous section. In this section, we outline the nature of the motivational beliefs and how they are related to both self-regulation and student outcomes.

EXPECTANCY COMPONENTS

Expectancy components are college students' "answer" to the question: "Can I do this task?". If students believe that they have some control over their skills and the task environment and that they have confidence in their ability to perform the necessary skills, they are more likely to choose to do the task, more likely to be involved in self-regulatory activities, and more likely to persist at the task. Various constructs have been proposed by different motivational theorists; they can be categorized as expectancy components. The main distinction is between how much control one believes one has in the situation and perceptions of efficacy to accomplish the task in that situation. Of course, these beliefs are correlated empirically, but most models do propose separate constructs for control beliefs and efficacy beliefs.

Control beliefs. A number of constructs and theories have been proposed about the role of control beliefs for motivational dynamics. For example, early work on locus of control (e.g., Lefcourt, 1976; Rotter, 1966) found that students who believed that they were in control of their behavior and could influence the environment (an internal locus of control) tended to achieve at higher levels. Deci (1975) and de Charms (1968) discussed perceptions of control in terms of students' belief in self-determination. De Charms (1968) coined the terms "origins" and "pawns" to describe students who believed they were able to control their actions and students who believed that others controlled their behavior. Connell (1985) suggested that control beliefs have three aspects: an internal source, an external source (or powerful others), and an unknown source. Students who believe in internal sources of control are assumed to perform better than students who believe powerful others (e.g., faculty, parents) are responsible for their success or failure and better than those students who don't know who or what is responsible for the outcomes. In the college classroom, Perry and his colleagues (e.g., Perry, 1991; Perry and Dickens, 1988; Perry and Magnusson, 1989; Perry and Penner, 1990) have shown that students' beliefs about how their personal attributes influence the environment — which they label "perceived control" — are related to achievement and to aspects of the classroom environment (e.g., instructor feedback).

In self-efficacy theory, outcome expectations refer to individuals' beliefs concerning their ability to influence outcomes, that is, their belief that the environment is responsive to their actions, which is different from self-efficacy (the belief that one can do the task; see Bandura, 1986; Schunk, 1985). This belief that outcomes are contingent on their behavior leads individuals to have higher expectations for success and should lead to more persistence. When individuals do not perceive a contingency between their behavior and outcomes, this can lead to passivity, anxiety, lack of effort, and lower achievement, often labeled learned helplessness (cf., Abramson, Seligman, and Teasdale, 1978). Learned helplessness is usually seen as a stable pattern of attributing many events to uncontrollable causes, which leaves the individual believing that there is no opportunity for change that is under their control. These individuals do not believe they can "do anything" that will make a difference and that the environment or situation is basically not responsive to their actions.

The overriding message of all these models is that a general pattern of perception of internal control results in positive outcomes (i.e., more cognitive engagement, higher achievement, higher self-esteem), while sustained perceptions of external or unknown control result in negative outcomes (lower achievement, lack of effort, passivity, anxiety). Reviews of research in this area are somewhat conflicting, however (cf., Findley and Cooper, 1983; Stipek and Weisz; 1981) and some have argued that it is better to accept responsibility for positive outcomes (an internal locus of control) and deny responsibility for negative or failure outcomes (an external locus of control, see Harter, 1985). Part of the difficulty in interpreting this literature is the different ages of the samples and the use of different definitions of the construct of control, different instruments to measure the construct, and different outcomes measures in the numerous studies. In particular, the construct of internal locus of control confounds three dimensions of locus (internal vs. external), controllability (controllable vs. uncontrollable), and stability (stable vs. unstable). Attributional theory proposes that these three dimensions can be separated conceptually and empirically and that they have different influences on behavior (Weiner, 1986).

Attributional theory proposes that the causal attributions an individual makes for success or failure mediates future expectancies, not the actual success or failure event. A large number of studies have shown that individuals who tend to attribute success to internal and stable causes like ability or aptitude will tend to expect to succeed in the future. In contrast, individuals who attribute their success to external or unstable causes (i.e., ease of the task, luck) will not expect to do well in the future. For failure situations, the positive motivational pattern consists not of an internal locus of control, but rather of attributing failure to external and unstable causes (difficult task, lack of effort, bad luck) and the negative motivational pattern consists of attributing failure to internal and stable causes (e.g., ability, skill). Lyndsay and Mike show different attributional patterns to explain their failures, with Lyndsay having a much more adaptive pattern. This general attributional approach has been applied to numerous situations and the motivational dynamics seem to be remarkably robust and similar (Weiner, 1986).

It should also be noted that in an attributional analysis, the important dimension linked to future expectancies (beliefs that one will do well in the future) is stability, not locus (Weiner, 1986). That is, it is how stable you believe a cause is that is linked to future expectancies (i.e., the belief that your ability or effort to do the task is stable over time, not whether you believe it is internal or external to you). Attributional theory generally takes a situational view of these attributions and beliefs, but some researchers have suggested that individuals have relatively consistent attributional patterns across domains and tasks that function somewhat like personality traits (e.g., Fincham and Cain, 1986; Peterson, et al, 1993). These attributional patterns seem to predict individuals' performance over time. For example, if college students consistently attributed their success to their own skill and ability as learners, then it would be predicted that they would continually expect success in future classes. In contrast, if students consistently attribute success to other causes (e.g., the instructors are excellent, the material is easy, luck), then their expectations might not be as high for future classes.

Individuals' beliefs about the causes of events can be changed through feedback and other environmental manipulations to facilitate the adoption of positive control and attributional beliefs. For example, some research on attributional retraining in achievement situations (e.g., Foersterling, 1985; Perry and Penner, 1990) suggests that teaching individuals to make appropriate attributions for failure on school tasks (e.g., effort attributions instead of ability attributions) can facilitate future achievement. Of course, a variety of issues must be considered in attributional retraining, including the specification of which attributional patterns are actually dysfunctional, the relative accuracy of the new attributional pattern, and the issue of only attempting to change a motivational component instead of the cognitive skill that also may be important for performance (cf., Blumenfeld, Pintrich, Meece, and Wessels, 1982; Weiner, 1986).

In summary, individuals' beliefs about the contingency between their behaviors and their performance in a situation are linked to student outcomes (E) and self-regulation (D) in Figure 1. In a classroom context, this means that college students' motivational beliefs about the linkage between their studying and self-regulated learning behavior and their achievement will influence their actual studying behavior. For example, if students believe that no matter how hard they study, they will not be able to do well on a chemistry test because they simply lack the aptitude to master the material, then they will be less likely to actually study for the test (the case of Mike). In the same fashion, if students believe that their effort in studying can make a difference, regardless of their actual aptitude for the material, then they will be more likely to study the material (the case of Lyndsay). Accordingly, these beliefs about control and contingency have motivational force because they influence future behavior.

Self-efficacy beliefs. In contrast to control beliefs, self-efficacy concerns students' beliefs about their ability just to do the task, not the linkage between their doing it and the outcome. Self-efficacy has been defined as individuals' beliefs about their performance capabilities in a particular domain (Bandura, 1982, 1986; Schunk, 1985). The construct of self-efficacy includes individuals' judgments about their ability to accomplish certain goals or tasks by their actions in specific situations (Schunk, 1985). This approach implies a relatively situational or domain specific construct rather than a global personality trait. In an achievement context, it includes college students' confidence in their cognitive skills to perform the academic task. Mike starts to doubt his self-efficacy for college work, while Lyndsay seems to believe that she can learn and improve. Continuing the example from chemistry, a college student might have confidence in her capability (a high self-efficacy belief) to learn the material for the chemistry test (i.e., "I can learn this material on stoichiometry") and consequently exert more effort in studying. At the same time, if the student believes that the grading curve in the class is so difficult and that her studying won't make much difference in her grade for the exam (a low control belief) she might not study as much. Accordingly, self-efficacy and control beliefs are separate constructs, albeit they are usually positively correlated empirically. Moreover, they may combine and interact with each other to influence student self-regulation and outcomes.

One issue in most motivational theories regarding self-efficacy and control beliefs concerns the domain or situational specificity of the beliefs. As noted above, self-efficacy theory generally assumes a situation specific view. That is, individuals' judgment of their efficacy for a task is a function of the task and situational characteristics operating at the time (difficulty, feedback, norms, comparisons with others, etc.) as well as their past experience and prior beliefs about the task and their current beliefs and feelings as they work on the task. However, there may be generalized efficacy beliefs that extend beyond the specific situation and influence motivated behavior. Accordingly, college students could have efficacy beliefs not just for a specific exam in chemistry, but also for chemistry in general, for natural science courses in contrast to social science or humanities courses, or for learning and school work in general. An important direction for future research will be to examine the domain generality of both self-efficacy and control beliefs. Nevertheless, it has been shown in many studies in many different domains, including the achievement domain, that college students' self-efficacy beliefs (or, in more colloquial terms, their self-confidence in their capabilities to do a task) are strongly related to the outcomes in Figure 1 (E) including their choice of activities, their level of engagement, and their willingness to persist at a task (Bandura, 1986; Pintrich and Schrauben, 1992; Schunk, 1985)

In our own research at Michigan, we have examined the role of self-efficacy beliefs and college student self-regulated learning and achievement in the college classroom. We have been involved in research in college classrooms since 1982 and have collected data on over 4,000 students from a variety of disciplines and courses including mathematics, biology, chemistry, English literature, English composition, sociology, and psychology (see Garcia and Pintrich, 1994, 1996; Pintrich, 1988a, b, 1989; 1999; Pintrich and Garcia, 1991, 1993; Pintrich, Smith, Garcia, and McKeachie, 1993; VanderStoep, Pintrich, and Fagerlin, 1996). In addition, these studies have been carried out at Research I institutions like Michigan, but also at comprehensive universities, small liberal arts colleges, and community colleges, increasing the generalizability of our findings. These studies have been correlational in design and used the Motivated Strategies for Learning Questionnaire (MSLQ, Pintrich et al, 1993) to assess student motivation and self-regulated learning in the classroom. We have used other measures such as student grades on course assignments (papers, midterms, final exams, quizzes, lab projects) as well as their final course grade as measures of achievement outcomes.

The MSLQ is a self-report instrument designed to measure student motivation and self-regulated learning in classroom contexts. The items and scales from the MSLQ focus on motivation and self-regulation at the course level. That is, college students are asked about their motivation and self-regulation for a specific course. It is not task or assignment specific (e.g., midterm exams, papers), nor is it more global with items about their motivation or self-regulation for college in general. In these correlational studies, we have assessed motivation and self-regulation at the beginning of the semester (a few weeks after the start of class) and then again at the end of the term, and in some studies we have used the MSLQ at three time points over the course of a 15-week semester. This type of design allows us to examine the relative role of different motivational beliefs over time within the course and how these beliefs predict various achievement outcomes.

In terms of self-efficacy beliefs, our results are very consistent over time and are in line with more experimental studies of self-efficacy (Bandura, 1997). Self-efficacy is one of the strongest positive predictors of actual achievement in the course, accounting for 9% to 25% of the variance in grades (an outcome, E in Figure 1), depending on the study and the other predictors entered in the regression (Pintrich, 1999). College students who believe they are able to do the coursework and learn the material are much more likely to do well in the course. Moreover, in these studies, self-efficacy remains a significant predictor of final achievement, albeit accounting for less total variance, even when previous knowledge (as indexed by performance on earlier tests) or general ability (as indexed by SAT scores) are entered into the equations in these studies.

Finally, in all of these studies, we also find that self-efficacy is a significant positive predictor of student self-regulation (D in Figure 1) and cognitive engagement in the course. College students who are confident of their capabilities to learn and do the coursework are more likely to report using more elaboration and organizational cognitive strategies (D in Figure 1). These strategies involve deeper cognitive processing of the course material, where students try to paraphrase the material, summarize it in their own words, or make outlines or concept maps of the concepts, in comparison to just trying to memorize the material. Lyndsay uses these strategies; Mike does not. In addition, college students who are higher in their self-efficacy for learning also are much more likely to be metacognitive, trying to regulate their learning by monitoring and controlling their cognition as they learn. In our studies, we have measures of these cognitive and self-regulatory strategies at the start of the course and at the end of the course, and self-efficacy remains a significant predictor of cognitive and self-regulatory strategy use at the end of the course, even when the earlier measure of cognition is included as a predictor along with self-efficacy. Accordingly, positive self-efficacy beliefs (C in Figure 1) can boost cognitive and self-regulatory strategy use (D in Figure 1) over the course of a semester.

In summary, our first generalization about the role of motivational beliefs in self-regulated learning emphasizes the importance of self-efficacy beliefs.

Generalization 1 - *Self-efficacy beliefs are positively related to adaptive cognitive and self-regulatory strategy use as well as to actual achievement in the college classroom.*

Accordingly, college students who feel capable and confident about their abilities to do the coursework are much more likely to be cognitively engaged, to try hard, to persist, and to do well in the course (C predicts outcomes E in Figure 1 as well as self-regulation D processes). In fact, the strength of the relations between self-efficacy and these different outcomes in our research as well as others' (Bandura, 1997; Pintrich and Schunk, 1996; Schunk, 1991) suggests that self-efficacy is one of the best and most powerful motivational predictors of learning and achievement. Given the strength of the relations, research on the motivational aspects of college student learning and performance needs to include self-efficacy as an important mediator between classroom contextual and personal factors and student outcomes. In terms of pedagogical implications, this generalization suggests that faculty need to be aware of how different aspects of the classroom environment can facilitate or constrain self-efficacy beliefs. More discussion of this issue will follow in the section on classroom context factors.

Value Components

Value components of the model incorporate individuals' goals for engaging in a task as well as their beliefs about the importance, utility, or interest of a task. Essentially, these components concern the question: Why am I doing this task? In more colloquial terms, value components concern whether students "care" about the task and the nature of that concern (see opening paragraph regarding faculty concerns that students do not care about, or are not interested in, course material). These components should be related to self-regulatory activities as well as to outcomes such as the choice of activities, effort, and persistence (Eccles, 1983; Pintrich, 1999). Although there are a variety of different conceptualizations of value, two basic components seem relevant; goal orientation and task value.

Goal orientation. All motivational theories posit some type of goal, purpose, or intentionality to human behavior, although these goals may range from relatively accessible and conscious goals as in attribution theory to relatively inaccessible and unconscious goals as in psychodynamic theories (Zukier, 1986). In recent cognitive reformulations of achievement motivation theory, goals are assumed to be cognitive representations of the different purposes students may adopt in different achievement situations (Dweck and Elliott, 1983; Dweck and Leggett, 1988; Ford, 1992).

In current achievement motivation research, two general classes of goals have been discussed under various names such as target goals and purpose goals (e.g., Harackiewicz, et al 1998; Harackiewicz and Sansone, 1991), or task specific goals and goal orientations (e.g., Garcia and Pintrich, 1994; Pintrich and Schunk, 1996; Wolters, Yu, and Pintrich, 1996; Zimmerman and Kitsantas, 1997). The general distinction between these two classes of goals is that target and task specific goals represent the specific outcome the individual is attempting to accomplish. In academic learning contexts, it would be represented by goals such as "wanting to get a 85% out of 100% correct on a quiz" or "trying to get an A on a midterm exam", etc.. These goals are specific to a task and are most similar to the goals discussed by Locke and Latham (1990) for workers in an organizational context such as "wanting to make 10 more widgets an hour" or to "sell 5 more cars in the next week."

In contrast, purpose goals or goal orientations reflect the more general reasons why individuals perform a task; these goals are related more to the research on achievement motivation (Elliot, 1997; Urdan, 1997). Here, it is a matter of the individual's general orientation (or "schema" or "theory") for approaching the task, doing the task, and evaluating performance on the task (Ames, 1992; Dweck and Leggett, 1988; Pintrich, 2000a, b, c). In this case, purpose goals or goal orientations refer to why individuals want to get 85% out of 100%, why they want to get an A, or why they want to make more widgets or sell more cars, as well as the standards or criteria (85%, an A) they will use to evaluate their progress towards the goal. Given the focus of our own work, we will limit our discussion to the role of goal orientation in learning and achievement in this chapter.

Several different models of goal orientation have been advanced by different achievement motivation researchers (cf., Ames, 1992; Dweck and Leggett, 1988; Harackiewicz, et al, 1998; Maehr and Midgley, 1991; Nicholls, 1984; Pintrich, 1989; Wolters et al, 1996). These models vary somewhat in their definition of goal orientation and the use of different labels for similar constructs. They also differ on the proposed number of goal orientations and the role of approach and avoidance forms of the different goals. Finally, they also differ on the degree to which an individual's goal orientations are more personal, based in somewhat stable individual differences, or the degree to which an individual's goal orientations are more situated or sensitive to the context and a function of the contextual features of the environment. Most of the models assume that goal orientations are a function of both individual differences and contextual factors, but the relative emphasis along this continuum does vary between the different models. Much of this research also assumes that classrooms and other contexts (e.g., business or work settings; laboratory conditions in an experiment) can be characterized in terms of their goal orientations (see Ford, Smith, Weissbein, Gully, and Salas, 1998 for an application of goal orientation theory to a work setting), but for the purposes of this chapter the focus will be on individuals' personal goal orientation.

Most models propose two general goal orientations that concern the reasons or purposes individuals are pursuing when approaching and engaging in a task. In Dweck's model, the two goal orientations are labeled learning and performance goals (Dweck and Leggett, 1988), with learning goals reflecting a focus on increasing competence and performance goals involving either the avoidance of negative judgments of competence or attainment of positive judgments of competence. Ames (1992) labels them mastery and performance goals with mastery goals orienting learners to "developing new skills, trying to understand their work, improving their level of competence, or achieving a sense of mastery based on self-referenced standards" (Ames, 1992, p. 262). In contrast, performance goals orient learners to focus on their ability and self-worth, to determine their ability in reference to besting other students in competitions, surpassing others in achievements or grades, and to receiving public recognition for their superior performance (Ames, 1992). Harackiewicz and Elliot and their colleagues (e.g., Elliot, 1997; Elliot and Church, 1997; Elliot and Harackiewicz, 1996; Harackiewicz, et al, 1998) have labeled them mastery and performance goals as well. Nicholls (1984) has used the terms task-involved and ego-involved for similar constructs (see Pintrich, 2000c for a review). In our own work, we have focused on mastery and performance goals and will use these labels in our discussion in this chapter.

In the literature on mastery and performance goals, the general theoretical assumption has been that mastery goals foster a host of adaptive motivational, cognitive, and achievement outcomes, while performance goals generate less adaptive or even maladaptive outcomes. Moreover, this assumption has been supported in a large number of empirical studies on goals and achievement processes (Ames, 1992; Dweck and Leggett, 1988; Pintrich, 2000c; Pintrich and Schunk, 1996), in particular the positive predictions for mastery goals. The logic of the argument is that when students are focused on trying to learn and understand the material and trying to improve their performance relative to their own past performance, this orientation will help them maintain their self-efficacy in the face of failure, ward off negative affect such as anxiety, lessen the probability that they will have distracting thoughts, and free up cognitive capacity and allow for more cognitive engagement and achievement. Lyndsay adopts a mastery goal of learning and understanding and certainly shows this adaptive pattern of outcomes. In contrast, when students are concerned about trying to be the best, to get higher grades than others, and to do well compared to others under a performance goal, it is possible that this orientation will result in more negative affect or anxiety, or increase the possibility of distracting and irrelevant thoughts (e.g., worrying about how others are doing, rather than focusing on the task), and that this will diminish cognitive capacity, task engagement, and performance.

In our own empirical research at Michigan, we have found similar patterns in our data with college students. Mastery goals have been positively related to cognitive strategy use and self-regulation as well as performance. These studies have shown that college students who report higher levels of mastery goals are more likely to use elaboration and organizational strategies as well as to be more metacognitive and regulating (as shown by Lyndsay), with mastery goals accounting for up to 16% of the variance in these outcomes. College students who adopted mastery goals and tried to focus on learning also tended to achieve at higher levels in terms of grades, albeit the variance accounted for was lower (only about 4%). These relations are not as strong as those for self-efficacy, but they were still statistically reliable across a number of samples and studies.

In terms of performance goals, we have not measured them on the MSLQ as they are traditionally defined in terms of outperforming others and trying to get the highest grades relative to peers. In contrast, we have assessed students' focus on general extrinsic goals for doing their coursework such as wanting to get good grades in general (both Lyndsay and Mike had this type of goal) and wanting to do well to satisfy parents and other adults. Using this measure of extrinsic goal orientation, we generally find that it is unrelated to, or is negatively related to, the use of cognitive strategies and self-regulation in college students. That is, students who are focused on grades, not learning, are less likely to be cognitively engaged and self-regulating (as was the case with Mike). In contrast, for performance, we do find some positive relations between an extrinsic goal orientation and grades, with extrinsic goal orientation accounting for 4% of the variance in some studies. In this case, it appears that students who have set a goal of getting good grades do get somewhat better actual grades than other students. Nevertheless, the results for extrinsic goals are not as stable or reliable as those for mastery goals.

More recently, some empirical evidence has emerged to indicate that performance goals are not necessarily maladaptive for all outcomes (Harackiewicz et al., 1998; Pintrich, 2000a, b, c). In this research, performance goals — the competitive urge or goal (where students are trying to approach the goal of doing better than others), seems to be positively related to actual performance at least in terms of final course grade (Harackiewicz, et al., 1998). In addition, these studies seem to show that there is not necessarily a decrement in cognitive engagement or self-regulation as a function of adopting a performance goal (Pintrich, 2000a, b, c). Finally, studies with younger students in junior high classrooms also have shown that students high in approach performance goals and high in mastery goals are not more anxious, do not experience more negative affect, and are equally motivated as those low in approach performance goals and high in mastery (Pintrich, 2000b). This recent research is leading to some reconceptualization of the general theoretical assumption that mastery goals are adaptive and performance goals are maladaptive, but there is still a need for much more research on the stability of these findings for performance goals.

In summary, the research on goal orientation suggests that at this point in time only one stable generalization is valid. Our second generalization is:

Generalization 2 - *Mastery goals are positively related to adaptive cognitive and self-regulatory strategy use as well as actual achievement in the college classroom.* Students who adopt a mastery goal and focus on learning, understanding, and self-improvement are much more likely to use adaptive cognitive and self-regulatory strategies as well as to achieve better results (C predicts outcomes in E, in Figure 1, as well as self-regulation processes D). Accordingly, classroom contexts that foster the adoption of mastery goals by students should facilitate motivation and learning. For example, college classrooms that encourage students to adopt goals of learning and understanding through the reward and evaluation structures (i.e., how grades are assigned, how tasks are graded and evaluated), rather than just getting good grades or competing with other college students, should foster a mastery goal orientation.

Task value. Goal orientation can refer to students' goals for a specific task (a midterm exam) as well as their general orientation to a course or a field. In the same way, students' task value beliefs can be fairly specific or more general. Three components of task value have been proposed by Eccles (1983) as important in achievement dynamics: the individual's perception of the importance of the task, their personal interest in the task (similar to intrinsic interest in intrinsic motivation theory), and their perception of the utility value of the task for future goals. These three value components may be rather parallel in children and college students, but can vary significantly in adults (Wlodkowski, 1988).

The perceived importance of a task, the importance component of task value, refers to the individuals' perception of the task's importance or salience for them. It is related to a general goal orientation, but importance could vary according to goal orientation. An individual's orientation may guide the general direction of behavior, while value may relate to the level of involvement. For example, some college students may believe that success in a particular course is very important (or unimportant) to them, regardless of their intrinsic or extrinsic goals. That is, the students may see success in the course as learning the material or getting a good grade, but they still may attach differential importance to these goals. Importance should be related to the individuals' persistence at a task as well as choice of a task.

Student interest in the task is another aspect of task value. Interest is assumed to be an individual's general attitude or liking of the task that is somewhat stable over time and a function of personal characteristics. In an educational setting, this includes the individual's interest in the course content and reactions to the other characteristics of the course, such as the instructor (cf., Wlodkowski, 1988). Both Lyndsay and Mike find some of their classes interesting and others less interesting (or even boring). Personal interest in the task is partially a function of individuals' preferences as well as aspects of the task (e.g., Malone and Lepper, 1987). However, personal interest should not be confused with situational interest, which can be generated by simple environmental features (e.g., an interesting lecture, a fascinating speaker, a dramatic film) but which are not long-lasting and do not necessarily inculcate stable personal interest (Hidi, 1990). Schiefele (1991) has shown that students' personal interest in the material being studied is related to their level of involvement in terms of the use of cognitive strategies as well as actual performance. There is a current revival in research on the role of interest in learning (see Renninger, Hidi, and Krapp, 1992).

In contrast to the means or process motivational dynamic of interest, utility value refers to the ends or instrumental motivation of the student (Eccles, 1983). Utility value is determined by the individual's perception of the task's usefulness for them. For students this may include beliefs that the course will be useful for them immediately in some way (e.g., help them cope with college), in their major (e.g., they need this information for upper level courses), or their career and life in general (e.g., this will help them somehow in graduate school). At a task level, student may perceive different course assignments (e.g., essay and multiple choice exams, term papers, lab activities, class discussion) as more or less useful and decide to become more or less cognitively engaged in the tasks.

Lyndsay does try to see how the course material may be useful to her, even if she does not find it very interesting.

Although these three components of task value can be separated, conceptually, in our work at Michigan with the MSLQ they have tended to factor together into one scale, which we have labeled task value. In our work with college students, task value is positively related to self-reports of cognitive strategy use including elaboration, organizational, and metacognitive strategies (Pintrich, 1999; Pintrich and Garcia, 1991; 1993). In these studies, task value accounted for between 3% to 36% of the variance in these different measures of cognitive engagement and self-regulation (C in Figure 1 predicts self-regulation process D). In addition, task value also was positively related to performance in these studies, albeit much less strongly. The general strength of the relation between task value and self-regulation was weaker than the relation between self-efficacy and self-regulation, but the positive association was still statistically reliable across studies. In other words, students who valued the course believed it was important to them and who were interested in the course material were more likely to be cognitive engaged and self-regulating as well as achieving at higher levels. These findings lead us to the next generalization.

Generalization 3 - *Higher levels of task value are associated with adaptive cognitive outcomes, such as higher levels of self-regulatory strategy use as well as higher levels of achievement.* This generalization may not be surprising, but it is important to formulate because constructs like value, utility, and interest are often considered to be unrelated to cognitive outcomes or achievement, and to be important noncognitive outcomes. It is of course important to foster value, utility, and interest as outcomes in their own right, but the generalization suggests that by facilitating the development of task value in the college classroom, an important byproduct will be more cognitive engagement, self-regulation, and achievement (C predicts both E outcomes in Figure 1 and self-regulation processes, D). For example, the use of materials (e.g., tasks, texts, articles, chapter) that are meaningful and interesting to college students can foster increased levels of task value. In addition, class activities (demonstrations, small group activities) that are useful, interesting, and meaningful to college students will facilitate the development of task value beliefs.

Affective Components

Affective components include students' emotional reactions to the task and their performance (i.e., anxiety, pride, shame) and their more emotional needs in terms of self-worth or self-esteem, affiliation, self-actualization (cf., Covington and Beery, 1976; Veroff and Veroff, 1980). Affective components address the basic question, how does the task make me feel? There is considerably less research on the affective components, except for student anxiety.

Anxiety. There is a long history of research on test anxiety and its general negative relationship to academic performance (Covington, 1992; Zeidner, 1998). Test anxiety is one of the most consistent individual difference variables that can be linked to detrimental performance in achievement situations (Hill and Wigfield, 1984). The basic model assumes that test anxiety is a negative reaction to a testing situation that includes both a "cognitive" worry component and a more emotional response (Liebert and Morris, 1967). The worry component consists of negative thoughts about performance while taking the exam (e.g., "I can't do this problem. That means I'm going to flunk; what will I do then?") which interfere with the students' ability to actually activate the appropriate knowledge and skills to do well on the test. These "self-perturbing ideations" (Bandura, 1986) can build up over the course of the exam and spiral out of control as time elapses, which then creates more anxiety about finishing in time. The emotional component involves more visceral reactions (e.g., sweaty palms, upset stomach) that also can interfere with performance.

In our own research program, we have examined the role of the worry component of test anxiety in the college classroom. Our results generally show a small relation between student's responses on the MSLQ items on test anxiety and their reports of strategy use, such as rehearsal, elaboration, or organizational strategies (correlations are in the range of .03 to .15, but include both low negative and low positive correlations). For metacognitive strategies, the correlations again are low (.07 to .17), but in the negative direction (Pintrich and Garcia, 1993; Pintrich et al, 1993). Given that there may be curvilinear relations between test anxiety and these cognitive and self-regulatory processes, the linear correlation estimates may not adequately capture the nature of the relations.

Zeidner (1998), in his review of the research on test anxiety and information processing, notes that anxiety generally has a detrimental effect on all phases of cognitive processing (see Figure 2). In the planning and encoding phase, people experiencing high levels of anxiety have difficulty attending to and encoding appropriate information about the task. In terms of actual cognitive processes while doing the task, high levels of anxiety lead to less concentration on the task, difficulties in the efficient use of working memory, more superficial processing and less in-depth processing, and problems in using metacognitive regulatory processes to control learning (Zeidner, 1998). Of course, these difficulties in cognitive processing and self-regulation will usually result in less learning and lower levels of performance.

In summary, test anxiety is generally not adaptive and gives us **Generalization 4** - *High levels of test anxiety are generally not adaptive and usually lead to less adaptive cognitive processing, self-regulation and lower levels of achievement.*

This generalization is based on a great deal of both experimental and correlational work as reviewed by Zeidner (1998). Of course, Zeidner (1998) notes that there may be occasions when some aspects of anxiety lead to some facilitating effects for learning and performance. For example, Garcia and Pintrich (1994) have suggested that some students, called defensive pessimists (Norem and Cantor, 1986), can use their anxiety about doing poorly to motivate themselves to try harder and study more, leading to better achievement. The harnessing of anxiety for motivational purposes is one example of a self-regulating motivational strategy that students might use to regulate their learning.

Nevertheless, in the case of test anxiety, which is specific to testing situations, the generalization still holds that students who are very anxious about doing well do have more difficulties in cognitive processing and do not learn or perform as well as might be expected. One implication is that faculty need to be aware of the role of test anxiety in reducing performance and should try to reduce the potential debilitating effects in their own classroom.

Other affective reactions. Besides anxiety, other affective reactions can influence choice and persistence behavior. Weiner (1986), in his attributional analysis of emotion, has suggested that certain types of emotions (e.g., anger, pity, shame, pride, guilt) are dependent on the types of attributions individuals make for their successes and failures. For example, this research suggests that an instructor will tend to feel pity for a student who did poorly on a exam because of some uncontrollable reason (e.g., death in family) and would be more likely to help that student in the future. In contrast, a instructor is more likely to feel anger at a student who did poorly through a simple lack of effort and be less willing to help that student in the future. In general, an attributional analysis of motivation and emotion repeatedly has been shown to be helpful in understanding achievement dynamics (Weiner, 1986) and there is a need for much more research on these other affective reactions in the college classroom.

Emotional needs. The issue of an individual's emotional needs (e.g., need for affiliation, power, self-worth, self-esteem, self-actualization) is related to the motivational construct of goal orientation, although the needs component is assumed to be less cognitive, more affective and, perhaps, less accessible to the individual. Many models of emotional needs have been proposed (e.g., Veroff and Veroff, 1980; Wlodkowski, 1988), but the need for self-worth or self-esteem seems particularly relevant. Research on student learning shows that self-esteem or sense of self-worth has often been implicated in models of school performance (e.g., Covington, 1992; Covington and Beery, 1976). Covington (1992) has suggested that individuals are always motivated to establish, maintain, and promote a positive self-image. Given that this hedonic bias is assumed to be operating at all times, individuals may develop a variety of coping strategies to maintain self-worth but, at the same time, these coping strategies may actually be self-defeating.

Covington and his colleagues (e.g., Covington, 1984; Covington and Berry, 1976; Covington and Omelich, 1979a,b) have documented how several of these strategies can have debilitating effects on student performance. Many of these poor coping strategies hinge on the role of effort and the fact that effort can be a double-edged sword (Covington and Omelich, 1979a). Students who try harder will increase the probability of their success, but also increase their risk of having to make an ability attribution for failure, followed by a drop in expectancy for success and self-worth (Covington, 1992).

There are several classic failure-avoiding tactics that demonstrate the power of the motive to maintain a sense of self-worth. One strategy is to choose easy tasks. As Covington (1992) notes, individuals may choose tasks that insure success although the tasks do not really test the individuals' actual skill level. College students may choose this strategy by continually electing "easy" courses or deciding upon "easy" majors. A second failure-avoiding strategy involves procrastination. For example, a college student who does not prepare for a test because of lack of time can, if successful, attribute it to superior aptitude. On the other hand, this type of procrastination maintains an individual's sense of self-worth because, if it is not successful, the student can attribute the failure to lack of study time, not poor skill. Of course, this type of effort-avoiding strategy increases the probability of failure over time which will result in lowered perceptions of self-worth, so it is ultimately self-defeating.

In summary, although less researched, affective components can influence students' motivated behavior. Moreover, as the analysis of the self-worth motive shows (Covington, 1992), the affective components can interact with other more cognitive motivational beliefs (i.e., attributions) as well as self-regulatory strategies (management of effort) to influence achievement. However, we do not offer any generalizations for these components given that they have not been subject to the same level of empirical testing as the other motivational components.

THE ROLE OF PERSONAL CHARACTERISTICS (A)

There are many different personal characteristics that college students bring with them to the college classroom. Of course, there are important personality differences (e.g., the Big Five personality traits) or more trait-like differences in implicit motives such as the need for achievement (Snow, et al, 1996). In this chapter, due to space considerations, we will note just three of the main personal differences — age, gender, and ethnicity (see A in Figure 1). These personal characteristics can have a major effect on the motivational and self-regulatory processes as well as outcomes as indexed by mean level differences in these variables. At the same time, and perhaps more importantly, these personal characteristics may moderate the relations between motivation (C in Figure 1) and outcomes (E in Figure 1), or motivation and self-regulation (D), or self-regulation (D) and outcomes (E).

Age

Generally stated, important age-developmental differences in motivational beliefs and self-regulatory processes develop over the course of the life-span (Eccles, Wigfield, & Schiefele, 1998; Pintrich and Schunk, 1996). The overall trend is in line with general developmental assumptions that both motivational and self-regulatory processes become more differentiated with age and that individuals become more capable of self-regulation with age. Most of the work that has explicitly focused on developmental differences has been concerned with age-related changes that occur before college, particularly in elementary and secondary school-age samples. The research with college students has not been explicitly developmental and has rarely used longitudinal designs that are needed to estimate developmental changes over the course of college, rather than simple cross-sectional designs.

In our own work on college student motivation, we have used relatively homogeneous samples with age ranges between 17 and 25, not a large span, for examining developmental differences. Moreover, we have not used longitudinal designs but have focused on student motivation within specific college classroom contexts, which of course change over the years in college. However, within our studies, we have collected short-term longitudinal data within a course for a semester or over a year-long course (e.g., two-semester calculus course, two-semester chemistry course). These designs have used two or three waves of data collection on student motivation, providing some estimates of how student motivation changes over the length of a course.

In all of our studies that have used multiple waves of data, the results have been fairly consistent, with various motivational beliefs decreasing over the course of the semester or year. Average levels of self-efficacy and task value, in particular, show reliable drops over time within a course. This may be expected as, at the beginning of the course, most students may have relatively high perceptions of self-efficacy, but as the course progresses and they receive feedback on their work, and there is the inevitable distribution of grades, then some students will lower their efficacy perceptions, resulting in a lower overall average. In the same manner, task value may be somewhat higher at the beginning of a course, as students report that they are interested in the course material and think that it will be important and useful to them. However, as the course progresses, some of the students come to find that some of the material is less than interesting, important, or useful to them. These students then rate the course lower and the overall average for the course decreases.

The results for use of self-regulatory strategies have been less consistent in our research, but given their generally positive relation with motivational beliefs, they would be expected to decrease as well within a course, over a semester. On the other hand, as students develop expertise in the use of self-regulatory strategies in the college context, one could expect that they would become more proficient in the used of various self-regulatory strategies. First year college students often may not even know very much about the different self-regulatory strategies that are available to them (e.g., Mike's case) or, even if they are able to use some self-regulatory strategies (e.g., Lyndsay's case), they still have to adjust and adapt their use to the college context. Accordingly, over the course of a four- or five-year college career, students will become more adept at self-regulating their cognition, motivation, behavior, and their context.

Of course, as we have worked with college faculty in our research, they generally find these decreases in motivation over the semester discouraging, and to some extent the drops in motivation are disappointing. However, it is important to recall that these are average decreases over all students, and that, given the variance in ratings, there are also some students who report increases in their motivation over time. Accordingly, it seems more important to consider the potential role of age as a moderator of the relations between motivation and self-regulation, rather than the average mean level differences that occur as a function of age. This also reminds us of the importance of aptitude-treatment interactions (ATIs) in which different students perceive, react to, and learn differentially in different college classroom contexts. That is, some students might be motivated in a classroom context that is structured a certain way or involves a certain type of material, while other students in the exact same course are less motivated and may even be bored by it. As in our two examples, both Lyndsay and Mike were bored by some of their classes, but it is likely that other students found those classes very interesting.

In terms of age as a moderator, within the age range of the traditional 17- to 25-year-old college student, it is unlikely that there will be many differences in the relations between motivation and self-regulation as a function of age. However, there is a need for research on potential age moderators effects, even within this traditional college group. More importantly, if one considers non-traditional college students who are over 25, then there may some important moderating effects. For example, these non-traditional students may have much higher levels of task value for their school work (C in Figure 1), be more focused on learning and not grades (C in Figure 1), and be much more willing to engage in the important types of self-regulatory activities (D, in Figure 1) focused on academic tasks, given they may be less distracted by other social activities in comparison to more traditionally-aged college students. In this case, the second and third generalizations regarding mastery goals and task value may not be as strong for these older students, essentially because there is little variance in mastery goals or task value in older college students. In the same manner, self-efficacy may not work in line with the first generalization given that older college students may be less confident of their academic skills, yet still self-regulate quite well. Research is needed on these types of moderator effects of age with diverse samples.

In summary, age may be an important personal characteristic that can change the nature of the student motivation and self-regulation in college classrooms. Certainly, students who have been in college longer and are older, even if they are within the traditional 17- to 25-year-old group, should be able to self-regulate better than new college students. To some extent, third and fourth year college students who are still enrolled in college have learned "the game" and have a repertoire of self-regulatory strategies that they can use to adapt to college demands. New college students often have to learn how to adapt their "high school" cognitive strategies and regulation processes to fit the increased demands in college (as is the case for both Mike and Lyndsay). Moreover, there are many high school students who have been "other-regulated" by parents or high school teachers and now find they have to self-regulate in the absence of these supports. There will be an age-related developmental progression in how students learn to cope and self-regulate their cognition, motivation, and behavior as they enter and progress through college. In addition, research is needed on the potential moderator effects of non-traditional aged college students on the general relations proposed between motivation and self-regulation.

Gender

Researchers have contended for many years that males and females possess varied academic strengths, that males and females differ in mathematical and verbal skills and that these different capabilities, in turn, partially account for the disparities in achievement levels between the sexes in certain academic domains (Maccoby and Jacklin, 1974). While such views are still pervasive in popular culture, recent research on gender differences in academic achievement and motivation would suggest otherwise.

First, the explanation concerning varied cognitive abilities between males and females has been called into question. There is very little evidence to support the notion that males and females possess different academic aptitudes. Researchers generally have found no gender differences in mathematical and verbal abilities. Moreover, when they did find differences, as in the case of spatial ability, they found that the differences were limited to specific types of tasks — in this case, mental rotation (Linn and Peterson, 1985).

Second, the statement that a gender-related achievement gap exists is apparently no longer accurate. Recent meta-analytic reviews of the research in this area have reported minimal, if any, gender differences in academic achievement (Hyde, Fennema, and Lamon, 1990; Linn and Hyde, 1989). Studies examining gender differences in mathematics generally discredit the notion of male superiority in mathematics. In fact, in some cases, females were found to outperform males on tests of mathematical ability (cf., Eisenberg, Martin, and Fabes, 1996). Similar findings were found in other academic domains. Hyde and Linn (1988), for example, maintain that sex-related differences in language competence, if they ever truly existed, certainly no longer exist.

This is not to say, however, that there are absolutely no gender-related differences. While there may be no variation between males and females in actual achievement levels, there are certainly differences in other outcome variables, namely choice and persistence (E in Figure 1). The percentage of females who choose to pursue natural science and/or mathematics majors in college, although increasing, is still modest at best, particularly in the fields of physical science and engineering. Moreover, while females comprise approximately half of the graduates who receive baccalaureates in life sciences and mathematics, less than one-fifth of all doctoral degrees in these fields are awarded to women (Rayman and Brett, 1995). Accordingly, women remain severely underrepresented in the fields of science, engineering, and mathematics.

The interesting question, of course, is why? If it is the case that women and men obtain comparable achievement test scores, then why do not more women pursue careers in science and mathematics? Motivational theorists generally explain this finding in terms of self-efficacy theory. Researchers have found that females generally have lower perceptions of competence (i.e., self-efficacy) than males in subjects such as mathematics and science, even when their actual performance is just as high, if not higher, than males' (Eccles, 1983; Meece and Eccles, 1993). That is, females are generally less confident that they can perform well on mathematics and science tasks. Researchers have also found that such disparities in self-efficacy levels are not limited to adolescents and college-aged women; gender related differences in self-efficacy beliefs have been found even among early elementary age girls (Entwisle and Baker, 1983; Frey and Ruble, 1987; Phillips and Zimmerman, 1990). Thus, it is believed that females' low self-perceptions of their competence influences, or rather deters them their pursuit of science-related career trajectories. After all, why would any student pursue a career in an area where she believed that she did not have the competence to learn or to do well in the academic domains related to that career?

Nevertheless, such findings should not imply that nothing can be done to counter this female fatalism. Lenney (1977), for example, suggests that this gender difference in self-efficacy levels may be influenced by certain contextual variables. In his review of the research, he concluded that variables such as the provision of clear and objective evaluative feedback, the sex-typing of academic tasks, and the emphasis on social comparison moderate the gender difference in self-confidence levels. In addition, some researchers have posited that perhaps the mean level differences in students' ratings of their efficacy beliefs are really a manifestation of response bias. Investigators believe that males have a tendency to over-inflate their ratings of confidence levels while females have a tendency toward modesty (Pajares and Graham, 1999; Wigfield, Eccles, MacIver, Reuman, and Midgley, 1991).

In addition to the research on self-efficacy beliefs, there is some limited evidence to suggest that females show comparatively lower levels of other components of motivation (C in Figure 1) than males. The research on attributions, for example, suggests that girls have a tendency to make maladaptive attributions. Numerous studies have demonstrated that females display decreased achievement strivings, especially under failure conditions, and often blame themselves (i.e., make internal causal attributions) for poor academic performance (in our two cases, Mike shows this debilitating pattern more than Lyndsay does). Even in situations where they are successful, researchers have found that females more often attribute their success to external and/or unstable causes. In contrast, males generally have been found to make more adaptive attributions, often attributing their performance to lack of effort or bad luck and even showing improvements in performance after failure (Dweck and Reppucci, 1973; Meece, Parsons, Kaczala, Goff, and Futterman, 1982). At the same time, however, Eccles and her colleagues caution against making such generalizations about the attributional styles of males and females, as studies often employed different methodologies when measuring attributions. Correspondingly, more recent research findings contradict the claim that females make maladaptive attributions. Roberts (1991), for instance, found that women in her study on gender differences in responsiveness to evaluations were not more self-disparaging in response to negative feedback.

Thus, the research on gender differences in motivational beliefs to date has proved somewhat inconclusive, with the possible exception that females generally tend to have lower self-perceptions of their academic ability. The research examining differences by gender of students' self-regulatory processes (D, in

Figure 1) has been even more inconsistent. First, there are very few studies on self-regulation that have specifically sought to test whether these processes vary by gender. Additionally, what few studies that do exist on this topic have focused on students in middle school grades or younger (Ablard and Lipschultz, 1998; Anderman and Young, 1994; Nolen, 1988; Zimmerman and Martinez-Pons, 1990). At present, we do not know of any study that has found conclusive evidence that gender differences exist in college students' self-regulated learning. Even in our own studies at Michigan, although we have at times found mean level differences, these differences were never consistent across studies and we believe were not indicative of any systematic pattern. Of those studies that focused on younger pre-collegiate students, however, researchers generally have found mixed results. Some researchers report that females display higher levels of self-regulated learning (e.g., Zimmerman and Martinez-Pons, 1990) while others contend that females are no more likely than males to self-regulate their learning (e.g., Meece and Jones, 1996). Clearly, more research is needed before definitive conclusions can be drawn about how gender might possibly moderate the relations between motivational and self-regulatory processes and the various outcome measures. On the other hand, if one were to speculate based on the stereotype that girls are more diligent note-takers and generally more studious, it would not be entirely unreasonable to expect females to display more self-regulatory behavior than males.

ETHNICITY

Despite having emerged primarily from research on White, middle-class youths, most current models of psychology generally make assumptions about the applicability of psychological research and generalizations to students from various cultures, contexts, and ethnicities. The models of self-regulation and motivation are certainly no exception. Unfortunately, however, very little research has been done to test these assumptions. The dearth of studies examining ethnic differences in students' motivational (C, in Figure 1) and self-regulatory processes (D, in Figure 1) is especially troublesome as the need for such research is quite apparent. As the ethnic minority enrollment continues to increase on college campuses across the country, college instructors are constantly confronted with issues concerning how to teach these students better. Consequently, it is imperative that our models of learning and motivation address potential variation according to ethnicity.

Similar to the research on gender differences, studies examining group differences in motivation and self-regulated learning generally address the following two questions. First, are there mean level differences across various ethnic groups in their levels of academic performance, motivation, and self-regulated learning? Second, do the relations between these various constructs differ across minority group students? That is, do we need to modify our general models of self-regulated learning and motivation to accommodate ethnic differences? Or, can we conclude that our models can be generalized more or less and that the constructs operate similarly among the various ethnic groups?

In terms of the first question, pronounced ethnic differences in mean achievement levels (E in Figure 1) have been found. In comparison to students from other ethnic minority groups and, in certain cases, Caucasian students, Asian American students have attained a relatively high level of academic success. Not only do they outperform other minority students on standardized test measures, the percentage of Asian American students who continue on to post-secondary education is greater than either African American or Hispanic students (Hsia and Peng, 1998). In contrast, researchers have found that African American and Hispanic students display the lowest levels of academic achievement and performance (e.g., Graham, 1994).

Motivational theorists have largely accounted for these disparities in achievement levels by suggesting that a) Asian American students have higher levels of achievement motivation and that b) African Americans, in contrast, are generally amotivated toward academic goals. As Graham (1994) points out in her review of African American achievement motivation, traditional research on this subpopulation intimated that African American students' low achievement levels can be attributed not to deficits in cognitive abilities, but rather their low expectations for future success as well as their low academic self-concept. The exact opposite has been said for Asian Americans. Researchers on Asian-Americans have suggested that these students are more likely to make effort attributions, to believe in the importance of education, as well as have high expectations for academic success (Hess, Chang, and McDevitt, 1987; Holloway, Kashiwagi, Hess, and Azuma, 1986; Stevenson and Lee, 1990).

However, recent research on both of these populations suggest that such explanations are too simplistic. Graham (1994), for example, found no evidence that African Americans display lower expectancies for success, nor did she find support for the notion that African American students have lower concepts of their academic ability. In fact, she states that the vast majority of studies report African American students to have higher expectations for success as well as higher self-concept beliefs. Similarly, the research on Asian Americans has also proved to be somewhat inconclusive. Studies on causal attributions have found that Asian Americans are prone to make internal and stable attributions especially in the face of failure which, according to attribution theory, should make one more susceptible toward learned helplessness and should not, by any means, lead to increased achievement levels. The research examining Asian-American self-efficacy beliefs has been equally troublesome. Numerous researchers have documented Asians and Asian American students' comparatively lower levels of self-efficacy and self-concepts of ability, even though their actual achievement test scores were often higher than non-Asians (Eaton and Dembo, 1997; Stigler, Smith, and Mao, 1985; Whang and Hancock, 1994).

Such findings bring us to our second question regarding how widely we can generalize our model to other populations. These studies certainly suggest that specific motivational constructs, like attributions and self-efficacy (C, in Figure 1), might not operate in a similar fashion for Asian American and African American students. More specifically, these findings imply that the magnitude of the relationships between these motivational variables and outcomes (E, in Figure 1) may not be as great for these two ethnic groups as it may be for Caucasian students. For example, the relationship between self-efficacy and achievement for both Asian American and African American students seems to be an inverse one, albeit in different directions. African American students have higher perceptions of their competence yet lower achievement test scores. Asian-American students, on the hand, have lower perceptions of their competence and higher achievement levels. In both cases, researchers have attempted to explain this discrepancy in terms of task value beliefs. Numerous researchers (e.g., Steele, 1997; Fordam and Ogbu, 1986; Graham, Taylor, and Hudley, 1998) suggest that in the case of African-American students, repeated school failures have led these students to devalue education and therefore self-efficacy beliefs do not come into play as much as it does for other students. In a similar fashion, Eaton and Dembo (1997) have proposed that Asian American students focus less on their situational perceptions of competence (i.e., self-efficacy) and more on the importance of successfully completing an academic task (i.e. value).

Another plausible explanation for this discrepancy is calibration — that is, the extent to which students' ratings of their motivational beliefs accurately reflect their true level of motivation. Similar to the research on gender differences in self-efficacy beliefs, there is evidence to suggest that African-Americans generally over-estimate their ability to perform an academic task while Asian-Americans may underestimate their ability. Given our model of self-regulation, which relies on monitoring of cognition and performance for regulatory efforts, if students are not calibrated then they will be less likely to seek to regulate and repair their cognition or behavior. More concretely, if some college students, such as African Americans, believe they are doing well and yet are not achieving at the appropriate level, they may be less likely to attempt to regulate their behavior. These students would not put forth more effort to change their cognition or behavior in order to improve their performance. In the long run, this lack of calibration, monitoring, and regulation would lead to lowered levels of performance and achievement.

In addition to the above research, a select group of researchers has proposed alternative models that focus more on the influence of social factors on the relations between the various motivational constructs. Steele and his colleagues, for example, have demonstrated how stereotypes can have deleterious effects on African American college students' academic achievement (Steele and Aronson, 1995; Steele, 1997). Steele's model rests on the notion of stereotype threat: he argues that in any evaluative situation, as a result of widespread negative stereotypes about the academic competence of African Americans, these students confront the threat of potentially being judged according to the stereotype as well as the threat of possibly fulfilling the stereotype. He further contends that this threat can interfere with students' cognitive processes, thus resulting in lower achievement levels. In support, Steele found in his series of empirical studies with college students that African American students indeed performed relatively poorly in comparison to a matched sample of European American college students, when they were told that a test was diagnostic of their true academic capabilities (Steele and Aronson, 1995).

In addition, the recent work of Shih and her colleagues extends the stereotype vulnerability framework by not only applying the model to another cultural group, but also by examining the potential effects of "positive" stereotypes on subsequent achievement. Interestingly, their research findings suggest that the mere activation of a "positive" stereotype (i.e., Asian Americans possess superior mathematical abilities) can serve to heighten Asian American college students scores on standardized measures of mathematics achievement (Shih, Pittinsky, and Ambady, 1999).

Finally, in terms of ethnic differences in self-regulated learning variables, there are very few studies that have examined how the process of self-regulated learning might be moderated by ethnicity. In terms of strategy use, however, there is some evidence to suggest that Asian-Americans have a tendency to employ what researchers have called surface-processing strategies when studying (i.e., memorization and rehearsal), rather than deep-processing strategies like metacognitive strategies (Marton, Dall'Alba, and Kun, 1996). However, such claims run counter to the assertion that the use of deep-processing strategies should lead to the highest levels of achievement.

In summary, there are potential age, gender, and ethnicity differences in both mean levels of motivation (C) and self-regulation (D), and more importantly potential moderator effects of these personal characteristics on the relations between motivation and self-regulation. There is a clear need for much more research on how these personal characteristics facilitate the development of motivation and self-regulation. In addition, it is important to consider how these personal characteristics might conditionalize the four generalizations offered in this chapter. At this point, it seems that these four generalizations can be taken as applying to all groups of college students, but there is a need for much more research on how age, gender, or ethnic differences may change the nature of these generalizations.

THE ROLE OF CLASSROOM CONTEXTUAL FACTORS (B)

A multitude of classroom contextual factors (B in Figure 1) may influence student motivation (C) and self-regulation (D) in the college classroom. However, four general factors can have a dramatic effect in these two areas: the nature of the task, the reward and goal structure of the classroom, the instructional methods, and the instructor's behavior. At the same time, there is not as much empirical research on how these classroom contextual factors (B) may influence student motivation (C) and self-regulation (D). One limitation of the model of motivation and self-regulation presented in this chapter is that it tends to concentrate on the individual college student, and not give enough consideration to how the context can situate motivation and self-regulation. There is a clear need for more research on how different aspects of the college classroom influence college student motivation and learning. Accordingly, this section on classroom contextual factors is not as detailed as the previous sections, but it does provide a sketch of potential relations and many directions for future research efforts.

NATURE OF ACADEMIC TASKS

Classroom research on teaching often focuses on what the instructor says and does in class and how that can have an influence on student motivation. However, the types of tasks that students are asked to complete also can have a dramatic influence. The academic tasks that students confront in the college classroom include multiple choice and essay exams, library research papers, expository essay papers, solution of problem sets, performing and writing up results from experiments, reading a text and discussing it in class, and other variations on assignments and assessment tasks. It has become an important assumption of research in cognitive psychology (cf., Brown, Bransford, Ferrara, and Campione, 1983; Crooks, 1988; Doyle, 1983) that the features of these different tasks (B in Figure 1) help to organize and guide students' cognition (D). For example, multiple choice tests that require only recognition of the course material often do not lead to deeper levels of cognitive processing in comparison to essay exams that require not only recall of information but also transformation of the information. In the same fashion, features of the academic tasks (B) may influence student motivation (C).

Two important components of tasks are content and product (Blumenfeld, Mergendoller, and Swarthout, 1987). Content refers to the actual course content that is embedded in the task. For example, two courses could cover the same basic material and concepts, but in one class students read secondary sources (e.g., a standard textbook) and in the other course they read primary sources (e.g., original writings in the field). The nature of these two types of readings could influence motivation in several ways. First, the primary source material may be written in a more engaging style and be more interesting to students, thereby fostering personal interest on the part of students which could lead to more motivated behavior (Garner, Brown, Sanders,, and Menke, 1992). On the other hand, the primary source material may be much more difficult for students to read in contrast to the standard textbook, which could result in lower self-efficacy perceptions for understanding the course material and less-motivated behavior. This simple example suggests that how the content is structured and organized in terms of both its difficulty level and interest can influence student motivation.

The product dimension of academic tasks involves what the students actually have to produce to complete the assignment or task. For example, tasks where students have some choice over what they do (e.g., choosing topics for research papers, choice of essays on exams) may foster higher control beliefs because students actually do have some personal control over the assignment. Of course, the difficulty level of the cognitive activities that students must carry out to complete the product can influence students' self-efficacy beliefs and interest levels. A too difficult task may elicit low self-efficacy beliefs and high anxiety, a too easy task may engender feelings of boredom, not interest. Accordingly, the key is to develop tasks that are within the range of most students' capabilities, but are still challenging to them (Pintrich and Schunk, 1996). Other features of exams (type of questions, time allowed to complete it) can increase test anxiety and have detrimental features on motivated behavior. Although these examples follow from theoretical predictions, there is very little empirical research on the role of academic tasks in college classrooms and there is a need for more research on tasks and their links to student motivation and cognition.

Reward and Goal Structures

The academic tasks that students confront in college classrooms are embedded in a larger classroom context that includes the overall reward and goal structures of the classroom. Reward structure refers to how "rewards" (i.e., grades) are distributed among students. The goal structure refers to how the different tasks are designed to be accomplished by the students (e.g., alone, cooperatively). These two structures may be related to one another in practice, but theoretically they can be orthogonal (Good and Brophy, 1987). Reward structures can be independent (grades are assigned based only on an individual's performance in relation to some standard or criteria, not on other students' performance), cooperative (grades are linked to other students' performance because a group of students have done a project or paper together and they all get the same grade for the one product), or competitive (grading on some type of curve where grades are assigned based on a "zero-sum game" which limits the number of high grades, where higher scores by some students automatically mean other students receive lower grades). Some research suggests that competitive reward structures have a detrimental influence on students' motivation by increasing anxiety and lowering students' self-efficacy and self-worth beliefs (Ames, 1992; Covington, 1992; Johnson and Johnson, 1974; Slavin, 1983).

However, research on the use of rewards in general, not just in competitive structures, has become very controversial again. There have been meta-analyses by Cameron and Pierce (1994) and Eisenberger and Cameron (1996, 1998) that suggest that rewards have few detrimental effects. In contrast, Deci, Koestner, and Ryan (1999), in another meta-analysis that re-analyzed the same studies, suggest that rewards can have detrimental effects on students' intrinsic motivation. The controversy has spawned a new edited book (Sansone and Harackiewicz, 2000) where various authors discuss the issues related to the use of rewards and their effects on student motivation and learning. The issues are complicated and it does not appear that any simple generalization like "rewards are good/rewards are bad" can be made, based on the research, although rewards that convey information to students about their capabilities seem to foster positive outcomes (Pintrich & Schunk, 1996). It is more important to note that activities and their accompanying rewards can have multiple effects on both the intrinsic and extrinsic motivation of students and that future research should attempt to understand the relations between contextual factors like rewards and both college student motivational and cognitive processes.

In terms of the goal structure of the classroom, again the structure can be individualistic, cooperative, or competitive in terms of how students are organized to accomplish the tasks. Most college classrooms are probably individualistic, where students basically work by themselves to master and understand the material. There may be occasions when college students are asked to cooperate formally (lab partners, writing groups, or formal study groups). Of course, students often cooperate informally in studying for exams. Students also may compete with one another in class discussion, competing for the floor and the presenting of ideas in the discussion. The evidence is overwhelmingly in favor of having students work together cooperatively to accomplish the tasks, because of increased self-efficacy and interest, lower anxiety, more cognitive engagement, and generally better performance (Ames, 1984, 1992; Covington, 1992; Slavin, 1983). Of course not all tasks can be done in a cooperative manner, but the evidence suggests that, if possible, instructors should provide opportunities in class for cooperative work or encourage students to work together outside class. It also should be noted that some of the research suggests that the most beneficial arrangement is to have students work together on the task (a cooperative goal structure), but to maintain an individualized reward structure where individual students are held accountable for their own work. For example, students may study together for a test, but they all are graded independently. Even more important, the research (Pintrich & Schunk, 1996) suggests that if students are put into groups to work together on a project (cooperative goal structure), they should still be required to produce a separate write-up or paper that is then graded independently (individualized reward structure). This allows students to work together, but still requires individual accountability which helps avoids the problem of "free riders" (students who do not contribute to the group).

Instructional Methods and Instructor Behavior

The general instructional methods that can be used in the college classroom (e.g., lectures, discussions, recitations, lab activities, simulations, etc.) may influence student motivation (see McKeachie, 1986; Perry, 1991), but research seems to be moving beyond simple comparisons of the relative effectiveness of these different methods, to focus on how the "quality" of these methods influences different cognitive and motivational processes and in turn how these processes mediate achievement (Murray, 1991; Perry, 1991). For example, it may be that student-centered discussions generally promote more student involvement and motivation than lectures (McKeachie, 1986), but it seems clear that lectures that are delivered in an interesting and stimulating manner can also increase student motivation. The key to understanding the relative effects of these different instructional strategies is to begin to examine how they may influence different components of students' motivational beliefs. Discussion methods do allow students more "control" over the class in terms of the pace and the "content" presented and therefore might be expected to facilitate motivation by increasing students' control beliefs. On the other hand, interesting and stimulating lectures could facilitate motivation by activating students' situational and personal interest in the subject. Accordingly, a consideration of the different components of motivation and how they might be related to different features of the classroom context suggests that there may be multiple pathways to the same general goal of facilitating student motivation. The instructional methods set the context and constraints that allow for more or fewer opportunities for certain motivating events to occur, but the actual occurrence of these events is a function of the instructor and the students' behaviors.

This general focus on the quality and process of the actual instructional context highlights the importance of instructor behavior. It seems clear that the ways in which the different instructional methods are used and implemented by the instructor can have dramatic effects on student motivation. For example, if small cooperative groups are used and implemented in the classroom in an unstructured, disorganized, "anything goes" manner, it is likely that not only actual student learning will suffer, but student motivation in terms of interest and self-efficacy will be diminished. Moreover, research on different instructor characteristics (e.g., clarity, organization, enthusiasm, rapport, expressiveness, etc.) has shown that these features are related to students' ratings as well as their actual learning, cognition, and motivation (see Feldman, 1989; Murray, 1991, Perry, 1991). For example, Perry and Penner (1990) found that instructor expressiveness (physical movement, eye contact, voice inflection and humor) had a positive influence on students' learning and motivation. Moreover, instructor expressiveness interacted with the control beliefs of students with expressiveness showing a larger effect for external locus of control students. There is still much research to be done, but this type of research that attempts to link different features of instructor behavior to different cognitive and motivational outcomes will have the most benefit for our understanding of college teaching and learning.

At the same time, the research will have to take into consideration that these instructor behaviors are embedded in classroom context that includes different task, goal, and reward structures as well as different instructional methods which may moderate the direct effects of instructor behaviors. Clearly, what will emerge from this type of research is a much more complex picture of how the classroom context can influence student motivation (see McKeachie, 1990), but it also will be a much more realistic view that eschews simplistic answers and "pat" solutions to the problems of teaching and student motivation.

CONCLUSION

Student motivation and self-regulation both have important roles to play in college student learning and achievement. The four generalizations offered in this chapter serve as good first principles for understanding how student motivation can facilitate or constrain self-regulated learning and achievement in the college classroom. Students who feel efficacious about their ability to learn and to do the work are more likely to be engaged and to do better. Likewise, students who are focused on learning, mastery, and self-improvement are more likely to be involved in learning and perform better. Finally, a third facilitating factor of engagement and achievement is task value with students who think the material is interesting, important, and useful more likely to be engaged and learning. A constraining factor on engagement and learning is test anxiety with higher levels of test anxiety interfering or impeding cognitive engagement, learning, and achievement.

These generalizations seem to apply to all groups of students, but there is a clear need for more research on how different personal characteristics may moderate or delimit how these four principles can be generalized. Finally, classroom context factors can certainly influence student motivation and cognition. Moreover, the classroom context factors discussed here are inherently open to manipulation and change, offering hope to faculty members who want to make improvements in their classrooms and in the nature of their instruction to facilitate student motivation and learning. Much research remains to be done, but the general model offered here should provide a conceptual framework for future research as well as practice.

REFERENCES

Ablard, K. E., and Lipschultz, R. E. (1998). Self-regulated learning in high achieving students: Relations to advanced reasoning, achievement goals, and gender. *Journal of Educational Psychology*, 90(1), 94-101.

Abramson, L., Seligman, M., and Teasdale, J. (1978). Learned helplessness in humans: A critique and reformulation. *Journal of Abnormal Psychology*, *87*, 49-74.

Ajzen, I. (1988). *Attitudes, personality, and behavior*. Chicago: Dorsey Press.

Ajzen, I. (1991). A theory of planned behavior. *Organizational Behavior and Human Decision Processes*, *50*, 179-211.

Alexander, P., Schallert, D., and Hare, V. (1991). Coming to terms: How researchers in learning and literacy talk about knowledge. *Review of Educational Research*, *61*, 315-343.

Ames, C. (1984). Competitive, cooperative, and individualistic goal structures: A cognitive-motivational analysis. In R. Ames and C. Ames (Eds.). *Research on motivation in education* (Vol. 1, pp. 177-207). New York: Academic Press.

Ames, C. (1992). Classrooms: Goals, structures, and student motivation. *Journal of Educational Psychology*, *84*, 261-271.

Anderman, E., and Young, A. (1994). Motivation and strategy use in science: Individual differences and classroom effects. *Journal of Research in Science Teaching*, 31, 811-831.

Bandura, A. (1982). Self-efficacy mechanisms in human agency. *American Psychologist*, *37*, 122-147.

Bandura, A. (1986). *Social foundations of thought and action: A social cognitive theory*. Englewood Cliffs, NJ: Prentice Hall.

Bandura, A. (1997). *Self-efficacy: The exercise of control*. New York: W.H. Freeman.

Baron, J. (1994). *Thinking and deciding*. New York: Cambridge University Press.

Baumeister, R.F., and Scher, S.J. (1988). Self-defeating behavior patterns among normal individuals: Review and analysis of common self-destructive tendencies. *Psychological Bulletin*, *104*, 3-22.

Bereiter, C., and Scardamalia, M. (1987). *The psychology of written composition*. Hillsdale, NJ: Lawrence Erlbaum Associates.

Berglas, S. (1985). Self-handicapping and self-handicappers: A cognitive/attributional model of interpersonal self-protective behavior. In R. Hogan and W.H. Jones (Eds.), *Perspectives in personality: Theory, measurement, and interpersonal dynamics* (pp. 235-270). Greenwich, CT: JAI Press.

Blumenfeld, P., Pintrich, P.R., Meece, J., and Wessels, K. (1982). The formation and role of self-perceptions of ability in the elementary classroom. *Elementary School Journal*, *82*, 401-420.

Blumenfeld, P., Mergendoller, J., and Swarthout, D. (1987). Task as a heuristic for understanding student learning and motivation. *Journal of Curriculum Studies*, *19*, 135-148.

Boekaerts, M. (1993). Being concerned with well-being and with learning. *Educational Psychologist*, *28*, 148-167.

Boekaerts, M., and Niemivirta, M. (2000). Self-regulated learning: Finding a balance between learning goals and ego-protective goals. In M. Boekaerts, P.R. Pintrich, and M. Zeidner (Eds.), *Handbook of Self-regulation: Theory, research, and applications*, (pp. 417-450). San Diego, CA: Academic Press.

Boekaerts, M., Pintrich, P.R., and Zeidner, M. (2000). *Handbook of self-regulation.* San Diego, CA: Academic Press.

Brown, A.L. (1997). Transforming schools into communities of thinking and learning about serious matters. *American Psychologist, 52*, 399-413.

Brown, A.L., Bransford, J.D., Ferrara, R.A., and Campione, J.C. (1983). Learning, remembering, and understanding. In J.H. Flavell and E.M. Markman (Eds.), *Handbook of child psychology: Cognitive development* (Vol. 3, pp. 77-166). New York: Wiley.

Butler, D.L., and Winne, P.H. (1995). Feedback and self-regulated learning: A theoretical synthesis. *Review of Educational Research, 65*, 245-281.

Cameron, J., and Pierce, W. (1994). Reinforcement, reward, and intrinsic motivation: A meta-analysis. *Review of Educational Research, 64*, 363-423.

Connell, J. P. (1985). A new multidimensional measure of children's perceptions of control. *Child Development, 56*, 1018-1041.

Corno, L. (1989). Self-regulated learning: A volitional analysis. In B.J. Zimmerman and D.H. Schunk, (Eds.), *Self-regulated learning and academic achievement: Theory, research and practice* (pp. 111-141). New York: Springer-Verlag.

Corno, L. (1993). The best-laid plans: Modern conceptions of volition and educational research. *Educational Researcher, 22*, 14-22.

Covington, M.V. (1992). *Making the grade: A self-worth perspective on motivation and school reform.* Cambridge: Cambridge University Press.

Covington, M. (1984). The motive for self-worth. In R. Ames and C. Ames (Eds.), *Research on motivation in education* (Vol. 1, pp. 77-113). New York: Academic Press.

Covington, M., and Beery, R. (1976). *Self-worth and school learning.* New York: Holt, Rinehart and Winston.

Covington, M.V., and Omelich, C.L. (1979a). Are causal attributions causal? A path analysis of the cognitive model of achievement motivation. *Journal of Personality and Social Psychology, 37*, 1487-1504.

Covington, M.V., and Omelich, C.L. (1979b). Effort: The double-edged sword in school achievement. *Journal of Educational Psychology, 71*, 169-182.

Crooks, T. (1988). The impact of classroom evaluation practices on students. *Review of Educational Research, 58*, 438-481.

Deci, E.L. (1975). *Intrinsic motivation.* New York: Plenum.

Deci, E.L., Koestner, R., and Ryan, R.M. (1999). A meta-analytic review of experiments examining the effects of extrinsic rewards on intrinsic motivation. *Psychological Bulletin, 125*, 627-668.

Deci, E.L., and Ryan, R.M. (1985). *Intrinsic motivation and self-determination in human behavior.* New York: Plenum.

de Charms, R. (1968). *Personal causation: The internal affective determinants of behavior.* New York: Academic Press.

Doyle, W. (1983). Academic work. *Review of Educational Research, 53*, 159-199.

Dweck, C.S., and Elliott, E.S. (1983). Achievement motivation. In P.H. Mussen (Series Ed.,) and E.M. Hetherington (Vol. Ed.) *Handbook of child psychology: Vol 4. Socialization, personality, and social development.* (4th ed., pp. 643-691). New York: Wiley.

Dweck, C.S., and Leggett, E.L. (1988). A social-cognitive approach to motivation and personality. *Psychological Review, 95*, 256-273.

Dweck, C., and Repucci, N. (1973). Learned helplessness and reinforcement responsibility in children. *Journal of Personality and Social Psychology, 25*, 109-116.

Eaton, M. J., and Dembo, M. H. (1997). Differences in the motivational beliefs of Asian American and Non-Asian students. *Journal of Educational Psychology, 89*(3), 433-440.

Eccles, J.S. (1983). Expectancies, values, and academic behaviors. In J.T. Spence (Ed.), *Achievement and achievement motives* (pp. 75-146). San Francisco: Freeman.

Eccles, J.S., Wigfield, A., and Schiefele, U. (1998). Motivation to succeed. In W. Damon (Series Ed.,) and N. Eisenberg (Vol. Ed.) *Handbook of child psychology: Vol 3. Social, emotional, and personality development.* (5th ed., pp. 1017-1095). New York: Wiley.

Eisenberg, N., Martin, C. L., and Fabes, R. A. (1996). Gender development and gender effects. In D. C. Berliner and R. C. Calfee (Eds.), *Handbook of educational psychology.* New York: Simon and Schuster Macmillan.

Eisenberger, R., and Cameron, J. (1996). Detrimental effects of reward: Reality or myth? *American Psychologist, 51*, 1153-1166.

Eisenberger, R., and Cameron, J. (1998). Reward, intrinsic interest, and creativity: New findings, *American Psychologist, 53*, 676-679.

Elliot, A.J. (1997). Integrating the "classic" and "contemporary" approaches to achievement motivation: A hierarchical model of approach and avoidance achievement motivation. In M.L. Maehr and P.R. Pintrich (Eds.), *Advances in motivation and achievement.* (Vol. 10, pp. 143-179). Greenwich, CT: JAI Press.

Elliot, A.J., and Church, M. (1997). A hierarchical model of approach and avoidance achievement motivation. *Journal of Personality and Social Psychology, 72*, 218-232.

Elliot, A.J., and Harackiewicz, J.M. (1996). Approach and avoidance achievement goals and intrinsic motivation: A mediational analysis. *Journal of Personality and Social Psychology, 70*, 461-475.

Entwisle, D. R., and Baker, D. P. (1983). Gender and young children's expectations for performance in arithmetic. *Developmental Psychology, 19*, 200-209.

Feldman, K. (1989). The association between student ratings of specific instructional dimensions and student achievement: Refining and extending the synthesis of data from multisection validity studies. *Research in Higher Education*, 30, 583-645.

Fincham, F.D. and Cain, K.M. (1986). Learned helplessness in humans: A developmental analysis. *Developmental Review, 6*, 301-333.

Findley, M., and Cooper, H. (1983). Locus of control and academic achievement: A review of the literature. *Journal of Personality and Social Psychology, 44*, 419-427.

Fiske, S., and Taylor, S. (1991). *Social cognition.* New York: McGraw-Hill.

Flavell, J.H. (1979). Metacognition and cognitive monitoring: A new area of cognitive-developmental inquiry. *American Psychologist, 34*, 906-911.

Foersterling, F. (1985). Attributional retraining: A review. *Psychological Bulletin, 98*, 495-512.

Ford, J.K., Smith, E.M., Weissbein, D.A., Gully, S.M., Salas, E. (1998). Relationships of goal orientation, metacognitive activity, and practice strategies with learning outcomes and transfer. *Journal of Applied Psychology, 83*, 218-233.

Ford, M. (1992). *Motivating humans: Goals, emotions, and personal agency beliefs.* Newbury Park, CA: Sage Publications.

Fordham, S., and Ogbu, J. (1986). Black students' school success: Coping with the burden of "acting white". *Urban Review, 18*, 176-206.

Frey, K., and Ruble, D. N. (1987). What children say about classroom performance: Sex and grade differences in perceived competence. *Child Development, 58*, 1066-1078.

Garcia, T., McCann, E., Turner, J., and Roska, L. (1998). Modeling the mediating role of volition in the learning process. *Contemporary Educational Psychology, 23*, 392-418.

Garcia, T., and Pintrich, P.R. (1994). Regulating motivation and cognition in the classroom: The role of self-schemas and self-regulatory strategies. In D.H. Schunk and B. J. Zimmerman (Eds.), *Self-regulation of learning and performance: Issues and educational applications* (pp. 127-153). Hillsdale, NJ: Lawrence Erlbaum Associates.

Garcia, T., and Pintrich, P.R. (1996). Assessing students' motivation and learning strategies in the classroom context: The Motivated Strategies for Learning Questionnaire. In M. Birenbaum (Ed). *Alternatives in assessment of achievements, learning processes, and prior knowledge* (pp. 319-339). Boston, MA: Kluwer Academic Publishers.

Garner, R., Brown, R., Sanders, S., Menke, D. (1992). "Seductive details" and learning from text. In K.A. Renninger, S. Hidi, and A, Krapp (Eds.), *The role of interest in learning and development* (pp. 239-254). Hillsdale, NJ: Lawrence Erlbaum Associates.

Gollwitzer, P. (1996). The volitional benefits of planning. In P. Gollwitzer and J. Bargh (Eds.), *The psychology of action: Linking cognition and motivation to behavior* (pp. 287-312). New York: Guilford Press.

Good, T., and Brophy, J. (1987). *Looking in classrooms.* New York: Harper and Row.

Graham, S. (1994). Motivation in African Americans. *Review of Educational Research, 64*, 55-117.

Graham, S., Taylor, A., and Hudley, C. (1998). Exploring achievement values among ethnic minority early adolescents. *Journal of Educational Psychology, 90*, 606-620.

Harackiewicz, J.M., Barron, K.E., and Elliot, A.J. (1998). Rethinking achievement goals: When are they adaptive for college students and why? *Educational Psychologist, 33*, 1-21.

Harackiewicz, J.M., and Sansone, C. (1991). Goals and intrinsic motivation: You can get there from here. In M.L. Maehr and P.R. Pintrich (Eds.), *Advances in motivation and achievement: Goals and self-regulation* (Vol. 7, pp. 21-49). Greenwich, CT: JAI Press.

Harter, S. (1985). Competence as a dimension of self-evaluation: Toward a comprehensive model of self-worth. In R. Leary (Ed.), *The development of the self* (pp. 95-121). New York: Academic Press.

Heckhausen, H. (1991). *Motivation and action.* New York: Springer Verlag.

Hembree, R. (1988). Correlates, causes, effects and treatment of test anxiety. *Review of Educational Research, 58*, 47-77.

Hess, R. D., Chang, C. M., and McDevitt, T. M. (1987). Cultural variations in family beliefs about children's performance in mathematics: Comparisons among People's Republic of China, Chinese-American, and Caucasian-American families. *Journal of Educational Psychology*, 79(2), 179-188.

Hidi, S. (1990). Interest and its contribution as a mental resource for learning. *Review of Educational Research, 60*, 549-571.

Hill, K., and Wigfield, A. (1984). Test anxiety: A major educational problem and what can be done about it. *Elementary School Journal, 85*, 105-126.

Hofer, B., Yu, S., and Pintrich, P.R. (1998). Teaching college students to be self-regulated learners. In D.H. Schunk and B.J. Zimmerman (Eds.), *Self-regulated learning: From teaching to self-reflective practice* (pp. 57-85). New York: Guilford Press.

Holloway, S. D., Kashiwagi, K., Hess, R. D., and Azuma, H. (1986). Causal attributions by Japanese and American mothers and children about performance in mathematics. *International Journal of Psychology, 21*, 269-286.

Hsia, J., and Peng, S. S. (1998). Academic achievement and performance. In L. C. Lee and N. W. S. Zane (Eds.), *Handbook of Asian American Psychology*. Thousand Oaks: Sage.

Hyde, J. S., Fennema, E., and Lamon, S. J. (1990). Gender differences in mathematics performance: A meta-analysis. *Psychological Bulletin, 107*, 139-155.

Hyde, J.S. and Linn, M.C. (1988). Gender differences in verbal ability: A meta-analysis. *Psychological Bulletin, 104*, 53-69.

Johnson, D., and Johnson, R. Instructional goal structure: Cooperative, competitive, or individualistic. *Review of Educational Research, 44*, 213-240.

Karabenick, S., and Knapp, J.R. (1991). Relationship of academic help seeking to the use of learning strategies and other instrumental achievement behavior in college students. *Journal of Educational Psychology, 83*, 221-230.

Karabenick, S., and Sharma, R. (1994). Seeking academic assistance as a strategic learning resource. In P.R. Pintrich, D. R. Brown, and C.E. Weinstein (Eds.), *Student motivation, cognition, and learning: Essays in honor of Wilbert J. McKeachie* (pp. 189-211). Hillsdale, NJ: Lawrence Erlbaum Associates.

Koriat, A., and Goldsmith, M. (1996). Monitoring and control processes in the strategic regulation of memory accuracy. *Psychological Review, 103*, 490-517.

Krapp, A., Hidi, S., and Renninger, K.A. (1992). Interest, learning and development. In K.A. Renninger, S. Hidi, and A. Krapp (Eds.), *The role of interest in learning and development* (pp. 3-25). Hillsdale, NJ: Lawrence Erlbaum Associates.

Kuhl, J. (1984). Volitional aspects of achievement motivation and learned helplessness: Toward a comprehensive theory of action control. In B. Maher and W. Maher (Eds.), *Progress in experimental personality research*. (Vol. 13, pp. 99-171). New York: Academic Press.

Kuhl, J. (1985). Volitional mediators of cognition-behavior consistency: Self-regulatory processes and action versus state orientation. In J. Kuhl and J. Beckman (Eds.), *Action control: From cognition to behavior* (pp. 101-128). Berlin: Springer-Verlag.

Lefcourt, H. (1976). *Locus of control: Current trends in theory research*. Hillsdale, NJ: Erlbaum.

Lenney, E. (1975). Women's self-confidence in achievement settings. *Psychological Bulletin, 84*, 1-13.

Liebert, R., and Morris, L. (1967). Cognitive and emotional components of test anxiety: A distinction and some initial data. *Psychological Reports, 20*, 975-978.

Linn, M. C., and Hyde, J. S. (1989). Gender, mathematics, and science. *Educational Researcher, 18*, 17-19, 22-27.

Linn, M. C., and Petersen, A. C. (1985). Emergence and characterization of sex differences in spatial ability: A meta-analysis. *Child Development*, 56(1479-1498).

Locke, E.A., and Latham, G.P. (1990). *A theory of goal setting and task performance*. Englewood Cliffs, NJ: Prentice Hall.

Maccoby, E. E., and Jacklin, C. N. (1974). *The psychology of sex differences*. Stanford, CA: Stanford University Press.

Maehr, M.L., and Midgley, C. (1991). Enhancing student motivation: A school-wide approach. *Educational Psychologist, 26*, 399-427.

Malone, T., and Lepper, M. (1987). Making learning fun: A taxonomy of intrinsic motivations for learning. In R. Snow and M. Farr, (Eds.), *Aptitude, learning, and instruction: Vol. 3. Cognitive and affective process analyses* (pp. 223-253). Hillsdale, NJ: Erlbaum.

Marton, F., Dall'Alba, G., and Kun, T. L. (1996). Memorizing and understanding: The keys to a paradox? In D. Watkins and J. Biggs (Eds.), *The Chinese learner: Cultural, psychological, and contextual influence*. Hong Kong: Comparative Education Research Centre, The Australian Council for Educational Research Ltd.

McKeachie, W.J. (1986). *Teaching tips: A guidebook for the beginning college teacher.* Lexington, MA: Heath.

McKeachie, W.J. (1990). Research on college teaching: The historical background. *Journal of Educational Psychology, 82*, 189-200.

McKeachie, W.J., Pintrich, P.R., and Lin, Y.G. (1985). Teaching learning strategies. *Educational Psychologist, 20*, 153-160.

Meece, J., Parsons, J., Kaczala, C., Goff, S., and Futterman, R. (1982). Sex differences in math achievement: Toward a model of academic choice. *Psychological Bulletin, 91*, 324-348.

Meece., J., and Eccles, J. (1993). Introduction: Recent trends in research on gender and education. *Educational Psychologist, 28*, 313-319.

Meece, J. L., and Jones, M. G. (1996). Gender differences in motivation and strategy use in science: Are girls rote learners? *Journal of Research in Science Teaching, 33*(4), 393-406.

Midgley, C., Arunkumar, R., and Urdan, T. (1996). "If I don't do well tomorrow, there's a reason": Predictors of adolescents' use of academic self-handicapping strategies. *Journal of Educational Psychology, 88*, 423-434.

Miller, G., Galanter, E., and Pribram, K. (1960). Plans and the structure of behavior. New York: Holt.

Murray, H. (1991). Effective teaching behaviors in the college classroom. In J. Smart (Ed.), *Higher education: Handbook of theory and research* (Vol. 7, pp. 135-172). New York: Agathon Press.

Nelson, T., and Narens, L. (1990). Metamemory: A theoretical framework and new findings. In G. Bower (Ed.), *The psychology of learning and motivation* (Vol. 26, pp. 125-141). New York: Academic Press.

Nelson-Le Gall, S. (1981). Help-seeking: An understudied problem solving skill in children. *Developmental Review, 1*, 224-246.

Nelson-Le Gall, S. (1985). Help-seeking behavior in learning. *Review of research in education* (Vol. 12, pp. 55-90). Washington DC: American Educational Research Association.

Newman, R. (1991). Goals and self-regulated learning: What motivates children to seek academic help? In M.L. Maehr and P.R. Pintrich (Eds.), *Advances in motivation and achievement: Goals and self-regulatory processes* (Vol. 7, pp. 151-183). Greenwich, CT: JAI Press.

Newman, R. (1994). Adaptive help-seeking: A strategy of self-regulated learning. In D. H. Schunk and B. J. Zimmerman (Eds.), *Self-regulation of learning and performance: Issues and educational applications* (pp. 283-301). Hillsdale, NJ: Lawrence Erlbaum Associates.

Newman, R. (1998a). Adaptive help-seeking: A role of social interaction in self-regulated learning. In S. Karabenick (Ed.), *Strategic help-seeking: Implications for learning and teaching* (pp. 13-37). Hillsdale, NJ: Lawrence Erlbaum Associates.

Newman, R. (1998b). Students' help-seeking during problem solving: Influences of personal and contextual goals. *Journal of Educational Psychology, 90*, 644-658.

Nicholls, J. (1984). Achievement motivation: Conceptions of ability, subjective experience, task choice, and performance. *Psychological Review, 91*, 328-346.

Nisbett, R. (1993). *Rules for reasoning*. Hillsdale, NJ: Lawrence Erlbaum Associates.

Nolen, S. B. (1988). Reasons for studying: Motivational orientations and study strategies. *Cognition and Instruction, 5*, 269-287.

Norem, J.K., and Cantor, N. (1986). Defensive pessimism: Harnessing anxiety as motivation. *Journal of Personality and Social Psychology, 51*, 1208-1217.

Pajares, F., and Graham, L. (1999). Self-efficacy, motivation constructs, and mathematics performance of entering middle school students. *Contemporary Educational Psychology, 24*, 124-139.

Paris, S.G., Lipson, M.Y., and Wixson, K.K. (1983). Becoming a strategic reader. *Contemporary Educational Psychology, 8*, 293-316.

Pascarella, E., and Terenzini, P. (1991). *How college affects students*. San Francisco, CA: Jossey-Bass.

Perry, R. (1991). Perceived control in college students: Implications for instruction in higher education. In J. Smart (Ed.), *Higher education: Handbook of theory and research* (Vol. 7, pp. 1-56). New York: Agathon Press.

Perry, R., and Dickens, W. (1988). Perceived control and instruction in the college classroom: Some implications for student achievement. *Research in Higher Education, 27*, 291-310.

Perry, R., and Magnusson, J-L. (1989). Causal attributions and perceived performance: Consequences for college students' achievement and perceived control in different instructional conditions. *Journal of Educational Psychology, 81*, 164-172.

Perry, P., and Penner, K. (1990). Enhancing academic achievement in college students through attributional retraining and instruction. *Journal of Educational Psychology, 82*, 262-271.

Peterson, C., Maier, S., and Seligman, M. (1993). *Learned helplessness: A theory for the age of personal control*. New York: Oxford University Press.

Phillips, D., and Zimmerman, B. J. (1990). The developmental course of perceived competence and incompetence among competent children. In R. Sternberg and J. Kolligian (Eds.), *Competence considered*. New Haven, CT: Yale University Press.

Pintrich, P.R. (1988a). A process-oriented view of student motivation and cognition. In J. S. Stark and L. Mets (Eds.). *Improving teaching and learning through research. Vol. 57. New directions for institutional research* (pp. 55-70). San Francisco: Jossey-Bass.

Pintrich, P.R. (1988b). Student learning and college teaching. In R.E. Young and K.E. Eble (Eds.), *College teaching and learning: Preparing for new commitments. Vol. 33. New Directions for teaching and learning* (pp. 71-86). San Francisco: Jossey-Bass.

Pintrich, P.R. (1989). The dynamic interplay of student motivation and cognition in the college classroom. In C. Ames and M.L. Maehr (Eds.), *Advances in motivation and achievement: Motivation-enhancing environments* (Vol. 6, pp. 117-160). Greenwich, CT: JAI Press.

Pintrich, P.R. (1994). Student motivation in the college classroom. In K. Prichard and R. M. Sawyer (Eds.), *Handbook of college teaching: Theory and applications* (pp. 23-43). Westport, CT: Greenwood Press.

Pintrich, P.R. (1999). The role of motivation in promoting and sustaining self-regulated learning. *International Journal of Educational Research, 31*, 459-470.

Pintrich, P.R. (2000a). An achievement goal theory perspective on issues in motivation terminology, theory, and research. *Contemporary Educational Psychology, 25*, 92-104.

Pintrich, P.R. (2000b). Multiple goals, multiple pathways: The role of goal orientation in learning and achievement. *Journal of Educational Psychology, 92*, 544-555.

Pintrich. P.R. (2000c). The role of goal orientation in self-regulated learning. In M. Boekaerts, P.R. Pintrich, and M. Zeidner (Eds.), *Handbook of Self-regulation: Theory, research, and applications*, (pp. 451-502). San Diego, CA: Academic Press.

Pintrich, P.R., and De Groot, E.V. (1990). Motivational and self-regulated learning components of classroom academic performance. *Journal of Educational Psychology, 82*, 33-40.

Pintrich, P.R., and Garcia, T. (1991). Student goal orientation and self-regulation in the college classroom. In M.L. Maehr and P.R. Pintrich (Eds.), *Advances in motivation and achievement: Goals and self-regulatory processes* (Vol. 7, pp. 371-402). Greenwich, CT: JAI Press.

Pintrich, P.R., and Garcia, T. (1993). Intraindividual differences in students' motivation and self-regulated learning. *Zeitschrift fur Padagogische Psychologie, 7*, 99-187.

Pintrich, P. R., Marx, R., and Boyle, R. (1993). Beyond cold conceptual change: The role of motivational beliefs and classroom contextual factors in the process of conceptual change, *Review of Educational Research, 63*(2), 167- 199.

Pintrich, P.R., McKeachie, W., and Lin, Y-G. (1987). Teaching a course in learning to learn. *Teaching of Psychology, 14*, 81-86.

Pintrich, P. R., Smith, D., Garcia, T., and McKeachie, W. (1993). Predictive validity and reliability of the Motivated Strategies for Learning Questionnaire (MSLQ). *Educational and Psychological Measurement, 53*, 801-813.

Pintrich, P.R., and Schrauben, B. (1992). Students' motivational beliefs and their cognitive engagement in classroom tasks. In D. Schunk and J. Meece (Eds.), *Student perceptions in the classroom: Causes and consequences* (pp. 149-183). Hillsdale, NJ: Erlbaum.

Pintrich, P.R., and Schunk, D.H. (1996). *Motivation in education: Theory, research and applications.* Englewood Cliffs, NJ: Prentice Hall Merrill.

Pintrich, P.R., Wolters, C., and Baxter, G. (2000). Assessing metacognition and self-regulated learning. In G. Schraw and J. Impara (Eds.). *Issues in the measurement of metacognition.* Lincoln, NE: Buros Institute of Mental Measurements.

Pressley, M., and Afflerbach, P. (1995). *Verbal protocols of reading: The nature of constructively responsive reading.* Hillsdale, NJ: Lawrence Erlbaum Associates.

Pressley, M., and Woloshyn, V. (1995). *Cognitive strategy instruction that really improves children's academic performance.* Cambridge, MA: Brookline Books.

Rayman, P., and Brett, B. (1995). Women science majors: What makes a difference in persistence after graduation? *The Journal of Higher Education, 66*(4), 388-415.

Renninger, K.A., Hidi, S., and Krapp, A. (1992). *The role of interest in learning and development.* Hillsdale, NJ: Erlbaum.

Roberts, T.-A. (1991). Gender and the influence of evaluations on self-assessments in achievement settings. *Psychological Bulletin*, 109(2), 297-308.

Rotter, J. B. (1966). Generalized expectancies for internal versus external control reinforcement. *Psychological Monographs*, 80, 1-28.

Ryan, A., and Pintrich, P.R. (1997). "Should I ask for help?" The role of motivation and attitudes in adolescents' help seeking in math class. *Journal of Educational Psychology*, 89, 329-341.

Sansone, C., and Harackiewicz, J. (2000). *Intrinsic and extrinsic motivation: The search for optimal motivation and performance*. San Diego, CA: Academic Press.

Sansone, C., Weir, C., Harpster, L., and Morgan, C. (1992). Once a boring task, always a boring task? The role of interest as a self-regulatory mechanism. *Journal of Personality and Social Psychology*, 63, 379-390.

Schiefele, U. (1991). Interest, learning, and motivation. *Educational Psychologist*, 26, 299-323.

Schneider, W., and Pressley, M. (1997). *Memory development between 2 and 20*. Mahwah, NJ: Lawrence Erlbaum Associates.

Schoenfeld, A. (1992). Learning to think mathematically: Problem solving, metacognition, and sense making in mathematics. In D. Grouws (Ed.), *Handbook of research on mathematics teaching and learning* (pp. 334-370). New York: Macmillan.

Schraw, G., and Moshman, D. (1995). Metacognitive theories. *Educational Psychology Review*, 7, 351-371.

Schunk, D. (1985). Self-efficacy and school learning. *Psychology in the Schools*, 22, 208-223.

Schunk, D.H. (1989). Social cognitive theory and self-regulated learning. In B.J. Zimmerman and D.H. Schunk (Eds.), *Self-regulated learning and academic achievement: Theory, research, and practice* (pp. 83-110). New York: Springer-Verlag.

Schunk, D.H. (1991). Self-efficacy and academic motivation. *Educational Psychologist*, 26, 207-231.

Schunk, D.H. (1994). Self-regulation of self-efficacy and attributions in academic settings. In D. H. Schunk and B. J. Zimmerman (Eds.), *Self-regulation of learning and performance: Issues and educational applications* (pp. 75-99). Hillsdale, NJ: Lawrence Erlbaum Associates.

Shih, M., Pittinsky, T. L., and Ambady, N. (1999). Stereotype susceptibility: Identity salience and shifts in quantitative performance. *Psychological Science*, 10(1), 80-83.

Simpson, M., Hynd, C., Nist, S., and Burrell, K. (1997). College academic assistance programs and practices. *Educational Psychology Review*, 9, 39-87.

Slavin, R. (1983). *Cooperative learning*. New York: Longman.

Snow, R., Corno, L., and Jackson, D. (1996). Individual differences in affective and conative functions. In D. Berliner and R. Calfee (Eds.), *Handbook of Educational Psychology* (pp. 243-310). New York: Macmillan.

Steele, C.M. (1988). The psychology of self-affirmation: Sustaining the integrity of the self. *Advances in Experimental Social Psychology*, 21, 261-302.

Steele, C.M. (1997). A threat in the air: How stereotypes shape intellectual identity and performance. *American Psychologist*, 52, 613-629.

Steele, C. M., and Aronson, J. (1995). Stereotype threat and the intellectual test performance of African Americans. *Journal of Personality and Social Psychology*, 69(5), 797-811.

Sternberg, R. (1985). *Beyond IQ: A triarchic theory of intelligence.* New York: Cambridge University Press.

Stevenson, H. W., and Lee, S.-Y. (1990). *Contexts of Achievement.* (Vol. 55). Chicago: The University of Chicago Press.

Stigler, J. W., Smith, S., and Mao, L.-w. (1985). The self-perception of competence by Chinese children. *Child Development, 56,* 1259-1270.

Stipek, D., and Weisz, J. (1981). Perceived personal control and academic achievement. *Review of Educational Research, 51,* 101-137.

Tryon, G. (1980). The measurement and treatment of test anxiety. *Review of Educational Research, 50,* 343-372.

Urdan, T. (1997). Achievement goal theory: Past results, future directions. In M.L. Maehr and Pintrich, P.R. (Eds.), *Advances in motivation and achievement* (Vol. 10, pp. 99-141). Greenwich, CT: JAI Press.

VanderStoep, S.W., Pintrich, P.R., and Fagerlin, A. (1996). Disciplinary differences in self-regulated learning in college students. *Contemporary Educational Psychology, 21,* 345-362.

Veroff, J., and Veroff, J. B. (1980). *Social incentives: A life-span developmental approach.* New York: Academic Press.

Weiner, B. (1986). *An attributional theory of motivation and emotion.* New York: Springer-Verlag.

Weiner, B. (1992). *Human motivation: Metaphors, theories, and research.* Newbury Park, CA: Sage Publications.

Weiner, B. (1995). *Judgments of responsibility: A foundation for a theory of social conduct.* New York: Guilford Press.

Weinstein, C.E., and Mayer, R. (1986). The teaching of learning strategies. In M. Wittrock (Ed.) *Handbook of research on teaching and learning* (pp. 315-327). New York: Macmillan.

Whang, P. A., and Hancock, G. R. (1994). Motivation and mathematics achievement: Comparisons between Asian-American and Non-Asian students. *Contemporary Educational Psychology, 19,* 302-322.

Wigfield, A. (1994). Expectancy-value theory of achievement motivation: A developmental perspective. *Educational Psychology Review, 6,* 49-78.

Wigfield, A., and Eccles, J. (1989). Test anxiety in elementary and secondary school students. *Educational Psychologist, 24,* 159-183.

Wigfield, A., and Eccles, J. (1992). The development of achievement task values: A theoretical analysis. *Developmental Review, 12,* 265-310.

Wigfield, A., Eccles, J., MacIver, D., Reuman, D., and Midgley, C. (1991). Transitions during early adolescence: Changes in children's domain-specific self-perceptions and general self-esteem across the transition to junior high school. *Developmental Psychology, 27,* 552-565.

Wlodkowski, R. (1988). *Enhancing adult motivation to learn.* San Francisco: Jossey-Bass.

Wolters, C. (1998). Self-regulated learning and college students' regulation of motivation. *Journal of Educational Psychology, 90,* 224-235.

Wolters, C., Yu, S., and Pintrich, P.R. (1996). The relation between goal orientation and students' motivational beliefs and self-regulated learning. *Learning and Individual Differences, 8,* 211-238.

Zeidner, M. (1998). *Test anxiety: The state of the art.* New York: Plenum.

Zimmerman, B.J. (1986). Development of self-regulated learning: Which are the key subprocesses? *Contemporary Educational Psychology, 16*, 307-313.

Zimmerman, B.J. (1989). A social cognitive view of self-regulated learning and academic learning. *Journal of Educational Psychology*, 81(3), 329-339.

Zimmerman, B.J. (1990). Self-regulated learning and academic achievement: An overview. *Educational Psychologist, 25*, 3-17.

Zimmerman, B.J. (1994). Dimensions of academic self-regulation: A conceptual framework for education. In D. H. Schunk and B. J. Zimmerman (Eds.), *Self-regulation of learning and performance: Issues and educational applications* (pp. 3-21). Hillsdale, NJ: Lawrence Erlbaum Associates.

Zimmerman, B.J. (1998a). Academic studying and the development of personal skill: A self-regulatory perspective. *Educational Psychologist, 33*, 73-86.

Zimmerman, B.J. (1998b). Developing self-fulfilling cycles of academic regulation: An analysis of exemplary instructional models. In D. H. Schunk and B.J. Zimmerman (Eds.), *Self-regulated learning: From teaching to self-reflective practice* (pp. 1-19). New York: Guilford Press.

Zimmerman, B.J. (2000). Attaining self-regulation: A social cognitive perspective. In M. Boekaerts, P.R. Pintrich, and M. Zeidner (Eds.), *Handbook of self-regulation: Theory, research, and applications* (pp. 13-39). San Diego, CA: Academic Press.

Zimmerman, B.J., and Kitsantas, A. (1997). Developmental phases in self-regulation: Shifting from process to outcome goals. *Journal of Educational Psychology, 89*, 29-36.

Zimmerman, B.J., and Martinez-Pons, M. (1986). Development of a structured interview for assessing student use of self-regulated learning strategies. *American Educational Research Journal, 23*, 614-628.

Zimmerman, B.J., and Martinez-Pons, M. (1988). Construct validation of a strategy model of student self-regulated learning. *Journal of Educational Psychology, 80*(3), 284-290.

Zimmerman, B. J., and Martinez-Pons, M. (1990). Student differences in self-regulated learning: Relating grade, sex, and giftedness to self-efficacy and strategy use. *Journal of Educational Psychology, 82*, 51-59.

Zimmerman, B.J., and Schunk, D. (1989). *Self-regulated learning and academic achievement: Theory, research, and practice.* New York: Springer-Verlag.

Zukier, H. (1986). The paradigmatic and narrative modes in goal-guided inference. In R. M. Sorrentino and E.T. Higgins (Eds.), *Handbook of motivation and cognition: Foundations of social behavior* (pp. 465-502). New York: The Guilford Press.

3. College Students' Degree Aspirations: A Theoretical Model and Literature Review With a Focus on African American and Latino Students

Deborah Faye Carter
Indiana University

Quite a few comprehensive studies on undergraduate experiences and general models of degree attainment and attrition have highlighted the importance of measuring educational aspirations. Many researchers theorize that student educational aspirations have strong effects on (or strong relationships with) a variety of outcomes, particularly college choice, student retention, and graduate school enrollment (Astin, 1977; Tinto, 1993

However, educational aspirations are less often studied as *outcomes*. A few higher education researchers have studied the factors that influence educational aspirations (e.g. Astin, 1977, 1993; Hearn, 1987, 1991; Pascarella, 1984), but scholars and researchers still have cursory knowledge about why the aspirations of racial/ethnic minority students and White students differ significantly.

The purpose of this chapter is to review and synthesize the literature related to educational aspirations. This review attempts to summarize what is known about aspirations in general and the aspirations of African American and Latinos specifically. I also posit a research and conceptual model, based on empirical research and existing theory, for understanding what affects educational aspirations.

Much of the literature described in this chapter has its foundations in sociology. Students' educational goals are the function of several elements, including internal psychological processes, social interactions, and structural processes; in this chapter I will focus on the formation and change of aspirations as a result of social interactions and structural processes. The main reason for this emphasis is that the concepts presented can contribute to theoretical advances in the study of educational aspirations and have practical implications for campus programming and institutional policies.

J.C. Smart and W.G. Tierney (eds.), Higher Education: Handbook of Theory and Research, 129–171.

In a review of aspirations studies of the 1960s and 1970s, Pascarella (1984) stated that researchers tend to use methods relying on empirical examinations of aspirations as opposed to theoretical examinations of aspirations. Pascarella developed a model of affective outcomes that posits that individual characteristics and secondary school achievement will have stronger effects on later educational aspirations than institutional environment variables. Pascarella's model has proven useful in understanding the process by which students' aspirations change over time, but there is still a need for understanding the unique processes by which the aspirations of students of color change over time.

The study of aspirations in general can be characterized as lacking in clarity. One key area that researchers have noted as needing greater understanding and theoretical specificity is the formation and maintenance of educational aspirations — particularly in populations who continue to be underrepresented in higher education institutions (Kao & Tienda, 1998).

The aspirations of students of color often do not fall into easily predictable patterns. In several studies, African American students tend to have higher than expected aspirations (Astin, 1990; Hanson, 1994), which some researchers have called "unrealistic," while other researchers have found that high aspirations for African Americans are the mediating factor in whether they attend college (St. John, 1991).

As early as the 1960s, research comparing the college-going behaviors and attainments of African American and White youth discovered significant differences in the aspirations and aspirations-change process between the two racial groups. In some studies, the researchers found that African American youth had lower aspirations than White youth while in others, the aspirations of African American youth were higher than or similar to those of White youth (Portes & Wilson, 1976; St. John, 1991). Regardless of the direction (or lack) of difference in aspirations levels, it has been clear that the variables affecting aspirations can differ in magnitude and direction between the racial groups.

There has been much less research on the aspirations of Latino high school and college students. The educational attainment rates of Latinos are at crisis levels; Latinos (particularly Mexican Americans) have much lower high school completion rates and college-going rates than White students, and tend to be concentrated in two-year institutions.

Researchers have suggested that "increasing minority participation in graduate programs is an important national goal to be realized. . . . It is for the collective benefit of society that the representation of minority group persons among those earning advanced degrees be increased" (National Board on Graduate Education cited in Deskins, Jr., 1994, p. 144). Indeed, a recent study found that the racial representation of physicians affects available health care in poor and minority communities (Komaromy, Grumbach, Drake, Vranizan, Lurie,

Keane, & Bindman, 1996). Therefore, the aspirations and subsequent graduate degree attainments of minority students not only have an impact on individual factors such as income, but also can have an impact on the welfare of entire communities.

This chapter is organized in two parts: the first addresses theoretical foundations relating to the study of aspirations, and the second describes a model of educational aspirations and highlights the empirical studies that relate to aspects of the model.

THEORETICAL FOUNDATIONS FOR ASPIRATIONS STUDIES

STATUS ATTAINMENT

Status attainment literature in the field of sociology provides the main foundation for the study of the educational aspirations of high school and college students. Blau and Duncan (1967) developed the first status attainment model, which focused on the occupational attainments of males from White and African American populations. Blau and Duncan's model assumes that ascriptive characteristics (father's education and income) determine the male's occupational attainment. The model is quite parsimonious and is composed of the five following variables: father's educational attainment and father's occupational status, and the respondent's educational attainment and first-job status. The first two are predictors of the latter two, and all four variables are predictors of the respondents' eventual occupational attainment. Educational aspirations were not included in Blau and Duncan's original model, but subsequent status attainment research has developed the model to take aspirations into account.

Many researchers have noted one main weakness in Blau and Duncan's model: the relationships between the variables could not be sufficiently explained (Kerckhoff, 1984; Sewell, Haller, & Ohlendorf, 1970; Sewell, Haller, & Portes, 1969). The model has been criticized because there seems to be little theoretical support for the concept that fathers' education determines sons' occupational attainments besides a strict notion of social reproduction (that is, people's socioeconomic status is determined by the status of their parents and there is little mobility between generations). In attempting to further enhance Blau and Duncan's model by explaining the processes by which a parent's socioeconomic status can affect the status of the adult child, Sewell, et al. (1969) and others expanded the model to include social psychological variables. In developing this expanded model, called the social psychological model of status attainment, the "Wisconsin model", or a socialization model, it was the position of the researchers that social psychological variables, previously shown to be important to educational attainment, were valuable to examine as intervening variables with respect to educational and occupational attainment. Such variables as significant others, reference groups, self-concept, aspirations, and experience of school success are all constructs whose effects on attainments had been proven in research completed in the late 1950s and early 1960s (Sewell, et al., 1969). Measures of ability were particularly highlighted as important for researchers to take into account because mental ability (as measured by IQ and other standardized tests) was assumed to affect the student's "academic performance and the influence significant others have on him [or her]" (Sewell, et al., 1970, p. 1015).

The social psychological model of status attainment assumes that the socioeconomic status and ability of the student affect the encouragement and support the student receives from significant others, which in turn, affect the student's goals and aspirations (Kerckhoff, 1976). The Wisconsin model posits causal arguments "linking social origins and ability with educational and early occupational status attainments by means of intervening behavioral mechanisms" (Sewell, et al., 1970, p. 1015). In developing this theory, Sewell, et al. (1969) applied the work of previous psychological researchers who, as early as 1935, concluded that individuals obtain their "social behavior tendencies largely through the influence of others" (p. 85) and that "one's conception of the educational behavior others think appropriate to him [or her] is highly correlated with [the] level of educational aspiration" (p. 85).

Sewell, et al.'s (1969) model presents four sets of causal relationships in a 1957 study of a homogenous sample (all White, farm youth) of Wisconsin high school male seniors: 1) social structural (socioeconomic status, or SES) and psychological factors (mental ability) affect significant others' influences; 2) significant others' influences affect educational and occupational aspirations; 3) aspirations affect attainment; and 4) educational attainment affects occupational attainment. Significant others (in this study) refers to parents, peers, and instructors.

Sewell, Haller, and Ohlendorf (1970) describe the patterns of effects in greater detail. Generally, social structural and psychological factors affect young men's academic performance and the influences that significant others have on them. The influences of significant others and the students' academic ability affect their levels of educational and occupational aspiration. The levels of aspiration affect educational and occupational status attainment.

The social psychological (or socialization) model of status attainment views aspirations as a central element in the status attainment process and states that aspirations "are formed in social interaction" (Knotterus, 1987, p. 116). Knotterus (1987), in an examination of status attainment researchers' view of society, states that in the social psychological model of status attainment, "aspirations develop in response to the evaluations one receives from significant others and the self-assessment of one's potential based upon academic performance" (p. 116). The social psychological model assumes that social interaction is structured by socioeconomic status groups. The implication being that "significant others — for example, teachers and peers — tend to be drawn from socioeconomic positions somewhat similar to those of the youth's parents and provide encouragement from a similar value orientation" (Otto & Haller, 1979 cited in Knotterus, p. 116). This perspective seems to assume relative homogeneity in the socioeconomic statuses of the population of any given high school.

Status attainment research primarily has been conducted on high school student populations and shows that through interactions with parents, teachers, peers, and other "significant others," students are socialized as to the value of achievement and appropriate educational goals. In this way, the status attainment perspective views society as "a mass of social actors, motivated by universalistic values and functioning in an open structure, are free to pursue their goals" (Knotterus, 1987, pp. 116-7).

Therefore, in the late 1960s, two theories of the process of status attainment (and by implication the development of educational aspirations and degree plans) emerged: one perspective is that educational aspirations and attainment are the direct result of socioeconomic/ascriptive factors (the Blau & Duncan model). The modification of Blau & Duncan's model is the socialization model, which holds that a student's socioeconomic status affects the way he or she interacts with others (and in turn how others interact with the student), which affect aspirations and ultimately attainment (Sewell, et all, 1969). Both theories of the status attainment process were supported by the research completed through the early 1970s, but the social psychological models explain more of the variance in attainments than the ascriptive, Blau and Duncan model (Sewell, et al., 1970).

Another perspective on status attainment was developed in response to what some researchers felt were the theoretical shortcomings of the social psychological model. This perspective, first advanced by Kerckhoff (1976), is called social allocation. Kerckhoff's view is that the process of status attainment is not so much a process of socialization than it is a process of social allocation. Kerckhoff's criticism of the Wisconsin model is that the model views an individual as relatively free to move through society; attainment is determined by what the individual chooses to do and how well the individual does it. The social allocation perspective views the individual as constrained by social structure — an individual's attainments are determined by what he or she is allowed to do. Researchers have found strong associations between "ambition" and attainment; therefore, the socialization model assumes that a student's goals direct and motivate the student's efforts which lead to attainment (Kerckhoff, 1976). On the other hand, the measures of ambition used in past research do not measure motivation as much as they measure "knowledge of 'the real world'" (Kerckhoff, p. 370). Most questions measuring motivation and ambition ask for students' plans or expectations, not their wishes or aspirations (Kerckhoff, 1976). Kerckhoff feels that the difference between *wishes* and *plans* are the most important distinctions between the socialization and social allocation perspectives. The social allocation perspective purports that:

> Expectations are strongly associated with attainments because [students] become sufficiently knowledgeable to be able to estimate the probabilities of various outcomes. . . .People's observations of the attainments of others like themselves undoubtedly do have a feedback effect on their expectations. [Kerckhoff, 1976, p. 371].

It is assumed that individuals may *want* the same outcomes, but that they may *expect* different outcomes based on their assessments of their life chances. Therefore, while the social psychological model of status attainment views the individual as unconstrained by society and success as determined by the individual's abilities, the social allocation model views the individual as constrained by society. The social psychological model views aspirations as resulting from an individual's social interactions and abilities. An assumption of the model is that a reason certain students are not upwardly mobile is because they are of low ability and/or that they do not have the goals and motivation to succeed. The social allocation interpretation views individuals as constrained by their life circumstances. Individuals only have degree expectations that they think they can achieve given the system constraints in which they live. Kerckhoff (1976, 1984) admitted that it may be difficult to empirically distinguish between the socialization and the social allocation interpretations of the status attainment model. However, Kerckhoff considers the social allocation perspective a different explanation for the same phenomenon.

One problem with Kerckhoff's perspective is that few researchers have demonstrated clear empirical differences between what students' want to happen versus what they expect to happen. In addition, there has not been uniform measurement of aspirations — some measure aspirations as likes or wants (Agnew & Jones, 1988), expectations (Weiler, 1993), and plans (Pascarella, 1984).

A second problem with Kerchkoff's perspective is the role that the concept of "opportunity" plays in the national culture of the people in the United States. "From the earliest days of the Republic, Americans have possessed an abiding faith that theirs is a land of opportunity" (Brint & Karabel, 1989, p. 3). The

United States, unlike European societies, was founded on the belief that people have limitless opportunities and can succeed through hard work and ability (a notion that is referred to as "contest mobility" and will be described in greater detail in the next section of this chapter). The uniqueness of U.S. society bears out in modern times: when the U.S. is compared with other industrial nations, no other country sends as many individuals to postsecondary educational institutions as the United States (Brint & Karabel, 1989).

The issue is that millions more individuals in this country aspire to high levels of education and prestigious occupations than the educational and occupational systems can support. "For example, over half of high school seniors [in the early 1980s] 'planned' careers in professional/technical jobs. . . but in that same year, only 13 percent of the labor force was employed in such jobs" (Brint & Karabel, p. 8). Thus, drawing a distinction between what a student wants and expects may be a particularly difficult and unique problem, especially for a population of students who have already reached postsecondary education and are faced with a changing job market.

Contest versus Sponsored Mobility

Turner (1960) proposed a framework for understanding the differences in the educational systems of the United States and England. Turner's view is that the U.S. educational system resembles a "contest" system of mobility where access to elite status is an open contest. An established elite does not have control over the final outcome of who may attain upward mobility and therefore education is a field in which open competition is the means by which people can improve their statuses. On the other hand, sponsored mobility is a system in which the elite controls the process. "Elite status is *given* on the basis of some criterion of supposed merit and cannot be *taken* by any amount of effort or strategy" (emphasis in original, Turner, 1960, p. 856). Turner compares upward mobility in a sponsored system to gaining entrance into a private club:

> Each candidate must be 'sponsored' by one or more of the members. . . . The governing objective of contest mobility is to give elite status to those who earn it, while the goal of sponsored mobility is to make the best use of the talents in society by sorting persons into their proper niches [Turner, 1960, pp. 856-857].

Turner also discusses how the societies ensure and maintain loyalty to the social system. In a contest mobility system, individuals think of themselves as competing for positions in the elite. When individuals think of themselves as future members of the elite, they begin to identify with the members of the upper classes, view high status society members as "ordinary" people, and begin to form the conviction that they may become members of the elite in the future. A contest mobility system influences the internalization of high achievement values in most members of society — especially those in the lower socioeconomic strata. Those members of society who are unambitious are "individual deviants" and not a threat to the cohesiveness of society. In a contest mobility system, education is considered an "opportunity" whereby an individual who has strong initiative and drive may make the best use of it. Turner describes the fact that researchers found the "general level of occupational aspiration reported by high school students is quite unrealistic in relation to the actual distribution of job opportunities" (p. 858) as proof that the United States educational system is primarily a contest mobility system. Lower SES students' aspirations are not lowered (or kept low) early in the educational process, as would be predicted in a sponsored mobility system.

In a sponsored mobility system, social control is maintained by guiding the members of the lower socioeconomic classes to feel inferior to the elite. The future members of the elite are selected very early in their schooling so that the others can be "taught to accept their inferiority and to make 'realistic' rather than [f]antasy plans" (p. 859). Early selection of future members of the elite prevents the "masses" from raising their hopes and thereby becoming powerful members of a discontented force.

The assumptions of contest mobility systems are similar to the assumptions of a meritocracy and of the social psychological models of status attainment: individuals' achievement affect their educational aspirations, expectations, and attainments. Sponsored mobility, and the social allocation perspective of mobility, view the individual as constrained by what the members of the elite will allow the individual to do: individuals' achievement is largely dependent upon their statuses at birth.

CRITIQUES OF STATUS ATTAINMENT & CONTEST/SPONSORED MOBILITY

The status attainment model is the primary way in which aspirations have been studied over the past thirty years. This section discusses critiques of status attainment research (and therefore much of the research on aspirations that use the status attainment model). Status attainment research — Blau and Duncan's model and socialization models — have been found to work well for samples of White males. When the models have been tested on White females and students of color of both genders, the models explain little of the variance. This section posits some reasons for lack of success of the status attainment research in explaining the outcomes of minority students and White females.

One of the main criticisms of the status attainment model is that it offers little to explain gender and ethnic differences, and probably that is a reason why the social psychological status attainment model has been cited sporadically in research articles in the last ten years. The socialization model explained very little of the variance in aspirations and attainment for women of all ethnicities and minority men (Berman & Haug, 1979), and often the pattern of relationships between the White samples and the minority samples were completely different (Portes & Wilson, 1976). Campbell (1983) completed a critique of the status attainment models and concluded that an important and necessary direction for status attainment research is in the area of "minority group differences in achievement processes... [and] it will be possible to determine if there might be a 'minority group status attainment process' which applies to racial minorities... " (p. 59). In addition to the criticism that the model has limited application to minority populations and women, there are several other critiques of the model and studies of aspirations in general (Kerchoff, 1984).

A second criticism of status attainment research, which may be related to the model's limited explanatory power for White female students and minority students, is that one of the core assumptions of the status attainment model is that the United States society functions as a meritocracy. In other words, the researchers who study students using the attainment model view educational systems as functioning mostly on merit — the students who are the most able will have the highest aspirations and attain the highest degrees. Eckland (1964) responded to previous researchers who stated that SES affects who attends college but has little relationship to who graduates from college:

> ... Social-class differences will increasingly determine who graduates among the college entrants of the [future]. ... To the extent that higher education develops the same mass conditions as our system of secondary education in which dropout has been so closely associated with social status, a similar process will occur in our colleges [p. 50]

Other researchers emphasize that the unequal opportunities for lower SES students are encouraged by an educational system that purports to reward students based solely on merit. Educational institutions transmit inequality by legitimating ascriptive statuses through academic achievement (Morrow & Torres, 1995). Therefore, a student's life chances can be determined by the student's circumstances at birth. This is counter to the assumptions of a meritocracy.

Contest mobility may describe the educational opportunities of certain members of the United States population, but at the time Turner published his article, the *Brown v. Board of Education* decision concerning the unequal and biased nature of African American elementary education was barely six years old. "The American system of stratification and mobility has caused Black mobility to approximate Turner's sponsored mobility" (Porter, 1974, p. 313). African Americans had and continue to have legal battles to gain entrance to the educational institutions where the "meritocratic contests" were supposedly taking place. All members of United States society could not participate in an "equal contest" for upward mobility, and status attainment models assume that the United States is an open opportunity structure (Wilson-Sadberry, Winfield, & Royster, 1991). This assumption seems to be incorrect, especially when one considers occupational outcomes. Women earn lower salaries than men and the situation is particularly startling for African Americans and Latinos: in 1980, Black women and Black men tended to earn salaries that were, respectively, 46% and 68% of those earned by White men (Grubb & Wilson, 1989). It seems that the system of mobility in the United States cannot be broadly categorized as a "contest" for all groups, but the patterns of mobility may vary greatly by ethnicity, SES, and gender. Therefore, it is reasonable to say that the assumption of meritocracy may be one problem with the applicability of the status attainment model to different populations.

A third criticism of status attainment literature is the dated nature of the research. Much of the status attainment research was completed in the 1960s and 1970s and may not take into account the increasing diversity on college campuses. The effects of affirmative action programs and financial aid programs on increasing access (in the 1970s) and limiting access (in the 1980s to present) are not examined. There are policy and structural issues that have long-term impacts on college student outcomes that are not addressed in status attainment models.

A fourth criticism of the early status attainment literature (although this is less true of recent educational aspirations studies by higher education researchers) is the focus on individual characteristics and lack of or limited use of institutional variables. Researchers have suggested that status attainment studies should take into account the characteristics and effects of the educational institution in addition to individual characteristics (Kerckhoff, 1976). Educational institutions are not equal in terms of resources and they affect the outcomes of students differently. Studies need to take this into account as well as individual differences between students (Pascarella, 1984).

A final criticism of the status attainment literature is more pertinent for the social allocation analysis than for the socialization perspective. Social allocation tends to view the process of status attainment and aspirations development as deterministic. Structural constraints in society limit the aspirations and attainments of individuals such that those whose parents are from the lower socioeconomic statuses will, more likely than not, remain at the same status through adulthood. However, there are individuals in society who resist the mechanisms of reproduction and succeed. Resistance theory posits that individuals in the lower socioeconomic classes of society resist the upper classes' control of resources through subtle or direct means (Giroux, 1983). Resistance has taken the form of direct confrontation in student protests and in more subtle means by way of students' rejection of messages from others that claim they cannot succeed (Feagin, Vera, & Imani, 1996; Hurtado, 1990).

A key element of resistance theory is the transformation of institutional structures. High aspirations may help increased numbers of African Americans and Latinos to achieve high levels of educational attainment. Perhaps maintaining high aspirations is one way minority students refuse to internalize "do not succeed" messages. Indeed, in spite of economic inequality, African Americans have historically maintained high hopes of becoming upwardly mobile through the education process (Knight & Wing, 1995).

Cultural and Social Capital

Status attainment and contest and sponsored mobility are well-established theoretical frameworks within which to study educational aspirations. Another theoretical framework that is gaining more prominence in recent higher education literature is based on Bourdieu's work on cultural capital and on the concept of social capital.

The terms "social capital" and "cultural capital" have their origins in Marxist analyses of class conflict and in Bourdieu's publications about French society. Both are terms used in many sociological theories of reproduction, which assume that society reproduces status (particularly class) differences within particular institutions.

Social capital can be defined as the relationships and institutions that shape a social group's (or society's) interactions. Researchers have linked the status attainment research to the concept of social capital in that "children's achievement is facilitated by. . . social capital involving parent-child interactions in learning activities" (Hao & Bonstead-Bruns, 1998, p. 177). Therefore, the quality of the interactions between parents and children affect the children's achievement.

Cultural capital is knowledge transmitted from upper- and middle-class families to their children. This knowledge adds to the economic capital that is already transmitted in the families. Cultural and social capital perspectives have been applied to higher education relatively recently. Researchers have used Bourdieu's framework as a way of explaining why class is so significant in affecting student outcomes and discussing the application of cultural capital to various outcomes including retention and college choice (Berger, 2000; McDonough, 1997).

Cultural capital may explain why lower SES students have lower aspirations. More-educated parents may socialize their children early to prepare their children for professional careers. Middle- and upper-class students may have more information about their post-secondary options and therefore would be more likely not only to attend college, but to attend higher status institutions that may afford them greater benefits later.

A significant limitation of many reproduction theories (including the discussions of social and cultural capital) is that the notions of agency and resistance are not examined thoroughly. In addition, many of systems of oppression in U.S. society are gender- and race/ethnicity-based in addition to being class-based. Since most reproduction theories focus on class differences, there is a gap in the literature regarding theories that can account for complex relationships between gender, race, and class. Some researchers have begun to fill that gap, noting the specific interactions of gender and race in how groups relate to each other (Luttrell, 1989; Morrow & Torres, 1995).

EXPLANATIONS FOR THE LOW ASPIRATIONS OF MINORITY YOUTH

The previous sections described the three main theoretical explanations for aspirations: status attainment, contest and sponsored mobility, and social/cultural capital. This section of the chapter discusses theories explaining why African American and Latino students have lower aspirations (and lower attainments) than White students.

African Americans

In the United States, African Americans have low educational and occupational attainments in comparison to White individuals. One explanation is the cultural deficit perspective. This perspective assumes that "Black cultural values, as transmitted through the family and specifically the parents, are dysfunctional, and therefore the reason for Blacks' low educational. . . attainment" (Solorzano, 1992, p. 30). The cultural deficit perspective also assumes that some African Americans do not place as high a value on education as do White individuals. Although Black parents tend to communicate to their children the need to work hard, Black children do not put a lot of effort into their schooling for three reasons:

> (a) perseverance at academic tasks has not developed as a part of their cultural tradition; (b) the actual texture of their parents' lives of unemployment, underemployment, and discrimination convey a powerful message that counteracts parental verbal encouragement; and (c) children learn from observing older members of their community that school success does not necessarily lead to jobs and other necessary and important things in adult life [Ogbu, 1983, p. 181].

Ogbu argues that because of the history of poor education of African American youth in this country, Black parents and children have a deep distrust for schooling. This distrust prevents Black children from internalizing the "values of the schools, accept[ing] school criteria for success, or follow[ing] school rules of behavior for achievement" (p. 181). Thus, because Black children do not internalize the values of schools, they tend to do much more poorly than White students.

Ogbu's research on the educational experiences of African American students has led to the development of the caste theory explanation of school failure. This theory asserts the following: (1) there is a caste system in the United States based primarily on race/ethnicity; (2) there is a typology of experiences of minority group members whereby "involuntary" minorities and "voluntary" minorities have historical differences with respect to their relationships with the country and the negative historical experiences that "involuntary" minority group members endured continue in the present; (3) in response to oppression and limited opportunities, "involuntary" minority group members develop various adaptive or survival strategies that are quite often negative adaptations (Foley, 1991; Ogbu, 1983).

Ogbu identifies Mexican Americans, Native Americans (American Indians), and African Americans as the primary involuntary minority groups in the United States. Ogbu feels that involuntary and voluntary minority group members "perceive their historical deprivation" quite differently (Foley, p. 65). Ogbu's thesis is that recent immigrant groups ("voluntary" minority group members) "do not perceive the racial barriers and the lack of opportunity in. . . American society" and therefore they view the United States as a "land of opportunity" in comparison to their country of origin. Because of this, voluntary minority group members have a sense of optimism about their future and do better in schools (Foley, p. 65). On the other hand, involuntary minority group members have negative views of society and of their chances to succeed in society. Ogbu's primary emphasis is on the negative adaptive strategies of involuntary minority group members:

> [Involuntary minority group members] are overwhelmed by the 'community forces' of a job ceiling and racial oppression, and by a variety of 'school forces.' Their typical psychological and cultural adaptation is self-defeating in several ways. They succumb to the dominant societies' myths about them as inferior. They are unable to create a folk theory of schooling that is optimistic about their future. They develop a dysfunctional oppositional culture that leads them to believe that they cannot be both academically successful and ethnically different. . . Caste theory makes a powerful case that involuntary minorities are not likely to succeed in school or in life [Foley, 1991, p. 67].

In addition, Fordham and Ogbu (1986) postulate that Black students, who are capable of doing well in school, do not do well because they do not want to be accused of "acting White." Certain behaviors are conceptualized by Black students as inappropriate because those behaviors are characteristic of White students.

Although there have been several critiques of Ogbu's research, one critique is the most salient for this chapter: Ogbu's emphasis on the negative adaptive patterns of involuntary minority group members (Foley, 1991). Ogbu theorizes that oppressed minority group members develop oppositional cultures, and these oppositional cultures come "trapped in a counterproductive pattern of reacting to racial stereotypes and myths" (Foley, p. 76). In this way, Ogbu's conception of African American school behavior resembles the oft-maligned "culture of povery" concept. However, in the "culture of poverty" perspective of African Americans in inner cities, African Americans are psychologically damaged: they have low self-esteem, pessimism, and a sense of fatalism. Ogbu's view of African Americans is not so much that the group is psychologically damaged, but that African Americans are "discouraged and trapped in the racist myths of the dominant society. They are unable to see that they can be both successful and Black" (Foley, p. 77). Caste theory does tend to ignore the ways in which oppressed groups engage in "positive" resistance. Thus, caste theorists tend to "underestimate the capacity of ethnic resistance movements to empower individuals" (Foley, p. 78).

Ogbu's research has parallels to the social allocation model of status attainment: members of involuntary minority group members see their opportunities as constrained by society, and that affects their behavior in schools. Ogbu's research in the United States has primarily focused on the school *failure* of African American children. Given that postsecondary education attendees are already successful by many standards, Ogbu's caste theory may have limited applicability to college students.

Latinos

The discussion of Ogbu's work has parallels for Latino students, who (particularly Mexican Americans) are considered involuntary minorities. As such, they are similar to African Americans in status and in educational attainment patterns. Therefore, Mexican American students may tend to feel negatively toward society and have a distrust of schooling. In addition to Ogbu's work, the work of Barrera is particularly applicable in explaining racial inequality.

Barrera (1997) describes three major deficiency theories of racial inequality: biological, cultural, and social structural. Biological theories assert that there are essential differences between members of racial groups that explain the respective gaps in levels of educational achievement, attainment, and socioeconomic success. Social structural theories argue that historical and social structure factors in the U.S. society have produced weak family structures for some racial/ethnic minority group members (e.g. African American, Latinos, American Indians) and have led to emotional problems and low educational attainment. Cultural deficiency theories argue that it is the culture of minority groups that contribute to their lower attainment rates and lower SES. These theorists have characterized African Americans and Latinos as having a "culture of poverty" where they have a "present orientation rather than [a] future orientation, a lack of work discipline, and so on" (Barrera, p. 5). "Individuals who share this 'culture' do poorly in school, and their educational attainment creates conditions of poverty and powerlessness, which interact with each other and create a vicious circle to perpetuate educational inequalities" (p. 5). In particular, theorists argue that Latinos suffer from a "language handicap" and lack of a success orientation, and because of their relatively lower SES, they suffer from a "cultural disadvantage." Chicano culture is often portrayed as "highly traditional and nonadapted to the requirements of upward mobility in an industrial society" (p. 6).

Barrera concludes that "as an approach to explaining racial inequality, then, deficiency models based on social structure are inelegant methodologically — different deficiencies have to be found for each racial group" (p. 7). While negative traits of the cultures of racial/ethnic minority groups are accentuated in such theories, the theories often do not examine accompanying positive traits (see Foley's critique of Ogbu in the previous section). Furthermore, thorough examinations of the positive and negative traits of the dominant cultural group are often not taken into account.

Ethnic Differences in Aspirations Studies

Latinos

Few studies have been done comparing the aspirations of Latino populations to other groups. However, two studies do provide some understanding of the issues that are particular to Latinos' aspirations. In a comparison of the aspirations of African American, Latino, Asian American, and White students using the National Educational Longitudinal Study (NELS) dataset, Latino youth had the lowest aspirations of the four groups (Kao & Tienda, 1998). Kao and Tienda supplemented their quantitative analyses with focus group interviews with African American and Latino youth. Based on their analyses, they conclude that Latino youth had optimistic educational aspirations — taking into account the lower socioeconomic status of their parents. Despite their relatively high aspirations, Latino youth in general did not have adequate information about college options and financial aid packages: "some students believed that their parents' financial status makes college an impossible dream, while others believe they can obtain a full scholarship simply because they are [Latino] or athletes" (p. 379).

Kao and Tienda also assert (as do other scholars who study the effects of aspirations on attainments — see St. John, 1991) that "educational aspirations mediate the influence of family backgrounds and significant others on ultimate educational attainments" (p. 380). What remains a question after years of research in this area is: if the deficit theories are accurate and there are negative pressures in the schools and cultures of African Americans and Latinos that limit attainments, why don't these pressures similarly constrain aspirations?

One answer to this question is the role that Latino parents play in the aspirations of their children. So (1987) found that Latino parents "have high aspirations for their children and want their children. . . to go to college as much as White parents want their children to do so" (pp. 49-50). So further found that Latino parents "started forming aspirations for college attainment when their children were still in elementary school" (p. 52).

African Americans

Researchers typically cannot pinpoint why the patterns of relationships between variables in models explaining African Americans' aspirations differ so greatly from the relationships in White student samples. When African Americans students have high aspirations, they have been referred to as "unrealistic;" and when lower-income students and/or African Americans inflate their educational expectations it has been labeled an adaptation to deprivation (Agnew & Jones, 1988). Students categorized as having "unrealistic expectations" do achieve their dreams (attend college, or complete a college degree, for instance), though perhaps in smaller numbers than their higher-income, higher-scoring peers (Agnew & Jones, 1988). Referring to African Americans specifically as having "unrealistic" aspirations seems especially unnecessary given the high aspirations of the people of the U.S. and that researchers have noted that low SES White students have had higher than "realistic" aspirations for several decades (Brint & Karabel, 1989). In fact, research indicates that high aspirations may at least partially mitigate the negative effects of low SES on college attendance (St. John, 1991). Therefore, high aspirations have assisted African American students in achieving their goals.

In the 1960s, African Americans were thought to have lower levels of aspirations than White students, but in studies where socioeconomic class is controlled, African Americans were found to have as high or higher aspirations within socioeconomic stratification groups (Portes & Wilson, 1976). These findings have led researchers to conclude that White students' higher attainments is due to their advantages in background variables and characteristics (Portes & Wilson, 1976). In fact, while minority students have "the aspirations, the ability, and the qualifications to go to a four-year college, they do not attend the college of their choice to the degree that Whites do." (Labovitz, 1975, p. 248).

In addition, the cultural deficit view of attainment "has become the social scientific norm even though little empirical evidence exists to support many of its claims" (Solorzano, 1992, p. 31). As has been discussed, African American students tend to have as high or higher aspirations than White students — especially when SES characteristics are controlled (St. John, 1991). Thus, the cultural deficit model seems to have little foundation in empirical research. The assumptions of the cultural deficit model may hold true for some selected groups of African Americans (Ogbu, 1983), but has yet to be demonstrated to be a universal norm, especially through national databases (Solorzano, 1992).

What is especially lacking in discussions of the educational aspirations of African American, Latino, and White students is the role that educational institutions play in the development and maintenance of aspirations. Focusing on the ways in which institutions contribute to the development of aspirations moves the discussion away from cultural and individual characteristics and toward the types of educational environments that are most conducive for student achievement. In this way, the literature on college impact and on the experiences of college students informs status attainment research.

College Students' Degree Aspirations and College Impact

The literature on college students' degree aspirations, that is, the literature on college students' plans to attend graduate school, is more sparse than the high-school-to-college literature. Pascarella (1984) both applauds and criticizes previous studies of college students' aspirations. On the one hand, Pascarella contends that the research of Astin (1977) and his colleagues make some contributions to an understanding of the institutional characteristics that influence students' aspirations. On the other hand, these research publications "have a number of methodological problems. . . the most important of these. . . is the orientation toward an empirical rather than theoretical framework for the data analyses" (Pascarella, 1984, p. 753). Few researchers have theorized why and how the characteristics of an institution impact an individual student's degree plans.

The social psychological status attainment model is the foundation of college student aspirations studies. College students are considered individual actors who have access to several parts of the campus and interact with the individuals they choose. Many researchers do recognize the ways in which institutional structures can constrain the behavior of individuals (Astin, 1993), but why is it that some institutions have higher proportions of student degree completion than others? Particular institutional characteristics and students' college experiences work to produce positive student educational outcomes. For example, African American students who attend historically Black colleges and universities (HBCUs) tend to go to graduate school in greater numbers than African Americans who attend predominantly White institutions (PWIs). Women who attend women's colleges attend graduate school in greater numbers and have more positive affective development than women attending coeducational institutions (Smith, 1990).

College choice literature also centers on the discussion of aspirations. The literature has evolved over the years into the formulation of a three-stage model: predisposition, search, and choice (Hossler & Gallagher, 1987). The predisposition stage has particular parallels to the study of aspirations. Predisposition is described as "a developmental phase in which students determine whether or not they would like to continue their education beyond high school" (Hossler & Gallagher, 1987, p. 209). The theoretical underpinnings for the predisposition stage is grounded in the status attainment literature (Hossler, Braxton, & Coopersmith, 1989). Much of the research on the predisposition stage finds significant relationships between level of aspirations and ethnicity, size of family, parents' education attainments, parents' income, student academic ability and achievement, and peer and teacher influences (Paulsen, 1990).

Person-environment fit — the degree to which an individual belongs in (is congruent with) an environment — has been a popular explanation for why some students seem to succeed and some fail in a given institution (Feldman & Newcomb, 1969).

> Students from lower status backgrounds differ from those of higher status backgrounds in ways that presumably produce greater incongruence between the lower status group and the demands and opportunities of the college environment. Thus entering students of lower socioeconomic status, in comparison to their higher status counterparts, (1) are less culturally sophisticated. . . ; (2) have had a more restricted range of experiences. . . ; and (3) are more likely to be oriented to college in terms of vocational or professional training and less likely to be oriented in terms of intellectual growth [Feldman & Newcomb, p. 277].

One problem with the traditional person-environment fit perspective is that the burden of congruence is placed on the student. Little responsibility is placed on the members of the campus community who have constructed and maintained the campus environment. The person-environment fit explanation of college impact — especially as it relates to SES — corresponds best with the contest view of social mobility (as described in previous sections). Those persons who are most like the environment they enter will be the most successful — although, since lower SES students tend to be less successful, perhaps a form of sponsored mobility is at work.

AFRICAN AMERICANS IN HIGHER EDUCATION

Although there are few articles that specifically test models of degree aspirations on African American college students, the author of this chapter has been able to locate very few published studies that test models of degree aspirations on Latino college students. The following section describes previous empirical research on African American college students' aspirations.

The models that have been tested on Black students are substantially different from models tested on White students. Therefore, it is important to understand the processes by which students develop and maintain educational aspirations and expectations, if only to understand the educational experiences of African American students. In a study of High School and Beyond (HSB) participants who graduated from college, Weiler (1993) found that roughly the same percentage of minority and White students who enrolled in graduate school initially did not expect to attend. However, there were large differences between the numbers of minority and White students who had expected to attend graduate school and then did not. Weiler concluded that "the key reason for lower post-baccalaureate attendance of minorities is the fact that a relatively large fraction of them who planned to continue their education beyond the baccalaureate at the time they entered college changed their minds" (p. 446). It is important to study the individual and institutional attributes of the process by which some college students are "cooled out" from graduate study. The process of cooling out is one in which the "socializing agents" in colleges — faculty and peers, the curriculum, and administrative procedures — all influence the lowering of educational plans (Clark, 1960; Pascarella & Terenzini, 1991).

Feagin, et al. (1996) detail some of the negative experiences African Americans have in PWIs. A central theme in the study is that of Black invisibility. Much like the main character of Ralph Ellison's book, African American students in Feagin, et al.'s study are not seen by "White professors, students, staff members and administrators. . . as full human beings with distinctive talents, virtues, interests and problems" (p. 14). Black students at PWIs often feel anxiety and fear at being the only one or one of a few African Americans in a particular environment. This anxiety can mean that African Americans look for the increased company of other African Americans for their support. Feagin, et al. also report that "a recent survey of Black students at mostly White universities found they were so concerned about intellectual survival that they were unable to devote as much attention to their personal, social, and cultural development as they should" (p. 75).

As with high school studies, researchers studying college students have implied that African Americans have unrealistic educational aspirations. Astin (1990) stated that Black students' aspirations are inconsistent with their career choices given the fact that 15.7%, 14.3%, and 37.7% of African Americans planned to earn doctoral, advanced professional (MD, JD), or Master's degrees respectively, while only 11%, 10.1%, and 36.9% of White students planned to earn such degrees. In addition, African Americans planned to be businesspersons or computer programmers 4%-6% more than White students. Doctorates are not necessarily required for such professions as businesspersons and computer programmers, and thus Astin feels Black students have unrealistic educational aspirations.

In a study using prestige scores for occupations (instead of discrete categories), White students tended to have nearly the same short-range occupational expectations as Black students at HBCUs and PWIs, and the long-range occupational expectations of White students tended to be slightly higher or about the same as the expectations of Black students (Dawkins, 1982). So, perhaps the career expectations of African American college students are not found to be so inconsistent when different measures and statistical controls are employed.

The degree to which college students' aspirations for graduate education are "unrealistic" is perhaps difficult to determine, particularly since students who attend postsecondary institutions have already demonstrated success. They completed secondary education and have the personal goals, initiative, and achievement necessary to apply to college and be admitted. College students are successful, talented, and capable — even likely — to earn graduate degrees. However, as research reviewed in this section demonstrates, there are significant patterns of stratification within higher education: African American students disproportionately attend less "prestigious" institutions, drop out of postsecondary institutions and tend not to go on to earn graduate degrees in similar numbers as White students (Carter & Wilson, 1996).

DESCRIPTION OF A THEORETICAL MODEL

The competing assumptions of educational mobility focus on conceptions of individual students' aspirations and attainment as being functions of social constraints (social allocation or sponsored mobility theoretical perspectives) or as being free of social constraints and subject to individual agency (status attainment or contest mobility theoretical perspectives). Empirical evidence supports both assumptions, but in addition, it seems evident that the processes of aspirations development are different for African American, Latino, and White students. Although it may be possible to develop a theoretical model of aspirations development that encompasses the experiences of African American, Latino, and White students, the model should be tested *separately* for each group because African American, Latino, and White students begin college with different backgrounds, attend different types of institutions, and have different experiences in college (Carter, 1999b; Kao & Tienda, 1998).

In addition, the theoretical conceptualizations of the role of institutions in the development of students' aspirations are lacking. Pascarella (1984) critiqued educational aspirations research as being atheoretical, and found few direct effects of institutional measures on students' degree aspirations. A few studies show that the structural characteristics of institutions do have direct effects on students' aspirations and that the role of institutional characteristics in the development of students' degree goals needs to be linked with the theoretical perspectives of status attainment (Carter, 2001).

Therefore, students' degree goals are a function of their own individual backgrounds and circumstances, their institutional choices (such as they are), and the socializing influences of institutions. Theories of students' degree aspirations and achievement that encapsulate the multi-faceted nature of student decision-making as well as the ways in which institutional environments affect students' decisions can better conceptualize the processes by which students make decisions about their futures.

Figure 1 shows a theoretical model based on the findings of previous studies and theoretical foundations previously discussed. This section of the chapter will focus on previous empirical research; the theoretical frameworks discussed in the first half of the chapter are the lenses through which these relationships in the model can be interpreted.

The research and conceptual model posed is perhaps most appropriate for quantitative research where the specific effects of variables can be tested on an outcome. However, there is a need for extensive qualitative work on students' degree aspirations (Kao & Tienda, 1998) and the model presented may assist qualitative researchers in studying about how students' aspirations are shaped.

Figure 1. Theoretical and Conceptual Model of Factors Influencing College Students' Degree Aspirations

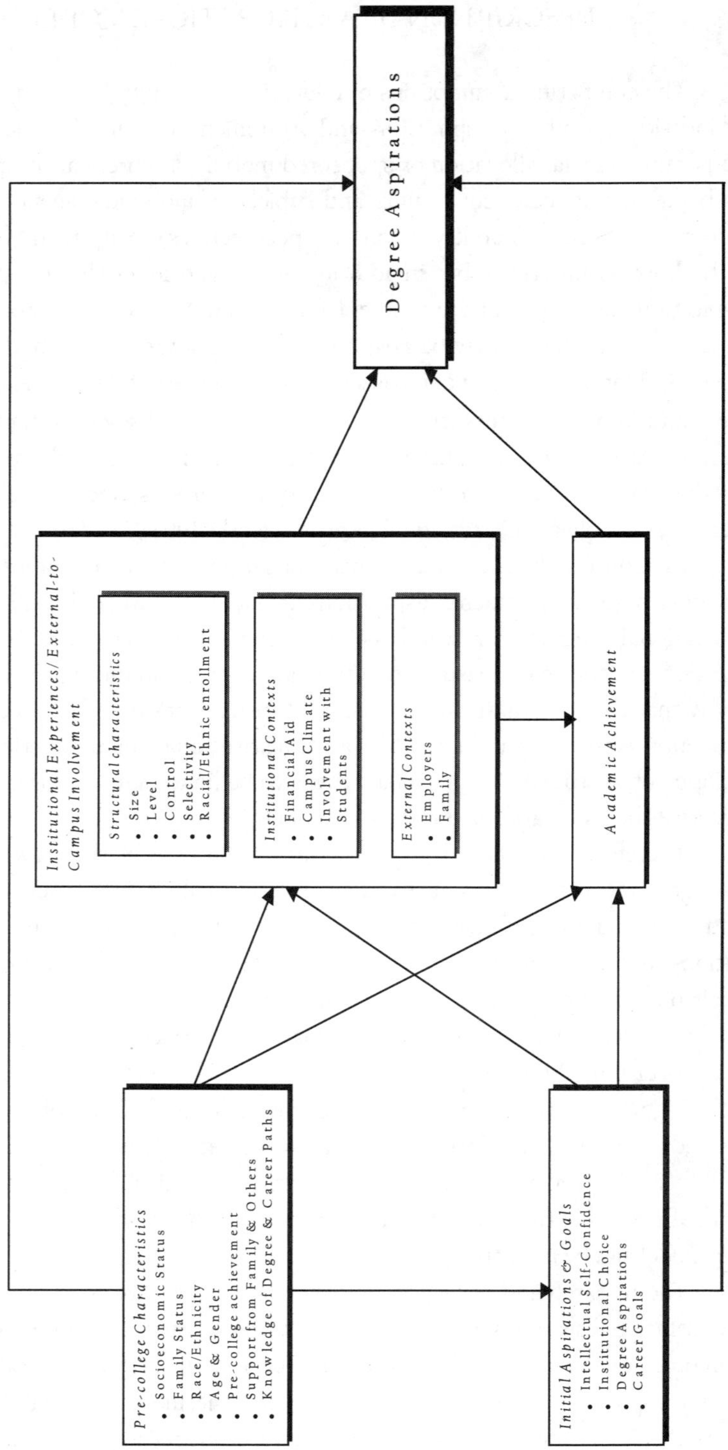

The model represents race/ethnicity as an exogenous variable in the model, but we may need to consider it specifically since the aspirations of racial/ethnic groups differ to such a degree. Generally, the ways in which students' degree aspirations are influenced can be described in four stages:

1. *Pre-college characteristics* (e.g. socioeconomic status, age, gender, family status, pre-college achievement, support from family and peers, knowledge of degree and career path) affect *students' initial aspirations and goals* (e.g. self-confidence, college choice behavior, initial degree aspirations, career goals).
2. *Pre-college characteristics* and *initial aspirations and goals* affect *institutional experiences and involvement.*
3. All three groups of variables in turn affect *academic achievement.*
4. Finally, *pre-college characteristics, initial aspirations, institutional experiences, and academic achievement* all affect later *degree aspirations.*

First, pre-college characteristics in the form of SES, age, family status, and pre-college achievement affect initial aspirations, students' career and life goals, levels of intellectual self-confidence, and college choices. There is significant evidence that socioeconomic status affects students' degree goals. Since many researchers argue that both contest and sponsored mobility processes affect the ways in which students develop their aspirations, pre-college achievement is an important measure to incorporate. Age and family status are variables that specifically distinguish between traditional and nontraditional students in higher education. Close to 50% of the higher education population are more than 24 years old, and older students tend to be married and/or have children (Choy & Premo, 1995). Since such a significant population of our higher education institutions is so different from traditional 18-year-old students who have been the focus of higher education research, considerations that uniquely affect the aspirations of nontraditional students needs to be taken into account as well. In addition, the support individuals receive from family and peers regarding their academic and career goals and the knowledge students have about career and degree paths all need to be considered as affecting students' initial aspirations and goals upon college entry.

Initial orientations, goals, aspirations, and institutional choice measures are important to incorporate into a model of degree aspirations because they can show the students' levels of intellectual and academic self-confidence, their initial degree and career goals, and the reasons they chose the institution they are attending (e.g. students' choice of institution was constrained by financial or social circumstances).

Second, pre-college characteristics and initial aspirations/goals affect institutional experiences and involvement. Students are not randomly assigned to higher education institutions. Pre-college characteristics and initial aspirations and goals affect the kinds of institutions students attend. The results of previous studies show that students interact in particular institutional contexts that influence their aspirations (Allen, 1992). For instance, the type of institution students attend (four-year or two-year, high cost vs. low cost, high percentage of minority enrollment, faculty-student ratio) affects the kind of financial assistance they can receive, their perceptions of campus climate, and their involvement with students and faculty. The financial aid students receive (especially students with work study awards, working on- or off-campus) affect the students' involvement with faculty, staff, and students on campus and their involvement with individuals external to the campus community. Student perceptions of the campus climate and the structural characteristics of the campus jointly can influence students' interactions with individuals off-campus — particularly if the students are nontraditional students or have interests that are not well-represented on-campus. Perceptions of campus climate may have indirect effects on aspirations by affecting the level of involvement students have with other students, faculty, and staff. In addition, students' involvement in communities that are external to the campus community also may be important factors affecting students' aspirations. In predominantly White institutions, African American and Latino students may have frequent interactions with their families, friends and others that may counteract the negative experiences.

Third, all three groups of variables in turn affect academic achievement. Students' experiences in institutional and external-to-the-institution contexts may affect their levels of college achievement. *Finally, all of the preceding variables affect later aspirations.* The following section details the empirical findings for each section of the model.

PRE-COLLEGE CHARACTERISTICS

Higher education research suggests several background characteristics affect student aspirations. African American students have been found to have aspirations as high as, or higher than, those of White students over several years of studies (Allen, 1991; Astin, 1977, 1993). However, the aspirations models tend not to work as well for African American populations (Blau & Duncan, 1967; Epps & Jackson, 1985; Portes & Wilson, 1976). Portes and Wilson (1976) found that African Americans out-perform White students (i.e. Black students receive higher grades and have higher aspirations, when SES is controlled) at each stage of the attainment process. Given this finding, they suggest that White students' advantage in attainment "depends directly on their initial advantages in the input variables" (p. 423).

As mentioned earlier, Latino students tend to have lower aspirations than

White or African American students, and statistical models tend to predict their aspirations well (Carter, 1999b; Kao & Tienda, 1998). Labovitz (1975) studied the effect of ethnicity, SES and fulfillment of college aspirations. Labovitz's model included measures of IQ, SES, college plans, GPA, school SES, and neighborhood SES as predictors of college attendance for 1966 San Diego high school seniors. Minority students were found to "have the aspirations, the ability, and the qualifications to go to a four-year college, [but] they do not attend the colleges of their choice to the degree that White [students] do" (p. 248). Again, the notion of contest mobility with respect to minority students is questioned. In Labovitz's study, attendance at a four-year college is not simply the result of an even "contest" based on ability and goals. There are other factors — unexamined in the study — that seem to disadvantage minority students in the college attendance process. This is particularly true when you consider that the students in Labovitz's study graduated from high school thirty years ago.

Women have lower aspirations than men, on average (McClelland, 1990), tend to be more adversely affected by delays in entry to higher education (Kempner & Kinnick, 1990), have more unexplained variance in aspirations models than men (Hearn, 1987), and tend to be less likely to pursue a post-baccalaureate degree immediately after college graduation (Isaac, Malaney, & Karras, 1992). Astin (1977) found that over a four-year period, almost uniformly women had lowered aspirations. However, women who attend women's colleges significantly raise their degree aspirations over a four-year period (Smith, 1990).

Socioeconomic status is the variable most often studied in status attainment models. Sewell and Shah (1967) completed a study to determine which affects college-going and completion more: ability or socio-economic status. They found that SES and intelligence have positive relationships to college attendance for both males and females. Further, for men, the effect of SES decreases over time, and SES has comparably lower effects on college outcomes than intelligence does. However, the same is not true for females. SES has a much greater effect on the outcome measures than intelligence (measured by scores on the Henmon-Nelson Test of Mental Maturity). The main point of their study is "that along with intelligence, socioeconomic status continues to influence college graduation even after socioeconomic selection has taken place in the process of determining who will attend college" (p. 20). Therefore, socioeconomic status plays a part in determining who can participate in the contest for upward mobility. It is known from the literature that lower income students, and students whose parents achieved lower levels of education, tend to have lower aspirations and expectations than higher SES students. SES seems to affect the aspirations and achievement of women and minority students more than it affects the aspirations and achievement of White male students (Burke

& Hoelter, 1988). Other researchers have concluded that the educational attainment of the same-sex parent is what most affects the educational behaviors of the student (Isaac, Malaney, & Karras, 1992).

The research on ability reveals complicated effects on aspirations. Ancis and Sedlacek (1997) state that "SAT scores tend to under-predict women's grades" and the use of other variables "provides for a more accurate and complete understanding of women's educational development" (p. 6). When colleges and universities rely on SAT scores to make academic decisions (financial aid based on "merit," and admissions decisions) they may be limiting the extent to which talented women students can obtain financial aid or participate in certain programs, and may restrict the admission of women students to certain institutions (Ancis & Sedlacek, 1997). In addition, academic advisors may have lower expectations of women students' achievement if they judge ability only by SAT scores. This has direct implications to the socialization view of social mobility: Significant others influence the goals of students. If the basis by which significant others' expectations of what women students are able to do is not a "true" measure of their ability (e.g. the SAT score), this could unnecessarily constrict students' future goals. When ability is measured by aptitude tests and grade point average, ability seems to have mostly indirect effects on educational aspirations. Perhaps this is because aptitude has been found to be strongly related to socioeconomic status (Thomas, Alexander, & Eckland, 1979). However, another study found that ability (as measured by IQ and GPA) has clear direct effects on the aspirations of White students, but no direct effects on the aspirations of African American students (Burke & Hoelter, 1988). Several researchers have found significant relationships between high college GPAs and high aspirations (Astin, 1977; Hearn, 1987; Pascarella, 1985), though in other studies, grade point average had no significant relationship to aspirations (Burke & Hoelter, 1988). These conflicting results suggest that tests of direct effects taking into account other background characteristics are important in determining the relationship of ability measures to aspirations.

Age and family status have not often been considered in models of degree aspirations. Two studies found that age is a significant predictor of White students' degree aspirations but not a significant predictor of African American and Latino students' aspirations. Younger White students tended to have higher aspirations after two and four years of college than older White students. Therefore, nontraditional students seem to have their aspirations constrained over time (Carter, 1999a; 1999b).

Knowledge of career and degree paths is an important element to consider in aspirations models. If students are not knowledgeable about the paths to graduate degrees and/or the necessary educational requirements for certain professions, their aspirations may change considerably over time. There is some evidence that African American students spend a shorter time preparing for college than White students. In a study conducted by the American College Testing (ACT) organization — the organization that administers one of the two most-used standardized tests for college admission — African American students attending their first-choice college tended to have lower ACT scores than those attending second- or third- or other-choice colleges. Explanations offered for this finding are that "students receiving higher scores on the ACT lift their aspirations, are recruited by other colleges, or find that financial aid opportunities have increased for them" (Maxey, Lee, & McClure, 1995, p. 101). This is not surprising, given that 81% of African American students were in twelfth grade when they took the ACT, as opposed to less than 70% of White students. African Americans may need more support than White students in developing postsecondary education plans (Maxey, et al., 1995).

Initial Aspirations and Goals

Burke and Hoelter (1988) use identity theory to conceptualize their approach to status attainment. They assert that people choose behaviors that correspond to their self-concept or identities. Thus, they assume that people who have strong, positive academic self-concepts should have higher educational aspirations and goals. Burke and Hoelter also take the same approach to studying aspirations as the Wisconsin (or social psychological) model, in that social psychological variables (e.g. academic identity/self-concept) mediate the effects of SES on educational intentions (Sewell, et al., 1969). They found that academic identity (as defined by students' evaluation of work independent of grades, perceived academic ability, and perceived ability to achieve high grades) mediates the effects of the main predictor variables — IQ and grade point average, for instance — on the educational plans of three of their sub-groups. Academic identity impacted the educational plans of White males and females, and African American females, but not of African American males.

The researchers offer very little explanation for the different findings for African American males, noting only that the meaning of educational expectations may differ for this particular group, and that the source of academic identity differs for the groups. Teacher influence has effects for the three groups, but not for Black males, and family background impacts White students' academic identity but not the identity of Black students. Burke and Hoelter suggest that "many of the variables of the traditional Wisconsin model are thus not relevant for [African Americans], even though, for [African American] females, academic identity is" (p. 41).

Burke and Hoelter believe that their study provided support for the notion that different models may be needed for separate ethnic and gender populations and showed support for their assumption that identity theory can be used successfully to broaden the Wisconsin model. Given that the researchers could not explain why the African American male students did not fit their identity theory assumptions, the usefulness of self-concept measures with respect to predicting aspirations may be limited. Burke and Hoelter's recommendation that self-concept variables should be incorporated into the Wisconsin status attainment model — without verifying the utility of the construct for African American males — remains an insupportable conclusion of their research.

The explanatory power of the social psychological model (the Wisconsin model) for the African American young men in the sample is much lower than for the young White men (Portes & Wilson, 1976). The correlations between self-esteem (measured in part by the Rosenberg Self-Esteem scale) with educational aspirations is .24 for White students, in contrast to the .13 value for African American students. The model explains 35% of the variance in educational aspirations for White students as opposed to 13% of the variance for African Americans. Portes and Wilson believe that African Americans are able to move through the educational and occupational systems due to self-reliance and ambition, while White students also use these attributes as well as benefiting from a social structural system that can "carry them along to higher levels of attainment" (p. 430). Portes and Wilson's findings seem to support a notion that aspirations are a function of individual attributes (contest mobility) as well as structural limitations (sponsored mobility).

There is some evidence in aspirations studies that the longer a student holds an aspiration, the more likely he or she will meet that goal. Alexander and Cook (1979) found that students who, before the 10th grade, planned to go to college were about 47% more likely to attend college as students who decided in the 12th grade to go to college. Therefore, early and sustained aspirations are important in the future attainments of students.

Astin (1977) incorporated analyses of students' degree aspirations in his study of the four-year effects of college. Astin found that "the student's degree aspirations at the time of college entrance are the most potent predictors of enrollment in graduate or professional schools" (p. 112). In terms of change in students' aspirations, several of Astin's findings (1977) are particularly interesting: Astin found that students' degree aspirations increase after college entrance — at the time of the study, 51% of first year students planned to achieve a postgraduate degree and four years later, this percentage increases to 65% of the students. What is also important about the findings of Astin's study is that students' changes in degree plans increase gradually over the four years. About 4% of students increase their aspirations each year of the study.

Astin updated his 1977 study in 1993 and found that 63 percent of students entering college in 1985 planned to earn a post-baccalaureate degree. By the fourth year of college, the number of students with postgraduate degree aspirations were 68 percent. In addition, there is only a .35 correlation between 1985 and 1989 aspirations, which suggests that most of the students change their aspirations over time, or that changes in aspirations are due primarily to college experiences. There continues to be a positive correlation between those who have high 1985 aspirations and graduate school attendance. The positive predictors of high aspirations are intellectual self-esteem, and "[indicating] 'to prepare for graduate or professional school' as an important reason for attending college" (p. 265). Astin's findings seem to support the previous findings that academic identity is related to educational aspirations (Burke & Hoelter, 1988).

The college choice literature acknowledges the effects of individual attributes and structural limitations. As was explained earlier, college choice literature intersects with aspirations literature in many ways, and there are direct implications of college choice on college student outcomes. The type of institution a student attends has significant implications for the student's future degree attainment and future occupational earnings. The process by which students choose institutions is an important element of understanding the process of educational aspirations development. A significantly lower proportion of African American students compared with White students attend their first choice institution (Hurtado, Inkelas, Briggs, & Rhee, 1997; (Maxey, et al., 1995).

Institutional Characteristics

Institutional characteristics and experiences can mediate or counteract background characteristics (Alwin, 1974), and can independently affect several educational outcomes including academic achievement and aspirations. This is especially true for African American students:

> The educational goals and activities of Black students are acted out in specific social environments that influence not only their ambitions, but also the possibility that they will realize their goals. Actors or agents in a particular setting — indeed, the setting itself — can either facilitate or frustrate the academic achievement of Black students. [Allen, 1992, p. 40]

Researchers have tried to broaden the status attainment models by introducing measures of students' experiences in educational institutions. Otto (1976) sought to expand Blau and Duncan's model by investigating the extent to which social integration (as defined by participation in school activities) affects educational attainment. According to Otto, past research on high school effects on educational attainment have found that within-school effects are far more important than between-school effects. Since Spady (1970) hypothesized that membership in extracurricular activities can provide opportunities for students to acquire, develop and rehearse attitudes and skills, Otto decided to study whether extracurricular involvement impacts educational attainment.

Studying a sample of 1957 Michigan high school graduates who participated in a follow-up study in 1972, Otto (1976) hypothesized that prior social integration (participation in extra-curricular activities) facilitates the "acquisition, development, and rehearsal of achievement-related attitudes" (p. 1379) and that the benefits of social integration should apply to outcomes other than educational attainment. Otto's hypothesis is partially supported by the research. Social integration is the only variable in the model that has a significant total effect on the three main outcomes: educational attainment, income, and occupational attainment. However, most of the effect of social integration on occupational attainment and income is mediated by educational attainment. The explanation for the mixed results is that social integration may be a proxy for aspirations and that a study of the effect of social integration needs to be completed while aspirations are controlled. This suggests that aspirations studies should take into account college experiences where students benefit from peer socialization.

In addition to college experiences, particular aspects of environments seem to affect student outcomes. Tuition cost is an institutional characteristic that affects attainment. Pascarella, Smart, and Smylie (1992) found that the cost of an institution had an independent effect on occupational attainment. Students who attended high-cost institutions tended to have higher occupational attainments than students who attended lower-cost institutions. High tuition has also been shown to influence persistence (educational attainment) negatively. The higher the tuition, the less likely students will persist (St. John, Oescher, & Andrieu, 1992).

Astin, Tsui, and Avalos (1996) found that private universities (as compared to religious colleges, private colleges, and public colleges and universities) have the highest nine-year degree attainment rates for every racial/ethnic group (72% overall). Catholic institutions have the second highest attainment rates at 54.9%. Therefore, attendance at a private university more than attendance at other institutional types can insure that a student earns a Bachelor's degree. Since the link between attendance at a private university and degree achievement is so strong, perhaps institutional type has an impact on the development of degree aspirations.

Attending a large college (in terms of size of student body) tends to lower educational aspirations of African American men in predominantly White institutions (PWIs) and historically Black colleges and universities (HBCUs) (Smith, 1988). Highly selective institutions tend to have a positive effect on aspirations for White students and Latinos (Carter, 1999b; Pascarella, 1985). In a national study of undergraduates, Astin (1977) found that students attending more highly selective institutions tend to increase their aspirations over time, while students attending selective, public institutions and large institutions tend to lower their aspirations. In a follow-up study in 1993, Astin also found that the percentage of women in the student body was a positive predictor of increased aspirations among students. In contrast, a study of the effects of institutional type on educational aspirations found that many of the institutional effects on aspirations were modest, leading to assertions that institutional environments have primarily indirect effects on aspirations, being mediated by variables like achievement (Pascarella, 1984).

There are clearly conflicting conceptions of the ways in which institutional differences affect individual students' aspirations. The effect of community colleges on the aspirations and attainments of students has been a point of controversy for several decades. Clark (1960) discussed the role of the community college in the educational and occupational attainment of students. Clark believed that lower SES students were directed to two-year colleges and were thus "cooled out" (lowered their aspirations) as a result of their experiences in the institutions. As stated before, the process of cooling out is one in which the "socializing agents" in the two-year college — faculty and peers, the curriculum, and administrative procedures — all influence the lowering of educational plans (Pascarella & Terenzini, 1991). There is considerable evidence that the mere fact that a student attends a two-year college as opposed to a four-year college lowers that student's chances of attaining a Bachelor's degree by 19% (Brint & Karabel, 1989; Vélez, 1985).

> Community colleges are significantly less able than four-year colleges to facilitate the educational and economic attainment of the approximately 30 to 40 percent of community college entrants seeking bachelor's degrees. . . [G] enerally baccalaureate aspirants entering community colleges secure significantly fewer bachelor's degrees, fewer years of education, less prestigious jobs and in the long run, poorer paying jobs than comparable students entering four-year colleges. . . [Dougherty, 1987, pp. 99-100]

In this way, community colleges function as a form of "tracking" in higher education, such that the more able, higher SES students go directly to four-year colleges and institutions while the lower SES, less able students attain two-year degrees. The function of community colleges in terms of lowering attainment (and presumably aspirations) has been described by some researchers as part of society's role in "managing ambition": the United States society generates more ambition than the opportunity structure can support; therefore, the attendance of lower SES students at community colleges is one structural way of depressing high ambitions (Brint & Karabel, 1989).

The institutional effects of HBCUs and PWIs on African American student achievement has been the focus of several studies over the past two decades. Given the fact that HBCUs comprise 9% of the nation's baccalaureate-granting institutions, but "account for more than 30 percent of the all Bachelor's degrees awarded" (Trent, 1991, p. 56) to African Americans, it seems that there is something unique about the way HBCUs facilitate aspirations and attainment. Many of the studies find that African American students tend to experience social isolation and suffer identity problems in PWIs that may interfere with academic achievement (Jackson & Swan, 1991). On the other hand, HBCUs have been described as providing a "very mediocre educational experience," given their comparative lack of resources (Jackson & Swan, 1991, p. 127). However, some researchers suggest that despite HBCUs' relative disadvantages with respect to resources, the colleges have "been able to create a social-psychological campus climate that not only fosters students' satisfaction, sense of community, and adjustment to college, but also increases the likelihood of persistence and degree completion" (Bohr, Pascarella, Nora, & Terenzini, 1995, p. 82).

Research showing the positive effects of HBCUs on students' achievement has been contrasted with the research on African American students' educational experiences in PWIs:

> Black students on White campuses, compared with their counterparts who graduate from [HBCUs], generally have lower grade-point averages, lower persistence rates, lower academic achievement levels, higher attrition rates, less likelihood of enrolling in advanced degree programs, poorer overall psychological adjustment, and lower post-graduate attainments and earnings. [Darden, Bagaka's, & Kamel, 1996, p. 56]

According to Fleming (1984), HBCUs facilitate students' academic development in three ways: friendship among peers, faculty, and staff; participation in the life of the campus; and feelings of academic success. HBCUs encourage African American students to interact with peers, faculty and staff to a greater degree than PWIs; African American students hold more positions of leadership in HBCUs than in White colleges; finally, the academic successes of African American students are more encouraged (and perhaps *noticed*) by faculty in HBCUs than in PWIs (Fleming, 1984).

In addition, attendance at HBCUs has been shown to enhance the life circumstances of students. African American students who attend HBCUs tend to have higher incomes twenty years later than students who attended other kinds of postsecondary institutions (Constantine, 1995). As far as educational aspirations, one study found that African American students attending HBCUs tend to aspire to doctoral degrees in greater numbers than African American students at PWIs — although the students at PWIs tend to aspire to more "prestigious" professional degrees (e.g. law and medical degrees) than the students at HBCUs (Allen & Haniff, 1991).

Besides research on the comparative experiences of African American students at PWIs and HBCUs, there is very little knowledge on the degree to which the percentage enrollments of racial/ethnic minority students affect their educational outcomes. The structural diversity of an institution (the numerical representation of various racial/ethnic groups) is an important characteristic of colleges and universities. College environments with very high percentages of White students (in comparison to students of color) tend to provide few cross-race interactions for White students, tend to treat students from minority groups as symbols rather than as individuals, and tend to convey the message that maintaining a campus multicultural environment is a low institutional priority (Loo & Rolison, 1986; Hurtado, Milem, Clayton-Pederson, & Allen, 1999). In addition, minority students have experienced significant levels of alienation and harassment based on their ethnic group membership (Loo & Rolison, 1986). Minority students have been described as highly "visible" on campus and "often viewed as outsiders and isolated from the mainstream" (Nagasawa & Wong, 1999, p. 81). Students of color at PWIs can experience minority status stress and alienation from the campus community (Loo & Rolison, 1986; Smedley, Myers, & Harrell, 1993). Thus, the racial composition of the students in a postsecondary educational institution can affect students' outcomes independent of other characteristics.

There are competing views as to whether large numbers of racial/ethnic minority group members will positively or negative affect student outcomes. On the one hand, in environments that have lower numbers of certain groups, underrepresented minority group members may be viewed as "tokens" — symbols rather than as individuals — which can heighten the visibility of the group members and exaggerate differences between groups (Hurtado, et al., 1999). On the other hand, large numbers of minority group members "can hinder their absorption into the campus culture" (Nagasawa & Wong, 1999, p. 87). What seems clear is that a critical mass of underrepresented minority group members is necessary for students to form supportive peer groups and feel comfortable on college campuses (Smedley, et al., 1993; Nagasawa & Wong, 1999). Having a larger number of racial/ethnic minority students on a college campus may communicate the message that the campus is committed to the success of minority students (Hurtado, 1990; Loo & Rolison, 1986). This may be true, since one study found that African American, Latino, and White students attending campuses with higher minority enrollments — taking into account the selectivity of the institutions — tended to have higher aspirations after four years (Carter, 1999b).

In addition, it is important to consider how the students at particular institutions differ. Students are not randomly distributed throughout the different college levels and types; different colleges attract different types of students

(Feldman & Newcomb, 1969). A student's socioeconomic status is significantly related to the type of college he or she attends. Karabel and Astin (1975) studied the effect of SES, academic ability and college selectivity and found that a "student's social origin is significantly related to the status of the college he [sic] attends" (p. 394). The lower the SES, the more likely a student will go to a less-expensive, public, and less-selective institution (Karabel & Astin, 1975; Pascarella, Smart, & Smylie, 1992). Hearn (1991) studied the types of colleges 1980 high school graduates attended and concluded that "the most stubborn barriers to meritocracy seem to be those that are directly and indirectly based in SES, rather than those that are based in race, ethnicity, or gender" (p. 168). In other words, although more students are attending postsecondary institutions, lower SES students attend less selective institutions more often than higher SES students. African Americans may have had comparable access to educational institutions in Hearn's study, but their educational and occupational outcomes are far lower than White students.

The college choice theoretical perspective coupled with the above research showing the relationship between SES and type of college a student attends may indicate that income plays an indirect role in the development of degree aspirations and that institutional characteristics play a direct role in developing or constraining students' aspirations. However, after finding few significant effects of institutional type on degree aspirations, Pascarella (1984) suggests that institutional characteristics play an indirect role in affecting students' aspirations. Whether the effect of institutional type is direct or indirect, these findings of studies on the effect of institutional characteristics on student outcomes highlight the importance of controlling for background characteristics in order to assess the true effect of institutional characteristics.

THE EFFECT OF FINANCIAL AID VARIABLES

There is very little research on the effect of financial aid on educational aspirations. Financial aid can be seen as representative of both institutional financial support and of individual financial need. Traditionally, broad financial aid support for students to attend college was intended to lessen any financial difficulties students may have in paying tuition. The Higher Education Act of 1965 is the first example of broad federal support for attendance at postsecondary institutions. This act featured grants and low-interest government-insured loans (Rippa, 1997). Therefore, financial aid awards to lower SES students should mediate the financial limitations of their backgrounds and increase the probability they will attend four-year institutions and desire to continue on to post-baccalaureate education. The type of aid students receive, and the degree to which their financial need is met, may impact their degree expectations. Institutional type and individual characteristics should both influence financial aid measures.

Very few studies incorporate financial aid variables into their models of educational outcomes. Unfortunately, quite a few of the financial aid studies are a decade or more old, which means that we will not know the effect of recent federal policies limiting financial aid for several years. The United States government policies from the 1960s and 1970s, geared toward increasing access to higher education by offering aid to financially needy students, were significantly weakened in the 1980s (Baker & Vélez, 1996). The result of the weakening in financial support to low income postsecondary students is that fewer funds for grants and more aid in the form of loans were made available to students. This study does examine the effect of financial aid on the degree aspirations of college students in the late 1980s and early 1990s.

St. John and Noell (1989) found that all types of financial aid packages had positive impacts on student enrollment decisions, particularly minority student enrollment. However, a review of the literature on access to postsecondary education noted that one reason for the decline of African American college attendees in the 1980s is that "African Americans are less willing to borrow for higher education for purely economic reasons. . . given that African American students are increasingly from low-income families in which a typical $10,000-12,000 debt will often be larger than his or her annual family income" (Baker & Vélez, 1996, p. 88).

What is known about the effect of financial aid (in unspecified forms) is that it facilitates students' peer social interactions (Cabrera, Nora, & Casteñeda, 1992). "Financial aid may provide recipients with enough freedom to engage in social activities. . . [or] remove anxieties, time, and effort associated with securing additional funds to finance their education" (p. 589). Students in work study programs may benefit in particular because they tend to have more frequent contact with faculty, staff and institutional policies (Hossler, 1984). Increased interaction with faculty and staff may increase students' knowledge of degree options and may encourage students to aspire to post-baccalaureate degrees.

Since financial aid has been found to affect access, retention, and degree progress, it is likely that aid will affect students' degree expectations. Perhaps, more importantly, the form of aid (loans vs. grants) may deter students from pursuing (or wanting to pursue) advanced degrees.

ACADEMIC ACHIEVEMENT

Several researchers have found significant, positive relationships between college GPAs and aspirations (Astin, 1977; Carter, 2001; Hearn, 1987; Pascarella, 1985). Clearly, the status attainment framework suggests that a student's educational aspiration level is affected by his or her prior academic performance. Thus, it seems that students may adjust their aspiration levels in college based on their college academic performance. Examining the role of academic ability in the development of degree aspirations is particularly important in determining what affects the patterns of mobility for African American, Latino, and White students.

CONCLUSIONS

The main theoretical framework described in this chapter can be summarized by discussing three themes presented in this paper: 1) the roles of ascribed status or merit in influencing students' aspirations; 2) the effects of institutional characteristics and experiences, and 3) the unique experiences and characteristics of African American and Latino students in higher education.

The social psychological status attainment model (Sewell, et al., 1969; 1970), Turner's (1960) contest vs. sponsored mobility, and cultural capital are the main lenses through which the roles of ascribed status and merit in affecting students' aspirations are examined. The status attainment model, Turner's theory of the mobility processes, and cultural capital hold significant assumptions about the ways in which students achieve (or acquire) status and how their aspirations are affected over time.

Institutional characteristics and experiences can have as strong an effect on students' aspirations as socioeconomic status or individual achievement. Each institution (or institutional type) has particular social environments that can independently affect academic outcomes. Specifically, certain characteristics of institutions may increase access to students from lower SES backgrounds and may particularly affect the educational goals of African American students.

African American and Latino students are populations of students who tend to come from lower income backgrounds and have lower rates of college enrollment than White students. Furthermore, researchers have not been wholly successful in explaining what affects African American and Latino students' degree aspirations. Future research needs to explain better the reasons why there are racial/ethnic group differences in educational aspirations.

The model posed in this chapter advances previous perspectives on college students' degree aspirations by incorporating previous empirical research into the dominant theoretical frameworks used in sociology. The unique experiences of African American and Latino students have not been explained well by existing research. Elements of the proposed model should help researchers explore the racial/ethnic differences between groups and, perhaps, given the proper data, will illuminate appropriate institutional responses to increasing students' degree goals and therefore increasing students' educational attainments. More research is also needed on the role of institutional environments on students' degree aspirations. Aspirations are individually and socially constructed; the pre-college elements of the social and individual construction are well-identified — theoretically, if not empirically. However, the gap remains in explaining how institutions affect students' degree goals and why racial/ethnic groups differ in their degree goals. This chapter and the proposed model take the first step by synthesizing previous research and theoretical perspectives to explain the changes in college students' aspirations over time — with emphasis on institutional environments.

There remain several significant gaps in current research on students' educational aspirations. First, as researchers and practitioners, we need to identify and make clear our assumptions about educational aspirations. For instance, although the lowering of aspirations may not be ideal, it ultimately might be a positive result given a student's circumstance. If a student from a low SES background aspires to be a physician, but achieves "only" a Bachelor's degree, that still is a success for the student. Understanding our assumptions about aspirations may help clarify models and theories that can explain the processes by which students' change their educational goals.

A second, related gap in research on students' aspirations is in what affects nontraditional students' aspirations. Nontraditional students are a majority of the individuals attending post-secondary institutions and additional research needs to be done to understand influences on their degree goals. It would be inappropriate to use theoretical models that assume direct high school-to-college mobility for college students who are in their late 20s and above.

Third, the existing theoretical frameworks discussed in this chapter, in conjunction with the empirical research reviewed, need to be supplemented with other theoretical approaches. Other disciplinary approaches (e.g. organizational theory, anthropology, psychology, racial identity theory) may help explain student aspirations in addition to the theoretical approaches from sociology. For example, racial identity theory may account for the negative characteristics related to minority group status but also may account for positive behavior like the effect of role models on student outcomes.

A final gap in the research on students' educational aspirations results from the methodology used in many studies. Much of the research on students' aspirations has been done using quantitative data analyses. The contribution of this body of work as a whole is significant, because researchers have been able to demonstrate the differences that occur between different student groups and have shown various direct and indirect effects on aspirations. However, qualitative research is a necessary new direction for study in this field. The process by which students set educational goals and change them over time is complex. Understanding *why* students change their goals and the many factors that affect their educational goals are important future directions for aspirations research.

REFERENCES

Agnew, R. & Jones, D.H. (1988). Adapting to deprivation: An examination of inflated educational expectations. *The Sociological Quarterly*, 29(2), 315-337.

Alexander, K.L. & Cook, M.A. (1979). The motivational relevance of educational plans: Questioning the conventional wisdom. *Social Psychology Quarterly*, 42(3), 202-213.

Allen, W.R. (1991). Introduction. In W.R. Allen, E.G. Epps, and N.Z. Haniff (eds.) *College in Black and White: African American students in predominantly White and in historically Black public universities* (pp. 1-14). Albany: State University of New York Press.

Allen, W.R. (1992). The color of success: African-American college student outcomes at predominantly White and historically Black public colleges and universities. *Harvard Educational Review*, 62(1), 26-44.

Allen, W.R. & Haniff, N.Z. (1991). Race, gender, and academic performance in U.S. higher education. In W.R. Allen, E.G. Epps, and N.Z. Haniff (eds.) *College in Black and White: African American students in predominantly White and in historically Black public universities* (pp. 95-109). Albany: State University of New York Press.

Alwin, D. F. (1974). College effects on educational and occupational attainments. *American Sociological Review*, 39(April), 210-223.

Ancis, J.R. & Sedlacek, W.E. (1997). Predicting the academic achievement of female students using the SAT and noncognitive variables. *College and University*, 72(3), 2-8.

Astin, A.W. (1977). *Four critical years*. San Francisco: Jossey-Bass Publishers.

Astin, A.W. (1990). *The Black undergraduate: Current status and trends in the characteristics of freshmen*. Los Angeles: Higher Education Research Institute.

Astin, A.W. (1993). *What matters in college?: Four critical years revisited*. San Francisco: Jossey-Bass Publishers.

Astin, A.W., Tsui, L., & Avalos, J. (1996). *Degree attainment rates at American colleges and universities: Effects of race, gender, and institutional type*. Los Angeles: Higher Educational Research Institute, University of California.

Baker, T.L. & Vélez, W. (1996). Access to and opportunity in postsecondary education in the United States: A review. *Sociology of Education*, (Extra Issue), 82-101.

Barrera, M. (1997). A theory of racial inequality. In A. Darder, R.D. Torres, and H. Gutíerrez (eds.), *Latinos and Education: A Critical Reader* (pp. 3-44). New York: Routledge.

Berger, J. B. (2000). Optimizing capital, social reproduction, and undergraduate persistence: A sociological perspective. In J. M. Braxton (ed.) *Reworking the Student Departure Puzzle* (pp. 95-124). Nashville, TN: Vanderbilt University Press.

Berman, G.S. & Haug, M.R. (1975) Occupational and educational goals and expectations: The effects of race and sex. *Social Problems*, 23, 166-181.

Blau, P.M. & Duncan, O.D. (1967). *The American occupational structure*. New York: John Wiley & Sons, Inc.

Bohr, L, Pascarella, E.T., Nora, A., & Terenzini, P.T. (1995). Do Black students learn more at historically Black or predominantly White colleges? *Journal of College Student Development*, 36(1), 75-85.

Brint, S. & Karabel, J. (1989). *The diverted dream: Community colleges and the promise of educational opportunity in America, 1900-1985*. New York: Oxford University Press.

Burke, P.J. & Hoelter, J.W. (1988). Identity and sex-race differences in educational and occupational aspirations formation. *Social Science Research*, 17, 29-47.

Cabrera, A.F., Nora, A., and Castañeda, M.B. (1992). The role of finances in the persistence process: A structural model. *Research in Higher Education*, 33(5), 571-593.

Campbell, R.T. (1983). Status attainment research: End of the beginning or beginning of the end? *Sociology of Education*, 56(January), 47-62.

Carter, D.F. (2001). *A Dream Deferred? Examining the Degree Aspirations of African American and White College Students*. New York: Garland.

Carter, D.F. (1999a). The impact of institutional choice and environments on African American and White students degree expectations. *Research in Higher Education*, 40(1), 17-41.

Carter, D.F (1999b). *Institutional diversity and the degree expectations of college students.* Paper presented at the meeting of the Association for the Study of Higher Education, Miami, FL.

Carter, D.J. & Wilson, R.T. (1996). *Minorities in higher education: 14th annual status report.* Washington, D.C.: American Council on Education.

Choy, S.P. & Premo, M.K. (1995). *Profile of older undergraduates: 1989-90.* National Center for Education Statistics, Statistical Analysis Report 95-167. Washington, D.C.: U.S. Department of Education, Office of Educational Research and Improvement.

Clark, B. (1960). The "cooling out" function in higher education. *American Journal of Sociology*, 65, 569-576.

Constantine, J.M. (1995). The effect of attending historically Black colleges and universities on future wages of Black students. *Industrial and Labor Relations Review*, 48(3), 531-546.

Darden, J.T., Bagaka's, J.G., & Kamel, S.M. (1996). Historically Black institutions and desegregation: The dilemma revisited. *Equity & Excellence in Education*, 29(2), 56-68.

Dawkins, M.P. (1982). Occupational prestige expectations among Black and White college students: A multivariate analysis. *College Student Journal*, 16(3), 233-242.

Deskins, Jr., D.R. (1994). Prospects for minority doctorates in the year 2000: Employment opportunities in a changing American society. In M. Holden, Jr. (ed.) *The challenge to racial stratification: National political science review* (volume 4) (pp. 98-148). News Brunswick: Transaction Publishers.

Dougherty, K. (1987). The effects of community colleges: Aid or hindrance to socioeconomic attainment? *Sociology of Education*, 60(April), 86-103.

Eckland, B.K. (1964). Social class and college graduation: Some misconceptions corrected. *American Journal of Sociology*, 70, 60-72.

Epps, E.G. and Jackson, K.W. (1985). *Educational and occupational aspirations and early attainment of Black males and females.* Atlanta, Georgia: Southern Education Foundation.

Feagin, J.R., Vera, H, and Imani, N. (1996). *The agony of education: Black students at White colleges and universities.* New York: Routledge.

Feldman, K. & Newcomb, T. (1969). *The impact of college on students.* San Francisco: Jossey-Bass.

Fleming, J. (1984). *Blacks in college.* San Francisco: Jossey-Bass.

Foley, D.E. (1991). Reconsidering anthropological explanations of ethnic school failure. *Anthropology & Education Quarterly*, 22, 60-86.

Fordham, S. & Ogbu, J.U. (1986). Black students' school success: Coping with the "burden of 'acting White'". *The Urban Review*, 18(3), 176-206.

Giroux, H.A. (1983). Theories of reproduction and resistance in the new sociology of education: A critical analysis. *Harvard Education Review*, 53(3), 257-293.

Grubb, W.N. & Wilson, R.H. (1989). Sources of increasing inequality in wages and salaries, 1960-80. *Monthly Labor Review*, 112(4), 3-13.

Hanson, S.L. (1994). Lost talent: Unrealized educational aspirations and expectations among U.S. youths. *Sociology of Education*, 67(July), 159-183.

Hao, L. and Bonstead-Burns, M. (1998). Parent-child differences in educational expectations and the academic achievement of immigrant and native students. *Sociology of Education*, 71(3), 175-198.

Hearn, J.C. (1987). Impacts of undergraduate experiences on aspirations and plans for graduate and professional education. *Research in Higher Education*, 27(2), 119-141.

Hearn, J.C. (1991). Academic and nonacademic influences on the college destinations of 1980 high school graduates. *Sociology of Education*, 64(July), 158-171

Hossler, D. (1984). *Enrollment management.* New York: College Entrance Examination Board.

Hossler, D., Braxton, J., & Coopersmith, G. (1989). Understanding student college choice. In Smart, J.C. (Ed.). *Higher Education: Handbook of Theory and Research* (volume 5). New York: Agathon Press.

Hossler, D. & Gallagher, K.S. (1987). Studying student college choice: A three-phase model and the implications for policymakers. *College and University*, 62(3), 207-221.

Hurtado, S. (1990). *Campus racial climates and educational outcomes.* Unpublished doctoral dissertation, University of California, Los Angeles.

Hurtado, S., Inkelas, K.K., Briggs, C., & Rhee, B. (1997). Differences in college access and choice among racial/ethnic groups: Identifying continuing barriers. *Research in Higher Education*, 38(1), 43-75.

Hurtado, S., Milem, J.F., Clayton-Pedersen, A.R., & Allen, W.R. (1999). Enacting diverse learning environments: Improving the climate for racial/ethnic diversity. *ASHE-ERIC Higher Education Report* Volume 26, No. 8. Washington, D.C.: The George Washington University, Graduate School of Education and Human Development.

Isaac, P.D., Malaney, G.D., & Karras, J.E. (1992). Parental educational level, gender differences, and seniors' aspirations for advanced study. *Research in Higher Education*, 33(5), 595-606.

Jackson, K.W. & Swan, L.A. (1991). Institutional and individual factors affecting Black undergraduate student performance: Campus race and student gender. In W.R. Allen, E.G. Epps, and N.Z. Haniff (eds.) *College in Black and White: African American students in predominantly White and in historically Black public universities* (pp. 127-141). Albany: State University of New York Press.

Kao, G. & Tienda, M. (1998). Educational aspirations of minority youth. *American Journal of Education*, 106(5), 349-384.

Karabel, J. & Astin, A.W. (1975). Social class, academic quality, and college "quality". *Social Forces*, 53(3), 381-398.

Kempner, K. & Kinnick, M. (1990). Catching the window of opportunity: Being on time for higher education. *Journal of Higher Education*, 61(5), 535-547.

Kerckhoff, A.C. (1976). The status attainment process: Socialization or allocation? *Social Forces*, 55 (2), 368-381.

Kerckhoff, A.C. (1984). The current state of social mobility research. *The Sociological Quarterly*, 25 (Spring), 139-153.

Knight, W.H. & Wing, A. (1995). Weep not, little ones: An essay to our children about affirmative action. In J.H. Franklin & G. R. McNeil (eds.) African *Americans and the living Constitution.* Washington: Smithsonian Institution Press.

Knotterus, J.D. (1987). Status attainment research and its image of society. American *Sociological Review*, 52(February): 113-121.

Komaromy, M., Grumbach, K., Drake, M., Vranizan, K, Lurie, N, Keane, D., & Bindman, A.B. (1996, May 16). The role of Black and Hispanic physicians in providing health care for underserved populations. *New England Journal of Medicine*, 334(20), 1305-1310.

Labovitz, E.M. (1975). Race, SES, contexts and fulfillment of college aspirations. *The Sociological Quarterly*, 16, 241-249.

Loo, C.M & Rolison, G. (1986). Alienation of ethnic minority students at a predominantly White university. *Journal of Higher Education*, 57(1), 58-77.

Luttrell, W. (1989). Working-class women's ways of knowing: Effects of gender, race, and class. *Sociology of Education*, 62(1), 33-46.

Maxey, J., Lee, J.S., & McLure, G.T. (1995). Are Black students less likely to enroll at their first-choice college? *Journal of Blacks in Higher Education*, 7, 100-101.

McClelland, K. (1990). Cumulative disadvantage among the highly ambitious. *Sociology of Education*, 63(April), 102-121.

McDonough, P.M. 1997. *Choosing colleges: How social class and schools structure opportunity.* Albany, NY: State University of New York Press.

Morrow, R.A., & Torres, C.A. (1995). *Social theory and education: A critique of theories of social and cultural reproduction.* Albany, NY: State University of New York Press.

Nagasawa, R. & Wong, P. (1999). A theory of minority students' survival in college. *Sociological Inquiry*, 69(1), 76-90.

Ogbu, J.U. (1983). Minority status and schooling in plural societies. *Comparative Education Review*, 27 (2), 168-190.

Otto, L.B. (1976). Social integration and the status attainment process. *American Journal of Sociology*. 81(6), 1360-1383.

Pascarella, E.T. (1984). College environmental influences on students' educational aspirations. *Journal of Higher Education*, 55(6), 751-771.

Pascarella, E.T. (1985). Students' affective development within the college environment. *Journal of Higher* Education, 56(6), 640-663.

Pascarella, E.T., Smart, J.C., & Smylie, M.A. (1992). College tuition costs and early career socioeconomic achievement: Do you get what you pay for? *Higher* Education, 24(3), 275-291.

Pascarella, E.T. & Terenzini, P.T. (1991). *How college affects students.* San Francisco: Jossey-Bass.

Paulsen, M.B. (1990). College choice: Understanding student enrollment behavior. *ASHE-ERIC Higher Education Report No. 6.* Washington, D.C.: The George Washington University, School of Education and Human Development.

Porter, J.N. (1974) Race, socialization and mobility in educational and early occupational attainment. *American Sociological Review*, 39(June), 303-16.

Portes, A. & Wilson, K.L. (1976). Black-White differences in educational attainment. *American Sociological Review*, 41(June), 414-431.

Rippa, S.A. (1997). *Education in a free society: An American history.* (8th ed.). New York: Longman.

Sewell, W.H., Haller, A.O., & Ohlendorf, G.W. (1970). The educational and early occupational status attainment process: Replication and revision. *American Sociological Review*, 35, 1014-1027.

Sewell, W.H., Haller, A.O., & Portes, A. (1969). The educational and early occupational attainment process. *American Sociological Review*, 34(February), 82-92.

Sewell, W.H. & Shah, V.P. (1967). Socioeconomic status, intelligence, and the attainment of higher education. *Sociology of Education*, 40(1), 1-23.

Smedley, B.D., Myers, H.F., & Harrell, S.P. (1993). Minority-status stresses and the college adjustment of ethnic minority freshmen. *Journal of Higher Education*, 64(4), 434-452.

Smith, A.W. (1988). In double jeopardy: Collegiate academic outcomes of Black females vs. Black males. *National Journal of Sociology*, 2, 3-33.

Smith, D.G. (1990). Women's colleges and coed colleges: Is there a difference for women? *Journal of Higher Education*, 61(2), 181-195.

So, A.Y. (1987). The educational aspirations of Hispanic parents. *Educational Research Quarterly*, 11, 47-53.

Solorzano, D.G. (1992). An exploratory analysis of the effects of race, class, and gender on student and parent mobility aspirations. *Journal of Negro Education*, 61(1), 30-43.

Spady, W.G. (1970). Lament for the letterman: Effects of peer status and extracurricular activities on goals and achievement. *American Journal of Sociology*, 75(January), 680-702.

St. John, E.P. (1991). What really influences minority attendance?: Sequential analyses of the High School and Beyond sophomore cohort. *Research in Higher Education*, 32(2), 141-158.

St. John, E.P. & Noell, J. (1989). The effects of student financial aid on access to higher education: An analysis of progress with special consideration of minority enrollment. *Research in Higher Education*, 30(6), 563-581.

St. John, E.P, Oescher, J. & Andrieu, S. (1992). The influence of prices on within-year persistence by traditional college-age students in four-year colleges. *Journal of Student Financial Aid.* 22(1), 27-38.

Thomas, G.E., Alexander, K.L. & Eckland, B.K. (1979). Access to higher education: The importance of race, sex, social class, and academic credentials. *School Review*, 87(2), 133-156.

Tinto, V. (1993). *Leaving college*. Chicago: University of Chicago Press.

Trent, W.T. (1991). Focus on equity: race and gender differences in degree attainment, 1975-76; 1980-81. In W.R. Allen, E.G. Epps, and N.Z. Haniff (eds.) *College in Black and White: African American students in predominantly White and in historically Black public universities* (pp. 41-59). Albany: State University of New York Press.

Turner, R.H. (1960). Sponsored and contest mobility and the school system. *American Sociological Review*, 25, 855-867.

Vélez, W. (1985). Finishing college: The effects of college type. *Sociology of Education*, 58(July), 191-200.

Weiler, W.C. (1993). Post-baccalaureate educational choices of minority students. *The Review of Higher Education*, 16(4), 439-460.

Wilson-Sadberry, K.R., Winfield, L.F., & Royster, D.A. (1991). Resilience and persistence of African-American males in postsecondary enrollment. *Education and Urban Society*, 24(1), 87-102.

4. UNDERSTANDING AND USING EFFICIENCY AND EQUITY CRITERIA IN THE STUDY OF HIGHER EDUCATION POLICY

Stephen L. DesJardins[1]
The University of Iowa

INTRODUCTION

Policy makers often have to make decisions about how resources are to be used in furthering societal objectives. Because resources are scarce, one of the objectives that decision-makers strive for is to allocate these resources among alternative uses in an efficient manner. Another objective that public policy-makers often pursue is to distribute scarce resources among individuals and groups in an equitable manner. In their analysis and deliberation, policy makers often view "efficiency" in allocation and "equity" in distribution as criteria that guide them in their decision-making.[2]

Efficiency and equity have long been the subjects of articles and books by political philosophers and economists. The classical economists like John Stuart Mills, Jeremy Bentham, and Adam Smith wrote extensively about efficiency in the marketplace. But these philosophers also spent a great deal of time discussing the just or equitable distribution of society's resources. For instance, in *The Wealth of Nations* (1776) Adam Smith stated, "But what improves the circumstances of the greater part can never be regarded as an inconvenience to the whole. No society can surely be flourishing and happy, of which the far greater part of the members are poor and miserable" (Book I, Chapter VIII).

In more recent times, the "equity-efficiency quandary" (see Schultz, 1972) has been a topic of discussion among economists interested in how the benefits

[1] I would like to thank Associate Editor Michael Paulsen for his assistance in the preparation of this manuscript. Without his valuable help, this project would not have been possible. Any errors or omissions are, however, my responsibility.

[2] There are, of course, other societal values and objectives that are important. For instance, political and economic liberty, opportunity, individual and collective security, and freedom (of speech, assembly, etc.). The focus of this paper is, however, on efficiency and equity as social values or objectives.

J.C. Smart and W.G. Tierney (eds.), Higher Education: Handbook of Theory and Research, 173–219.

and costs of a college education are distributed. In the 1960's and 1970's, a number of economists like Theodore Schultz, Gary Becker, Samuel Bowles, W. Lee Hansen, Burton Weisbrod and Edward Denison wrote extensively on whether the financing of higher education was efficient and whether the distribution of the benefits (especially in terms of personal income) were equitable. Schultz (1972) concluded that "(t)he allocation of resources to provide the instructional services of higher education in the United States is neither socially efficient nor equitable" (p. 2). Hansen noted that "(t)he objective of promoting greater equity might well conflict with such other objectives as economic efficiency" (Hansen, 1972, p. 262).

Today, efficiency and equity considerations permeate many writings on higher education policy. For example, Longanecker (1978) finds that "federal policy has been focused primarily on achieving three goals: promoting equality of educational opportunity, reducing the burden of college costs (efficiency), and assuring a strong system of higher education" (p.1). Hearn and Longanecker (1985) discuss efficiency and equity as policy criteria by suggesting that some policy analysts believe that "low postsecondary tuition as public policy is both inefficient and inequitable" (p. 488). McMahon (1991) states that "increased efficiency is one means of sustaining and improving quality and access" in higher education (p.143). McMahon also suggests that there are important interactions between the three "pillars" of higher education policy [efficiency, quality, and access (or equity)] and that weaknesses in one of these areas can have detrimental effects on the other two. McMahon's discussion of the interaction between these policy values or objectives suggests that they are linked and that policy makers may sometimes need to trade one objective (i.e., increased efficiency) for another (equity) and vice versa.

Even though efficiency and equity are often inextricably related, and these objectives are often cited as educational goals, very few education policy analysts discuss these criteria in detail. When these objectives *are* discussed it is often assumed that the audience understands the philosophical and economic foundations of these concepts, how they are defined, and the implications that they have for public policy-making. Unfortunately, the conceptual and theoretical foundations underlying equity and efficiency criteria — grounded in moral and political philosophy as well as economics — may not be widely understood. Also, social objectives are often poorly defined and not applied to policy discussions in a consistent manner. To properly account for efficiency and equity objectives "in the formulation of economic and social policy requires that they be specified in as precise a fashion as possible" and that these objectives be "both sufficiently general to command broad consensus and sufficiently specific to permit useful application" (LeGrand, 1991, p. 1).

The purpose of this chapter is to present some of the philosophical and economic issues related to efficiency and equity as decision-making criteria.[3] As a precursor, a discussion of the philosophical concepts underlying these criteria will be presented. After laying the philosophical groundwork, the concepts of economic efficiency and social welfare theory will be presented. Following the section on economic efficiency will be a discussion about equity. In the final section a higher education policy issue will be examined in order to demonstrate the practical applications of the key concepts discussed in this chapter. This chapter will demonstrate that it is helpful to think about how we can improve higher education by searching for ways to improve *both* efficiency and equity considerations.

UNDERLYING PHILOSOPHICAL CONCEPTS

Terminology

Before proceeding, it may be helpful to discuss the meanings of terms that are often used in philosophical discussions and that frequently arise in discussions of educational policy. Also, because some of these terms are often used interchangeably in the literature, it is important to clarify how they are used in this chapter.

The terms *equity*, *justice*, *fairness*, and *equality* are often used interchangeably in policy discussions and in scholarly writings. For instance, there is some agreement that access to higher education should be "equitable" and this term is often treated as being synonymous with "fairness" or "justice." However, in moral and political philosophy, these terms often have very specific meanings. For instance, in *A Theory of Justice*, John Rawls (1971) develops the notion of "justice as fairness" and this definition permeates much of recent moral and political philosophy on this subject. Rawls, however, is very specific in his definition of what this notion means. Some analysts believe that the key distinction between equity and broader conceptions of justice is that equity is related to the notion that individuals and groups get what they deserve through hard work and ambition.[4] Even though there may be very real differences in the definitions of equity, justice, and fairness, I will follow LeGrande's (1990; 1991) lead and treat these terms as synonyms throughout this chapter.

Distinguishing between equity and equality is another matter. These "two concepts are in fact quite distinct. Equality has a descriptive component, whereas equity is a purely normative concept. Partly as a consequence, equality

[3] Because some of the concepts and issues discussed are too complex to be fully treated in this chapter, references to additional literature are provided.

[4] These are known as "desert-based theories of justice" and will be discussed below.

does not necessarily imply equity, or equity equality. Equality of various kinds may be advocated for reasons other than equity; equitable outcomes may be quite inegalitarian" (LeGrand, 1991, p. 11). An example may help. Assume there is a fixed sum of scholarship money to be distributed to three students. Student A is awarded 25 percent of the total, student B is given 45 percent, and student C is allocated 30 percent of the funds. This distribution is clearly unequal; however, is the distribution of the scholarship funds also inequitable? What if we found out that the students were given grants in proportion to public service they did during the summer? The distribution would remain unequal, but given this additional information about the allocation of these resources, the distribution may not necessarily be considered inequitable.

COMPETING MORAL PHILOSOPHIES[5]

Before discussing equity and efficiency as evaluative criteria, it is important to briefly describe some of the moral philosophies that are the foundation of these social objectives. For instance, much of the analysis of welfare that is done by economists is rooted in competing views about the nature of the *well-being* of the individual and society. "All plausible moral views assign an important place to conceptions of individual good, utility, welfare, or well-being" (Hausman and McPherson, 1996, p. 71). There are, however, different opinions about how these conceptions are defined and how they interrelate. As Hausman and McPherson (1996) note, "(t)he theory of well-being is a messy area of philosophy. It is difficult even to categorize the various theories, and they all face serious difficulties" (p. 72). But welfare economists and others cannot "avoid addressing these philosophical problems if they want to be able to judge when welfare increases or decreases" (Hausman and McPherson, 1996, p. 72). The following sections briefly describe some of these foundational theories.

THEORIES OF "WELL-BEING"

Theories of well-being can be classified as either formal or substantive theories. Formal theories do not inform us about *what* things are intrinsically good for people, rather, these theories give us guidance on *how to discover* what is good for people through observation. One way that economists (and others) attempt to discover what is good for people is by observing what individuals prefer. This is often called the "*preference-satisfaction*" or "*preference-utilitarianism*" view of well-being, where satisfaction of preferences is considered intrinsically good

[5] Some of the information about the moral philosophies discussed in this section comes from Lamont, 2000. This "dynamic" encyclopedia of philosophy is a valuable resource to learn more about the fundamental concepts of moral and political philosophy.

and something that we should attempt to maximize. This view is appealing to economists because they often rely on utility theory to explain human choices. For many economists, utility is equated with preference satisfaction, and utility, well-being, and happiness are often considered synonymous.[6]

On the other hand, substantive theories of well-being tell us *what* things are intrinsically good for people. For example, ethical hedonism is a substantive theory that says that our fundamental *moral obligation* is to maximize pleasure or happiness (and reduce pain) and that pleasure is desired for its own sake (see Sidgwick, 1907, for details). This theory specifically indicates what is good for people — pleasure, and indicates that our moral objective is the pursuit of pleasure.[7] Many economists are, however, "attracted to a formal theory of well-being" because "they appear to involve fewer philosophical commitments. In particular, economists are reluctant to make substantive claims about what is good or bad for people" (Hausman and McPherson, 1996, p. 72).

Utilitarianism

Utilitarianism is a moral theory according to which an action is right if (and only if) it conforms to the principle of utility. Jeremy Bentham formulated the principle of utility in *Introduction to the Principles of Morals and Legislation* in 1789. An action is in keeping with the principle of utility if (and only if) this action leads to more pleasure or happiness, or less pain or unhappiness, than any other alternative. (Instead of "pleasure" and "happiness," the word "welfare" is sometimes used).

Since the main concern of utilitarians is welfare, utilitarianism is often called a "welfare-based theory." Because the focus is on welfare, utilitarianism is only tangentially concerned with the primary foci of other theories (e.g., liberty, equality, how the least advantaged are treated, resources and desert-based theories; all discussed below). The main concerns of these alternative theories are

[6] "One reason why economists are attracted to a formal theory of well-being is that formal theories *appear* to involve fewer philosophical commitments" (Hausman and McPherson, 1996, p. 72; emphasis added). However, Hausman and McPherson discuss the implications of equating well-being with the satisfaction of preferences and find that this supposition is "questionable in itself. It mistakenly suggests that social policy should attend to all preferences, even if they are expensive, anti-social, or the results of false beliefs, manipulations or problematic psychological processes" (p. 83). Preference satisfaction as well-being is also problematic when preferences change or conflict with one another. Equating well-being with preferences is also questionable because utility is very often not easy to measure. For more on this issue see Chapter 6 in Hausman and McPherson, 1996.

[7] Though it may appear to be the case, formal and substantive theories are not necessarily incompatible. "For example, if happiness is the ultimate object of preference, then it could be true both that well-being is the satisfaction of preference and that well-being is happiness" (Hausman and McPherson, 1996, p. 72).

only important in the ways that they *contribute* to increasing the welfare of individuals and society.

Another characteristic feature of Bentham's theory is the idea that the rightness of an action depends on the value of its consequences. This is why the theory is also sometimes described as "consequentialist." Bentham's theory of utilitarianism differs from other varieties in its assumption that the standard of value is pleasure and the absence of pain; that the *value of the consequences* of a particular act is what counts in determining whether the act is right;[8] and by its maximizing assumption that an action is not right unless it tends towards the optimal outcome (Zalta, 2000). The fact that the consequences matter counters the complaint that some individuals have that utilitarianism focuses only on materialistic values.

RAWLS' DISTRIBUTIVE JUSTICE

In recent years, one of the most widely discussed theories of distributive justice has been that proposed by John Rawls. In *A Theory of Justice* (1971), Rawls set the stage for recent discussions about justice by developing the following principles:

1) "Each person is to have an equal right to the most extensive total system of equal basic liberties compatible with a similar system of liberty for all" (p. 266). This is sometimes known as the *priority of liberty* principle.
2) "Social and economic inequalities are to be arranged so that they are both:
   (a) to the greatest benefit of the least advantaged, consistent with the just savings principle" (known as the *Difference Principle*),[9] and
   (b) "attached to offices and positions open to all under conditions of fair equality of opportunity" (p. 266).

Rawls specifies that the first principle (number 1 above) must be satisfied prior to (2), and that principle (2b) must be satisfied prior to (2a). Principle (1) governs how liberty is distributed and Principle (2b) governs the distribution of opportunities. Looking at justice in this way makes all principles of justice relate to distributive justice.

Some philosophers, like Rawls, feel that the key problem with utilitarian-

[8] Known as "act-utilitarianism." There are other types of utilitarianism, for instance "rule utilitarianism" and "indirect utilitarianism" (see Zalta, 2000, for details).

[9] Rawls' Difference Principle has been criticized by some philosophers who espouse other moral approaches. For instance, egalitarians (advocates of strict equality) argue that inequalities permitted by the Difference Principle are unacceptable even if they do benefit the least advantaged. Strict utilitarians object to the Difference Principle because its main focus is not on utility maximization.

ism is that a violation of an individual's rights is acceptable if the consequences of this violation are that society is made better off. Rawls believes his social contract-based theory of justice avoids this problem. Rawls titles his view "justice as fairness," which simply means that the rules of justice are agreed to in an initial contractual situation that is fair for everyone. This "original position" is just an idea (like Hobbes' state of nature) to help frame and motivate the discussion about the principles that should underlie a just society. In the original position, individuals imagine what it would be like without a government. Then they discuss among themselves what kind of government could be established and supported by a social contract and still achieve justice. The original position is negotiated under a "veil of ignorance," which means that individuals choose the social structure they would like without knowing their eventual place in society. Individuals will act in their self-interest, but will be motivated toward a "just" society because they are not sure what their position will be in the eventual social structure. The idea of using the original position is not to justify the authority of some particular government, rather, Rawls uses this mental exercise to try to come to an agreement about the basic principles that should be the foundation of a just society.

Rawls' main concern is with the absolute position of the least advantaged group rather than their relative position. For example, if a system of strict equality of income maximizes the absolute position of the least advantaged in society, then Rawls would advocate strict income equality. However, if the well-being of the least advantaged is improved by an unequal distribution of resources (like income), then principle (2a) prescribes inequality up to the point where the absolute position of the least advantaged can no longer be improved. In this way Rawls' theory is a welfare-based theory like utilitarianism.

With regard to efficiency, Rawls adopts the economic concept of Pareto efficiency (discussed below). He notes, however, that there are many difficulties if one uses the Pareto criterion to attempt to order different states of the world. For instance, there are many social arrangements that are efficient but not all of them are just. Therefore we need to invoke a theory of justice to select among the most just arrangements.

Economists usually group utilitarianism and Rawlsian philosophy under a broad mantle — *social welfare philosophy* (welfarism for short). This is the theory of justice that underlies modern welfare economics. At the heart of welfarism are the following: that end state results are typically evaluated in terms of how they affect the utility of society, and that the assets of society (i.e., labor, ability) can be used for redistribution if doing so would improve the welfare of society.[10]

[10] Known as "asset egalitarianism."

However, welfarism justifies redistributive policies only if they maximize welfare, and individual rights are justified only "in terms of their contribution to social welfare and not as absolutes" (Boadway and Bruce, 1991, p. 176).

Social welfarism is the philosophical basis for the "ability to pay" principle often used in discussions of redistributive policies. An example from higher education might be that financial aid is largely distributed based on the financial resources of a student's family (or the student, if financially independent).

A criticism of social welfare philosophy is that it ignores, and in fact cannot even make sense of, claims that people deserve certain economic benefits in light of their actions. This criticism is based on the concern that various forms of welfarism do not adequately deal with the fact that individuals are responsible for their actions and that their choices often determine their well-being.[11]

Libertarianism

In general, libertarians believe in individualism — that individuals are the basic units of social organization and that their rights are natural — that is, they are inherent in all human beings or are rights that do not depend on consequences (Nozick, 1974). "For philosophical libertarians, acts and policies are just if and only if they do not violate anyone's rights" (Hausman and McPherson, 1996, p. 130). Libertarians believe that the combination of the rule of law, defending natural rights, and limiting government will enhance individual and social well-being.

Libertarianism not only focuses on the rights of individuals (natural and property rights), but also emphasizes people's responsibilities. Although some critics believe libertarians are endorsing purely selfish motives, libertarians argue that charity and benevolence can be social objectives if these ideals are reached without infringing on individual liberty. Generally libertarians do not subscribe to redistributive policies (like Rawls' Difference Principle) because they feel that forced redistribution infringes on liberty. However, if redistribution did not infringe on individual liberty, then libertarians would not be opposed.

Resource-based Theories of Justice

Advocates of resource-based theories of justice believe that people should have to accept the consequences of their choices. For instance, people who gain more in resources (e.g., income) through the fruits of their labor should not have

[11] For more information about ideas of social welfare, see Hardin, 1982, 1988; Elster and Roemer, 1991; and Glover, 1990

to subsidize individuals who *choose* leisure over labor. Resource-based philosophers also believe, however, that circumstances that are beyond the control of individuals, like poor health, disabling conditions, or little natural ability, should not lead to disadvantage with regard to their life chances.

Resource-based principles are relatively new and were developed mainly as an attempt to improve upon Rawls' Difference Principle. For instance, advocates of resource-based principles aim to make the Difference principle more "endowment" or "ambition" sensitive. (Lamont, 2000). Ronald Dworkin (1981a, 1981b), probably the most well-known proponent of the resource-based approach, argues that people should begin with equal resources, but that due to the choices they make they may end up with different benefits. "Of course, there is a problem with natural inequalities – they are not distributed according to people's choices, nor are they justified by reference to some other morally relevant fact about people" (Lamont, 2000). To deal with this problem, Dworkin proposes a hypothetical scheme like Rawls' veil of ignorance. One difference is that under Dworkin's approach, individuals can (behind the veil) choose to buy "insurance" against being disadvantaged. The insurance "payments" are then used to provide a pool of money from which the disadvantaged can be compensated.[12]

Because the motivation behind resource-based theories is similar to that of the Difference Principle, the moral criticisms of the two theories are also similar. Unlike the Difference Principle, however, it is not at all clear what would constitute an implementation of many resource-based theories in the real world. It is at minimum difficult, and some say impossible, to measure differences in people's natural talents. Therefore, it would be hard to determine to whom compensation should be provided because of natural ability disadvantage.[13] Nonetheless, a system of compensation for the physically and mentally disabled would be a partial implementation of such a system. The problem is that under this arrangement natural inequalities would not be remedied, yet the theory requires that such inequalities be compensated for. In short, it is not clear how resource-based theories would be implemented; therefore, it is difficult to see how they improve on the Difference Principle.

Advocates of resource-based principles criticize the Difference Principle because they believe it does not provide sufficient rewards for ambition or the consequences of peoples' choices. With regard to the latter, some people choose leisure over labor, and resource-based theorists believe that the more ambitious should not have to subsidize the less ambitious. Conversely, they also argue that the Difference Principle does not adequately compensate people for natural ine-

[12] For more on this see Dworkin, 1981a and 1982a.

[13] Also, how would one determine natural talent from developed talent?

qualities (like low levels of natural endowments, poor health, or other disabling conditions) over which people have no control.[14]

DESERT-BASED THEORIES OF JUSTICE

There are a number of different desert-based principles but most of these proposals have to do with rewarding people because of their effort or contribution to the social product. Philosophers who advocate desert-based principles feel that some groups deserve more resources because they work hard to obtain them. Desert theorists argue that the Difference Principle does not explain the *process* by which some groups become more or less advantaged and that these explanations are relevant to the fairness of these positions.[15]

The main moral objection to desert-based principles is that these principles make economic benefits dependent on factors over which people have little control, like natural ability. John Rawls (1971) has made one of the most widely discussed arguments to this effect. The problem is that productivity is a function of many factors, some related to the choices that individuals make, others that a person has little or no control over. The main argument by Rawls and other philosophers who object to desert-based principles is that individuals should not be economically disadvantaged because of factors that they have no control over.

In general, libertarianism, resource- and desert-based theories tend to be Kantian philosophical notions. That is, the emphasis is on absolute rights. A particular implication of Kantian theory is the benefit principle of taxation, whereby taxes are levied in accordance with the benefits received. This theory is often the basis of arguments used by some economists to defend the existing distribution of wealth (see Buchanan, 1954; Nozick, 1974). It is also the basis of many "user fees" that are now popular in institutions of higher education to finance facilities like computer laboratories. The basic notion is "those who benefit pay."

Given the differences between social welfare and Kantian theories of justice, these theories appear to be "fundamentally irreconcilable" (Boadway and Bruce, 1991, p. 176). Nonetheless, since economists often reside in different philosophical "camps," it is instructive to understand the moral and political philosophy underlying many of their beliefs.

[14] Rawlsian principles, especially the Difference Principle, have been critiqued at length elsewhere (Barry, 1973; Daniels, 1975; Pettit, 1980) therefore I include only the brief critiques noted above.
[15] Additional readings on this subject can be found in Feinberg, 1970 and Lamont, 1994.

THE CONCEPTUAL BASIS OF INDIVIDUAL CHOICE

Political and moral philosophers and economists have long discussed efficiency and equity criteria. In fact, a special branch of economics emerged within which these issues are commonly studied. This field, known as welfare (or normative) economics, goes beyond the study of positive economics which is typically "concerned with the effects of an event on objectively measurable economic variables such as price and quantity" (Boadway and Bruce, 1991, p. 1). Positive economics is concerned with what "is" whereas welfare economics is concerned with what "ought" to be. A welfare economist attempts to determine the "desirability of a particular policy — not in terms of his or her own values, but in terms of some *explicitly stated ethical criteria*" (Boadway and Bruce, 1991, p. 1; emphasis added). That is, the objectives of social policy are *ideological*, whereas the methods by which we achieve (or attempt to achieve) these goals remain a matter for positive economic analysis.

For instance, in the United States public (and to a lesser extent private) higher education is subsidized. Society has determined that higher education "ought" to be publicly subsidized. Whether or not higher education is a social objective that ought to be subsidized is an ideological or normative question that has been (and continues to be) debated in the political sphere. Once society has made the normative determinations about public policies (like subsidizing higher education) welfare economics can help us to answer how these social objectives can be reached and the consequences of our actions in pursuit of these objectives. Many times economists (and others) forget that ethics and value judgments have long been, and continue to be, an integral part of welfare economics.

UTILITY THEORY

As mentioned above, utility has often been equated with happiness, satisfaction, or well-being. This is especially true in the writings of the classical economists. Because of conceptual problems, however, many modern economists assume that utility is a subjective concept and reflects nothing more than an ordinal (or rank ordering) of preferences.

For instance, assume a student has a choice to attend a private college that costs $25,000 per year or a public institution that costs $5,000 per year. We cannot tell anything about the utility differences between these two options since utility is really unobservable. We can, however, make inferences about the utility that this student derives by observing her choice. If she chooses the private school, we can infer that she derived more utility from that choice than the alternative. But calculating the magnitude of utility differences is problematic.

Does this student receive five times as much utility by choosing the private institution compared to the public college? This is a difficult question and one that is skirted by focusing on the *order* or ranking of utilities instead of their differences in magnitude. In this case, we know from observation that the student preferred the private college to the public institution. In such instances, economists assume that rational individuals, attempting to maximize their welfare, choose to consume "bundles" (or combinations) of goods — products and services, including colleges — that provide the greatest utility.[16]

PREFERENCES AND THE AXIOMS OF CONSUMER THEORY

In order to make our complex world amenable to study, economists (and other social scientists) often make simplifying assumptions in their models. A number of assumptions are often used when economists study the behavior of consumers. One assumption is that consumers' choices are indicative of their preferences. Another assumption is that economic theory typically "portrays agents as choosing rationally" (Hausman and McPherson, 1996, p. 27). Choices are rational if they are transitive and complete.[17] Transitivity means that if a student thinks that Harvard University (X) is at least as good as Cal Tech (Y), and that Cal Tech (Y) is as least as good as Princeton (Z), then Harvard (X) is as least as good as Princeton (Z). Completeness refers to the assumption that any two "bundles" of goods can be compared. Basically this axiom says that goods can be compared, and that the individual will be able to decide whether one good is better than another. Another possibility is that the consumer would be just as satisfied with one good as another. In this case we say that the individual is "indifferent" with respect to these goods. Transitivity and completeness are two of the three "axioms" of consumer theory. The third axiom, reflexivity, means that any bundle of goods is assumed to be at least as good as itself.[18]

In addition to the axioms of consumer choice described above, another assumption made about utility is that additional units consumed provide less *additional* satisfaction — that is, marginal utility (MU) — relative to previous units consumed. This assumption is known as the "law of diminishing marginal utility." This assumption also implies that consumers prefer "bundles" (or combinations) of goods and services that contain some variety (known as the principle of

[16] Modern welfare economists often assume that "the preferences of the consumer are the fundamental description useful for analyzing choice, and utility is simply a way of describing preferences" (Varian, 1996, p. 55).

[17] Some question whether completeness is a condition of rationality. See Levi, 1980 for a discussion.

[18] More information about preferences, the axioms of consumer theory, and objections to these concepts can be found in Varian, 1996.

"diversity in consumption"), rather than all of one particular good.

Economic models that are often used to understand and describe the behavior of individuals (or sometimes other agents, like households) are based on the concept of utility maximization. These models can be represented algebraically as:

$$\max U = f(A,B)$$

where "U" represents the utility of the individual (or a household) and "A" and "B" represent measurable quantities of a good or service. The practical problem is that utility is not observable. Thus we use individual preferences for "A" and "B" to indirectly represent, or act as a proxy for, the utility gained from consumption of these items.

Indifference Curves

One way to describe preferences is in graphical form by using indifference curves. These analytic tools provide us with a visual representation of the combinations of the two goods (in our case, "A" and "B") that provide equal levels of satisfaction.[19] For example, in Figure 1 assume that Good $_A$ represents studying (student work) and Good $_B$ leisure-related activities (i.e., going to a hockey game or to a concert). All points on any one of the individual indifference curves displayed (U_1-U_3) represent combinations of studying and leisure that provide equal levels of utility. That is, the individual is indifferent about the consumption of any of the combinations of goods represented along any one of these curves. However, all combinations of studying and leisure on a higher indifference curve — such as U_3 — are preferred to all combinations on a lower curve — such as U_2. In other words, studying-leisure combinations associated with U_3 provide the student with more utility than the combinations represented by U_2, and by the same logic U_2 is everywhere preferred to U_1. Preference directions are north and east because "a rational utility maximizing consumer will want to achieve the highest indifference curve possible" (Browning and Browning, 1987, p. 503-504).

The indifference curves in Figure 1 have negative slopes in keeping with our assumption about more being preferred to less.[20] Also, because individuals generally prefer some combination of goods and not all of one good, the indifference curves are convex to the origin. Given these characteristics, the indifference

[19] Indifference curves and other functions used in economic analysis can also be represented mathematically. I will refrain from such representations in this article. Readers interested in examining appropriate mathematical formulations of this model could consult Varian (1996) and Hirshleifer (1980), and similar texts.

[20] If, however, studying (Good A) were an economic "bad", the slope of the indifference curves would be positive.

curves displayed in Figure 1 are known as "well-behaved."

Mapping out different combinations of consumptive bundles that individuals are indifferent about can help us to make ordinal statements about the relative well-being of individuals under different states of the world. As we will see later in the chapter, having information about the preferences of many individuals will help us make judgments about social issues.

THE BUDGET CONSTRAINT

In Figure 1, there are many different combinations of studying and leisure that the individual might prefer to consume. For instance, preferences are defined for all combinations of Good $_A$ (studying) and Good $_B$ (leisure) within the space bounded by the vertical and horizontal axes. This means that there are indifference curves covering this whole space. However, individuals (and society) are constrained in their consumption by their income and the prices of the goods in question (P_A and P_B). In Figure 1 the budget line A_0-B_0 represents the resource constraint. In this case the individual can consume any combination of the goods in question in the space bounded by — that is, on or below — the budget line.

Figure 1: The Analysis of Consumer Choice

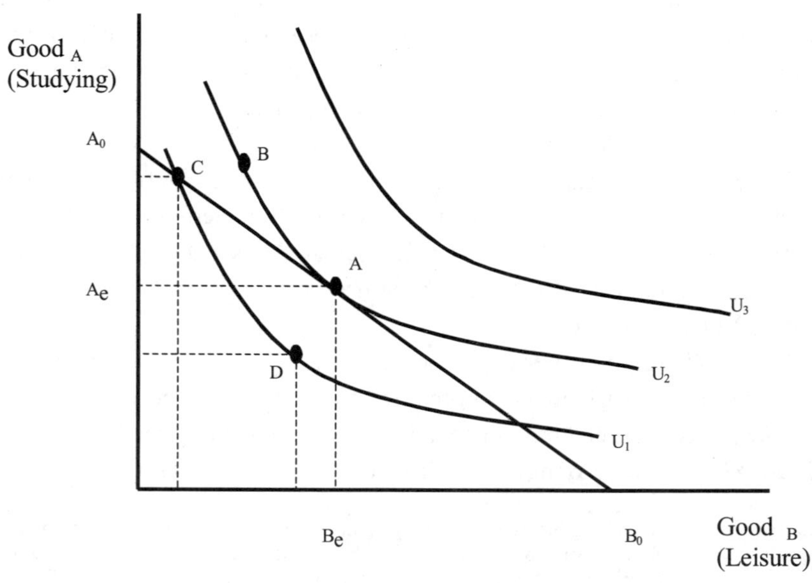

Combining the budget line with indifference curves provides us with analytic tools to make comparisons of alternative states of the world. In this case, the tools can be used to examine a student's decision-making process in choosing the combination of studying and leisure that yields the highest utility subject to income and price constraints. For instance, any point (like D) down and to the left of the budget line represents an inefficient use of resources because a student could obtain more of each good and higher levels of utility or satisfaction by moving from D to A. The key idea is that any consumptive point inside the budget frontier is inefficient.

Although point C lies on the budget line, this combination of goods is not optimal. The slope (in absolute value) of the budget constraint (P_B / P_A) indicates the "external" or market-based rate at which the student must give up studying to obtain additional units of leisure, while fully spending, but not exceeding, the budget. The slope of the indifference curve (MU_B / MU_A) — called the marginal rate of substitution (MRS) between studying and leisure — indicates the "internal" rate at which the student is willing to forego studying in order to obtain more leisure, while maintaining the current level of satisfaction. At point C, the slope of the budget constraint is less than the slope of indifference curve U_1 . Therefore, the amount of studying the student is willing to forgo exceeds the amount that must be given up to obtain an additional unit of leisure. This situation means that there are possible welfare gains to the student by reallocating income to consume more of Good $_B$ (leisure) and less of Good $_A$ (studying). This reallocation is displayed as a movement *along* the budget constraint from point C to point A, and on to a higher indifference curve (U_2). It is at point A that the consumer (student) has found an optimum where the amount of studying the student "will" and "must" give up to obtain more leisure — that is, the slopes of the indifference curve and budget line — are equal. Or, alternatively, the marginal utilities of each good are just equal to the prices of each good. The condition for a consumer optimum is therefore where the budget line and an indifference curve are tangent.[21]

The conclusion noted above can be extended to all consumers (students). The Pareto criterion in terms of *exchange efficiency* requires that all consumers (students) have equal MRS's. To simplify the analysis above, we have assumed that there are competitive markets in which all consumers will face the same price ratios for the two goods. And, even though each consumer may have a different set of preferences (and therefore different indifference curves), they all maximize utility by choosing the combination of goods that equates their MRS

[21] Note that any combination of goods on U_3 would provide more satisfaction than the combinations represented by U_1 or U_2. However, U_3 lies outside the consumers' budget set and is therefore not feasible.

with the price ratios of the two goods as determined in the marketplace. That is, the slopes of consumers' indifference curves and budget constraints will be equal, and all consumers will have the same MRS yet consume different quantities of the two goods consistent with their different preferences.

PRODUCTIVE EFFICIENCY

In order to achieve total economic efficiency (Pareto optimality) we must not only be efficient in the way goods and services are *exchanged*, we must also be efficient in the way they are *produced*, and the *product mix* must reflect societal preferences. Exchange efficiency was discussed above. In this section we discuss *efficiency in production*, the second criterion that must be met to achieve economic efficiency.[22] To continue our education-related example, let us assume that two variable inputs, teacher time and student time, are used in the production of student learning.[23] This example is graphically displayed in Figure 2 with teacher time on the vertical axis and student time on the horizontal axis. There are many different combinations of teacher and student time that can produce a given level of student learning. Plotting these input combinations produces an *isoquant* (meaning "same quantity") that indicates the combination of teacher and student time (inputs) that will yield a given level of student learning (output). Three isoquants ($Q_1 - Q_3$) are displayed in Figure 2, with isoquant Q_3 everywhere above and to the right of Q_2, and Q_2 everywhere above Q_1. This ordering indicates that Q_2 produces higher levels of student learning than Q_1, and Q_3 higher output than Q_2.[24] Isoquants have a negative slope indicating that if less (more) teacher time (student time) is used in the production of student learning then more (less) student time (teacher time) must be employed to achieve the same level of output (learning). The rate at which these two inputs can be substituted in order to keep output constant is known as the *marginal rate of technical substitution* (MRTS).

The MRTS is the slope of the isoquant at any point, and moving from left to right, the MRTS declines along an isoquant.[25] The *law of diminishing marginal product* indicates that as we increase the use of one input relative to another, the

[22]Productive efficiency is also sometimes called "internal" efficiency.

[23]It is questionable whether institutions of higher education, or their faculty, combine inputs (teacher time and student time) and resources to achieve results (student outcomes, research, and public service) in an efficient way. This example is simply used to illustrate the idea of efficiency in production and should not be construed as anything more than that.

[24]An infinite number of these curves could be traced in the space bounded by the two axes.

[25]When inputs are perfect substitutes the isoquants are straight lines and the MRTS is constant and equal to the slope of the line. The law of diminishing returns produces the convexity of the isoquants displayed in Figure 2 and the resultant non-constant MRTS.

Figure 2: Efficiency in the Production of Student Learning

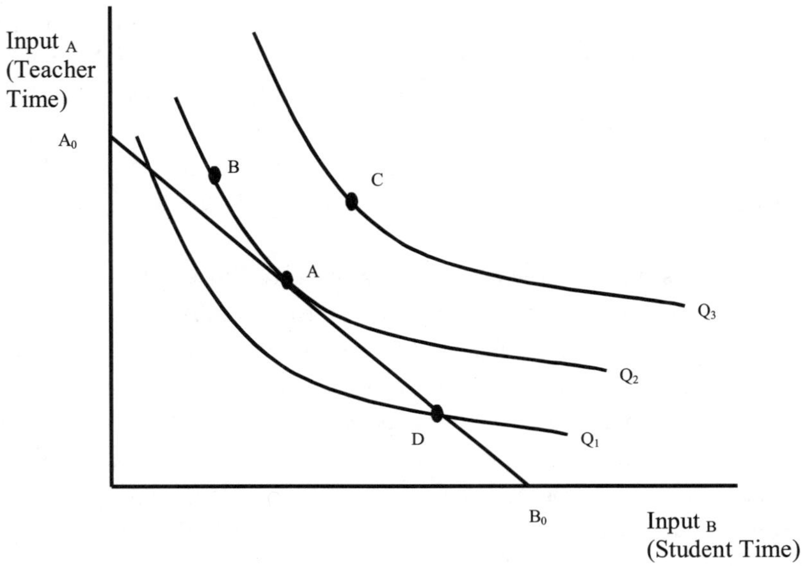

additional output produced by that input (the marginal product or MP) will tend to decline. With regard to our example, the marginal product of student time (teacher time) is the amount of additional learning (output) that is produced by employing one more "unit" of student time (teacher time) in the production of student learning. For example, less teacher time (depicted as a movement from point B to point A in Figure 2) can be used to produce a given level of student learning (depicted by Q_2), if use of student time is increased sufficiently. The substitution of student for teacher time results in an increase in the marginal product of teacher time (MP_T), and a decrease in the marginal product of student time (MP_S). The rate at which student time must be substituted for teacher time to maintain output on the same isoquant depends on changes in the relative marginal products of the two inputs. Therefore, the slope of the isoquant (MRTS), at a given point, equals the ratio of the marginal products of the two inputs (MP_S / MP_T) at that point.

Isoquants are useful analytic tools but they only provide information about output possibilities. Decision-makers must also have information about how much can be spent to achieve a given level of student learning (output) and about the relative costs of the inputs being used (teacher and student time) in order to make decisions about the optimum level of inputs and output. Information about cost constraints and the relative prices of the inputs being used are provided by the *isocost* (meaning "same cost") curve (depicted as A_0-B_0 in Figure 2). The (absolute value of the) slope of the isocost curve represents the rate at which teacher and student time must be substituted to avoid exceeding the expenditure (indicated by the isocost line) allocated to student learning. This rate depends on the relative prices of teacher and student time. The "price" of teacher time (P_T) is the teacher's salary and the "price" of employing student time (P_S) in the production of learning is assumed to be their foregone earnings. The level of expenditure available to produce student learning is the area bounded by the isocost curve, and the slope of the isocost curve equals the input-price ratio (P_S / P_T).

Since we assume that the cost of educating a student is determined in the marketplace, our optimization problem is how to maximize output given the exogenously determined level of expenditure available.[26] The objective is, therefore, to move to the highest isoquant given our expenditure constraint.

Figure 2 indicates that given our expenditure constraint, point C on output level Q_3 is not attainable. Conversely, output level Q_1 is not an efficient outcome since a higher level of student learning is obtainable given the amount of resources available (represented by the isocost curve). Thus, any movement from Q_1 to Q_2 would be an efficiency-enhancing move. For instance, point D could be improved upon since a large amount of student time, and a relatively small amount of teacher time, is being used to produce student learning. This means that the marginal product of an additional dollar's worth of student time is less than the marginal product of an additional dollar's worth of teacher time. Reallocating these inputs in different proportions by employing more teacher and less student time would allow us to remain within our budget constraint (stay on A_0-B_0) yet achieve a higher level of output (from Q_1 to Q_2). The reallocation of inputs improves the way we use teacher and student time and is therefore an efficiency improvement. Subsequent reallocations of student and teacher time eventually results in movement to point A, where the isoquant and isocost curves are tangent. This is the only point on Q_2 (the highest output achievable given the expenditure constraint) where the rate at which the two inputs can be substituted for each other (MRS) equals the rate at which they must be substituted along the given expenditure constraint (P_S / P_T). At point A, the MRTS (the ratio of marginal products, MP_S/ MP_T) and the relative input prices (P_S /

[26] Another optimization problem is often discussed in production theory: how to choose input combinations that minimize the cost of production for a given level of output. Graphically this could be represented by a single isoquant curve and multiple isocost curves. The optimization problem would be to attain the lowest possible isocost curve given the level of output chosen.

P_T) are equal and we have achieved our second criteria needed for Pareto optimality, *efficiency in production.*[27]

As was true for exchange efficiency, in this example we also assume that input prices are determined in the competitive marketplace. This means that all universities employ teacher and student time at the same input-price ratio. Because universities choose to produce efficiently, where their isoquant and isocost curves are tangent, their MRTS's will all be equal.

One may note that the study of productive efficiency parallels our analysis of exchange efficiency in that indifference curves are analogous to isoquants; isocost curves to budget lines; marginal utility to marginal product; and that the MRS and MRTS are similar concepts. A major conceptual difference between the two approaches is, however, that utility is not observable or measurable when evaluating exchange efficiency, but production or output is typically ascertainable.

PRODUCT-MIX EFFICIENCY

In order to achieve full economic efficiency we must not only be efficient in the way goods and services are produced and exchanged, the mix of these goods must also reflect the preferences of consumers. This latter type of efficiency is known as *product-mix efficiency*.

Let us assume that Good $_A$ and Good $_B$ in Figure 3 represent educational outputs like teaching and research, respectively. By allocating time and effort to these activities in different ways there are many different combinations of research and teaching that institutions (faculty) can produce and that society can consume. The set of output combinations that are possible is known as the production possibilities set. The shape of the production possibilities set is a function of the types of technologies that are available in the production of teaching and research. The boundary of this set (depicted by A_0-B_0 in Figure 3) is known as the *production possibilities curve* (PPC). This boundary indicates the maximum quantities of teaching and research that can be produced with the available resources (inputs) and technology. The PPC has a concave shape implying diminishing returns in productive transformation[28] and the (negative) of the slope of the PPC indicates the marginal rate of (productive) transformation (MRT_{TR}) of teaching for research. The MRT_{TR} measures the rate at which teaching can be

[27] As was true for our discussion of exchange efficiency above, we again assume competitive markets to simplify the analysis. When markets are competitive, all firms face the same input prices which translates into all firms equating the MRTS of student time for teacher time.

[28] Teaching and research may be complimentary goods, which would imply a slightly different shape for the PPC. See McKenzie (1979) for more about the economics of the educational process and McKenzie and Staaf (1974) for an economic analysis of student learning.

Figure 3: Product Mix Efficiency

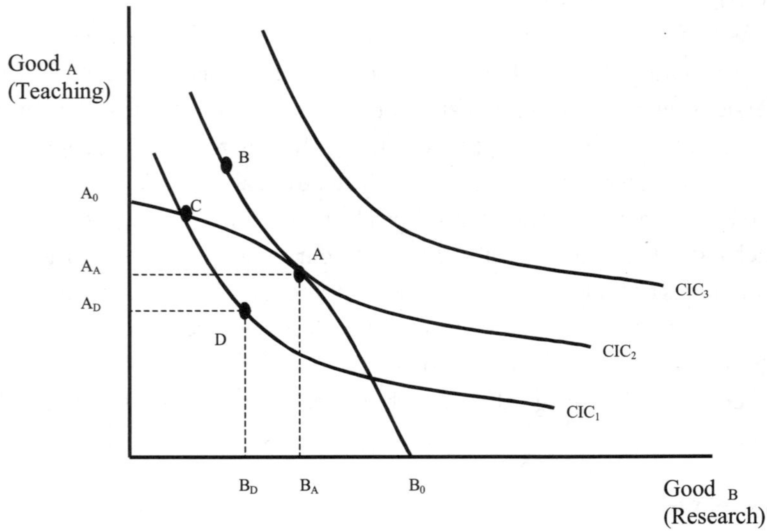

traded for research using given quantities of productive inputs (like student and teacher time).

The indifference curves displayed in Figure 3 (CIC_1-CIC_3) are known as *community indifference curves* (CIC).[29] Each curve represents combinations of teaching and research (output) that produce an equal aggregate level of utility. Different combinations of teaching and research can be produced, and the rate at which these outputs can be traded off is known as the marginal rate of substitution of teaching for research (MRS_{TR}). Mathematically, the MRS_{TR} is the absolute value of the slope of the CIC.

These analytic devices (the PPC and the CIC's) can be used to help us determine if inputs and outputs are being used in an efficient manner. Given the PPC constraint, our hypothetical community cannot achieve CIC_3 since it lies everywhere above the PPC. Likewise, point B is unattainable since it also lies outside the production possibilities frontier. Any point (like D) down and to the left of the PPC is not efficient in the way output is being produced in that more of each good (or both) could be produced (by moving north, east, or northeast of the origin, respectively). For instance, using D as the starting point, a lot more teaching could be produced, as depicted by a movement from D to C. This movement does not reduce aggregate utility since C remains on CIC_1. Even though C represents *technical efficiency* in production of the two goods (since it lies on the

[29] The CIC was formulated by Lerner, 1932. Another aggregate indifference curve often used is the Scitovsky indifference curve (SIC) introduced by Scitovsky, 1942. For a more recent explanation of the derivation of these types of indifference curves see Just, Hueth, and Schmitz, 1982.

PPC), it is not a fully (economically) efficient solution. Factors of production could be reallocated so that a more preferred mix of teaching and research is produced (depicted by a movement from C to A). A move like this is *allocatively efficient* because it produces the mix of the two goods most preferred by consumers of higher education. The combination of technical and allocative efficiency (as represented by the tangency of CIC_2 and the PPC) results in an economically efficient outcome. By moving from point D to point A the efficiency criterion is met in that the marginal rate of transformation between teaching and research (MRT_{TS}) equals the marginal rate of substitution between these two outputs (MRS_{TS}).

Efficiency in Exchange, Production, and Product Mix: Pareto Optimality

As noted above, economic efficiency is not, as some individuals believe, "fundamentally a matter of saving time or materials in production or distribution. An efficient state of affairs is one in which it is impossible to make someone better off (in terms of preference satisfaction) without making someone else worse off" (Hausman and McPherson, 1996, p. 84). To achieve this state of affairs, known as *Pareto optimality*, three conditions must be met *simultaneously*. First, productive activities need to be organized so as to maximize output given the inputs used (*efficiency in production*). This type of efficiency is often the focus of operations researchers and production engineers and is depicted in Figure 2. Second, there must be *efficiency in consumption and exchange*, as displayed in Figure 1. The general idea is that goods and services produced by the economy are distributed efficiently among individuals. The third condition that needs to hold is *product mix efficiency*. This means that "the optimal combinations of goods should be produced given existing production technology and consumer tastes" (Barr, 1998, p. 71), as depicted in Figure 3. For instance, even though society may have the technical know-how to build a new community college, this does not provide a justification for doing so. Society must be willing to forgo other uses of the resources dedicated to the construction of this institution (the notion of *opportunity cost*). Thus, there must be some agreement that this is a societal objective.

The discussion above indicates that the notion of economic efficiency has as its underlying principles two value judgments: individualism and the Pareto principles. Individualism has to do with the idea that people are the best judges of their well-being or preferences. Individualism is in contrast to the idea of paternalism, an idea that many advocates of individualism believe has a distinctly "antidemocratic element" (Browning and Browning, 1987, p. 14). As might be expected there are critics of individualism. Some critics of individualism believe that there are individuals who are unable to make utility judgments and that someone needs to make these judgments for them.[30] Other critics of individualism note that there are many people who are not yet alive therefore their preferences remain unknown, thus agents who are now alive must protect these individuals' interests. To counter these criticisms economists often refer "interchangeably to the basic decision-maker as an individual and a household, thereby allowing for the fact that parents may determine preferences on behalf of their children" (Boadway and Bruce, 1991, p. 2). This is especially true when examining primary education policies where the unit of analyses is often minor children.

The second value judgment, the Pareto principle, says that a state of the world in which no improvement is feasible is defined as Pareto optimal. Even though this concept may sometimes conflict with other value judgments (such as equity, liberty, or freedom of speech), as we have seen above the Pareto principle is often used to rank different states of the world. As a guide to making policy decisions, the Pareto criterion[31] is subject to criticisms on at least two fronts. In the real world policy decisions typically result in some individuals being made better off at the expense of others. In these cases the Pareto criterion is not useful in helping to guide decision-makers. A second criticism is that a complete ranking of all social states is often not possible so we are unable to use the Pareto criterion to help make decisions. These two weaknesses of the Pareto criterion mean that "the decision maker is forced to choose between policies that trade off one persons welfare against another's, and the Pareto criterion gives him no help" (Stokey and Zeckhauser, 1978, p. 272-273). Because of these problems economists have developed an alternative approach to studying individual and social welfare.

SOCIAL WELFARE THEORY

PREFERENCE AGGREGATION

In order to make use of the individualism and Pareto principles to evaluate public policy we must have an idea of how to aggregate preferences into social

[30] For instance, American society apparently believes that children should be educated to a specified age (often 16 years old), even though some children (or their parents) may not want to go to school until age 16. Some educators and philosophers believe this requirement is paternalistic.

[31] There is a distinction that needs to be made. A Pareto optimum is any point that satisfies the three conditions mentioned earlier. The Pareto criterion just means that the direction for welfare improvement is, in general, north and east of the origin.

orderings so that we can rank different states of the world. However, sometimes we are unable to order and compare outcomes (known as Pareto non-comparable states) and this is an important limitation of welfare theory. Even though this limitation is sometimes present, the appeal of using the Pareto approach is that by adding *weak* value judgments[32] we are able to rank *many* states of the world, thus giving us measures by which we can *describe* policy implications and *prescribe* specific actions.

One way to move from a discussion of individual choice to one of social decision-making is to aggregate individual preferences into a social utility function. There are many different ways to do this[33] but one common way is to simply sum up all individual utilities into an "aggregating function" often known as a "social welfare function" (SWF).[34] For instance, the classical utilitarian or Benthamite[35] welfare function is the simple summation of individual utility functions. Another welfare function is the Rawlsian or maximin function. The Rawlsian welfare function indicates "that the social welfare of an allocation depends only on the welfare of the worst off agent — the person with the minimal utility" (Varian, 1996, p. 549). Other social welfare functions can also be defined, each of which assume different ethical or moral judgments about how to aggregate the welfare of different individuals. Once we have chosen a welfare function we can begin to use this analytic tool to evaluate different policy scenarios.

EFFICIENCY- AND/OR EQUITY-ENHANCING CHANGES IN POLICIES

For example, Figure 4 can be used to help us evaluate whether higher education policies are efficiency-, equity-enhancing, or both. The area bounded by A_0 and B_0 is a utilities possibilities set and the curve A_0-B_0 is the possibilities frontier reflecting scarce resources that can be dedicated toward higher education. In this example each axis is assumed to represent the utility levels of students. For instance, Utility $_A$ represents how satisfied one group of students (e. g., the rich) are with their education and Utility $_B$ might represent another group's (e.g., the poor) satisfaction level.

Because we are now dealing with decisions about social welfare, W_1-W_3

[32] Weak value judgments might be thought of as those that are generally accepted (at least in welfare economics) whereas strong value judgments are typically thought of as being more controversial. Two examples of weak value judgments are 1) individualism and 2) the weak form of the Pareto principle. An example of a strong value judgment is Rawls' difference principle (see Boadway and Bruce, 1991 for more about strong and weak value judgments).

[33] See Boadway and Bruce, 1991, for details.

[34] Aggregating functions are often defined to be increasing in each individual's utility. This restriction assures us that if all individuals prefer A to B then the social ordering will also prefer A to B. Also, social welfare functions are sometimes called the social choice rule (Sen, 1970).

[35] Named for Jeremy Bentham (1748-1832) the founder of the utilitarian school of moral philosophy.

are defined as isowelfare (or equal welfare) curves that represent the preferences of decision-makers, like college administrators. By defining the isowelfare curves in this way we are assuming that college administrators are "omniscient ethical observers" and, as agents for society, they have made an ethical or moral determination about what constitutes welfare improvements in higher education.[36] The objective for the economist is to "maximize this function subject to the relevant economic and institutional constraints" (McMahon, 1982, p. 6). Some situations improve *efficiency*, some improve *equity*, and sometimes *both* are simultaneously improved.

For instance, assume that initially we are at point B, where the rich are more satisfied with higher education than the poor, as evidenced by the relative amount of utility they each have (A_1B_1). There are possibilities to improve this situation. For example, a policy change that causes a move from point B (which is a socially inefficient situation) to point C (which is on the possibilities curve) increases efficiency. In this case, rich students' (Group A) satisfaction with higher education is improved but at the expense of no one (the poor's level of satisfaction remains the same as at point B). Because nobody is made worse off from this movement, the Pareto criterion is met. As McMahon (1982) has noted, however, pure efficiency moves like this "have pitfalls" (p. 7). Increases in efficiency can often "expand" the amount of resources available (as evidenced by the move from B to C), but sometimes these changes create a more inequitable dis-

Figure 4: Social Welfare Functions

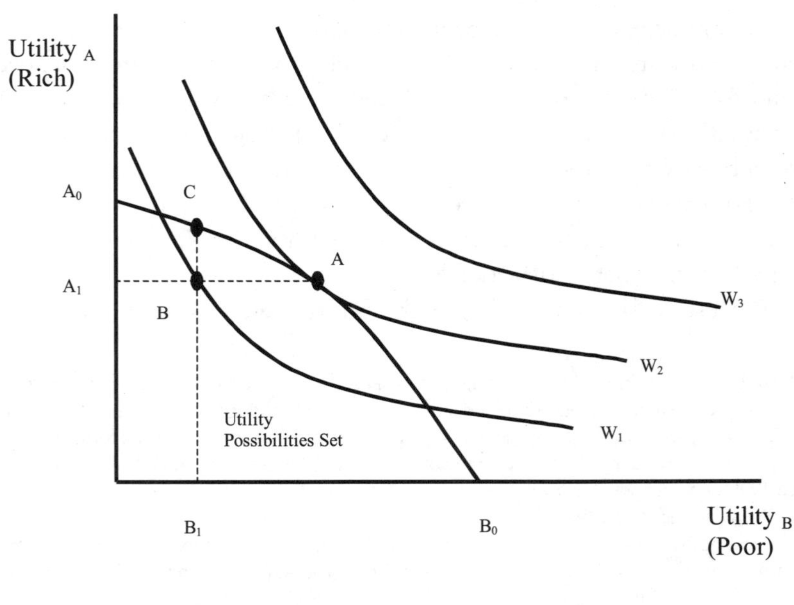

[36] For more on the subject of the "omniscient ethical observer" see McMahon, 1982.

tribution. For instance, in this case the rich are the only ones who gained, which actually worsens an already inequitable distribution of satisfactions with higher education between students from rich and poor family-income backgrounds.

However, if society (as represented by our omniscient administrator) is not satisfied after observing that the policy change yielded a gain for the rich and not for the poor, resources could be redistributed. For instance, a move from C to A indicates a redistribution from rich to poor students and moves society onto a higher social welfare curve (W_2). The fact that social welfare actually improves is a clear indication that the redistribution is a valued social objective. Point A is on the utility possibilities constraint indicating that higher education resources are being used efficiently. This example also suggests that policies that improve efficiency can sometimes "be a source for financing improvements in equity" (McMahon, 1982, p. 14), in this case because some of the redistribution (C to A) is paid for by the increase in efficiency (B to C).

It is important to reiterate that the position of the social welfare curves are determined by what society — in terms of the ethical omniscient observers (college administrators) — thinks about how higher education resources ought to be distributed. The analytic approach is to start with specific moral judgments and then examine their implications for the distribution of resources. "The welfare function approach is a very general way to describe social welfare. But because it is so general it can be used to summarize the properties of many kinds of moral judgments" (Varian, 1996, p. 552). The objective of the economic analyst is to attempt to help decision-makers get to an optimum, like the one at point A.[37]

Another Way to Measure Welfare Change: The Compensation Principle

"The strength of the Pareto criterion lies in the fact that it does not require the utilities of different households to be compared or 'weighted'. Its weakness lies in the fact that it yields an incomplete ordering" (Boadway and Bruce, 1991, p. 96). One way to deal with this incompleteness is to extend the Pareto principle by invoking the compensation principle.[38] This principle "was introduced much later than the Pareto principle in the hope that it would be a more powerful device for choosing among policies" (Just, Hueth, and Schmitz, 1982, p. 33). The compensation principle has "emerged as the criterion that is empirically the most widely applicable" (Just, Hueth, and Schmitz, 1982, p. 45). This principle states that if two resource allocations are Pareto non-comparable, we may be

[37] A direct move from B to A would, of course, be a simultaneous improvement in both efficiency and equity.

[38] First discussed by Hicks (1939) and Kaldor (1939) and sometimes referred to as the Kaldor-Hicks criteria or compensation test.

able to devise a scheme where individuals who are made better off by a policy change *could* (potentially) compensate those who are made worse off, thereby improving the welfare of society. An important point is that the compensation criterion does not require the redistribution to actually take place, there simply needs to be the *potential* for the payment of compensation.

Like the Pareto principle, the compensation criterion also involves making value judgments. The decision to compensate individuals who are harmed by a policy or policy change is a subjective judgment, whether the payment is made or not. In fact, a decision to undertake a policy and *not* compensate the losers may be a subjective decision "of a more serious nature" (Just, Hueth, and Schmitz, 1982, p. 34). That these value judgments need to be made should not, however, keep us from attempting to analyze the distributional impacts of policy changes.

In the real world, the compensation principle is often operationalized by calculating two statistical measures. These measures, known as compensating variation (CV) and equivalent variation (EV), are often used in welfare economics to study the distributional impacts of different policy scenarios. These measures are used as proxies for utility because utility itself is not directly observable or measurable. These measures are often important in determining how much individuals are *willing to pay* to improve their welfare or to avoid having their utility reduced. The "intuitive appeal of this criterion is that in a sense there are potential gains from trade" among the winners and losers of a policy change (Boadway and Bruce, 1991, p. 15).

A specific example may help illustrate the compensation principle, CV, and EV. Assume that the staff in a registrar's office in a large university processes student registrations by hand. This process is very labor intensive and therefore requires a sizeable staff to perform this important function. Assume an automated web-based registration system is introduced, and as a result, a large number of staff are displaced from their jobs. Using the compensation criterion, the introduction of the new registration system is a *potential* Pareto improvement if the gainers (i.e., staff who run the new system, organizations who provide the software/hardware, students who can register from home) *could* compensate the losers (staff who lost their jobs). If, however, no actual compensation takes place there really are losers and winners, even though there are *potential* gains to society as a whole. The value judgment that comes into play is whether society (through decision makers) actually wants to compensate the losers. The new technology scenario represents a *potential* Pareto improvement if the amount of compensation that the gainers are willing to pay to get to their new welfare position is greater than the minimum amount that the losers would have to be paid to accept losing their jobs. *Compensating variation* is the dollar amount required to restore the staff who lost their jobs to the welfare level they experienced before the new registration system was introduced. *Equivalent variation* is the minimum dollar amount that would have to be paid to the beneficiaries of the new system if the web-based system were never introduced.[39]

These two willingness-to-pay measures are foundational in applied welfare economics. They are directly related to the theories of consumer choice outlined above and allow us to make determinations about whether the welfare increase to individuals who gain from a policy change is enough to compensate the losers and still improve the welfare of those who gain.[40]

Other Types of Decision Criteria

Compensating and equivalent variation are used to help decision-makers evaluate the distributional impacts of policy changes. There are also other criteria that education analysts often use to evaluate whether policies are achieving their goals. Some of these have their roots in disciplines other than economics, but some have also been the purview of welfare economics. It may be helpful to provide a brief discussion of a few of these criteria.

McMahon (1982) suggests that there is a hierarchy of criteria used to evaluate the effects of changes in education policies. The lowest level criterion, *accountability*, allows a determination of whether the outputs that are being paid for are actually being produced. However, this criterion does not address whether the outputs are being produced *effectively*. The second level of efficiency is known as *production function analysis*. This type of analysis attempts to provide some insight into the factors that produce desired educational outcomes. Attempts to derive educational production functions have not been very successful and even if they were, they are defective because they typically do not consider the costs of the inputs relative to the value of the outputs. *Cost-effectiveness analysis* does consider the cost of inputs relative to the value of the outputs, and is therefore an improvement on the production function methodology. *Benefit/cost analysis*, the next concept in the hierarchy, also considers costs relative to the value of outputs, but uses the *expected value* of outputs, thereby introducing a probabilistic and temporal dimension. Benefit/cost ratios, the net present value, and internal rates of return are often calculated in an effort to determine the merits of the policy under consideration. Often times, when used in calculating the returns to higher education, only individual and monetary measures are in-

[39] For a graphical display of CV and EV see Just, Hueth, and Schmitz, 1982. For a more complete treatment see Boadway and Bruce, 1991.

[40] For more information about the compensation principle and some of the problems in applying this test see Boadway and Bruce, 1991 or Just, Hueth, and Schmitz, 1982.

cluded, thereby mis-specifying the true educational costs and benefits. To remedy this potential problem, some benefit/cost analyses include a consideration of the individual, psychic and social costs and benefits of higher education. Only by "going the full distance to include some qualitative evaluation of all the private and social benefits and their relative weights can full social efficiency (Pareto optimality) be attained" (McMahon, 1982, p. 11).

EQUITY AS A SOCIETAL OBJECTIVE

In the discussion above we have focused on the determination of efficiency and some of the conceptual problems of classical and modern welfare economics. Even though our focus has been on efficiency, many philosophers and economists believe that society also needs to be concerned with the way its resources are distributed. As noted above, there are times when economically efficient outcomes are not consistent with the values and objectives of society. In this section we turn to some of the concepts that underlie and inform analyses of the effects of policies on the equity of the distribution of resources.

Before proceeding, however, we must address a fundamental question: Should equity be an objective of social policy? Even though most observers believe that it should, there are some moral philosophers and economists who do not believe that it should be. Typically they cite four reasons for their objections. The first reason is *impracticality* and it is cited by some[41] because they believe that "agreement on the definition of equity is impossible" (LeGrand, 1991, p.14). The second reason often cited is that the use of equity is *inappropriate* because "matters of equity involve value-judgments and hence are not amenable to positive analysis" (LeGrand, 1991, p.14). However, as we have noted above, efficiency criteria are also laden with value judgments. Even though positivist approaches are often used to determine whether policies are efficient, the key is establishing a definition of the meaning of efficiency and then determining (according to the definition) whether the policy is efficient. There seems no logical reason why this approach cannot also be used to determine the *equity* of social objectives. As LeGrande (1991) notes, "The problem lies in a lack of agreement concerning the definition of equity, not in an alleged inapplicability of positive analysis" (p.15).

Another reason often cited for why equity should not be used as a social objective is offered by Peter Bauer (1982, 1983). He suggests that using equity is *immoral* because "it stems from an unworthy motivation: that of envy" (LeGrand, 1991, p.15). However, promotion of equity as a social objective may be based on a variety of reasons other than envy (i.e., self-interest or even empathy). Also, the source of the motivation for promoting equity should not necessarily exclude it

[41] For an example see Hayek, 1976.

from being an objective of society any more than the reasons for promoting efficiency should keep it from being a social goal.

Finally, as Hayek notes (1976), the use of equity (which Hayek calls "social justice") as a criterion for social decision-making is an *arbitrary* and *meaningless* idea because it results from a spontaneous process: market forces. Hayek and his followers believe that a myriad of individuals and organizations interact to produce outcomes, and that describing these outcomes as "just" or "equitable" is illusory, just as "describing as unfair the fact that one area was wet while another was sunny" (LeGrand, 1991, p.17). Critics of Hayek's notion of social justice note that resource distribution is often a result of government action, and *not* the result of a spontaneous process. Thus, it appears that social justice or equity does have meaning when applied to non-spontaneous processes. Hayek even admits that the concept of equity does have meaning when applied to non-spontaneous processes. If this is the case, then application of equity as a social objective is not an illusion, even though it may be elusive (LeGrand, 1991).

Types of Equity

Using efficiency criteria and the social welfare function approach are similar ways to describe social well-being. Another way to examine the impact of policies on the well-being of society is to study "fair" allocations or "just" distributions. The search for a fair or just distribution of resources is an attempt to achieve social goals that reflect the values of society. However, our attempt to judge whether or not distributions are just must "start with a definition of what might be considered a fair way to divide bundles of goods, and then use our understanding of economic analysis to investigate its implications" (Varian, 1996, p. 552). Thus it is important for us to understand how this concept is defined and used in discussions about distributional issues.

Even though we noted above the differences between equity and equality, the former is "frequently interpreted as requiring *equality* of outcome in either of two kinds: *equality of income* and *equality of utility*" (LeGrande, 1991, p. 64). With regard to the former, LeGrande notes, "there can be no automatic identification of unequal incomes with inequity; nor equal incomes with equity" (LeGrande, 1991, p. 64). This is because incomes are determined by many interacting factors; how much one works, whether a person is discriminated against in employment, and one's ability are a few of these factors.

Also, there are differences in how economists and others define and measure income. Some definitions include only wages or salaries; others add non-wage income like dividends and interest. Other definitions include job satisfaction, health, and the value of one's own production as forms of non-monetary income. Still others may include the value of how much a person enjoys his or her leisure time. The value of leisure time is especially important because even though some individuals have similar opportunities, they may have different incomes because of the labor/leisure tradeoffs that they make.

How labor/leisure tradeoffs impact one's level of income is described in Figure 5; income is represented on the vertical axis, and the amount of labor/leisure that each individual chooses is represented on the horizontal axis. Two scales are used to measure the labor/leisure tradeoff. The top scale measures leisure with the origin representing no leisure and the 24 hour point (maximum time-in-a-day constraint) representing all leisure. The bottom scale measures labor, with the origin indicating that one works for 24 hours per day and the time-in-a-day constraint represents all work and no leisure. The opportunities that Tom and Jane have are represented by the straight (constant slope) *opportunity constraints.* Tom's opportunity constraint is the steeper function while Jane's opportunity constraint is the flatter straight line. These opportunity constraints measure "the individual's *potential* consumption, including leisure" (Barr, 1998, p. 131; emphasis his). Tom has more potential "full income" (which includes leisure) than Jane does and this is indicated by the fact that his opportunity constraint intersects the vertical (income) axis at a higher point than does Jane's

Figure 5: Poor by Individual Choice, or by Opportunity Constraint? (Adapted from Barr, 1998, p. 131)

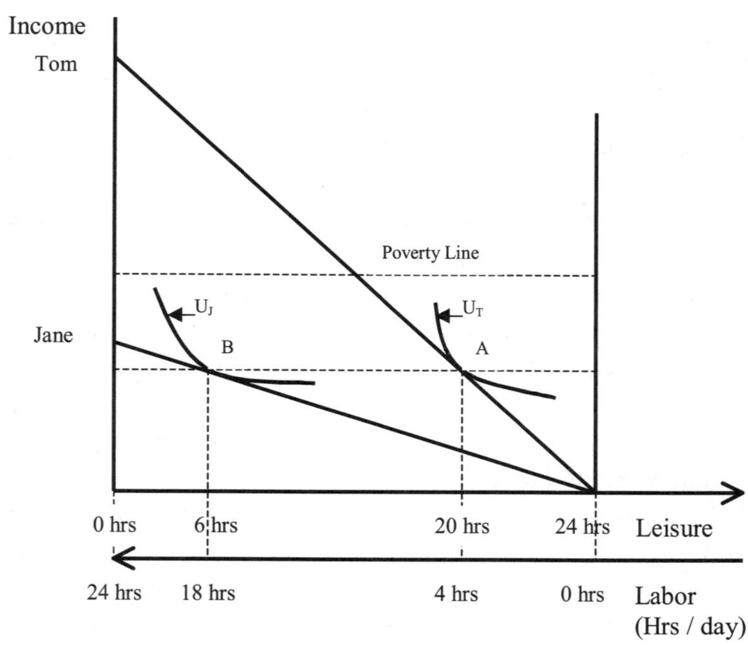

opportunity constraint. The curves labeled U_T and U_J are indifference curves representing how Tom and Jane trade off income and labor/leisure. Tom and Jane maximize their utility (at points A and B) where their opportunity constraints are tangent to their indifference curves. At these points Tom and Jane's utilities are equal, but each individual maximizes utility (and income) by combining labor and leisure in different amounts.

Tom and Jane are both "poor" because their actual income levels (at points A and B, respectively) are below the poverty line. But the reason why Tom is poor is that he chooses leisure (20 hours per day) over labor (four hours per day). He has the *opportunity* to choose much more labor and by doing so could earn full income above the poverty line. Tom's situation is in contrast to Jane's; she labors 18 hours per day and has only 6 hours of leisure time per day. Even if Jane worked 24 hours per day, she still would not increase her income enough to move out of poverty. Thus, it is important to keep in mind the importance of individual choice, especially with regard to the labor/leisure tradeoff, when considering whether the incomes of individuals or groups are equitable.

Given the problems with using the distribution of income as an equity measure, some philosophers (Sen, 1973 and Hammond, 1976) argue that we should focus on equating utilities. The argument is that individuals who have different incomes could have equal utilities (as was the case in Figure 5 above) by combining different amounts of labor and leisure. However, focusing on equating utilities is problematic because it requires that we be able to observe, measure, and compare utilities between individuals. Also, Dworkin (1981a; 1981b) and others note that it may be very difficult or expensive to equate the preferences of individuals with very different tastes. For instance, "suppose there are two students with the same education, skills and family background, one of whom works hard for her final exams while the other spends most of his time playing poker" (LeGrande, 1991, p. 66). The former gets a higher grade than the latter and this may result in utilities that are unequal; "yet it is hard to see that there is much unfairness in this situation" (LeGrande, 1991, p. 66). The important point to remember is that "we cannot simply observe inequality in either incomes or utilities and thereby judge, *on the basis of that inequality alone*, whether the distribution concerned is inequitable or not. We need to have further information. . . about the circumstances in which those distributions arose" (Le Grande, 1991, p. 66; emphasis added).

Horizontal equity is the idea that equals should be treated equally. Examples from education are: allocating equal expenditures per student, equal admissions probabilities for like students, and equal financial aid for students with like needs. Some of the measures that are often used to assess the degree of inequality (especially in educational finance) are the range of the differences, the restricted range (95th to 5th percentile range), the variance, the coefficient of variation, the mean deviation, the Atkinson index, and the Gini coefficient.[42] For instance, tests of horizontal equity might include comparing the financial resources available to similar institutions (four-year publics), collegiate units (colleges of education), or departments (e.g., all higher education programs).

Two other kinds of equity that are often discussed are vertical and intergenerational equity (sometimes known as *mobility*). The former is the idea that unequals should be treated unequally, and the latter involves distributing resources to achieve equity across generations. These equity measures are interrelated because both "are concerned with the unequal treatment of unequals" (McMahon, 1982, p. 19-20). For instance, the provision of Pell grants to low-income students is an example of vertical equity, but this redistribution may also improve the socioeconomic mobility of students, thereby reducing intergenerational inequities. Vertical equity can take place by various means, ranging from leaving inequalities produced by inheritance and by the marketplace undisturbed (*commutative equity*), to the Rawlsian notion of *positivism*, which attempts to right social wrongs through strict redistributive policies. Intergenerational equity is a concept that is critically important in education, since one of the stated goals of education is to break the link between parents' wealth and a student's future prospects or opportunities. For example, in their recent study of class-based differences in how students experience the costs of college, Paulsen and St. John (in press) found substantial evidence of class-based production of postsecondary educational opportunities in the American system of higher education. Such class-based reproduction of postsecondary opportunities promotes the intergenerational transmission of inequities, and therefore, it is one way in which the principle of intergenerational equity would be violated.

Some observers believe that horizontal and vertical equity have intuitive appeal. As Hausman and McPherson (1996) note, "it is difficult to imagine anyone taking issue with these requirements as they stand. But they do so at the expense of specificity. Precisely who are equal and who unequal? What is meant by treatment? What form should the different treatment of unequals take?" (p. 72). Until these questions are answered, it is difficult to apply these principles. The problem is that when we attempt to answer these questions (especially

[42] For applications of these measures to education see Berne and Stiefel, 1984. Berne, 1978, discusses the implications of the use of these different measures. For an example of the calculation of a Gini coefficient to whether educational attainment is equitable in developing countries, see Lewis and Dundar, forthcoming.

[43] A number of economists have been working on a way around this dilemma, especially with regard to horizontal equity. One such approach is to examine the consequences of a policy change (like an increase in taxes), and establish whether there have been any reversals in the rank ordering of individuals. If there are changes in the rankings, then the policy is held to be inequitable (see Atkinson, 1980; or Plotnick, 1981, 1982, 1985 for details).

with regard to vertical and intergenerational equity) "consensus is likely to disappear" (Hausman and McPherson, 1996, p. 72).[43]

Equal access to various goods and services (e.g., a college education) has also been discussed as an equity objective. As is true of definitions of efficiency, "it is not at all clear what many people who express a concern about unequal access to a good really care about. Explicit definitions are rare" (Olsen and Rogers, 1991, p. 92). For instance, Olsen and Rogers believe that some analysts who discuss equal access to goods and services are really concerned with *equal consumption* of these goods and services among groups. For example, Olsen and Rogers note that in their study of college access, Alexander, Pallas and Holupka (1987) seem to be concerned with equal access, yet they focus on differences in the average consumption of college. However, Olsen and Rogers note that there are differences in access and consumption.

For example, assume that individuals have equal access to public universities because of the subsidies provided, yet some prospective students choose to attend college while others do not. Under this scenario, access to (public) institutions is equal but the consumption of this good — that is, a college education — is not. The public policy question is: Is this situation inequitable or not? Olsen and Rogers believe that equal access to a good should be defined in terms of whether individuals are *able* to consume *equal quantities* of the good. There are, as one might expect, problems with this definition. For instance, assume that there are two students who want to attend a particular college,]. These students have to pay the same tuition, and there are no subsidies or other forms of financial aid. Assume also that one student is "richer" than the other. These students will be differentially impacted by the costs of college even though the prices they face are equal. This happens because the "poorer" individual will have to pay a higher proportion of his or her budget to consume an equal amount of college education (they have different budget constraints).

The scenario described above can be graphically depicted, as in Figure 6 below. We assume there are two individuals and two types of goods and services that can be consumed. One of these goods is higher education (on the horizontal axis) and the other is a composite of all other goods (displayed on the vertical axis). One prospective student is "richer" and her budget line is A_{rich} B_{rich}. The "poorer" student's budget constraint is A_{poor} B_{poor} and lies everywhere inside of the richer student's constraint. The fact that the two budget lines are parallel indicates that the (relative) prices they face are equal. Thus, if equality of access is defined as equal prices, these students have equality of access. However, if equality of access is defined as Olsen and Rogers suggest it should be, then equality of access has not been achieved because the richer individual can consume more of higher education than the poorer person can. Equality of access as defined by Olsen and Rogers could be achieved if the price of higher education was reduced for the poor student. Such a reduction in price is depicted by a rotation of the initial budget line ($A_{poor}B_{poor}$) to a new position at ($A_{poor}B_{rich}$). Of course, under this scenario, the definition of equality of access as equal prices would be violated.

Another way equity is defined is based on whether or not resource distri-

Figure 6: Equal Access Under Different Tuition and Budget Scenarios

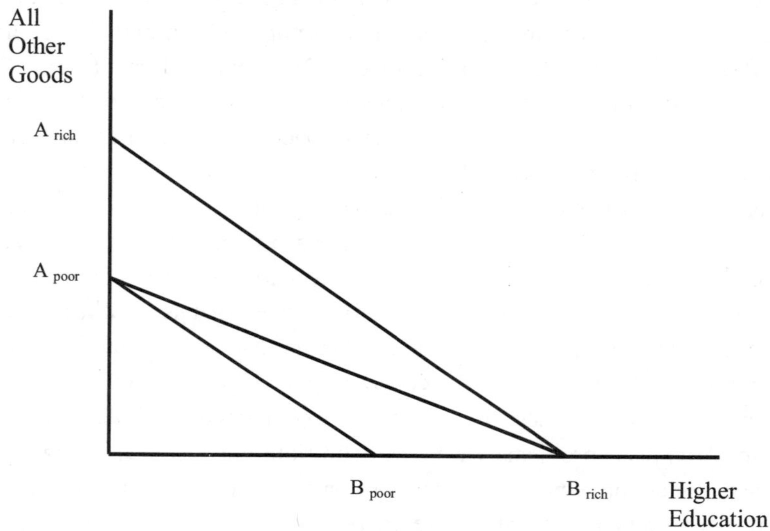

butions are "envy-free." Foley (1967) is credited with this concept, but the concept has its origins in "how to cut a cake fairly." The envy-free way to distribute cake between two individuals is for one person to cut the cake and the other person to choose the first piece. Equal divisions may not, however, be Pareto efficient if individuals have different preferences for the good in question. If individuals have different preferences for the good in question, a Pareto improvement is often possible through trade. As noted above, however, the question then becomes whether the Pareto efficient outcome is a "fair" one. If equal division is considered fair, then a Pareto efficient solution — which requires unequal prices — may not be equitable. Again, it depends on how equity is defined.[44]

There are different *degrees* to which the goal of equity, especially in higher education, can be pursued. McMahon (1982) notes that one option is known as *commutative equity* and this principle leaves the results of the marketplace undisturbed. In an educational financing context this principle emphasizes pure competition for student aid based on ability and would not permit need-based finan-

[44] For a formal treatment of these topics, see Varian, 1996.

cial aid. This "remedy" does little to alleviate inequalities and permits considerable intergenerational transmission of inequities.

The second level of equity, *fiscal neutrality*, uses subsidies and other transfer payments to students for the purpose of promoting greater social equity. The intention is to level the *financial* playing field for students thereby reducing *one* source of inequality. By using grants, scholarships, need-based aid, low-interest loans, and work-study programs to assist students, higher education goes beyond the rather weak commutative principle.

Proportionality, the third equity principle, requires equal payments in relation to ability to pay and emphasizes that benefits should be proportional to needs. However, proportionality is a difficult concept to operationalize because measuring need is often problematic. Proportionality would allow for differential amounts of educational resources to be spent on citizens because some students are relatively shortsighted (do not attend college or fail to complete) while others are more farsighted (choose the high-return programs, demand greater quantities of higher education) about investments in human capital. Proportionality is the concept that "most closely corresponds to equality of educational opportunity" (McMahon, 1982, p. 21). Also, it appears that proportionality would "severely reduce but not eliminate intergenerational transmission of inequality of earnings" (McMahon, 1982, p. 21).

As alluded to above, *positivism* implies progressive rates on both the tax and benefit sides of the financing equation. This Rawlsian notion is designed to remedy past injustices and inequities by helping the disadvantaged. With regard to higher education, imposition of this principle would attempt to eliminate intergenerational inequities by providing full-cost aid to students who are unable to finance their higher education. Also, the application of this principle would require that students with shortsighted higher education investment horizons be highly compensated in order to entice them to attend college. Some philosophers believe that policies designed using a positivist approach would ultimately eliminate vertical and intergenerational inequities and result in a state of distributive justice.

Finally, there is the *equal sacrifice (at the margin), equal marginal benefit doctrine.* By assuming diminishing marginal utility of income and benefits, it can be shown that maximization of social benefits occurs when marginal social benefits equal marginal social costs. This is the basis of benefit/cost studies that are often used to evaluate the efficiency of educational programs. Some economists believe that to equalize these costs and benefits "at the margin requires progressive tax and benefit rates — or positivism" (see McMahon, 1982 for details).

APPLYING THESE CRITERIA TO EDUCATION ISSUES

Virtually everyone agrees that educational efficiency and equity are important goals for higher education. However, "they disagree on how best to achieve them" (Hearn and Longanecker, 1985, p.487). As discussed above, efficiency and equity can be used to help us evaluate how to achieve social objectives. These criteria could be used, for instance, to help us understand better the high tuition-high aid proposals that have been discussed lately in higher education circles.

The present system of public financing of higher education subsidizes students by providing resources to institutions to cover much of the cost of instruction of students. There are some observers who believe there is a more efficient and equitable approach to higher education finance (see Hearn and Longanecker, 1985, for a discussion). Known as the "high tuition-high aid" approach, this policy would substantially raise tuition at public universities and redistribute some of the increased tuition revenue to needy students in the form of increased financial aid. This approach is, in effect, an application of the classic economic notion of price discrimination. Also dubbed "tuition rationalization" (Hearn and Longanecker, 1985, p.489), this approach would permit students in different financial circumstances to be, in effect, charged different tuition rates. In general, middle- and upper-income families would experience a rise in their net price of attendance. Proponents of tuition rationalization believe that access for middle- and upper-income students would not be adversely affected because these students tend to be relatively unresponsive to changes in net price (St. John, 1991a; Heller, 1997). Conversely, there is evidence that low-income students are more responsive to changes in price (especially in the form of grants) so the provision of increased subsidies to low-income students disadvantaged by the tuition increase would induce positive enrollment effects and gains in college access.

Of course, some students facing increased tuition would undoubtedly decide not to attend college. Proponents of high tuition-high aid believe this result would actually be an efficiency-enhancing policy outcome. For instance, after the general tuition increase, students who are "at the margin" with regard to their college attendance decision may no longer believe a college education is worth the increased cost. Thus, their investment decision is not distorted because of the general subsidy and their decision may be social welfare-enhancing because resources are likely to be redirected to more highly valued uses.

The proponents of high tuition-high aid (sometimes known as "revisionists") believe that institutional subsidization of higher education violates our higher-order equity criteria because "it spends more money on the middle class and rich than on the poor" (Hearn and Longanecker, 1985, p.489). Other analysts have also noted that even though state income taxes are generally progressive, students with affluent parents tend to send their children to college at much higher rates than do the relatively poor. Thus, an inequitable distribution of educational benefits occurs, with low-income students paying taxes to finance the higher education of the (relatively) well-off (Hansen and Weisbrod, 1969).

Advocates of the high tuition-high aid policy believe that equity would be enhanced because the present method of financing higher education (through general subsidies to institutions) is more beneficial to upper income students. They believe this is the case because 1) wealthier students tend to have higher participation rates than their low-income counterparts and 2) the combination of participation rates and state tax schemes used to finance higher education produce a regressive distribution of higher education benefits which disproportionately impacts low-income families. The high tuition-high aid proposal is also supposed to be more equitable because it targets public subsidies toward individuals who are typically not able to afford a college education (i.e., these students presumably have the willingness but not the ability to pay).[45]

Proponents of this financing arrangement often use moral arguments to defend this system. Revisionists believe a high tuition-high aid strategy is the best way to encourage intergenerational equity through social mobility, thereby providing for the nation's needs for an educated society. They also use a vertical equity argument when advocating unequal treatment (increased subsidies) for low-income students. Some advocates of the high tuition-high aid policy also use the paternalistic argument that students are unwilling or unable to make rational choices about college education. Others argue that higher education enrollments would be less than socially optimum if there were no subsidies. In contrast, advocates of the present financing arrangement think that state funding of institutions provides leverage that may help legislators nudge institutions to provide academic and public programs that support state goals (Cohn and Geske, 1990).

A Graphical Display of the Economic Effects of Subsidies to Higher Education

Much of the discussion surrounding the high tuition-high aid debate is related to how general subsidies affect student choice. We can use some of the tools of the economist (discussed above) to analyze the effects of direct subsidies to public higher education.

Typically the average tuition at public institutions of higher education usually covers only a small proportion of the true cost of educating a student, with the difference made up by tax revenues generated by federal and (mostly) state

[45] See Johnstone, 1999, for more detail and criticisms of this proposal.

governments. One of the reasons why societies subsidizes higher education is because they wish to increase consumption of this good. A society may do this because it is paternalistic or because of a belief that higher education provides benefits over and above those that individuals obtain.[46] The subsidies provided to higher education are, in effect, a reduction in the "price" of education. The effects of general subsidies can be displayed graphically, as in Figure 7.

Assume the status quo optimum is at point B, where the indifference curve W_0 is tangent to the budget line A_0 B_0. The subsidy, or reduction in price, rotates the budget line from its original position (A_0 B_0) to a new position (A_0 B_1). The new consumptive optimum is depicted by A, where the new (expanded) budget line A_0 B_1 and new (higher) indifference curve W_1 are tangent. The decrease in tuition (price) leads to an increase in the consumption of higher education from e_0 to e_1.

Figure 7: The Effect of a Subsidy to Higher Education
(Adapted from Hirshleifer, 1980, p. 119)

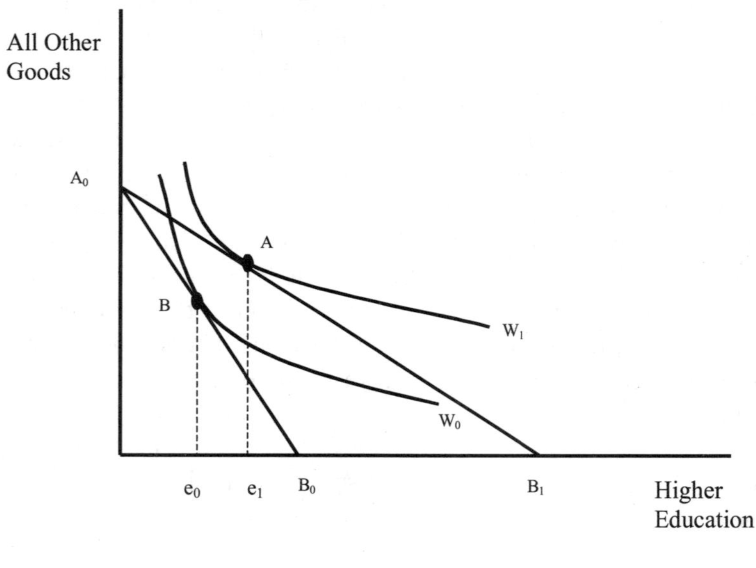

As is often the case, the analysis may not be this simple. In academic year 1999-2000 the average tuition and fees at public four-year institutions was about $3,300 (*Chronicle of Higher Education*, 1999) and this covers about 30% of the actual cost of educating a student at these institutions (thus, the actual cost of instruction is about $10,000). Figure 8 provides a graphical description of the

[46] This implies that there are "external benefits" in higher education production and that there would be underconsumption of higher education if this market were left to the private demand of individuals. See Browning and Browning (1987) for a discussion of externalities.

economic effects of this "fixed quantity" subsidy. A fixed quantity subsidy provides a "certain quantity of a good. . . to a consumer at no cost; or perhaps at a cost below the market price. The essential characteristic of this particular type of subsidy is that the quantity of the good being subsidized is beyond the control of the consumer" (Browning and Browning, 1987, p. 92) and therefore, it is hard to supplement.

For example, assume that the budget line facing the student is initially represented by A_0E_0. The state provides E_{state} units of higher education to students who choose to attend public universities and the tuition these students pay ($3,300) is represented by the vertical distance A_0A_1. This amount, however, does not cover the full cost of attendance (represented by A_0A_2). The difference (A_1A_2) represents the amount of the subsidy. The provision of the subsidy changes the original budget line (A_0E_0) to one represented by A_0ABCE_0 (the heavy line). Under these circumstances, students who elect to receive the fixed quantity subsidy will maximize utility on indifference curve W_1 at point B where there is a point of tangency with the new fixed-subsidy-based budget constraint. However, if a student wanted to obtain more — or what he perceived to be a better "quality" — college education by attending a private college (depicted by E_1), he must forego the subsidy. Thus, he is subject to the CE_0 por-

Figure 8: The Effects of a Fixed Quantity Subsidy

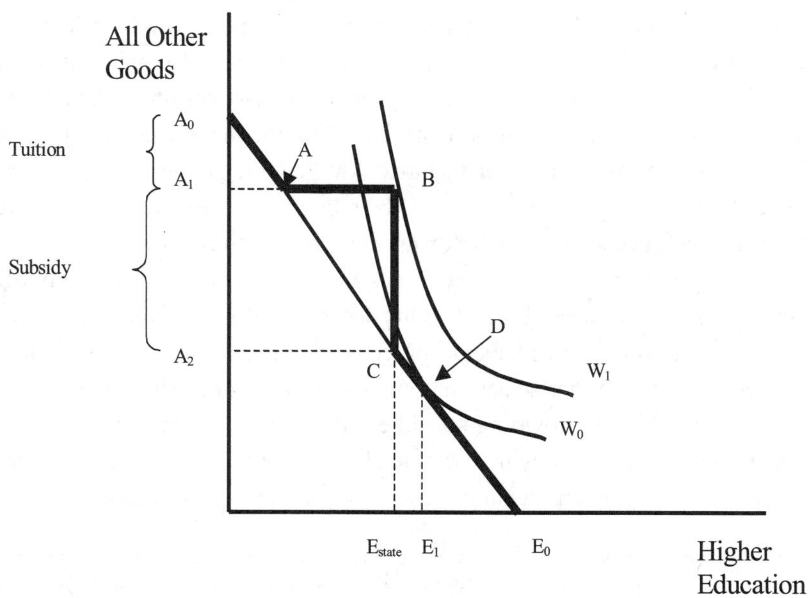

tion of the budget line, where the student incurs the full cost of the college education.[47] Foregoing the subsidy results in a welfare reduction as depicted by the movement from point B on indifference curve W_1 to a new equilibrium point at D on curve W_0.

In general, (and other things being equal) students would consume *less* higher education if a fixed quantity subsidy was not provided. Some students — with indifference curves not represented in Figure 8 — would choose to obtain less than E_{state} units of education, reaching maximum utility somewhere along the A_0C portion of the original budget constraint (the one operative before the fixed quantity subsidy was available). The subsidy, however, entices these students to improve their welfare (a move to point B on a higher indifference curve) where more education is consumed than would have been the case without the subsidy. There are many reasons why society supports subsidies to higher education and we will now turn to a discussion of some of the arguments for and against subsidization.

ARGUMENTS SUPPORTING SUBSIDIES TO HIGHER EDUCATION

There are different reasons cited for why society finances public higher education in the way described above. One of the reasons is to promote equality of educational opportunity. A value judgment widely held by American society is that citizens who have the ability to succeed in college should not be hampered from attending college because of financial reasons. How best to ensure equal opportunity is a policy issue of great importance but also one that is controversial. Some individuals contend that subsidies to institutions, subsidization of student loans, and direct grants to students are not the optimum way to assure educational opportunity. For instance, low-income students may be loan-averse and therefore unwilling to incur debt in order to finance college, even though the payoff in the future may (on average) be worth the investment.

Another reason why society seems to want to finance public colleges the way it does is because of affordability issues. College is expensive, and in recent years tuition increases have outpaced increases in the general price level. Some observers believe that society has an obligation to keep the cost of college education affordable by providing subsidies. We must keep in mind, however, that the provision of a subsidy in and of itself does not reduce the cost of higher education to society, it only changes the way the benefits and costs of higher

[47] This is, of course, a simplification of reality. Some states provide subsidies to students that can be used at private institutions. Some states even provide subsidies to students who choose to attend institutions outside of the state of residence. The general point is not lost, however. Fixed quantity subsidies make it hard for a student, or a family, to supplement the quantity (or quality, if one believes private colleges are better quality) of higher education.

education are distributed. For instance, a subsidy, as noted above, changes the price of education to individuals within society, but the cost of a given quantity of higher education remains the same. There are no free lunches; society must pay for higher education whether in the form of taxation to provide general subsidies, or in the form of higher tuition if there are no subsidies. As Browning and Browning (1987) note, "So the real issue is why people other than those who receive the educational services should bear part of the cost" (Browning and Browning, 1987, p. 154).

Another widely cited reason for subsidization of higher education is that students often encounter problems with borrowing to finance college. Capital markets often will not finance investments in human capital to the same extent that they will finance investments in other capital goods. The argument is that, because it is difficult for students to utilize their future earnings as collateral in the private capital market, demand for education will be lower than socially desirable if college education is not subsidized.

As mentioned earlier in this chapter, some individuals believe that the provision of higher education results in positive externalities, that is, that benefits accrue to society as well as the individual when citizens are college educated. External benefits often cited are the imparting of a common language, knowledge of the legal system, acceptance of a common set of social values (that may make the social system more stable), and a better informed electorate. Other positive externalities often cited are increased productivity and a higher national product since the college-educated are thought to be more productive.[48] But students' increased productivity is often reflected in the higher wages they receive. Since this is a substantial pecuniary benefit captured largely by the individual consumer of college education, it is debatable whether there are external benefits due to (alleged) increased productivity.[49] Often forgotten but nonetheless important are the *negative* externalities that may also be generated by the public subsidization of higher education. For example, some authors cite the student unrest of the 1960s and 1970s and an excess supply of Ph.D.s in some disciplines as examples of the external costs of higher education.

With regard to externalities, strict economic efficiency does not require that social benefits be "internalized" (paid for by society) unless the failure to do so would reduce their production. Often policy analysts neglect to discuss whether the above-mentioned externalities would occur *regardless* of societal subsidization. In the economic literature this concept is known as the *relevance of externalities* (Buchanan and Stubblebine, 1962). In our high tuition-high aid ex-

[48] Whether a college education results in increased productivity in individuals is debatable. See Cohn and Geske, 1990 for the issues.
[49] True external benefits are effects that are not captured within the price system.

ample, if some students would attend college without a tuition subsidy (as is certainly the case), then the externalities (positive and negative) produced by these students are deemed irrelevant because they would have been produced anyway. Thus, the social benefits of a low tuition policy may be overstated.

Another aspect of externalities often overlooked is the possibility that subsidization of students in primary and secondary schools could also make the externalities of higher education irrelevant (in a technical sense). For instance, if society were better able to prepare students for higher education, the underprivileged may not *need* subsidies to entice them to attend college. Reducing educational inequities may change the rational cost calculations of the underprivileged, thereby making college attendance a more viable option. The understanding that they can improve their welfare (and maybe that of their offspring) at a lower cost (college would not be as difficult as when a person is underprepared) may entice these students to enter college at higher rates than would otherwise be the case. Focusing more resources on students early in primary school may create a situation whereby students would be more willing and able to self-finance their higher education through loans or other methods because the individual costs of college attendance would be brought more in line with the perceived benefits. If this scenario were realized, we might need fewer subsidies at the higher education level. Thus, improved education at primary and secondary levels could set in motion a developmental path that increases students' willingness to pay for college, gives individuals the human capital necessary to become productive members of society, and produces intergenerational benefits to the individual and society. From a social point of view this scenario implies that one way to improve efficiency in higher education may be to target more resources at the primary and secondary levels.

Another area that is typically not addressed in the high tuition/high aid debate is the influence on enrollment demand relative to academic programs. The high tuition-high aid proposal would provide blanket subsidies to students deemed needy. However, there are two dangers in targeting subsidies in this manner. First, blanket subsidies may not encourage students to enter academic programs that are socially desirable. Second, as mentioned above, we must be careful not to bestow subsidies on students who would enroll in these programs without the subsidy. This error "results in foregone opportunities for increasing other enrollments or for using the resources to achieve other goals" (Hoenack, 1982, p.411).

For example, the high tuition/high aid proposal would not provide differential subsidies based on program-specific demand nor would it differentiate based on the cost of instruction *within* an institution. The relative uniformity of tuition charges in public institutions has made for large variations in subsidies for specific academic programs (as a function of instructional cost). A uniform tuition policy is less efficient than it could be because money is being spent in areas with relatively low returns, and it may be inequitable because the relatively well-off are more likely to be in disciplines with relatively high rates of return. Thus, if society is really interested in effectively targeting subsidies, maybe we should be moving to target subsidies at an even more micro level than the revisionists suggest. For instance, policy analysts should examine the efficiency- and equity-enhancing effects of targeting higher education subsidies toward specific academic areas where there is insufficient demand but high social returns. A targeted approach could also be used to encourage disadvantaged students to enroll in certain programs. For instance, aid awards in excess of need could be given to encourage minorities and/or low-income students to enroll in areas where there has been historical under-representation (a positivist approach).

There seems to be some concern that political forces will make movement to a high tuition-high aid policy unlikely (Griswold, 1996; Johnstone, 1998). Because it will cost them more to attend college, the middle class is not likely to endorse the proposal and this group has a lot of political power. Also, the educational system has created extensive political power and the stakeholders in higher education are often prepared to exercise their influence (Windham, 1976). Since legislators tend to be vote maximizers, and interest groups are "unlikely to forego subsidies for themselves in the interest of economic efficiency" (Hoenack, 1982, p. 414), a new higher education financing policy may be difficult to implement. However, financial considerations may make this action inevitable. When tax revenues fall (when, not if, the next recession hits), or higher education financing loses in the competition for available funds (to prison construction and care of the elderly), then legislators and education analysts may be *forced* to rethink higher education financing strategies. Understandably, some policy analysts (St. John, 1991b) would prefer to see the higher education enterprise move ahead of the curve on higher education financing instead of waiting for a crisis to force the issue.

CONCLUSIONS

One thing that is very important to remember is that equity and efficiency are not necessarily mutually exclusive objectives. Progress on equity and efficiency grounds is sometimes achievable. "For example, if it should be determined that increasing the access of relatively high ability students from disadvantaged groups to higher education results in enhanced social mobility, and if this outcome is generally acknowledged to be a benefit to society, subsidies for such students can be desirable to increase efficiency" (Hoenack, 1982, p. 408). Hopefully the discussion provided in this chapter will help us understand better how the analytics of welfare economics and moral philosophy can help move us toward the central objective of welfare economics: to build a framework that will allow us to make "meaningful statements about whether some economic situations are socially preferable to others" (Boadway and Bruce, 1991, p.137).

As this chapter documents, there are many moral and theoretical problems that make the search for a unified framework especially challenging. In its present state, welfare economics does not provide us with all of the tools necessary to resolve all policy issues and social problems. "To argue that applied welfare economics has all the answers to solving real-world problems is a mistake, just as it is a mistake to argue that political science or moral philosophy has all the answers" (Just, Hueth, and Schmitz, 1982, p. 336). Nevertheless, even with all of its problems, welfare economics is still useful in helping to evaluate policy decisions, like those that are often made with regard to how higher education is or will be configured. As noted above, economists and educational policy analysts believe the concepts of efficiency and equity provide "useful starting points in the search for a set of operational norms to be used in the pricing and financing of higher education" (Hansen and Weisbrod, 1969, p.102).

Also, I hope this chapter has demonstrated that researchers who evaluate education policy are "going to have to get their feet wet in the swamps of moral philosophy" (Hausman and McPherson, 1993, p. 712). Only when value judgments (and hence, policies) enjoy widespread support will ranking social states form the basis of legitimate policy, a necessary condition in a democratic society (Boadway and Bruce, 1991). As Lester Thurow stated, "I don't think you can forever move toward inequality and still maintain a democracy. They're incompatible principles" (*Star Tribune*, March 7, 1996). And even though "economic reasoning is better at helping to choose among ways to *accomplish* a distributional objective than at helping to *choose* objectives" (Schelling, 1984, p. 18; emphasis added), this should not prevent us from considering ways to do both. The study and application of moral philosophy is difficult, and even though I've tried to "provide a rough map of the terrain" there are "no guarantees that those who venture in will not find some surprises. It's a tough and tangled territory" (Hausman and McPherson, 1993, p. 712).

Hopefully, the philosophical ideas and analytic tools described above will help education researchers and their clients to find new ways to study our higher education system. As demonstrated above, it may be helpful to think about how we can improve education by searching for ways to improve *both* efficiency and equity considerations. For if we can hold this up as a social objective we can "contribute to better education for all, and through this to humane growth in society (McMahon, 1982, p.3).

REFERENCES

Alexander, K.L., Pallas, A.N., and Houlupka, S. (1987). Consistency and change in educational stratification: Recent trends regarding social background and college access. *Research in Social Stratification and Mobility* 6: 161-185.

Atkinson, A.B. (1980). Horizontal equity and the distribution of the tax burden. In H. Aaron, M. Boskin (eds.), *The Economics of Taxation*, Washington D.C.: Brookings Institution.

Barr, N. (1998). *The Economics of the Welfare State*. Stanford, CA: Stanford University Press.

Barry, B. (1973). *The Liberal Theory of Justice*. Oxford: Clarendon Press.

Bauer, P. (1982). *Equality, the Third World, and Economic Delusion*. London: Methuen.

Bauer, P. (1983). The grail of equality. In W. Letwin (ed.) *Against Equality: Readings on Economic and Social Policy*. London: Macmillan Press.

Bentham, J. (1789). *Introduction to the Principles of Morals and Legislation* (Reprinted 1967, W. Harrison, ed. Oxford: Basil Blackwell).

Berne, R. (1978). Alternative equity and equality measures: Does the measure make a difference? In E. Tron (ed.), *Selected Studies in School Finance*. Washington, DC: U.S. Office of Education.

Berne, R. and Stiefel, L. (1984). *The Measurement of Equity in School Finance: Conceptual, Methodological, and Empirical Dimensions*. Baltimore, MD: Johns Hopkins University Press.

Boadway, R., and Bruce, N. (1991). *Welfare Economics*. Cambridge: Basil Blackwell.

Browning, E.K., and Browning, J.M. (1987). *Public Finance and the Price System*. New York: Macmillan.

Buchanan, J.M. (1954). Individual choice in voting and the market. *Journal of Political Economy* 62: 334-343.

Buchanan, J.M., and Stubblebine, W.C. (1962). Externality. *Economica* 29: 371-384.

Cohn, E., and Geske, T. (1990). *Economics of Education*. New York: Pergamon Press.

Daniels, N. (1975). *Reading Rawls*. Oxford: Blackwell.

Dworkin, R. (1981a). What is equality? Part 1: Equality of welfare. *Philosophy and Public Affairs* 10(3): 185-247.

Dworkin, R. (1981b). What is equality? Part 2: Equality of resources. *Philosophy and Public Affairs* 10(4): 283-345.

Elster, J. and Roemer, J.E. (eds.) (1991). *Interpersonal Comparisons of Well-Being*. Cambridge: Cambridge University Press.

Feinberg, J. (1970). *Doing and Deserving: Essays in the Theory of Responsibility*. Princeton, NJ: Princeton University Press.

Foley, D. (1967). Resource allocation and the public sector. *Yale Economic Essays* Spring: 45-102.

Glover, Jonathan (ed.) (1990). *Utilitarianism and Its Critics*. New York: Macmillan Publishing Co.

Griswold, C.P. and Marine, G.M. (1996). Political influences on state policy: Higher-tuition, higher-aid, and the real world. *Review of Higher Education* 19(4): 361-389.

Hammond, P.J. (1976). Equity, Arrow's conditions and Rawls' difference principle. *Econometrica* 44 (4): 793-804.

Hansen, W.L. (1972). Equity and the finance of higher education. In T.W. Schultz, (ed.), *Investment in Education: The Equity-Efficiency Quandary*. Chicago: The University of Chicago Press.

Hansen, W.L. and Weisbrod, B.A. (1969). *Benefits, Costs, and Finance of Public Higher Education*. Chicago: Markam.

Hardin, R. (1982). *Collective Action*. Baltimore, MD: Johns Hopkins University Press.

Hardin, R. (1988). *Morality Within the Limits of Reason*. Chicago: University of Chicago Press.

Hausman, D.M. and McPherson, M.S. (1993). Taking ethics seriously: Economics and contemporary moral philosophy. *Journal of Economic Literature* XXXI: 671-731.

Hausman, D.M. and McPherson, M.S. (1996). *Economic Analysis and Moral Philosophy*. Cambridge: Cambridge University Press.

Hayek, F.A. (1976). *Law, Legislation and Liberty, Vol. II: The Mirage of Social Justice.* Chicago:University of Chicago Press.

Hearn, J.C., and Longanecker, D. (1985). Enrollment effects of alternative postsecondary pricing policies. *Journal of Higher Education* 56: 485-508.

Heller, D. E., (1997). Student price response in higher education: An update to Leslie and Brinkman. *Journal of Higher Education* 68(6): 624-659.

Hicks, J.R. (1939). *Value and Capital.* London: Oxford University Press.

Hirshleifer, J. (1980). *Price Theory and Applications.* Englewood Cliffs, NJ: Prentice-Hall, Inc.

Hoenack, S.A. (1982). Pricing and efficiency in higher education. *Journal of Higher Education* 53(4): 401-418.

Johnstone, D.B. (1998). Patterns of finance: Revolution, evolution, or more of the same? *The Review of Higher Education* 21(3): 254-255.

Johnstone, D.B. (1999). Financing higher education: Who should pay? In P.G. Altbach, R.O. Berdahl, P.J. Gumport, (eds.), *American Higher Education in the Twentieth Century: Social, Political, and Economic Challenges.* Baltimore: Johns Hopkins University Press.

Just, R.E., Hueth, D.L., and Schmitz, A. (1982). *Applied Welfare Economics and Public Policy.* Englewood Cliffs, NJ: Prentice-Hall, Inc.

Kaldor, N. (1939). Welfare propositions and interpersonal comparisons of utility. *Economic Journal* XLIX: 549-552.

Lamont, J. (1994). The concept of desert in distributive justice. *The Philosophical Quarterly* 44: 45-64

Lamont, J. (2000). Distributive Justice. In Zalta, E.N. (ed.). *The Stanford Encyclopedia of Philosophy* (Summer Edition). URL = http://plato.stanford.edu/contents.html

LeGrand, J. (1990). Equity vs. efficiency. *Ethics* 10(3): 554-568.

LeGrand, J. (1991). *Equity and Choice: An Essay in Economics and Applied Philosophy.* London: Harper Collins Academic.

Lerner, A.P. (1932). The diagrammatical representation of cost conditions in international trade. *Economica* 12: 346-56.

Levi, I. (1980). *The Enterprise of Knowledge.* Cambridge, MA: MIT Press.

Lewis, D.R. and Dundar, H. (forthcoming). Equity effects of higher education in developing countries. In D.W. Chapman, A.E. Austin (eds.), *Higher Education in the Developing World.*

Longanecker, D. (1978). *Federal Assistance for Postsecondary Education: Options for Fiscal Year 1979.* Washington: Government Printing Office.

McKenzie, R.B. (1979). *The Political Economy of the Educational Process.* Hingham, MA: Martinus Nijhoff Publishing.

McKenzie, R.B. and Staaf, R.J. (1974). *An Economic Theory of Learning: Student Sovereignty and Academic Freedom.* Blacksburg, VA: University Publications.

McMahon, W. (1982). Efficiency and equity criteria for educational budgeting and finance. In W. McMahon, T. Geske, (eds.), *Financing Education: Overcoming Inefficiency and Inequity.* Urbana: University of Illinois Press.

McMahon, W. (1991). Improving higher education through increased efficiency. In D. Finifter, R. Baldwin, and J. Thelin, (eds.), *Financing The Uneasy Public Policy Triangle in Higher Education: Quality, Diversity, and Budgetary Efficiency.* New York: Macmillan.

Nozik, R. (1974). *Anarchy, State, and Utopia.* New York: Basic Books.

Olsen, E.O. and Rogers, D.L. (1991). The welfare economics of equal access. *Journal of Public Economics* 45: 91-105.

Paulsen, M.B. and St. John, E.P. (in press). Social class and college costs: Examining the financial nexus between college choice and persistence. *The Journal of Higher Education* 72.

Pettit, P. (1980). *Judging Justice: An Introduction to Contemporary Political Philosophy*. London: Routledge and Kegan Paul.

Pigou, A.C. (1932). *Economics of Welfare, 4th Edition*. London: Macmillian.

Plotnick, R. (1981). A measure of horizontal inequity. *Review of Economics and Statistics* 63(2): 283-288.

Plotnick, R. (1982). The concept and measurement of horizontal inequity. *Journal of Public Economics* 17 (3): 373-391.

Plotnick, R. (1985). A comparison of measures of horizontal inequity. In M. David, T. Smeeding (eds.), *Horizontal Equity, Uncertainty, and Economic Well-being*. Chicago: The University of Chicago Press.

Rawls, J. (1971). *A Theory of Justice*. Cambridge, MA: Harvard University Press.

St. John, E.P. (1991a). The impact of student financial aid: A review of recent research. *Journal of Student Financial Aid* 21(1): 118-132.

St. John, E.P. (1991b). A framework for reexamining state resource-management strategies in higher education. *Journal of Higher Education* 62(3): 263-267.

Sen, A. (1970). *Collective Choice and Social Welfare*. San Francisco: Holden, Day.

Sen, A. (1973). *On Economic Inequality*. Oxford: Oxford University Press.

Schelling, T.C. (1984). *Choice and Consequence*. Cambridge, MA: Harvard University Press.

Schultz, T.W. (1972). Optimal investment in college instruction: Equity and efficiency. In T.W. Schultz, (ed.), *Investment in Education: The Equity-Efficiency Quandary*. Chicago: The University of Chicago Press.

Scitovsky, T. (1942). A reconsideration of the theory of tariffs. *Review of Economic Studies* 9: 89-110.

Sidgwick, H. (1907). *The Methods of Ethics*. London: Macmillan.

Smith. A. (1776). *An Inquiry into the Nature and Causes of the Wealth of Nations*. Reprinted 1981. Indianapolis: Liberty Classics.

Stokey, E. and Zeckhauser, R. (1978). *A Primer for Policy Analysis*. New York: W.W. Norton and Co.

The Chronicle of Higher Education. (1999). *Almanac Issue*. Washington, DC

Thurow, L. (1996). Author/MIT economist says U.S. faces dire threats. *Minneapolis Star Tribune*, March 7: D1 and D8.

Varian, H.R. (1996). *Intermediate Microeconomics: A Modern Approach*. New York: W.W. Norton and Co.

Windham, D. (1976). Social benefits and the subsidization of higher education: A critique. *Higher Education* 5: 237-252.

Zalta, E.N. (ed.) (2000). *The Stanford Encyclopedia of Philosophy* (Summer Edition). URL = http://cdl.library.usyd.edu.au/stanford/entries/justice-distributive/.

5. THE POLICY SHIFT IN STATE FINANCIAL AID PROGRAMS

Donald E. Heller
Pennsylvania State University

I. INTRODUCTION

The last three decades have seen important changes in how states finance higher education. Rising public sector tuition prices, constrained growth in state appropriations to institutions, and the development of new types of student financial aid programs have altered the funding landscape in many states. These changes have occurred as other factors — including demographic shifts, increased accountability demands, and the transformational influence of technology — have placed new pressures on public higher education institutions and systems.

The affordability of higher education has received much attention in recent years.[1] Parents, students, policymakers, and college leaders alike are concerned with how affordable college is, both in reality as well as in perception. Perhaps at least partially because of media trumpeting the "$1,000-a-week price tag" of college (Morganthau and Nayyar, 1996), studies have shown that the public overestimates the true cost of college. For example, in a 1998 survey conducted for the American Council on Education, respondents overestimated the average tuition charge at a community college by 180 percent and at a public four-year institution by 212 percent (Ikenberry and Hartle, 1998).[2] What is more disturbing is that lower-income parents overestimated the true cost of college more than did parents from higher-income families. In another indication of the extent of the problem of public perception of college costs, respondents grossly *underestimated* the amount of financial aid that was available nationally.

[1] For an overview of recent trends in the affordability of public higher education, see Heller (2001).
[2] To ensure that the survey respondents were able to distinguish between tuition charges and total costs (including room and board), the survey also asked them to estimate total costs at both types of institutions. They overestimated total costs at a community college by 193 percent, and at a public four-year institution by 99 percent.

J.C. Smart and W.G. Tierney (eds.), Higher Education: Handbook of Theory and Research, 221–261.

In the same survey, the cost of a college education was rated a top concern by parents in greater numbers than were issues such as "their children being a victim of crime, health care for their children, or quality of public schools" (Ikenberry and Hartle, 1998, p. 6). The "good" news from this portion of the survey is that respondents from all income groups had roughly similar concerns about paying for college.[3]

In response to these concerns, the federal government has commissioned numerous studies of college costs and prices in the last decade (see, for example, National Commission on Responsibilities for Financing Postsecondary Education, 1993; National Commission on the Cost of Higher Education, 1998; United States General Accounting Office, 1998). The most visible effort was likely that of the National Commission on the Cost of Higher Education, created by Public Law 105-18 in 1997. The Commission's report, *Straight Talk About College Costs and Prices*, was widely awaited by many observers both within and outside the higher education community. Yet after a year of study, the Commission's conclusions were less than definitive:

> After providing pages of statistical and testimonial data regarding each potential cause, they hedge in their conclusions. After posing the question, "Have increases in college and university administrative costs affected tuition increases?" their answer was a definitive "Possibly" (p. 248). In response to the question "Have costs to construct and renovate campus facilities affected tuition increases?' their answer is "Probably" (p. 266). And, their answer to "Have technology costs driven tuition up?" was "Possibly" (p. 266). Such answers, of course, are less than satisfying (Mumper, 2000, p. 41).

While many expected the report to point the finger at the villain in the college affordability melodrama, it conspicuously avoided singling one out.

Public college and university affordability is the result of a number of factors, including the direct or "sticker" price of college, the level of state appropriations to institutions, and the availability of student financial aid. Financial aid is provided by many sources — state governments, the federal government, institutions, and private sources — and through multiple mechanisms — grants, loans, vouchers, and work study. In recent years, financial aid has been an important factor in assessing affordability. Thirty-five years ago less than half of the states had student aid programs, and public colleges and universities had

[3] This finding needs to be interpreted with caution, however. The survey did not ask what *type* of college the respondents were concerned about paying for. One interpretation could be that higher-income parents were concerned about paying private college tuition (where, based on existing research, their children are most likely to attend), while lower-income parents were concerned about paying for a public community college or 4-year institution.

very small, if any, financial assistance programs of their own. Today, every state in the union has some type of aid program, and many public institutions have developed their own grant and loan programs.

This chapter describes how the provision of state financial aid has shifted in recent years, and what some of the impacts of this shift have been. Following this introduction, I provide a brief history of how states have financially supported public higher education institutions through direct appropriations to the institutions as well as through support to students. Public higher education has a long and illustrious history in this country, and understanding how it has been financed is critical to comprehending the current state of affairs. The next section traces the recent increases in public college and university tuition prices, along with changes in the pattern of state appropriations to institutions, and the resulting shift in the burden of paying for college from the taxpayers towards students and their families.

The fourth section describes how the structure of state financial aid programs has changed in recent years, primarily through the development of merit-based programs. A description of a number of the larger state merit aid programs is provided. That section also describes the growth in institutionally-funded financial aid, which has served to supplement the resources available from the federal and state governments. The final section of the chapter provides some concluding thoughts and some issues for consideration in the future.

II. A BRIEF HISTORY OF STATE SUPPORT FOR HIGHER EDUCATION

THE COLONIAL ERA THROUGH WORLD WAR II

State support of higher education in the United States began with public allocations to private, largely church-chartered institutions.[4] This support was often in the form of the granting of public lands, and authorization for the running of lotteries to benefit the institution. Many state governments in the late 18th and early 19th centuries began to provide direct financial support from general tax revenues to support a number of private colleges and universities.

The first truly "public" institutions of higher education were initially chartered in the late 18th century, primarily in the South and Midwest. These institutions received direct state subsidy, though their control can best be described as "quasi-public" because of the degree of autonomy generally granted to their trus-

[4] Brubacher and Rudy (1976) and Rudolph (1990) provide good summaries of the early history of state support for private institutions.

tees. In some institutions, the trustees were self-perpetuating, thus putting the overall control of the institution beyond public reach. Brubacher and Rudy (1976) note that it was well into the 19th century before many state legislatures began asserting governance control over these public universities by reserving the right to appoint trustees. Brubacher and Rudy designate the University of Virginia, founded by Thomas Jefferson in 1819, as the "first real state university" (p. 147) for the following reasons:

- The university had a board of visitors appointed by the governor of the state.
- The state provided initial capital and ongoing funds for the operation of the university.
- The university was founded to be free of "domination by any and all religious sects" (p. 149).
- Provisions were made for the provision of free tuition to selected poor students from throughout the state.

This mixing of state support for both public and private institutions of higher education continued into the early 19th century. A turning point, however, was the famous *Dartmouth College* case of 1819, in which the state of New Hampshire tried to assert control over Dartmouth College because of its chartering and support of the institution. The New Hampshire Superior Court found in favor of the state, ruling that Dartmouth was a public institution. Upon appeal to the U.S. Supreme Court, the defense of the college and its independence from the state was passionately argued by Daniel Webster, in an oft-quoted speech before the Court:

> This sir, is my case. It is the case, not merely of that humble institution, it is the case of every college in the land. . . for the question is simply this: Shall our state legislature be allowed to take that which is not their own, to turn it from its original use, and apply it to such ends or purposes as they, in their discretion shall see fit? Sir, you may destroy this little institution. . . but if you do. . . you must extinguish, one after another, all those great lights of science, which, for more than a century, have thrown their radiance over the land! (quoted in Rudolph, 1990, pp. 209-210).

The Supreme Court ruled in favor of Dartmouth, thus effectively closing the door on any further attempts by the states to gain control of private institutions. The *Dartmouth* case clarified the distinction between public and private colleges and universities in the United States. Following *Dartmouth*, states began to focus their financial support for higher education on the publicly-controlled and -supported institutions, and phased out most of the direct appropriations to private institutions.

The most important event in the expansion of state support for higher education was the passage of the Morrill Act in 1862. Sponsored by Representative Justin Morrill of Vermont, the act provided federal land grants to states which created colleges and universities for the purpose "to teach such branches of learning as are related to agriculture and the mechanic arts" (quoted in Rudolph, 1990, p. 252). The federal land grants allowed the states to sell the land, with the proceeds to be turned over to the colleges. The Morrill Act led to the founding of a great number of public colleges and universities, all funded primarily through direct appropriations from the state.

While the 19th century public institutions were funded primarily through the revenues from the land grants, supplemented by appropriations from state general fund tax revenues, there were other sources of revenues. Some colleges and universities were the beneficiaries of donations from individuals. In addition, these public institutions did often charge tuition directly to the individual, though the charges were generally well below the level of those charged by private institutions and were not universal. An early 20th century study on the subject of public tuition charges concluded,

> Yet the idea of fees or tuition was not entirely absent from the state university plan even in the beginning. The Federal Land Grant Act does not make any restriction against fees. . . . However, in the majority of cases no tuition as such was introduced in the new type [public] of institution and such fees as were created were nominal in amount. Probably the boards found then, as now, that other sources of income were not sufficient and that a charge of some kind against the student was a necessity. Probably they felt that the student would appreciate his work more if he paid something for it (Morey, 1928, pp. 185-186).

Another study confirmed the nominal nature of early tuition rates at public institutions, noting mid-19th century annual tuition and fee rates of $12 at the University of Wisconsin (1855), $10 at the University of Tennessee (1866), $5 at the University of Illinois (1868), $15 at Ohio State (1874), and $5 at the University of Missouri (1874) (Sears, 1923).

Even with relatively low tuition charges, there was a recognition that the charging of *any* tuition at public institutions left open the possibility that such an action would effectively close out certain students from attending.

> In the application of any scale of fees it must be kept in mind that there will be some who will desire the privileges of the school and are entitled to it, but who can not pay. All agree that for these individuals provision should be

> made so that they will not be deprived of the opportunity. Scholarships and loans are the established and practical methods by which this condition can, to some extent, be met. The funds for these purposes are now generally inadequate even for the present range of expense (Morey, 1928, p. 188).

This view echoed that noted earlier, of Thomas Jefferson and the founding of the University of Virginia, which had provisions for free tuition to selected poor students from throughout the state. Similarly, when Iowa State University opened in 1855, it established 50 free scholarships (Sears, 1923).

The Morrill Act and the founding of public higher education institutions in many states helped lead to large increases in enrollments in the latter half of the 19th and first half of the 20th century. Figure 1 shows the number of institutions and total enrollment in higher education from the post-Civil War era up to the beginning of World War II. While the number of institutions (public and private combined) increased threefold during this period, enrollments grew almost 30 times. Not only was the country seeing more colleges and universities, it was seeing great increases in the size and scope of the institutions.

Tuition fees in public colleges and universities climbed after the Civil War and throughout the first half of the 20th century. Average rates were reported to be approximately $50 per year in the 1920s (Holst, 1923; Sears, 1923), rising to $80 by the start of World War II (President's Commission on Higher Education, 1947, Volume II).

Figure 1: Number of Higher Education Institutions and Total Enrollment
Source: *National Center for Education Statistics (2000a), Table 174*

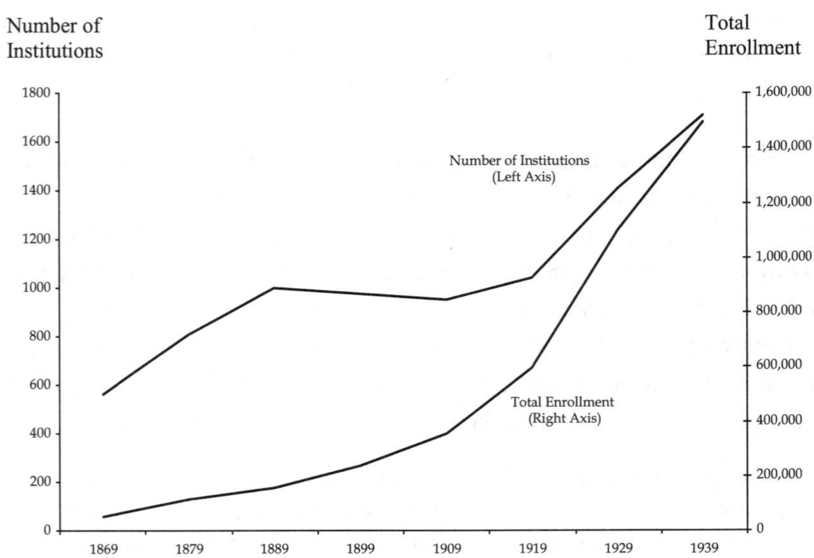

THE GI BILL AND THE POST-WORLD WAR II ERA

The end of World War II, preceded shortly before by the passage of the Servicemen's Readjustment Act of 1944 (commonly referred to as the GI Bill), began what is often referred to as the "golden age" in American higher education (Freeland, 1992). While the GI Bill is often noted as the first broad-based, government-funded financial aid program, the motivation for its passage was very different. After World War I, returning veterans rallied in Washington to protest the federal government's failure to award them bonuses that they felt they were promised. Franklin Roosevelt, who was assistant secretary of the navy during World War I, well remembered the fate of the veterans of that war. Early in World War II, with the support of the American Legion, Roosevelt began formulating plans for the reentry of veterans into American society. Anxious to avoid the "bonus riots" of World War I, and to avoid prolonged idleness and spells of unemployment for the newly-returned veterans, he spearheaded the passage of the GI Bill through Congress.[5]

Higher education enrollments continued the expansion begun earlier in the century, swelled by the generous benefits afforded to returning GIs. The GI Bill provided tuition benefits of $500 per year, plus $75 per month for living expenses (Goodwin, 1994). This was during an era when the average annual tuition at a public college (for resident students) was under $100 and under $300 at a private college (President's Commission on Higher Education, 1947, Volume II, p. 17). Enrollment in higher education expanded from 1.5 million students before World War II to over two million immediately after the war, and upwards from there (Figure 2). The bulk of the expansion occurred in public institutions, which saw their enrollment increase almost tenfold in the fifty years following the war (enrollment at private institutions increased only 170 percent in the same period).

Even with the support provided to returning veterans by the GI Bill, state higher education policy, with few exceptions, focused on providing access to college via the mechanism of universal low tuition. State budgetary support for public colleges and universities was used primarily to heavily subsidize the price of college for all attending, regardless of their financial need. The child of the wealthy doctor received the same "financial aid" — distributed through the general state subsidy — as did the child from a poor family. The policy was seen as efficient, in that it required minimal bureaucratic and administrative mechanics beyond the decisions regarding the size of the appropriation for each institution.

[5] For excellent summaries of the events that led up to the passage of the GI Bill, and its impact on society, see Bennett (1996) and Greenberg (1997).

Figure 2: Total Higher Education Enrollment by Sector
Source: *National Center for Education Statistics (2000a), Table 175*

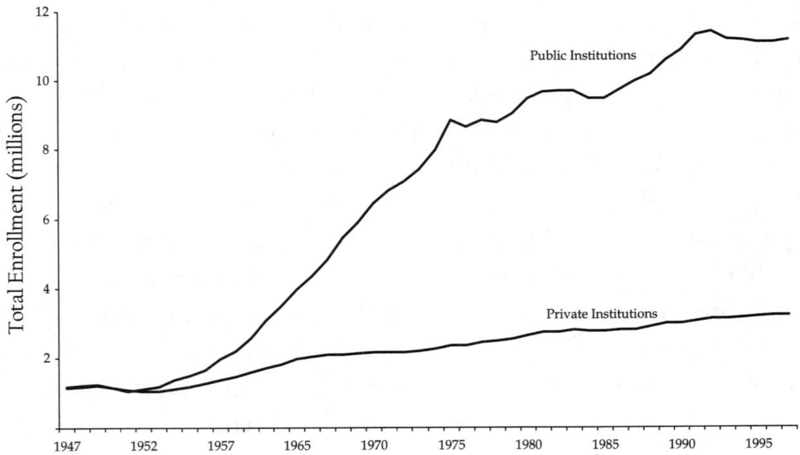

It was also deemed to be equitable, as all citizens of the state attending a single institution received an equal subsidy, and therefore paid the same price.

While public sector tuition prices remained low relative to those of private colleges, they were an increasingly important source of support. Student fees provided about 12 percent of total revenues to public colleges and universities in 1927, increasing to 20 percent in 1940 (Morey, 1928; President's Commission on Higher Education, 1947, Volume VI). The GI Bill helped reduce the share of total revenues paid by students to 14 percent in 1947, though the combination of student-paid tuition and GI Bill-paid tuition totaled 36 percent of total revenues in public institutions (President's Commission on Higher Education, 1947, Volume VI, Table 46). Thus, the GI Bill benefited both students, by lowering the share of the cost of education they had to bear, and institutions, by increasing the share of total costs borne by students and the federal government together.

Public sector tuition prices continued their climb in the post-war era, reaching an average of $261 in 4-year institutions and $99 in community colleges in 1964 (National Center for Education Statistics, 2000a). Some states began limited scholarship programs to award financial aid to help defray the cost of tuition, but these programs often targeted their aid based on the academic achievement, rather than financial need, of the student and her family. The Truman Commission on Higher Education, in its review of the financing of higher education, noted the New York state scholarship program (the nation's first large-scale state program), which awarded grants based on performance in the

Regents examinations (President's Commission on Higher Education, 1947, Volume II). While the Commission did encourage states to develop their own scholarship programs to help meet its stated goal of equal opportunity in higher education, its primary recommendation was the creation of a federally-funded program because of its belief that the states would not or could not step up to their obligation:

> Irrespective of, and in addition to whatever program of grants-in aid the Federal Government may decide to adopt, this Commission urges generous extension of State scholarship provisions. Nevertheless, it is realistic to concede that in the immediate future many States will not feel that they can afford to embark upon such a program. . . . In other words, however intrinsically desirable it is to extend such a program within the States, this Commission believes that such scholarships would not represent a sufficiently comprehensive or adequate attack upon the problem; and especially would this be true in the less prosperous states (Volume II, p. 47).

Notwithstanding the pessimism of the Truman Commission, a number of states did join New York in developing their own scholarship programs.[6] By the end of the 1960s, the Carnegie Commission on Higher Education reported that there were nineteen state-run scholarship programs, and in the 1969-1970 academic year they awarded a total of almost $200 million in grants to 488,000 students (Carnegie Commission on Higher Education, 1971). The programs ranged in size from Maine's, which appropriated $61,000 and served 150 students, to the oldest program in New York, where $59 million was divided among 263,000 students.

THE HIGHER EDUCATION ACT OF 1965 AND CREATION OF THE STATE STUDENT INCENTIVE GRANT PROGRAM IN 1972

The passage of the Higher Education Act of 1965 (HEA) ushered in a new era in student financing of higher education. The HEA authorized the first broad-based, federally-funded financial aid programs. Title IV of the act created the Educational Opportunity Grant program (EOG), the Guaranteed Student Loan Program, and the College Work-Study program.

[6] It should be noted that the federal government's adherence to the Truman Commission recommendations was not immediate. As described in the next section, it took almost two decades for passage of the Higher Education Act of 1965, which authorized the first large-scale, need-based grant and loan programs by the federal government.

While these key federal programs were first authorized with the passage of the HEA in 1965, they had little impact on students at first. Michael Mumper (1996) points to a number of reasons for this failure. Part of the problem was the way in which the grant funds were distributed to states, which was based on total college enrollments rather than on the financial need of students in the state. In addition, Mumper points out that the political and social climate was not supportive of the funding and implementation of the programs:

> In the face of the fiscal and political constraints imposed by the Vietnam War, national policy-makers were generally not in the mood to expand the Great Society commitments. In addition, student rioting and general campus unrest had soured many people on aid to higher education in general and on student aid in particular. The Title IV programs remained in place, but they proved only to be small first steps toward insuring equal educational opportunity (p. 81).

The reauthorization of the HEA in 1972 was an important step in changing the structure and funding of the Title IV programs to ensure that they better met the goals of improving equity and opportunity in higher education. Largely through the initiative of Rhode Island Senator Claiborne Pell, the EOG program was revamped (and renamed the Basic Educational Opportunity Grant program, later renamed Pell Grants in 1980) in order to target the aid on the neediest students. The funding for the program was expanded, so that by 1974-1975, the program's first full year of operation, over one million students (16 percent of all undergraduates) received grants of up to $1,400 to help pay for college (Mumper, 1996).

Another important feature of the 1972 reauthorization was the creation of the State Student Incentive Grant (SSIG) program, which provided federal matching funds for state-run, need-based grant programs. This proved to be a critical catalyst to the development and expansion of the state programs. While in 1969 19 states appropriated just under $200 million for these programs, by 1974 this had expanded to 36 states and $423 million (Fenske and Boyd, 1981). By 1979, every state (and the District of Columbia) reported at least one grant program, and the total appropriated had increased to over $800 million (National Association of State Scholarship and Grant Programs, various years). A 1975 survey conducted by the National Association of State Scholarship Programs commented that, "Growth represented in '74-75 and '75-76 in the historical summary table above, to a large degree, is a response to the new

SSIG Program which permits up to a $1,500 annual student award (equal shares of $750 Federal/State) in this new form of State/Federal partnership" (Boyd, 1975, p. 2). The growth in total appropriations for the state grant programs is shown in Figure 3.

While the SSIG program (renamed the Leveraging Educational Assistance Partnerships program in the 1990s) may have been a catalyst for the development of the state scholarship programs, it is hard to credit it for the subsequent funding growth of those programs. In its first year of operation (1974-1975), the SSIG program distributed $19 million to the states, a small portion of the $423 million spent by the states on student aid that year. While state grant appropriations grew almost 750 percent (in current dollars) from 1974 to 1998, funding for the SSIG program topped out at $78 million in 1981, an increase of just over 300 percent (College Board, 1999b). Funding for SSIG/LEAP stayed in the range of $60-$70 million through most of the 1980s and 1990s, before being cut back to a level of $25 million in 1998. Despite recent annual attempts by the Clinton Administration to kill the program, Congress has kept it on fiscal life support. It is hard to demonstrate a linkage between the level of funding for SSIG/LEAP and the actions states took to expand their own grant programs to the extent they did.

Figure 3: Total Appropriations for State Grant Programs
Source: *Author's calculations from Fenske and Boyd (1981); National Association of State Scholarship and Grant Programs (various years); National Center for Education Statistics (2000a), Table 38.*

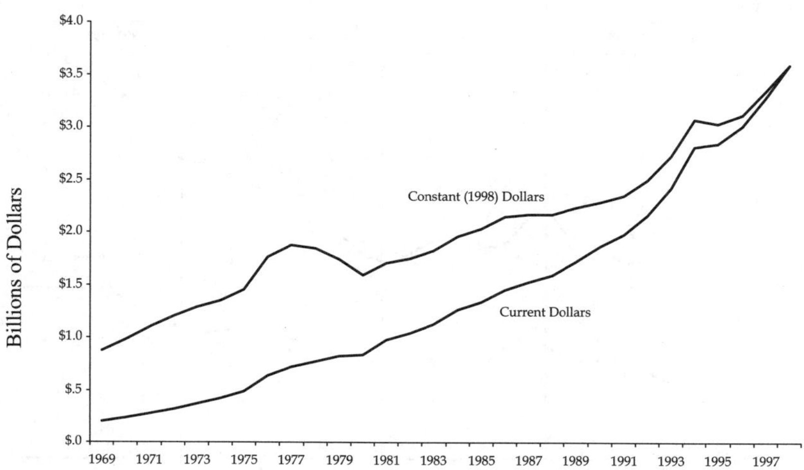

III. TUITION INCREASES AND THE SHIFTING BURDEN OF PAYING FOR COLLEGE

TUITION INCREASES SINCE THE 1960S

The slow but steady pace of tuition increases imposed by public colleges and universities began to accelerate in the mid-1960s. Analysts have proposed a number of explanations for the increases, including: the increase in demand for higher education, driven primarily by the entrance of baby boomers into college; increased costs, due to new services and facilities being provided; and a lack of productivity growth in higher education, due largely to the labor-intensive nature of the enterprise. The era from the Great Society onwards can be divided into four periods, as shown in Figure 4.

From 1964 to 1972, real prices increased at a rate of 4.5 percent annually in 4-year institutions and 7.0 percent in community colleges. The Vietnam War era was also a period of great expansion in incomes; median family income grew 3.2 percent in real terms during these years (United States Bureau of the Census, 2000b). Thus, students and their families were at least partially protected from the price increases by rising incomes. In the remainder of the 1970s, smaller nominal tuition increases combined with higher rates of inflation served to lower the real price of college in both sectors.

The 1980s brought in a new era in public college pricing. Annual tuition increases returned to their earlier, pre-1970s levels, growing 4.3 percent in 4-year institutions and 3.1 percent in community colleges. To exacerbate the afforda-

Figure 4: Average Public Sector Tuition Prices (1998 Dollars)
Note: *The annual tuition change in each sector is shown for each of the four designated periods. Prices were deflated using the school year Consumer Price Index.*
Source: *Author's calculations from National Center for Education Statistics (2000a), Tables 38 and 317.*

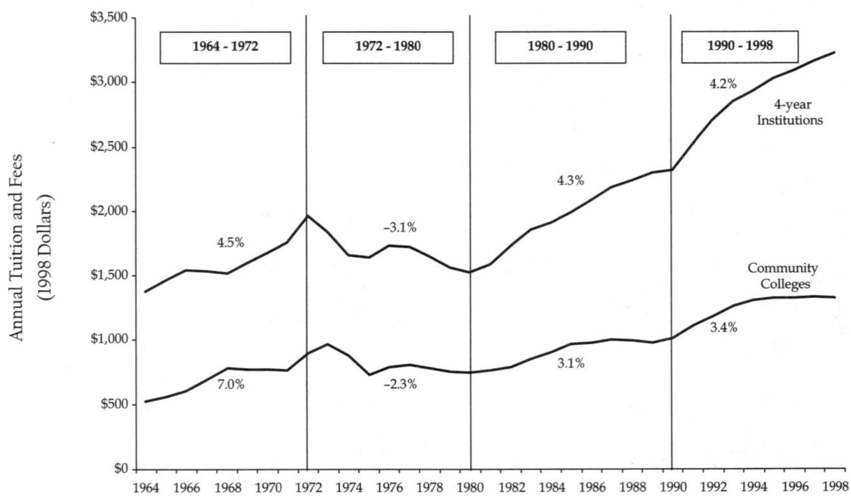

bility problem, family incomes in the country stagnated during this decade, growing only 0.6 percent annually in real terms. While in 1980 it took the median family 3.7 percent of its annual income to pay the tuition at a 4-year institution, by 1990 this had grown to 5.3 percent.

The 1990s saw a similar pattern as the previous decade. Tuition prices continued to climb at approximately the same rate, and family income growth continued to be elusive. The two trends worked together to push the average 4-year tuition up to 6.9 percent of median family income in 1998.

CHANGES IN STATE SUPPORT

While tuition prices were eating up more of the typical family's income, the pattern of state support of higher education was also changing. Figure 5 displays two measures of state support: total state and local appropriations per headcount enrollment in public institutions (across all fifty states), and state and local appropriations plus state scholarship program appropriations per headcount enrollment in public institutions (both measures are shown in constant dollars).[7] Over the three decades since the mid-1960s, there have been five

Figure 5: State Support per Student (1998 Dollars)

Note: *The annual change is shown for each of the five designated periods. Prices were deflated using the school year Consumer Price Index, and the per-student amounts were calculated using headcount enrollments.*

Source: *Author's calculations from National Association of State Scholarship and Grant Programs (various years); National Center for Education Statistics (2000a), Tables 38 and 176; Quantum Research Corporation (2000)*

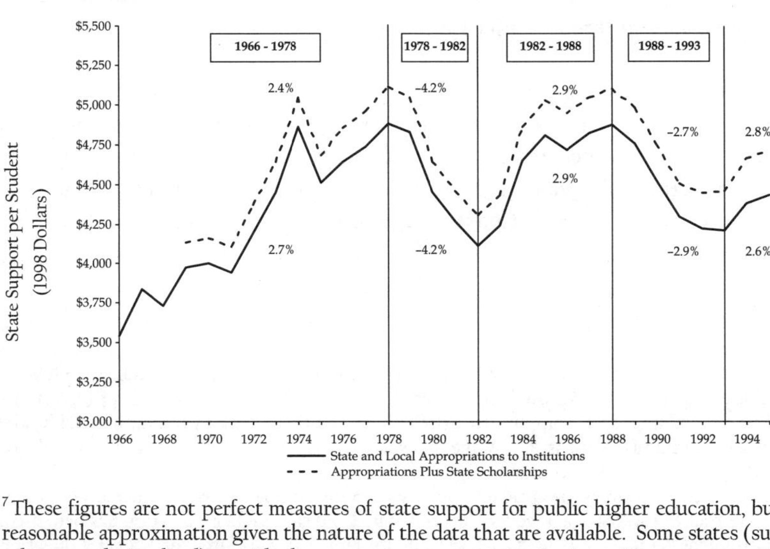

[7] These figures are not perfect measures of state support for public higher education, but they are a reasonable approximation given the nature of the data that are available. Some states (such as Pennsylvania and Maryland) provide direct support to private institutions. However, over 99 percent of state and local appropriations in 1995-1996 went to public institutions (author's calculations from Quantum Research Corporation, 2000). Local appropriations in most states are targeted at community colleges.

distinct "boom and bust" cycles.

From 1966 through 1978, there were steady real increases in state support per student, with the exception of a one-time decrease in 1975.[8] The period from the late 1970s to the early-1980s was an era of double-digit inflation, as well as continued increases in enrollment. While appropriations increased in nominal terms, the combination of high inflation and enrollment increases served to decrease the state support per student during this period.

The period beginning in 1982 was characterized by economic recovery, with appropriations increasing and inflation decreasing. In addition, the enrollment surge began to level off, as the last of the baby boomers were completing their college education. These factors helped to return the growth in state support to the levels enjoyed during the earlier era. Once again, this boom was followed by a five-year bust, where real declines in state appropriations and a renewed increase in enrollments combined to decrease overall support by just under 3 percent per year.

The most recent period for which data are available shows that a recovery is once again in effect. Enrollments have leveled off, and as state budgets have enjoyed a recovery from the dismal conditions of the late 1980s and early 1990s, states are once again targeting resources at higher education. Even with this recovery, however, state support per student (in real dollars) is still below the level of two decades earlier.[9]

The recent increases in state support should be viewed with a cautious eye. A recent forecast of state fiscal conditions in the early 21st century conducted for the National Center for Public Policy and Higher Education found that the future may hold a very different reality for higher education:

> Based on national averages, state spending for higher education will have to increase *faster* than state spending in other areas — just to maintain current services. . . . Since the percentage of the state budget dedicated to higher education has actually *declined* over the past decade, continuing to fund current service levels for higher education would represent a significant shift in state budget trends (Hovey, 1999, p. vii).

[8] The large spike in support in the 1974-1975 academic year (and the subsequent decline the following year) is due to a large reported growth (17 percent in real terms) in state and local appropriations that year. The data on appropriations are from the HEGIS and IPEDS surveys, administered by the National Center for Education Statistics. While this spike may appear unusual, there is no evidence that the data for that year are not accurate.

[9] While data from these sources are available only up through the 1995-1996 academic year, other sources indicate that the state fiscal recovery has continued and that higher education has benefited. Information from the Grapevine project at Illinois State University (Center for Higher Education and Educational Finance, 2000) indicates that state appropriations have grown at a real rate of 4.7 percent since 1996, while the most recent data from the National Center for Education Statistics show that enrollments have continued to be stable.

This forecast is based both on projections of the fiscal status of state budgets, as well as projected increases in the demand for higher education. The National Center for Education Statistics has estimated that public college enrollments are projected to increase at a rate of 1.3 to 1.8 percent annually (National Center for Education Statistics, 2000b). This compares with enrollment growth of 1.1 percent annually in public institutions over the most recent ten years. The cautionary note sounded by Hovey was repeated in a report from the American Association of State Colleges and Universities (2000), which warned that

> A number of indicators reveal that while residents are more affluent than ever before and state governments are spending more than ever before, the portion of state funds allocated to colleges and universities has not recovered the levels posted before the recession of 1990-92. The question of fiscal priority is an increasingly important one, given that institutions in many states will face unprecedented demands for higher education access at the same time that demands in other areas, especially those related to health care, are likely to grow. As the competition for state resources intensifies, the pressure on institutions to raise revenues via tuition and other means will undoubtedly mount, raising a number of difficult questions for state policymakers (p. 4).

The net effect of these two trends — increasing tuition prices and stagnating levels of state support — has been an important shift in the burden of paying for public higher education. Figure 6 shows the percentage share of the educational and general expenditures in public institutions borne by taxpayers (in the form of state appropriations and state scholarship programs) and by students and their families (paying tuition and fees).[10] In 1969, the state covered 60 percent of the expenditures share, and tuition and fees provided 15 percent. By 1978, the difference between these shares had widened to over 47 percent, largely due to the increasing state support during this period (Figure 5) and the decrease in real tuition prices in the mid-1970s (Figure 4). From 1978 on, the difference narrowed as tuition prices increased and state support fluctuated. In 1995 students and their families were paying 23 percent of expenditures, while state support had dropped to 47 percent. The difference of 24 percent was little more than half the level of 1978.

[10] It should be noted that a portion of the tuition and fees paid by students and their families is covered by federal Pell Grants and other forms of non-state financial aid. Even if these other sources are subtracted from gross tuition and fees, the shift in the funding pattern over time described in this section is similar. One can also argue that this funding pattern still represents a shift of the burden from the state to students, with students responsible for securing their resources for paying for college from their own earnings and savings, those of their parents, and financial aid from non-state sources.

Figure 6: State Support and Tuition and Fees as a Share of Educational and General Expenditures in Public Institutions

Source: *Author's calculations from National Association of State Scholarship and Grant Programs (various years); Quantum Research Corporation (2000)*

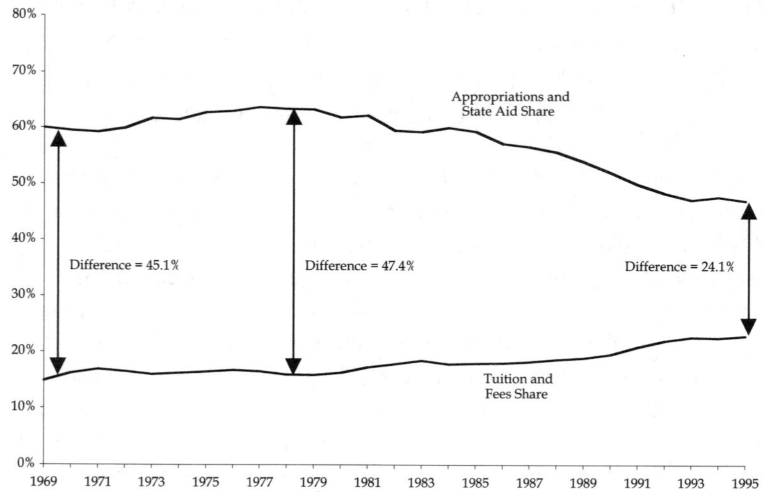

IV. THE DEVELOPMENT AND GROWTH OF NEW FORMS OF FINANCIAL AID

PROGRAM STRUCTURE THROUGH THE EARLY 1990S

The federal State Student Incentive Grant (SSIG) program appears to have spurred the creation of many of the state scholarship programs. Before the authorization of SSIG in 1972, 24 states had scholarship programs. By five years later, every state had developed one. Yet as described earlier, the funding for SSIG could not have been the sole factor in spurring the expansion of the state programs, as state funding increases far outpaced what Congress and each administration were willing to provide to SSIG.

The original state aid programs were focused primarily on providing grants to financially needy students, though, as in the New York State program earlier in the 20th century, some programs required students to demonstrate some form of academic achievement.[11] Even with achievement included as a criterion in some states, however, most programs mirrored the goals of the federal Title IV programs of providing access to college, and to a lesser extent, choice of institutions:

[11] The terms "scholarships" and "grants" are used interchangeably here to designate financial aid for college that the student does not have to repay nor provide work to receive. Some writers distinguish the two, with "scholarships" being awarded for meritorious achievement, and "grants" for financial assistance.

> Access and choice are two principal themes in student aid that have become familiar through frequent and thorough discussion over the past 20 years as they unfolded first in hortatory statements, then in large and growing funded student aid programs. The expressed goal of such programs has been to benefit young persons in the society by providing wide access to their choice of postsecondary education institutions. . . . The goal of wider access was achieved by changing the nature and purpose of monetary awards from prizes recognizing accomplishments or potential, to assistance granted almost solely to offset financial need (Fenske and Boyd, 1981, pp. 2-3).

An early survey of the National Association of State Scholarship Programs found that 16 of the 42 states had scholarship programs that used some measure of academic merit as a criterion for awarding grants, and that these programs totaled 23.7 percent of the $500 million awarded that year (Boyd, 1975).

There is no question that assuring access remained the primary goal of most programs in the 1970s and early 1980s. The 1980-1981 survey of state grant programs asked the scholarship agencies, "What specific decisions highlight the purpose of 'access' in your program?" (Reeher and McKelvey, 1981, p. 98). A sample of the responses is shown in Table 1 (p. 238). As can be seen, the focus in most states was on targeting aid at the neediest students. In that same survey, of the 84 programs that were targeted at undergraduate students, 44 used exclusively financial need-based criteria, one used exclusively merit criteria, 29 used measures of both financial need and merit, and 10 were unclassifiable from the information provided.[12] The criteria used to determine academic achievement or merit varied from state to state. Included in the list were such measures as high school or college grade point average, class rank, SAT or ACT score, and recommendations.

In the 1981-1982 survey, the National Association of State Scholarship and Grant Programs began to more systematically track the grant programs that did *not* use financial need as a selection criteria (Reeher, 1983). Many of these programs were targeted at specific populations, such as the children of deceased or permanently disabled firefighters or law enforcement officers (Delaware, Georgia, Idaho, Massachusetts, New Jersey), descendents of Confederate soldiers and sailors (Florida), and children of deceased or disabled war veterans (Florida, Massachusetts). Most of these highly-targeted programs were very small, awarding fewer than 100 scholarships annually. Other programs, which gener-

[12] Many states had more than one undergraduate scholarship program, so the total number of programs exceeds 51 (50 states plus the District of Columbia). A number of programs required that the student demonstrate "satisfactory academic progress" while in college in order to maintain eligibility for the grant; this was not considered to be a measure of merit.

Table 1: Policies to Promote Access in Selected State Scholarship Programs, 1980-1981 Academic Year
Note: *The policies are copied verbatim from the source.*
Source: *Reeher and McKelvey (1981), p. 98.*

State	Policy
Alabama	The $300 awards are sufficient to cover the cost of tuition at state/junior community colleges. Therefore, reasonable access is assumed.
Arkansas	Proposed increase in the maximum award will enable the student to choose the college of his/her choice, public or private.
California	Taking into consideration the student's low income and disadvantaged background in the selection process.
Florida	Students are allowed to attend the accredited Florida postsecondary institution of their choice and are selected on the basis of unmet need.
Georgia	The requirements of "substantial unmet need" and the purpose of the program to meet a portion of that amount to help assure "access" to some postsecondary school is emphasized on the application forms, brochures, etc.
Maine	Awards to all students with need.
New Jersey	Higher awards given to students with high financial need.
North Carolina	Program is directed to neediest students who apply within the deadline dates.
Ohio	Priority to low income students. Larger grants to low income students.
Oregon	The decision to always give priority to neediest students emphasizes and continues the state's commitment to providing access.
Tennessee	In ranking, neediest students are assisted first.
Virginia	The College Scholarship Assistance Program is designed to assist the neediest students at both public and private schools.

ally served many more students, did award scholarships based on academic merit. In that survey, which was the first to track the total dollars awarded in non-need programs for the first time, the distribution of award dollars to undergraduates was: 60.3 percent based on need alone; 30.7 percent based on a combination of financial need and non-need based criteria; and 9.0 percent based on non-need criteria alone.

Over the next dozen years, both need-based and non-need programs grew substantially and at similar rates, keeping the proportion of the award dollars at approximately the same levels. While the total dollars awarded to undergraduates grew from $975 million in 1981-1982, to $2.4 billion in 1993-1994, the percentage of dollars awarded without using financial need as a measure fluctuated between 8.9 percent and 11.1 percent of the total (National Association of State Scholarship and Grant Programs, various years).

The Creation of the Georgia HOPE Scholarship Program

A turning point in the structure of the state financial aid programs came in 1993, when Governor Zell Miller created the Georgia HOPE Scholarship program.[13] The HOPE, or Helping Outstanding Pupils Educationally, program was developed by Miller from one of the key promises made in his 1990 campaign for governor. He proposed Georgia's first lottery, with the revenues earmarked for funding improvements to the state's educational system in three areas: prekindergarten programs, educational technology, and college scholarships. In introducing the details of the lottery to voters, Miller stressed the scholarship component as focusing on college access:

> In an effort to increase the percentage of Georgia high school graduates who attend college, Mr. Miller said he would establish a scholarship fund "to assist any high school student who achieves a grade-point average of a certain level, who enrolls at an accredited college or university in Georgia, and whose family meets a certain income requirement." He did not spell out income or grade-point average requirements (Sherman, 1991, p. A1)

Miller was successful in persuading both the Georgia Assembly and the voters to make Georgia only the second state in the South (after Florida) to enact a lottery.[14]

Merit scholarships were not new to Georgia; it was one of the half dozen or so states that put the majority of its state scholarship dollars into non-need based programs. But the development of HOPE established a new standard for the funding of merit programs.

The initial HOPE scholarship program implemented in the 1993-1994 academic year had both a merit and need component. Students needed to graduate from high school with a B average, and have a family income of below $66,000. In return for meeting these criteria, students would be awarded a scholarship to cover the full cost of their tuition at any public institution in Georgia for two years, or $500 to attend a private institution in the state. Students had to maintain the B average in their freshman year to retain the scholarship for the second year. In its first year, HOPE awarded $21.4 million to 43,000 students (Georgia Student Finance Commission, 2000b).

Since its founding, the structure of the HOPE program has undergone a number of revisions. The family income cap was raised in the second year to

[13] For an excellent review of the creation of the HOPE program, see Mumper (1999).
[14] The Georgia state constitution prohibited a lottery, so the legislature and voters had to approve a constitutional amendment.

$100,000, and then eliminated in 1995, thus removing financial considerations as a criterion for the awards. Award amounts for students attending public institutions were expanded to cover mandatory fees and a $300 per year book allowance, in addition to tuition, and payments to students attending private colleges and universities in the state were increased in three steps to $3,000. The scholarships were expanded to include up to four years of support. In addition, the high school grade eligibility criterion was changed so that students had to earn a B average in a set of core academic courses, excluding non-core courses.

By the 1998-1999 school year, the impact of HOPE had greatly expanded. Scholarships totaling $189 million were awarded to over 141,000 students that year. The distribution of awards for the first seven years of the program's existence is summarized in Table 2. While 41 percent of the students were enrolled in public 4-year institutions or community colleges, they received 60 percent of the dollars awarded, largely due to the higher tuition and fee rates at these institutions as compared to the public technical institutes. The average award to the over 500,000 students who have benefited from HOPE scholarships is just under $2,000.

The expansion of HOPE occurred simultaneously with large cutbacks in Georgia's need-based scholarship programs. In 1993-1994, the first year of the HOPE Program, Georgia allocated $5.3 million to its need-based programs. By 1998-1999, it had decreased appropriations to these programs to $0.5 million, cutting them by over 90 percent during those five years.

HOPE has become the dominant merit aid program in the nation. In its

Table 2: Distribution of HOPE Scholarship Awards, 1993 through 1999
Note: *A student receiving an award each year for four years is counted as four students; thus, the average award per student is the amount received each year.*
Source: *Author's calculations from Georgia Student Finance Commission (2000c)*

	Students		Awards		
Sector	*Number*	*% of Total*	*Amount (millions)*	*% of Total*	*Average Award per Student*
University system*	206,377	40.7%	$588.90	59.7%	$2,854
Technical institutes	224,383	44.2	193.80	19.6	864
Private institutions	76,511	15.1	204.20	20.7	2,668
Total – All institutions	507,271	100.0	986.90	100.0	1,946

**The university system includes all public 4-year institutions and community colleges in the state.*

first year, the HOPE program alone represented nine percent of all the merit dollars awarded by the states. By its fourth year of operation, the program had grown to the extent that it awarded one of every three merit dollars awarded by all fifty states. As other states moved more aggressively into the merit scholarship game (documented below), HOPE's share of all merit awards has declined somewhat. Data from the most recent year available (1998-1999), however, indicate that HOPE still grants more than 25 percent of the merit dollars awarded by all the states.[15]

From Governor Zell Miller's initial motivations for HOPE, which focused on expanding college access for students from families below a particular income level, the focus of the program has shifted. The lifting of the income cap as a criterion for the awards opened the program to upper-middle and upper-income families that were excluded from most financial aid programs. In fact, the state of Georgia trumpeted this achievement in a press release issued in 2000:

> The National Association of State Student Grant and Aid Programs' (NASSGAP) 30th Annual Survey Report also shows that for the third consecutive year Georgia distributed more student financial aid not based on family income than any other state. . . . "We are very pleased that Georgia is doing more than any other state to make a college or technical institute education available and affordable to all Georgia students and their families," said Glenn Newsome, executive director of the Georgia Student Finance Commission (Georgia Student Finance Commission, 2000a, p. 1).

The elimination of the income cap is not the only aspect of HOPE that targets spending toward students in higher income brackets. Since its inception, the program has required that students use federal Pell Grants as a source of financial aid *before* they are allowed to receive the tuition and fee payments allowed under HOPE. Since tuition and fees in public institutions in Georgia have been below the Pell Grant maximum since HOPE was created, and HOPE dollars cannot be used to pay for other costs of attendance such as room, board, and travel expenses, this has meant that the lowest income Georgians (those eligible for the maximum Pell Grant from the federal government) receive nothing from HOPE other than the book allowance award (currently $300 per year). This has resulted in a program that Patrick Callan claims, "was structured to exclude the participation of low-income students who received federal Pell Grants, a kind of

[15] Georgia has a number of smaller merit grant programs, but in 1998-1999 HOPE represented 85 percent of all merit dollars in the state.

reverse means testing" (Callan, 2001, p. 88).[16]

This policy shift is a far cry from the accomplishments of most state programs in the 1960s and 1970s, when, to reiterate the words quoted earlier in this chapter, "The goal of wider access was achieved by changing the nature and purpose of monetary awards from prizes recognizing accomplishments or potential, to assistance granted almost solely to offset financial need" (Fenske and Boyd, 1981, p. 3). As Callan (2001) sums it up, "Basically, non-need-based programs give subsidies to students who are already college bound" (p. 88).

Another aspect of HOPE needs to be considered when examining the distributive aspects of the program. HOPE is funded entirely by the Georgia lottery, an aspect that is still somewhat unique among state-funded financial aid programs (though as described below, many states are beginning to follow Georgia's lead). Studies of state lotteries that have analyzed the nature of the implicit tax they impose have been consistent in concluding that the tax burden is very regressive, and in fact, more regressive than any other category of state taxes. Regressive taxes place more of the relative burden for paying them on lower-income taxpayers. Charles Clotfelter and Philip Cook (1991), in their detailed study of state lotteries, concluded that

> The evidence is quite clear that the implicit lottery tax is decidedly regressive. That is to say, an increase in the revenue from lotteries has exactly the same distributional impact as the imposition of or increase in the rate of a similarly regressive tax. . . . The fact that participation declines with education appears to support critics' charges that with their relatively high takeout rates, lotteries take advantage of the ignorance of bettors (pp. 227, 230).

Their last conclusion is particularly ironic, if in fact the benefits of the lottery playing in Georgia (i.e., the HOPE scholarship awards) are flowing disproportionately to middle- and higher-income recipients. Cook later noted the ironic nature of using lottery revenues to fund education programs: "An education lottery is an odd link between two government enterprises. One exploits the public ignorance, and the other is supposed to be helping that ignorance" (Selingo, 1999b, p. A38).

Mumper (1999) cites a more recent national study of gambling patterns, which found that while the percentage of the population playing the lottery does not vary greatly by either income or education levels, the dollar amount played does. The less education or income an individual had, the more was the total amount bet on lotteries in a year.

[16] In March 2000, the Georgia legislature passed a bill that changes this inequity. It allows HOPE recipients to use their HOPE award to pay for tuition and fees, and use Pell dollars to pay for room, board, and other expenses, thus increasing the total amount of grants for which low-income students are eligible.

Florida Follows Georgia's Lead

While HOPE was the first broad-based merit scholarship program operated by the states, it is by no means the last. The popularity of HOPE was noted nationwide, and in particular, by Georgia's southern neighbors. Since 1993, a number of merit scholarship programs in other states have been developed.

In 1997, the Florida legislature created the Bright Futures Scholarship program. Like Georgia, Florida had existing merit scholarship programs before the development of Bright Futures, and in fact, disbursed the largest amount of merit aid of any of the states before the development of HOPE in Georgia. Bright Futures consolidated Florida's existing merit programs into a single program, and lowered the academic standard that needed to be met to win an award.

As with HOPE, Bright Futures is funded from state lottery revenues, and it has no income eligibility cap. Since its creation, it has become the nation's second largest state-run merit program. It has three types of awards, two for traditional college students, and one for students attending vocational/technical postsecondary education. A summary of the awards and eligibility requirements is shown in Table 3 (p. 244).

In its initial year of operation in 1997-1998, the program awarded $69.6 million to 43,244 students, or an average award of $1,609 per student (Postsecondary Education Planning Commission, 1999). In its second year, the program expanded to award $93.3 million to 56,281 students, with approximately 57 percent of the dollars going to existing postsecondary students renewing their scholarships, and the remainder awarded to incoming students (Sue Jones, Florida Department of Education, personal communication, January 12, 2000). In 1999-2000, $131.5 million was distributed to over 70,000 students (Bureau of Student Financial Assistance, 2000).

Bright Futures has quickly become not just a popular program, but a fairly ubiquitous one as well. Data from the Florida Board of Regents show that almost 70 percent of the incoming resident students in Florida's public 4-year institutions in the fall of 1998 earned one of the three types of Bright Futures scholarships (Postsecondary Education Planning Commission, 1999). The rates ranged from a low of 33.4 percent of the incoming students at Florida A&M University, the state's historically Black institution, to a high of 99.3 percent at the University of Florida, the flagship campus. At the state's community colleges, 21 percent of incoming freshmen that year carried with them

Table 3: Florida Bright Futures Scholarship Award Amounts and Eligibility Criteria
Note: *There are alternative eligibility criteria for home-schooled students and GED recipients. All awards can be renewed for up to seven years or until a degree or a certain number of credit hours is attained.*
Source: *Postsecondary Education Planning Commission (1999)*

	Academic Scholars	Merit Scholars	Gold Seal Vocational
Award amount (public institutions)	100% of tuition and fees plus $600	75% of tuition and fees	75% of tuition and fees
Award amount (private institutions)	Pegged at 100% of tuition at comparable public institution	Pegged at 75% of tuition at comparable public institution	Pegged at 75% of tuition at comparable public institution
High school GPA	3.5 for college curriculum (15 courses)	3.0 for college curriculum (15 courses)	3.0 in college courses and 3.5 in vocational courses
Minimum test score	1270 SAT/28 ACT	970 SAT/20 ACT	Varies, depending on the test taken
Other requirements	75 hours of community service in high school	–	–
Postsecondary GPA (for renewal)	3.0	2.75	2.75

a Bright Futures scholarship.

The Florida Postsecondary Education Planning Commission (PEPC) conducted an initial evaluation of the Bright Futures program in 1999 at the request of the Florida legislature (Postsecondary Education Planning Commission, 1999). Staff at PEPC analyzed the racial/ethnic and income distribution of the awards. A summary of the findings is shown in Table 4. Both Black and Hispanic students, who totaled over one-third of all public high school graduates in the state in 1997, received only 17.5 percent of the Bright Futures initial scholarship awards. White and Asian-American students received a disproportionate share of the scholarships, as compared to their distribution among public high school graduates.

The median household income in the state of Florida in 1998 was approximately $35,000 (United States Bureau of the Census, 2000a). From the data shown in Table 4, a conservative estimate is that no more than 37 percent of the Bright Futures scholarships went to students in the half of Florida's families with income below the median. By taking the mid-point of the $30,000 to

$39,999 income category (i.e., the Florida median), a more realistic estimate is that less than 30 percent of the scholarships went to families below the median. Almost 40 percent of the scholarships went to students from families with incomes above $60,000 per year. The PEPC report also found that the majority of Bright Futures awardees in the states' public institutions did not have financial

Table 4: Distribution of Florida Bright Futures Scholarship Initial Awards, 1998-1999
Note: *The income distribution statistics were taken from a sub-sample of scholarship awardees, so the total is less than that of the race/ethnicity total.*
Source: *Author's calculations from Postsecondary Education Planning Commission (1999), Exhibits 6 and 9; National Center for Education Statistics (2000a), Tables 106 and 185*

	NUMBER OF AWARDS	% OF TOTAL	
Race/Ethnicity			% of Public High School Graduates, 1996-1997
Native American	55	0.2%	0.2%
Asian American	1,148	4.5	2.7
Black	1,893	7.5	20.2
Hispanic	2,527	10.0	13.9
White	19,335	76.2	62.8
Other	420	1.7	–
Income			Cumulative %
‹ $10,000	484	2.6%	2.6%
$10,000 - $19,999	1,433	7.7	10.3
$20,000 - $29,999	2,178	11.7	22.0
$30,000 - $39,999	2,792	15.0	37.0
$40,000 - $49,999	2,271	12.2	49.2
$50,000 - $59,999	2,327	12.5	61.7
$60,000 - $69,999	1,712	9.2	70.9
$70,000 - $79,999	1,545	8.3	79.2
$80,000 - $99,999	1,712	9.2	88.4
› $100,000	2,141	11.5	99.9

need for college, as defined by the federal needs analysis methodology. Only 21 percent of the scholarships went to students receiving a Pell Grant, and only 11 percent went to students receiving a Florida need-based scholarship.

Income was also an important predictor of whether Bright Futures recipients retained their scholarships in their second year in college. While less than 65 percent of all students from families with income below $20,000 per year retained their scholarships while in college, over 75 percent of students from families making more than $70,000 per year were able to renew their awards.

Bright Futures has received its share of criticism. A 1997 report by the Business/Higher Education Partnership in Florida noted that the state "engineered a popular wealth transfer from low- and mid-income people to the well-to-do" (quoted in "A not very bright idea," 1997, p. 2D). Charles Reed, former Chancellor of the state university system in Florida, echoed that criticism by describing the program as one where "you take from the poorest people of our state, the people who play the Florida lottery, and transfer their money to the wealthiest people in the state" ("Higher education group wants scholarship changes," 1997, p. 8) and "poor, dumb, public policy" ("Chancellor blasts scholarship program," 1997, p. B4). A newspaper in Palm Beach, one of Florida's most affluent communities, derided the program: "The program is not based on financial need. It takes from the poor, who play the lottery, and gives in full measure to the more affluent" ("Florida's dim bulbs," 1999, p. 14A).

Other criticisms of the program have centered around the standards initially used to determine academic merit. A controversy arose when *The Miami Herald* published an analysis of the first cohort of Bright Futures awardees that found that almost 10 percent of the students took remedial courses while in college (Wheat, 1999). This occurred even though the legislation authorizing the program stated that, "Funds from any scholarship within the Florida Bright Futures Scholarship Program may not be used to pay for remedial or college-preparatory coursework" (Florida Bright Futures Scholarship Program, Florida Statutes, 1997). Adam Herbert, who replaced Reed as the Chancellor of the state university system in 1998, used these figures to question the validity of the program. "If it's [Bright Futures] to move Florida toward being a no-tuition state, we're accomplishing that. If the policy is to encourage high levels of achievement, we still have a ways to go" (Wheat, 1999, p. 1A). A spokesman for Florida Lieutenant Governor Frank Brogan, who was former commissioner of education in Florida, said, "It's difficult to believe that you can get a 3.0 [grade point average] in a college preparatory curriculum and still not be where you need to be. That's very troubling" ("Almost 10 percent of scholarship recipients had to take remedial courses," 1999).

In response to these findings, the Florida legislature attempted to raise the minimum SAT score required for the Merit Scholar awards (which approximately 60 percent of the recipients receive) from 970 to 1020. This plan was vigorously opposed by minority lawmakers. According to Miami Senator Kendrick Meek, "Without this [the 970 SAT standard] . . . you might as well say to the majority of students at Florida A&M and FIU . . . that you will no longer have an opportunity to receive a Bright Futures scholarship. This is going to hurt the most needy people in this state, people who maybe didn't test well but are some of the best students" (Silva, 1999, p. 6B).[17]

Though lawmakers ultimately stalemated on their attempts to raise the SAT score, the issue is not dead even though the percentage of initial award recipients receiving remediation dropped from just under 10 percent in the first year to three percent in the second year of the program (Postsecondary Education Planning Commission, 1999).[18] The evaluation conducted by PEPC recommended that the minimum SAT for the Merit Scholars award be increased from 970 to 1020 and the high school grade point average increased from 3.0 to 3.1, even though it acknowledged that under the proposed standard, "the greatest percentage decrease [in awards] is for Black, Hispanic, and Native American students, as well as for students from lower income families" (p. 31).

Other States Jump on the Bandwagon

Georgia and Florida have become the dominant forces in state merit financial aid programs. The two states together increased their share of the total merit dollars awarded by all states from 26 percent in 1990 to 53 percent in 1998, the most recent year for which data are available. But other states have scrambled to jump on the merit aid bandwagon and capitalize on the popularity of broad-based merit programs.

In 1997, the Louisiana legislature created the Tuition Opportunity Program for Students (TOPS). Like Florida's Bright Futures program, TOPS has no in-

[17] As described earlier, Florida A&M University is the state's historically Black institution. Florida International University (FIU) is a Hispanic-serving institution, with Hispanics representing approximately 50 percent of its 30,000 students. It enrolls more Hispanics than any other 4-year institution in the country (National Center for Education Statistics, 2000a).

[18] The PEPC evaluation pointed to a change in the eligibility criteria for the vocational scholarships in the second year, which greatly reduced the number of Gold Seal recipients who took remedial courses. The percentage of Academic Scholars and Merit Scholars taking remedial courses was 2.5 percent in 1997-1998 and 1.7 percent in 1998-1999.

come eligibility requirements and has varying levels of awards, depending upon the academic achievement of the student. Unlike HOPE and Bright Futures, however, TOPS is funded from general revenues. The top level Honors Award (for those students achieving a score of 27 on the ACT test and a high school grade point average of 3.50) provides full tuition at any public institution in Louisiana, plus $800 for other expenses (Louisiana Office of Student Financial Assistance, 2000). For students attending private institutions in the state, the Honors Award provides an amount equivalent to tuition plus $800 at a comparable public college or university. The lowest level award provides full tuition at a public institution to students with an ACT score of 20 and grade point average of 2.50. Students can renew the awards for up to four years if they maintain a set college grade point average and number of credit hours earned.

The Louisiana Office of Student Financial Assistance initially estimated that approximately 15,000 students would be eligible for awards in the program's first year of operation, 1998-1999, and that the program would cost the state $36.2 million. However, its estimates were way below the actual qualification rates in that first year; 23,000 students qualified for a total of $62.4 million in TOPS awards (Louisiana Office of Student Financial Assistance, 1999; Selingo, 1999a). State officials pointed to three primary reasons for their underestimate: 1) the lack of hard data available, especially regarding high school grade point averages, to estimate scholarship eligibility rates; 2) a lack of staff available to "perform the in-depth research essential to the development of projections for complex programs such as TOPS" (Selingo, 1999a, p. A36); and 3) an increase in the number of students taking the ACT exam, including those who took the exam multiple times to try to achieve the minimum cutoff score. The program was expected to expand to 37,000 students at a cost of $86 million by the 2000-2001 year.

The popularity of TOPS put an unexpected strain on the Louisiana treasury, but its popularity has made it a difficult target for any changes geared at reining in its cost. Since its inception, legislative proposals have been discussed that would control the growth of the program's cost by: making students payback the grant if their college grades fall below a certain level; putting a cap on the amount of tuition the awards would cover, thus leaving students and their families to pick up the cost of future increases; reducing the award amount for students from families with incomes above $100,000; and raising the academic standards. All of these attempts have failed, as the popularity of TOPS has made it virtually politically untouchable.

On the funding side, one Louisiana legislator introduced a bill to implement a $0.25 surcharge on state lottery tickets, with the additional proceeds earmarked for the TOPS program. The same bill would tap $25 million from the state's tobacco lawsuit settlement fund to put towards TOPS. These legislative efforts also failed.

There is little data available on the impact of TOPS on college attendance in Louisiana. A 2000 study by the state's Office of Student Financial Assistance found that 15 percent of the awards in the 1999-2000 school year went to students from families earning incomes of at least $100,000 (Dyer, 2000). Information like that has generated the kind of criticisms made of other merit aid programs that have no income caps. According to Charles Reed, former chancellor of the state university system in Florida, "It's not the best use of state resources when you have families making $100,000 to $200,000 a year and their children are getting a full ride" (Selingo, 1999a, p. A36). David Breneman, dean of the Curry School of Education at the University of Virginia, recalled his attempt at trying to convince a group of legislators that college costs were an especially important issue for needy students. "I might as well have been talking to a brick wall. What affordability clearly meant to the legislators involved was how to pump more money to middle- and upper-income families" (Selingo, 1999a, p. A36).

In 1997, New Mexico began its Lottery Success Scholarship program. Funded by 40 percent of the proceeds of the state lottery, the program awards a grant equivalent to the full tuition at any public institution in New Mexico, with no income eligibility requirements. Students must be New Mexico residents, be enrolled full-time, and must achieve a 2.5 grade point average in their first semester in college. Even though students do not receive the awards until their second semester enrolled, the grants are renewable for up to eight semesters. Means-testing of recipients was excluded from the program, even though the New Mexico Commission on Higher Education in 1997 established a set of principles for financial aid that required that "state grant aid should continue to be based upon financial need of students" and "state grant aid should be targeted to the 'neediest of the needy' students" (New Mexico Commission on Higher Education, 1997, p. 1).

As with the other broad-based merit scholarship programs, the Lottery Success Scholarships have proven to be very popular. First year awards of $4.4 million to 5,378 students increased to $8 million and 8,232 students in the 1998-1999 year ("Lottery scholarships benefit wide array of N.M. students," 1998; New Mexico Commission on Higher Education, 1999). The rapid growth of the program, combined with stagnating revenues from the lottery, threatened its viability. A $2.7 million shortfall was estimated for the 2000-2001 year, rising to a projected deficit of $50 million by 2004. The New Mexico legislature has wrestled with both capping the size of the awards in the program, as well as diverting a higher percentage of lottery revenues towards it.

The state of Michigan chose to use a portion of its tobacco lawsuit settlement funds for the Michigan Merit Award Scholarship Program. It was expected to award approximately $80 million to 37,000 students in its initial year of operation in 2000-2001. The program provides one-time grants of $2,500 to students attending in-state public institutions, and $1,000 to those attending private or out-of-state institutions, with no income eligibility requirements. The awards are made to students who achieve a certain level on the state's standardized Michigan Educational Assessment Program (MEAP) tests.

Table 5: Qualification Rates for Michigan Merit Award Scholarships, 2000 - 2001

Note: *An ANOVA analysis of the scholarship qualification rates among the racial/ethnic groups and among the free or reduced lunch quartiles determined that the differences were statistically different from zero at a level of $p \leq .001$.*

Source: *Heller (2000)*

	% of Eligible Test-takers Qualifying for Scholarship
RACE/ETHNICITY	
Native American	19.4%
Asian American/Pacific Islander	39.7
African American	7.0
Hispanic	20.3
White	33.9
Multiracial	25.7
Other	23.8
Race/ethnicity missing or unknown	32.3
TOTAL	30.3
Quartile – % of Students in School on Free or Reduced Lunch (range, median)	
Highest (26.6% to 100%, 41.8%)	17.6%
Second (12.6% - 26.2%, 18.8%)	26.1
Third (5.9% - 12.6%, 9.1%)	34.8
Lowest (0.3% - 5.9%, 3.0%)	42.1
Free lunch percentage missing or unknown	13.8
TOTAL	30.3

An analysis of the MEAP test results for the first cohort of students eligible for the scholarships found that a disproportionate share of the scholarship awards would end up in the pockets of students from White, Asian American, and wealthier school districts. Table 5 summarizes the scholarship eligibility rates for students from different racial/ethnic groups, and from districts with varying percentages of students on free or reduced lunch.[19]

Besides the examples provided here, a number of other states, including Alabama, Kentucky, Maryland, Texas, and Washington have implemented broad-based merit scholarship programs in recent years. The result of the development and expansion of these programs has been a large increase in the dollars dedicated to merit aid by the states, relative to appropriations for need- and merit-based programs. The growth rates of both types of programs (in constant dollars) are shown in Figure 7.

Between 1982 and 1986, funding for need-based and merit aid programs increased proportionally at the same rates, both having increased approximately 25 percent over the four years. Beginning in 1987, however, the increase in appropriations for merit aid programs began to outpace the growth of need-based programs. After a short dip in the early 1990s, when states began to allocate

Figure 7: Growth of State Need-based and Merit Aid in Constant (1998) Dollars
Source: *Author's calculations from National Association of State Scholarship and Grant Programs (various years)*

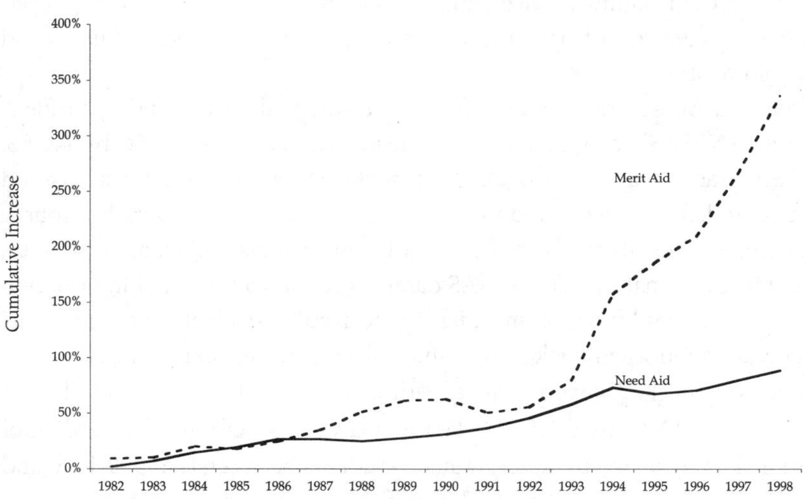

[19] The Michigan merit program was challenged in federal court by a coalition headed by the American Civil Liberties Union, the National Association for the Advancement of Colored People, and the Mexican American Legal Defense and Education Fund (Christian, 2000). The lawsuit, filed on behalf of a group of minority students in Michigan, alleged that the program violated Title VI of the Civil Rights Act of 1964 and the 14th Amendment to the U.S. Constitution. As of this writing, the case is still in the courts.

proportionally more money to the need programs, increases for merit programs began to accelerate. Since the development of the Georgia HOPE program in 1993, states have begun to emphasize more and more the merit aid programs. In the sixteen years since the National Association of State Scholarship Grant and Aid Programs began to separately track the merit programs, funding for these programs has increased 336 percent in real dollars, while funding for the need-based programs has increased only 88 percent. In 1982, the share of dollars in the merit programs was 9.3 percent of the total appropriated by the states; by 1998, this share had doubled to 18.6 percent.

THE DEVELOPMENT OF INSTITUTIONAL AID PROGRAMS TO SUPPLEMENT STATE SUPPORT

As described earlier, the affordability of college is determined by a number of factors, including the sticker price of the institution as well as the amount of financial aid that is awarded. And also described earlier was the fact that there are many sources of financial aid, including the federal and state governments, private sources, and institutions themselves.

There is limited aggregate information available on the allocation of institutional financial aid to undergraduate students. The National Center for Education Statistics (NCES), through its Integrated Postsecondary Education Data System, does collect information on scholarship expenditures from institutional sources as part of its annual college finances survey. The survey forms, however, do not ask colleges to distinguish between aid awarded to undergraduates and graduate students.

One valuable source of information is the National Postsecondary Student Aid Survey (NPSAS), conducted in four academic years since 1986 by NCES. The NPSAS surveys are a nationally representative sample of institutions and students enrolled in colleges and universities, and thus, present a rich resource for examining national trends in the awarding of financial aid from all sources, including institutional aid. The NPSAS datafiles contain a wealth of information about the sources and types of financial aid received by students in each year, as well as details about their background and college academic experiences.

In a study in the *Journal of Student Financial Aid*, Donald E. Heller and Thomas F. Nelson Laird (1999) used NPSAS data to analyze changes in the awarding of institutional financial aid to undergraduate students between the 1989-1990 and 1995-1996 academic years.[20] The findings of that study can be used to examine how the growth of institutional financial aid programs compares to changes in

[20] The study examined only full-time, dependent students attending four-year institutions, so it represents a subsample of all undergraduate students attending college in those years. However, these students received approximately two-thirds of the grant dollars awarded to all undergraduates each year.

other types of aid programs. Table 6 shows such a comparison for public and private 4-year institutions nationally.

In both sectors of higher education, total educational and general expenditures increased less than 50 percent between 1989 and 1995, while scholarship and fellowship expenditures from all sources increased 72 percent at public institutions and 80 percent at private institutions.[21] Pell Grants, which are awarded by the federal government exclusively to under-

Table 6: Financial Aid and Total Spending in 4-year Institutions, 1989-1990 and 1995-1996 Academic Years

Source: *Author's calculations from Quantum Research Corporation (2000); Heller and Nelson Laird (1999)*

	1989-1990	1995-1996	% Change
Public Institutions			
Total educational and general expenditures	$57,156,128,000	$79,650,716,000	39.4%
Scholarship expenditures — all sources	3,654,809,000	6,270,652,000	71.6
Pell Grants	1,609,314,000	1,968,094,000	22.3
Institutional grants to undergraduates	386,648,000	928,420,000	140.1
Institutional grants as % of total scholarship expenditures	10.58%	14.81%	40.0%
Institutional grants as % of total educational and general expenditures	0.68	1.17	72.3
Private Institutions			
Total educational and general expenditures	$37,184,113,000	$55,707,146,000	49.8%
Scholarship expenditures – all sources	4,845,435,000	8,711,855,000	79.8
Pell Grants	672,894,000	860,973,000	28.0
Institutional grants to undergraduates	1,856,073,000	3,806,248,000	105.1
Institutional grants as % of total scholarship expenditures	38.31%	43.69%	14.0%
Institutional grants as % of total educational and general expenditures	4.99	6.83	36.9

[21] As noted earlier, the scholarship and total expenditure data from the IPEDS surveys are for undergraduate and graduate programs combined.

graduates, increased less than 30 percent in each sector.

The data from NPSAS indicate that institutional spending on grants to undergraduates grew the fastest of any of these categories, increasing 140 percent in public institutions and 105 percent in private institutions. In 1989, just over 10 percent of the total scholarship dollars awarded by public 4-year institutions represented institutionally-funded grants to undergraduate students; by 1995, this proportion had increased to just under 15 percent. In private institutions, which historically have relied much more heavily on institutionally-funded financial aid, the proportion of total scholarship expenditures awarded to undergraduates from institutional funds grew from 38.3 percent to 43.7 percent. These figures indicate that institutionally-awarded grants are becoming an increasingly more important source of financial aid, especially in public institutions.

V. CONCLUSION

This chapter has documented recent changes in how states provide financial aid for college. Universal low tuition, a distinguishing feature of public higher education in this country for two hundred years, began to erode in the later years of the 20th century. In addition, the state financial aid programs, which since their inception have been focused primarily on promoting college access among the neediest students, have also seen important changes in structure and emphasis in the last decade.

These changes have had a large impact on college affordability, and how we evaluate it. In an era when public college tuition prices were very low, or in some institutions, even free, there were few concerns about college affordability. Even the poorest students were assumed to be able to scrape together the resources necessary for college, supplementing what they and their families could provide with support from other, largely private, sources.

The last two decades have seen a drop in the affordability of college for many students, with the burden falling especially heavily on those from families of lesser means. Donald E. Heller (2001) examined changes in the affordability of public institutions in the recent past, focusing on differences among varying groups of students. Dividing students into five groups by family income, he found that the proportion of family income necessary to pay the tuition and fees at the average 4-year public institution in the country increased the greatest for students in the lower income groups. For students in the lowest income quintile, the proportion of income increased from 11.7 percent in 1971 to 25.8 percent in 1997, an increase of almost 120 percent. For students in the wealthiest group, the share of their family's income necessary to pay the tuition increased from 1.6 percent to 2.3 percent, an increase of only 47 percent. Similar changes occurred in the relationship between incomes and tuition prices at community colleges.

Using data from the National Postsecondary Study Aid Survey, Heller also analyzed the gross, or sticker price of college paid by groups of students, along with the net price after subtracting all grants received. He found that students in the lowest and second income quintiles saw an average increase of 61 percent and 73 percent, respectively, in the net price they paid for college between 1989 and 1995 (measured in current dollars). Students in the fourth and highest income quintiles saw an increase of 49 percent and 55 percent, respectively. There were also large differences among students from different racial/ethnic groups. While White students saw an increase of 56 percent in the net price they paid, African American students experienced a net price increase of 208 percent and Hispanics 414 percent.

These trends appear to have impacted not just the affordability of college, but its accessibility as well. The College Board (1999a), in its annual survey of college prices, reported on the college entry rates of high school graduates in different income quartiles since the 1970s. These data can be used to examine how the college-going rates of students from different groups have changed over time.

Figure 8 shows the gap between the college entry rates of students from the highest income families, and those who are less well-off. The gap in the college entry rate between students from the highest earning families (income of greater than $74,584 in 1997 dollars) and poorest families (income less than $25,063) was just under 31 percentage points in 1971. By 1996, the gap had grown to over 34 percentage points. The other two groups either gained ground or maintained their position relative to the highest income students during this period.

Similar gaps exist in the college participation rates of White students compared to those of African Americans and Hispanics. An analysis of the undergraduate participation patterns of African Americans found that:

> African American college participation has historically lagged behind that of Whites, and the trend over the last two decades shows that the undergraduate participation of African Americans fell relative to Whites. In 1976, the African American rate of 16.4 percent was 4.4 percentage points below that of Whites; by 1996, the gap grew to 7.1 percentage points. . . . Recent trends in college-going behavior would have to continue for two more decades *just* for African Americans to reduce the current gap between their college participation and that of Whites to the level it was in 1976 (Heller, 1999, pp. 14-15, 27).

Figure 8: Gap Between the College Entry Rates of Students in the Top Family Income Quartile and Those in Other Quartiles

Note: *The rates used are the proportion of 18 to 24 year-old high school graduates who enter post-secondary education. Three-year moving averages were used to minimize the impact of year-to-year variation in measurement.*

Source: *Author's calculations from College Board (1999a), Table 10*

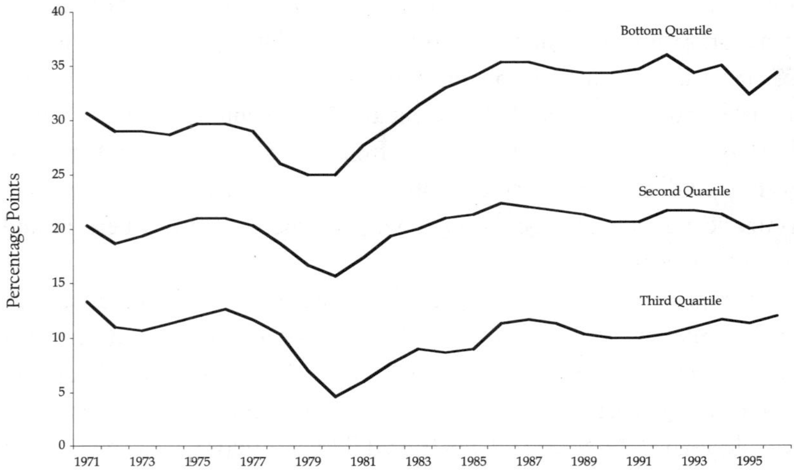

Hispanics also lost ground relative to White students between 1976 and 1996.[22]

All of the financial aid programs developed and dollars awarded during these 25 years — Pell Grants, State Student Incentive Grants, state scholarship programs, and institutional scholarships — have evidently done little or nothing to decrease the differences in college participation in this country between groups that have historically had high college-going rates, and those that have not participated as fully in college. One could argue that in the absence of all these programs, the gaps would be even greater. Yet if the primary purpose of the major state and federal aid programs, as articulated in the 1970s, was to eliminate financial need as a barrier to college attendance, then it appears that we have not yet achieved the condition articulated by Lloyd Morey nearly 75 years ago:

> In the application of any scale of fees it must be kept in mind that there will be some who will desire the privileges of the school and are entitled to it, but who can not pay. All agree that for these individuals provision should be made so that they will not be deprived of the opportunity. Scholarships and

[22] The undergraduate participation rates in this study were calculated differently, using the 18 to 29 population as the base. Thus, while comparisons among racial groups are valid, the rates shown here cannot be compared to those of the income groups described earlier.

> loans are the established and practical methods by which this condition can, to some extent, be met (Morey, 1928, p. 188).

This chapter has documented how state financial aid policy has changed in recent years, and what some of the implications of those changes are. Merit-based scholarship programs — with funding often from such sources as state lotteries and tobacco settlements, and with many of the benefits flowing to students who do not need assistance to pay for college — are receiving the bulk of the attention and marginal dollars that legislators and governors are willing to allocate to student aid. The reasons for this largesse for students from middle- and upper-income families is quite understandable; programs like HOPE Scholarships in Georgia, Bright Futures in Florida, Lottery Success Scholarships in New Mexico, and the Michigan Merit Award Scholarships, have proven to be quite popular with voters, especially among those who are influential in the political process. Charles Reed, former chancellor of the state university system in Florida, related a vignette that sums up his frustration with these policies:

> A man approached Chancellor Charles Reed in Miami recently to tell him what a wonderful university system Florida has. Reed asked him to explain. The man said his two children at the University of Florida were receiving new lottery-funded scholarships. But Reed was troubled when he learned that the man was an orthopedic surgeon who could easily afford university tuition without financial aid from the state. "Something is really wrong when you do that," Reed said. . . . "When you can give something away to the middle and upper-middle class, in politics, it doesn't get any better than that" (Dunkelberger, 1997, p. 1A).

Thomas Mortenson, a long-time observer of financial aid policy in the nation, criticizes merit scholarships for similar reasons:

> In the economic world of highly constrained social welfare maximization, giving scarce financial aid resources to people who do not need them is wasteful, unnecessary, unproductive, and comes at the price of adequate and appropriate student financial aid for others who could not afford to attend college without such assistance (Mortenson, 1997, p. 2).

One might expect the merit programs to be popular with colleges and universities, as they may be pumping additional money into the financial aid system that might not otherwise be available for need-based scholarships. Yet at least some observers recognize that while these policies may benefit higher education financially, they do not serve the best long-term interests of the nation. The American Association of State Colleges and Universities, a lobbying organization for public 4-year institutions, noted that,

> Many new generation programs are inefficient in that they provide significant benefits to students who already have the means and/or ability to leverage funds to cover college expenses. The recipients of merit-based scholarships are disproportionately from middle and upper income families; many such families can pay at least a portion of students' college expenses. Many of these same recipients are also the primary beneficiaries of other college affordability programs, such as federal tax credits/deductions, prepaid tuition plans, or college savings plans (Reindl and Brower, 2000, p. 2).

Policymakers need to reexamine the purposes of state financial aid, to determine whether public funds should be used to reward academic achievement and subsidize the behavior of many who would attend college anyway, or whether they should be used to provide critical support to those who desperately need it to attain a postsecondary education. If the former view prevails, then we should expect to see more states follow the lead of the pioneers in the state merit scholarship arena. If the supporters of the latter win out, then state policymakers will need to rededicate themselves to the financial aid principles espoused three decades ago with the passage of the Higher Education Act of 1965 and the creation of many of this nation's need-based financial aid programs.

References

Almost 10 percent of scholarship recipients had to take remedial courses. (1999, March 7). *The Associated Press State & Local Wire, BC cycle.*

American Association of State Colleges and Universities. (2000). *AASCU special report: State fiscal conditions*. Washington, DC: Author.

Bennett, M. J. (1996). *When dreams came true: The GI Bill and the making of modern America.* Washington, DC: Brassey's.

Boyd, J. D. (1975). *State/territory funded scholarship/grant programs to undergraduate students with financial need to attend public or private post-secondary educational institutions. Seventh annual survey, 1975-76 academic year.* Deerfield: Illinois State Scholarship Commission.

Brubacher, J. S., & Rudy, W. (1976). *Higher education in transition: A history of American colleges and universities, 1636-1976* (Third ed.). New York: Harper & Row, Publishers.

Bureau of Student Financial Assistance. (2000). *Bright Futures facts [On-line file]*, [http://www.firn.edu/doe/bin00072/bffacts.htm]. Tallahassee: Florida Department of Education.

Callan, P. M. (2001). Reframing access and opportunity: Problematic state and federal higher education policy in the 1990s. In D. E. Heller (Ed.), *The states and public higher education policy: Affordability, access, and accountability*. Baltimore, MD: The Johns Hopkins University Press.

Carnegie Commission on Higher Education. (1971). *The capitol and the campus: State responsibility for postsecondary education. A report and recommendations*. New York: McGraw-Hill.

Center for Higher Education & Educational Finance. (2000). *Appropriations of state tax funds for operating expenses of higher education for fiscal years 1994-95 through 1999-00 [On-line data file]* [http://coe.ilstu.edu/grapevine/table4.html]. Normal: Illinois State University.

Chancellor blasts scholarship program. (1997, December 18). *The Florida Times-Union* (Jacksonville, FL), p. B4.

Christian, N. M. (2000, June 28). A.C.L.U. sues Michigan, citing bias in giving college aid. *The New York Times*, p. A16.

Clotfelter, C. T., & Cook, P. J. (1991). *Selling hope: State lotteries in America.* Cambridge, MA: Harvard University Press.

College Board. (1999a). *Trends in college pricing 1999*. Washington, DC: Author.

College Board. (1999b). *Trends in student aid 1999*. Washington, DC: Author.

Dunkelberger, L. (1997, December 20). 'Bright Futures' dim for poor; The scholarships tend to benefit middle- and upper-income students, critics say. *Sarasota Herald-Tribune*, p. 1A.

Dyer, S. (2000, August 1). 15% of TOPS recipients from upper-income families. *The Advocate* (Baton Rouge, LA), p. 10A.

Fenske, R. H., & Boyd, J. D. (1981). *State need-based college scholarship and grant programs: A study of their development, 1969-1980*. New York: College Entrance Examination Board.

Florida Bright Futures Scholarship Program, Florida Statutes, 240.40201 §10 (1997).

Florida's dim bulbs. (1999, June 26). *The Palm Beach Post*, p. 14A.

Freeland, R. M. (1992). *Academia's golden age: Universities in Massachusetts, 1945-1970.* New York: Oxford University Press.

Georgia Student Finance Commission. (2000a, June 20). *Georgia no. 1 in student financial aid third year in row [On-line file]*, [http://www.gsfc.org/press_release/pr_06-20-2000.htm]. Tucker, GA: Author.

Georgia Student Finance Commission. (2000b). *Georgia's HOPE scholarship program [On-line file]*, [http://www.gsfc.org/press_release/hopefaq.cfm]. Tucker, GA: Author.

Georgia Student Finance Commission. (2000c). *HOPE scholarship program - Program totals [On-line file]*, [http://www.gsfc.org/gsfc/html_summary_grant_all_cov_H.htm]. Tucker, GA: Author.

Goodwin, D. K. (1994). *No ordinary time: Franklin and Eleanor Roosevelt: The home front in World War II.* New York: Simon and Schuster.

Greenberg, M. (1997). *The GI bill: The law that changed America.* New York: Lickle Publishing.

Heller, D. E. (1999). Racial equity in college participation: African American students in the United States. *Review of African American Education, 1*(1), 5-29.

Heller, D. E. (2000). *Affidavit and expert report of Donald E. Heller* (presented in *White et al. v. Engler et al.*). Detroit: The American Civil Liberties Union of Michigan.

Heller, D. E. (2001). Trends in the affordability of public colleges and universities: The contradiction of increasing prices and increasing enrollment. In D. E. Heller (Ed.), *The states and public higher education policy: Affordability, access, and accountability.* Baltimore, MD: The Johns Hopkins University Press.

Heller, D. E., & Nelson Laird, T. F. (1999). Institutional need-based and non-need grants: Trends and differences among college and university sectors. *Journal of Student Financial Aid, 29*(3), 7-24.

Higher education group wants scholarship changes. (1997, December 16). *The Tampa Tribune,* p. 8.

Holst, J. H. (1923). The imposition of fees in state-supported institutions. *Educational Review, 65* (January), 35-39.

Hovey, H. A. (1999). *State spending for higher education in the next decade: The battle to sustain current support.* San Jose, CA: National Center for Public Policy and Higher Education.

Ikenberry, S. O., & Hartle, T. W. (1998). *Too little knowledge is a dangerous thing: What the public thinks about paying for college.* Washington, DC: American Council on Education.

Lottery scholarships benefit wide array of N.M. students. (1998, October 30). *Albuquerque Tribune,* p. A5.

Louisiana Office of Student Financial Assistance. (1999). *6,218 TOPS recipients fail to meet renewal requirements [On-line file],* [http://www.osfa.state.la.us/ 110599renreq.htm]. Baton Rouge: Author.

Louisiana Office of Student Financial Assistance. (2000). *Louisiana's Tuition Opportunity Program for Students (TOPS) [On-line file],* [http://www.osfa.state.la.us/schgrt6c.htm]. Baton Rouge: Author.

Morey, L. (1928). Student fees in state universities and colleges. *School and Society, 28*(712), 185-192.

Morganthau, T., & Nayyar, S. (1996, April 29). Those scary college costs. *Newsweek,* 53-56.

Mortenson, T. G. (1997). Georgia's HOPE Scholarship Program: Good intentions, strong funding, bad design. *Postsecondary Education OPPORTUNITY, 56*(February), 1-3.

Mumper, M. (1996). *Removing college price barriers: What government has done and why it hasn't worked.* Albany: State University of New York Press.

Mumper, M. (1999, November). *HOPE and its critics: Sorting out the competing claims about Georgia's HOPE scholarship.* Paper presented at the annual meeting of the Association for the Study of Higher Education, San Antonio, TX.

Mumper, M. (2001). The paradox of college prices: Five stories with no clear lesson. In D. E. Heller (Ed.), *The states and public higher education policy: Affordability, access, and accountability.* Baltimore, MD: The Johns Hopkins University Press.

National Association of State Scholarship and Grant Programs (various years). *NASSGP/NASSGAP annual survey report.* Deerfield, IL; Harrisburg, PA; and Albany, NY: Illinois State Scholarship Commission; Pennsylvania Higher Education Assistance Agency; and New York State Higher Education Services Corporation.

National Association of State Student Grant & Aid Programs. (2000). *NASSGAP 29th annual survey report.* Albany: New York State Higher Education Services Corporation.

National Center for Education Statistics. (2000a). *Digest of education statistics, 1999.* Washington, DC: U.S. Department of Education.

National Center for Education Statistics. (2000b). *Projections of education statistics to 2010*. Washington, DC: U.S. Department of Education.

National Commission on Responsibilities for Financing Postsecondary Education. (1993). *Making college affordable again: Final report*. Washington, DC: Author.

National Commission on the Cost of Higher Education. (1998b). *Straight talk about college costs and prices: Report of the National Commission on the Cost of Higher Education*. Phoenix, AZ.: American Council on Education and the Oryx Press.

New Mexico Commission on Higher Education. (1997). *Principles to guide the restructuring of state funded student financial aid in New Mexico [On-line file]*, [http://www.nmche.org/publications/prncplsfa.html]. Santa Fe: Author.

New Mexico Commission on Higher Education. (1999). *The condition of higher education in New Mexico*. Santa Fe: Author.

A not very bright idea. (1997, December 21). *St. Petersburg Times*, p. 2D.

Postsecondary Education Planning Commission. (1999). *Florida's Bright Futures Scholarship Program: A baseline evaluation*. Tallahassee, FL: Author.

President's Commission on Higher Education. (1947). *Higher education for American democracy*. New York: Harper & Brothers.

Quantum Research Corporation. (2000). *CASPAR database system [On-line data file]* [http://caspar.nsf.gov/]. Bethesda, MD: Author.

Reeher, K. R. (1983). *National Association of State Scholarship and Grant Programs. 13th annual survey, 1981-82 academic year*. Harrisburg: Pennsylvania Higher Education Assistance Agency.

Reeher, K. R., & McKelvey, J. L. (1981). *National Association of State Scholarship and Grant Programs. 12th annual survey, 1980-81 academic year*. Harrisburg: Pennsylvania Higher Education Assistance Agency.

Reindl, T., & Brower, D. (2000). *State student financial aid: Tough choices and trade-offs for a new generation* (AASCU Perspectives, Vol. 2, No. 1). Washington, DC: American Association of State Colleges and Universities.

Rudolph, F. (1990). *The American college and university: A history* (1990 ed.). Athens, GA: University of Georgia Press.

Sears, J. B. (1923). Our theory of free higher education. *Educational Review, 65*(January), 27-34.

Selingo, J. (1999a, April 16). For fans of state merit scholarships, a cautionary tale from Louisiana *The Chronicle of Higher Education*, p. A36.

Selingo, J. (1999b, April 16). Seeking dollars to further their dreams, scholarship supporters push for lotteries. *The Chronicle of Higher Education*, p. A38.

Sherman, M. (1991, November 14). Miller reveals lottery plans for education; He anticipates easy referendum passage. *The Atlanta Journal and Constitution*, p. A1.

Silva, M. (1999, April 16). Minority lawmakers fail in effort to change Florida scholarship bill. *The Miami Herald*, p. 6B.

United States Bureau of the Census. (2000a). *Median household income by state: 1984 to 1998 [On-line data file]*, [http://www.census.gov/hhes/income /histinc/h08.html]. Washington, DC: Author.

United States Bureau of the Census. (2000b). *Regions--Families (all races) by median and mean income: 1953 to 1998* [On-line data file], [http://www.census.gov/hhes/income/histinc/f06.html]. Washington, DC: Author.

United States General Accounting Office. (1998). *Tuition increases and colleges' efforts to contain costs*. Washington, DC: Author.

Wheat, J. (1999, March 7). Scholarship winners deficient in basics. *The Miami Herald*, p. 1A.

6. Back to the Basics: Regression as It Should Be

Corinna A. Ethington
University of Memphis

Scott L. Thomas
University of Georgia

Gary R. Pike
University of Missouri-Columbia

INTRODUCTION

Sir Francis Galton (1885) introduced the idea of "regression" to the research community in a study examining the relationship of fathers' and sons' heights. In his study he observed that sons do not tend toward their fathers' heights but instead "regress to" the mean of the population. He thus formulated the idea of "regression toward mediocrity", and with the development of the method of least squares procedures by Carl Friedrich Gauss (Myers, 1990), multiple regression analysis using ordinary least squares procedures (OLS) has become one of the most common statistical techniques for investigating and modeling relationships among variables. Applications of regression occur in almost every field, and one can hardly pick up an issue of a higher education journal without running across at least one study in which OLS regression was the methodology of choice. Similarly, there is a plethora of work presented at the Association for the Study of Higher Education, Division J of the American Educational Research Association, and the Association for Institutional Research utilizing multiple regression techniques. Such widespread use of this powerful technique encourages us to revisit the basic principles underlying this "workhorse" of higher education research in an effort to identify ways in which it can be used to deliver more refined analyses, thereby further enhancing the credibility of our research.

This is not an introductory chapter on multiple linear regression. We assume the reader has a working knowledge of regression techniques. Rather, our intent in this chapter is to call attention to a number of important technical issues that, while covered in most introductory courses, are put to little use in higher education research. The issues we raise, while fundamental to the accu-

J.C. Smart and W.G. Tierney (eds.), Higher Education: Handbook of Theory and Research, 263–293.

rate application of this most useful technique, are frequently overlooked or not sufficiently reported in our published research. It is our hope that this chapter will refocus our awareness on some of the key issues that make multiple linear regression techniques so useful. Regaining a focus on these issues will allow us to refine in important ways our analyses using these techniques and to further improve our research on a variety of higher education outcomes.

USES OF REGRESSION ANALYSIS

The two predominant uses of multiple regression are for prediction and explanation, and the methodological approach taken in the analyses depends upon the purpose of the estimation of the model. Suppose, for example, that an institutional research office has been charged with determining whether a set of variables (e.g., ability, high school achievement, socioeconomic status, interests, motivation) can predict end-of-freshman-year grade point average. If the purpose is to optimize the prediction and to use such a prediction equation in making admission decisions, the goal is the development of the most parsimonious equation with the least errors of prediction so that the best estimates of yield rates from admission pools can be obtained. The aim is to eliminate superfluous variables, not to test theoretically based hypotheses. The use of theory is not required in the selection of variables for use in the development of such a predictive equation, and the parameter estimates are of little importance. Of more importance are economy, availability of data, ease of obtaining needed information, and accuracy of prediction. Various approaches may be used to identify the smallest number of variables necessary to produce the most accurate prediction estimates (see Montgomery & Peck, 1992 and Myers, 1990, for a presentation of the development of the regression equation for prediction). Different approaches using the same data may lead to the retention of different sets of variables, but any approach that meets the needs of the researcher and produces accurate estimation is sufficient.

While the higher education research literature is replete with regression studies using the prediction terminology, few actually use the methodological approaches involved in the development of the most efficient prediction equation. Almost all of the regression applications in higher education are for explanatory purposes, and it is this approach that we take in our development of this chapter, for explanation is the essence of behavioral research. Almost all of our research questions seek to understand and explain why some phenomenon under study varies from person to person, and most generally the phenomena studied in higher education are "multivariate" in nature. That is, the primary focus of a study (the dependent variable) is conceptualized as being related to and influenced by multiple interrelated factors (the independent variables). Rarely can simple bivariate relationships adequately capture and explain or model reality. The complexity of behavioral science phenomena demands that we study the covariation among the independent variables as well as that of the dependent variable with the independent variables. It is this variance and covariance that is the basis of multiple regression.

Our search for explanations of variability and attempts to model reality imply that there is a theoretical or conceptual basis for not only the anticipated relationships among variables, but for the selection of variables studied. In his classic text on the application of multiple regression in behavioral research, Pedhazur (1982) argues that "methods per se mean little unless they are integrated within a theoretical context" (p. 3) and goes on to state that "in explanatory research data analysis is designed to shed light on theory" (p. 11). This focus on theory in the application of multiple regression in behavioral research has been argued for since the 1950s when regression became commonly used in the social sciences. Ezekiel and Fox (1959) stress the necessity for "careful logical analysis, and the need both for good theoretical knowledge of the field in which the problem lies and for thorough technological knowledge of the elements involved in the particular problem" (p. 181). Thus, both good theory and methodological competence are required for the most effective application of multiple regression.

The Role of Theory

As noted above, the most general application of multiple regression in higher education research is to explain phenomena, and Kerlinger (1973) states that such explanations are called theories. Kerlinger defines theory as "a set of interrelated constructs (concepts), definitions, and propositions that present a systematic view of phenomena by specifying relations among variables, with the purpose of explaining and predicting the phenomena" (p. 9). Thus, the selection of variables to be used in explaining phenomena and the specific hypotheses to be tested are derived from the particular theory in which the research is grounded. The constructs and definitions within the theory lead to the operationalization of the constructs and the measurement of the variables subsequently used in testing the theoretical hypotheses. We assume, therefore, that the set of independent variables and the dependent variable used in the statistical analyses are directly specified by some underlying theory.

Using theory as the basis for the choice of independent variables in multiple regression also has implications for how the results of the regression analysis can be discussed. The interpretation of the estimated regression coefficients as *indices of effects* of independent variables on an outcome can *only* be applied within a theoretical context. Pedhazur (1982) argues that without theory as the basis for variable selection, *no* statement can be made about effects or meaningfulness of variables. He further argues that with an atheoretical selection of variables or with the use of statistical variable-selection procedures (e.g., stepwise procedures), the context of the research reverts to prediction, and in the predictive study, all that can be concluded about the independent variables is which combination of them will best predict the outcome. Thus, any use of stepwise techniques in developing explanatory models is *always* improper. Indeed, in an editorial statement in the journal *Educational and Psychological Measurement*, the editor, Bruce Thompson, delineated the major problems associated with stepwise procedures and suggested that studies utilizing such procedures should not be submitted to that journal (Thompson, 1995).

Variable selection for use in multiple regression also calls for parsimony. Multiple indicators of single constructs of the theory often lead to statistical problems. When these multiple indicators are highly inter-correlated among themselves, extreme multicollinearity may be introduced (discussed later in the chapter) which also precludes any meaningful interpretation of results. But even when extreme multicollinearity is not present in the data, Gordon (1968) argued that large numbers of "control" variables lead to the "partialing fallacy" and that the introduction of control variables should also be used only within an explicit theoretical context and not simply because they are available. From examples given in his paper, he goes on to show that using "odds-and-ends" type variables can often result in the regression coefficients of variables having weak relationships with the dependent variable and being statistically significant only because they are "less repetitively represented" (p. 598). Thus, the meaningfulness of the results of multiple regression analyses relies heavily on the use of an *appropriate theory* for variable selection and the *appropriate application* of multiple regression techniques. As Pedhazur (1982) noted, "Data do *not* speak for themselves but through the medium of the analytic techniques applied to them" (p. 4).

ELEMENTS OF MULTIPLE REGRESSION ANALYSIS

SETTING THE STAGE

The theoretical model and the operationalization of constructs in that model lead to data structure and the statistical model. The theoretical model describes the conceptual view of the researcher in studying the phenomena of interest and the statistical model gives a mathematical representation that is used to test the theory. The data structure and relationships specified through the statistical model determine in large part if regression is the appropriate tool for the analysis. While regression is an amazingly robust tool (i.e., it can withstand relatively egregious violations of its underlying assumptions) it is still susceptible to a number of characteristics of the data being analyzed. We therefore cannot stress enough the importance of "getting to know" the data being analyzed. This acquaintanceship process requires developing a familiarity with the source and structure of the data, the measurement characteristics of the variables, and the univariate and joint distributional characteristics of the variables.

DATA STRUCTURE

As with many statistical procedures, the inferential utility of multiple regression rests in large part on the assumption that the data being analyzed are drawn through some type of simple random sample. Implicit in this assumption is that the theoretical model itself can be operationalized using data from a single unit of analysis (e.g., students *or* institutions but not students *and* institutions). This assumption, however, is often unrealistic when modeling outcomes in higher education. For example, environmental effects play a central role in much of the theoretical work on a host of individual-level outcomes in our field (e.g., student outcomes). One only needs to consider thirty years of Astin's work for evidence of the role of college environments on individual behaviors and attitudes (Astin, 1993). In such a context, we presume students to be affected importantly by their shared environments — that is, the researcher is concerned with two distinct levels of analysis, the student and the institutional environment (e.g., the campus, the department, the classroom, etc.).

Conceptual frameworks such as Astin's I-E-O model often yield operationalizations incorporating data from more than one level of analysis. Generally speaking, such operationalizations are inappropriate for techniques that assume that each variable being analyzed comes from the same level of analysis (the multiple linear regression techniques we focus on here rely on this assumption). Data structures resulting from these operationalizations require "multilevel" techniques designed to capitalize on data from multiple levels of analysis (see Bryk & Raudenbush, 1992; Ethington 1997; Heck & Thomas, 2000).

A separate but related problem arises when using many large-scale data sets such as those collected by the National Center for Educational Statistics. Oftentimes these data rely on complex, multistage sampling strategies where institutions are randomly selected in a first stage and individuals are then randomly selected in a second stage — that is, for purposes of efficiency, individuals are clustered within institutions in the sampling design. While still a probability sample, this type of data collection scheme is anything but simple and has important consequences for results obtained through statistical techniques, such as multiple linear regression, that assume the data are obtained through simple random sample at a single level of analysis (see Thomas & Heck, 2001).

MEASUREMENT OF VARIABLES

Dependent Variables

While no consensus exists over the appropriate baseline level of measurement of independent variables, it is most desirable that the outcome in a linear regression model be measured at a continuous level (i.e., the interval or ratio level of measurement). Although a regression model with a non-continuously measured outcome will yield results, researchers interested in modeling non-continuous outcomes should not use regression procedures such as the one we focus on here. More appropriate procedures exist for analyzing such outcomes and researchers are encouraged to turn to generalized regression models such as binomial logit, multinomial logit, or probit models that are designed specifically for these types of outcomes (see Long [1997] for an excellent introduction to these models).

Independent Variables

One of the most appealing features of the linear regression model is the ease with which its results can be interpreted. Regardless of how the variables in the model are measured, the simple "one unit increase in x yields a 'b' unit increase/decrease in y" interpretation holds. Following from this, the most meaningful interpretations of multiple regression results will be realized when the independent and dependent variables are measured on scales where such unit increases or decreases are uniform.

Age and income are ideal examples of variables with rich interpretative properties — each one unit interval at any point on the scales is the same distance as any other and the 0 point on the scale represents the absence of the property being measured. Thus if one were to use a regression model to express the relationship between age and income, for example, it might be interpreted as a one-year increase in age being associated with a $9,700 increase in earnings (the value for the age slope coefficient), on average.

Things get a little murkier and less precise when the researcher replaces age with, say, a variable measuring agreement on a 5-point scale. While most people would concur that such scales can suggest one's general level of agreement or disagreement with a statement, it is also clear that the distances between the 5 points on the scale are not necessarily uniform (as was the case with age in the previous example). In interpretation, it then becomes impossible to show that a one unit increase from 1 to 2 on the scale is the same as a one unit increase from 4 to 5, for example. Clearly, interpretation of models using non-continuous independent variables becomes much less precise. Nonetheless, modeling non-continuous independent variables can still provide results sufficient for meaningful interpretation. The lesson here is that the highest the level of measurement precision is the best when using multiple regression models. Lower levels of measurement are usually accompanied by greater measurement error — a problem we focus on later in this chapter.

There exists a widely used special case of independent variables that deserves mention. Many variables, such as sex or religion, are scaled as nominal level measurements — that is, there is no ordering to the scale and the intervals between points are meaningless. Given the previous discussion pointing to the desirable properties of continuously measured variables, one might conclude, erroneously, that such nominal level measurements are problematic in multiple regression models. On the contrary, variables of this type can easily be converted into very useful measures that are actually superior to ordinally measured variables such as the attitude scale in the above example.

Consider the nominally measured variable capturing respondents' sex. It might be coded 1 for males and 2 for females. Such variables can be recoded into "dummy" or "indicator" variables by assigning a score of 0 to one group and a score of 1 to the other group. For example, let's say we recoded the sex variable above so that 0 represented males and 1 represented females. Variables employing such a coding scheme "trick" the regression model into providing an estimate of the net difference (on the outcome variable) between the two groups — a very useful result. Dummy coding can be used to a variety of creative ends in multiple regression models and we encourage the interested reader to further explore the ins and outs of this important topic (see Hardy [1993] for a good introduction and overview).

Before leaving issues of measurement properties of the variables, it is important to point out that a key assumption of the regression model is that the variables are all measured without error.[1] This of course is a tall order. Providing that the error associated with the measurement of the variables in the model is "random" (i.e., not systematically associated with values on any variables in the model or observations in the data set), the result is that the effects observed will be smaller than if there was no measurement error. In other words, in the absence of perfectly measured variables, the model likely understates the true relationship between any two variables, and can lead to erroneous interpretations and conclusions.

Given the importance of these measurement issues, the researcher should

[1] Several assumptions associated with the use of multiple linear regression will be enumerated later in the chapter.

take great care to ensure that the variables being used are sufficient to yield meaningful interpretations from the regression results. The astute researcher is cognizant of these level of measurement issues as well as the actual distributions of the variables being included in the model. For example, too often we discover that respondents report only 2 or 3 values on a 5-point Likert scale — greatly diminishing the range of interpretation with such a variable and oftentimes rendering the variable meaningless in the analysis. For this reason it is crucial that the actual distribution of each variable in the model be carefully examined in a univariate fashion to ensure that the variables being used possess the measurement properties that are expected of them.[2]

Such preliminary examinations are an important first line of defense when developing the regression model and can be conducted using the data exploration tools available in packages such as SPSS or SAS. Tests of joint distributional properties, every bit as important as examining univariate characteristics but more complex, are usually conducted through an analysis of the "residuals" from the regression and are considered later in this chapter.

Model Specification

Aside from these concerns over the precision of measurement, the researcher must also take great care when specifying the regression model. It must be assumed that the theoretical model is correctly specified in the statistical model being tested. There are two key dimensions to this assumption that will be revisited later in this chapter. The first is that the relationship between the independent variables and the outcome is in fact a linear one. In other words, it is assumed that the theoretical relationship can be expressed with a straight line. If this assumption is theoretically untenable then the multiple linear regression model is inappropriate. While technically the assumption is that the outcome can be expressed as a linear combination of the independent variables, a first check of this assumption might be through a simple bivariate scatterplot of theoretically important independent variables and the outcome.

Assuming that the researcher can reasonably conclude that the theoretical relationship can be adequately expressed with a linear function, another dimension of model specification that must be considered concerns the inclusion of all theoretically important variables and the exclusion of those that are unimpor-

[2] It is not uncommon at this stage for researchers to focus on the normality of each of the variables in the model. The only variable assumed to be normally distributed is the error term, ε, something that cannot be assessed at this point in the analysis. The observed variables in the regression model can have almost any kind of distribution. However, we remind the reader to pay careful attention to these distributions to develop a sense of how well the scales are actually functioning.

tant. The estimated effects of variables included in the regression model will be biased upward to the degree that other theoretically important variables have been excluded — that is, the researcher runs the significant risk of attributing the effects of important variables not included in the model to those that are present. Put simply, the theoretical and empirical models must be in congruence. Any deviation between the two will result in biased estimates and potentially misleading statistics, results, and conclusions. It is the researcher's responsibility to know where the theoretical and empirical models diverge and to assess the likely impact of such inconsistencies.

With these issues of measurement and model specification in mind, in the next section we lay out the basic mathematical properties of the regression model. After this, we turn our attention to a number of common assumptions necessary for the appropriate use of the multiple linear regression model.

The Statistical Model

Multiple linear regression falls into a class of linear models that is based on the statistical model known as the General Linear Model:

$$Y = X\beta + \varepsilon$$

The specific multiple linear regression model is:

$$y = \beta_0 + \beta_1 x_{1i} + \beta_2 x_{2i} + \ldots + \beta_k x_{ki} + \varepsilon_i \qquad (i = 1, 2, \ldots, n)$$

The outcome, y, is generated by two components. The first component defines the "best" linear relationship between the outcome (y) and the predictors ($\beta_0 + \beta_1 x_{1i} + \beta_2 x_{2i} + \ldots + \beta_k x_{ki}$). For any given level of x, there is a corresponding "predicted" level of y, ($E[y] = \beta_0 + \beta_1 x_{1i} + \beta_2 x_{2i} + \ldots + \beta_k x_{ki}$). The second component is ε_i, the stochastic or random source of variation. This error term, ε_i, is a random variable for which outcomes are governed by a probability distribution and it has the following properties:[3]

1. $E(\varepsilon_i) = 0$, the mean of the error term is always equal to 0,
2. $Var(\varepsilon_i) = \sigma^2$, the variance of the error is the same at any level of x,
3. $Cov(\varepsilon_i,\varepsilon_j) = 0$, the error terms for any two observations are uncorrelated,
4. ε_i is normally distributed.

While there are a number of methods that could be used to estimate this model, the procedure used in the original development of multiple regression analysis and the one most commonly used now is the method of least squares (often referred to as ordinary least squares [OLS]; it is the default method in

[3] In the next section, we will direct attention to the importance of understanding the properties and characteristics of the error term.

most statistical software packages).[4] The OLS procedure estimates the regression coefficients (β) such that the sum of the squared errors ($\Sigma\varepsilon^2$) is minimized. The βs are population parameters and the estimated coefficients are denoted by b. Mathematically, the regression coefficient measures the change in the dependent variable (y) for each one-unit increase in x, holding all other independent variables constant. A more common interpretation is that the coefficient for the variable x represents the net effect of x on y, and the magnitude of the coefficient depends on the metric in which the independent variable is measured. The intercept of the equation (β_0) most generally does not have substantive meaning because it represents the value of the dependent variable y when the value on each of the x is 0.

Most software programs also calculate standardized coefficient betas (not to be confused with the population parameters, βs). Betas represent the regression coefficients that would be produced had all variables been standardized. Thus, it is as if all variables were standardized, and they each have the same metric. Since the independent variables can be considered to have a common metric, the relative magnitude of the betas can be compared, unlike the bs.

Once the βs are estimated, the total sum-of-squares which constitutes the variability in the dependent measure can be decomposed into two parts: regression sum-of-squares (explained) and residual (error) sum-of-squares. These sums-of-squares are the basis for the statistical tests.

Tests of Significance

The omnibus test for significance of regression is an F-test that determines whether there is a linear relationship between the dependent variable y and any of the independent variables. The null and alternative hypotheses for this F test are

$$\text{Ho: } \beta_1 = \beta_2 = \ldots = \beta_k = 0$$
$$\text{Ha: } \beta_j \neq 0 \text{ for at least 1 } j$$

Rejection of the null hypothesis implies that at least one of the independent variables has a significant relationship to the dependent variable in the presence of the other variables in the model. This F-test is simply the ratio of the mean square regression divided by the mean square residual:

$$F = MSreg/MSres$$

When the F is significant, we then examine tests on the coefficients of the

[4] Our purposes in this chapter are not to give a thorough mathematical presentation of multiple regression complete with matrix algebra. We instead focus on the interpretation of the statistical results. The reader interested in the mathematics of regression is referred to any standard text on multiple regression for the mathematical formulae.

independent variables to determine which variables are contributing to the explanation of variance and have an effect on the dependent variable. These tests of the coefficients are t-tests and are equivalent to an F-test on the change in the amount of variance explained in the dependent variable that would result from adding the individual independent variable to an equation containing all other independent variables.

The ratio of the sum-of-squares regression to the sum-of-squares total is the coefficient of determination (R^2) and gives the proportion of the total variation in y that is explained by or attributable to the set of independent variables (most basically, the R^2 represents the square of the correlation between the observed and predicted values of y). This is referred to as the R-square and is an indicator of the model fit, ranging from 0 indicating no fit to 1.0 indicating a perfect fit.

$$R^2 = SSreg/SStotal$$

Many researchers attempt to decompose the proportion of variance explained by the set of independent variables into components uniquely attributable to each independent variable. The only situation in which this is possible is when all independent variables are uncorrelated, which is almost never the case. Numerous approaches have been developed attempting this decomposition, and depending upon which approach is taken, variance attributed to individual variables differs substantially. We refer readers to Pedhazur (1982) for a complete discussion of the difficulties in attempts at variance partitioning, and we agree with the eminent sociologist Otis Dudley Duncan who recommended dispensing with such efforts altogether:

> The simplest recommendation — one which saves both work and worry — is to eschew altogether the task of dividing up R^2 into unique causal components. In a strict sense, it just cannot be done, even though many sociologists, psychologists, and other quixotic persons cannot be persuaded to forego the attempt (1975, p. 65).

Substantive Importance vs. Statistical Significance

When statistical significance is found, one must then address the issue of the substantive importance of the findings. It is commonly known that large sample sizes contribute to the likelihood of finding statistically significant effects in any type of statistical analysis, and we often use survey data that represent responses by hundreds if not thousands of subjects. It is the researcher's responsibility to determine what magnitude of effect is substantively meaningful, given the nature of the data gathered and the question being addressed. Some authors seek to give guidelines for criteria of importance, but an effect of a certain magnitude that is important in one setting is not necessarily important in other settings. For example, Cohen (1977) suggests that an R^2 of .01 could be viewed as a small, meaningful effect, but few would agree that explaining only 1% of the variance in the dependent variable using a collection of independent variables is of any theoretical importance. Comparing the R^2 obtained in a study to R^2s reported in similar studies and careful consideration of the magnitude of the betas (standardized coefficients) can help place substantive importance on findings. Betas of .05 or less can hardly be argued to be meaningful given that this represents a 5/100 standard deviation change in the dependent variable for a 1 standard deviation change in the independent variable holding other effects constant.

THREATS TO THE UTILITY OF MULTIPLE REGRESSION

As with most inferential techniques, several assumptions must be made when using multiple linear regression models. Failure of the data to meet these assumptions undermines the validity of any results produced by the statistical model and may suggest that the multiple linear regression model is inappropriate for the data. While there exists general confusion about which assumptions are most appropriate for linear regression models, there does exist some consensus that there are several assumptions that can more or less impact the accuracy of results produced by the statistical model. We have already introduced the first two of these assumptions, specification and measurement, in an earlier section of the chapter. Violation of either of these two assumptions compromises the accuracy of the slope estimates from the multiple regression model. Another set of assumptions relates to the characteristics of the error term, ε_i (see assumptions numbered 3-6 in Table 1). Violation of this set of assumptions impacts estimates of the standard errors associated with the slope estimates and compromises subsequent tests of significance.

Admittedly, it is unlikely that each of the assumptions in Table 1 can be fully met and we therefore point out to the reader that the violation of these assumptions will always be a matter of degree. It is the responsibility of the researcher to gauge the degree to which the tenability of these assumptions encourage or discourage the use of the multiple regression model. With this in mind, the following section briefly considers each assumption, its potential impact on estimates produced by the model, and ways to determine the degree to which the assumption is met.

Table 1: Key assumptions associated with the use of multiple linear regression

1. Specification (linearity and independent variables):	Simply put, we assume the outcome can be best expressed as a linear function of the independent variables plus some error term and that all of the relevant independent variables are included in the model. This assumption was addressed in an earlier section of this chapter;
2. No measurement error:	We assume that each of the independent variables in the model is measured precisely;
3. Mean independence:	We assume that the average value of the error term is always equal to zero and that this value does not depend on the independent variables;
4. Homoscedasticity:	We assume that the variance of the error term is the same across all levels of the independent variables;
5. Uncorrelated errors:	We assume that the value of the error term for any one observation is not influenced by the value of the error term for other observations in the data set; and
6. Normally distributed errors:	The overall distribution of the error term is normally distributed.

Testing These Assumptions

Despite the groundwork that was laid in an earlier section of this chapter, encouraging the researcher to get to know the data, rarely does the researcher know in advance if the multiple linear regression model is appropriate. The only way such a determination can be made with any certainty is through a post hoc analysis of the model's residual — that random part that is left over after the model has been fit (ε_i in mathematical terms). More concretely, the residual is the difference between the value (y) predicted by a model for case i and the actual observed value for the case i. A better fitting model will yield a smaller aggregate residual than a model that fits less well (these residuals are in fact the basis for the "least-squares" in OLS).

Many regression assumptions can be better understood and tested through a relatively simple residual analysis. Any mainstream statistical package used in the social sciences (e.g., SAS, SPSS, or Stata) will provide an impressive and often overwhelming array of features to analyze OLS regression residuals. Below we outline several cursory examinations that should be conducted with any multiple linear regression analysis. Manuals accompanying most statistics packages provide the details of carrying out such analyses as well as additional tests and interpretations that might be useful. We expect the interested reader to become familiar with this documentation. While the first two assumptions have been considered earlier in this chapter, we revisit that earlier treatment to help establish a context for our focus on the properties of the error term in assumptions 3-6.

Assumption 1: Model Specification
Consequence of Violation: estimated coefficients will be subject to bias.

Earlier in the chapter when the assumption of linearity was first introduced it was suggested that a good place to start thinking about this assumption was with bivariate scatterplots of each key independent variable and the outcome, y. Of course, a shortcoming of such a rudimentary analysis is that the outcome, y, is presumed to be a linear function of the *combination* of independent variables — something that cannot be readily tested through bivariate considerations alone. Now armed with residuals, the researcher has a much more useful and accurate way to test the linearity assumption.[5]

Such an analysis, in the aggregate, is a relatively straightforward matter in most mainstream statistics packages. Most packages provide the researcher with the option of plotting the values predicted by the model with the residual associated with each prediction. If the relationship between the dependent and independent variables can be realistically expressed as a linear function, then this plot of the predicted values and residuals will lack any visible pattern. That is, the model will fit equally well across all predicted values, with the residuals randomly distributed in a band around 0 (the mean value of the residuals). Any systematic variations between the predicted values and residuals should suggest a violation of the linearity assumption.

Assumption 2: Measurement
Consequence of Violation: estimated slope coefficients can be biased toward zero.

As outlined earlier in the chapter, few variables in the social sciences are measured with a high degree of precision. As a result, this assumption is always compromised to some degree and the estimated slope coefficients are therefore smaller than they would be if the underlying variable could be perfectly measured. For single variable measures such as age or income, the researcher must rely on theory and intuition as gauges of likely precision. However, it is worth bearing in mind the earlier discussion concerning the precision of various levels

[5] Remedies for violations of the assumptions associated with multiple linear regression models are numerous and often complex. Although we occasionally offer an example of the simpler remedies for some of these violations, space limitations of this chapter prohibit a responsible and representative treatment of most of these remedies. We therefore refer the interested reader to detailed yet accessible considerations of these remedies that are found in many software manuals or texts such as Neter, Wasserman, and Kutner (1985).

of measurement. "Hard" measures such as age (calculated from reported year of birth) are arguably more reliable than soft measures such as agreement (measured on a Likert scale, for example). For composite scales, the researcher can use reliability measures such as Cronbach's alpha to get a sense of how precise the measurement really is. There is an entire field concerned with measurement issues and the reader is referred to varied but representative works such as Lord and Novick (1968), Nunnally (1978), or Bohrnstedt (1983), for more detailed treatments of the subject. For purposes of the current discussion, we call attention to the importance of this issue and point out that its neglect can lead to grossly misleading interpretations and conclusions.

Assumption 3: Mean Independence
Consequence of Violation: estimated slope coefficients can be biased toward zero.

While the first two assumptions deal with issues of model specification and measurement, these issues manifest themselves in the structure of the error term of the model. That is, variable mis-measurement and mis-specification leave their imprints on the error term and lead to violations of assumptions required for the appropriate use of the multiple regression model. While some statisticians (e.g., Lewis-Beck, 1980) argue that the assumption of mean independence is only of concern when the intercept estimates are important (rarely the case in the social sciences), others point out that the effects of all causes of y that are incorrectly omitted from the model are lumped into the error term, ε_i. Should any of these incorrectly omitted independent variables be correlated with other independent variables in the model, this would result in a correlation between the independent variables and the error term itself — a clear violation of the mean independence assumption. Similarly, to the extent that measurement error exists, this is also lumped into the error term, ε_i. This measurement error impacts the measured value of the independent variables in the model and therefore also correlates with the error term, ε_i. Again, a problem. There is no easy way to measure the degree of violation of the assumption of mean independence. As before, the reader is encouraged to carefully consider the congruence between theoretical and empirical models and to give careful thought to the measurement of variables operationalizing the theoretical model.

Assumption 4: Homoscedasticity
Consequence of Violation: estimated standard errors likely to be biased.

The plots of the predicted and residual values used to test the linearity assumption can also be used to test the homoscedasticity assumption — that is, that the error (as expressed by the residual values) is the same across all levels of the independent variables. In instances where this assumption does not hold, the spread of the residuals will either increase or decrease with the predicted values of y. For example, predictions of student performance (y) may, for some reason, be more accurate for students from lower SES backgrounds (x) than for those from higher SES backgrounds. That is, there will be more error in prediction for students from high SES backgrounds than those from low SES backgrounds. This prediction error (residual) plotted against predicted performance or family SES will fan out from one end of the graph to another, illustrating the heteroscedastic (as opposed to homoscedastic) nature of the error.

Violation of this assumption often results in standard errors being biased upwards, thereby decreasing the likelihood of rejecting a false null hypothesis — that is, all else being equal, the researcher will be less likely to declare a given coefficient as statistically significant. There are a number of remedies for heteroscedasticity, including weighted least squares regression techniques or the use of estimates of robust standard errors that some packages produce. The reader is again referred to the manuals accompanying specific software packages to learn more about these remedies.

Assumption 5: Uncorrelated Errors
Consequence of Violation: estimated standard errors likely to be biased downward.

We took time earlier in the chapter to call the reader's attention to simple random sampling assumptions undergirding multiple linear regression models. Such a sampling scheme rarely produces a sample in which the responses from any two observations might be systematically related. However, when time or clustering becomes part of the sampling scheme it becomes very possible that either 1) observations are correlated across time points (e.g., faculty attitudes across the semester or year), or 2) observations are correlated within sampling clusters (e.g., students within schools). Such samples will often yield observations that influence one another systematically and compromise the assumption of uncorrelated errors in the regression model. The consequence of such a violation is very similar to that of the presence of heteroscedasticity, but the bias in estimated standard errors will always be downward. That is, when modeling data with correlated error terms, the researcher will be more likely to mistakenly declare a coefficient significant when in fact it is not.

If time is the dimension of concern here, then a simple test for "serial-correlation" can be conducted using most software packages. Perhaps the most accessible of these tests is the Durbin-Watson autocorrelation statistic that looks for similarities among surrounding time-ordered observations in a data set. If the model yields correlated disturbance terms, the researcher should find a more appropriate "time-series" or "event-history" technique (e.g., see Ostrom, 1990, or Allison, 1985).

If a concern exists relating to the clustering of observations in the sample, then a separate set of tests and remedies, unfortunately less accessible, needs to be applied. See Thomas and Heck (2001) for a full consideration of these issues and remedies.

In the absence of either of these sampling conditions this assumption is less likely than the others to create problems for the researcher.

Assumption 6: Normally Distributed Errors
Consequence of Violation: varies by sample size.

The final assumption we consider in this section has to do with the distribution of the error term itself. Given a sufficient sample size, say over 100 (assuming fewer than five independent variables in the equation), this is the least critical of the assumptions associated with the use of multiple linear regression. When using smaller samples this assumption is certainly more important as it speaks directly to the researcher's ability to use the t-distribution for significance testing. With larger samples, however, the central-limit theorem overrides the need for normally distributed errors in the sample. There are several ways to test this assumption. Perhaps the two most straightforward are through the use of residual plots. In most software packages one can easily produce a histogram of the residuals to visually assess the distribution. Another useful depiction is realized through a "cumulative probability plot" available in many statistics packages. Alternatively, the researcher could save the residual scores and have the software package compute descriptive scores for the skewness and kurtosis of the residual distribution. In the worst case scenario where the researcher is using a sample of less than 100 and the distribution of residuals suggests non-normality, it is possible to transform the outcome variable by taking its natural logarithm, in the case of a positively skewed residual distribution, or squaring it in the case of a negatively skewed distribution.

In summary, while multiple linear regression is a relatively robust technique there are a number of assumptions that when compromised can degrade the utility of the method. Some of these assumptions are more crucial than others. Model specification and measurement issues are critical as are other assumptions concerning mean independence and homoscedasticity. Less critical but still worthy of the researcher's attention are assumptions dealing with uncorrelated errors and the distribution of the error term itself. It is highly unlikely that any model used in the behavioral sciences could meet these assumptions perfectly. However, slope estimates and hypothesis tests will be compromised to the degree that certain of these assumptions are abused. The researcher should always have a sense of where these weaknesses lie in the model and qualify any interpretations or conclusions accordingly.

OTHER CONSIDERATIONS

Outliers

Cases with exceptional values on either the dependent or independent variables can have dramatic effects on results produced by the multiple linear regression model. As mentioned earlier in the chapter, a good first line of defense against such exceptional influences is through the close examination of initial descriptive statistics and the distribution of the variables included in the model. Observations with extreme values should always be noted and carefully considered for removal from the multiple linear regression analysis. Another check for such influences is found through an analysis of the model's residuals. A residual analysis goes beyond simple univariate characteristics of the variables included in the model and instead provides a consideration of the joint effects of these variables. Highly unusual cases — those with extreme values or unlikely combinations of values — should be considered for removal from the analysis.[6]

Cases with extreme values, or outliers, can be easily identified on a plot of residuals (again, available in most mainstream statistical software packages). These cases will appear on the borders of the plot and most software packages provide ways by which the researcher can identify the offending case in order to conduct further analyses in hopes of remedying the problem. This type of analysis only considers the residual — that is, the predicted value minus the observed value — and therefore provides information about the fit of the outcome variable with the predictor variables. Ill-fitting cases will have larger residuals that often suggest the need for further consideration of extreme observations.

In addition to looking directly at the residuals, it is important to identify

[6] While the presence of obvious outliers erodes the explanatory power of the model and potentially leads to less than accurate estimates, the removal of these cases will admittedly create artificialities in the data. Often researchers faced with the removal of outlying observations will either report two sets of estimates (with and without the outlying case[s]), transform the variable to eliminate the problem, or gather more observations. However this problem is handled, it is incumbent upon the researcher to acknowledge any alteration of the dataset.

cases that have extreme values on one or more independent variables and the outcome variable — for cases with extreme values on the independent variables can have a dramatic impact on the outcome. Extreme values on the independent variables, assuming they are accompanied by extreme values on the outcome variable, would be potentially masked from detection in an analysis of the residuals. One way to locate potentially problematic observations that may not appear on a residual plot is by a measure of the distance of cases from the average values of all the independent variables in the model. This measure is known as the *Mahalanobis' Distance* and is readily available in most statistical packages. As with large residuals, extreme values on this measure often suggest the need for further analysis and consideration of the extreme observations.

Another way to think about the impact of extreme observations is directly in terms of the influence they may have on the estimates of the parameters in the multiple regression model. *Cook's Distance* is a very useful measure of influence and is readily available in most software packages. This measure provides the researcher with an index of the impact on the residuals of removing a particular observation from the data set. Relatively large Cook's Distance values suggest highly influential observations that may be disproportionately pulling the model's estimates in their direction. More often than not, cases with high Cook's Distance values will also have high values on the Mahalanobis' Distance measure introduced above. Again, observations with high values on these measures often suggest the need for further analysis and consideration of the offending cases.

The Special Case of Extreme Multicollinearity

While the multiple linear regression model has been shown to be robust in terms of modest violations to the assumptions outlined in the previous section, there is an additional assumption, a mathematical requirement actually, that must be met when using this model: the absence of perfect multicollinearity. If any of the independent variables in the model is perfectly correlated with another independent variable (or a linear combination of other independent variables) it is impossible to arrive at a solution for the model. And while a unique solution to the model can always be identified in the absence of perfect multicollinearity, the presence of very strong relationships among the independent variables (i.e., extreme multicollinearity) can create serious problems in interpreting the regression results.

As with all behavioral science research, most regression analyses in educational research include independent variables that are correlated to various degrees. For example, many of the studies of college students make use of independent variables such as academic involvement, social involvement, and perceptions of the college environment to explain learning outcomes. Theories explicating these relationships often specify theoretically important correlations among these constructs and accordingly, many of the variables used to operationalize these constructs are significantly correlated. Likewise, regression research focusing on faculty frequently includes independent variables such as gender, academic discipline, academic rank, and years of service, and many of these variables are likely to be correlated. Multicollinearity is often theoretically important and multiple linear regression performs well as long as the level of multicollinearity among the independent variables is not excessive (a relative term that we will consider subsequently).

Although an explanation of the statistics underlying multiple regression with correlated independent variables is beyond the scope of this chapter, a basic understanding of the logic of multicollinearity is important. Figures 1 — 3 depict possible relationships among the independent and dependent variables in a multiple regression model. Circles are used to represent the independent and dependent variables, and areas of overlap represent the correlations among the

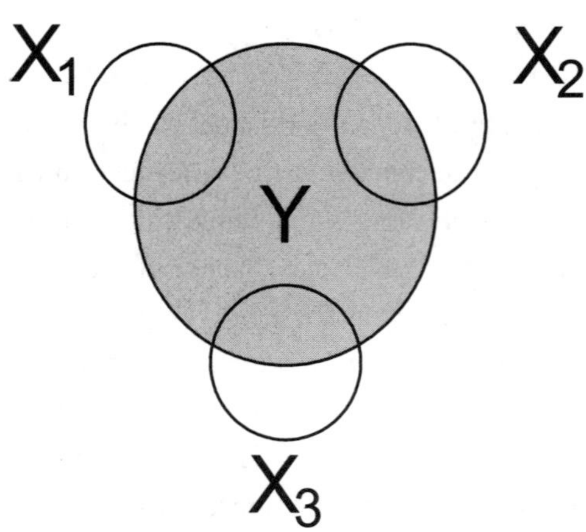

Figure 1. An Ideal Mathematical Situation — Uncorrelated Independent Variables

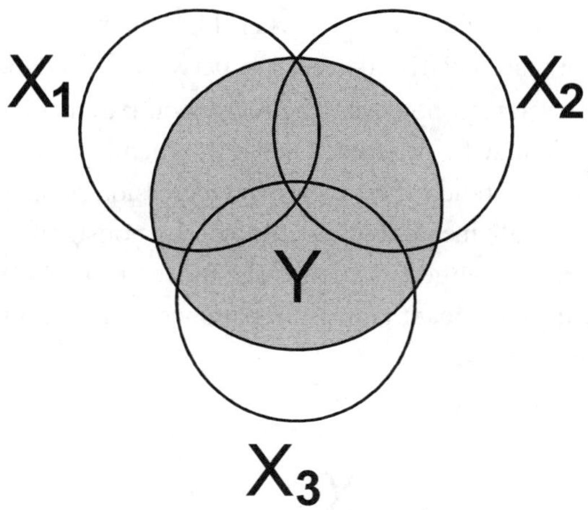

Figure 2. A Typical Situation — Moderately Correlated Independent Variables

variables. In the simplest situation, mathematically speaking (see Figure 1), the independent variables (x_i) are correlated with the dependent variable (y), but they are not correlated with each other. Estimation of the regression parameters is straightforward. In fact, in the absence of intercorrelations among the independent variables, the standardized regression parameters (β_i) will be identical to the correlations between the independent variables and the dependent variable (r_{xy}). While mathematically straightforward, rarely will such a condition be theoretically tenable or practically possible in the behavioral sciences.

Figure 2 depicts a more typical situation in higher-education research. In this instance, the three independent variables are correlated with the dependent variable. However, they are also correlated with each other. Estimation of the regression parameters for this model is possible, but the standardized regression parameters will not be equivalent to the correlations between the independent and dependent variables. In this case the standardized regression parameters will be less than the correlations between the independent and dependent variables.

The situation depicted in Figure 3 involves a high degree of multicollinearity among the independent variables. Although estimation of the model may still be possible, interpretation of the results of the multiple regression analysis will be problematic.[7] In situations where there is high multicollinearity among the independent variables, there will be marked inconsistencies between some, or all, of the regression parameters and the correlations between the independent and dependent variables. For example, when high multicollinearity is present there may be a moderate positive correlation between an independent variable and the dependent variable; however, the regression parameters (b, β) for that independent variable may be negative. Likewise, when high multicollinearity is present in the data, the standard errors for the regression parameters tend to be very large, and seemingly meaningful results will be nonsignificant. In fact, the presence of an unusually large F-value for the model as a whole, coupled with few or no statistically significant regression parameters, is usually a good indicator of high multicollinearity.[8]

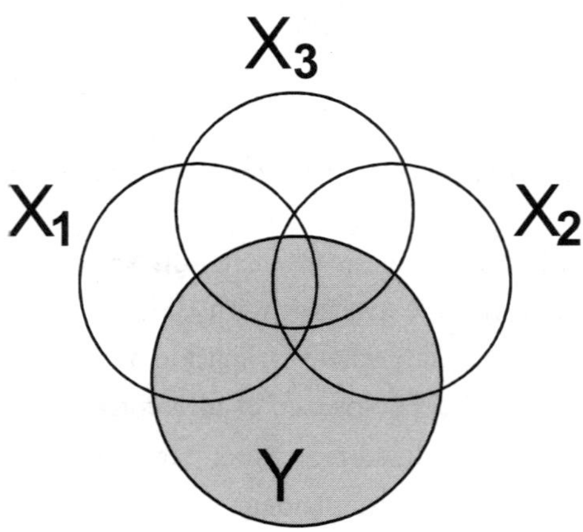

Figure 3. A Problematic Situation — Highly Correlated Independent Variables

[7] Again, when one of the independent variables is a linear combination (i.e., a weighted sum) of other independent variables in the model, perfect multicollinearity exists and estimation of the model is not possible.
[8] The inclusion of interaction terms (not covered in this chapter but frequently used in behavioral science research) can also create conditions of excessive multicollinearity, particularly if the interactions are cross products of two variables that are included in the regression model. Interaction terms will tend to have strong correlations with the "main effects" from which they were created. As a result, the regression parameters and significance tests of the regression parameters will not accurately represent the relationships of the interaction terms to the dependent variable. Researchers interested in including interactions in multiple regression models would be well advised to use R^2-change statistics to evaluate the importance of the interactions and to avoid attempts to interpret the regression parameters.

Table 2: Correlations, Means, and Standard Deviations for ACT Scores and First Year Grade Point Average

	ACT Composite	ACT English	ACT Math	ACT Reading	ACT Science	FY GPA
ACT Composite	1.00					
ACT English	0.84	1.00				
ACT Math	0.77	0.54	1.00			
ACT Reading	0.83	0.65	0.42	1.00		
ACT Science	0.82	0.54	0.59	0.60	1.00	
FYGPA	0.39	0.36	0.35	0.28	0.29	1.00
Means	25.80	25.94	25.03	26.59	25.01	2.92
SD	3.48	4.15	4.32	4.79	3.83	0.76

A concrete example may be helpful in understanding the effects of high multicollinearity in multiple regression analyses. Assume that a researcher wants to learn how well students' grades during their first year of college can be explained by their entering academic abilities. The dependent variable in the study is first-year college grade point average, and the independent variables are the English, Mathematics, Reading, and Science Reasoning subscores on the *ACT Assessment* examination, as well as the *ACT Assessment* composite score. For this study, the researcher regresses first-year grade point average on all five *ACT Assessment* scores using data from 1020 students.

Examining the correlations among independent and dependent variables is always a good place to start in understanding multiple regression results, and these correlations can also be useful in identifying potential problems with multicollinearity. Table 2 presents the correlations among the six variables from the hypothetical study. It is important to note that all five of the *ACT Assessment* scores have low to moderate positive correlations with first-year grade point average, ranging from a low of 0.28 for the reading subscore to a high of 0.39 for the composite score. The correlations among the four *ACT Assessment* subscores are also moderate and positive, with all but one of the correlations ranging from 0.54 to 0.65. The *ACT Assessment* composite score has large, positive correlations with all four ACT subscores, ranging from 0.77 to 0.84. While these correlations are quite large and raise suspicion, none is sufficiently large ($r_{xy} > 0.90$) to suggest clear problems of high multicollinearity in the regression model. As the reader will see, problems with high multicollinearity become apparent when the multiple regression analysis is performed.

Table 3. Results for the Regression of First-Year Grade Point Average on ACT Scores

Effect	b	Standard Error	t	p	β
Intercept	0.714	0.165	4.321	0.000	
ACT Composite	-0.028	0.081	-0.348	0.728	-0.129
ACT English	0.044	0.022	2.042	0.041	0.243
ACT Math	0.043	0.021	2.042	0.041	0.246
ACT Reading	0.012	0.021	0.584	0.559	0.077
ACT Science	0.015	0.021	0.584	0.488	0.075

Table 3 displays the results of the multiple regression analysis. What is most striking about these results is that the regression parameters for the composite score are negative, whereas the correlation between ACT composite scores and first-year grade point averages is positive. In fact, composite scores are more strongly correlated with first-year grades than are any of the ACT subscores. It is also important to note that while the result for the overall regression model is statistically significant ($F = 40.59$; $df = 5, 1014$; $p < 0.001$), regression parameters for only two of the ACT scores (English and Mathematics) are statistically significant. Moreover, these parameters are significant at the $p < 0.05$ level, but not at the $p < 0.01$ level. As previously noted, these results strongly suggest that the independent variables in the regression model are highly collinear. What is not clear, either from the correlations or the regression results, is the locus of the problem.

Most mainstream statistical analysis packages, such as SAS, SPSS, or Stata, provide a variety of techniques for detecting multicollinearity. Two closely related tests of multicollinearity are the tolerance and the variance inflation factor (VIF). Software packages calculate these statistics by first regressing each independent variable on the other independent variables in the regression model. For example, in the first step in calculating tolerance and VIF statistics for the *ACT Assessment* composite score variable, software programs regress composite scores on the four ACT subscores. The proportion of the variance in composite scores that is explained by the ACT subscores (R^2) is then used to calculate both the tolerance and VIF statistics that are ultimately reported by the statistics program. Tolerance is defined as:

$$T = (1 - R^2)$$

Whereas the VIF is the reciprocal of the tolerance:

$$VIF = 1 / (1 - R^2)$$

As a general rule, tolerances that are less than or equal to 0.10 can be seen as in-

Table 4. Results of the Multicollinearity Tests

Effect	Tolerance	VIF	Condition Index
Intercept			1.000
ACT Composite	0.006	166.229	262.787
ACT English	0.057	17.179	19.978
ACT Math	0.058	17.590	18.035
ACT Reading	0.047	21.244	23.667
ACT Science	0.071	14.179	27.870

dicators of high or extreme multicollinearity. Conversely, VIF statistics in excess of 10.0 are indicators of this same problematic condition. It is important to note that these thresholds are "rules of thumb," rather than absolute criteria for determining whether multicollinearity exists. Tolerance values that are less than 0.10 and VIF values greater than 10.0 may not indicate the existence of high multicollinearity. Researchers should always examine correlations and parameter estimates, as well as the standard errors of parameter estimates, when evaluating multicollinearity. Counterintuitive or theoretically inconsistent results are often signs that problematic levels of multicollinearity may exist as well as the presence of betas greater than 1.

Table 4 presents the results of the tolerance and VIF tests for the model involving the regression of first-year grades on all five ACT scores. In the table, all of the tolerance and VIF statistics exceed their thresholds, indicating that the degree of multicollinearity is a problem. In particular, the tolerance and VIF statistics for *ACT Assessment* composite scores are extreme (0.006 and 166.229, respectively). In fact, the tolerance statistic for composite scores indicates that 99.4% of the variance in composite scores can be explained by ACT subscores.

Actually regressing the independent variables on each other, rather than simply relying on the results provided by a statistical package, can help pinpoint the sources of high multicollinearity in a regression model. For example, regressing composite scores on ACT subscores reveals that all four subscores contribute significantly to the explanation of composite scores. Standardized regression parameters for the English, Mathematics, Reading, and Science Reasoning subscores are 0.31, 0.30, 0.34, and 0.27, respectively. These findings indicate that the observed multicollinearity problem is a product of the relationship of composite scores to a combination of all four ACT subscores.

Another statistical technique that can be used to assess the degree of multicollinearity in the data is the Condition Index. The Condition Index is defined as the square root of the ratio of the largest eigenvalue for a regression parameter to the eigenvalue of the regression parameter for the independent variable being tested.

$$CI_i = (\lambda_{max} / \lambda_i)^{1/2}$$

The Condition Index and VIF score, taken together, provide a powerful way to detect potentially problematic levels of multicollinearity. Both of these statistics are easily produced using most mainstream software packages. A frequently cited standard for detecting potential multicollinearity problems comes from Belsey, Kuh, and Welsch (1980) who suggest that variables with Condition Indexes in excess of 30 *and* VIF scores above 5 should be treated with caution. The number of Condition Indexes that are above the threshold indicates the number of linear relationships in the data. Again, these values are intended to be a "rule of thumb," rather than an absolute standard for assessing multicollinearity. In the hypothetical study, each of the subscores has a relatively high VIF value but the Condition Indexes for the four ACT subscores do not indicate the presence of problematic levels of multicollinearity (i.e., they are below the thresholds suggested above). In contrast both the VIF score (166.229) and the Condition Index for the composite scores (262.79) are well above the extreme multicollinearity threshold. Extreme values such as these should always catch the researcher's attention.

Because the tests for multicollinearity indicate that the inclusion of the composite score and ACT subscores is problematic, the prudent course of action is to eliminate the composite score from the model. Bear in mind however that, in reality, the theoretical model may prohibit the deletion of a variable from the statistical model. While the researcher's alternatives are limited in such cases, it is possible use different modeling procedures (e.g., ridge-regression) in an attempt to get around this problem (see Belsey, Kuh, & Welsch [1980] or Chatterjee & Price [1977] for excellent discussions of these and other alternatives).

Table 5 presents the regression results for a model in which first-year grade point averages are regressed on the four ACT subscores. The results clearly

Table 5. Results for the Regression of First-Year Grade Point Average on ACT Subscores

Effect	b	Std. Err.	t	p	β	Tol.	VIF	CI
Intercept	0.706	0.164	4.314	0.000				1.000
ACT English	0.037	0.007	4.980	0.000	0.204	0.490	2.040	18.506
ACT Math	0.036	0.007	5.486	0.000	0.206	0.583	1.715	16.494
ACT Reading	0.005	0.006	0.821	0.412	0.033	0.496	2.016	21.587
ACT Science	0.008	0.008	0.991	0.322	0.040	0.501	1.997	25.437

show that multicollinearity is not a problem in this model. Tolerance, VIF, and condition index values are not close to the thresholds indicating the presence of dangerously high multicollinearity. Likewise, the standard errors of the regression parameters are quite similar. One surprising result is that, despite the fact that Reading and Science Reasoning subscores are significantly correlated with first-year grades, the regression parameters for these variables are not statistically significant.

In order to understand this result, it is important to remember what the regression parameters represent. These parameters represent the relationship between the independent and dependent variables, after accounting for the effects of the other independent variables in the model. In the current analysis, the relationship between the Reading subscore and first-year grades is subsumed by the relationships of both ACT English and Mathematics subscores to first-year grades. The same is true for the ACT Science Reasoning subscore. In effect, the results presented in Table 5 indicate that including the Reading and Science Reasoning subscores in the regression model does not add to the explanatory power of the model beyond what is provided by the *ACT Assessment* English and Mathematics subscores. In effect, the strength of the relationships in the model suppresses the effects of Reading and Science Reasoning subscores on first-year grades.

We again return to our mantra that theory should play an important role in the modeling process. Theory is essential in identifying and understanding potentially problematic levels of multicollinearity in regression models. Researchers familiar with the literature on the prediction of college grades using standardized test scores would, most likely, be aware that the *ACT Assessment* composite score is a weighted linear combination of the test's four subscores. As a result, they would not make the mistake of including the composite score and the subscores in a multiple regression analysis. An understanding of theory and literature is also important in less obvious situations. Theory and research should guide researchers' expectations about relationships among independent variables, as well as relationships between independent and dependent variables. When results run counter to expectations, researchers who are familiar with the literature will have some basis for interpreting the results and identifying possible sources of problematic levels of multicollinearity. When results run counter to expectations, and multicollinearity is not a problem, researchers would be well advised to examine the measures they are using and to ask whether those measures accurately and appropriately represent the underlying constructs they are intended to portray.

SUMMARY AND CONCLUSION

In this chapter, we have attempted to call attention to some of the theoretical and technical issues that we feel have been too often neglected in multiple linear regression studies. What we have not addressed above is a question frequently asked prior to the conceptualization of the multiple regression model: How large does my sample need to be? We save this question for the end because its answer impacts all facets of the regression model considered in this chapter. This question is especially important since the size of the sample used in a regression study impacts the stability of results, attempts to meet the assumptions, and appropriateness of the statistical tests. Cohen and Cohen (1983) provide tables and formulae to assist the researcher in power analyses and determining adequate sample size for a study given a specified number of independent variables and an *a priori* estimate of effect size. Others give "rules of thumb" in terms of number of subjects per independent variable. For example, Stevens (1996) suggests that *generally* about 15 subjects per variable are adequate for reliable results that would cross-validate well. Hinkle, Wiersma, and Jurs (1998) argue that a sample size of greater than 100 is needed for five or fewer independent variables but offer no suggestion for larger numbers of variables. They note, however, that as the number of variables approaches the number of subjects the R^2 becomes artificially inflated. Regardless of the recommendation adopted, we urge researchers to pay careful attention to the sample size issue, but remember also that extremely large sample sizes can result in minuscule effects being statistically significant.[9]

This brings us again to the issue of substantive importance, and it is in the substance of the findings of a study that its worth and value are found. However, without the careful attention to research design and the appropriate applications of methods, findings are of little substantive importance regardless of the magnitude and statistical significance of results. The validity of findings becomes even more crucial when policy recommendations are an outgrowth or purpose of the study. Policy recommendations based on questionable research methods lead to poor and often incorrect policy which, when discovered to be incorrect, can be not only exceedingly embarrassing for the researcher but also very costly to remedy. Poor research also leads to comments such as that made by Hechinger (cited in Pedhazur, 1982), who as education editor for the *New*

[9] Researchers applying sample weights to correct for disproportionate sampling methods should always pay careful attention to the effect of these weights on the effective size of the sample. Application of raw weights supplied with many secondary data sets will artificially inflate the sample size and result in almost every coefficient becoming statistically significant in a multiple regression analysis. Researchers contemplating the use of sample weights are encouraged to see Thomas & Heck (2001) for suggestions on their proper use in regression models.

York Times suggested that social scientific research should be ignored altogether by policy makers. Pedhazur goes on to note that such actions "further erode the support for social science research as a means of studying social phenomena and destroy what little credibility it has as a guide for social policy" (p. 267). These statements, made twenty years ago, are as applicable today as they were then.

However, even the most carefully conducted study is less useful unless presented in a manner that allows readers to fully understand all aspects of the analysis. A full and complete description of the data used is crucial. In order for readers to adequately understand the characteristics of the sample used and to accurately interpret the results presented, they need a clear understanding of how the variables were measured and/or constructed. To that end, the researcher should always provide the estimated means, standard deviations, and correlations for all variables used in the analyses. Failure to present this information is equivalent to a researcher utilizing analysis of variance procedures and failing to provide group means and standard deviations. It is also important to present the complete results of the regression analyses — that is, a presentation of the standardized and unstandardized coefficients for *all* variables used in the regression model. While the researcher may be only interested in the effects of particular variables in the model, the reader should have the opportunity to examine the estimates for the full model.

As noted in the beginning of this chapter, our intent has been to refocus attention on several important and often neglected issues associated with the use of multiple linear regression models. We have done so with the assumption that the reader has a general working knowledge of regression techniques and have consequently omitted much of the mathematical and technical details of the development of regression procedures. Readers who have need for more technical details on the issues we have presented or for "fix-ups" for violations of assumptions are urged to go to the many references included herein. We have in this chapter sought to remind researchers of the need for,

(1) strong attention to theory in the development of the conceptual model,

(2) careful consideration of theory, measurement, and data structure in the development of variables used in specification of the empirical model, and

(3) examination of the key threats to the utility of multiple regression.

Careful attention to these points will better ensure the more accurate and responsible application of multiple linear regression in higher education research.

REFERENCES

Astin, A. W.. (1993). *What matters in college.* San Francisco: Jossey-Bass.

Allison, P D. (1985). *Event history analysis: Regression for longitudinal event data.* Thousand Oaks: Sage Publications, Inc.

Belsey, D. A., Kuh, E. & Welsch, R. E. (1980). *Regression diagnostics: identifying influential data and sources of multicollinearity.* New York: Wiley.

Bohrnstedt, G. W. (1983). Measurement. In P. H. Rossi, J. D. Wright, & A. B. Anderson (Eds.) *Handbook of survey research* (pp. 69-121). New York: Academic Press.

Bryk, A. S. & Raudenbush, S. W. (1992). *Hierarchical linear models.* Newbury Park: SAGE Publications, Inc.

Chatterjee, S. & Price, B. (1977). *Regression analysis by example.* New York: Wiley.

Cohen, J. (1977). *Statistical power analysis for the behavioral sciences* (Rev. ed.). New York: Academic Press.

Cohen, J., and Cohen, P. (1983). *Applied multiple regression/correlation analysis for the behavioral sciences,* second edition. Hillsdale, NJ: Lawrence Erlbaum Associates.

Duncan, O. D. (1975). *Introduction to structural equation models.* New York: Academic Press.

Ethington, C. A. (1997). A Hierarchical linear modeling approach to studying college effects. In J. Smart (ed.), *Higher education: Handbook of theory and research, XII* (pp. 165-194). New York: Agathon Press.

Ezekiel, M., & Fox, K. A. (1959). *Methods of correlation and regression analysis.* New York: John Wiley & Sons.

Galton, F. (1885). Regression toward mediocrity in heredity stature. *Journal of the Anthropological Institute, 15,* 246-263.

Gordon, R. A. (1968). Issues in multiple regression. *The American Journal of Sociology, 73,* 592-616.

Hardy, M. A. (1993). *Regression with dummy variables.* Thousand Oaks, CA: Sage Publications, Inc.

Heck, R. H. & Thomas, S.L. (2000). *An introduction to multilevel modeling.* New Jersey: Erlbaum & Associates.

Hinkle, D. E., Wiersma, W., & Jurs, S. G. (1998). *Applied statistics for the behavioral sciences,* fourth edition. Boston: Houghton Mifflin.

Kerlinger, F. N. (1973). *Foundations of behavioral research.* New York: Holt, Rinehart and Winston.

Lewis-Beck, M. S. (1980). *Applied regression: an introduction.* Beverly Hills: Sage Publications, Inc.

Long, J. S. (1997). *Regression models for categorical and limited dependent variables.* Thousand Oaks, CA: Sage Publications.

Lord, F. M. & Novick, M. R. (1968). *Statistical theories of mental test scores.* Reading, MA: Addison-Wesley.

Montgomery, D. C., & Peck, E. A. (1992). *Introduction to linear regression analysis,* second edition. New York: John Wiley & Sons.

Myers, R. H. (1990). *Classical and modern regression with applications,* second edition. Boston: PWS-KENT Publishing Co.

Neter, J., Wasserman, W., & Kutner, M. H. (1985). *Applied linear statistical models: Regression, analysis of variance, and experimental designs* (2nd Ed.). Homewood, IL: Richard D. Irwin.

Nunnally, J. (1978). *Psychometric theory* (2nd ed.). New York: McGraw-Hill.

Ostrom, C. W. (1990). *Time series analysis regression techniques.* Thousand Oaks, CA: Sage Publications, Inc.

Pedhazur, E. J. (1982). *Multiple regression in behavioral research: Explanation and prediction.* New York: Holt,

Rinehart & Winston.

Stevens, J. (1996). *Applied multivariate statistics for the social sciences,* third edition. Mahwah, NJ: Lawrence Erlbaum Associates.

Thomas, S. L. & Heck, R.H. (2001). Analysis of large-scale secondary data in higher education: potential perils associated with complex sample designs. *Research in Higher Education,* 42, 517-540.

Thompson, B. (1995). Stepwise regression and stepwise discriminant analysis need not apply here: A guidelines editorial. *Educational and Psychological Measurement*, 55, 525-534.

7. THE EVOLVING ROLE OF THE COMMUNITY COLLEGE: POLICY ISSUES AND RESEARCH QUESTIONS

Kevin J. Dougherty
Teachers College
Columbia University

Community colleges are much in the policy limelight these days. State and federal policymakers are looking especially at community colleges as a cost-effective way to serve the increasing number of students wishing to go to college (Phelan, 2000). Moreover, community colleges recommend themselves as key institutions to meet the training demands of the increasing sub-baccalaureate sector of the occupational structure (Grubb, 1996). And those concerned about remedial education and distance education naturally focus on community colleges since they are major purveyors of both forms of education (Spann, 2000).

For those who have long staffed and studied the community college, this attention by policymakers is in many ways gratifying. A key institution of higher education is finally getting the full measure of attention that it fully deserves by reason of social importance and share of student enrollments. Community colleges number about one thousand, comprising over one-quarter of all higher educational institutions in the United States.[1] In 1997, these nearly institutions enrolled 5.3 million students for credit, accounting for nearly 37% of all degree-credit college students and 42% of all first-time freshmen (American Association of Community Colleges, 2000a:11, 25, 27, 43; U.S. National Center for Education Statistics, 1999a:203, 211, 283).[2] Community colleges play key roles in

[1] The American Association of Community Colleges identified 968 community colleges in 1998, while the U.S. National Center for Education Statistics tallied 1,047 public two-year higher education institutions (American Association of Community Colleges, 2000a: 11; U.S. National Center for Education Statistics, 1999a: 283).
[2] These enrollment figures are drawn from the NCES figures for public two-year higher education institutions. These figures do not include nondegree credit enrollments, which are common at com-

J.C. Smart and W.G. Tierney (eds.), Higher Education: Handbook of Theory and Research, 295–348.

opening access to higher education to less advantaged students, providing training for sub-baccalaureate occupations, fostering economic development, and providing a wide range of adult non-vocational education and community services (Cohen and Brawer, 1996a; Dougherty, 1994; and Dougherty and Bakia, 1999).

But while basking in the policy limelight is pleasurable, it is also hazardous to good scholarship and policy. The policy limelight brings attention to certain facets of the community college but leaves other important facets in darkness. And even the spotlighted features often suffer from being illuminated in ways that distort their true features.

Hence, in this chapter, I would like to review several important aspects of the community college, beginning first with those now in the policy spotlight but moving to those at the edge or even totally left in obscurity. In this review, I will summarize the state of policy and research on a given topic and suggest what policy changes and research initiatives seem in order.

ISSUES IN THE POLICY SPOTLIGHT

Higher education enrollments are once again rising rapidly under the impetus of the baby boom echo and growing college ambitions among high school graduates (Schneider and Stevenson, 1999). State and federal policymakers are wary and even frightened of the demands this incoming tide of students will place on the costs of higher education. At a time, when states face major financial demands from other sectors (K-12 education, corrections, and Medicaid), policymakers and scholars are looking to the community college as a place to inexpensively house many students (Pascarella, 1999:13; Rouse, 1998:615). For example, economist Cecilia Rouse states: "As the importance of skills and college enrollments continues to increase, state policymakers should keep in mind that community colleges provide a potentially cost-effective way to increase both access to higher education and overall educational attainment" (Rouse, 1998:615).

This recommendation assumes that the community college is equal to the four-year college in its contribution to students' educational and occupational attainment. This issue has provoked considerable controversy among scholars (Brint and Karabel, 1989; Dougherty, 1994; Grubb, 1996; Pascarella, 1999; Rouse, 1999) but it has gone almost totally unmentioned among policymakers. Hence, I will take up the issue of the community college's impact on its students' educa-

munity colleges, especially in remedial education, adult education, or contract training. I estimate noncredit enrollments to be about half as big as credit enrollments, based on figures from the states of California, Illinois, Maryland, New York, and Washington for fall 1993.

tional and economic attainment below, under the rubric of topics largely outside the policy spotlight.

For our purposes here, it is important to note that for policymakers the real hindrance to an expanded role for the community college does not lie in its problematic impact on students but in its ability to handle increasing state accountability demands, newly aggressive competitors, and the demands of distance education and remedial education. Tony Zeiss, the 1999-2000 chair of the Board of Directors of the American Association of Community Colleges, states:

> We are in the midst of a learning explosion . . . public community colleges have increased their spending per full-time equivalent students by 52 percent since 1986. As expenditures increase, so do regulations and accountability pressures. . . . To capture our legacy, to meet the demands of our students, and to return value to taxpayers, we simply must face these challenges with optimism and action. The converging forces of (1) increased employer demands, (2) increased student demands, (3) technological advances, (4) decreased public funding, and (5) increased accountability are producing an extremely competitive education and training environment. (Zeiss, 1998:11)

Let us pursue several of these issues cited by Zeiss.

Growing Competition

In recent years, policymakers and scholars have been furiously discussing the rising role of for-profit educational providers, particularly those using distance education technologies such as the Internet (Levine, 1997; Marchese, 1998; Phipps, 1999; Strosnider, 1997, 1998; Winston, 1999). And this discussion has occurred within community college venues as well (Dillon and Cintron, 1997; Zeiss, 1998). Tony Zeiss, previously quoted, makes clear the sense of threat from private training providers: "If we don't meet the needs and expectations of students, the for-profit colleges and training organizations certainly will; indeed they already have the jump on us. . . . Just who are the competitors in postsecondary education? Public colleges and universities; private, nonprofit colleges and universities; proprietary for-profit colleges and universities; and corporate training organizations are all involved in the career development business and have been for many years" (Zeiss, 1998:8, 12). This sense that community colleges face a much more competitive environment has a strong basis. For example, a study of which colleges are most exposed to competition by for-profit providers identified 49% of public two-year colleges as particularly vulnerable (Winston, 1999:16).

Research Needed

Despite these alarums, we do not know how many potential community college students the new competitors have siphoned off or in the future might siphon off. It is quite possible that the competitive challenge is far smaller than many fear, primarily because the new competitors may be targeting students that community colleges may not be serving in any great numbers now: for example, mid-career adults pursuing advanced education. Moreover, we know particularly little about the precise location of the competitive challenge: in what particular curricular and geographical areas and among which particular clients is it greatest? Finally, we know very little about what steps community colleges are taking to counter their competition. Prompted by these data deficits, the Community College Research Center at Columbia University launched a research project in fall 2000 to look at, among other subjects, the new competition for community colleges: its magnitude and location and the community college response. The data for this study are being provided by 15 community colleges nationwide.[3]

Policy Questions

For many policymakers, the growing competition faced by community colleges is a good thing. More competition means more student choice and greater organizational and social efficiency. But at the same time, consideration needs to be given to whether the competing providers — if successful — indeed will be providing the same educational goods but at a lower price or higher quality. They may well be providing different educational goods. In particular, they may be loath to provide much general education, regarding this as an unnecessary ornament. Many students may well agree, especially if they can get a degree more quickly and more cheaply. But from a societal standpoint, this loss of general education may cost society considerably. We will return to the topic of general education toward the end of this chapter. In addition, community colleges may respond to greater competition by emulating for-profit providers in relying very heavily on part-time instructors. This will have major implications for the future of faculty governance, which is dependent on a strong corps of full-time faculty (Winston, 1999:18-19).

[3]The results of this project will be published in journals and books and on the CCRC website: http://www.tc.columbia.edu/ccrc. Inquiries can be addressed to ccrc@columbia.edu.

TOUGHER PUBLIC FUNDING

Community colleges face a more difficult fiscal environment not only because private competition has intensified but also because their public patronage is both stingier and more demanding. The public (federal, state, and local) share of total community college revenue dropped from 69.0% in 1991-92 to 67.8% in 1996-97, with the state share dropping most: 46.2% to 43.3% (American Association of Community Colleges, 2000a:108-109). In the late 1990s, public funding rebounded but the new millennium has brought back straitened finances. In 2001, some 20 states rescinded as much as 5% of the appropriations they had made to higher education the previous summer (Hebel and Selingo, 2001).

The early 1990s depression in state financing left a lasting legacy: the imposition of more stringent accountability standards. That is, funding has become predicated no longer just on input variables such as enrollments but is now based in part on measures of institutional output (Burke and Serban, 1998:53-54; Carnevale, Johnson, and Edwards, 1998). Federal funds under the Perkins Vocational Education Act and the Workforce Investment Act carry significant performance accountability requirements (Grubb and Badway, 1999). Moreover, at least 9 states have enacted performance-based funding in which a small pot of money — either as an addition to or deduction from their regular state appropriation — is disbursed according to how well community colleges meet certain performance standards (American Association of Community Colleges, 2000b; Burke and Serban, 1998:99; Burke and Modarresi, 1999:2, 10-11; Dougherty and Kim, 2001). States vary greatly in the number and content of these standards. Certain standards are fairly common: a community college's degree of accessibility (measured by portion of the population enrolled), persistence and retention rate, the rate at which students transfer to four-year colleges, graduation or completion rate, degree of success in placing students in jobs, performance on licensing exams, success in workforce development, and student satisfaction (American Association of Community Colleges, 2000b; Burke, 1997:48-49; Burke and Serban, 1998:51-55, 98; Dougherty and Kim, 2001).

Policy Questions

Performance funding is attractive in that it promises to ensure that community colleges pay close attention to the priorities of their federal and state patrons. However, there are reasons to doubt that, as currently constituted, it will be as effective as hoped. Certain of these problems are generic to performance funding, regardless of whether it is applied to community colleges or to four-year colleges. Performance funding introduces instability in college funding, making it hard for colleges to plan for the future and making them leery of taking chances on untried programs (Dougherty and Kim, 2001). Moreover, if already resource poor and poorly performing colleges lose funding, this may confirm and deepen their performance deficit (Grubb and Badway, 1999:2). Thirdly, performance funding can potentially produce perverse consequences. For example, does the demand for a high persistence rate result in colleges inflating grades and retaining students who should be allowed to leave (Grubb and Badway, 1999:19-20, 30; Ruppert, 1995:13, 20-21)? Moreover, given that most higher educational institutions pursue several different, not entirely compatible, missions, different performance standards may pull them in contradictory directions (Grubb and Badway, 1999; Layzell, 1999:238).

But in addition to these generic problems, there are problems that are specific to community colleges. Not infrequently the performance measures are not well matched to the mission of the community college. To begin, important missions are not always coupled with performance measures. A study of 11 states that then had performance funding for community colleges found that only 6 had a measure for transfer rate, only 4 had a measure for workforce development, and only 4 had measures for minority student access, retention, or graduation (Burke and Serban, 1998:51-53, 95-98). In addition, even when community college missions are coupled with performance measures, the fit may be quite loose. For example, several states base their performance funding on the community college's retention rate (Burke and Serban, 1998:50). But community college leaders frequently complain that this measure applies far less well to community colleges than to four-year colleges. Many two-year students enter college as an experiment to see if they are really interested in college and leave when they decide it is not to their taste. Should this be counted against the community college or should it be seen as a kind of successful learning (Burke and Serban, 1998:26; Grubb, 1996:62)?

These concerns suggest that the framing of performance standards should be approached carefully and deliberately, in full consultation with community college officials. Each of the major missions of the community college (including college transfer, occupational training, remedial education, general education, and perhaps adult nonvocational training) should be represented by a performance standard that is carefully calibrated and measured. Furthermore, policymakers need to be fully aware that these missions sometimes do conflict, thus causing the applicable performance standards and measures to whipsaw community colleges. For example, the stronger a community college's commitment to occupational training, the weaker on average its transfer rate (for more see below and Dougherty, 1994:186-188). As a result, community colleges strongly responding to incentives for more occupational training may, however, perform less well in the area of transfer and thus be financially penalized on that front. Finally, policymakers need to be mindful of the organizational repercussions of financially penalizing poorly performing community colleges. Rather than simply having their funds cut, such colleges need to be provided help in order to develop the organizational capacity to meet performance standards.

As Tony Zeiss has noted, the financial pressures attendant with tougher state financing and growing private competition have pushed community colleges to become very interested in workforce development and distance education. As it happens, these are topics that have also attracted great attention among higher education policymakers and researchers.

Workforce Development

Over the past 80 years, community colleges have carved a distinctive niche for themselves in the area of workforce development. Today, about three-fifths of community college students are pursuing vocational training for immediate entry into the labor market (Cohen and Brawer, 1996a:226-227; Grubb, 1996:52). As a result, nearly half of recent labor force entrants with some college, but not a bachelor's degree, begin at a community college (Grubb, 1996:54-56; U.S. National Center for Education Statistics, 1998:432).

There is every reason to believe that the community college's role in workforce development will be even greater in the coming years. The sub-baccalaureate labor market will continue to grow (Braddock, 1999; Grubb, 1996:2-4). State and federal policymakers and business leaders will remain keenly interested in workforce development, regarding it as a key, if not the key, mission of the community college. And community college leaders will continue to pursue workforce development both out of ideological conviction and because they see it as a key counterbalance to inadequate state aid and to the growing threat from private competitors.

Community colleges are actively involved in providing pre-employment training for a wide variety of occupations, ranging from the health professions to the construction trades (American Association of Community Colleges, 2000a:64-65; Cohen and Brawer, 1996a:chaps. 8, 10; Dougherty and Bakia, 2000; Grubb, 1996, 1999).

However, four fields dominate: health professions, business, protective services (police and fire), and engineering-related technologies.[4] For example,

[4] Two-thirds of all certificates and associate degrees awarded by community colleges are in vocational fields. In turn, two-thirds of these vocational certificates and degrees are given in just four fields: health professions and related sciences (32 percent of all vocational certificates and associate degrees in 1996-97), business management and administrative services (23 percent), protective ser-

three-fifths of those graduating from Registered Nursing programs in a given year do so with an Associate's degree, typically received from a community college (U.S. Census Bureau, 2000:124)

This pre-employment occupational training is often conceptualized as exclusively sub-baccalaureate. But graduates of occupational programs are increasingly able to go on to pursue baccalaureate degrees. Overall, among 1980 community college entrants involved in the High School and Beyond Survey, 23% of those receiving vocational associate's degrees ended up transferring to a four-year college by spring 1984 (Grubb, 1991:200-201).[5]

Students who graduate from community college vocational programs receive substantially better wages than do high school graduates, although lower payoffs than college graduates. For example, comparing students similar in race and ethnicity, education of parents, marital status, and job experience, students who attend community college but do not receive a certificate or degree lead high school graduates by about 5 to 10% in earnings for every year of community college they attend. Students graduating from community colleges with one-year certificates outpace high school graduates by about 10% in annual earnings. And community college students earning a vocational associate's degree earn 20 to 30% more than comparable high school graduates. However attractive these figures are, we need to keep in mind that, on average, the payoffs to a bachelor's degree are even higher. Baccalaureate recipients receive 40% higher incomes than comparable high school graduates (Grubb, 1996:90; idem, 1999:10-11 and Tables 6-9; Kane and Rouse, 1995, 1999).[6]

The community college's role in workforce development goes beyond preparing people for their first job. It also lies in upgrading the skills of current workers or retraining unemployed workers and welfare recipients for new jobs. Over 90% of community colleges now engage in contract training: that is, they contract with an outside group (such as a firm, industry association, or government agency) to deliver specified training, with the contractor being viewed as the main client for the training (students are secondary clients) and the contractor largely, if not entirely, determining who will receive the training, what will be the content of the training, and what will define success (Dougherty and Bakia, 2000; Grubb et al., 1997; Pincus, 1989).

vices (7 percent), and engineering-related technologies (6 percent) (American Association of Community Colleges, 2000a: 64-65).

[5] Despite the rising transferability of occupational degrees, the question nonetheless remains whether they are as transferable as academic degrees. Grubb (1991) finds major differences in transfer rate, but this study does not control for differences in social background, high school record, and educational and occupational ambitions. See below for more.

[6] We also need to keep in mind that these estimates are average effects. The payoff to a given community college credential varies by students' sex, social class background, and field of study and whether they find employment in a field related to their training (Grubb, 1996: 95, 99, 102).

Though the data are still sparse and not yet conclusive, the community college's contract training programs appear to have brought students higher incomes, firms greater productivity and profits, and community colleges more students, revenues, and political support. At the same time, there is also some evidence of a negative impact on the mission and structure of community colleges.

Rigorous studies of the impact of contract training on trainees are quite scarce. However, the data available show positive effects on graduation rates, placement rates, wages, and possibly, job upgrading (Dougherty and Bakia, forthcoming; Dougherty and Bakia, 1999:57-60; Krueger and Rouse, 1996; Lynch, 1992).

Equally sparse are hard data on the impact of contract training on employers. A study of two New Jersey firms did find that trainees less often left the company, had more job upgrades, were more often nominated for and received individual or group performance awards, and believed their supervisor would say they were doing a better job than a year ago (Dougherty and Bakia, forthcoming; Dougherty and Bakia, 1999:60-61; Krueger and Rouse, 1996). One very interesting impact of contract training on employers is that apparently it partially substitutes for inhouse training by employers themselves. To be sure, states often do require firms to put up as much as half the cost of the training in order to receive grants (Bosworth, 1999). And an evaluation of New Jersey's state aid program found that firms receiving grants for contract training stated that they planned to contribute an average of $2 for every dollar they received in state aid (Van Horn, Fichtner, Dautrich, Hartley, and Hebbar, 1998:11). Yet a study of the state aid program in New York State found that, when asked in 1987 what they would have done in the absence of state aid, 34% of recipient firms stated that they would have done the training with their own staff and 26% said they would have purchased training elsewhere (Winter and Fadale, 1990:5). This raises the nettlesome question of the degree to which state aid is unnecessarily subsidizing employee training efforts by firms. To date, there is little evidence that states have carefully examined this issue of unnecessary corporate welfare.

For community colleges, finally, contract training has wide-ranging and subtle impacts. On the positive side, it boosts enrollments and revenues and enlarges business's political support for community colleges. It also helps keep the regular vocational offerings of community colleges in closer touch with the changing demands of the labor market. However, contract training also carries negative consequences for the community college. It greatly enlarges business's influence on community college decisions. This is not bad in and of itself, but it may make it harder to maintain a focus on public interests that do not carry a definite business bottom line, such as general education. Also, the energetic pursuit of contract training may leave less administrative time, attention, and energy for such traditional missions as baccalaureate preparation and general education for citizenship. The transfer program may particularly feel the effects of a loss of administrative attention. It takes great administrative time and energy to construct and maintain effective articulation agreements with four-year colleges, as new courses appear at community colleges and four-year colleges and as the signatories to the initial agreement pass on and new principal actors have to be socialized. The traditional missions of community colleges may also be threatened by the diffusion of a "business-like" ethos of operation, as community colleges try to attract and retain training contracts from business. Less emphasis may be placed on transfer and general education because business is not very interested in it and community college administrators come to internalize this orientation (Dougherty and Bakia, 2000; idem, forthcoming).

Research Needed

As the tentative note of some of the findings above indicates, much important research remains to be done on the community college's role in workforce development. To begin, very few of the economic return studies rigorously compare the returns to training at community colleges and training at other two-year institutions such as proprietary schools and public vocational and technical schools. Moreover, there are far too few studies that examine the impact of contract training on students and on employers (including the issue of corporate welfare). And while we have more data on its impact on community colleges themselves, we need to closely investigate the impact of contract training on community college's commitment to transfer and general education.

Policy Recommendations

The strong differences in return among community college vocational credentials (by level and field) and between them and the baccalaureate degree suggest the importance of ensuring that students are aware of these differences and choose wisely. Yet students too often choose poorly paid and overcrowded fields because they, and not infrequently their teachers, are unaware of the great variability in returns to different levels of credentials and fields of study (Grubb, 1996:95; 1999:14-17). Working class and nonwhite students particularly need good vocational counseling, both because they are the least likely to receive adequate information to begin with and because they have fewer resources to cope with the consequences of making poorly informed choices. Some states are making notable efforts to improve students' ability to navigate the vocational education system. For example, the Florida community college and state university systems have been developing a statewide system for computer-assisted student advising that can be expanded to include career advising (Florida State Board of Community Colleges, 1998:39-40). What remains to be seen, however, is whether such systems reach working class, minority, and older students as well as they do more computer literate recent high school graduates from advantaged backgrounds.

But greater occupational knowledge will not overcome the difficult dilemma faced by community college students over whether to pursue a vocational versus an academic associate degree. On average, vocational associate degrees carry a greater economic payoff than do academic associate degrees (Grubb, 1996:94-95). But academic associate degrees are more transferable toward baccalaureate degrees, which carry a greater economic payoff (see below and Dougherty, forthcoming). This dilemma — of whether to pursue a smaller but more certain payoff (in the case of a vocational certificate or associate degree) or instead to pursue a larger but less certain return (in the case of a more transferable academic associate degree) — can be made less painful by state policy. Training programs should be connected vertically, so that graduates of programs providing lesser skills or short-term training could later enter program offering higher skills, longer training, and typically higher certificates or degrees (Grubb, 1996:123-128).[7] And as part of this vertical integration of degrees, efforts should be made to make vocational degrees more transferable toward the baccalaureate. This will be discussed in greater detail below.

It is not just community college students but also administrators who face an information gap concerning vocational education. Community college preservice preparation programs too often lack up-to-date intelligence on the changing contours of the labor market. Today, the problem is less that courses are offered for which there is very little demand, though that continues to be an issue.[8] The greater difficulty is course content and equipment that are not keeping pace with the often rapidly changing skill demands of employers. Tradition-

[7] This integration can also be used to bridge the strong divide within community colleges between traditional vocational education programs and job-training programs focused on job reentry for welfare recipients, dislocated workers, and displaced homemakers. Often these programs provide quite short-term training in simple skills. Hence, they would benefit immensely from having the option of feeding into community college certificate and associate programs that provide greater skills and bring greater economic returns (Grubb, 1996: 124-125; Grubb, Badway, Bell, and Castellano, 1999).

[8] Programs may be kept operating despite low employer demand because student enrollees have little knowledge about labor market conditions, and continue to enroll. And community colleges have had little strong incentive to keep track of the real demands of the labor market because, until recently, they have been funded almost exclusively on the basis of enrollments rather than outputs (Grubb, 1996: 187-190).

ally, community colleges have relied on a variety of devices to promote such alignment with the labor market, including business advisory committees and employer surveys. However, employers have felt little pressure to clearly communicate to community colleges what their skills needs are, because they often are hazy about what those needs really are, they draw on a wide variety of sources of skill training besides community colleges, and their hiring needs are unstable, varying greatly depending on the state of the business cycle (Grubb, 1996:196-198). The community college's contribution to lack of responsiveness to labor-market trends can be lessened by moving community colleges toward performance funding formulas that emphasize outputs such as job placement. Such formulas encourage community colleges to more actively track labor market requirements and close down programs with poor placement records (Dougherty and Kim, 2001; Grubb, 1996:198). This of course brings us back to the topic of accountability standards, which we discussed earlier. And as noted earlier, performance funding is not an unmixed blessing.

Finally, with respect to contract training, if further research does confirm that it often results in unnecessary corporate welfare and weakening the transfer and general education functions, ways must be found to minimize these negative impacts. With regard to corporate welfare, state governments should try to devise funding formulas that maximize employers' willingness to train their workers and yet minimize the substitution for reasonable business expenditures on training. And in the case of transfer and education, the negative effects of community college pursuit of contract training can perhaps be mitigated or eliminated by providing strong incentives — for example in state performance funding formulas — for community college efforts to bolster the general education and transfer opportunities of occupational students.

INSTRUCTIONAL TECHNOLOGY AND DISTANCE EDUCATION

Distance education has provoked tremendous interest among government policymakers, community college officials, and higher education researchers. For policymakers and researchers, distance education promises to widen access to higher education, meet the vocational training needs of adult workers, and yet cut instructional costs. Community college officials share these views but also see distance education as crucial to meeting the challenge from private training providers (American Association of University Professors, 1998:31; Blumenstyk, 1998; Gladieux and Swail, 1999; Phipps et al., 1998:15; U.S. National Center for Education Statistics, 1999b:2).

According to a national survey, 62% of public two-year colleges offered distance education in 1997-98 and another 20% were planning to offer it within the next three years.[9] These distance education offerings enrolled 714,160 students.[10]

It is important to keep in mind that distance education is by no means synonymous with the Internet. The most common distance education technology is one-way prerecorded video (used by 62% of public two-year colleges), followed by asynchronous Internet instruction (57%), and two-way interactive video (53%), All other technologies were utilized by less than one-sixth of public two-year colleges (U.S. National Center for Education Statistics, 1999b:12, 16, 38).

Moreover, distance education does not encompass all usage of instructional technology (American Association of University Professors, 1998:32). Even students resident on campus may be taught through non-direct instruction in such forms as closed circuit TV when certain courses are oversubscribed or asynchronous instruction when instructors wish to offer self-paced instruction.

Research Findings and Research Needs

Despite the great enthusiasm for distance education and proposals that it should be promoted even more, the research base is rather weak on its effectiveness and the optimal circumstances for use. There is a great need for research on the impact of distance education on student learning and on the faculty role.

A staple of commentary on distance education and of several reviews of the literature is that it has essentially the same impact on student academic achievement as does in person instruction (Moore et al., 1990; Russell, 1999). However, this conclusion should be resisted. Most research on the impact of distance education has been conducted at four-year institutions, raising questions about its applicability to community colleges (Phipps and Merisotis, 1999:34). More importantly, the vast majority of studies on the impact of distance education has been quite flawed methodologically, usually failing to use an experimental design (utilizing randomized assignment to experimental and control groups) or at least a good quasi-experimental design involving statistical controls for a large range of input variables. Better conducted studies are needed to answer

[9] In comparison, 34% of all postsecondary institutions (but 78% of public four-year institutions) offered distance education in 1997-98 (U.S. National Center for Education Statistics, 1999b: 12).

[10] This would represent just over 13% of the 5,360,686 students enrolled for credit in public two-year degree-granting institutions in fall 1997 (U.S. National Center for Education Statistics, 1999a: 200). If the base were total (credit and noncredit) enrollments, the percentage would be 8.7%, based on an estimate that noncredit enrollments are half as large as credit enrollments (see Dougherty and Bakia, 2000). However, only 3% of distance education enrollments reported by public two-year colleges are in noncredit programs (U.S. National Center for Education Statistics, 1999b: 16, 20, 26, 28).

why, for example, dropout rates are higher for distance education than for traditional instruction (Phipps and Merisotis, 1999:3-5, 19-21, 25). In addition, whatever its quality, the research extant has little to say about the conditional effectiveness of distance education (DE): that is, how its impact on students varies by the particular DE technology used, the kind of subject being taught, the characteristics of students (for example, their skills, personalities and learning styles), and the quality of the faculty teaching them. As it is, a number of studies indicate that the impact of distance education varies by such student characteristics as academic skills, personality (independence, persistence, and time management skills), and social background (such as sex and marital status) (Phipps and Merisotis, 1999:5-6, 16, 24, 26, 30-31; Powell, Conway, and Ross, 1990; Sherry, 1996). Finally, we know very little about the impact of entire programs using DE rather than just individual courses (Phipps and Merisotis, 1999:5, 23).[11]

If we have much to learn about the impact of distance education on students, we have virtually a whole world to learn about its impact on faculty and the social and administrative structure of colleges. For example, how does distance education change the nature of teaching and the role of faculty in institutional governance? There is a lot of concern that widespread use of distance education will result in faculty losing control of their intellectual property — in the form of course syllabi and lectures — as these are made public or as colleges increasingly demand ownership of course materials so that they can freely substitute teachers (American Association of University Professors, 1998:34-35; Rhoades, 1998:203). In fact, despite evidence that distance education courses disproportionately rely on part time faculty, very few faculty contracts provide for protecting full time faculty against job loss due to the spread of instructional technology (American Association of University Professors, 1998:35; Rhoades, 1998:195, 207). Moreover, the question has been raised whether the greater use of distance education weakens faculty self-governance. To begin with, very few faculty contracts stipulate a faculty role in approving distance education courses and the use of new instructional technology and provide for training faculty in the new technologies (Rhoades, 1998:186-188). Moreover, observers have wondered whether the greater use of faculty who are part time, untenured, and dispersed across sites may result in fewer opportunities for faculty to work together on institutional issues and therefore exercise a strong collective voice in institutional decision making (Eaton, 2000:4-5; Phipps et al., 1998:24).

[11]There are also questions about whether the rising use of distance education may weaken general education in the community college (Easton, 2000: 6-7; Phipps et al., 1998: 24-25). See the discussion of general education below.

Policy Recommendations

Given how much we do not know about the impact and effectiveness of distance education, it behooves community colleges to pursue it with caution. At the very least, they should be very aware that the effects of distance education may not be uniform, and that in certain circumstances distance education may be distinctly inferior to traditional education. This may be particularly the case for students, often from disadvantaged backgrounds, with poor academic skills and weak motivation. Such students seem to particularly benefit from a high degree of direct faculty-student and student-student contact because these provide motivation, deepen understanding, and promote retention (Eaton, 2000:9; Pascarella and Terenzini, 1991:98, 101-102, 104; Phipps et al., 1998:26; Tinto, 1987). Traditional instruction would be more likely to provide this contact, but there may be a great temptation to provide distance education out of a desire to keep down the cost. If distance education is used, however, efforts should be made nonetheless to ensure maximal faculty and student contact, even if not in person.

Given also the possibly negative effects of distance education on the faculty's role in institutional decision making, every effort should be made to protect the faculty role. Policies should be instituted to train faculty in new instructional technologies and to maximize faculty participation in setting rules for staffing distance education courses, selecting instructional technologies, and evaluating the effectiveness of distance education courses (American Association of University Professors, 1998; Eaton, 2000; Rhoades, 1998). Moreover, distance education means should be used to counteract the negative impact of distance education on collegial faculty interaction: for example, virtual academic senates can be established (Eaton, 2000:8-9).

Remedial Education[12]

Workforce preparation and distance education have not been the only facets of community college instruction that have interested policymakers in recent years. Albeit with a different valence, remedial education has attracted as much or more attention as distance education.

In a federal survey of higher education institutions in 1995, public two-year colleges reported that 41% of their freshmen enrolled in a remedial course that

[12]I use this term with reservations. It connotes repairing the defects of previous education. Yet, it is not really repair work in the not uncommon case of an adult who came out of high school with good academic skills many years ago but is now coming back to take college courses and needs a brush-up on high school math and writing skills. In this case, developmental education is the more appropriate term.

fall, while the figure reported by all higher education institutions was 29% (U.S. National Center for Education Statistics, 1996:6, 10). However high these figures may seem, they are probably underestimates. The NCES survey let institutions themselves define what constitute college-level skills and therefore what courses and students are remedial. Consequently, there was great variation in whether colleges categorized, for example, English as a Second Language as remedial: 55% of public two-year colleges, but only 38% of all colleges, did so (U.S. National Center for Education Statistics, 1996:2, 25). Moreover, the survey probably failed to pick up covert remediation in the form of courses that are not designated as remedial but are taught at below college level because of the poor skills of many students enrolled in them (Grubb, 2001; Levin, 1999). Moreover, many institutions may simply have misrepresented the true incidence of remediation out of a sense of shame (Phipps, 1998:vi, 5).

By all accounts, the incidence of remediation has been rising in community colleges. In the 1995 NCES survey, 55% of public two-year colleges stated that they had more students taking remedial education in 1995 than 5 years before (U.S. National Center for Education Statistics, 1996:11). Several factors appear to be driving this rise. First, the rising college going rate, when coupled with the open door policy of community colleges, has brought them increasing numbers of students from lower ranks in the high school class. But as or more important is the fact that state officials and even four-year college heads have been pushing to have remediation cut back or even entirely eliminated at four-year colleges and instead relegated to community colleges. Perhaps the best known case of this has been the 1998 decision by the New York City Board of Higher Education to almost entirely phase out remedial education at the four-year colleges of the City University of New York. But similar efforts have been made in Florida, Georgia, and California (Arenson, 1998a,b; Healy, 1995a,b; Lively, 1993; Shaw, 2001).[13]

Remedial education by community colleges has not been as controversial as it has been for four-year colleges, because remediation has long been seen by many as a fundamental mission of the community college. For example, 40% of states require and 11% encourage their community colleges to offer remediation (U.S. National Center for Education Statistics, 1996:30). But even so, there has

[13]Several different factors have entered into this repudiation of remediation at four-year colleges. Clearly at work have been a desire to cut public expenditures by shifting remediation from four-year colleges to cheaper education venues and to rectify a failure of the high schools to graduate college-ready students (Healy, 1995a,b; Lively, 1993; Shaw, 2001: 199). But less obvious and even more problematic motives are also at work. These include a desire to maintain the perceived economic and status value of baccalaureate degrees by restricting them to those deemed truly meritorious. Given the disproportionate number of remedial students who are poor and nonwhite, this sentiment slides more or less consciously into class and race prejudice. It is instructive that the opponents of university remediation are often the same as the opponents of affirmative action (Shaw, 2001: 194, 196).

been a rising chorus of dissatisfaction with remedial education even in the community college (Ignash, 1997:6).

Research Findings and Research Needs

Despite the great extent of remedial education in the community college, we have little indication of whether it is being done well. Very few institutions conduct systematic evaluations and states have little idea of how successful their program are (Phipps, 1998:10-11; Roueche and Roueche, 1999:53-54; Shaw, 2001:197). And the studies that are available typically have massive methodological flaws. For example, in a national survey of higher education institutions in fall 1995, public two-year colleges reported that a little over two-thirds of their students successfully completed remediation courses in reading, writing, and mathematics (U.S. National Center for Education Statistics, 1996:13). This finding is very flimsy. The survey relies on institutional reports and there is no way of knowing how institutions decided what was successful completion and whether it really entailed mastery of college-level skills. Similarly, another national study reported that 77% of those passing remedial math courses, and 91% of those passing remedial English, went on to get passing grades in college level courses in the same subjects (Boylan, Bonham, and Bliss, 1992). However, like most studies of remediation, this study does not use random assignment to experimental and control groups or, at least, control for differences among programs in student input characteristics. Furthermore, it fails to control for selective attrition from remedial programs by reporting outcome measures for program dropouts as well as program completors. As a result, good post-remedial performance may be largely due to the initial ability and motivation of program completers rather than anything a remedial course did. Finally, this study is reporting a pretty low level of accomplishment: 77% to 91% of remedial graduates are getting at least a D in subsequent college level courses whose rigor is not specified. (Grubb, 2001; Levin, 1999).

Given the absence of much good research on remediation, we need studies that carefully examine the impact of remedial courses using research designs featuring random assignment to experimental and control groups and/or careful measurement of academic aptitude, motivation, and social background. These studies need to measure outcomes for noncompletors and nonremedial students as well as remedial completors, controlling for student characteristics prior to remediation. Program impact should be measured not just in terms of completion of remedial programs but also levels of academic proficiency relative to nonremedial students, rates of graduation from the community college with a certificate or degree, transfer and baccalaureate attainment rates, and eventual economic attainment (Grubb, 2001; Levin, 1999).

There is evidence that teaching techniques differ in effectiveness according to student learning styles. For example, older students may be better able to handle accelerated courses or combined remedial/collegiate courses (Ignash, 1997:17). Moreover, students with deficiencies in only one subject may do well with computer assisted courses, but students with multiple deficiencies may need to interact with an instructor because they require a lot of guidance (McMillan et al., 1997:29). Hence, research on remediation needs to be attentive to how its impact varies by type of student and type of technique. As part of this, research needs to establish whether programmed instruction is good for all students. There is a great temptation to use it across the board because it is inexpensive, but it may work well with only certain kinds of students (Pascarella and Terenzini, 1991:103-104, 109).

Finally, given the strong drive in recent years to push remedial education out of four-year colleges and relegate it instead to community colleges (Phipps, 1998:1; Shaw, 2001:200-201), it is important to examine what impact that policy has had on the educational and economic attainment of remedial students. Do remedial students who once would have been able to enter a four-year college but now are required to go first to a community college end up with fewer years of education, poorer credentials, and less money than do comparable students who are allowed to remain at four-year colleges? Such a study could be conducted by comparing remedial students in states with more or less restrictive policies on remediation at four-year colleges or comparing baccalaureate oriented remedial students before and after a policy has been enacted (as at the City University of New York) requiring them to go first to community colleges for remediation.

Policy Recommendations

Effective remediation involves both improving the deficiencies students have when they arrive in the community college and reducing the need for remediation to begin with, by improving the skills of students even before they enter the community college. Returning to the former, effective remediation requires that community colleges know which students need help (through mandatory assessment at entrance to the community college) and ensure that those students indeed get remediation (through mandatory placement in remedial courses) (Phipps, 1998:23; Roueche and Roueche, 1999:23-24, 47-48). But mandatory assessment at entrance to the community college and mandatory placement in remedial courses are not universally practiced. In the fall 1995 federal survey of remediation, only two-thirds of public two-year colleges required students believed to need remediation to actually take remedial courses; the remainder only recommended remedial courses (U.S. National Center for Education Statistics, 1996:19). While undergoing remediation, students should be allowed to take regular college-level courses to the degree possible, in order to bolster their academic motivation by giving them a sense of progress. That is, if a student needs remediation in math, but not in reading and writing, it makes sense that he or she be allowed to take a college-level course in English, though of course not college-level math (McMillan, Parke, and Lanning, 1997:28; Roueche and Roueche, 1999:30-32). Another procedure that some studies indicate is effective is to pair college-level courses with remedial courses, creating learning communities (Grubb, 2001; Levin, 1999; Tinto, Russo, and Kadel, 1994).[14] Finally, it has been proposed that remedial courses be infused to the maximum degree possible with higher order thinking skills, thus preparing students for transition to regular academic courses (Levin, 1999; Shaw, 2001:198).

Whether policymakers can or should prescribe the method of remedial education is doubtful. A wide variety of pedagogies are in use in remedial education today, and there is no conclusive evidence on which is best (Boylan, Bonham, and Bliss, 1992; Grubb, 2001; Levin, 1999; McMillan et al., 1997). This lack of clarity may well be due to the fact that the efficacy of a given pedagogy is not universal, but specific to a particular type of student and subject matter. Whatever the pedagogy, it is important that faculty be well-trained and motivated and that remedial education not be relegated to the least prepared and motivated teachers (McMillan et all, 1997:28-29; Roueche and Roueche, 1999:26). Buttressing faculty efforts must be a wide range of support services including individualized counseling to help students deal with academic, career, and life contingencies (Phipps, 1998:10, 23; Roueche and Roueche, 1999:46).

However effective remedial education in the community college might become, it is important as well to act proactively to improve the academic skills of students even before they enter the community college (Ignash, 1997; Phipps, 1998; Roueche and Roueche, 1999). The need for such a policy is indicated by the fact that 40% of higher education institutions in 1989 did not make efforts to decrease the need for remedial education (U.S. National Center for Education Statistics, 1991:15). What initiatives might such a proactive policy take? The most important is establishing a closer alignment between high school graduation requirements and college expectations (Phipps, 1998:ix, 20-21; Roueche and Roueche, 1999:50). This can be done in several ways. One is to raise the requirements for high school graduation: for example, Texas has stiffened its require-

[14] However, Nora (2000) notes that, though learning communities clearly improve students' perception that their academic skills have improved, it is not clear whether they improve them in actuality.

ments and identified a core curriculum for public high schools (Breneman and Haarlow, 1998:12, 16; Ignash, 1997:18). But whatever the level of these requirements it is important that they be clearly understood. Hence, several states such as Colorado and Oklahoma have more clearly specified their college expectations and then made sure they articulate with the content and competency standards for high school graduates. Furthermore, states have established programs to inform high schools on how well their graduates are doing in college (Ignash, 1997:17-18; Phipps, 1998:21-22).[15] These general programs are being supplemented by federal and state efforts, such as GEAR UP, to provide disadvantaged students, well before they decide about college, with mentoring, tutoring, and a guarantee of college access and financial aid if they meet specific requirements such as completing a college prep curriculum and maintaining a certain minimum GPA (Breneman and Haarlow, 1998:16; Phipps, 1998:ix, 21-22). Buttressing these measures to clearly communicate higher standards are efforts to improve the capacity of teachers to reach those standards. As part of the now two decade old movement to improve the academic excellence of elementary and secondary schooling, many states are actively instituting measures of student performance and improving the preparation of teachers (Conley, 1997; Phipps, 1998:22; Shaw, 2001:199-200).

Though community colleges may well do a better job of remediation than four-year colleges, it is questionable that the bulk of postsecondary remediation should be relegated to community colleges. If four-year colleges almost wholly abandon remediation, this will drastically weaken the political support for adequate state and federal funding of remedial education. Moreover, requiring poorly prepared baccalaureate aspirants to begin their collegiate careers at community colleges is likely to substantially reduce their chances of eventually securing a baccalaureate degree. As will be explored in the next section, community college entrants with baccalaureate aspirations are significantly less likely to succeed in completing their degrees than comparable students entering four-year colleges.

ISSUES OUTSIDE THE SPOTLIGHT

As can be seen above, the community college issues that have commanded the attention of higher education policymakers and community college officials certainly deserve consideration. But there are other topics that also deserve policy attention but have received far less. These include the role of general educa-

[15]For example, Maryland's Student Outcome and Achievement Report (SOAR) informs high school and district personnel about how recent high school graduates are doing: how much remedial work they need; their performance in first college level courses in English and mathematics; their cumulative GPAs; and their persistence rates (Ignash, 1997: 17-18; Phipps, 1998: 21-22).

tion and community building as key missions of the community college and the question of whether the community college hinders the educational attainment of its baccalaureate entrants. These issues have attracted the interest of some researchers but they are effectively off the policy agenda. But that status is not a given, and must be challenged. Policy discourse should not be restricted to the conventional wisdom enunciated by political and economic elites.

Let us begin this process of widening the spotlight by considering the question of whether the community college helps or hinders educational attainment and, if so, what can be done about it.

EDUCATIONAL ATTAINMENT: DO COMMUNITY COLLEGES HELP OR HINDER?

For community college officials and most policymakers, the community college is a great engine of educational opportunity, especially for disadvantaged students. A typical statement of this faith in the community college comes from a policy paper recently issued by the Education Commission of the States:

> Community colleges' early history in expanding educational opportunity represents a uniquely American success story. Established in 1901, the first two-year "junior" colleges were dedicated to providing access and education to the mass population. . . . So successful were these new two-year institutions that demand and support for community colleges grew at an exponential rate. . . . From all indications, enrollment demands at community colleges are likely to continue expanding well into the new century. Over the next decade, many states will experience explosive growth in the number of high school graduates, many of whom will look to the community college for initial access to four-year colleges and universities or for specialized vocational training. The demographic profile of these students increasingly will reflect the population's growing ethnic diversity and ever-widening range of socioeconomic backgrounds. (Phelan, 2000:2)

There is considerable truth to the claim that community colleges provide an enormous boost to educational attainment by expanding access to higher education. Several studies find that states and localities that are highly endowed with community colleges have significantly higher rates of college going than states and localities with a smaller community college presence (Dougherty, 1994:50-51; Grubb, 1989; Rouse, 1998).[16]

But a major qualification must be attached to this finding, a qualification that goes entirely unmentioned in the Education Commission of the States pol-

[16]Several features of community colleges make them great avenues of college access. The colleges are widely distributed across the country. Their tuitions are usually lower than those of four-year colleges and, because they are nearer by, dormitory residence is not necessary (or even possible). And because of their open-door admissions ideal, they are more willing to take in "nontraditional" stu-

icy paper quoted above and in fact in virtually all official statements on the community college. Many different studies find that entering a community college rather than a four-year college significantly lowers the probability that a student will attain a baccalaureate degree and, degree aside, significantly lowers a student's educational attainment (Dougherty, 1994:52-61; Pascarella and Terenzini, 1991:372-373, 506-507; Whitaker and Pascarella, 1994).[17] Because of the hindering effect of community colleges on the educational attainment of their baccalaureate entrants, states with many community colleges enjoy a far smaller lead in baccalaureate attainment than they do in simple college entrance over states with few community colleges (Dougherty, 1994:51-52; Rouse, 1998). States with many community colleges have a somewhat higher (but not statistically significant) rate of baccalaureate production than do states with few community colleges largely because community colleges bring significantly more people into college than do other kinds of institutions. However, this democratizing effect is undercut by the fact that these "extra" students, once they enter the community college, are considerably less likely to actually get a baccalaureate than if they had entered a four-year college. In other words, the community college's contribution to baccalaureate production is small because its "diversion" effect largely, though not completely, cancels its "democratizing" effect. Because this is still for many people a difficult finding to swallow, let me review the evidence demonstrating the extent of this diversion effect and illuminating the mechanisms producing it. We can then turn to the research and policy questions suggested by that evidence.

Hindrances to Baccalaureate Success

Clearly, a major part of the explanation for why community college entrants get far fewer baccalaureate degrees than four-year college entrants lies in the fact that community college students on average tend to come from less wealthy families, be less well prepared academically, and have lower educational and occupational aspirations. Yet, when we control for these student differences, community college entrants still secure considerably fewer bachelor de-

dents: high school dropouts, the academically deficient, vocational aspirants, and adults interested in skill upgrading.

[17]However, partially counterbalancing this effect is the finding — which is tentative and by no means conclusive, because it is based on only a few studies — that community colleges are as or more helpful than four-year colleges to students who are older, come from disadvantaged backgrounds, and do not aspire to a bachelor's degree (Berkner, Cuccaro-Alamin, and McCormick, 1996: 16-20; Dougherty, 1994: 56; Pascarella et al., 1995: 90; Whitaker and Pascarella, 1994: 204).

grees. Even when we compare community college entrants and four-year college entrants with the same demographic background (social class, race, and sex), academic aptitude, high school grades, and educational and occupational aspirations, the community college entrants on average attain 11 to 19% *fewer* baccalaureate degrees than their four-year college peers (Dougherty, 1994:52-61; and Pascarella and Terenzini, 1991:372-373, 506-507).

Clearly, the fact of going to a community college has an impact on educational attainment, quite apart from what qualities students bring to college. On closer inspection, we find that baccalaureate aspirants who begin at a community college are more likely than comparable four-year college entrants to drop out during the first two years of college, not move on to become juniors, and drop out in the junior or senior year (Dougherty, 1994:chap. 4).[18] Let's examine how each of these factors hinders baccalaureate reception by community college entrants.

Dropout in the Community College

Community colleges have a particularly high rate of dropout. Among students who first entered higher education in fall 1995, 44% of the entrants to public two-year colleges had left college sometime before spring 1998 without any degree; the comparable percentage for four-year college entrants was 18% (Berkner, Horn, and Clune, 2000:9, 26, 43, 59). To be sure, many of those who leave community colleges without a degree are not dropouts. They may have left without a degree because they only wanted to take a few courses or attain certain delimited skills short of a degree. And if they come to try out college, find it is not to their taste, and then leave, this could well be counted not as a personal or institutional failure but a legitimate educational attainment (Grubb, 1996:80-81). That said, many students do come to community college aspiring to a degree and still fail to succeed.

Personal factors certainly play an important role in unnecessary dropout at community colleges because they do attract many students who are poorly prepared, have low or weak academic motivation, and have lives beset by crisis. At the same time, institutional hindrances also play an important role in student dropout. Studies controlling for family background, high school record, and educational and occupational ambitions still find that community college students more often drop out in the first two years of college than do their four-year col-

[18]The following pages draw on and elaborate the discussion in Dougherty (1994), which critically synthesizes the results of a large number of studies. In order to avoid bibliographic overload, in what follows I will cite the relevant pages in Dougherty (1994), supplemented by references to studies that have come out since the publication of that book.

lege peers (Dougherty, 1994:86). The reasons for this difference are not definitively settled but there is evidence that this dropout gap may be attributable to the fact that community colleges are less able to academically and socially integrate their students into the life of the college through such devices as campus dorms and being surrounded by academically oriented students and teachers (Dougherty, 1994:85-92).

Inadequate Transfer Rates

Community college students are much less likely to go on to the junior year in pursuit of bachelor's degrees than are students entering four-year colleges. The main reason is obvious: most community college entrants are not pursuing a baccalaureate and, even when they state this goal, it is often a matter of hope rather than expectation. Moreover, community college students on average come from less advantaged families and are less prepared academically than are four-year college entrants (Cohen and Brawer, 1996a:55-58; Dougherty, 1994:53; Grubb, 1996:61, 80-82).

Still, institutional factors play an important role in the low transfer rate for community college entrants. Though community colleges do "warm up" many students, many others are cooled out. Two multivariate statistical analyses find that baccalaureate aspirants entering community colleges are significantly more likely to lower their ambitions by the end of the second year than are students of similar background, ability, and aspirations entering four-year colleges (Pascarella et al., 1998).[19] What may explains this weakening of ambition? A key factor is the community college's commitment to sub-baccalaureate vocational education. The more vocational a community college, the lower its transfer rate (Armstrong and Mellisinos, 1994:88; Dougherty, 1994:94). Why is this so?

Apparently, strongly vocational community colleges pull many students who enter with baccalaureate ambitions or who are undecided into vocational education by spreading before students an array of well designed and attractively packaged vocational programs in fields such as nursing, allied health professions, computer operations, and engineering technology. These programs are well advertised in college catalogs and brochures. They are often housed in more modern facilities than the academic programs. And the colleges frequently proclaim that vocational-education graduates do as well as baccalaureates (although on the whole this is not true) (Dougherty, 1994:93-97).

[19]Though this study is carefully done, it should also be noted that it is based on a small sample of institutions: 5 two-year colleges and 18 four-year colleges in 16 states. Given the large number and variability of two- and four-year colleges across this country, a question has to be raised about the representativeness of this small sample. See below for more.

Moreover, as community colleges have become more vocational, faculty and staff have put less emphasis on transfer. At the very least, vocationalization has brought in a greater number of faculty members and staff who put more emphasis on workforce development and less on transfer. In a 1995-96 national survey of community college faculty, the vocational faculty put a much higher emphasis on workforce development and a much lower stress on transfer than their academic counterparts. When asked what, in their own view, was the primary mission of the community college, 48% of the vocational faculty responded with workforce development and 14% with transfer. This was far different from their academic counterparts: only 21% put workforce development first, while 37% rated transfer as primary (Brewer, 1999:16-17).

This is not to say that enrolling in a vocational program is an insurmountable hurdle to transferring to a four-year school. Many community college vocational students do transfer to four-year colleges. For example, a study of students in the High School and Beyond Survey who entered community colleges in 1980 found that 23% of those who received a vocational Associate degree and 7% of those receiving a vocational certificate ended up transferring to a four-year college by spring 1984. However, these figures are still far lower than the transfer rate for those graduating with an academic Associate degree: 49% (Grubb, 1991). And state figures from the mid-1990s back up this disparity. A Florida survey of 1993 community college entrants followed up in 1998 found that, whereas 20% of those majoring in academic subjects transferred, the figure was only 6% for vocational majors (Florida Department of Community Colleges, 2000). And an Illinois survey of 1990 entrants followed up five years later found the transfer rates for academic and vocational majors to be 35% and 12%, respectively. To be sure, a good part of this disparity is due to the fact that vocational entrants may not harbor baccalaureate ambitions. However, the Illinois survey found that, even among those with baccalaureate ambitions, the transfer rate for vocational majors was still considerably lower than for academic majors: 25% and 40%, respectively (Illinois Community College Board, 1998). For more on the subject of the transferability of vocational degrees, see Dougherty (forthcoming).

If community-college entrants do retain a desire to transfer, they encounter several organizational obstacles to actualizing this goal. As two-year colleges, community colleges do not control an upper division to which they can pass on whom they wish. Rather, they depend on four-year colleges to accept their transfer students. And there is evidence that four-year colleges are less willing to take in community-college transfers than to admit freshmen, especially if those would-be transfers are in vocational programs and/or largely minority community colleges. Universities' distaste for community college transfer students does not take the form only of simple denial of admission. It also evidences itself in the poorer financial aid they typically give transfer students than new freshmen and continuing students. This aid gap has an impact. A study of transfer applicants to the University of California who were accepted but did not matriculate (19% of those accepted) found that a major reason was finances (Dougherty, 1994:96-97). Even when four-year institutions are committed to accepting transfers, this does not mean that transfer students are home free. Eligible students may still be denied admission to the campus of their choice because of insufficient room in the junior year, particularly in highly popular majors. And if offered an alternate campus, many accepted transfer students refuse either because the second campus has different requirements or because they cannot move due to family and other obligations (Dougherty, 1994:97).

Attrition in the Upper Division

Even after transferring to four-year colleges, community-college entrants are still at greater risk of failing to secure a baccalaureate than are four-year college natives. Several state and national studies have found that community college transfers have a considerably higher rate of attrition than four-year-college natives entering the junior year. Five years after transfer, about two-fifths of transfer students have left higher education without a baccalaureate degree. Meanwhile, the comparable percentage for four-year college natives entering the junior year the same year as the community college transfers is about one-quarter (Dougherty, 1994:97-100).[20]

A good part of this difference in dropout rate is no doubt due to the lower average aptitude and weaker motivation of two-year-college transfers compared to four-year natives. But there is evidence that several features of the U.S. higher education system also contribute to the higher mortality of community-college transfers. Compared to four-year college natives, transfer students less often

[20] Based on an analysis of the High School and Beyond Survey, Lee et al. (1993) argue that community college transfers and four-year college natives have essentially the same rate of baccalaureate attainment. However, Lee et al. (1993) do not seem to control for how many credits the students have accumulated. As a result, they are comparing the persistence rate of community college transfers only over the years after transfer to that for four-year college natives over their entire undergraduate career (including the high dropout freshman year). A similar error seemingly occurs in the NCES analysis of the 1994 follow-up of the 1989-90 cohort of the Beginning Postsecondary Student Survey (McCormick, 1997: 26, 38-39). The better comparison would have been between community college transfers and four-year natives with comparable numbers of accumulated credits. For example, studies comparing community college transfers with four-year natives who have reached the junior year find that the transfers have considerably lower persistence and graduation rates than the four-year native juniors (Dougherty, 1994:109-111).

receive financial aid, their lower-division credits are less often recognized by senior colleges, and they are not as well integrated socially and academically into four-year colleges (Dougherty, 1994:97-101).

The fact that transfer students less often receive financial aid than native four-year college students increases the probability that transfer students will have to withdraw for lack of money and hinders transfer students' academic and social integration into four-year colleges (Dougherty, 1994:98). Secondly, a sizable number of transfer students lose credits in transit to four-year colleges, thus slowing their educational progress and endangering their ability to finance their college career. This credit loss appears to be particularly pronounced among students transferring from community college vocational programs. Students transferring with academic courses are often protected by state requirements that public universities accept community college general education courses. But nongeneral education courses get much tougher scrutiny (Cohen and Brawer, 1996a:331-332; Dougherty, 1994:98-101; Rifkin, 2000; Striplin, 2000). For example, a study of 26 California community colleges in 1998 found that their non-liberal arts courses were often not deemed transferable: 27% of the non-liberal arts courses were not regarded as transferable to the California State University system and, more ominously, 73% were not considered transferable to the University of California system (Striplin, 2000). For more on the causes of credit loss, see Dougherty (1994:100-101).

The third major obstacle transfer students encounter is difficulty integrating themselves into the social life of four-year colleges. Because of less adequate financial aid, transfer students more often have to work to support themselves and thus have less time to mix with their peers on campus. Orientation programs directed specifically to transfer students are rare, and clubs and other extracurricular activities at four-year colleges usually focus their recruitment efforts on freshmen. In addition, transfer students often fail to get campus housing because many four-year colleges give priority to freshmen. These various impediments often lead transfer students to complain that they find it difficult to join student activities and take part in the general social life of the college. Poorer social integration has been found to cause, in turn, greater likelihood of academic failure (Dougherty, 1994:101-102).

Finally, transfer students run afoul of obstacles to integrating themselves academically into four-year colleges. Studies repeatedly find that they tend to suffer a sharp drop in grades in the first year after transfer (Cohen and Brawer, 1996a:65; Dougherty, 1994:102).[21] Clearly, a good part of the grade shock encountered by transfer students may stem from a collision between their abilities and the tougher standards of the four-year colleges. But it also stems from institutional factors: particularly, less access to financial aid and, perhaps, poorer academic preparation in the community college. Greater unmet financial need has been found to be associated with poorer upper-division grades (Dougherty, 1994:98-103). In addition, there is also reason to believe that community-college transfers may also get poorer upper-division grades than four-year-college natives because their lower-division preparation is, on average, inferior (Dougherty, 1994:103). However, there is some controversy over this point.

Calling into question how well community college transfers are prepared for their upper-division studies is a 1991 survey by the Washington State Board for Community and Technical Colleges of 1604 students who had entered community college in 1988 and transferred by 1991. The researchers found that, while 85% of the transfer students said that their classes gave them adequate preparation for junior/senior course work, 55% said the four-year college faculty were more challenging, 70% said their four-year college courses demand more analysis, 70% said more reading, and 65% said more writing (Washington State Board for Community and Technical Colleges, 1994:11, 16-17). This survey is buttressed by an analysis of the 1993 National Study of Postsecondary Faculty. It found that, among full-time instructional staff and faculty who taught credit classes at public two-year colleges, 47% said they *never* used essay mid-term or final examinations in *any* of their classes and 51% stated that they never used term or research papers in any of their classes (Palmer, 2000:48-49, 87-88).[22]

On the other hand, Pascarella, Bohr, Nora, and Terenzini (1995) argue that community colleges do not provide inferior academic preparation. They found that two-year college students perform just as well as comparable four-year college students — similar in social background, precollege ability and aspirations, and various college experiences — on tests of reading comprehension, mathematics, and critical thinking (at the end of the first year) and writing and science reasoning (at end of second year). This study deserves very careful attention, given the high quality research that Pascarella et al. are known for. Still,

[21]It is frequently claimed that transfers' upper-division grades soon recover from "transfer shock," but this is misleading. It is based on comparing the grades of students two or three years past transfer to those of students in the first year of transfer. Even when the same cohort is involved, no correction is made for the fact that the older students no longer include the many students who did badly after transfer and dropped out. In fact, a study of Illinois transfers found that, while those who eventually graduated with a baccalaureate largely did rally from their transfer shock, those who dropped out never did recover (Illinois Community College Board, 1986)

[22]The comparable figures for part-time instructors were 53% and 59%. The figures varied by the instructors' teaching field. Among full-timers, 73% of the instructors in health sciences never used essay exams but the figure for humanities instructors was only 17% (Palmer, 2000: 48).

there are reasons to resist Pascarella and his colleagues' conclusion (1995:93-94). The sample includes only five two-year colleges (yielding 280 students the first year and 147 the second year) and eighteen four-year colleges. Given the great variability among both two- and four-year colleges, there has to be serious doubt about how well such a small sample of institutions could represent the entire universe of nearly 1800 two-year colleges and 2300 four-year colleges. Secondly, Pascarella et al. (1995) themselves raise the question of how well the standardized multiple-choice tests they administered measure the skills actually needed to succeed in a four-year college (Pascarella et al., 1996:93-94). To these issues I would add a third problem: the study controls for the average precollege academic ability of first-year students at each college and whether the students resided on campus or not. This could have substantially reduced differences between four-year and two-year colleges by eliminating two advantages four-year college students have: greater exposure to high ability peers and greater access to campus residence (which is a potent source of academic and social integration). These methodological concerns about the Pascarella et al. (1995, 1996) study — when coupled with other studies showing differences in academic rigor between community colleges and four-year colleges (Dougherty, 1994:103-104) — raise the possibility that on average community colleges are less academically rigorous than four-year colleges and that this contributes to the higher attrition of community college transfers as versus four-year college natives in the junior and senior years of college.

Policies for Improving Educational Attainment

In order to improve the educational attainment of community college entrants, efforts must be made to reduce attrition, increase degree completion, and where useful encourage the pursuit of the baccalaureate. A myriad of proposals and a host of policy efforts have been made to accomplish these desiderata, but these have not commanded nearly as much policy and even research attention as they deserve. Given the widespread conviction among policymakers that the community college should be perhaps the major device for absorbing future increases in college enrollments, there is little interest in hearing about or dealing with community colleges' deficiencies in providing educational opportunity. Yet, this attention is crucial, particularly if we are to serve the interests of working class and minority students, who depend heavily on the community college for access and opportunity in higher education (Nora, 2000; Rendon and Garza, 1996).

Reducing Attrition

As discussed above, not all leaving of community college without a credential is truly academic failure, but a considerable part is. How can we reduce the cases of students leaving community colleges without realizing their ambitions? One important way is to strengthen the integration of community college students into the academic and social life of their institutions. Academic integration can be enhanced by encouraging greater faculty/student interaction both inside and outside of class. In addition, students' work lives should be integrated with their academic lives. Outside jobs absorb a great part of students' attention and time and may lead them to leave college entirely. Colleges can try to neutralize this competing influence by providing more jobs on campus and by academicizing outside work through paid internships (Dougherty, 1994:252-253). Because students' social ties are also important in binding them to their colleges, observers have suggested encouraging the formation of student clubs and study groups; keeping students on campus longer through cultural and social events in the evenings and on weekends; and holding weekend or even weeklong retreats for students (Dougherty, 1994:253; Tinto, Russo, and Kadel, 1994). Learning communities appear to be a particularly potent means of pursuing academic and social integration simultaneously. Student interaction with each other and with faculty appears to be significantly intensified by scheduling related courses in blocks so students move en masse from one to the other or by offering team taught mega-courses that meet several days a week for several hours at a time (Tinto, Russo, and Kadel, 1994).[23]

Besides making efforts to better integrate students generally, community colleges particularly need to reduce the high dropout rate among disadvantaged students. As discussed above in the section on remedial education, community colleges need to work with the secondary school system to improve the competence and motivation of students before they even reach the community college. And once in the community college disadvantaged students need to be offered strong remedial education programs, coupled with intensive counseling (Dougherty, 1994:253-254). This academic support and counseling should be backed up by close monitoring — perhaps through a computerized advising system — of students' grades and course taking patterns to make sure that they take the right courses, not register for courses beyond their ability, and receive academic counseling when necessary (Dougherty, 1994:254). In addition, especially for minority and working class students, strong efforts must be made to

[23]Another strategy to encourage social and academic integration would be for community colleges to provide dormitories. This suggestion may appear quixotic, since only 5% of community colleges have dormitories. But this number has been growing as community colleges build dorms in order to attract students who would otherwise go to four-year colleges and to house students who normally live outside the locality (such as international students) (Lords, 1999).

make the community colleges as welcoming as possible, opening themselves to the cultures, concerns, and abilities of non-dominant groups. This openness needs to show up in the content of the curriculum, the methods of instruction, and the attitudes, behavior, and composition of teachers, administrators, and student service staff (stretching from admissions and financial aid to academic support and student life) (Banks, 1995; Rendon and Garza, 1996:300-301). We will return to this issue below, in the context of multiculturalism and the building of social solidarity.

Increasing Credentials Attainment and Baccalaureate Transfer

But retention is not enough if it does not lead to a credential that fits students' interests and abilities. These need not be transfer-oriented degrees. Certain vocational certificates and associates' degrees can lead to quite good incomes: for example, for men, those in engineering or computers and for women, ones in health, business, or public service (Grubb, 1996:94-96).

At the same time, it is important to encourage all those capable to pursue the baccalaureate degree, because of its higher payoff. In order to finesse the dilemma discussed above between the lower but more certain payoff of pursuing a terminal vocational associate's degree and the higher but less certain payoff (for community college entrants) of pursuing the baccalaureate, strong efforts should be made to enhance the transferability of vocational credits toward baccalaureate degrees (Dougherty, forthcoming).

In order to enhance the transfer chances of all students, changes need to be made at several different points, particularly raising transfer aspirations and then facilitating the transfer process, which includes ensuring success after transfer.

Encouraging transfer aspirations. Community colleges should aim to strengthen and even awaken transfer interest by approaching those students who might be or should be interested in transfer with extensive and up-to-date information about transfer opportunities. Certainly the general faculty role in transfer advising must be revived, but community colleges should also follow the California community colleges in establishing transfer centers that stock all available information on transfer, house special transfer counselors, and provide a place to meet admissions officials from the universities. Meanwhile, in the case of disadvantaged students who are more likely to enter the community college not wishing to pursue a baccalaureate degree, efforts should be made to intercept them very early, even before they enter the community college, in order to build up their aspirations (Dougherty, 1994:253-254; Palmer, 1998:5; Rifkin, 2000:6).

In order to overcome students' fears of having to move away from the community college to an entirely new college, it is useful to have them experience four-year college life in advance. Community colleges should encourage their students to take courses at four-year colleges, participate in university cultural events, and simply visit university campuses. And four-year colleges should be encouraged to offer upper-division courses or even entire baccalaureate programs at community colleges (more on this below).

Facilitating the transfer process. In order to insure the success of transfer students, it is necessary to minimize the possibility that they lose credits in transfer, be denied financial aid, fail to be integrated socially into the four-year college, or be poorly prepared for upper-division work

To reduce the loss of credits, many recommend — and several states have mandated — that general education courses be accepted in a blanket fashion: approved community college general education courses should be accepted as meeting university general education requirements, or an associate's degree in approved majors should be made sufficient for junior-level standing (Dougherty, 1994:257; Illinois State Board of Higher Education, 1997; Rifkin, 2000:3; Schmidt, 1997).[24] The transferability of nongeneral education courses can be furthered through course equivalency guides and common course numbering systems connecting community college and four-year college courses (Dougherty, 1994:257; Knoell, 1996:58; Rifkin, 2000:4). This information can be embedded in computerized advising systems that list the courses that four-year colleges currently require, generate recommended course plans, and in some cases keep track of how well students are meeting those requirements (Dougherty, 1994:258; Nussbaum, 1997).

Occupational students face particularly hard problems in transferring credits, necessitating efforts tailored to their needs. It is helpful that states such as Florida have mandated that community colleges and public four-year colleges work together to ease the transfer of occupational degrees (Horine, 1998; Pitter, 1999:1, 6-7). But to be effective, this mandate needs to be backed up by particular devices that make it practicable. One such device is to establish "capstone" programs, in which occupational education courses in community colleges are credited by four-year colleges against a major in a technical field and the bulk of students' upper-division course load is devoted to meeting four-year colleges' general education requirements (Dougherty, 1994:255; Pitter, 1999:10-11; Rifkin, 2000:5; Washington State Board for Community and Technical Colleges,

[24]A particularly elaborate effort to identify a set of general education courses that are guaranteed transferability is the Illinois Articulation Initiative. Based on a collaboration between four-year and community college faculty, a statewide General Education Core Curriculum has been defined that consists of 12 to 13 courses in five fields: oral and written communication, math, humanities and fine arts, social sciences, and natural sciences (Illinois State Board of Higher Education, 1997).

1997:10).[25] Another promising device is to introduce more general education into occupational programs so that they are more transferable and to ensure that the general education courses already required in those programs are meeting state requirements for transferable general education courses (Pitter, 1999:6; Rifkin, 2000:6).

While state universities are particularly important partners for community colleges efforts to facilitate transfer, so are private colleges, including for profit schools. Traditional private colleges may welcome occupational transfers as a means of shoring up their enrollments in a more competitive higher education economy. And for-profit colleges may particularly be open to new transfer arrangements because of their desire for rapid growth and their weak or nonexistent academic traditions. As it happens, the League for Innovation in the Community College — a compact of 19 leading community colleges nationwide — has forged an agreement with several nontraditional colleges to set up transfer processes. These partners include Western Governors University, the University of Phoenix, and United States Open University (League for Innovation in the Community College, 2001).

After transfer, financial aid often remains a problem for transfer students. Financial aid that is more plentiful and better tailored to transfer students' changing needs can help these students more fully integrate themselves socially into the four-year school by lessening their need to work to pay their bills (Dougherty, 1994:258; Rifkin, 2000:7). At the same time, transfer students need other help as well. They need orientation programs directed solely to them, rather than ones that lump them with freshmen and other new students (Dougherty, 1994:258).

Many transfer students suffer a sharp drop in grades between community college and four-year colleges, and this is not a minor and transitory experience, as is often claimed. If indeed inadequate preparation in the community college is a factor, this can be alleviated by closer parallelism between university and community college standards. University and community college faculty should be encouraged to teach the same courses, perhaps on each other's campuses. Moreover, potential transfer students need to be made aware — perhaps by taking university courses in advance of transfer — that university work often will be tougher and require more self-directed work. Also standards for entry into and graduation from transfer programs should be made tougher and transfer courses should be made more rigorous, requiring reading of more complex materials and engaging in more analytic writing (Dougherty, 1994:259-260; Rifkin, 2000:3).

[25]A variant on this is 2 + 2 + 2 articulation, as in California, in which high schools, community colleges, and four-year colleges forge explicit agreements for moving vocational students through the three levels (Helm and de Anda, 1993).

All of these efforts to enhance transfer rates and post-transfer success can be given a strong boost if states financially reward community colleges and state four-year colleges that have higher transfer rates. In fact, this is occurring through the increasingly popular device of performance based funding, in which a certain portion of state funding depends on institutional performance in certain areas such as transfer rate (Burke and Serban, 1998; Dougherty and Kim, 2001; Rifkin, 2000:6).

Beyond ensuring that the ambitions of baccalaureate aspirants are not thwarted, community colleges must also increase their efforts to "warm up" those who have sub-baccalaureate aspirants but have the ability to pursue a baccalaureate degree. This is particularly important in the case of disadvantaged students who are more likely to enter the community college not wishing to pursue a baccalaureate degree. They need to be intercepted very early, as they enter or even before they enter the community college, to suggest the idea of pursuing a baccalaureate degree and to develop the skills and motivation that would make it possible. A notable example of such a program has been the Puente Project, a collaboration between the University of California and the California Community Colleges targeted to Mexican-American students (Laden, 1999). And if students feel that they cannot pursue a baccalaureate degree — perhaps because their economic needs are more immediate, requiring them to secure a short-term vocational degree — then they need to be shown how a vocational degree can be later made transferable toward a baccalaureate degree.

The Need for Structural Reforms

Though the reforms sketched above are eminently worth pursuing, I would argue that they are also limited because they do not eliminate the fundamental institutional obstacles that hinder the baccalaureate attainment of community college entrants. The reforms leave the community college as a two-year, commuter institution that is structurally separate from the four-year colleges. As long as community colleges remain commuter institutions, they will never be able to integrate their students academically and socially to the same degree as four-year colleges, which are much more often residential. Devices such as arranging more events on campus and requiring faculty to interact more with students do enhance social cohesion, but they cannot begin to match college residential life in involving students in the life of a college. As long as community colleges remain two-year institutions, their baccalaureate aspirants will have to overcome the psychological difficulty that to pursue their degree they have to transfer to a new and foreign institution. And as long as community colleges remain institutionally separate from universities, transfer students will always run into difficulty in getting admitted, receiving financial aid, transferring their community college credits, and preparing themselves for upper-division courses. Because of their institutional separation from community colleges, four-year colleges will continue to prefer admitting new freshmen rather than older transfers and giving them priority in getting financial aid. Four-year college faculty and officials will continue to favor their courses over those offered by community colleges and thus to be reluctant to accept community college credits. And because they are not members of the same institutions, university and community-college faculty will continue to find it hard to keep up with each others' academic expectations. Visits, exchanges, and negotiations can partially bridge this gulf, but they cannot substitute for the regular contact that occurs between teachers of upper-division and lower-division courses within a single institution. These structural limitations may explain why college transfer rates have not risen as much as reformers would hope (Center for the Study of Community Colleges, 1988:108, 110, 144, 146, 156, 160).

The limitations of the nonstructural changes discussed above suggest the need for reforms that would transform the very structure, and not just operations, of the community college. These structural changes can be ranged along a continuum of how deeply they change the very organization of community colleges and four-year colleges.

Community colleges and four-year colleges can be brought into closer physical relationship through university centers at community colleges. For example, Macomb Community College in Michigan and North Harris Montgomery Community College District in Texas provide space on their own campuses for universities to offer baccalaureate courses taught by university faculty and some community college faculty (Cook, 2000:3; Martorana, 1994; Washington State Board for Community and Technical Colleges, 1997:13).

Dual-enrollment programs pull community colleges and four-year colleges together social psychologically rather than physically. Students are admitted into both institutions simultaneously and are treated as members of both. If they satisfactorily complete a lower-division transfer program in the community college, they are guaranteed transfer to the four-year college (Dougherty, 1994:255; Knoell, 1996:59; Rifkin, 2000:5; Washington State Board for Community and Technical Colleges, 1997:12-13).

But the most radical structural reform of the relationship between community colleges and four-year colleges is to allow community colleges themselves to become de facto four-year colleges, by allowing them to offer baccalaureate degrees (Cook, 2000; Dougherty, 1994:263-266). Students could move between the lower and upper divisions, without any of the difficulties attendant today with transfer between community college and senior college. Students would not be crossing a chasm between mutually suspicious colleges but traversing a barely discernible line within the same institution. They would take their financial aid and credit with them since the same student-assistance and registration systems are involved. Their lower-division academic preparation would be much better attuned to the demands of upper-division courses because the faculty in the two divisions would often be one and the same and, in any case, would be housed within the same organization. And if they were to take any vocational courses, these would usually be creditable toward their baccalaureate degree, since the baccalaureate degrees would often be built on vocational associate degree programs.

The suggestion of giving community colleges the right to offer baccalaureate degrees is controversial and many policymakers simply dismiss it.[26] However, the idea has been slowly spreading. Florida has decided to allow a community college to award a baccalaureate degree if no four-year college will agree to offer baccalaureate programs at the community college (MacDonald, 1999; Schmidt, 1999). Arkansas, meanwhile, has given Westark Community College the right to offer a baccalaureate degrees in nine areas (Cook, 2000:4). Furthermore, calls have been made in Arizona and New York to have two year colleges offer baccalaureates in applied technology (Call, 1997; Healy, 1998).

A policy of allowing community colleges to offer baccalaureate degrees does face some important questions. One is resources and cost. To what degree and at what cost will community colleges need to upgrade their faculty, libraries, labs, and so forth to meet baccalaureate accreditation requirements (Cook, 2000:6; Pitter, 1999:9)? This issue of resources immediately raises the question of finance. How will these new programs be financed within a state and local structure oriented to different financing of two-year and four-year education, with bigger local and smaller student contributions in the case of community colleges as versus four-year colleges (Cook, 2000:6)? And finance issues necessarily raise governance issues. Who will govern and accredit the new BA programs (Cook, 2000:6)? Finally, will the rise of community college granted baccalaureates harm the non-BA missions of community colleges by diverting time, attention, and money (Cook, 2000:5)? These are all major questions but they should not preclude exploring the benefits of having community colleges themselves grant baccalaureate degrees, in place of the current cumbersome and often inefficient system of having to pass on students to four-year colleges if they are to get baccalaureates.

[26] For a review and rebuttal of typical objections to the idea of community colleges being able to offer baccalaureate degrees, see Dougherty (1994: 263-266).

Research Needed on Educational Attainment

Though excellent research has been done on the impacts of the community college on educational attainment, there are several important areas in which there is little good research. These under-studied areas include variations in community college effects and some aspects of the process by which community colleges hinder the educational attainment of their baccalaureate aspirants.

Variations in Community College Effects

The research extant has focused on the average effects of community colleges, but as we have seen above there is suggestive evidence that community college effects may vary considerably depending on students' traits and community colleges' characteristics (Dougherty, 1994:56; Pascarella et al., 1995:90; Whitaker and Pascarella, 1994:204). However, these variable effects have been given far too little attention by researchers and policymakers.

On the student side, aspirations and social background shape what impact community colleges have on academic, educational, and economic attainment. White, middle class, and female students seemingly experience greater cognitive growth and attain more education if they attend four-year colleges rather than community colleges, but the reverse appears to be true for nonwhite, working class, and male students (Dougherty, 1994:56; Pascarella et al., 1995:90; 1996:38-39). Similarly, students with high educational or occupational aspirations attain significantly more educationally or occupationally if they enter four-year colleges rather than community colleges, but those with low aspirations seemingly do as well or better attending community colleges (Dougherty, 1994:56; Whitaker and Pascarella, 1994:204-206).[27] Given this suggestive evidence, we need to examine rigorously — using large national samples with extended followups — how community college effects vary by students' social background (social class, race, sex), age, educational and occupational aspirations, and so forth. Such investigations will help clarify for whom and in what circumstances the community college is a particularly helpful or unhelpful institution.

On the institutional side, we know that community colleges vary greatly among themselves in their declared missions, degree of support for college transfer, financial resources, and so forth (Bailey and Morest, 2001; Shaw and London, 1998). And again we have suggestive evidence that variations in the characteristics of community colleges produce variations in their students' educational and occupational attainment. For example, the more vocational a community college is the lower its transfer rate (Dougherty, 1994:94; Dougherty, forthcoming).

[27]Similar variation occurs in the area of economic attainment. Women get higher returns for vocational associates' degrees and certificates than do men, if one controls for family background, marital and family status, labor force experience, and a number of other variables (Grubb, 1996: 90, 262).

Again, this suggests the need to disaggregate community colleges and examine whether different types produce different results for their students.

More Data on How Baccalaureate Aspirants Are Hindered

Though we have detailed explanations of why baccalaureate aspirants entering community colleges are less successful than their peers entering four-year colleges, we still could learn more about how this differential effect is produced. To begin, we have only a few studies that examine differences between community colleges and four-year colleges in rates of attrition, controlling for differences in background, ability, motivation, and so forth and these studies are from the 1970s (see Dougherty, 1994:85-92).

Similarly, the finding that community college students have a higher rate of failure to continue on to the upper-division than do comparable students who first entered four-year colleges is based on studies that do not control for a wide range of possible differences between these two kinds of students (see Dougherty, 1994:92-97). Hence, there is a need for careful multivariate studies in order to conclusively establish that there is a significant *institutional* contribution to the lower transfer rate of community college entrants.

The extent and causes of post-transfer attrition also needs further attention. The study by Lee et al. (1993) should be replicated, perhaps with the Beginning Postsecondary Student Survey, with the proviso that transfer students are compared with native students with the same number of credits as the transfer students brought in. Moreover, we need a large scale national survey to definitively settle remaining doubts about whether community college students on average receive an inferior academic preparation prior to transfer. Also more studies need to be conducted, especially using national data sets, on the precise power and mode of operation of inadequate financial aid and post-transfer academic and social malintegration in the higher attrition of transfer students.

Finally, it would be very useful to have studies that examine the impacts all at once of all the career contingencies (lower-division attrition, failure to transfer, and attrition in the upper division) facing B.A. aspirants. By examining them all within one data analysis, rather than having to paste together several different pieces of data, we can determine the relative weights of these career contingencies.

Besides more research to deepen our understanding of the community college's impact on educational attainment, we also need more research evaluating the effectiveness of the policies proposed to increase the baccalaureate attainment rates of community college entrants. Virtually all the policy proposals could use more evaluation, but two recent proposals are particularly in need of careful scrutiny. The call to encourage the transferability of vocational credits should be examined in terms of what efforts are really being made to advance this goal and how successful those efforts are proving in easing the transferability of vocational credits. Secondly, we need to examine the impact on baccalaureate attainment of university centers established at community colleges, programs of dual enrollment at community colleges and four-year colleges, and community colleges themselves offering baccalaureate degrees.

GENERAL EDUCATION

General education is a recurrent subject in discussions about the purposes of education. It also a term that covers quite different concepts. A traditional definition, associated with the concept of liberal education, centers around transmitting a common culture, whether it is a national culture or certain ways of thinking about the world. But another definition, rooted in Progressive education, focuses on preparing for life by fostering skills that are of broad utility, such as communication skills and critical thinking (Levine, 1978:8-9; Zeszotarski, 1999). As it happens, higher education faculty and officials tend to combine these two elements. This can be seen in two analyses, reported in Table 1 below. The first is a 1987 national survey of 2487 higher education institutions (with a response rate of 50%). Using open-ended questions, it found six identifiable dimensions of general education. Two clearly pertain to liberal education: (1) heritage: providing a common core of great ideas and passing on a common Western heritage; (2) counterpoint: exposing students to subjects outside their majors. The other four dimensions involve general education as opposed to liberal education: (3) instrumental skill development e.g. writing, speaking, critical thinking; (4) empowerment: developing the whole learner and the capacity to be a lifelong learner; (5) social agenda: serving social purposes such as global awareness and environmentalism; and (6) valuing: learning to perceive values operating in different situations and how values are determined (Smith, 1993:246-247).

Since 1987, it is clear that the definition of general education has broadened. The dimensions of heritage and of social agenda have broadened, as multicultural understanding has become more valued. Moreover, the dimension of instrumental skills development has broadened to include computer literacy (Zeszotarski, 1999:45-47).

Community colleges define general education in ways that are quite similar to the dimensions identified in Smith's (1993) general survey of higher education institutions. As Table 1 below indicates, similar dimensions of general education were found in an analysis by the Center for the Study of Community Colleges at

Table 1: Dimensions of General Education

1987 Survey of Higher Education Institutions (Smith, 1993): dimensions identified	Center for the Study of Community Colleges Analysis of Catalogs of 32 Community Colleges (Zeszotarski, 1999): dimensions identified	
Heritage	Core knowledge of cultural heritage	34%
Counterpoint	Academic breadth	13%
Instrumental skills	Basic skills	44%
Empowerment	Lifelong learning	16%
	Personal growth	31%
	Interpersonal skills	22%
Social agenda	Appreciate diversity	25%
	Citizenship	22%
Valuing	Moral development	13%

UCLA of the catalogs of 32 community colleges nationwide (Zeszotarski, 1999).

Moving from goals to actual programmatic efforts, it is clear that these general education goals are by no means lip service. According to the analysis of community college catalogs, all 32 of the colleges analyzed had some kind of general education requirement for their transfer programs and at least 90% of them had some general education requirement for their nontransfer programs (Zeszotarski, 1999:45-47).[28] Moreover, community colleges have been actively involved in service learning, with 30% of colleges reporting in 1995 that they had service learning offerings and another 45% proposing to establish them (Barnett, 1996:10).

Though these figures of community college involvement in general education are impressive, we also need to be aware that they exaggerate the actual degree to which community college students receive general education. For example, among the 90% of community colleges that had core curriculum requirements for their nontransfer programs, half of those requirements varied from program to program, raising question about just how "core" those general education requirements are. In addition, 50% of the colleges did not require their nontransfer students to take even one course in U.S. government and 43% did not require a U.S. history course (though over 90% of them did require such courses of their transfer students). Finally, only 31% of the 32 community colleges required a course in ethnic studies or multiculturalism for students in transfer programs and only 21% required it of students in nontransfer programs

[28]In addition, a nationwide survey of college faculty in 1997 found that community college faculty put nearly identical emphasis as faculty generally on such forms of general education as oral and written communication skills (89% of community college faculty versus 88% of all faculty put this as very important), analysis and problem-solving abilities (86% vs. 85%), and science and technological literacy (43% vs. 41%) (Huber, 1998: 69-71).

(Zeszotarski, 1999:45-47). In fact, the attention to multicultural education may be even lower than this. In an annual survey of college administrators, only 15% of community college administrators stated that their college required specific courses focusing on multicultural issues (El-Khawas, 1992). Similarly, another survey found that community colleges were less likely than four-year colleges to have multicultural general education requirements, courses in ethnic and gender studies, and changes in the disciplines, faculty programs, advising, or centers and institutes (Levine and Cureton, 1992).

These apparent gaps in the provision of general education are not surprising because community colleges face great difficulties in providing general education for all their students. These colleges enroll students so varied in backgrounds, interests, and ways of utilizing the college that it is very hard to give them a common core of general education. The decline of transfer education and the rise of occupational education has meant that community colleges now enroll many students whose primary purpose is likely to be preparation for a job rather than preparation for a variety of life roles. This problem is exacerbated if employers are paying for the training. They are likely to doubt the utility of general education. In fact, even within the community college, contract training is often driven by an ethos quite different from, and even opposed to, general education. A 1993-94 national survey of directors of contract training operations at community colleges found that when they praised certain community colleges as running exemplary contract training programs, a frequent theme was that these colleges ran their operations in a very business-like way, which was strongly contrasted with the way typical for education (Johnson, 1995:139, 154).[29] As a result, contract training programs typically are narrowly focused on providing skills and devote little or no attention to broader social knowledge and life skills (Dougherty and Bakia, 2000).[30] In addition, the rise of distance education complicates general education. Distance education courses are often focused on narrow competencies, in part because of the desires of vocationally oriented clients (Phipps et al., 1998:24-25). Moreover, much distance education is organized around single courses or small packages of courses rather than entire programs, making it difficult to include general education (Eaton, 2000:6).

Policy Recommendations

For general education to thrive, it needs forceful advocacy by policymakers and not just community college educators. As in precollegiate education, the importance of education for citizenship and other important social roles needs to be

[29]For example, the community college receiving the most mention, Johnson County (Kansas) Community College, was praised by one observer for running "their contract training and business services like a business. . . . They are marketers first and educators a distant second" (quoted in Johnson, 1995: 139).

resolutely reaffirmed. Given the fact that general education thrives best within a milieu of organized programs rather than a smorgasbord of individualized courses, it is also important to stress again the importance of the degree as an organizing principle for the supply and demand of education (Eaton, 2000:7-8).

One of the most important areas in which general education needs to be strengthened is in the nontransfer curriculum, where general education requirements tend to be the weakest (Zeszotarski, 1999:45-46). Besides more often requiring general education courses similar to those for transfer students, there are other techniques for infusing general education into occupational and remedial education that have been suggested under the rubric of academic-vocational integration. These include applied academics courses, incorporation of academic skills (particularly in communications and math) into occupational programs, incorporating academic modules into expanded occupational courses, multidisciplinary courses combining academic and occupational perspectives and concerns, and tandem and cluster courses (Cohen and Brawer, 1996a:359-364; Grubb and Associates, 1999:chap. 7; and Perin, 1998). However, it is important to realize that what is often billed as academic and vocational integration fails to bear up under close inspection (Perin, 1998).

In order to strongly encourage these efforts, states should make extensiveness and effectiveness of general education one of the indicators they use in performance-based funding. This would be best done in the form of output measures really measuring general education acquired. However, this will only work if agreement is reached on what is meant by general education and if valid measures of its acquisition are developed. Hence, in the interim, states may want to consider performance indicators that tap how extensively community colleges are providing general education.

Research Needs

There is a great need for research on how extensively, how well, and in what ways community colleges discharge their role in general education. A survey by the National Center for Education Statistics on general education would

[30]There are some exceptions to this pattern. The auto service technician programs developed by General Motors, Ford, and others do lead to an associate's degree incorporating a number of general education courses. Furthermore, recent contract training for inservice workers not infrequently devotes a significant amount of attention to "soft skills" such as problem solving, team work, and communication that approach the life competencies and understandings enunciated by some forms of general education. However, these general education elements are circumscribed by their focus on work problems. For example, at one community college, the auto repair program restricted the required general education course in social science to a course in human relations in organizations (Dougherty and Bakia, 2000).

be very important both to illuminate the extent and forms of general education and to call attention to its importance. Such an assay of the state of general education should examine whether students in different programs within the community college receive very different amounts and kinds of general education. Moreover, research on general education in the community college should try to pinpoint different conceptualizations and pedagogies of general education used in community colleges and how well they work in different program areas and with different kinds of students.

MULTICULTURAL EDUCATION AND COMMUNITY BUILDING

The general education function of the community college borders on another function that also goes virtually unmentioned among policymakers: the creation of community. Community colleges are an important means of generating a vibrant "civil society," by providing a place for citizens of diverse backgrounds to come together — whether as students in courses or participants in public events on campus (such as art performances and exhibitions or public affairs forums) — to learn about each other and search for over-arching commonalities (Cohen and Brawer, 1996a:284-286; Rhoads and Valadez, 1996). Community colleges are better able to do this than either four-year colleges or high schools because their student bodies are typically more socially diverse than those of four-year colleges and more chronologically diverse than those of high schools. Moreover, community colleges typically have a stronger commitment to serving their local communities (Dougherty and Bakia, 1999; Grubb et al., 1997).

And indeed the American Association of Community Colleges and many of its members have embraced the role of building community solidarity (American Association of Community Colleges, 1988:6-7, 29-31; Pierce, 1996). As many as 250 community colleges have participated in the Beacon Project of the American Association of Community Colleges, in which community colleges across the country explore different forms of community engagement (Barnett, 1995).

Beyond the question of how strongly community colleges are pursuing the community building mission is the fact that it has not become a policy goal for government and other policymakers. Though they may welcome it and occasionally fund it, it is given little push, as evidenced by the fact that none of the performance based funding systems have it as an indicator (American Association of Community Colleges, 2000b; Burke, 1997; Burke and Serban, 1998).

Policy Recommendations

Just as policymakers have established various programs to encourage and assist elementary and secondary schools to build solidarity across social divisions, so should there be programs to do the same within community colleges. In fact, given the high degree of racial and class segregation in high school in many parts of the country, the community college is today as important as the high school as a place for fostering racial and ethnic understanding and integration.

One of the most potent ways of fostering inter-group understanding and solidarity is through sustained and relaxed interaction among students of different backgrounds. Clubs, associations, and teams have traditionally been devices to facilitate this interaction. However, rather than leave this to chance, efforts need to be made to consciously guide student groups toward intercultural mixing. Moreover, these co-curricular and extra-curricular activities should be supplemented by specifically curricular activities such as learning communities and cooperative learning that also foster sustained interaction. Learning communities, where students share the same class or are together for extended periods of learning time, can provide opportunities for a multitude of interactions built around common tasks (Tinto, Russo, and Kadel, 1994). Meanwhile, smaller communities can be created within classrooms via cooperative learning groups (Mahony, 1992).

The building of multi-cultural community solidarity is much enhanced if group differences in achievement are minimized. Hence, teaching techniques should be utilized that facilitate the success of students of varied backgrounds: for example, cooperative learning techniques seem particularly useful for Black and Mexican-American students.[31] Moreover, colleges need to change educational structures and practices — such as biased assessment instruments, teacher expectations, or staffing patterns — that unfairly produce achievement differences among students differing in race, ethnicity, class, or gender.[32]

Research Needs

The community-building function, though described and celebrated by community college observers, has not been systematically studied except in recent research by Kathleen Shaw and Howard London (1998). We have little solid information on how successful the community college has been in fostering understanding and social solidarity across students and community members of different backgrounds. Moreover, to the degree community colleges have been at least partially successful, information is needed on the various techniques community colleges have used and how successful each has been both generally and with specific kinds of participants.

SUMMARY AND CONCLUSIONS

We have traversed a wide variety of issues involving the community college. We began with ones in the policy limelight, that is, issues under active discussion by government officials, policy oriented researchers, and other members of the policymaking community. We discussed the growing competition faced by community colleges from proprietary schools, the weakening support of state governments and their increasing attachment of performance standards to a portion of that support, and various areas of instructional activity that are attracting great interest: workforce development (especially in such forms as contract education), distance education, and remedial education. But then we moved to issues that lie at the edge of, or even outside, the policy limelight. These include general education, community building, and the hindering effect of community colleges on baccalaureate attainment.

The point of this journey from policy spotlight to policy twilight is to show that the issues deemed important by the policy community do not encompass all important issues facing the community college. Therefore, it is important that those who seek to understand and improve the community college not restrict themselves only to those issues that are of current interest to policymakers. To be sure, addressing the issues of concern to policymakers is valuable because those issues often are important and, in any case, will be acted upon, for good or for ill. It is important to think carefully and do probing research on topics such as accountability and distance education because done badly they could have a quite deleterious impact. Poorly conceptualized accountability indicators could badly distort how community colleges pursue their missions. A utopian, uncritical pursuit of distance education could damage the educational opportunities of students who would most benefit from traditional education.

But if researchers constrict their attention to issues in the policy limelight, they may well fail to address issues that are key to properly guiding the community college. Many important issues fall outside the policy spotlight for reasons other than their importance. As John Kingdon, Charles Lindblom, Claus Offe, Deborah Stone, and other analysts of the policy process have noted, the atten-

[31]Miami-Dade Community College has made a particularly notable effort to carefully think out its instructional program in order to open room for a variety of learning and teaching styles (Jenrette and Adams, 1992).

[32]Joliet Junior College in Illinois and Miami-Dade Community College have attracted attention for their efforts to pluralize the racial and ethnic backgrounds of their teaching staffs and to broaden faculty awareness of cultural differences and their impact on learning (Jenrette and Adams, 1992).

tion given to a social problem or policy issue is not just a function of its degree of social importance. Whether an issue enters the policy arena and is put on the issue attention and decision agenda also depends on the presence of policy entrepreneurs who will advocate that issue or offer solutions to it, the culture of the society and the structure of the polity (which selectively favor and disfavor certain issues), the interests of powerful economic and political groups, the state of the economy (a good economy provides resources to take on more problems), the novelty of the issue, and the stage of the electoral and policymaking cycle (Hilgartner and Bosk, 1988).

Because social importance does not alone determine policy centrality and because policy centrality is a socially constructed result, policy relevant research must be guided not just by the current definitions of policymakers but also by considerations of the general interests of society, interests that often are articulated only by groups well outside the inner circles of power. Policy oriented researchers must not allow themselves to be constrained by the fact that policymakers do not talk about and seemingly do not want to hear about the fact that the community college, even while it expands college access, also hinders the opportunities of baccalaureate aspirants. Rather, policy oriented scholars need to note this impact, investigate its ramifications, and offer alternatives if community colleges are to make their best contribution to educational opportunity, especially for disadvantaged students. Similarly, while policymakers may pay little attention to the community college's potentially major contribution to multicultural education, it is important that scholars attend to it because the community college can play a major role in building social solidarity in a diverse society that is forever risking fragmentation.

REFERENCES

American Association of Community Colleges. (1988). *Building Communities: A Vision for a New Century*. Washington, DC: Author.

American Association of Community Colleges. (2000a). *National Profile of Community Colleges: Trends and Statistics*. (3rd ed.) Washington, DC: Author.

American Association of Community Colleges. (2000b). *Performance Based Funding — A Review of Five States*. Washington, DC: Author. http://www.aacc.nche/headline/082399/head1.htm

American Association of University Professors. (1998.) "Distance Learning." *Academe* 84: 30-38.

Anderson, K. (1981). Post-high school experiences and college attrition. *Sociology of Education* 54: 1-15.

Anderson, K. (1984). Institutional differences in college effects. ERIC Document Reproduction Service No. ED 256 204. Boca Raton, FL: Florida International University.

Arenson, K.W. (1998a). With new admissions policy, CUNY steps into the unknown. *New York Times* May 28: A1,B6.

Arenson, K.W. (1998b). Classes are full at catch-up U. *New York Times* May 31: sec. 4, p. 4.

Armstrong, W.B. and Mellissinos, M. (1994). Examining the relationship between the liberal arts, course levels, and transfer rates. *New Directions for Community Colleges* #86 (Summer): 81-91.

Bailey, T. and Morest, V.S. (2001). *Multiple Missions of Community Colleges*. New York: Community College Research Center, Teachers College, Columbia University. http://www.tc.columbia.edu/ccrc

Banks, J.A. (1995). Multicultural education: Historical development, dimensions, and practices. In J. A. Banks and C.A.M. Banks (eds.), *Handbook of Research on Multicultural Education* (pp. 3-24). New York: Macmillan.

Barnett, L. (1995). *A Climate Created: Community Building in the Beacon College Project*. ERIC Document Reproduction Service No. ED 393 494. Washington, DC: American Association of Community Colleges.

Barnett, L. (1996). Service learning: Why community colleges? *New Directions for Community Colleges* #93 (Spring): 7-15.

Berkner, L.K., Cuccaro-Alamin, S., and McCormick, A.C. (1996). *Descriptive Summary of 1989-90 Beginning Postsecondary Students: Five Years Later*. NCES 96-155. Washington, DC: U.S. National Center for Education Statistics.

Berkner, L., Horn, L., and Clune, M. (2000). *Descriptive Summary of 1995-96 Beginning Postsecondary Students: Three Years Later*. NCES 2000-154. Washington, DC: U.S. National Center for Education Statistics.

Blumenstyk, G. (1998). Western Governors' University takes shape as a new model for higher education. *Chronicle of Higher Education* (Feb. 6): A21.

Bosworth, B. (1999). Unpublished tabulations from "The 1998 Survey of State-Funded, Employer-Focused Job Training Programs." Belmont, MA: Regional Technology Strategies, Inc

Boylan, H.R., Bonham, B., and Bliss, L. (1992). The impact of developmental education programs. Paper presented to the First National Conference on Research in Developmental Education. Charlotte, NC.

Braddock, D. (1999). Occupational employment projections to 2008. *Monthly Labor Review* 122 (11): 51-77.

Breneman, D.W., and Haarlow, W.N. (1998). *Remediation in Higher Education*. Washington, DC: Thomas B. Fordham Foundation.

Brewer, D.J. (1999). *How Do Community College Faculty View Institutional Mission? An Analysis of National Survey Data*. New York: Community College Research Center, Teachers College, Columbia

University. http://www.tc.columbia.edu/ccrc

Brint, S.G., and Karabel, J.B. (1989). *The Diverted Dream*. New York: Oxford University Books.

Burke, J.C. (1997). *Performance-Funding Indicators: Concerns, Values, and Models for Two- and Four-Year Colleges and Universities*. ERIC Document Reproduction Service No. ED 407 910. Albany, NY: State University of New York, Rockefeller Institute of Government.

Burke, J.C., and Serban, A.M. (eds.) (1998). *Performance Funding for Public Higher Education: Fad or Trend?* New Directions for Institutional Research #97. San Francisco: Jossey-Bass.

Burke, J.C., and Modarresi, S. (1999). *Performance Funding and Budgeting: Popularity and Volatility — The Third Annual Survey*. Albany, NY: State University of New York, Rockefeller Institute of Government.

Call, R.W., and Associates. (1997). *The Applied Baccalaureate: A New Option in Higher Education in the United States*. ERIC Document Reproduction Service No. ED 409 038. Alfred, NY: University College of Technology.

Carnevale, A.P., Johnson, N.C., and Edwards, A.R. (1998). Performance-based appropriations: Fad or wave of the future? *Chronicle of Higher Education* April 10: B6.

Center for the Study of Community Colleges. (1988). *An Assessment of the Urban Transfer Opportunity Program. The Ford Foundation's Second Stage Transfer Opportunity Awards. Final Report*. ERIC Document Reproduction Service No. ED 293 573. Los Angeles: University of California.

Cohen, A.M., and Brawer, F.B. (1996). *The American Community College*. (3rd ed.) San Francisco: Jossey-Bass.

Cohen, A.M. and Brawer. F.B. (1996b). *Policies and Programs that Affect Transfer*. Washington, DC: American Council on Education.

Conley, D.T. (1997). *Roadmap to Restructuring*. Eugene, OR: University of Oregon, ERIC Clearinghouse on Educational Management.

Cook, A. (2000). *Community College Baccalaureate Degrees: A Delivery Model for the Future?* Policy Paper. Denver, CO: Education Commission of the States, Center for Community College Policy.

Derry, W. (1997). Interview by Kevin Dougherty with Auto Tech Coordinator, Broward Community College. Ft. Lauderdale, FL.

Dillon, C., and Cintron, R. (eds.) (1997). *Building a Working Policy for Distance Education*. New Directions for Community Colleges #99. San Francisco: Jossey-Bass.

Dougherty, K.J. *The Contradictory College: The Conflicting Origins, Impacts, and Futures of the Community College*. Albany: State University of New York Press, (1994).

Dougherty, K.J. (In press.) The community college. In J.J.F. Forest and K. Kinser (eds.), *Encyclopedia of Higher Education in the United States*. ABC-CLIO Publishing.

Dougherty, K.J. (Forthcoming). Maintaining the transfer function in an occupationally oriented institution. New York: Community College Research Center, Teachers College, Columbia University.

Dougherty, K.J., and Bakia, M.F.. (1999). *The New Economic Development Role of the Community College*. ERIC Document Reproduction Service No. ED439 750. New York: Community College Research Center, Teachers College, Columbia University. http://www.tc.columbia.edu/ccrc

Dougherty, K.J., and Bakia, M.F. (2000). Community colleges and contract training: Content, origins, and impacts. *Teachers College Record* 102 (1): 197-243.

Dougherty, K.J. and J. Kim. (2001). *Performance-Based Funding and Community Colleges: Forms, Origins, and Impacts*. New York: Community College Research Center, Teachers College, Columbia University. http://www.tc.columbia.edu/ccrc

Eaton, J.S. (1994). *Strengthening Collegiate Education in Community Colleges*. San Francisco: Jossey-Bass.

Eaton, J.S. (2000). *Core Academic Values, Quality, and Regional Accreditation: The Challenge of Distance Learn-*

ing. Washington, DC: Council for Higher Education Accreditation.

Ecker, P., and Calhoun-French, D. (1999). General education at Jefferson Community College: Accountability and integrity. *New Directions for Community Colleges* #92. San Francisco: Jossey-Bass.

El-Khawas, E. (1992). *Campus Trends*. Washington, DC: American Council of Education.

Florida State Board of Community Colleges. (1998). *The Florida Community College System: A Strategic Plan for the Millennium, 1998-2003*. Tallahassee: Author.

Florida Department of Community Colleges. (2000). *Outcomes: A Longitudinal Look at the Class of 1993*. Tallahassee, FL: Author. ERIC Document Reproduction Service No. ED 440 708.

Gladieux, L., and Swail, W.S. (1999). *The Virtual University and Educational Opportunity: Issues in Equity and Access for the Next Generation*. Policy Perspectives. Washington, DC: The College Board. http://www.collegeboard.org/policy/html/virtual.html.

Grubb, W.N. (1989). The effects of differentiation on educational attainment: The case of community colleges. *Review of Higher Education* 12: 349-374.

Grubb, W.N. (1991). The decline of community college transfer rates: Evidence from national longitudinal surveys. *Journal of Higher Education* 62: 194-217.

Grubb, W.N. (1996). *Working in the Middle: Strengthening Education and Training for the Mid-Skilled Labor Force*. San Francisco: Jossey-Bass.

Grubb, W.N. (1999). *Learning and Earning in the Middle: The Economic Benefits of Sub-Baccalaureate Education*. New York: Community College Research Center, Teachers College, Columbia University. http://www.tc.columbia.edu/~iee/ccrc/public.htm

Grubb, W.N. (2001). *From Black Box to Pandora's Box: Evaluating Remedial/developmental Education*. New York: Community College Research Center, Teachers College, Columbia University. http://www.tc.columbia.edu/~iee/ccrc/public.htm

Grubb, W.N., Badway, N., Bell, D., Bragg, D., and Russman, M. (1997). *Workforce, Economic, and Community Development: The Changing Landscape of the 'Entrepreneurial' Community College*. Mission Viejo, CA: League for Innovation in the Community College.

Grubb, W.N., and Badway, N. (1999). Performance measures for improving California community colleges: Issues and options. Unpublished paper, University of California at Berkeley, School of Education.

Grubb, W.N., Badway, N., Bell, D., and Castellano, M. 1999. Community colleges and welfare reform. *Community College Journal* 69 (June/July): 31-36.

Grubb, W.N., Worthen, H., Byrd, B., Webb, E., Badway, N., Case, C., Goto, S., and Villeneuve, J.C. (1999). *Honored But Invisible: An Inside Look at Teaching in Community Colleges*. New York and London: Routledge.

Healy, P. (1995a). Stiffer requirements in Georgia. *Chronicle of Higher Education* April 21: A36.

Healy, P. (1995b). Georgia adopts tougher entrance standards for state colleges. *Chronicle of Higher Education* June 30: A22.

Healy, P. (1998). Arizona considers landmark plan to allow community colleges to offer baccalaureate degrees. *Chronicle of Higher Education* Jan. 16: A30.

Hebel, S. and J. Selingo. (2001). For public colleges, a decade of generous state budgets is over. *Chronicle of Higher Education* (April 20): A10.

Helm, P. and R. deAnda. (1993). *2 + 2 + 2 Evaluation and Report*. Sacramento, CA: California Community Colleges, Office of the Chancellor. ERIC Document Reproduction Service No. ED 352 093.

Hilgartner, S., and Bosk, C. 1988. The rise and fall of social problems: A policy arenas model. *American Journal of Sociology* 94: 53-78.

Horine, Don. 1998. Associate degrees to start going further: Some will transfer to all Florida universities. *Palm Beach Post* (July 26): p. 14A.

Huber, M.T. (1998). *Community College Faculty Attitudes and Trends, 1997*. Stanford, CA: Stanford University, National Center for Postsecondary Improvement.

Ignash, J. (1997). Who should provide postsecondary remedial/developmental education? *New Directions for Community Colleges* #100: 5-20.

Illinois Community College Board. (1986). *Illinois Community College Board Transfer Study: A Five Year Study of Students Transferring from Illinois Two Year Colleges to Illinois Senior Colleges in the Fall of 1979*. ERIC Document Reproduction Service No. ED 270 148. Springfield, IL: Author.

Illinois Community College Board. (1989). *Current Issues in Transfer Articulation between Community Colleges and Four Year Colleges in Illinois*. ERIC Document Reproduction Service No. ED 304 168. Springfield, IL: Author.

Illinois Community College Board. (1998). *Illinois Community College System Transfer Study*. Springfield, IL: Author. ERIC Document Reproduction Service No. ED 422 048.

Illinois State Board of Higher Education. (1997). *Illinois Articulation Initiative: Policy and Procedures Manual*. ERIC Document Reproduction Service No. ED 416 930. Springfield: Author.

Jenrette, M.S., and Adams, J.Q. (1992). Community college contexts for diversity: Miami-Dade Community College and Joliet Junior College. *New Directions for Teaching and Learning* #52.. San Francisco: Jossey-Bass.

Kane, T.J., and Rouse, C.E. (1995). Labor-market returns to two- and four-year colleges. *American Economic Review* 85: 600-614.

Kane, T.J., and Rouse, C.E. (1999). The community college: Educating students at the margin between college and work. *Journal of Economic Perspectives* 13 (1): 63-84.

Knoell, D. M. (1996). Moving toward collaboration in transfer and articulation. *New Directions for Community Colleges* 96 (Winter): 55-63.

Krueger, A., and Rouse, C.E. (1996). *The Effect of Workplace Education on Earnings, Turnover, and Job Performance*. Princeton, NJ: Princeton University, Center for Economic Policy Studies.

Laden, B.V. (1999). Socializing and mentoring college students of color: The Puente Project as an exemplary celebratory socialization model. *Peabody Journal of Education* 74 (2): 55-74.

Lavin, D.E., Alba, R., and Silberstein, R. (1981). *Right versus Privilege: The Open Admissions Experiment at the City University of New York*. New York: Free Press.

Layzell, D. (1999). Linking performance to funding outcomes at the state level for public institutions of higher education. *Research in Higher Education* 40 (2): 233-246.

League for Innovation in the Community College. (2001). League announces articulation agreement between member colleges and four-year universities. *League Connections* 2 (2).

Lee, V.E., Mackie-Lewis, C., and Marks, H.M. (1993). Persistence to the baccalaureate degree for students who transfer from community college. *American Journal of Education* 102 (1): 80-114.

Levin, H.M. (1999). Remediation in the community college. Paper presented to Social Science Research Council Workshop on the Multiple and Changing Roles of Community Colleges, New York, February 11-12, 1999.

Levine, A. (1978). *Handbook on Undergraduate Curriculum*. San Francisco: Jossey-Bass.

Levine, A.. (1997). How the academic profession is changing. *Daedalus* 126 (4): 1-20.

Levine, A. and Cureton, J. 1992. The quiet revolution: Eleven facts about multiculturalism and the curriculum. *Change* 24(1): 25-29.

Lynch, L. (1992). Private-sector training and the earnings of young workers. *American Economic Review* 82: 299-312.

Lively, K. (1993). States try to end remedial courses at 4-year colleges. *Chronicle of Higher Education* Feb. 24: A28.

Lords, E. (1999). More community colleges are building dormitories. *Chronicle of Higher Education* Nov. 12: A54.

MacDonald, Mary. 1999. FCCJ sees hope on degree; Legislation key to 4-year program. *Florida Times-Union* (Jacksonville) (April 29): p. A-1.

Mahony, E. (ed.). (1992). *Building Community through Diversity: Connecting Students to their Learning Environments: An Anthology of Classroom Projects Undertaken for the Kellogg Beacon Grant. Final Report.* ERIC Document Reproduction Service No. ED 349 064. St. Louis, MO: St. Louis Community College.

Marchese, T. (1998). Not-so-distant competitors: How new providers are remaking the postsecondary marketplace. *AAHE Bulletin* (May).

Martorana, S.V. 1994. *Upper-Division Collegiate Course Offerings on Community College Campuses and Implications for Restructuring American Postsecondary Education.* University Park, PA: Pennsylvania State University, Center for the Study of Higher Education. ERIC Document Reproduction Service No. ED 370 643.

McCormick, A. (1997). *Transfer Behavior among Beginning Postsecondary Students: 1989-1994.* NCES 97-266. Washington, DC: U.S. National Center for Education Statistics.

McMillan, V.K., Parke, S.J., and Lanning, C.A. (1997). Remedial/developmental education approaches for the current community college environment. *New Directions for Community Colleges* 100: 21-32.

Moore, M.G., Thompson, M.M. Quigley, B.A., Clark, G.C., and Goff, G.G. (1990). *The Effects of Distance Learning: A Summary of Literature.* ERIC Document Reproduction Service No. ED 330 321. University Park, PA: American Center for the Study of Distance Education

Nora, A. (2000). *Re-examining the Community College Mission.* White Papers for the New Expeditions Project. Washington, DC: American Association of Community Colleges. http://www.nche.edu/initiatives/newexpeditions/White-Papers/accesswhite.htm

Nora, A., and Rendon, L. (1990). Determinants of predisposition to transfer among community college students: A structural model. *Research in Higher Education* 31: 235-255.

Nussbaum, T.J. (1997). *Enhancing Student Transfer: Memorandum of Understanding.* ERIC Document Reproduction Service No. ED 414 965. Sacramento, CA: Office of the Chancellor, California Community Colleges.

Ohio adopts measures for financing of 2-year colleges. *Chronicle of Higher Education* June 29, 1994: A21.

Palmer, J.C. (1998). *Fostering Student Retention and Success at the Community College.* Policy Paper. Denver, CO: Education Commission of the States, Center for Community College Policy.

Palmer, J.C.. (2000). *Instructional Faculty and Staff in Public Two-Year Colleges.* NCES 200-192. Washington, DC: National Center for Education Statistics.

Pascarella, E.T. (1999). New studies track community college effects on students. *Community College Journal* 69 (10): 8-14.

Pascarella, E.T., and Terenzini, P.T. (1991). *How College Affects Students.* San Francisco: Jossey-Bass.

Pascarella, E.T., Bohr, L., Nora, A., and Terenzini, P.T. (1995). Cognitive effects of 2-year and 4-year colleges: New evidence. *Educational Evaluation and Policy Analysis* 17: 83-96.

Pascarella, E.T., Edison, M., Nora, A., Hagedorn, L., and Terenzini, P.T. (1996). Cognitive effects of attending community colleges. *Community College Journal* 66 (4): 35-39.

Pascarella, E.T., Edison, M., Nora, M., Hagedorn, L.S., and Terenzini, P.T. (1998). Does community college versus four-year college attendance influence students' educational plans? *Journal of College Student Development* 39: 179-193.

Perin, D. (1998). *Curriculum and Pedagogy to Integrate Occupational and Academic Instruction in the Community College.* ERIC Document Reproduction Service No. ED 428 793. New York: Community College Research Center, Teachers College, Columbia University. http://www.tc.columbia.edu/

ccrc.

Phelan, D.J. (2000). *Enrollment Policies and Student Access at Community Colleges.* Policy Paper. Denver, CO: Education Commission of the States, Center for Community College Policy.

Phipps, R.A. (1998). *College Remediation: What It Is, What It Costs, What's at Stake.* Washington, DC: The Institute for Higher Education Policy.

Phipps, R.A., Wellman, J.V., and Merisotis, J.P. (1998). *Assuring Quality in Distance Learning.* Washington, DC: Council for Higher Education Accreditation.

Phipps, R.A., and Merisotis, J.P. (1999). *What's the Difference? A Review of Contemporary Research on the Effectiveness of Distance Learning in Higher Education.* Washington, DC: The Institute for Higher Education.

Pierce, D. (1996). Building communities on firm foundations: Remarks at a conference sponsored by the Kellogg Foundation. Washington, DC: American Association of Community Colleges. http://www.aacc.nche.edu/initiatives/COMMBLDG/firm.html.

Pincus, F.L. (1989). Contradictory effects of customized contract training in community colleges. *Critical Sociology* 6: 77-93.

Pincus, F.L., and Archer, E. (1989). *Bridges to Opportunity? Are Community Colleges Meeting the Transfer Needs of Minority Students?* New York: College Board.

Pitter, Gita Wijesinghe. 1999. "Ladders to Success: Enhancing Transfer from Technical Associate in Science Degrees to Baccalaureates." Paper presented to Annual Forum of the Association for Institutional Research. ERIC Document Reproduction Service No. ED 433 764.

Powell, R., Conway, C., and Ross, L. (1990). Effects of student predisposing characteristics on student success. *Journal of Distance Education* 5 (1): 20-37.

Rendon, L., and Garza, H. (1996). Closing the gap between two- and four-year institutions. In Rendon, L., Hope, R.O., and Associates (eds.), *Educating a New Majority.* San Francisco: Jossey-Bass.

Rhoades, G. (1998). *Managed Professionals.* Albany, NY: State University of New York Press.

Rhoads, R.A., and Valadez, J.R.. (1996). *Democracy, Multiculturalism, and the Community College.* New York: Garland.

Rifkin, T. (2000). *Improving Articulation Policy to Increase Transfer.* Policy Paper. Denver, CO: Education Commission of the States, Center for Community College Policy.

Roueche, J.E., and Roueche, S.D. (1999). *High Stakes, High Performance: Making Remedial Education Work.* Washington, DC: Community College Press.

Rouse, C.E. (1998). Do two-year colleges increase overall educational attainment? Evidence from the states. *Journal of Policy Analysis and Management* 17: 595-620.

Ruppert, S. (1995). Roots and realities of state-level performance indicator systems. *New Directions for Higher Education,* #91 (Fall): 11-23.

Russell, T.L. (1999). *The No Significant Difference Phenomenon.* Raleigh, NC: North Carolina State University, Office of Instructional Telecommunications.

Schmidt, P. (1997). States press their colleges to make transferring easier. *Chronicle of Higher Education,* July 18.

Schmidt, P. (1999). Florida's 2-year colleges allowed to offer B.A.'s. *Chronicle of Higher Education* July 2: A29.

Schneider, B., and Stevenson, D.L. (1999). *Ambitious Generation.* New Haven, CT: Yale University Press.

Shaw, K.M. (2001). Reframing remediation as a systemic phenomenon: A comparative analysis of remediation in two states. In B.K. Townsend and S.K. Twombly (eds.), *Community Colleges: Policy in the Future Context* (pp. 193-221). Westport, CT: Ablex.

Shaw, K.M., and London, H.B. (1998). The interplay between ideology, culture, and educational mobility: A typology of urban community colleges with high transfer rates. Unpublished paper, Temple University, School of Education.

Sherry, L. (1996). Issues in Distance Learning. *International Journal of Educational Telecommunications* 1(4): 337-365. (http://www.cudenver.edu/-lsherry/pubs/issues.html.)

Smith, V. (1993). New dimensions for general education. In Arthur Levine (ed.), *Higher Learning in America, 1980-2000* (pp. 243-258). Baltimore, MD: Johns Hopkins University Press.

Spann, M.G., Jr. (2000). *Remediation: A Must for the 21st-Century Learning Society.* Policy Paper. Denver, CO: Education Commission of the States, Center for Community College Policy.

Striplin, J.C. (2000). ERIC review: An examination of non-liberal arts course transferability in California community colleges. *Community College Review* 28 (4) 67-77.

Strosnider, K. (1997). For-profit university challenges traditional colleges. *Chronicle of Higher Education* June 6: A32.

Strosnider, K. (1998). For-profit higher education sees booming enrollments and revenues. *Chronicle of Higher Education* Jan. 23:

Tinto, V. (1987). *Leaving College.* Chicago: University of Chicago Press.

Tinto, V., Russo, P., and Kadel, S. (1994). Constructing educational communities: Increasing retention in challenging circumstances. *Community College Journal* 64 (4): 26-29.

Townsend, B.K. (1995). Community college transfer students: A case study of survival. *Review of Higher Education* 18: 175-193.

United States Bureau of the Census. (2000). *Statistical Abstract of the United States: 2000.* Washington, DC: Government Printing Office.

United States National Center for Education Statistics. (1991). *College-Level Remedial Education in the Fall of 1989.* NCES 91-191. Washington, DC: US GPO.

United States National Center for Education Statistics. (1994). *Report on the State of Remedial Education, 1992-1993.* Washington, DC:. U.S. Department of Education.

United States National Center for Education Statistics. (1996). *Remedial Education at Higher Education Institutions in Fall 1995.* NCES 97-584. Washington, DC: U.S. Author.

United States National Center for Education Statistics. (1997). The *Condition of Education, 1997.* Washington, DC: U.S. Government Printing Office.

United States National Center for Education Statistics. (1998). *Digest of Education Statistics, 1998.* NCES 99-036. Washington, DC: U.S. Department of Education.

United States National Center for Education Statistics. (1999a). *Digest of Education Statistics, 1999.* NCES (2000)-031. Washington, DC: U.S. Department of Education.

United States National Center for Education Statistics. (1999b). *Distance Education at Postsecondary Institutions: 1997-1998.* NCES (2000)-013. Washington, DC: Author.

Van Horn, C., Fichtner, A., Dautrich, K., Hartley, T, and Hebbar, L. (1998). *First-Year Interim Report, Evaluation of the Workforce Development Partnership Program: Executive Summary.* New Brunswick, NJ: Rutgers University, Heldrich Center for Workforce Development.

Washington State Board for Community and Technical Colleges. 1994. *Transfer Outcomes in Washington Community Colleges.* Operations Report #94-1. Olympia, WA: Author. ERIC Document Reproduction Service No. ED 365 395.

___. 1997. *1997-98 Articulation and Transfer in the State of Washington.* Olympia, WA: Author. ERIC Document Reproduction Service No. ED 416 922.

Whitaker, D.G., and Pascarella, E.T. (1994). Two-year college attendance and socioeconomic attainment. *Journal of Higher Education* 65: 194-210.

Winter, G.M. and Fadale, L.M. (1990). Impact of economic development programs in SUNY community colleges: A study of contract courses. *Community Services Catalyst* 20 (2): 3-7.

Winston, G.C. (1999). For-profit higher education: Godzilla or chicken little? *Change* 31 (1): 13-19.

Zeiss, T. (1998). The realities of competition: Will our students become theirs? *Community College Journal* 68 (8): 8-13.

Zeszotarski, P. (1999). Dimensions of general education requirements. *New Directions for Community Colleges* #109: pp. 39-48. San Francisco: Jossey-Bass.

8. REEXAMINING DOCTORAL STUDENT SOCIALIZATION AND PROFESSIONAL DEVELOPMENT: MOVING BEYOND THE CONGRUENCE AND ASSIMILATION ORIENTATION

James Soto Antony
University of Washington

Introduction

In the spring of 2000, hundreds of national leaders in graduate education from colleges and universities around the nation gathered to talk about ways of reforming doctoral training in the arts and sciences (Re-envisioning the Ph.D. Conference, Seattle, 2000). The meeting, sponsored by the Pew Charitable Trusts, underscored a growing crisis in American doctoral education. Up until recently, traditional disciplinary Ph.D. programs were assumed to be training students to enter the professorate. For a variety of reasons, the availability of academic posts in many fields has declined in recent years (Chronicle *of Higher Education*, 1999) and a larger percentage of doctoral degree recipients have, as a result, begun to look for employment in sectors outside of academe (Sanderson & Dugoni, 1997). The reduced availability of academic posts in many fields, along with the increased migration of a variety of doctoral degree recipients to the private sector, has forced many doctoral training programs to consider reforming the structure and outcomes of doctoral training.

Certainly, the changing employment prospects and professional aspirations of doctoral degree recipients beg the question of how doctoral education in the disciplines might be reformed. Such reform would be functional in assisting students in becoming more employable, and would also increase the breadth of learning that occurs in doctoral programs. In effect, such reform is centered on the question, "What might be done to equip doctoral students for the 21st century?"

J.C. Smart and W.G. Tierney (eds.), Higher Education: Handbook of Theory and Research, 349–380.

Any discussion about what students need to know speaks to closely held conceptions about how doctoral students should be professionally developed or socialized. Of the many frameworks for understanding student professional development and socialization, two theoretical propositions have received focused attention in the literature: (1) the psychological and sociological frameworks of career choice and professional decision-making (Katz, 1963; Klein and Weiner, 1977; Holland, 1966; 1973; 1985; 1997; Williamson, 1965; Zaccaria, 1970), and (2) frameworks of professional socialization (Bragg, 1976; Merton, Reader, & Kendall, 1957; Tierney and Rhoads, 1994; Weidman, 1989; Weidman, Twale, & Stein, 2001).

It may seem odd to examine career choice literature as a pathway to a discussion on graduate student socialization. As I make clear in this chapter, career choice theorists lay the foundation for all future research on both career decision-making and professional career development and socialization. Career choice theorists have attempted to explain the factors that operate on the individual level to motivate career decision-making and development. Socialization theorists have attempted to explain how the organization (either work or academic) has motivated individuals' career decision-making and development. The career choice and socialization theorists share the goal of explaining career decision-making and development. Where career choice theorists do so from the standpoint of the individual, socialization theorists do so from the standpoint of the organization.

Regardless of the orientation researchers in these fields adopted, both traditions have provided a sound theoretical basis for understanding a process conceptually similar to career choice and professional development — why one chooses to pursue doctoral education and what drives the professional socialization that occurs during doctoral training. I will argue that even though these frameworks accurately describe the type of socialization that occurs in doctoral programs, too often the socialization described by these frameworks (and actually practiced in doctoral programs) is skewed toward a "congruence and assimilation" orientation. As I will elaborate, this orientation is problematic for many reasons. Chief among them is that an adherence to traditional notions of congruence and assimilation poses challenges to individuals who might be quite dissimilar from the organization to incorporate their own unique identities into graduate work. Moreover, this orientation ignores the possibility of a socialization process that is more unique, individualistic, and reflective of the diverse nature of more recent incumbents to academic and professional roles. Lastly, this orientation attenuates our ability to increase the overall breadth of doctoral students' knowledge; the extent of their practical experiences; and the applicability of their competencies to non-research institutions and to the private sector.

As with others (Fordham, 1988; Taylor and Antony, in press; Tierney, 1997; Turner and Thompson, 1993; Weidman, Twale, and Stein, 2001), the challenge I attempt to address is to advance a framework for graduate student socialization that accounts for the increasing numbers of women and minorities entering professional and academic degree programs. I submit that such a framework should not require congruence and assimilation in order for the student to be considered successfully socialized. Therefore, my purpose here is to discuss graduate student socialization broadly, and to provide an alternative way of thinking about how socialization can be conceived theoretically, and practiced. I submit that any focused discussion of the topic must first trace the paradigmatic roots of popular theories of student socialization. And, as I have already hinted, these roots are found embedded in the psychological and sociological frameworks of career choice and decision-making, both of which ultimately shaped the primary assumptions underlying current professional socialization theory.

In appreciating the connections among these various theoretical traditions, it becomes possible to illuminate how socialization, both in theory and practice, adopted a congruence and assimilation orientation that was derived from the earlier assumptions of career choice and development theorists.

In my presentation of the psychological and sociological theories of career choice, and in my subsequent presentation of socialization theory, I aim to expose the manner in which the congruence and assimilation orientation operates. I then will demonstrate how this orientation spills over into current thinking about how graduate students are, and should be, socialized. Ultimately, my goal is to discuss the theoretical and practical reasons why the congruence and assimilation orientation is problematic and proffer the lineaments of a modified framework for graduate student socialization. I will argue that an alternative framework might more profitably guide the type of structural reform necessary for increasing the overall breadth of doctoral students' knowledge, the extent of their practical experiences, and the applicability of their competencies to non-research institutions and the private sector.

For the purposes of this chapter I focus exclusively on Ph.D. programs in the arts and sciences. Although there are many similarities between professional doctoral programs and what I discuss here, my intent is to focus on what we have thought of as the traditional disciplines; once that foundation has been laid, in future work I will turn to the similarities and differences for the professions.

The Traditional Psychology of Career Choice and Aspiration Development

An Historical Perspective

Psychological theories of career choice and aspiration development began to appear in the early 1900s. Most notably, Parsons (1909) developed a schema that summarized the conceptual framework that career guidance counselors should follow in helping people make career decisions (Brown, Brooks, and Associates, 1984). When Parsons conducted his research, the United States was becoming an industrialized nation with a rapidly increasing population due to the influx of immigrants. The education received in schools was seen primarily as inappropriate for the world of work. As a result, vocational guidance and vocational education emerged to assume the role of helping individuals make career or occupational decisions (Brown, et al., 1984). Parson's approach to choosing an occupation had three basic tenets. First, an individual should establish a clear understanding of his or her aptitudes, abilities, interests, ambitions, resources, limitations, and of their causes. Second, an individual should establish knowledge of the requirements and conditions of success, advantages and disadvantages, compensation, opportunities, and prospects in different lines of work. Third, an individual should establish true reasoning on the relations between these two groups of facts (Parsons, 1909).

According to Brown et al. (1994), because the growing industrial sector in the United States provided many employment opportunities, vocational guidance and education concentrated upon the study of occupations. This focus was rooted in the belief that adequate information about occupations provided a sufficient foundation upon which an individual could base occupational aspirations. Guiding individuals' occupational aspirations through the systematic study of various occupations, a method based upon Parsons' second tenet, was the predominant model until the 1940s (Brown, et al., 1984).

During the Great Depression, American industry no longer provided the plentiful job opportunities that it had in earlier times, and the primary concern of vocational and occupational counselors became the retraining of displaced workers (Brown, et al., 1984). This shift in America's economy caused vocational research to shift as well. No longer was the exclusive study of occupational opportunities (which were by then few and far between) in vogue. With the advent of factor analysis and the emergence of psychometrics, the systematic study of individuals began. The Depression, along with World War II, helped to create the perceived need to select individual workers for the training required by specific jobs. To aid in the new effort to place workers with certain attributes and aptitudes into the most appropriate of the available jobs, numerous tests (e.g., the Minnesota aptitude tests and the Army General Classification Tests) and occupational interest inventories were developed (Antony, 1996).

The testing movement, guided in part by the earlier study of occupations, formed the basis of many psychological and social-psychological theories guided by what has been called the "trait and factor" approach to understanding occupational choice and decision-making (Brown, et al., 1984). Perhaps the best known derivative theory among all trait and factor theories of occupational decision-making is Holland's structural-interactive theory of career choice (Holland, 1966; 1973; 1985; 1997). Before launching into a full discussion of Holland's theory, I will provide a brief description of trait and factor theory. I do so in order to account for the origins of the congruence and assimilation orientation (which I ultimately intend to critique in this paper) and how this orientation lies at the heart of Holland's theoretical assumptions. As I discuss below, trait and factor theory, and the manner in which it ultimately shaped Holland's thinking, has significant implications for how we organize doctoral study.

Trait and Factor Theory — Matching Personality and Occupations

The first well-articulated theory of occupational aspiration and decision-making, the trait and factor approach, is derived from the psychology of individual differences (Zaccaria, 1970). Trait and factor theory is based upon the assumption, as explained by Williamson (1965), that each individual is characterized by a unique pattern of capabilities and potentialities (traits). These traits and capabilities can be correlated with the requirements of specific jobs, and successful persons in any given job will tend to possess those traits and capabilities (Katz , 1963; Klein and Weiner, 1977; Williamson, 1965; Zaccaria, 1970). According to Klein and Weiner (as cited in Brown, et al., 1984), four primary assumptions drive trait and factor theory. These are: (1) each individual has a unique set of traits that can be measured reliably and validly; (2) occupations require that workers possess certain traits for success, although a worker with a rather wide range of characteristics can be successful in a given job; (3) the aspiration of an occupation is a rather straightforward process, and matching is possible; and (4) the closer the match between personal characteristics and job requirements, the greater the likelihood for success, productivity, and satisfaction.

Although trait and factor theory led to the development of numerous tests, instruments, inventories, and scales, the application of the theory has not been without its critics. Many accuse counselors who utilize the trait and factor method of ignoring the individual's input in interpreting the validity of testing results. Others argue that trait and factor approaches are overly deterministic, ignoring interactions between personality and environment (Brown, et al., 1984). Despite these criticisms, trait and factor theory had a profound impact upon early career research. Specifically, trait and factor theory formed the foundation for a host of career and interest inventories — many of which are still used today. Trait and factor theory also influenced the development of more refined theories grounded in some of the theory's primary assumptions. The most widely cited example is Holland's structural-interactive theory of career choice (Holland, 1966; 1973; 1985; 1997).

Holland's Theory — A Personality-Occupation Typology

A product of many of the pioneers in trait and factor theory, Holland developed a structural-interactive theory of career choice (Holland, 1966; 1973; 1985; 1997) guided by one overarching notion. Specifically, Holland's theory is derived from the notion that human behavior is a function of the interaction between individuals and their environments (Smart, Feldman, & Ethington, 2000). Holland's theory finds its roots in earlier trait and factor theories. This is evident in Holland's assertions that individuals' occupational interests are one aspect of personality and that descriptions of one's occupational interests provide insight into that person's personality (Brown, et al., 1984). More specifically, Holland (1982) contends that the aspiration of a particular occupation is an expression of personality rather than being something independent of personality. But it is Holland's accounting of the interaction between individuals and their environments that most distinguishes his theory from earlier trait and factor approaches.

In sum, there are three components making up Holland's theory: individuals, environments, and the fit or consonance between the two. Holland's theory forwards three basic assumptions (Smart, et al. 2000). The first assumption is that individuals will choose academic or work environments that are compatible with their own personalities (what Smart, et al. (2000) refer to as the "self selection" assumption). The second assumption is that academic or work environments reinforce and reward different patterns of student abilities — what Smart, et al. (2000) refer to as the "socialization" assumption. The third assumption is that individuals will flourish in environments that are consonant, or fit with, their personalities — what Smart, et al. (2000) refer to as the "congruence" assumption.

Holland developed six basic personality types used to describe both individuals' personalities and environments — realistic, investigative, artistic, social, enterprising, and conventional. Salient attributes of Holland's personality types

Table 1: Salient Attributes of Holland's Six Personality Types for Individuals
Source: *Smart, Feldman, & Ethington (2000)*

People who are:	*Prefer activities that involve the:*	*Acquire competencies that are:*	*Perceive themselves to be:*	*Value:*
Realistic	Explicit, ordered, and systematic manipulation of objects, tools, machines, and animals	Manual, mechanical, agricultural, electrical, and technical as opposed to educational or social	Practical, conservative, mechanical, technical, athletic, and lacking in social skills	Material rewards (money, power, and status) for tangible accomplishments
Investigative	Observational, symbolic, systematic, and creative investigation of physical, biological, and cultural phenomena. Avoid persuasive, social, and repetitive activities	Scientific and mathematical as opposed to persuasion and leadership oriented	Cautious, critical, complex, curious, independent, precise, rational, and scholarly	Development or acquisition of knowledge
Artistic	Ambiguous, free and unsystematic manipulation of physical, verbal, or human materials to create art forms or products. Avoid routine activities and conformity to established rules	Artistic — language, art, music, drama, and writing— as opposed to clerical or business oriented	Expressive, original, intuitive, nonconforming, introspective, independent, emotional, and sensitive	Creative expression of ideas, emotions, or sentiments
Social	Manipulation of others to inform, train, develop, cure, or enlighten others. Avoid explicit, ordered, systematic activities involving materials, tools, or machines	Interpersonal (human relations-oriented) and educational as opposed to manual and technical	Cooperative, empathic, generous, helpful, idealistic, responsible, tactful, understanding, and warm	Fostering the welfare of others and social service
Enterprising	Manipulation of others to attain organizational goals or economic gain. Avoid scientific and intellectual activities	Leadership oriented, interpersonal, speaking and persuasion oriented as opposed to scientific	Aggressive, ambitious, domineering, energetic, extroverted, optimistic, popular, self confident, sociable, and talkative	Material accomplishment and social status
Conventional	Explicit, ordered, systematic manipulation of data. Avoid ambiguous or unstructured activities	Clerical, computations, and business system-oriented as opposed to artistic	Careful, conforming, orderly, and as having clerical and numerical ability	Material and financial accomplishment, and power in social, business, and political arenas

Table 2: Salient Attributes of Holland's Six Personality Types for Environments
Source: *Smart, Feldman, & Ethington (2000)*

	Emphasize activities that are:	*Promote the acquisition of competencies that are:*	*Encourage individuals to perceive themselves as:*	*Reward people for:*
Realistic	Concrete, practical, and use machines, tools, or materials	Manual, mechanical, and technical as opposed to human relations oriented	Having practical, productive, and concrete values	Conforming behavior and practical accomplishments
Investigative	Intellectual, analytical, and use knowledge	Analytical, scientific, and mathematical as opposed to persuasive or leadership oriented	Cautious, critical, complex, curious, independent, precise, rational, and scholarly	Skepticism, persistence in problem solving, documentation of new knowledge, and understanding solutions of common problems
Artistic	Ambiguous, free and unsystematic and involve expressive interactions with others	Innovative and creative as opposed to clerical or business oriented	Possessing unconventional ideas of manners and aesthetic values	Imagination in literary, artistic, or musical accomplishments
Social	Centered on the mentoring, treating, healing, or teaching of others	Interpersonal (human relations-oriented) and educational as opposed to manual and technical	Cooperative, empathic, generous, helpful, idealistic, responsible, tactful, understanding, and warm	Empathy, humanitarianism, sociability, and friendliness
Enterprising	Focused on the manipulation of others to attain organizational goals or economic gain	*Leadership oriented, interpersonal, speaking and persuasion oriented* Environments that are: as opposed to scientific	Aggressive, ambitious, domineering, energetic, extroverted, optimistic, popular, self confident, sociable, and talkative	Initiative in the pursuit of financial or material accomplishments; dominance, and self-confidence
Conventional	Focused on explicit, ordered, systematic manipulation of data	Clerical, computation oriented, and business system-oriented as opposed to artistic	Having a conventional outlook and concern for orderliness and routines	Dependability, conformity, and organizational skills

for individuals are shown in Table 1. Similarly, salient attributes of Holland's personality types for environments are shown in Table 2.

The *realistic* personality prefers, or environment supports, activities involving the manipulation of machinery, tools, or animals, and those that place a lower premium on social skills. The *investigative* personality prefers, or environment supports, activities that are analytical and require one to be curious, methodological, precise, and less interested in demonstrating leadership skills. The *artistic* personality prefers, or environment supports, activities that tend to be expressive, nonconforming, original, introspective, and do not require clerical skills. The *social* personality prefers, or environment supports, working with and helping others — activities that are not necessarily ordered, systematic activities requiring mechanical and scientific abilities. The *enterprising* personality prefers, or environment supports, activities that require leading others, attaining organizational goals or economic gain — activities that are not necessarily systematic or require scientific ability. Finally, the *conventional* personality prefers, or environment supports, activities involving the systematic manipulation of data, records, files, and materials.

According to Holland, individuals can usually be viewed as belonging predominantly to one of these personality types, and environments are typically composed of individuals who share dominant personality characteristics. Ultimately, the more one resembles any particular personality type, the more likely he or she will be to exhibit the characteristics associated with that type, and the more likely he or she will be to choose to work in a job environment that is congruent with that personality type. Moreover, the environments will tend to support the activities of individuals who more closely match the predominant personality type of others working in the environment. This match or consonance between individual and environment facilitates socialization in that individuals whose personalities are consonant with the environment are more likely to behave in ways that get rewarded, and are more likely to be accepting of the culture and norms of the environment (Smart, et al., 2000). Lastly, the consonance between individual and environment is a primary determinant of successful achievement, satisfaction, and development. Individuals who are in environments that match their personalities are more likely to change or develop in ways that are consistent with the fundamental values and norms of the environment (Smart, et al., 2000). Said differently, academic or work environments are more likely to develop individuals in ways that are functional for professional success to the extent that there is a degree of consonance between the individual and the environment. One wonders how such a theory influences graduate student socialization; and to this we now turn.

Holland's Theory and Graduate Student Socialization

Researchers have successfully validated Holland's theory as a tool for explaining patterns of stability or change among undergraduates in various academic environments (see Smart, et al., 2000). However, researchers have been slow to use Holland's theory specifically to study graduate student socialization, with only one study (Smart, 1987) showing that congruence between undergraduate and graduate majors was related to satisfaction with graduate education. Notwithstanding, Holland's three basic assumptions of self-selection, socialization, and consonance have heuristic value and face validity in the context of how graduate student socialization actually occurs. As any former graduate student or current faculty member knows, graduate students and academic departments select one another based upon a mutual fit between one another's interests and orientations (Holland's assumption of self-selection). It is also commonly known that those graduate students who behave in ways that are consistent with the norms and values of the academic department, and who excel in ways that are deemed appropriate by faculty, are more likely to be rewarded (Holland's socialization assumption). Lastly, these two prior conditions undoubtedly allow graduate students to flourish in academic environments that closely match their interests and orientations (Holland's assumption of congruence).

Holland's theory advanced our thinking about how individuals choose, and succeed in, academic and professional environments by taking into account the manner in which aspects of the individual interact with environmental characteristics to produce stability or change. In a way, Holland's theory moved traditional psychological approaches to career aspiration development away from the highly deterministic trait and factor camp — a movement that was, in part, a response to the general dissatisfaction career theorists began to have with traditional psychological approaches. While Holland refined his structural-interactive theory, many sociologists developed their own theoretical perspectives on how individuals choose careers. I will discuss this movement next, as it partially forms the foundation of traditional theories of graduate student socialization.

Sociological Perspectives on Career Choice and Development

The sociological approach to career choice and development is based upon the assumption that circumstances external to an individual, or elements beyond his or her control, have a profound influence upon career aspiration. Osipow (1973) was one of the first sociologists to begin examining career choice from a sociological perspective. According to Osipow, the sociological approach is grounded in the assumption that the degree of freedom an individual has in choosing a career is small, and that any person's self-expectations for career attainment are largely consonant with the expectations others in society have for that person. Therefore, society is assumed to present occupational opportunities in a manner that is in line with the expectations it carries for the individual (Osipow, 1973).

A sociological theory of career aspiration takes into account the manner in which circumstances impose career aspirations upon individuals. Of the many circumstances that have been examined in the sociological literature, the influence of an individual's social class upon educational and career aspirations has been extensively examined by sociologists. In numerous studies of the influence of social class membership upon occupational attainment, a strong association between social class and the types of careers chosen by individuals has been established (e.g., see Alwin, 1974; Berman and Haug, 1975; Blau and Duncan, 1967; Dawkins, 1982; Deskins, 1994; McClelland, 1990; Morrow and Torres, 1995; Sewell, Haller, & Ohlendorf, 1970; Sewel, Haller, & Portes, 1969; Solorzano, 1992). Specifically, individuals from lower social class backgrounds tend to choose (or be directed towards) occupations carrying less social status or prestige (Havighurst, 1964; Hollingshead, 1949; McClelland, 1990; Morrow and Torres, 1995; Osipow, 1973; Sewell, Haller, & Ohlendorf, 1970; Sewell, Haller, & Portes, 1969; Solorzano, 1992). One mechanism through which the association between social class and occupational aspiration operates is "career inheritance" (i.e., when individuals choose careers that are identical or similar to their parents'). Students tend to choose the particular occupations of their fathers (Antony, 1996; 1998a; 1998b; Brown, et al., 1984; Werts, 1968). Specifically, this was found to be the case for physicians' and dentists' sons — these students tended to be more likely to enter those same occupations than would be expected in the general population (Antony, 1996; 1998a; 1998b).

Additionally, the relationship between social class and occupational aspiration has also been reported in research by Blau and Duncan (1967), Lipsett (1962) and Sewell and Shah (1968), who concluded that variables such as race, gender, parental occupation, family income, place of residence, and parental marital status (all indicators of, or otherwise correlated with social class) profoundly affect opportunities, training, life experiences, and preparation (both academic and occupational). In trying to determine what influences an individual's career aspiration, these researchers concluded that the social position at which the individual begins (i.e., his or her family's social class) plays the most influential role. Carter (1999) has written an extensive review of the literature on these sociological paradigms of status attainment, and has found that these paradigms are useful in promoting a model that explains such phenomena as educational aspirations and degree attainment — particularly for minority student populations.

Social class membership likely influences career aspirations because parents' levels of educational attainment (a component of social class) are associated with particular levels of resources and experiences. These are resources and experiences upon which one can draw during childhood and adolescence (the time during which many of the foundational values, beliefs, and goals might be formed regarding occupations and the self).

Family income, another indicator of a family's social class, has been shown to be strongly related to students' occupational aspirations and career expectations (Osipow, 1973). Specifically, students will choose occupations that are at similar salary and prestige levels to those of their parents. Additionally, family income has been found to have profound effects upon students' expectations of a future salary and the availability of future opportunities (Osipow, 1973; Sharp and Weidman, 1989), possibly shaping their self-conceptions regarding their efficacy toward attaining a particular career.

One wonders how such findings regarding social class influence graduate student socialization. One might not be surprised, for example, that individuals from low-income families are more likely to attend lower status colleges and universities for undergraduate studies, and are less likely to have parents who have attained graduate or professional degrees (McDonough, 1997). Given the findings presented above regarding career inheritance, students from lower social-class backgrounds are less likely to aspire to careers that require graduate and professional education (Antony, 1998a; 1998b; Pascarella, Brier, Smart, & Herzog, 1987). Moreover, graduate and professional students from lower social-class and/or minority backgrounds are more likely to feel obligations to apply their learning in practical ways — typically in the service of their communities. This orientation fundamentally shifts the type of socialization students receive during graduate or professional school, at times placing them at a distinct disadvantage if faculty believe these orientations are antithetical to the academic or professional enterprise in which students are training (Antony and Taylor, in press; Becker, Geer, & Hughes, 1965; Cooley, Cornell, & Lee, 1991; Fordham, 1988; Fries-Britt, 1998; Taylor and Antony, in press). My point here is not to be overly deterministic, but rather to point out the strong influence that social class can have on one's choices and on one's socialization during graduate school.

Perhaps one of the most exciting developments coming out of the sociological tradition is that of socialization theory. Socialization theory is an attempt to account for the interaction between individual and social or organizational factors in the production of both occupational attainment and professional development. Its primary focus lies in the description of the stages or processes that individuals undergo as they evolve from neophyte to full member of an occupation.

A diverse body of work on socialization has recently been brought together to specifically address the socialization of collegiate faculty (Tierney and Rhoads, 1994) and undergraduates (Weidman, 1989). In the next section, I will briefly summarize the work of these classical socialization theorists. Because socialization theory is a useful way to organize our thinking about graduate student socialization, I will then relate this summary of socialization theory to the topic of graduate student socialization.

Socialization Theory

Socialization is typically viewed as a process of active social engagement in which one individual (or an organization) directly influences the perceptions, behavior, and skill acquisition of another individual. In educational settings, this socialization occurs as a function of direct communications between teachers and students, and also occurs indirectly — or at least in a more latent fashion — through interactions between peers, and the perceptions students develop regarding how to engage the curriculum and how to earn positive evaluations.

According to Daresh and Playko (1995), the socialization process culminates in students' abilities to answer three key questions: (a) What do I do with the skills I have learned?; (b) What am I supposed to look like and act like in my professional field?; and (c) What do I, as a professional, look like to other professionals as I perform my new roles?

In a helpful text that summarizes socialization theories relevant to graduate education, Weidman, Twale, and Stein (2001) speak metaphorically about the socialization process, indicating that graduate students undergo a sort of "metamorphosis" during the graduate school years. This change implies a period of discomfort. Cahn (1986) and Staton (1990) have described this discomfort as a process in which the graduate student becomes more insecure and uncertain while acquiring new information throughout the graduate school experience.

Weidman, et al. (2001) also describe socialization as an upward moving spiral carrying the new graduate student through recurring processes toward the goal of role acquisition. According to their metaphor, as the student ascends the spiral, he or she becomes more accomplished than at entry, having changed

Table 3: Stages and Core Elements of Socialization
Source: *Weidman, Twale, & Stein (2000)*

Stages	Core Elements		
	Knowledge Acquisition	*Investment*	*Involvement*
Anticipatory	Learns general role expectations through mass media and observation of role incumbents. Accuracy of knowledge a factor because of outsider status.	States interest in role and its status by applying to/ enrolling in school and rejecting alternatives (Becker, 1960; Geer, 1966). Financial and temporal (full- vs. part-time status) investment.	Admission and matriculation create sense of involvement in role. Becomes an "insider." Begins to think of self in role (Mortimer & Simmons, 1978). May "shadow" a professional in the field.
Formal	Didactic instruction primary source of knowledge of argot, heritage, etiquette of role. Begins to achieve some competence in required knowledge and skills. Expectations of these dimensions are clear. Begins to understand why alternative roles/ institutions were rejected (Thornton & Nardi, 1975; Mortimer & Simmons, 1978). Sorting and selecting of students by faculty.	Specialized knowledge, educational policies, social value of consistency, pride and self-esteem make change difficult (Geer, 1966; Becker & Carper, 1956a; 1956b). Includes values, attitudes, ethics and beliefs of the profession.	Interacting with others provides opportunity to compare own skill and competence in performing role and motives for choosing profession with role incumbents and other students. Reflects on own performance. Demonstrates competence in some role tasks. Sometimes treated as role incumbent (Thornton & Nardi, 1975; Becker & Carper, 1956a; 1956b). Rites of passage, exams passed, fellowships, internships.
Informal	Learns informal (implicit) role expectations (Thornton & Nardi, 1975). Attains status within student or other informal group.	Tenure in role and sponsorship of incumbents and faculty make giving up role increasingly difficult. Claim of being in role forces novice to act as if it were true (Goffman, 1961). Development of faculty-student bonds.	Increasing involvement with role incumbents leads to learning implicit role dimensions. Participation in role activities increases perception of competence. Mechanical solidarity with other students (Huntington, 1957)
Personal	Can perform cognitive dimensions of role with adequate skill and competence. Preparation for exams, oral defenses of work.	Sponsorship based on professional competence as well as manner in which role tasks are performed. Creates an increasing sense of obligation to live up to expectations (Thornton & Nardi, 1975; Sherlock & Morris, 1967). One-on-one mentoring.	Increasing sense of solidarity with role incumbents. Clinical experience, joint presentations and publication with faculty.

in specific ways at each step, and ultimately having been prepared to assume new professional roles.

Socialization theorists such as Tierney and Rhoads (1994) and Mario (1997) have indicated that graduate and professional fields and disciplines in higher education exhibit the same structural dimensions of organizational socialization originally described by Van Maanen and Schein (1979). Borrowing from these same organizational socialization roots and from the work of Thornton and Nardi (1975), Weidman, et al. (2001) describe two assumptions of socialization: (1) that socialization is a developmental process, and (2) that certain core elements of socialization can be linked to the development of role commitment or identity. It is to a description of this developmental process and these core elements that I turn next.

Socialization as a Developmental Process

Thornton and Nardi (1975) used the term stage in an effort to describe role acquisition and identity formation (the key outcomes of socialization) as a developmental process. Although beyond the scope of the present chapter, it is important to point out here that socialization theorists did not corner the market on the idea of stage-oriented development of identity. These theorists owe a great deal to the earlier work of a generation of developmental psychologists, too numerous to cite here. Additionally, the concept of a sequential process of distinct stages driving identity formation was also simultaneously being explored by the earliest of student development theorists, as a way of describing student identity formation (for a thorough review of these theories, see Evans, Forney, & Guido-DiBrito, 1998). In any case, the implication of socialization theorists' borrowed concept of stage-oriented development is that socialization occurred via a serial passage (i.e., through a sequence of stages). Like their theoretical predecessors, socialization theorists believe that as a student progresses from one stage to another, there is an identifiable increase in the commitment to (and adoption of) the identity necessary to be successful in the new role. Weidman, et al. (2001) correctly point out that identity and role commitment are not accomplished completely during professional preparation, but rather continue to evolve after individuals begin professional practice. Nonetheless, four stages (as described in Table 3) have been represented throughout the socialization literature as the organizing framework for understanding how novices develop identity and commitment.

In the *anticipatory* stage of role acquisition, an individual becomes aware of the behavioral, attitudinal, and cognitive expectations held for a role incumbent.

This stage covers the preparatory and recruitment phases as the student enters graduate and professional programs (Weidman, et al., 2001). During the anticipatory stage, novices enter their programs of study with stereotypes, preconceived notions, and certain expectations about the professional role. Bucher and Stellings (1977) have indicated that during this stage, new students may make a commitment to being graduate students and to the idea of becoming a member of the profession.

During the *formal* stage, the student is able to learn about normative role expectations. At this stage, there is general consensus between students and faculty about the normative expectations (Weidman, et al., 2001). Students are inducted into the program, practice role rehearsal, and thereby determine their degree of fitness, observe and imitate expectations through role-taking, and become familiar faces in the program (Stein, 1992).

During the *informal* stage of socialization and role acquisition, the student learns of the informal or hidden role expectations which "arise and are transmitted by interactions with others" in the program (Thornton and Nardi, 1975). Students respond to behavioral clues, observe acceptable behavior, and are aware of the degree to which their own behavior is acceptable. While some of this information comes from faculty, students tend to develop their own peer culture and social and emotional support system among classmates (Staton and Darling, 1989; as cited in Weidman, et al., 2001).

The *personal* stage of socialization is that in which the role is internalized or adopted. Students form a professional identity, and reconcile the dysfunction and incongruity between their previous self-image and their new professional image as they assume their new role (Weidman, et al., 2001). Students must accept the norms and value orientation of the field, and resolve any conflict (i.e., between their own values and norms and that of the field) that could impede a total role transformation (Bullis and Bach, 1989; Gottlieb, 1961).

In summary, thinking about socialization as a developmental process essentially ascribes a serial nature to the development of identity, commitment, and role acquisition. This serial development takes the neophyte from the earliest thinking about what it might be like to be a member of a particular role and, through interactions with the training or professional preparation process, socializes him to become an accepted member of that profession or role. Throughout that socialization process, the neophyte's conceptions of self and the role are challenged. These classical stage theories of socialization see the ultimate end of socialization as being one in which the neophyte has adopted not only the identity of the role, but also the values and norms of the profession.

Core Elements of Socialization

According to socialization theorists (e.g., Baird, 1990, 1992; Bragg, 1976; Merton, Reader, & Kendall, 1957; Tierney, 1997; Tierney and Rhoads, 1994; Van Maanen and Shein, 1979; Weidman, 1989; Weidman, et al., 2001), the transmission of normative role dimensions to students is a goal of socialization, and can occur as an institutional-level or individual-level process. Regardless of whether socialization is seen as an institutional or individual process, the core elements of socialization are *knowledge acquisition*, *investment*, and *involvement*. These core socialization elements (outlined in Table 3) are related to the development of role identity and commitment — important indicators of successful socialization that results in the internalization of professional norms and values, and role acquisition (Stein, 1992; Thornton and Nardi, 1975).

Based upon the work of Stein (1992), Weidman, et al. (2001) illuminate two ways in which knowledge acquisition is relevant to socialization. Obviously, a sufficient knowledge of a field is required so an individual is able to perform the role and, ultimately, be considered both competent and professional. The second way in which knowledge acquisition is relevant to socialization is through awareness of the expected dimensions of the professional role, the ability to act successfully in that role, and of others' assessments of one's performance in the role (Stein, 1992).

During socialization, knowledge will move from being general to being specialized and complex. The novice first develops an understanding of the problems and ideology characteristic of the chosen profession and an understanding of why alternative professions were rejected (Weidman, et al., 2001. Moreover, the novice becomes aware of his or her capacity to participate in a professional culture as he or she learns its language, heritage, and etiquette (Weidman, et al, 2000). In short, this development leads the novice to begin to act and feel like a person who occupies the role (an incumbent). This sense of incumbency leads to identification with the role, an idea first introduced by Becker and Carper (1956a; 1956b) and Sherlock and Morris (1967).

The second core element of socialization is that of *investment*. Investment in a role is "committing something of personal value such as time, alternative career aspirations, self-esteem, social status, or reputation to some aspect of a professional role or preparation for it" (Weidman, et al., 2001). This investment stands to increase during the time spent in a graduate program. According to Geer (1966), as the novice begins developing a commitment to a particular professional role and its related status, contemplating a change in educational institutions or professional aspirations becomes increasingly difficult. Moreover, Stein

(1992) has indicated that investment involves learning specialized material and skills that are not usually transferable to other occupations. Stein goes on to suggest that this investment can be considerable, and as more specialized knowledge is acquired the investment on the part of the student increases dramatically.

Sherlock and Morris (1967) also point out that the support and mentoring received from an advisor or other faculty member can create a tie (or identification) between the student and the institution or field. This tie or identification can develop into a sense of obligation to live up to the expectations of the mentor, thus increasing commitment to the role. Thus, accepting sponsorships results in deeper commitments to the professional role (Weidman, et al., 2001).

The third element of socialization is *involvement*. The application of involvement to thinking about socialization makes sense, given the long tradition of involvement theory in the theoretical work on other forms of student development and achievement. Not unlike Durkheim's (1961) idea that shared group values and friendship support can reduce suicide, Spady (1970a; 1970b), Tinto (1975), and Pascarella (1980) viewed higher levels of social and academic integration as the key to reducing attrition. Each of these theorists, either directly or indirectly, invoked the concept of involvement as the vehicle through which social and academic integration is attained. Most notably, Astin (1984) defined involvement as the mechanism through which commitment to the institution, and the goal of graduation, are developed.

In terms of socialization, involvement intensity varies as students progress through their program (Astin, 1984; Brown, 1970), and involvement with teachers and older students gives the novice insights into professional ideology, motives, and attitudes (Weidman, et al., 2001). Olesen and Whitaker (1968) indicate that involvement in the role brings about professional role identification.

Socialization Theory and Graduate Student Socialization

The conceptions of the socialization process I have reviewed underscore the fact that, during the socialization process, neophytes (or in the case of this chapter, graduate students) explore aspects of themselves and ideas about the career or field that go beyond their own original conceptions. These new conceptions may be uncomfortable at times, but socialization theory makes it clear that it is through a reconciliation of these newer ideas and, eventually, an adoption or integration of these ideas, that an individual becomes socialized into a field.

In the case of graduate students, socialization can be thought of as a developmental process. In the initial stages of program identification and entry, the student carries great expectations and anticipations about what it will be like to be a student in a particular field and in a particular institution. During this initial anticipatory stage, a student becomes aware of the behavioral, attitudinal, and cognitive expectations held for a graduate student, as well as for a professional in the chosen field. Role acquisition and identity formation occur in a serial nature. Through interactions with fellow students, faculty, and the overall professional preparation process, the new graduate student is taken from the earliest thinking about what it might be like to be a member of a particular field to becoming an accepted member of that field. Along the way, the student picks up new skills, makes increased commitments and investments to the field, and becomes increasingly involved in the field. As knowledge increases, investments continue, and as involvement intensifies the student gains insights into professional ideology, motives, and attitudes. Ultimately, adopting these motives, attitudes and ideologies brings about professional role identification. This role identification becomes the hallmark of socialization, and allows the student to actually want to become, and be successful as, a member of the profession — an indicator of the student having been successfully socialized into the profession.

Like Holland's conceptions described above, socialization theory, with its developmental structure and core elements, has face validity. Graduate students do seem to travel through these various stages, making increased levels of investment and commitment along the way to identity formation and role acquisition. I have therefore attempted up to this point to not merely describe psychological theories of career choice and the basic elements of socialization theory, but to relate these descriptions to our thinking about the structure of graduate education. Having done so, I must now advance the primary argument I intend to make. This argument is, essentially, that both socialization theories and psychological theories of professional career choice and development share many aspects of what I refer to as the "congruence and assimilation" orientation.

The Congruence and Assimilation Orientation Defined

In my presentation of the psychological and sociological theories of career choice, and in my subsequent presentation of socialization theory, I aimed to expose the manner in which the congruence and assimilation orientation operates. Up until this point, however, I have not offered a formal definition of what I mean by the congruence and assimilation orientation.

In short, the congruence and assimilation orientation found throughout psychological and sociological theories of career choice, and in socialization theory, requires the internalization or adoption of a profession's norms, values, and ethics so that the neophyte's own professional identity and self-image are defined by them. This internalization or adoption is, in reality, described as a replacement of one's own norms and values with those of the field one aspires to enter. To the extent one's own values are *congruent* with those of the field, one will be a successful professional in that field. Other researchers have criticized this assimilation demand, and it may be useful to say a word about this now.

Perhaps the earliest recognition of the congruence and assimilation demands of socialization theory can be found in the work of Bess (1978). In this work, Bess discusses the differences between socialization and professionalization. These two terms are, I believe, mistakenly used interchangeably throughout the socialization literature. This belief is supported by Bess, who points out,

> Professionalization is the process by which students learn the skills, values, and norms of the occupation or profession, while socialization. . . refers to the process of adopting the values, norms, and social roles which constrain behavior in an organizational setting such as a graduate school or the college or university where faculty are employed.

Other researchers have drawn a similar distinction (i.e., merely learning skills, values, and norms versus adoption of those elements) between professionalization and socialization (e.g., see Becker, Hughes, and Strauss, 1961; Bragg, 1976; Friedman, 1967; Tierney and Rhoads, 1994). Despite this important difference, professionalization and socialization share many traits. In particular, both are continuous and social learning processes (Bess, 1978). Moreover, by elaborating upon the work of Bragg (1976), professionalization and socialization can be viewed as different parts of the same five-stage continuum. Specifically, the processes of professionalization and socialization both require the following elements: (1) observation — the identification of a role model(s); (2) imitation — the 'trying on' of a role model's behavior; (3) feedback — the evaluation of the 'trying on' of behavior; and (4) modification — the alteration or refinement of behavior as a result of evaluation. I believe that socialization distinguishes itself from the process of professionalization by requiring a fifth stage, internalization or adoption — the incorporation of the role model's values and behavior patterns in the individual's self-image.

Weidman, et al. (2001) indirectly adopt a similar view of the distinction between professionalization and socialization, although they use the word socialization to describe the entire process included in Bragg's continuum introduced above. They see the early stages of a graduate or professional program (what I would term the years of "professionalization") as differing from those at the conclusion (what I would call the years of "socialization"). Specifically, they acknowledge a difference both in terms of challenge and in terms of demands for the integration of professional values and ethics as the student progresses through the graduate school years. This is what has been called the dialectic aspect of socialization (Bragg, 1976; Staton, 1990; as cited in Weidman, et al., 2001) in which "socialization [becomes] a subconscious process whereby persons internalize behavioral norms and standards and form a sense of identity and commitment to a professional field."

Therefore professionalization should be viewed as the transmission of content knowledge; the informing about professional norms, ethics, and values; and the teaching of technical skills. Socialization distinguishes itself from the process of professionalization, however, by requiring the *internalization* or *adoption* of the profession's norms, values, and ethics to the point of defining the neophyte's own professional identity and self-image — what I refer to as the congruence and assimilation orientation.

Looking back at the psychological theories of career choice, and the classical structure of socialization theories, it is clear that the congruence and assimilation orientation is in operation. In the next two sections, I will briefly outline how this orientation operates in psychological theories of career choice, and in the classical structure of socialization theories.

The Congruence and Assimilation Orientation of Career Choice Theories

Recalling the origins of psychological theories of career choice, trait and factor theory, it becomes clear that psychological theories of career choice adopt the congruence and assimilation orientation. In the case of trait and factor theory, its primary assumptions were that each individual has a unique set of traits that can be measured reliably and validly; that occupations require that workers possess certain traits for success; and that the aspiration of an occupation is a rather straightforward process, and matching is possible. However, it is the fourth assumption of trait and factor theory that most clearly illuminates its reliance upon a congruence and assimilation orientation — that the closer the match between personal characteristics and job requirements, the greater the likelihood for productivity, satisfaction and success. Obviously, the implications for such an assertion with regard to graduate students is that the match between students' personal characteristics and those common among individuals within the academic discipline for which they are training directly influences students' likelihood for productivity, satisfaction and success.

This fourth assumption of trait and factor theory had an important influence on the thinking of future career researchers, and also influenced the manner in which future socialization theorists structured their thinking about socialization. Specifically, in the case of Holland's connection to graduate student socialization, the congruence and assimilation orientation is fully evident. According to Holland's theory, graduate students and academic departments select one another based upon a mutual fit between one another's interests and orientations (Holland's assumption of self-selection). Graduate students who behave in ways that are consistent with the norms and values of the academic department, and who excel in ways that are deemed appropriate by faculty, are more likely to be rewarded (Holland's socialization assumption). Lastly, these two prior conditions allow graduate students to flourish in academic environments that closely match their interests and orientations (Holland's assumption of congruence).

Holland makes no secret of congruence being at the center of his theory, and there is a great deal of research that supports his contention. However, my purpose here is to think about the manner in which psychological theories of career choice shaped socialization theorists' conceptions of how individuals develop identifications with, and ultimately go on to attain, professional roles. In the next section, I will briefly describe how the congruence and assimilation orientation also lies at the center of socialization theory.

The Congruence and Assimilation Orientation of Socialization Theory

The conceptions of the socialization process I have reviewed underscore the fact that, during the socialization process, neophytes experience a reconciliation of their own conceptions and ideas about the profession and professional role with newer ideas — ideas that are acquired during graduate study. Eventually, an adoption or integration of these newer ideas into one's own thinking, along with acquiring the skills of the profession, are what distinguishes an individual who has becomes socialized into a field.

In the case of graduate students, socialization can be thought of as a developmental process aimed toward the end of congruence and assimilation. In the initial stages of program identification and entry, the student carries great expectations and anticipations about what it will be like to be a student in a particular field and in a particular institution. During this initial anticipatory stage, a student becomes aware of the behavioral, attitudinal, and cognitive expectations held for a graduate student, as well as for a professional in the chosen field. As knowledge increases, investments continue, and involvement intensifies the student gains insights into professional ideology, motives, and attitudes. Ultimately, adopting these motives, attitudes and ideologies brings about professional role identification. This role identification becomes the hallmark of socialization, but socialization theories assert that it is the level of congruence with, and assimilation into, the professional field that remains the primary determinant of whether a student has been successfully socialized into the profession. Boiled down, those who argue for socialization theory assert that the degree to which a student assimilates is the degree to which he or she is successfully socialized. As I will argue in the next section, even though this assertion is an accurate description of how socialization is practiced in most graduate school programs, this form of socialization remains problematic. This is because many students who have the potential to be successful are unable to make the uncomfortable decision to replace their own values with the values and norms graduate programs attempt to inculcate through socialization.

Why the Congruence and Assimilation Orientation is Problematic

As I have indicated above, socialization theory traditionally assumes that in order for an individual to be successfully socialized, two conditions must be satisfied. First, the individual must develop characteristics that are congruent with others' in the field of choice. Second, the individual must assimilate his or her values to be congruent with the norms of the profession. I have demonstrated how this congruence and assimilation orientation finds its roots in the psychology of career choice and development. What is problematic with the congruence and assimilation orientation of traditional socialization theory?

Researchers have long been dissatisfied with the "linear" nature of traditional socialization theories. Linear models of socialization are models that assume all individuals progress through the socialization process in a singular way. All individuals progress through each of the stages and core elements of socialization (see Table 3) in a step-by-step incremental fashion. The normative congruence and assimilation expectations common to most traditional socialization theories are, by definition, a primary feature of linear models of socialization theory. This linear nature has been criticized by researchers (e.g., Fordham, 1988; Taylor and Antony, in press; Tierney, 1997; Turner and Thompson, 1993) for four reasons. First, critics of this traditional linear view of socialization claim that it ignores the effects of graduate students' perceptions (Wentworth, 1980) and gender on the way individuals perform a professional role (Gilligan, 1978). Second, critics (e.g., Thornton and Nardi, 1975) believe that linear approaches to socialization fail to account for change in normative role expectations over extended periods of time. Third, researchers (e.g., Feldman, 1974; Gilligan, 1978) charge that the linear nature of socialization theories assume students are all the same. Fourth, this homogeneity assumption, and the normative consensus orientation required by traditional socialization perspectives, have also been shown to limit women's opportunities for equal access to professional roles and networks (McClelland, 1990; Weidman, et al., 2001).

Weidman's earlier conceptual framework for undergraduate socialization (Weidman, 1989) has made valuable contributions to socialization theory. However, Tierney (1997) argues that this framework for undergraduate socialization ignores the possibility of a socialization process that is unique, individualistic, and reflective of the diverse nature of more recent recruits to academic and professional roles.

Recognizing many of the problems associated with traditional linear approaches to conceptualizing socialization, Stein and Weidman (1989; 1990) developed a modified conceptual view of socialization that affords an alternate way to think about, and hence shape, graduate student socialization. This view maintains that socialization is a complex, developmental process in which the relationships among student background characteristics, university experiences, socialization outcomes, and mediating elements such as personal and professional communities prior to and during the graduate school experience come into play (Weidman, et al., 2001). Contrary to the linear relationship between socialization elements in traditional models, the elements in Stein and Weidman (1989; 1990) framework are assumed to be linked in a bi-directional fashion (Weidman, et al., 2001). These newer frameworks recognize "a reciprocity of influences on the student such that the context and processes of the educational experience influence each other and the socialization outcomes affect the normative context of the higher education environment experienced by students" (Weidman, et al., 2001). The socialization process is conceived to indicate the interaction between and among the various constituent elements rather than being strictly linear, causal phenomenon, and to illustrate that socialization is developmental (Weidman, et al., 2001).

In describing their own conceptual advancements over traditional socialization theorists' approaches, Weidman, et al., (2001) follow the conceptual lead of Thornton and Nardi (1975) and suggest that socialization occurs in four stages: anticipatory, formal, informal, and personal. The Weidman, et al., (2001) revised framework suggests that:

> . . . socialization into the professions may be conceived as a process whereby the novice enters the graduate educational program with values, beliefs, and attitudes about self and anticipated professional practice. . . [; the novice is then] exposed to various socializing influences while pursuing a graduate degree, including normative pressures exerted by faculty and peers, from society, professional organizations, professional practice, and personal reference groups. . . [; the novice must assess] the salience of the various normative pressures for attaining personal and professional goals. . . [; finally, the novice must] assume, change, or maintain those values, aspirations, identity, and personal commitments that were held at the onset of the socializing experience.

Weidman, et al., (2001) state that a student can (through his or her own socialization outcomes) shape the norms and values of an academic department. Moreover, by acknowledging in their final theoretical statement that the novice must ultimately "assume, change, or maintain those values, aspirations, identity and personal commitments that were held at the onset of the socializing experience," their framework moves us away from a simple, linear view of socialization. Additionally, similar to what I have argued for here, their last theoretical statement supports the idea that socialization theory should divest itself from a strict congruence and assimilation orientation. What I offer in the final section of this chapter builds upon this initial beginning by offering what I consider to be the lineaments of a socialization theory that divests itself of the congruence and assimilation orientation.

The Lineaments of a Framework for Graduate Student Socialization

My concern about traditional approaches to socialization, with their dependence upon a congruence and assimilation orientation, centers on three aspects. First, they assume there is only one way of socializing graduate students or shaping their experiences. Second, they assume that all graduate students should be socialized into the same type of career as others in the discipline or field. Third, they assume that future success is measured not only by the extent to which content is mastered, but also by the extent to which the traditional norms and standards of the profession are internalized. These three assumptions lie at the heart of the congruence and assimilation orientation.

What might a modified framework for graduate student socialization — one that divests itself from the congruence and assimilation orientation — look like? I offer the following three points to guide our thinking:

1. Socialization should instill an awareness of a field's values and norms without expecting a student to accept those values and norms as one's own;

2. Socialization should take many forms as there is more than one method for socializing graduate students; and

3. Socialization should enhance, and support the assertion of, intellectual individuality.

What follows is an elaboration of each of these points, with a provision of examples.

A Modified Framework for Graduate Student Socialization

A modified framework for graduate student socialization distinguishes between developing an awareness of, versus developing a personal acceptance of, a field's content, values, and norms. This type of socialization recognizes that an individual can master content and develop the acumen to work within the traditional norms, values, and standards of a profession without having to internalize, or accept as one's own, those norms, values, and standards. A graduate student socialized in this way learns about the values and norms that drive a profession, but is not expected to adopt those values and norms as his or her own in order to be considered successfully socialized.

An example of how this modified form of socialization works can be found in an earlier study of African American doctoral student socialization (Antony and Taylor, in press). African Americans who identified strongly with graduate school and the idea of becoming a university professor were interviewed about their socialization experiences and their approaches to ensuring attainment of an academic career. All of these students developed high levels of competence academically, and mastered the skills and techniques of their field. What distinguished those who successfully continued to pursue an academic career from others was the fact that they had been actively socialized (usually by empathic mentors) to learn how to navigate the normative expectations of the field without co-opting their own values. Those students who were socialized to believe that the field's norms and values needed to be adopted in order to succeed felt a great amount of cognitive and emotional dissonance. This ultimately led these students to assume that an academic career was not for them, and that the personal sacrifices one needed to make in order to attain an academic career were insurmountable and unacceptable. From this example, it is clear that socializing students to learn about the values, norms, and expectations of a field can be accomplished while refraining from suggesting to students that the field's normative position should replace one's own values.

A modified framework for graduate student socialization should accept that there is more than one way to socialize graduate students. Although mainstream content and techniques are likely to be taught in relatively standard or traditional ways, socialization can still shape students' learning and development through a variety of experiences. These varied experiences might entail modification of pedagogy or curricular content. Students might be socialized into their field by being exposed to alternative forms of education — forms that familiarize them with different applications of the field's knowledge, or alternative careers within the field. In any case, there are a variety of experiences that could be folded into the graduate school years that, in sum, would socialize students in ways that go beyond traditional notions.

Moreover, departments that recognize the need for flexibility in how students are socialized could develop socialization approaches that broaden students' intellectual and practical experiences in ways that extend beyond the traditional disciplinary foci. One example brings this idea to life.

In most graduate school environments, a graduate school advisor typically educates someone within the traditional values and norms of a discipline as well as his or her own personal predilections. However, the disciplines and professions are changing rapidly. Knowledge advances at an astronomical rate, and newer ways of thinking about traditional ideas will continue — as they always have done — to shape who enters a field and what activities guide practice or research in that field. Many graduate departments now believe that what is needed is a form of graduate school socialization that encourages more interdisciplinary work. Through such interdisciplinary work, students develop competencies that push beyond the parameters of the socialization their mentors or departments can offer. Such diversified socialization can contribute to students applying their knowledge to solving broader (i.e., interdisciplinary) problems, or working in new fields or sectors.

A modified framework for socialization should enhance, and support the assertion of, intellectual individuality. It is through expressions of intellectual individuality that a field expands. History is replete with examples of individuals who, despite considerable pressure to conform to normative ideas within a field, nonetheless pushed beyond those boundaries, making incalculably valuable advances and contributions to the field.

Intellectual individuality is not an expression of complete departure from the normative intellectual values and accepted content of a field. Rather, intellectual individuality — at its best and most productive — is afforded only to those who have completely mastered what is known, and use that knowledge as the foundation for creating new intellectual approaches. Such individuality is the expression of one's own voice toward the end of advancing traditional intellectual notions in attempt to improve the field. As such, it is one's expression of intellectual individuality — not intellectual conformity — that is most valuable to a field. For this reason, graduate students should be socialized to develop this individuality.

Conclusion

I have attempted to make a fairly simple argument, which might be summarized in the following manner. First, our present theoretical and practical approaches to graduate student socialization unnecessarily rely upon a congruence and assimilation orientation. Second, this orientation — which finds its roots in traditional psychological theories of career choice — is problematic. Chief among the many problems is that an adherence to traditional notions of congruence and assimilation poses challenges to individuals who might be quite dissimilar from the organization to incorporate their own unique identities into graduate work. Moreover, this orientation ignores the possibility of a socialization process that is more unique, individualistic, and reflective of the diverse nature of more recent incumbents to academic and professional roles.

Finally, the congruence and assimilation orientation attenuates our ability to increase the overall breadth of doctoral students' knowledge; the extent of their practical experiences; and the applicability of their competencies to non-research institutions and to the private sector. Future thinking about socialization will benefit from a proactive divestiture from this orientation — one that is guided by the three ideas for a new socialization framework that I propose.

In offering the three ideas for a new socialization framework, my intent is to broaden our conversations about socialization in a way that encourages an explicit recognition of how the notions of congruence and assimilation play themselves out in our everyday socialization of students. As these three points illustrate, a socialization process that does not rely upon congruence and assimilation of course recognizes the need for students to master the knowledge, content, and techniques of a field, and to learn about the norms and political realities of a profession. Where a congruence and assimilation non-dependent view of socialization takes us, however, is toward an appreciation of individuality. This modified view of socialization honors students' different personal expectations and orientations. Furthermore, it guides our efforts to work closely with students to tailor the graduate school experience in a way that maximizes their chances of successfully attaining the goals and aspirations they have set for themselves.

In the introduction, I described a national meeting on graduate education. Among the outcomes of this conference, scholars and practitioners agreed that graduate education needed to be reformed in order to increase the overall breadth of doctoral students' knowledge; the extent of their practical experiences; and the applicability of their competencies to non-research institutions and to the private sector. The modified approach to socialization that I have offered here will move us closer toward achieving the outcomes of this conference.

REFERENCES

Alwin, D.F. (1974). College effects on educational and occupational attainments. *American Sociological Review, 39*(April), 210-223.

Antony, J.S. (1998a). Exploring the factors that influence men and women to form medical career aspirations. *Journal of College Student Development*, 39(5): 1-10.

Antony, J.S. (1998b). Personality-career fit and freshman medical career aspirations: A test of Holland's theory. *Research in Higher Education*, 39(6): 679-698.

Antony, J.S. (1996). Factors influencing college students' abandonment of medical career aspirations. Unpublished Ph.D. dissertation. University of California, Los Angeles.

Antony, J.S. & Taylor, E. (in press). Graduate student socialization and its implications for the recruitment of African American education faculty. In Tierney, W.G. (Ed.), Faculty Work in Schools of Education: *Rethinking Roles and Rewards for the 21st Century*.
Albany, NY: SUNY Press.

Astin, A.W. (1984). Student involvement: A developmental theory for higher education. *Journal of College Student Personnel*, 25(4): 297-308.

Baird, L.L. (1992). The stages of the doctoral career: Socialization and its consequences. San Francisco: Paper presented at the annual meeting of the American Educational Research Association. ERIC Document Number ED 348 925.

Baird, L.L. (1990). The melancholy of anatomy: The personal and professional development of graduate and professional students. In Smart, J.C. (Ed.), *Higher Education: Handbook of Theory and Research.* Vol VI. New York: Agathon Press.

Becker, H.S. (1960). Notes on the Concept of Commitment. *American Journal of Sociology*, 66 (1): 32-40.

Becker, H.S., and Carper, J. (1956a). The development of identification with an occupation. *American Journal of Sociology*, 61(4): 289-298.

Becker, H.S., and Carper, J. (1956b). The elements of identification with an occupation. *American Sociological Review*, 21(3): 341-348.

Becker, H.S., Geer, B., Hughes, E.C., and Strauss, A. (1961). *Boys in White: Student Culture in Medical School.* Chicago: University of Chicago Press.

Berman, G.S. & Haug, M.R. (1975). Occupational and educational goals and expectations: The effects of race and sex. *Social Problems, 23*, 166-181.

Bess, J.L. (1978). Anticipatory socialization of graduate students. *Research in Higher Education*, 8, 289-317.

Blau, P.M. & Duncan, O.D. (1967). *The American occupational structure.* New York, NY: John Wiley & Sons, Inc.

Bragg, A.K. (1976). *The Socialization Process in Higher Education.* ERIC/AAHE Research Report No. 7. Washington, DC: The George Washington University, School of Education and Human Development.

Brown, R.E. (1970). *Professional Orientations of Graduate Students and Determinants of Membership in the Graduate Students' Union at University of California.* Final report. Berkeley: Center for Research and Development in Higher Education.

Brown, D., Brooks, L., & Associates. *Career choice and development.* San Francisco, CA: Jossey-Bass Inc.

Bucher, R., & Stellings, J. (1977). *Becoming a Professional.* London: Sage Publications.

Bullis, C., and Bach, B. (1989). "Socialization Turning Points: An Examination of Change in Organizational Identification." Paper presented at the annual meeting of the Western Speech Communication Association, Spokane, WA. ERIC Document Number ED 306 607.

Cahn, S. (1986). *Saints and Scamps.* Totowa, NJ: Rowman and Littlefield.

Carter, D.F. (November, 1999). *College students' degree aspirations: A theoretical model and literature review with a focus on African American and Latino students.* Paper presented at the annual meeting of the Association for the Study of Higher Education (ASHE), San Antonio, TX.

Chronicle of Higher Education. (1999). *The almanac of higher education.* Chicago, IL: University of Chicago Press.

Cooley, M.R., Cornell, D.G., and Lee, C. (1991). Peer acceptance and self-concept of Black students in a summer gifted program. *Journal of Education of the Gifted,* 14: 166-177.

Daresh, J., and Playko, M. (1995). "Alternative Career Formation Perspectives: Lessons for Educational Leadership from Law, Medicine, and Training for the Priesthood." Paper presented at the annual meeting of the University Council for Educational Administrators, Salt Lake City, UT. ERIC Document Number ED 387 909.

Dawkins, M.P. (1982). Occupational prestige expectations among Black and White college students: A multivariate analysis. *College Student Journal, 16*(3), 233-242.

Deskins, D.R. (1994). Prospects for minority doctorates in the year 2000: Employment opportunities in a changing American society. In M. Holden (Ed.). *The challenge to racial stratification: National political science review, Volume 4,* (pp. 99-148). New Brunswick: Transaction Publishers.

Durkheim, E. (1961). *Suicide.* Translated by J. Spaulding and C. Simpson. Glencoe, IL: Free Press.

Evans, N.J., Forney, D.S., & Guido-DiBrito, F. (1998). *Student Development in College: Theory, Research, and Practice.* San Francisco, CA: Jossey Bass.

Feldman, S. (1974). *Escape from the Doll's House: Women in Graduate and Professional Education.* New York: McGraw Hill.

Fordham, S. (1988). Racelessness as a factor in Black students' school success: Pragmatic strategy or pyrric victory? *Harvard Educational Review,* 58: 43-84.

Friedman, N.L. (1967). Career stages and organizational role decisions of teachers in two public junior colleges. *Sociology of Education, 40* (2), 120-134.

Fries-Britt, S. (1998). Moving beyond black achiever isolation: Experiences of gifted black collegians. *Journal of Higher Education,* 69(5): 557-576.

Geer, B. (1966). Occupational commitment and the teaching profession. *School Review,* 74: 31-47.

Gilligan, C. (1978). *In a Different Voice: Psychological Theory and Women's Development.* Cambridge: Harvard University Press.

Goffman, E. (1961). *Asylums: Essays on the Social Situation of Mental Patients and other Inmates.* Garden City, NY: Anchor Books.

Gottlieb, D. (1961). Processes of Socialization in American Graduate Schools. *Social Forces,* 40(2), 124-131.

Havighurst, R.J. (1964). Youth in exploration and man emergent. In Borow, H. (Ed.), *Man in a world at work.* Boston, MA: Houghton Mifflin.

Holland, J.L. (1966). *The psychology of vocational choice.* Waltham, MA: Blaisdell.

Holland, J.L. (1973). *Making vocational choices: A theory of careers.* Englewood Cliffs, NJ: Prentice Hall.

Holland, J.L. (1985). *Making vocational choices: A theory of vocational personalities and work environments.* (2nd ed.). Englewood Cliffs, NJ: Prentice Hall.

Holland, J.L. (1982). The SDS helps both females and males: A Comment. *Vocational Guidance Quarterly, 30*(3), 195-197.

Holland, J.L. (1997). *Making vocational choices: A theory of vocational personalities and work environments.* (3rd ed.). Odessa, FL: Psychological Assessment Resources.

Hollingshead, A.B. (1949). *Elmstown's youth.* New York: Wiley.

Huntington, M.J. (1957). The Development of a Professional Self-image. In Merton, R.K., Reader, G. G., & Kendall, P.L. (Eds.). *The Student-Physician: Introductory Studies in the Sociology of Medical Educa-*

tion. Cambridge, MA: Harvard University Press.

Katz, M. (1963). *Decisions and values: A rationale for secondary school guidance.* New York, NY: College Entrance Examination Board.

Klein, K.L., and Weiner, Y. (1977). Interest congruency as a moderator of relationship between job tenure and job satisfaction and mental health. *Journal of Vocational Behavior, 19*, 91-98.

Lipsett, L. (1962). Social factors in vocational development. *Personnel and Guidance Journal, 40*, 432-437.

Mario, M. (1997). *Professional Socialization of University Lecturers in Mozambique.* Unpublished Ph.D. dissertation. University of Pittsburgh.

McClelland, K. (1990). Cumulative disadvantage among the highly ambitious. *Sociology of Education, 63*(April), 102-121.

McDonough, P.M. (1997). Choosing Colleges; How social class and schools structure opportunity. Albany, NY: SUNY Press.

Merton, R.K., Reader, G. and Kendall, P.L. (1957). *The Student Physician.* Cambridge, MA: Harvard University Press.

Morrow, R.A. & Torres,C.A. (1995). *Social theory and education: A critique of theories of social and cultural reproduction.* Albany, NY: SUNY Press.

Mortimer, J.T. & Simmons, R.G. (1978). Adult Socialization. *Annual Review of Sociology, 4*, 421-454.

Oleson, V.L., and Whittaker, E. (1968). *The Silent Dialogue: A Study of the Social Psychology of Professional Socialization.* San Francisco: Jossey-Bass.

Osipow, S.H. (1973). *Theories of career development* (2nd ed.). Englewood Cliffs, NJ: Prentice-Hall Inc. Parsons, F. (1909). *Choosing a vocation.* Boston, MA: Houghton Mifflin.

Pascarella, E.T. (1980). Student-faculty informal contact and college outcomes. *Review of Educational Research, 50*, 545-595.

Pascarella, E. T., Brier, E. M., Smart, J. C., & Herzog, L. (1987). Becoming a physician: The influence of the undergraduate experience. *Research in Higher Education*, 26(2): 180-201.

Re-envisioning the Ph.D. Conference. (April, 2000). Sponsored by the Pew Charitable Trusts, Seattle, Washington. http://depts.washington.edu/envision/.

Sanderson, A.R. & Dugoni, B. (1997). *Doctorate recipients from United States universities: Survey of earned doctorates.* Summary Report, 1997. Chicago, IL: National Opinion Research Center.

Sewell, W.H., Haller, A.O., & Ohlendorf, G.W. (1970). The educational and early occupational status attainment process: Replication and revision. *American Sociological Review, 35*, 1014-1027.

Sewell, W.H., Haller, A.O., & Portes, A. (1969). The educational and early occupational attainment process. *American Sociological Review, 34*, 82-92.

Sewell, W.H., & Shah, V.P. (1968). Social class, parental encouragement, and educational aspirations. *American Journal of Sociology, 73*, 559-572.

Sharp, L.M. & Weidman, J.C. (1989). Early careers of undergraduate humanities majors. *Journal of Higher Education, 60*(September/October), 544-564.

Sherlock, B., and Morris, R. (1967). The Evolution of the Professional: A Paradigm. *Sociological Inquiry, 37*(1): 27-46.

Smart, J.C. (1987). Student satisfaction with graduate education. *Journal of College Student Personnel, 28*, 68-77.

Smart, J.C., Feldman, K.A., & Ethington, C.A. (2000). Academic disciplines: Holland's theory and the study of college students and faculty. Nashville, TN: Vanderbilt University Press.

Solorzano, D.G. (1992). An explanatory analysis of the effects of race, class, and gender on student and parent mobility aspirations. *Journal of Negro Education, 61*(1), 30-43.

Spady, W. (1970a). Dropouts from higher education: An interdisciplinary review and synthesis. *Interchange, 1*, 64-85.

Spady, W. (1970b). Dropouts from higher education: Toward an empirical model. *Interchange*, *2*, 38-62.

Staton, A. (1990). *Communication and Student Socialization.* Norwood, NJ: Ablex Publishing.

Staton, A. & Darling, A. (1989). Socialization of teaching assistants. In Nyquist, J., Abbott, R. & Wulff, D. (Eds.). *Teaching Assistant Training in the 1990s.* New Directions for Teaching and Learning No. 39. San Francisco: Jossey-Bass.

Stein, E.L. (1992). Socialization at a protestant seminary. Unpublished Ph.D. dissertation. University of Pittsburgh.

Stein, E.L., and Weidman, J.C. (1990). The socialization of doctoral students to academic norms. Paper presented at the Annual Meeting of the American Educational Research Association, Boston, MA.

Stein, E.L. and Weidman, J.C. (1989). Socialization in graduate school: A conceptual framework." Paper presented at the Annual Meeting of the Association for the Study of Higher Education, Atlanta, GA.

Taylor, E. and Antony, J.S. (in press). Wise schooling and stereotype-threat reduction: Successful socialization of African American doctoral students in education. *Journal of Negro Education.*

Thornton, R., and Nardi, P.M. (1975). The dynamics of role acquisition. *American Journal of Sociology*, 80(4): 870-885.

Tierney, W.G., and Rhoads, R.A. (1994). *Faculty Socialization as Cultural Process: A Mirror of Institutional Commitment.* ASHE-ERIC Higher Education Report No. 93-6. Washington, DC: The George Washington University, School of Education and Human Development.

Tierney, W.G. (1997). Organizational socialization in higher education. *Journal of Higher Education*, 68 (1): 1-16.

Tinto, V. (1975). Dropout from higher education: A theoretical synthesis of recent research. *Review of Educational Research*, *45*, 89-125.

Turner, C.S.V., and Thompson, J. (1993). Socializing women doctoral students: Minority and majority experiences. *Review of Higher Education*, 16(3): 355-370.

Van Maanen, J., and Shein, E. (1979). Toward a theory of organizational socialization. In B. M. Straw (Ed.), *Research in Organizational Behavior*, 1: 209-264.

Weidman, J.C. (1989). Undergraduate socialization: A conceptual approach. In Smart, J.C. (Ed.). *Higher Education: Handbook of Theory and Research*, Vol. V. New York: Agathon Press.

Weidman, J.C., Twale, D.J., and Stein, E.L. (2001). Socialization of graduate and professional students in higher education: A perilous passage? ASHE-ERIC Higher Education Report. Washington, DC: The George Washington University, School of Education and Human Development.

Wentworth, W.M. (1980). *Context and Understanding: An Inquiry into Socialization Theory.* New York: Elsevier.

Werts, C.E. (1968). Parental influence on career choice. *Journal of Counseling Psychology*, *15*, 48-52.

Williamson, E.G. (1965). Vocational counseling: Trait and factor theory. In B. Stefflre (Ed.). *Theories of counseling.* New York, NY: McGraw-Hill Book Company.

Zaccaria, J.S. (1970). *Theories of occupational choice and vocational development.* Boston, MA: Houghton Mifflin Company.

9. Implementation Analysis in Higher Education

Åse Gornitzka, Svein Kyvik and Bjørn Stensaker
Norwegian Institute for Studies in Research and Higher Education (NIFU)

INTRODUCTION

Revisiting the Missing Link — Implementation Analysis in Higher Education

In many countries higher education is currently undergoing fundamental changes concerning its governance, structure, funding and organization. Often-mentioned forces triggering these changes are effects of the post-industrial society on higher education and the current invasion of "the market" in higher education (Williams, 1995; Slaughter and Leslie, 1997). These change processes seem to point in the direction of a future for higher education institutions that is likely to consist of more self-regulated, dynamic and innovative organizations. Consequently, in the attempts to analyze and document the current changes in higher education, there is a tendency not to focus on the analysis of governmental policies. This is understandable, due to the current attention given to other forces affecting change in higher education, e.g., the possibilities of new technologies in teaching and learning, corporate based life-long learning schemes blurring the boundaries between education and employment, and the effects of globalization on higher education.

However, governments are far from silent and paralyzed by the developments described above. Even though over the last few years the way in which politicians and public authorities have participated in shaping the future of higher education has changed, the involvement as such has not become less (Neave and van Vught, 1991; Neave, 1998). Under labels such as "managerialism" (Henkel, 1991), "new public management" (Pollitt, 1993) and "the evaluative state" (Neave, 1988), one can find new policies, ideas and

J.C. Smart and W.G. Tierney (eds.), Higher Education: Handbook of Theory and Research, 381–423.

concepts on how politicians and public authorities would like to see higher education develop. Even though many observers seem to agree that the role of the state in higher education is changing (Neave and van Vught, 1991; Dill and Sporn, 1995; Neave, 1998; Henkel and Little, 1999), this fact does not imply that the role and impact of the state on higher education is less relevant than before. A look at the pace and scope of the many public reforms and policy initiatives in higher education throughout the OECD area gives strong indications of a rather proactive state, where new actions are taken continuously as a response to the changing environment for higher education. There are many examples of such reform initiatives during the last decade. In the UK, for example, public reforms have influenced the funding of higher education and research, introduced several reforms that have changed the way higher education institutions are steered and managed, and launched comprehensive national assessment to ensure and secure the quality of teaching and learning (Kogan and Hanney, 2000). There are claims that these policy initiatives are evidence of a state with tighter control over higher education (Bauer and Henkel, 1999). In Sweden, several large reforms have been implemented during the 1990s, in which de-regulation, the introduction of quasi-market mechanisms and a national quality assurance system for higher education have been introduced (Bauer and Henkel, 1999). Similar policy initiatives and public reforms are taking place in other West European countries (Maassen and van Vught, 1996), former Eastern European countries (Westerheijden and Sorensen, 1999), and in the US. The increasing role higher education institutions seems to play in the socio-economic and technological development of our societies is, in addition, an indication that the public interest in influencing higher education will continue in the years to come.

Not surprisingly, this public interest in higher education is often combined with concerns about the efficiency, quality and effectiveness of this sector. In the end, it is exactly these objectives that guide public policy making in higher education. In a situation where tight public budgets, accountability claims due to new social demands, and output of higher education are on the agenda, policy analysis and, in particular, implementation analysis should be squarely at the center of the research interest of students of the sector.

However, it could be questioned whether this is the case. Even if policy analysis still interests many researchers in higher education, and policy documents, white papers and other policy initiatives often are analyzed and commented upon, there are few thorough studies that analyze and "follow" a given policy through the implementation process. When Pressman and Wildavsky coined the term "implementation studies" in political science with their seminal book *Implementation*, in 1973, it was argued that well founded and theoretically based implementation analysis, i.e., what happens after decisions have been made and policies are put into action, was a "missing link" in policy studies conducted at that time (cf. Hargrove, 1975). Over 25 years later this still seems to be a valid argument with respect to research in higher education. Implementation studies could, however, be particularly interesting in the present situation for higher education, since it seems evident that public policy, to a great extent, still is shaped during the implementation process.

First, with the amount of resources spent on higher education and with the social expectations now being put on higher education, there is a need for analysis that informs the public on the effectiveness of policy processes that distribute these resources in the sector. To know what those resources are being used on, and their effects, is of great interest to the society in general and stakeholders in higher education in particular. Second, even if the state and public officials are active in policy making and in reform-initiating activities, it is likely that current globalization, "technification" and "marketization" processes in the sector influence the policy implementation process in new and less known ways. And when the environment for public policy making is changing, it should be more important than ever to analyze how policy is affected by these forces, and to try to identify factors that stimulate or hinder the policy initiatives taken. Third, with new stakeholders entering and influencing higher education, i.e., new categories of students, new forms of knowledge producing actors, and new types of "consumers" of higher education, a new territory for policy making is being shaped where little knowledge about cause and effect relationships exists — something that a thorough analysis of the implementation process could help to uncover.

The aims of higher education researchers attracted to this field should, thus, perhaps still echo those that initiated this kind of research (O'Toole, 1986): to contribute to the development of theories of effective implementation of policy goals, and to aid those involved in policy formulation and implementation processes by developing empirically-based recommendations on how the aims of programs and reforms could be accomplished. Therefore, this article will explore the practice and potential of applying implementation analysis for studying change processes in higher education.

An Outline of the Chapter

The purpose of this chapter is to review the theoretical, empirical, and practical advances of the implementation approach in higher education policy studies. In part two, it discusses the development of implementation studies in higher education with some references to the general literature in the field. This section starts by presenting the most seminal implementation study conducted in higher education to date, a study of nine higher education reforms in six European countries conducted by a multi-national research team led by Paul Sabatier, one of the leading American scholars of implementation theory, together with Ladislav Cerych, one of the most central European higher education researchers (Cerych and Sabatier, 1986). Their study is still the most comprehensive in its field, and few studies using an explicit implementation approach have later been published. The study is based on a top-down approach, i.e., a perspective where policy objectives are taken as a starting point for the analysis. Our presentation of the Cerych and Sabatier study gives us the possibility to present and discuss the general strengths and weaknesses of using a top-down perspective for analyzing public policy. We pay special attention in this discussion to the so-called bottom-up perspective, i.e., a criticism of how a top-down perspective often overlooks the needs and special characteristics of those that are in the front-line in implementing public policy, or are affected by it in one way or another. This critique is particularly relevant in the context of higher education policy given the structural and cultural characteristics of this sector. The section ends with a theoretical discussion on how these two basic perspectives might be combined in various hybrid-models.

In part three, the relationship between policy studies and policy making is explored. This section starts by asking why there seems to be so little interest in implementation analysis in current higher education research. Even if several reasons for this can be listed, we argue that a major factor is the changes experienced in the form, content and objectives in public policy that have led to changing the label of implementation studies in addition to displacing the central foci of the studies conducted. The argument put forward is that changes in policy type and policy content in turn have affected the current research focus, and thus made the classic top-down and bottom-up perspectives in implementation analysis less suitable as analytical tools. Three dominant themes of current higher education policy making are listed and discussed: the dominant place of evaluation in policy-reformulation, the focus on the adaptive higher education institution, and the increased interest in private instead of public solutions to perceived higher education problems.

In part four, the discussion from the previous section is continued by reviewing some major current policy studies in higher education and their way of handling and exploring the described changes in higher education policy. However, questions and some comments are made regarding the potential relevance of using some of the basic insights of an implementation perspective in current research efforts.

Part five closes the chapter with a discussion of the extent to which a renewed interest in implementation analysis could be of practical relevance to policy makers in higher education. Related to this, some suggestions are given on what kind of research is still needed in this area to fill our existing gaps in knowledge, and some recommendations are given to guide future research activities in the implementation field.

HISTORY, PERSPECTIVES AND CRITIQUE RELATED TO IMPLEMENTATION ANALYSIS IN HIGHER EDUCATION

Introduction

Although there is a long tradition in higher education research, as in other social sciences, for studying the relationship between goals and outcome and explaining what went wrong, it is fair to say that the explicit focus on the implementation process as a distinct field of study in social science first took off in the mid-1970s. The book by Pressman and Wildavsky, *Implementation*, first published in 1973, represents a benchmark in this respect. Based on a study of the Economic Development Administration's employment effort in Oakland, California, two general policy recommendations were put forward in order to facilitate implementation of public program goals. First of all they showed that an implementation process can include a large number of decision points, and that each required clearance point adds to the probability of stoppage or delay. The number of such points should therefore be minimized wherever possible. Secondly, the authors recommended that as much attention should be paid to the creation of organizational machinery for executing a program as for launching one. Another important contribution of this book was its emphasis on an adequate underlying causal theory of the relationship between means and ends in a reform process. This and other case studies, which drew rather pessimistic conclusions about the ability of governments to effectively implement their programs, were followed by a large number of papers that aimed to investigate the conditions necessary for trying to achieve the objectives of a particular policy.

Various attempts were undertaken to build general theories on effective implementation, or how public agencies should proceed to secure that their policy objectives could be accomplished. Still, empirical evidence on the effectiveness of these models was in general missing. One could, therefore, say that the tendency of trying to identify implementation failure and the related lack of thorough empirical investigations into how implementation processes actually could succeed was one of the major reasons why a large multi-national research project on policy implementation in higher education in Europe was launched in the late 1970s and early 1980s (Cerych and Sabatier, 1986). In the context of this chapter, this study merits special attention. Not only is it still the most comprehensive and explicit analysis using an implementation approach, it is also a central study in the implementation literature in general. A major question guiding this research project, led by Ladislav Cerych and Paul Sabatier, was: Are contemporary societies really as incapable of planned change in higher education as the pessimists suggest? In their own comment to this question, they concluded that centrally initiated reform initiatives indeed were possible, and that such initiatives also could be characterized as a success under certain conditions (op. cit. 1986: 242-254).

However, research efforts such as the Cerych and Sabatier study, mainly built on a top-down perspective, clearly illustrate the complexity of analyzing policy implementation. The latter study could still be criticized for underestimating these problems. Those who argued for developing theoretical models that tried to incorporate the complexity related to implementation processes focused instead on how those who actually worked with putting the policy into action experienced the process. Not surprisingly, this way of analyzing implementation soon became known as the bottom-up perspective. A debate by those favoring a top-down or a bottom-up perspective when analyzing implementation processes then followed for years. Some attempts at combining these two perspectives were later undertaken, before the theoretical development seemed to come to a halt.

Premfors (1984) has shown that the top-down/bottom-up distinction has been used in three rather different contexts. First, the scholarly debate has concerned the most appropriate way of *describing* implementation processes. Is the top-down perspective more relevant than the bottom-up approach? A second and related question concerns the *methodology* used in implementation research. How should research be undertaken? Finally, much implementation research has a *normative* purpose. How can research help governments to attain the goals of programs or reforms? The differences in approaches in what became the field of implementation studies, are centered upon the following aspects:

1. What is implementation? Is there a start and a finish to it? And if so, where do you draw the line?
2. What constitutes a "policy", or what is the object of implementation?
3. What is failed and what is successful implementation?
4. What are the best instruments for implementation?

With these questions in mind, in this section we will give a brief overview of the perspectives, models and critiques of higher education implementation research (for a more extensive overview, see e.g., Sabatier, 1986; Lane, 1993; Parsons, 1995).

Cerych and Sabatier — The Classic Implementation Study in Higher Education

The major contribution to the field of implementation research in higher education is undoubtedly the book *Great Expectations and Mixed Performance. The Implementation of Higher Education Reforms in Europe*, by Ladislav Cerych and Paul Sabatier. This book was published in 1986 and was the final outcome of a large research project encompassing nine specific reforms initiated during the 1960s. Separate case-studies were undertaken as part of this project: the British Open University (Woodley, 1981), the Swedish 25/5 Admission Scheme (Kim, 1982), the University of Umeå in Sweden (Lane, 1983), the Polish Preferential Point System, the University of Tromsø in Norway (Bie, 1981), the Norwegian Regional Colleges (Kyvik, 1981), the French *Instituts Universitaires de Technologie* (Lamoure, 1981), the University of Calabria in Italy (Coppola-Pignatelli *et al*, 1981), and the German *Gesamthochschule* (Cerych *et al.*, 1981).

All these reforms sought explicitly to make important changes in the higher education systems of their countries. Three types of objectives predominated in these reforms: a) to widen access to higher education, b) to increase the relevance of higher education to regional development, and c) to develop more vocationally oriented and short-term higher education. The main purpose of the project was to analyze reasons for the success or failure of these reforms by applying policy implementation analysis (see also Cerych, 1992).

In the conceptual framework that guided the research project, Cerych and Sabatier distinguished between policy formulation, policy implementation, and policy reformulation as the three stages major changes in public policy pass through (1986:10):

1) A period of policy formulation involving an awareness of inadequacies in the existing system, followed by the examination of one or more means of redressing the situation, and culminating in a formal (legal) decision by the cabinet or parliament to establish a new program or institution.
2) The program is then assigned to one or more organizations for implementation. In higher education reforms, these will almost always include the Ministry of Education and the affected establishments of higher education. Other institutions such as local governments or private employers may also be included, if the program involves the creation of new universities or efforts to employ graduates. Within the implementation stage one can normally distinguish an initial phase involving the elaboration of regulations and the creation of new structures necessary to translate the cabinet-parliamentary decision into actual practice from a subsequent phase involving day-to-day applications and adjustments of the initial decisions.

3) Based upon various actors' evaluations of the implementation experience and reactions to changing conditions, there will follow what may be termed the reformulation stage, in which efforts are made to revise program goals, to change the implementing institutions or, in extreme cases, to abandon the program altogether. Such reformulation may be based on elaborate studies of the outcomes of the program or simply on perceptions of such effects or on changes in the general political climate. Whereas major revisions will often involve formal decisions by the cabinet or the parliament, they may sometimes proceed solely from the discretionary authority vested in the education ministry or the affected institutions of higher education. Program reformulation may also be the product of a more subtle process involving cumulatively important changes largely imperceptible to people outside the implementing institutions.

Special emphasis was laid on the analysis of goals, their comparisons with outcomes, and the factors affecting policy implementation, particularly the attainment of formal goals. These factors were listed as follows:

1. Legal (official) objectives
    a. Clarity and consistency
    b. Degree of system change envisaged
2. Adequacy of the causal theory underlying the reform
3. Adequacy of financial resources provided to implementing institutions
4. The degree of commitment to various program objectives among those charged with its implementation within the education ministry and the affected institutions of higher education
5. Degree of commitment to various program objectives among legislative and executive officials and affected groups outside the implementing agencies
6. Changes in social and economic conditions affecting goal priorities or the program's causal assumptions.

This list is fairly similar to those presented in the general implementation literature by Sabatier (1986) and others.

With respect to the goals of the reforms, the authors took as a starting point that their success or failure was dependent upon two aspects of the goals themselves: the amount of system change envisaged and their internal clarity and consistency. The larger the change decided upon, the lower the degree of accomplishment of the reform, and the more clarified and consistent the aims of the change are, the more easily the objectives could be fulfilled. However, Cerych and Sabatier also suggested that vague and somewhat conflicting goals are often the price to be paid for obtaining agreement in the policy formation process, and that ambiguity facilitates adjustments to changing circumstances during the implementation stage.

On the basis of the analyses of the various higher education reforms, the authors came to the conclusion that ambiguity and conflict in goals are in many cases unavoidable, and in addition that a precise goal does not guarantee superior implementation.

They therefore suggested that instead of focusing on clear and consistent objectives, implementation analyses ought to identify an "acceptable mix of outcomes" (p. 243).

In another work, Sabatier (1986) states that the emphasis on clear and consistent policy objectives among those scholars adhering to the top-down perspective was a mistake. He adds that (p. 29): "This does not, however, preclude the possibility for assessing program effectiveness. Instead, it simply means that effectiveness needs to be reconceptualized into the 'acceptability space' demarcated by the intersection of the ranges of acceptable values on each of the multiple evaluative dimensions involved". He illustrates his point by referring to the Norwegian regional colleges which had a multitude of conflicting aims: "While the institutions after a decade were receiving 'excellent' ratings on very few of these dimensions, the evidence suggests they were satisfactory on all of them" (p. 29).

With respect to the effect of degree of change on the outcome, Cerych and Sabatier stated that a more complex conceptualization of the scope of change was necessary to capture the processes. They suggested a three-dimensional framework that they called depth of change, functional breadth of change, and level of change. *Depth of change* indicates the degree to which a new policy implies a departure from existing values and practices. *Functional breadth* of change refers to the number of functional areas in which a given policy is expected to introduce modifications, while *level of change* indicates the target of the reform: the system as a whole, a particular sector of the system, or a single institution.

Lessons learned from the comparative study indicated some interesting conclusions:

- Policies implying far-reaching changes can be successful if they aim at one or only a few functional areas of the system or an institution.
- It is easier to change a single (or to create a new) institution than a whole system.
- Reforms projecting a very low degree of change both in terms of depth and functional breadth are often unsuccessful, essentially because they do not galvanize sufficient energy to overcome inertia in the system.

In the theoretical outline of their project, Cerych and Sabatier also stressed the importance of an adequate causal theory or a set of assumptions about means and ends. "If goals are to be realized, it is important that causal links be understood and that officials responsible for implementing the program have jurisdiction over sufficient critical linkages to make possible the attainment of objectives. Only when these two conditions have been met can the basic decision establishing the reform be said to 'incorporate' a valid causal theory" (p.15). They concluded that it was startling to observe how many of the reforms examined were based on wrong assumptions. However, they also admit that not everything can be foreseen in advance and advocate that systematic evaluation ought to be an integral part of implementation as a means of correcting errors, reformulating implementation strategies or even goals.

Another policy recommendation that came out of their analyses was that leaders or strong personalities — so-called "fixers" (Bardach, 1977) committed to the reform play an important role in the accomplishment of goals: "Such individuals were engaged in most reforms linked to the system as a whole. Usually their role was limited to policy formulation and adoption and to the very early phase of implementation. We suggest that many difficulties, distortions, and conflicts that arose later could have been overcome had real 'fixers' been there for a longer period." (p. 251).

The Central Debate: Top-Down Or Bottom-Up?

The complexity issue raised, *inter alia*, by the Cerych and Sabatier study, serves as a good introduction to the central debate in implementation research: what are the essential factors furthering or hindering the fulfillment of the objectives of a given reform initiative? The effort made by Cerych and Sabatier to create a set of "critical" variables in understanding implementation success, was a procedure followed by many researchers involved in implementation analysis, both inside and outside higher education. The central characteristic for these kinds of studies was the belief that implementation processes could be centrally controlled and steered if just the number of relevant variables and their interconnectedness were disclosed.

An earlier study by Van Meter and Van Horn (1975) is an illustrative example of this type of thinking. In their model of how to analyze the implementation process, "critical" variables were a) *policy standards and objectives*, and b) *policy resources*. In addition, four other factors were included: inter-organizational communication and enforcement activities; the characteristics of the implementing agencies; the economic, social, and political environment affecting the jurisdiction or organization within which implementation takes place; and the disposition of implementers:

- Policy standards and objectives

The objectives of the reform are obviously the starting point for the analysis of implementation processes. As Pressman and Wildavsky (1973:xiv) noted, "implementation cannot succeed or fail without a goal against which to judge it." In general, clear and unambiguous goals are easier to implement than a set of vague, complex and contradictory goals. In addition, if general guidelines are the foundation for a reform, the probability is relatively high that different interpretations will make implementation difficult. In addition, Van Meter and Van Horn assumed that implementation will be most successful where only marginal change is required and where goal consensus is high. Furthermore, of these two variables, goal consensus will have a greater effect on effective implementation than will the level of change. The likelihood of effective implementation will accordingly depend in part on the nature of the policy to be carried out, and the specific factors contributing to the realization or non-realization of policy objectives will vary from one policy type to another. Thus, characteristics of the objectives of an initiative may be assumed to be important for the possibilities for implementing an initiative in line with its objectives.

- Policy resources

Policies also make available resources for the implementation of a reform, through funds or other incentives, which facilitate the administration of a program. It is general wisdom that funds are usually not adequate, making the accomplishment of policy objectives difficult to achieve.

- Inter-organizational communication and enforcement activities

In the context of inter-organizational relations, two types of follow-up activities are most important. First, technical advice and assistance should be provided. Second, superiors should rely on a wide variety of sanctions — both positive and negative.

- The characteristics of the implementing agencies

This factor consists of both the formal structural features of organizations and the informal attributes of their personnel. Van Meter and Van Horn mention the competence and size of an agency's staff, the degree of hierarchical control of processes within the implementing agencies, etc.

- Economic, social, and political conditions

General economic, social and political conditions have been shown to be important for the relationship between objectives and results. Political measures are often undertaken without sufficient analysis of financial consequences. Furthermore, economic conditions change continuously, and it is not unusual that it will be difficult to put through a measure in line with its original intentions. Political support for a reform can also change over time, due to new power constellations or to changes in priorities.

- The disposition of implementers

This could concern the motivation and attitudes of those responsible for implementing the reform. Experience has shown that key persons in an organization, or "fixers" in Bardach's (1977) terminology, can be very influential for the success or failure of a reform.

A number of papers followed in the wake of the Van Meter and Van Horn contribution, and they were basically aimed at improving the list of factors important for the effective implementation of program goals. Sabatier and Mazmanian (1981), for example, listed seventeen variables within three major categories that were believed to affect policy implementation:

- Tractability of the problem
  a. Availability of valid technical theory and technology
  b. Diversity of target-group behavior
  c. Target group as a percentage of the population
  d. Extent of behavioral change required
- Ability of statute to structure implementation
  a. Clear and consistent objectives
  b. Incorporation of adequate causal theory
  c. Financial resources
  d. Hierarchical integration with and among implementing institutions
  e. Decision-rules of implementing agencies
  f. Recruitment of implementing officials
  g. Formal access by outsiders
- Non-statutory variables affecting implementation
  a. Socio-economic conditions and technology
  b. Media attention to the problem
  c. Public support
  d. Attitudes and resources of constituency groups
  e. Support from sovereigns
  f. Commitment and leadership skill of implementing officials

Several of these first attempts at developing theoretical contributions in the field of implementation analysis were to a large extent confined to discussions of which factors were important to study in implementation processes. O'Toole (1986) lists more than 100 studies from the late 1970s and early 1980s that were merely dedicated to identify important variables. In some cases, the authors also linked the variables in more complex theoretical models (e.g. Sabatier and Mazmanian, 1981).

The first wave of implementation researchers' attempts at developing conceptual and methodological frameworks for theoretical and practical implementation purposes were soon heavily criticized. One line of criticism was that these approaches mainly identified important variables or a checklist of factors without specifying a model of implementation (see O'Toole, 1986). Others argued that the number of variables were too long and that there was a need for research which could identify which variables were most important and under which circumstances (see Lester *et al.*, 1987). In the following we will go through the points that were raised in the discussions and point to the relevance of these issues in a higher education policy setting.

The emphasis on clear and consistent policy objectives as a precondition for effective implementation was soon criticized. Several scholars argued that the lack of clear and consistent program goals is more the rule than the exception. Instead, "objectives are characteristically multiple (because we want many things, not just one), conflicting (because we want different things), and vague (because that is how we can agree to proceed without having to agree also on exactly what will be done)" (Majone and Wildavsky, 1978). However, this fact does not necessarily preclude the possibility of implementing public policy reforms. There are numerous examples of successful reforms whose initial goals were manifold and non-consistent. The focus on goal clarity as a condition for successful implementation was probably in hindsight the least productive both in terms of scholarly contribution and policy advice. During the 1970s and the early 1980s key scholars in decision making theory and organization theory were leading a fierce debate on the status of goals as a main element in determining human action. The early implementation literature somehow seems to have bypassed this discussion. Furthermore, insisting on clear goals and making that a central element of the research outcome could be interpreted as an expression of a certain political naïveté on the part of the researchers. Nonetheless, we believe that the discussion on the status of "goal clarity" is highly relevant to the higher education sector. Several authors have pointed to the increase in expectations directed at higher education systems and institutions over the last 20-30 years, even to the extent to one can talk of demand overload for such institutions

(Clark, 1998). In this respect it is safe to assume that policy goals in this sector are increasingly complex and situations of inconsistency in policy goals are very likely to occur.

The same kind of naïveté is also present in the insistence on the role of an "adequate causal theory" as a policy recommendation to practitioners. In many policy areas the cognitive demands put on policy making are very high. Arriving at the "adequate causal theory" is not only difficult in face of political controversy, but also when cause and effect relations are disputed in professional or scientific communities. The list of difficulties for those who want to build policy upon an adequate policy theory is rather long. Still, the early implementation researchers were right in trying to unravel the underlying logic of policy decisions, and the attention given to this aspect of policy (but not the conclusions drawn) fits the later "cognitive turn" in the social sciences (cf. DiMaggio and Powell 1991 and Scott 1995). The attention given to underlying "policy theory" is certainly worth keeping in mind. In essence this point brings up the issue of what constitutes the knowledge basis for policy making. In the present context it gives grounds for higher education researchers to reflect on their own role as information and knowledge providers for decision-makers.

Still another criticism was related to the relative short time frame of top-down implementation studies. The many examples of program failure reported were based on studies undertaken too early after the launching of the reform. In a longer time perspective, the overall evaluation of the outcome might be more favorable. This is a simple yet important methodological point for anyone attempting to study the effects of policy initiatives.

The main criticism, however, was that these studies represented a "top-down" approach to implementation analysis, which was not very adequate in explaining real-life implementation processes (Hjern, Hanf and Porter, 1978; Barrett and Fudge, 1981; Hjern and Hull, 1982). Thus, the top-down approach represented an instrumental and rational understanding of organizations. Certain goals are to be realized through particular measures. It is presumed that changes in organizational structure, authority relations, decision-making principles and communication patterns will lead to desired results. The studies applying a bottom-up approach would refer to and distance themselves from the top-downers before presenting an alternative way of addressing the issue of implementation. They represented a break with the earlier implementation approach theoretically, methodologically and normatively, to the extent that they took great pains to avoid a "hierarchical" terminology and focus. Clearly, such a critique should be at the heart of the interests of higher education policy researchers that devote their scholarly attention to a sector that traditionally has been viewed as particularly "bottom-heavy" and where core functions of the institutions are seen as naturally defying hierarchical structures.

One line of criticism aimed at the top-down perspective was attacking the belief in the implementation process as a technical procedure. Sabatier (1986) summarized this as a three-part problem. The first problem is the emphasis on central objectives and decision-makers and the tendency to neglect initiatives coming from local implementing officials, from other policy subsystems and from the private sector. Second, top-down models are difficult to use in situations where there is no dominant policy or agency, but rather a multitude of governmental directives and actors. Third, top-down models are likely to underestimate the strategies used by street level bureaucrats and target groups to divert central policy to their own purposes. In this respect, Dunleavy (1981) stressed the important role of professionals in the implementation chain. Teachers, doctors, planners, engineers, social workers, etc. all have discretion in how they carry out their work. The relevance of such an observation to the policy and practice in higher education should be obvious to anyone familiar with how colleges and universities work.

In contrast to the top-down approach, the bottom-up researchers start by mapping the network of actors at the bottom of the implementation chain and ask them about their goals, strategies, activities, and contacts. The contacts are then used as a means to identifying the network of actors involved in the execution of a public policy at the local level. A key proponent of this approach is Elmore (1980). He argues for a backward mapping approach as an alternative to forward mapping which is basically identified as the "the conventional model". Backward mapping is the strategy by which participants create common purposes out of essentially multiple goal environments (cf. Calista, 1994:136). He challenges the mythology of the top-down perspective on grounds that it is an inappropriate way of describing real life policy implementation, and because central control over processes at local level is not necessarily desirable. In implementation processes bargaining is claimed to be crucial not only to adjust but also to create the goals of social programs. The disparity between formal policy decision and practice that in the first wave of implementation studies was seen as erring behavior and "goal displacement" is now considered as a natural part of implementing policy. It is also put forward as a prescriptive strategy for researchers and for decision-makers. In a bottom-up perspective the "intentions in Oakland" are not hierarchically subordinate to the "goals in Washington".

One further illustration of such an approach is found in the work of Hjern and his colleagues. In the introduction to a presentation of a study of Swedish and German labor market training programs Hjern *et al.* (1978:304) state: "The research reported here explores the possibilities for developing a framework which is appropriate for the administering within a multi-organizational setting, where national and local objectives, public and private interests can be simultaneously satisfied." Their point of departure is an unraveling of "the illusions of central control" (Hanf and Scharpf, 1978:113) and explicit rejection of the adequacy of unitary administration and a clear chain of command from central to local level. Hjern *et al.* focus on the local networks that are at work in the area of labor market training, and how these contributed to reducing unemployment. They conclude that program success was far more dependent on the skills of street-level implementers than upon the efforts of central governmental officials. Also in other studies (e.g. Hjern and Hull, 1985) Hjern and his colleagues chose to make a societal problem their analytical focus rather than a public policy program. The ordering principle of implementation research from this perspective is not "policy problems as defined and addressed by the 'political system' but policy problems as defined and addressed by relevant societal actors" (Hjern and Hull, 1982:105). Thus the object of implementation is not a given entity. Second, they enter into their analysis on equal terms, as they put it, private actors and resources (Hjern and Hull, 1985:153). Finally they include non-mandated actors who take part in program administration. It is part of the research task to uncover the actual implementation structures, i.e., those actors, organizations and individuals that are involved in problem solving.

The bottom-uppers' research question is thus rather different from the top-downers'. They ask how actors go about solving societal problems in different areas and see what role government measures play in that. The criteria of successful implementation is then not focused on a degree of match or mismatch between formal intentions and actions of the implementers, or on the possible "deviant behavior" of the agencies that are trusted to put policy into practice. Their democratic ideal also comes across as different, in the sense that they see the "local" flair in handling societal problems as an expression of a well-functioning democracy, and not as undemocratic actions of agencies that run wild or undermine the decisions made by democratically elected bodies. Here we can draw a useful parallel to the discussion on legitimacy in higher education relationship with the state and other stakeholders. The attention given to the traditional concept of institutional and individual academic freedom sets this sector apart from other sectors of society where governments have exerted a stronger steer.

However, heavy criticism was directed at the bottom-up approach for allegedly underestimating the role of governmental objectives and implementing strategies in major reform efforts. Critiques referred to numerous examples of public reforms that had achieved their goals. Still, it is fair to say that the early attempts at building theories on effective implementation largely ignored the problems that might emerge in cases where local level implementers and those affected by the reform opposed the directives. The emphasis on rational steering processes and top-down system control and communication does not take properly into account the role of those organizations or actors that are the target of the reform. However, organizational culture and traditions are important for understanding the relationship between intentions and results. Organizations have a history, and over time key norms and values become incorporated in their organizational identity and patterns of behavior. The culture, which is institutionalized in an organization, often represents a conservative element when internal or external actors attempt to change the organization's behavior. Traditions and culture are attributed a special value which makes it difficult to undertake extensive changes. When public measures strongly contradict the norms and values of an organization, and which the majority of its members share, it will be difficult to carry out the implementation process in line with its intentions.

Adjusting to Complexity — The Development Of Combined Models

Partly as a result of the discussion between top-downers and bottom-uppers, and partly as a result of obvious weaknesses in the early top-down approaches, various attempts at building more comprehensive hybrid models took place — see, for example, Lane (1993) or Parsons (1995) for an overview.

In the later editions of Pressman and Wildavsky's *Implementation* (1979 and 1984), Wildavsky and colleagues incorporate some of the criticisms of the top-down approach to present a revised view on implementation. They reject the idea that goals and programs are reifications: goals should not be viewed as static. Goals often change over time, partly because of weaknesses in the ideas themselves, partly because of the fact that ideas change, and also because of new circumstances. On the other hand they are not willing to reduce the status of policies to only a collection of words, and they reject the interactionist idea that the function of the implementation process is to satisfy the needs of the participants regardless of the actual policy results. Majone and Wildavsky point to an essential problem when they state that (1978:114):

> Implementation is evolution. Since it takes place in a world we never made, we are usually in the middle of the process, with events having occurred before and (we hope) continuing afterward. At each point we must cope with new circumstances that allow us to actualize different potentials in whatever

policy ideas we are implementing. When we act to implement a policy, we change it.

Implementation thus often implies both the carrying out of goals as well as the reformulation and re-design of original intentions and plans. Implementation in this sense has also been conceptualized as *mutual adaptation* (Browne and Wildavsky, 1984a) and a *learning process* (Browne and Wildavsky, 1984c).

An implementation model put forward by Barrett and Fudge (1981) is in line with this way of reasoning. They argue that implementation may be best understood in terms of a policy-action continuum, in which an interactive and negotiative process is taking place over time, between those seeking to put policy into effect and those upon whom action depends. They strongly object to the "recipe book approach" to successful implementation, e.g. as found in Sabatier and Mazmanian (1979), that in their view obfuscates the inherent political aspects of implementation: "We would thus argue that it is essential to look at implementation not solely in terms of putting policy into effect, but also in terms of observing what actually happens or gets done and seeking to understand how and why. This kind of action perspective takes "what is done" as central, focuses attention on the behavior or actions of groups and individuals and the determinants of that behavior, and seeks to examine the degree to which action relate to policy, rather than assuming it to follow from policy" (Barrett and Fudge 1981:12-13).

Another model has been suggested by Elmore. In his work from 1985 Elmore combines the approaches "forward mapping", which is essentially a top-down perspective, and "backward mapping" — a bottom-up perspective — in an effort to overcome the inadequacies of either approach. "Specifying the expected relationship between implements and their effects is only half of the story — the forward mapping, if you will. The other half consists starting with the consequences of those choices back through the sequence of decisions to first choices — the backward mapping half, if you will" (Elmore, 1985:37). He then goes on to describe policy making and implementation as bargaining processes. Where policy makers deliberately anticipate the responses of other actors, and their actions and interests, they are using what Elmore terms "reversible logics". "Policy makers make strategic errors when they confuse their aspirations about what should happen with their calculated judgments about what will happen." (Elmore, 1985:39). So from a policy maker's perspective implementation involves two types of problems. First there is the issue of choosing the correct combination of implements that is likely to produce the desired effect (forward mapping). Second, one should turn the system around to look at the set of decisions that policy would have to affect and anticipate the effect of parochial solutions to the outcomes of a policy.

The later work of Sabatier (1986), one of the leading proponents of the top-down framework, has suggested that implementation studies could be undertaken within "an advocacy coalition framework". This approach is based on the premise that the most useful aggregate unit of analysis for understanding policy change is a policy subsystem or policy segment, i.e., those actors from a variety of public and private organizations who are actively concerned with a policy problem or issue, such as higher education. Sabatier proposes to adopt the bottom uppers' unit of analysis assuming that "actors can be aggregated into a number of advocacy coalitions which share a set of normative and causal beliefs and which dispose of certain resources." Together with a keen focus on the legal instruments and socio-economic conditions that constrain behavior as the legacy from the top-down perspective, he suggests a synthesized model for the study of implementation processes.

Some Concluding Comments

The body of scholarly literature on implementation presented above has provided rather disparate answers to the questions we outlined earlier. First there is a distinction between those who see implementation as a rather narrow process with a start and a finish, versus those who view implementation as a process without a decision to launch it nor a goal line that marks the ending of putting policy into practice. And second, there is a distinction to be made between viewing processes in terms of phases or stages it goes through, versus seeing policy implementation and formation as intertwined where the defining and negotiating over intentions and objectives is continuous and infinite. For the latter scholars what is to be accomplished is something to be bargained over and not a given attribute of policies/programs under implementation. That is to say, policy intentions are not fully developed until they are negotiated. Consequently the criteria for determining policy success or failure differ significantly according to the approach you use. Likewise for the issue of what is "democratic" or not. The difference between the two approaches becomes most apparent with respect to the policy recommendations that they carry. Where top-downers prescribe an adequate policy theory, more control, goal clearance, and fixers to push the policy through, the bottom-uppers would recommend local knowledge and user control and policy outcomes measured against local objectives. Given this state of affairs, implementation research has been criticized for its theoretical pluralism, for its restricted nature, and for being non-cumulative (Lester *et al.*, 1987). Lane has summarized the state of the art in this field in the following way (1993:100-101):

> Implementation theory has thus far been the search for some interaction pattern or way of structuring the process of implementation in such a manner as to achieve a high probability of policy accomplishment. This has resulted in a controversy between those who believe in control, planning and hierarchy on the one hand and those who believe in spontaneity, learning and adaptation as implementation techniques on the other. . . . Whereas the top-down models emphasize responsibility, the bottom-up models underline trust.

Furthermore, Jan Erik Lane claims that a useful reorientation of implementation theory would be to examine how accountability might be upheld in the implementation of policies and how much trust can be placed in policy implementers if they are still to be accountable. He furthermore argues that no single model of policy implementation will guarantee policy accomplishment. "Sometimes control and hierarchy may be conducive to successful implementation, sometimes exchange and interaction are crucial in implementation." (1993:106).

The top-down emphasis on central control as a means to secure successful implementation, could be seen as a scholarly anachronism in the sense that such government strategies are both ideologically and in practice increasingly replaced by, or modified by, indirect means of control. Nevertheless, one of the major contributions of the first wave of implementation studies was the emphasis on the importance of inter-organizational arrangements and the characteristics of the formal ties between program/policy issuers and the implementing institutions.

Studying the impact of formal hierarchical arrangements between institutions is important both from a scholarly (echoing the neo-institutional theory development) and a practical perspective. For students of higher education policy it is crucial. Clearly implementation in times of new relations between agencies/public institutions and central authorities will continue to arouse interest. What are the consequences for implementation when the formal levers of control between government and underlying institutions have been changed? This is a highly pertinent issue that should lead to careful examination of the actual changes in formal arrangements and the consequences of such changes. A focus on decisions and legal resolutions does not represent an obsolete area of interest. Rather it directs attention to central determinants of political administrative action, also with respect to higher education. Furthermore, national governments continue to formulate policies for higher education with the expectation that such initiatives are translated into practice in the field. Also supra-national organizations, such as the EU and NAFTA in North America, have ambitions of effectiveness with the programs and policies they formulate with respect to higher education. The point we try to make is simply that the relationship between policy issuers and the units that policies are directed at in the higher education sector is in many cases undergoing formal alterations. And as such the attention to such arrangements are important to incorporate into a study of implementation of specific policies.

A lasting and important contribution of the bottom-uppers is the highlight they put on the organic aspects of implementation, the informal processes and spontaneous constellations that spring out of processes, the strong element of negotiation and the political aspects of processes also outside the central political apparatus. However, not unlike other behavioral approaches in the study of politics, it tends to overlook the weight carried by institutions as a powerful frame of human action.

The bottom-uppers' change of focus from the policy decision-fixation to organic processes clearly served to sensitize the student of implementation processes to the danger of reifying policy and add mythical properties to the power of a policy decision and program. However, the complete relaxation of a special focus on authoritative policy decisions at a central level is also ill advised. A policy decision then has the same status as other "environmental factors" that play a role, with no higher rank order. It is not the trigger of the processes one is studying, as it would for the top-downers. This might be a good approach in areas where government initiatives are many and scattered, but "ignoring" the importance of formal government decisions and the momentum that such decisions carry both symbolically and as a driving force in implementation processes seems empirically errant.

THE POLICY CHANGE — FROM IMPLEMENTATION TO EVALUATION, ADAPTATION AND PRIVATIZATION

Introduction

A search for comprehensive implementation studies in higher education using criteria originally launched by Pressman and Wildavsky (1973:167) is a rather disappointing affair. It is not an easy task to find studies that carry the word "implementation" or a reasonable synonym in the title. Even if one may find the word implementation in many higher education texts appearing since the Cerych and Sabatier study, the word is often not defined or analytically specified, indicating that the implementation process is not of main interest of the studies conducted.

In a discussion of why implementation research in higher education has not boomed after the seminal work offered by Cerych and Sabatier, several reasons could be identified, including the complexity of the research task and the lack of a unified perspective in the field due to the debate between bottom-uppers and top-downers. Furthermore, studies of the implementation of higher education reforms have also to a large extent been undertaken in a European context. The relatively few studies of American reforms applying an explicit implementation approach have been explained by system differences. Clark (1986) states that reforms in American higher education, in contradiction to Europe, typically are not planned and enacted through the national center. Because the American system is so large and decentralized, reforms are usually generated at lower levels. In Clark's words: "If authority is extensively decentralized, then opportunities to innovate are decentralized; higher levels find levers of change usually beyond their reach" (1986:260). Instead, reforms occur incrementally, have small expectations, depend considerably on local initiative, and are often market-driven.

In addition, implementation of higher education reforms may be more difficult to accomplish than reforms within other sectors of society, let it be transportation, health care, agriculture, or military defense. Cerych and Sabatier (1986:256) have discussed this question. They argue that the special problems posed by higher education reform implementation are set primarily by the many autonomous actors present, and by the diffusion of authority throughout the structure. Even in a centralized state, higher education is more "bottom-heavy" than most social sub-systems and certainly more than lower education levels. Policy implementation then becomes very interactive, and implementation analysis becomes a study of the respective interactions. Higher education policy implementation is increasingly complicated by its ambiguous and multiple goals. Although the system is concerned primarily with knowledge, it has been called upon to assume many new functions only indirectly related to its traditional responsibility for producing, extending, and transmitting knowledge. It is now supposed to actively promote social equalization, to provide more vocational training, to assist in regional development, to cater increasingly for adults, and so on. Cerych and Sabatier conclude that there is no general consensus regarding these new functions and, if and when they become specific policy objectives, they are immediately questioned and openly contested.

Implementation studies of higher education reforms might to a larger extent than in other sectors have been undertaken in other contexts and under other labels, for example, evaluation studies. This is an argument also raised in general by Ham and Hill (1988:111), who criticize the search criteria used by Pressman and Wildavsky. They argue that there are many studies with a policy focus but without the implementation label, that could be of great relevance to the implementation field. The latter explanation brings us to the possibility that policy studies, in which implementation analysis is a central part, also depend very much on the content and type of policy that is produced and put into action. Not least could the lack of perceived interest in implementation analysis in higher education be a result of changes in public policy in higher education from the mid 1980s and during the 1990s. One major change is, e.g. the shift towards New Public Management doctrines emphasizing privatization, deregulation and evaluation (see e.g. Henkel, 1991; Neave, 1988). As a consequence, it is possible to identify a change in the way public policy is framed, i.e., that only broad frameworks and objectives are specified, leaving much discretion to local organization and implementing agencies (see van Vught, 1989).

Even if it may be difficult to differentiate sharply between internal and external forces in the developments within policy studies, we will argue that changes in public policy have influenced policy and implementation studies. This development has resulted in a change in the way policy and implementation studies are conducted, and not in a declining interest in the implementation "theme" as such, even if the label has changed. Three statements are put forward and will be discussed in the following:

- The change in public policy in higher education has led to an increased interest for program evaluations and research-based evaluations.
- The increased interest in the self-regulation model of public steering of universities and colleges has led to an increased attention towards the adaptive and innovative higher education institution.
- The ideological shift in policy, towards customers and consumers, market and deregulation has led to an increased interest in studying new forms of policy formation and implementation acknowledging the blurring boundaries between higher education and industry, employment and economy.

Although the statements are clearly interrelated, they will for reason of clarity be discussed separately in the following section.

From Implementation to Evaluation Studies

In one way, it could be argued that implementation studies are victims of their own success (cf. Wittrock, 1985:17). The attention early implementation studies got when illustrating the limitations of the top-down model paved the way, especially in higher education, for including evaluation methods and studies during the implementation phase to identify the potential null-effects, perverse effects and side-effects of given reform attempts (Vedung, 1997). Implementation studies headed in the direction of evaluation research, when the former started including a focus on "problems" rather than on policy decisions and including an attention on "outcomes" as well as on "outputs". At the same time, the field of evaluation was also expanding its scope, methods and theoretical position away from that of the "rational" paradigm of organization theory and the "scientific" paradigm of positivist philosophy of science, into advocating multiple theoretical positions (Cook, 1985), triangulation of different methods (Albæk, 1995), and questioning the formal policy objectives which they once took for granted (Guba and Lincoln, 1989). The traditional distinction between implementation and evaluation studies, emphasizing that evaluation studies had a tendency to concentrate only on effect measurements studies (see e.g. Hargrove, 1975), were soon to be irrelevant due to these developments in the evaluation field.

The development showed a refinement of the evaluation instrument, ending up with evaluation models that answered the need for more process and theory-driven approaches, the need to take account of the context surrounding reform implementation, and perspectives that could handle the more pluralistic society with multiple forces shaping and influencing reform attempts (Chen, 1990; Guba and Lincoln 1989; Vedung, 1997).

In sum, evaluation research expanded into and blurred with traditional implementation research, and the direction that implementation studies took, also contributed to blurred distinctions. This development may be detected when it comes to how implementation and evaluation research is defined and demarcated. For example, Rossi and Freeman (1989: 18) include implementation research when they define evaluation research as "the systematic application of social research procedures for assessing the conceptualization, design, implementation, and utility of social intervention programs." And even if there are still proponents of a formal separation between implementation and evaluation studies (Vedung, 1997:7), it is questioned today whether it is fruitful or possible in practice to separate between implementation and evaluation research at all (Albæk, 1989:99, Calista, 1994:137).

The only difference the latter scholars detect between implementation and evaluation research is that, while implementation studies have some characteristics of being an academic discipline, evaluation research has traditionally been more practice oriented, focusing on giving advice and being relevant for policy makers. Moreover, while implementation research has been populated by political scientists and organizational analysts, evaluation research has attracted people from sociology, psychology and education (cf. also Albæk, 1989: 100).

However, the integration of evaluation and implementation studies is not unproblematic (Browne and Wildavsky, 1984b:203). The reasons for keeping the analytical distinction between implementation and evaluation, even if they overlap in practice, are those of methodological and analytical coherence, to avoid that "the seamless web of public policy might thus reassert itself with a vengeance, converting all rival conceptual dominions into an imperialized hodgepodge" (Wildavsky, 1984: xvii). Still, by advocating the need for implementation approaches that highlight evolution, adaptation and learning, it may be said that Wildavsky himself contributed to the confused situation that emerged in implementation and evaluation research (see the contributions by Browne and Wildavsky in Pressman and Wildavsky, 1984).

Tight research funds due to decreasing resources in higher education have in addition led to a growth in and a demand for more applied research. The practical nature of most evaluative research has, therefore, had an advantage in this situation. The downside of this development, at least in Europe, is that few large and theoretically based research-driven evaluations have been carried out in the 1990s. However, a closer look at how different kinds of evaluations are designed and carried out reveals that learning and development are often incorporated in the different evaluations (Peters and Olsen, 1996). In that respect, it is possible to identify a combination of the top-down and the bottom-up perspective that was recommended as one way out of the stalemate situation between the perspectives (Browne and Wildavsky, 1984a:230-231).

In higher education, this development may be most clearly visible in the quality assessment movement. Even if there has been a heated debate about the pros and cons of evaluation systems with a focus either on accountability or on improvement, most national evaluation systems in Europe incorporate both purposes to some degree (Westerheijden *et al.*, 1994), and empirical studies indicate that it is possible to develop evaluation systems that combine these two purposes in a joint procedure (Saarinen, 1995; Stensaker, 1997; see also Massy, 1999; Dill, 2000).

From Steering to Adaptation

The change in public policy in the direction of decentralization and self-regulation (van Vught, 1989) has in turn contributed to a change in the focus of "implementation studies". The theoretical foundation of this new policy is that implementation as such is better left to the targeted organization, and that the only aspects policy makers should specify are the objectives and frames of the policy. The control aspects and steering possibilities of the traditional top-down approach are, in other words, often changed to an approach that emphasizes the adaptive or innovative capacity of the organization or agency that is the target for public policy initiatives (van Vught, 1989; Neave and van Vught, 1991; Clark, 1998). In a Nordic context, for instance, implementation as learning has become a common way of designing public policy and the evaluatory aspect is an explicit part of the implementation process. Public measures are designed as limited small-scale experiments. If the outcome of such a trial period is deemed successful, then the policy initiative can be turned into general policies.

Growing internationalization of higher education and the emergence of a supra-national level of governance in Europe (European Union) are affecting higher education institutions more and more. These developments have enhanced the trend towards studying the adaptive organization. Thus, while traditional implementation studies often took public policy as the sole starting point of any investigation, adaptation studies also take socio-economic and structural developments in society, changes in public demands, and public expectations into account (see e.g. Dill and Sporn, 1995, Sporn, 1999, Maassen *et al.*, 1999).

Compared to the traditional implementation studies, the new adaptation framework has little to do with the top-down approach. Instead, we can find many characteristics of the bottom-up approach applied in the research that is carried out under this umbrella. While the top-down approach underlined responsibility and control, and where the subsequent implementation studies tried to identify under which conditions this could take place, studies of adaptive organizations are more concerned with the trust element, arguing that there are different organizational paths to reach identical political objectives (Lane, 1995:111).

From Public to Private Solutions

The third noticeable development in public policy that has affected implementation studies is a shift in the belief in public solutions to policy problems. Both the illusions of central control and public control came under ideological attack. The rise of the "new right" in Western politics in the 1980s is a significant development in this respect, where it was questioned to what extent applying public solutions to policy problems always was the right thing to do. Thus, advocates of the private initiative argued for, and carried out, policies that to a larger extent opened up for different kinds of privatization, marketization, quasi-marketization and deregulation. This ideological shift is identifiable both in the public sector in general (Olsen and Peters, 1996), and also in higher education (Williams, 1995; Slaughter and Leslie, 1997).

Neave and van Vught (1991:252) argue that this development does not necessarily lead to a reduction in the product or outcome control by governments, but that process or "through-put" control is limited. Thus, for traditional implementation research that had a focus on the process of putting policy into action, this development in public policy removed parts of the very core of the studies within the implementation area. Suddenly, what was on the political and research agenda was how to develop systems of evaluation for increased information utilization and a revival of the old *ex ante* implementation analysis, i.e., when and where should public policy be exposed to means of privatization, marketization and deregulation (see e.g. Niklasson, 1996; Williams, 1995).

The "democratization" of policy making that is inherent in the developments toward more privatization, deregulation and use of market mechanisms is also paving the way for a growing interest in studying policy making and implementation in a multi-organizational setting in which "national and local objectives, public and private interests, are simultaneously advanced by representatives of a variety of organizational actors" (Hanf and Toonen, 1985:vi). To study policy making and implementation as a top-down process is less relevant in this framework. The increased interest in policy networks, policy communities (Lane, 1995) or organizational fields (DiMaggio and Powell, 1991) in which it is difficult to pinpoint the originator of a given policy is, therefore, understandable. Network analysis does not have a hierarchical starting point, and represents a shift away from a master/subordinate relationship to one where policy makers and implementers are more equal and the interaction between them becomes the focus of the study (Barrett and Fudge, 1981:258). However, there is a marked difference between the political ideology underlying the 1970s and 1980s bottom-up studies and the market ideology that largely ignores the political-democratic aspects of user orientation or user focus.

In addition, we also start to see the first attempt to use market-type models in analyzing change processes in higher education. Thus, Dill and Sporn (1995:7) have argued for the advances of the industrial organization approach, where higher education is treated as just another industry sector. Even if higher education does possess some special characteristics, Dill and Sporn claim that the sector still can be analyzed by examining the conditions that shape the amount of competition in an industry. Among these, the identification of forces other than that of government regulation, i.e., the behavior of consumers, suppliers, substitutes and potential new entrants to the higher education industry. Using Porter's argument, they state that "it is more illuminating to consider how government affects competition than treating government regulation as a separate force" (Dill and Sporn, 1995:7).

Conclusion

The development in political ideology described above sets the focus on rather different aspects of policy making and implementation compared to the analytical focus of the first wave of implementation studies. Rather, one could see the interest in new research questions as related to changes in public policy making. How, for instance, is policy shaped in this new multi-organizational framework in which different stakeholders try to affect policy and policy realization (Neave, 1995)? What are the efficient policy instruments in a situation where the degree of governmental control is loosened (van Vught 1997)? Undoubtedly this represented a significant shift of the ideology of public policy, and such policy developments impinge on the definition of relevant research issues. However, if we look beyond the rhetoric of "self-regulation" the transition from one state to the other is not unequivocal. At the level of actual policy in many Western countries the formal structures of the former state control models linger on alongside the ideological and practical decentralized and autonomized structures (Gornitzka and Maassen, 2000). Most of these systems are still in a "hybrid" state where remnants of old systems are blended with the new. The complexity of public policy and political (sub)systems poses serious challenges to the student of implementation, when ideas of self-regulation mix with continued aspirations and practices of central control, and when structures of responsibility and governance are unclear. Consequently, the new policy developments have undoubtedly had an impact on policy studies, yet the "old" issues are not obsolete and irrelevant within new landscapes of public policy and models of state governance.

BUILDING ON THE PAST? CURRENT EMPIRICAL POLICY RESEARCH IN HIGHER EDUCATION

Introduction

Given the changes in higher education policy described above, the question then becomes how current policy studies handle this changing policy landscape.

A search through the current higher education literature with a special attention to studies that try to analyze the relationship between a formally defined or specified policy or reform on the one side and institutional responses, adaptation or practice on the other, do show that these questions are at the very core of many studies. On the European scene, it is possible to identify several research projects that are of great interest to the implementation field. However, many studies seem to have a normative purpose when analyzing public policy initiatives, without much empirical evidence. Other studies often lack a theoretical framework to structure the analysis, and thus represent empirical descriptions with little contribution in terms of generalizable knowledge. Still, as a result of changes in higher education policy, current empirically oriented "implementation studies" seem to change according to the development outlined earlier. Some typical examples of recent studies are given below.

The Pragmatic Approach

One of the participants in the Cerych and Sabatier study, Jan Erik Lane, continued to study implementation processes in higher education, an interest that resulted in the book *Institutional Reform. A Public Policy Perspective*, in 1990. The study had an explicit, but broad, policy implementation approach, where the author tried to "combine a public policy perspective on the decision-making of organizational development and the implementation of top-down reforms with an institutional approach to the internal life of academia that underlines the profound importance of the value system of the academic professions" (Lane, 1990: xiv). In this respect Lane's research is built on some of the most essential lessons from the earlier wave of implementation literature and the scholarly debate that followed in the 1970s and 80s.

The book gives a theoretical review of general policy models available for analyzing policy implementation, and at the same time it provides the reader with an overview of models of the policy sector in focus: higher education. Not surprisingly, Lane argues that if one is to understand policy making and policy implementation, a general model of these processes is not sufficient. As such, this study uses an approach often applied in evaluation studies, i.e., to use different theories and concepts that relate to the specific problem to be solved. Analyses of policy processes require detailed insight into the object of reform, thus knowledge about institutions, people and behavior of the given policy sector is important (Lane, 1990: 39). In the pursuit of such knowledge, the author uses a new institutionalist approach to guide the search (cf. March and Olsen, 1984; March, 1988; Olsen, 1988). The factors important in this approach, and which influence implementation, are physical structure, demographic structure, historical development, development of personal networks, and temporal structure (decision points in time) (Olsen, 1988:35).

The questions guiding the study are also very much of general interest (Lane, 1990: xii): a) Can policy making be comprehensive, or only marginal? b) To what extent does policy making deviate from a rational choice model towards foolishness and pathology? c) Does top-down policy-implementation work? d) Is successful implementation a fiction? The questions indicate assumptions that policy making and policy implementation often display a number of deficiencies: ambiguous goals, unreliable means, policy failure and policy inefficiency.

The empirical background for the book was several attempts by Swedish authorities to redirect and change higher education in the period between 1975-77. However, the method for studying whether implementation of these goals had occurred, can be said to be somewhat unusual. Instead of the case-study method often used in implementation studies, several national surveys targeting academics made up the empirical data together with secondary data from other studies of the same reforms. Summarized, the reforms initiated had the following goals (Lane, 1990:142):

- decentralization
- equalization of institutional statuses
- responsiveness to labor market demands
- participation and codetermination
- possibilities for recurrent, "life long" education.

The findings regarding the realization of these goals suggest both policy failures and policy successes. When it comes to policy failure, several factors seem important. The occurrence of policies with ambiguous objectives is identified (cf. Cerych and Sabatier, 1986). Moreover, policies with what the author claim are unimplementable objectives were found, i.e., the attempt to abolish elements of the traditional concept of the university as exemplified in the search for a completely new internal decision-making structure and for a system of curricula with no liberal arts type of training (Lane, 1990:236). When it comes to unintended outcomes of the implementation process, Lane claims that the number and comprehensiveness of the reform attempts created an implementation bureaucracy. To quote: "The more numerous the reforms of higher education, the larger the size of coordinating bodies above local units, and the more rapid the growth in bureaucratic personnel within the system's local institutions" (Lane, 1990:181).

Of the policy successes mentioned, Lane points out that even if "garbage can" type of processes were found during implementation, they were hardly extensive, and that "public policy is possible, not only in the incrementalist notion of marginal change, but also in the form of comprehensive social change by means of social reform" (Lane, 1990:238). The important guideline when implementing, according to a new institutionalist perspective, is that change is possible as long as the institutional core is not threatened. As long as the reform policies were enacted that intended to change the size of the units, the mix of the student body, the organizational structure and the system of undergraduate and graduate curricula, the implementation process could proceed without pathological ingredients (Lane, 1990:237).

Even if the book contains a broad theoretical overview and interesting empirical data, it is still the methodological aspects of carrying out implementation studies that is of particular interest to the reader. The provision of a set of conceptual distinctions, both with respect to the applicability of various organizational models to higher education decision-making and the evaluation of reform outcomes, is a tool that will offer much to the student of various implementation processes in higher education. Not least, the book gives a careful treatment of questions with respect to criteria for determining "policy success" versus "policy failure". What is successful implementation to one group may be policy failure to another group, because groups perceive or interpret the ends, the means and the outcomes differently. Lane's distinction between the feasibility and desirability of a given policy is, therefore, a useful reminder for everyone doing implementation studies. And even if one manages to distinguish between these two concepts, there will still be problems attached to handling descriptive indeterminacy in every implementation study (Lane, 1990:231). Instead of providing prescriptive advice about the chances of a successful implementation process, Lane's book is most of all a valuable inventory of the complexity involved when one is to study the process of putting policy into practice, and may be seen as an early attempt to combine several frameworks in analyzing policy implementation.

The Organizational Theory Approach

The use of organization theory for studying change in higher education is hardly a new development. One could actually reverse the statement, claiming that several important studies in organization theory rather have grown out of studies of higher education (Rhoades, 1992:1884). In recent studies of "putting policy into practice" that are framed by organization theory, the investigation has focused not merely on the implementation of higher education policy or reform; rather, implementation is seen as a case of organizational change in higher education institutions.

The most novel element when it comes to applying organization theory to the study of change is an expansion of the analytical scope of the studies carried out. While organization theorists traditionally analyzed changes *within* organizations, such theoretical frameworks are today often used to study inter-organizational relationships, i.e., between organizations and different stakeholders in the organizational environment. The recognition that organizations are dependent on their environment is the main factor behind this development. For organization theory to be applicable to the study of policy implementation, the latter recognition is essential.

Even if the Lane study may be said to be one of the earliest attempts to use organization theory in understanding how policy affects practice in higher education, the application of the theoretical framework is nonetheless rather weak. A more consistent study in that respect is that of Goedegebuure (1992), where a resource dependency perspective is applied to understand merging activities in the college sector in Australia and the Netherlands. In both countries the initiative to amalgamate small institutions into larger ones came as a direct result of governmental policies, with the governments spelling out certain incentives to guide the merging process, i.e., increasing institutional size would trigger increased funding (Goedegebuure, 1992: 3-6).

On the basis of the political objectives, and by outlining theoretical propositions on the basis of the resource-dependency framework, these are then tested empirically using a range of data. The results of the analysis show, *inter alia*, that governmental policies relating funding mechanisms to the mergers in the two countries were highly successful (Goedegebuure, 1992:225). However, the study also argues that the merging activity depended on other environmental factors in addition, and that the extent to which a given institution engaged in a merger depended on "the overall environmental situation as perceived by the institutions" (Goedegebuure 1992:226). This result could be interpreted positively both by top-downers and bottom-uppers in an implementation perspective. For top-downers, the existence of well-defined policy means, i.e., economic incentives that guided the successful implementation of the mergers, must certainly be encouraging. For bottom-uppers, the notion that successful implementation depended on how institutions perceived their general situation could be an argument for analyzing potential merging activity by some form of backward mapping.

In general, the resource dependency framework proved to be a fruitful perspective for analyzing and understanding the institutional behavior that took place after the policy initiatives in the two countries, accounting for the role of the environment in producing organizational change as well as focusing on the organizational capacity to influence environmental conditions under which they have to operate (Goedegebuure, 1992: 223-224).

A current project with great relevance for students interested in implementation is a large comparative study of governmental policies and programs for strengthening the relationship between higher education institutions and the national economy (TSER-HEINE project) (see also Gornitzka, 1999). The main research question is how higher education organizations change in response to or in interaction with government policies and programs. The research involves an examination of how government policies and programs act as impetuses for change in higher education organizations. The approach used is not identical to the set-up of a top-down implementation study. It does not follow a given policy from formation to implementation, to the effects of the policy in question, assuming a linear causal chain of events. The focus of this study is on public policy initiatives as possible inputs to organizational change processes at an institutional level.

The conceptual framework applied in this study is built around two theoretical perspectives on organizational change, resource dependence theory and neo-institutional theory. The framework rests on two main assumptions. First, organizational response to environmental expectations is shaped by inter-organizational factors, such as power distributions and institutional values, identities and traditions. Second, organizational actors seek actively to interact with environmental constituents in order to shape and control dependency relations. The TSER-HEINE project framework echoes the classic implementation studies in the sense that it incorporates a special attention to characteristics of government policies that are directed at institutions in higher education. It assumes that such aspects are of importance in the study of how state action serve as an impetus for organizational change. Policies are more than just "a collection of words". Furthermore, their approach does not see the state as "just another actor". The research takes as a point of departure that governments are essential in furnishing and maintaining an overall governance system within which the day-to-day relationship between higher education and government takes place. Such system-level characteristics are studied as part of the significant institutional and historical context within which policies and programs are developed and organizational change processes are positioned. Methodologically, the TSER-HEINE project takes a two-step comparative approach to the study of institutional change. National policies within the selected subject area are studied and compared in an independent analysis (cf. Gornitzka and Maassen, 2000 and Fulton *et al.*, 2002). Second, the main empirical basis is found in a set of case studies at an institutional level in the seven European countries that are part of the project, which in turn are analyzed cross-nationally. Here, the government policies of the national level policy analysis reappear in the analysis to the extent that they have impacted on the dynamics of the change processes studied at an institutional level.

This study exemplifies a multi-level comparative approach, with an explicit focus on government decisions and actions as part of a frame of order within which organizational adaptation takes place. The approach used is also compatible with an interest in issues of implementation in the sense that types of policy and systems of state control and steering are seen as important to understanding the responsiveness of universities and colleges. One of the outcomes of the study demonstrates that most of the governmental policies that were studied were not directly linked in a linear-causal way to outcomes at the institutional level. Nonetheless, the value of national policies for institutional level change processes is more than "just" symbolic. The normative and cognitive content of policies certainly affects the sets of values and norms of the institutional actors involved in institutional adaptation and change. Furthermore, a central conclusion refers to the importance of viewing the success or failure of implementing specific policies in relation to the governmental steering approach within which these policies are embedded (van Heffen *et al.*, 1999:291).

The Network Approach

Central to these types of studies are the attempts to couple actor and structure relationships, establishing the "missing link" between the micro and macro level of analysis. In the words of Lane (1990: 39), these models are high on realism, but have weaknesses when it comes to analytical stringency.

One of the projects using a network/field approach to study policy change is a comparative research study, where national policy developments in Swedish, Norwegian and UK higher education are analyzed and compared over the last decades, with a special focus on the extent to which public reforms have affected the values and behavior of academics within higher education institutions (see Kogan and Hanney, 2000; Henkel, 2000; Bleiklie *et al.*, 2000; Bauer *et al.*, 1999, Kogan *et al.*, 2000).

The theoretical foundations for these studies can be pinpointed quoting Kogan and Hanney (2000:20-21), when they state that "it has proved virtually impossible to make an adequate match between micro analysis, in which the verities of close-grained empirical studies can be demonstrated, and macro analysis, in which more generally applicable propositions can be announced and interrogated. The world of knowledge has increasingly accepted that more than one incommensurate or apparently inconsistent proposition can be advanced simultaneously. In the social domain, in particular, reality does not pile up in well-connected hierarchies of paradigms and theorems". Thus, it is argued that the problem of traditional implementation studies of both a top-down and a bottom-up character is the question of how the levels are related to one another. Consequently, both the top-down and the bottom-up perspectives are rooted in a hierarchical model limiting the dynamics of policy making and policy shaping (Bleiklie *et al.*, 2000:15). To fully understand the changes higher education has gone through in the three countries, the authors instead develop theoretical frameworks using metaphors like arenas, frames and space of action (Bauer *et al.*, 1999: 31), or "fields of social action" (Bleiklie *et al.*, 2000:15).

Even if it may be difficult to disagree with the arguments put forward, one could claim that this type of policy analysis is (again) entering some of the classical problems in the history of implementation analysis, where the number of independent variables is difficult to limit, especially since the dependent variable that the comparative project aims at explaining — change in higher education — is difficult to operationalize. As such, these studies are not restricted to the process where policies are put into practice, but also have an interest in studying how policies come about.

The political context is quite different in the three countries studied. The UK policy direction is perhaps the most exceptional, where higher education institutions shifted from state-subsidized independence to increased dependence on, and deference to, state policies (Kogan and Hanney, 2000:234). Nonetheless political similarities can also be detected. Thus, rather identical conclusions can be identified between the countries when it comes to how policies and reform attempts seem to have been created, being a product of a complex interplay of context, ideologies, ministers and bureaucracies. The findings in the UK disclose that it is difficult to identify a traditional policy community in this country (Kogan and Hanney, 2000:237). A point they make is that in the UK the processes of national policy do not interact directly with the academic system so much as they act as separate systems producing fields of force between them (p. 238). The factor explaining much of the developments seems to be that of historical continuity — in all the three countries. Because of the longitudinal character of the studies, the processes of historic continuation may be followed more easily, showing extensive explanatory power (Kogan and Hanney, 2000:238; see also Bleiklie *et al.*, 2000:307, Bauer *et al.*, 1999:266).

When it comes to identifying the forces of change, quite similar conclusions are also reached. To quote the conclusion from the Norwegian study, "Changes that have taken place were not the outcome of political reforms alone. They should be considered part of more comprehensive demographic, sociostructural and political-institutional processes of change. Within this context the reforms have been both the driving forces behind and the responses to change" (Bleiklie *et al.*, 2000:307).

Conclusion

Policy realization and political reform are predominantly studied as a part of a comprehensive change process, and not as the sole cause of change. Apparently policy studies in Europe to an increasing degree take the same path as current studies of organizational change in the US. In the eye of an American observer, this is a theoretical position where "people (and organizations) are understood to be constructed and to act in the light of socially constructed and defined identities, which are understood to be made up of cultural ideas. . . Their sovereignty, boundaries, and control systems are similarly embedded in cultural material" (Meyer 1996:243). These observations are valid also for many of the studies of policy and change in the area of higher education. The empirical studies referred to above point to the following directions of current and future studies. First, the development is clearly going from a single theoretical framework towards applying a multi-theoretical framework. The direction of change is seen as non-linear rather than linear. Institutional and systemic change are analyzed as a result of dynamic interactive processes rather than as the product of a centrally determined design. The theoretical perspectives applied have gone from viewing implementation as a separate process towards seeing policy making and implementation as integrated processes. Similarly we note a renewed interest in the formal structures that frame action.

CONCLUSIONS AND CHALLENGES FOR FUTURE RESEARCH

In the field of higher education, research the interest in studying implementation "peaked" in the mid-1980s, with Cerych and Sabatier's study as the highlight. While, since then, a large number of studies on higher education policy issues have been conducted, explicit implementation studies have become rare phenomena in the field. How can this be explained? We have pointed to changes in the type of governmental policy and the introduction of new governmental steering strategies with respect to higher education as key factors that can enter as part of the explanation.

However, the knowledge that governments still keep up their reform tempo in higher education — leading in some cases to success and in others to failure — should still trigger interest by researchers in studying the processes that bring about the effects of governmental policies. While the nature of the relationship between government and higher education has changed over the last decade or so, this change was not an expression of the withdrawal of the government from higher education, or the end of public reforms in higher education. Instead it can be argued that the overall relationship between governments and higher education institutions has changed, leading to different conditions for putting governmental policies into effect. This obviously poses challenges to research into implementation processes. While these challenges are by no means novel in the field of implementation studies in general, specific developments in higher education make it even more urgent to deal with them seriously.

Related to the rise of the "stakeholder society" (Maassen, 2000), policy making and reform implementation tend to take place more and more in a network structure that replaces traditional bilateral relationships between the government and higher education institutions. Instead of looking at implementation process in the traditional (causal) way, now implementation processes should be perceived as an *interactive* process. Furthermore, 30 years of implementation research has amply demonstrated the lack of realism in assuming that policies and reform initiatives move from government to objects of implementation unaffected by the road they travel. Assumptions of governmental omniscience and omnipotence are not helpful as a point of departure for implementing policies in practice, nor for studying such processes. Also, in many cases, a policy or a given reform is not the start of change, but a reflection of it; in other words, the government may "legitimize" changes by developing policies or new laws responding to developments in the higher education system. Understanding implementation in higher education is taking notice of how policies and reforms often are formal political confirmation of developments in the field, and not some kind of alien phenomenon that is thrust upon "unsuspecting" institutions.

Based on these considerations, future research should pay attention to the following topics. Policy and reform studies in higher education should in principle use a multi-level approach. This implies that implementation studies have to be transformed, for example, into studies that examine the relationship between the authority responsible for policy making and the policy object, i.e., from policy implementation to policy interaction. Implementation studies should include a much more careful analysis of the processes of formulating governmental policies, and ask e.g. how the nature of the policy relationship affects the way the policy object is involved in the policy making, feels responsible, and feels committed to the agreed upon policy. Also one should give special attention to the different interests of institutions in higher education and who the winners and losers are in the process of shaping government policies and reforms. Certainly, the structures of policy making may be seen as a network, but that does not make issues of power, interests and conflicts over policy irrelevant in explaining institutional responses to initiatives from government or supra national bodies.

Furthermore, we would once again underline what we see as one of the most interesting trajectories of future research in this field, i.e., the process of putting specific policies and larger reforms into effect within a framework of a changed steering model. When government is "steering at a distance", it nonetheless designs the frame within which higher education can more or less autonomously work on realizing the main higher education goals. In principle, self-regulation cannot be easily identified with implementation in the narrow sense of the term. As we have pointed to earlier, governments still have aspirations of affecting the actions of higher education institutions in specific ways, through grand scale reform programs, limited policies or other initiatives. How can they do that within a system where many of the traditional levers of implementation and instruments of government formally have been "decentralized"? Maybe the mismatch between aspirations of governments in connection with specific reforms or policies and the governance models represents the modern governmental "implementation deficit". Or, maybe it is the research conducted that is out of focus. If "old" policy and reform instruments such as central planning and other input-oriented measures are abandoned by governments, there should be a more thorough investigation of the kind of measures that have replaced them as well as how these function as the new levers of implementation. One tendency seems to be that "hard" policy instruments are replaced or combined with "softer" ones during reform. To a greater extent than before, governments also seem to trust their persuasive power, their ability to create meaning and to provide guidance to human behavior both prior to and during reform efforts. One can find this tendency in many governmental white papers and policy plans that advocate reform, where the need for a renewed identity for higher education, a cultural shift, and a reshaping of the roles of higher education are highly advocated, but without any well defined objectives or specified "programs" guiding implementation. If this is the "new" form of policy making with respect to higher education, implementation analysis must focus more on mechanisms through which governmental persuasion and meaning creation take place, and how these are influenced by interaction with the field.

We believe this general question to be a worthwhile endeavor to which researchers of higher education policy could devote serious and systematic attention. Serious efforts along this line require a firm theoretical underpinning that can be drawn from some of the current studies in higher education policy we have referred to earlier, coupled with an empirically solid investigation into "real-life" processes in higher education. More specifically, it calls out for using "softer" models of implementation analysis where attention is not so much on causal models like the one Cerych and Sabatier advocated. Instead, there is a need for an approach that identifies how power and influence can be studied in processes when communication and persuasion are central variables. Since attempts at pushing the implementation field forward by continuously adding to the long list of potentially important variables to be studied have not gained as much as expected, perhaps we should give a more holistic, cultural and cognitive approach a chance?

REFERENCES

Albæk, E. (1989). *Fra sandhed til information. Evalueringsforskning in USA — før og nu.* Viborg: Akademisk forlag.

Albæk, E. (1995). Policy evaluation: design and utilisation. In R. Rist, (ed.), *Policy Evaluation. Linking Theory to Practice.* Aldershot: Edward Elgar Publishing Limited.

Baier, V.E., March, J.G. and Sætren, H. (1994). Implementation and ambiguity. In D. McKevitt. and A. Lawton (eds.), *Public Sector Management. Theory, Critique and Practice.* London: Sage Publications.

Bardach, E. (1977). *The Implementation game.* Cambridge: MIT Press.

Barrett, S. and Fudge, C. (1981). Examining the policy-action relationship. In S. Barrett and C. Fudge (eds.), *Policy and Action.* London: Methuen.

Bauer, M, Askling, B., Marton, S.G. and Marton, F. (1999). *Transforming Universities. Changing patterns of governance, structure and learning in Swedish higher education.* London: Jessica Kingsley Publishers.

Bauer, M. and Henkel, M. (1999). Academic response to quality reforms in higher education: England and Sweden compared. In M. Henkel and B. Little (eds.), *Changing Relationships between Higher Education and the State.* London: Jessica Kingsley Publishers.

Bie, K.N. (1981). *Creating a New University: The Establishment and Development of the University of Tromsø.* Oslo: Institute for Studies in Research and Higher Education.

Bleiklie, I., Høstaker, R. and Vabø, A. (2000). *Policy and Practice in Higher Education. Reforming Norwegian Universities.* London: Jessica Kingsley Publishers.

Browne, A. and Wildavsky, A. (1984a). Implementation as mutual adaptation. In J. Pressman and A. Wildavsky, *Implementation.* Berkeley: University of California Press.

Browne, A. and Wildavsky, A. (1984b). What should evaluation mean to implementation? In J. Pressman and A. Wildavsky, *Implementation.* Berkeley: University of California Press.

Browne, A. and Wildavsky, A. (1984c). Implementation as exploration. In J. Pressman and A. Wildavsky, *Implementation.* Berkeley: University of California Press.

Calista, D.J. (1994). Policy Implementation. In S.S. Nagel (ed.), Encyclopedia of Policy Studies. New York: Marcel Dekker.

Cappola-Pignatelli, P. et al. (1981). *Rapporto sull'universita della Calabria.* Roma: Gruppo di Ricerche sull'edilizia per l'Istruzione Superiore (GREIS).

Cerych, L. (1992). Reforms and higher education: Implementation. In B.R. Clark and G. Neave (eds.), *The Encyclopaedia of Higher Education,* Volume 2. Oxford: Pergamon Press.

Cerych, L. and Sabatier, P. (1986). *Great Expectations and Mixed Performance. The Implementation of Higher Education Reforms in Europe.* Stoke-on-Trent: Trentham Books.

Cerych, L., Neuse, A., Teichler, U. and Winkler, H. (1981). *Gesamthochschule — Erfahrungen, Hemmnisse, Zielwandel.* New York: Campus Verlag.

Chen, H. (1990). *Theory-Driven Evaluations.* Newbury Park, California: Sage.

Clark, B.R. (1986). Implementation in the United States: A comparison with European higher education reforms. In L. Cerych and P. Sabatier: *ibid.*

Clark, B. (1998). *Creating Entrepreneurial Universities: Organizational Pathways of Transformation.* Oxford: Pergamon Press.

Cook, T. D. (1985). Postpositivist critical multiplism. In R. L. Shotland and M. M. Mark (eds.), *Social Science and Social Policy.* Beverly Hills: Sage.

Dill, D.D. (2000). Designing Academic Audit: Lessons Learned in Europe and Asia. *Quality in Higher Education* 6(3):187-207.

Dill, D.D. and Sporn, B. (eds.) (1995). *Emerging Patterns of Social Demand and University Reform: Through a*

Glass Darkly. Oxford: Pergamon Press.

DiMaggio, P. and Powell, W. W. (1991). *The New Institutionalism in Organizational Analysis*. Chicago: University of Chicago Press.

Dunleavy, P. (1981). Professions and policy change: notes toward a model of ideological corporatism. *Public Administration Bulletin* 36: 3-16.

Elmore, R. (1978). Organizational models of social program implementation. *Public Policy* 26: 185-228.

Elmore, R. (1985). Forward and backward mapping: Reversible logic in the analysis of public policy. In K. Hanf and T.A.J. Toonen (eds.), *Policy Implementation in Federal and Unitary Systems*. Dordrecht: Martinus Nijhoff Publishers.

Fulton, O., Gornitzka, Å. and Maassen, P. (eds.) (2002). *Higher Education, the State and the Economy: Relationships and Policies in Eight European Countries*. Dordrecht: Kluwer Academic Publishers

Goedegebuure, L.C.J. (1992). *Mergers in Higher Education*. Utrecht: Uitgiverij LEMMA B.V.

Gornitzka, Å. (1999). Governmental policies and organisational change in higher education. *Higher Education* 38:5-31

Gornitzka, Å. and P. Maassen (2000). National policies concerning the economic role of higher education. *Higher Education Policy* 13: 225-230

Guba, E. and Lincoln, Y. (1989). *Fourth Generation Evaluation*. Newbury Park, California: Sage.

Ham, C. and Hill, M. (1988). *The policy process in the modern capitalist state*. Brighton: Wheatsheaf Books.

Hanf, K. and Scharpf, F.W. (1978). *Interorganizational Policy Making. Limits to Coordination and Central Control*. London: Sage Publications.

Hanf, K. And Toonen, T.A.J. (1985). *Policy implementation in federal and unitary systems. Questions of analysis and design*. Dorndrecht: Martinus Nijhoff Publishers.

Hargrove, E. C. (1975). *The Missing Link. The Study of the Implementation of Social Policy*. Washington: The Urban Institute.

Henkel, M. (1991). *Government, Evaluation and Change*. London: Jessica Kingsley Publishers.

Henkel, M. (2000). *Academic Identities and Policy Change in Higher Education*. London: Jessica Kingsley Publishers.

Henkel, M. and Little, B. (eds.) (1999). *Changing Relationships between Higher Education and the State*. London: Jessica Kingsley Publishers.

Hjern, B., Hanf, K. and Porter, D. (1978). Local networks of manpower training in the Federal Republic of Germany and Sweden. In K. Hanf and F.W. Scharpf (ibid.)

Hjern, B. and Hull, C. (1982). Implementation research as empirical constitutionalism. *European Journal of Political Research* 10: 105-115.

Kim, L. (1982). *Widened Admission to Higher Education in Sweden — the 25/5 Scheme. A Study of the Implementation Process*. Stockholm: National Board of Universities and Colleges.

Kogan, M., Bauer, M., Bleiklie, I. and Henkel, M. (2000). *Transforming Higher Education — A Comparative Study*. London: Jessica Kingsley Publishers.

Kogan, M. and Hanney, S. (2000). *Reforming Higher Education*. London: Jessica Kingsley Publishers.

Kyvik, S. (1981). *The Norwegian Regional Colleges: A Study of the Establishment and Implementation of a Reform in Higher Education*. Oslo: Institute for Studies in Research and Higher Education.

Lamoure, J. (1981). *Les Instituts Universitaires de Technologie en France*. Paris: Institute of Education.

Lane, J.E. (1983). *Creating the University of Norrland. Goals, Structures and Outcomes*. Umeå: CWK Gleerup.

Lane, J.E. (1990). *Institutional Reform. A Public Policy Perspective*. Aldershot: Dartmouth.

Lane, J.E. (1993). *The Public Sector: Concepts, Models and Approaches*. London: Sage.

Lane, J.E. (1995). *The Public Sector: Concepts, Models and Approaches*. London: Sage. 2nd edition

Lester, J.P., Bowman, A.O'M., Goggin, M.L. and O'Toole, L.J. (1987). Public policy implementation:

Evolution of the field and agenda for future research. *Policy Studies Review* 7: 200-216.

Maassen, P. (2000). The changing roles of stakeholders in Dutch university governance. *European Journal of Education*. 35:449-464.

Maassen, P. and van Vught (1996). *Inside Academia.* Utrecht: Tijdstroom.

Maassen, P., Neave G. and Joengbloed B. (1999). Introduction: Organisational adaptation in higher education. In B. Joengbloed, P. Maassen and G. Neave (eds.), *From the Eye of the Storm — Higher Education's Changing Institution*. Dordrecht: Kluwer Academic Publishers.

Majone, G. and Wildavsky, A. (1978). Implementation as evolution. *Policy Studies Review Annual* 2: 103-117.

March, J.G. (1988). *Decisions and Organizations*. Oxford: Blackwell.

March, J.G. and Olsen, J.P. (1984). *Rediscovering Institutions*. New York: The Free Press.

March, J.G. and Simon, H.A. (1958). *Organizations*. New York: John Wiley.

Massy, B. (1999). Energizing Quality Work: Higher Education Quality Evaluation in Sweden and Denmark. NCPI Technical Report No. 6-06. Stanford: National Center for Postsecondary Improvement.

Meyer, J.W (1996). Otherhood: The promulgation and transmission of ideas in the modern organizational environment. In B. Czarniavska and G. Sevón (eds.), *Translating Organizational Change*. New York: Walter de Gruyter.

Neave. G. (1988). On the cultivation of quality, efficiency and enterprise: an overview of recent trends in higher education in Western Europe 1986-88. *European Journal of Education* 23:7-23.

Neave, G. (1995). The stirring of the prince and the silence of the lambs: The changing assumptions beneath higher education policy, reform and society. In D.D. Dill and B. Sporn (eds.), *Emerging Patterns of Social Demand and University Reform: Through a Glass Darkly*. Oxford: Pergamon Press.

Neave, G. (1996). Higher education policy as an exercise in contemporary history. *Higher Education* 32: 403-415.

Neave, G. (1998). The evaluative state reconsidered. *European Journal of Education* 33: 265-284.

Neave, G. and van Vught, F.A. (eds.) (1991). *Prometheus Bound. The Changing Relationship Between Government and Higher Education in Western Europe*. Oxford: Pergamon Press.

Niklasson, L. (1996). Game-like regulation of universities: will the new regulative framework for higher education work? *Higher Education*, 32: 267-282.

Olsen, J.P. (1988). Administrative reform and theories of organization. In C. Campbell and B.G. Peters (eds.), *Organizing Governance, Governing Institutions*, Pittsburgh: University of Pittsburgh Press.

Olsen, J. P and Peters, G. (eds.) (1996). *Lessons From Experience*. Oslo : Scandinavian University Press.

O'Toole, L.J. (1986). Policy recommendations for multi-actor implementation: an assessment of the field. *Journal of Public Policy* 6: 181-210.

Parsons, W. (1995). *Public policy. An Introduction to the Theory and Practice of Policy Analysis.* Aldershot: Edward Elgar.

Pollitt, C. (1993). *Managerialism and the Public Services: Cuts or Cultural Change in the 1990s?* Oxford: Blackwell.

Pressman, J.L. and Wildavsky, A. (1973). *Implementation.* Berkeley: University of California Press.

Pressman, J.L. and Wildavsky, A. (1984). *Implementation.* Berkeley: University of California Press. 3rd edition.

Premfors, R. (ed.) (1984). *Higher Education Organization. Conditions for Policy Implementation.* Stockholm: Almqvist & Wiksell International.

Rossi, P.H. and Freeman, H.E. (1989). *Evaluation: A Systematic Approach.* Newbury Park, California: Sage.

Saarinen, T. (1995). Systematic higher education assessment and departmental impacts: translating the efforts to meet the needs. *Quality in Higher Education* 1: 223-234.

Sabatier, P. (1986). Top-down and bottom-up approaches to implementation research: a critical analysis and suggested synthesis. *Journal of Public Policy* 6: 21-48.

Sabatier, P. and Mazmanian, D. (1979). The conditions of effective implementation. *Policy Analysis* 5: 481-504.

Sabatier, P. and Mazmanian, D. (1981). The implementation of public policy: A framework of analysis. In D. Mazmanian and P. Sabatier (eds.), *Effective Policy Implementation*. Lexington: Lexington Books.

Scott, P. (1999). The research-policy gap. *Journal of Education Policy* 14: 317-338.

Slaughter, S. and Leslie, L.L. (1997). *Academic Capitalism: Politics, Policies, and the Entrepreneurial University*. Baltimore: Johns Hopkins University Press.

Sporn, B. (1999). *Adaptive University Structures. An Analysis of Adaptation to Socio-Economic Environments of US and European Universities.* London: Jessica Kingsley Publishers.

Scott, W. R. (1995). *Institutions and Organizations*. Thousand Oaks, California: Sage.

Stensaker, B. (1997). From accountability to opportunity: the role of quality assessments in Norway. *Quality in Higher Education* 3: 277-284.

van Heffen, O., Verhoeven, J. and De Wit, K. (1999). Higher education policies and institutional response in Flanders: Instrumental analysis and cultural theory. In B. Jongbloed, P. Maassen and G. Neave (eds.), *From the Eye of the Storm — Higher Education's Changing Institution.* Dordrecht: Kluwer Academic Publishers.

Van Meter, D.S. and Van Horn, C.E. (1975). The policy implementation process. A conceptual framework. *Administration and Society* 6:445-488.

van Vught, F.A. (1997). The effects of alternative governance strategies. In B. Steunenberg and F.A. van Vught (eds.), *Political Institutions and Public Policy. Perspectives on European Decision Making.* London: Kluwer Academic Publishers.

Vedung, E. (1997). *Public Policy and Program Evaluation.* London: Transaction Publishers.

van Vught, F. A. (ed.) (1989). *Governmental Strategies and Innovation in Higher Education.* London: Jessica Kingsley Publishers.

Westerheijden, D. F., Brennan, J. and Maassen, P. A. M. (eds.), (1994). *The Changing Context of Quality Assessment. Recent Trends in West European Higher Education.* Utrecht: Lemma.

Westerheijden, D. F. and Sorensen, K. (1999). People on the bridge: Central European higher education institutions in a storm of reform. In B. Jongbloed, P. Maassen and G. Neave. (eds.), *From the Eye of the Storm. Higher Education's Changing Institution.* Dordrecht: Kluwer Academic Publishers

Williams, G.L. (1995). The "marketization" of higher education: Reforms and potential reforms in higher education finance. In D.D. Dill. and B. Sporn (eds.), *Emerging Patterns of Social Demand and University Reform: Through a Glass Darkly.* Oxford: Pergamon Press.

Wittrock, B. (1991). Social knowledge and public policy: Eight models of interaction. In P. Wagner (ed.), *Social Sciences and Modern States: National Experience and Theoretical Crossroads.* Cambridge: Cambridge University Press.

Woodley, A. (1981). *The Open University of the United Kingdom.* Paris: European Cultural Foundation.

10. Academic Careers for the 21st Century: More Options for New Faculty

Judith M. Gappa
Purdue University

As American colleges and universities move into the twenty-first century, their faculty members now number approximately one million (Kirshstein, Mattheson & Jing, 1997). This expansion in the numbers of faculty has been accompanied by changes in the traditional academic career to accommodate numerous and varied institutional and individual needs. Today, the majority of faculty members no longer occupy tenure-eligible positions. Twenty-eight percent of the full-time faculty members are not eligible for tenure, and 42% are part-time (Gappa, 2000). The proliferation of faculty careers and employment arrangements raises a critically important question: how do colleges and universities make and keep the academic career attractive to the most promising current and potential faculty members?

Making the academic career attractive to talented people is fundamental to the health and long term stability of higher education, and of society. As Bowen and Schuster (1986) have pointed out, the nation's faculties educate about a third to a half of every age cohort of young people and increasingly contribute to the life-long learning of older Americans as well. They train virtually the entire leadership of American society in the professions, government, business and the arts. They provide the basic research and scholarship, philosophical and religious inquiry, public policy analysis, social criticism, cultivation of the arts and technical consulting upon which American society depends. In sum, faculty members through their teaching, research and service exert an enormous influence on the economic and cultural development of the nation (p. 3). Yet Bowen and Schuster suggest that interest in the academic career, especially among the exceptionally talented, is waning (p.229). Tierney and Bensimon (1996) find

J.C. Smart and W.G. Tierney (eds.), Higher Education: Handbook of Theory and Research, 425–475.

that the extent of common negative experiences during the probationary period is indicative of a system needing change.

Of course, the academic career has always been a subject of enormous interest to faculty, especially during the late 1960s and 1970s (Jencks & Riesman, 1968; AAUP/AAU Commission on Academic Tenure, 1973; O'Toole, Van Alstyne, & Chait, 1979; Smith & Associates, 1973). But discussion of the academic career at the beginning of the twenty-first century differs from that of a generation ago when tenure reform was also a "hot topic". During the 1990s scholarly inquiries have focused on the attractiveness of the academic career by exploring two major subjects: potential problems with and modifications to traditional tenure systems and alternative academic careers outside the tenure system (Austin & Rice, 1998; Trower, 1996; Chait, 1998; Chait & Trower, 1997; Tierney & Bensimon, 1996: Gappa, 1996; Gappa & Leslie, 1997, 1993; Baldwin & Chronister, 2001). While debates about the pros and cons of tenure continue, the nature of the academic career has fundamentally and irreversibly changed. External and internal pressures have caused colleges and universities to seek additional flexibility in faculty positions. Colleges and universities have opted for faculty appointments that allow flexibility because of: heightened public criticism of higher education and its faculty members, the end of mandatory retirement, shrinking federal and state support, consumer demands for education that meets their needs, and increasing use of technology (Massy & Wilger, 1992; Heydinger & Simsek, 1992; Rhoades, 1998; Levine, 1997).

It does not appear that higher education will return to its former "golden years" (as the period from the mid 1950s to the 1970s has been called) any time soon. Instead, to cope with change and meet their particular needs, individual colleges and universities are revising tenure policies and practices, making decisions regarding how to fill previously tenured positions, and developing new career tracks and employment arrangements to accommodate the rising numbers of new faculty members who are not eligible for tenure. The emphasis upon good institutional practices for faculty employment of a generation ago (AAUP/AAU Commission, 1973; Chait & Ford, 1982) has been expanded to include non-tenure eligible faculty (Gappa & Leslie, 1993; Chronister & Baldwin, 1999; Gappa, 1996). Institutional and individual choices and flexibility have eroded the earlier vision of a uniform career. Policy makers such as national organizations, labor unions, or other organized change efforts (Rhoades, 1998), have been replaced by colleges and universities, no longer as willing to adhere to guidelines promulgated nationally.

Faculty members also differ from their counterparts a generation ago. There are more women and members of minority groups (Tierney & Bensimon,

1996). They do not necessarily find tenure track positions attractive, because of the current tenure process and criteria and because of their lifestyle needs (Massy & Wilger, 1992; Austin & Rice, 1998; Rice, 1996; Boice, 1992). Tenured faculty are experiencing changes in their decision-making roles, governance prerogatives, and workloads (Rhoades, 1998; Kennedy, 1997; Bowen & Schuster, 1986; Levine, 1997). Even definitions of academic freedom and tenure are no longer universal. Individual faculty at different types of institutions and with different types of assignments define academic freedom from their perspectives, and individual institutions are modifying traditional tenure systems (Tierney & Bensimon, 1996; Clark, 1987; Trower, 1996).

There are now so many faculty members who are off the tenure track that attention has shifted to making alternative career paths attractive to them. As the numbers of tenure track faculty continue to decline vis-à-vis those who are non-tenure eligible, the need for attractive and legitimate career alternatives to tenure increases (Chronister & Baldwin, 1999, Baldwin & Chronister, 2001; Gappa & Leslie, 1993, 1997; Breneman, 1997). Careers outside academe are being scrutinized for models, structures and characteristics applicable to higher education (Trower, 1998; Heydinger & Simsek, 1992; Waterman, Waterman & Collard, 1994, Edgerton, 1993). Studies of differences among faculty by discipline and type of institution are sought (Clark, 1997, 1987; Benjamin, 1998; Leslie, 1998b).

This chapter explores the academic career by looking at what changes may make it more attractive to people of talent. Specifically, it focuses on tenure-track faculty in the probationary period and on non-tenure eligible faculty, emphasizing these themes:

- Studies of generational similarities and differences among faculty members show that while faculty attitudes about the value of tenure and the desirability of an academic career have not changed much, their satisfaction with some aspects of the career have.
- Faculty demographics have changed remarkably over the past generation. Increasingly, institutions are using non-tenure eligible positions, and this trend will not be reversed any time soon.
- New tenure-track faculty members or aspirants differ in important respects from those who entered the career a generation ago. They seek balance between their careers and lifestyles, and a collegial working environment.
- Faculty members on and off the tenure track seek flexibility and options in their careers.

The exploration of these themes begins by looking at generational similarities and differences between the early 1970s and the 1990s and at current faculty demographics. The chapter then examines recent research on the probationary period itself, and on probationary faculty members' working conditions, attitudes, and satisfaction levels. Recommendations for various reforms of the probationary period are also explored. The chapter then explores the academic career from the perspective of faculty who are outside the tenure system, e.g. non-tenure eligible. After a brief overview of workplace trends outside the academy, different employment arrangements for both part- and full-time non-tenure eligible faculty members are examined, along with various exemplary strategies and models in use in different institutions. The chapter concludes with recommendations for making the academic career more attractive to all current and potential faculty members in tenured, tenure-track or probationary, and non-tenure eligible positions.

GENERATIONAL DIFFERENCES AND SIMILARITIES

How much change in academic careers has there been over the last generation and what has changed? This section looks at generational differences and similarities in faculty perceptions of the academic career, faculty attitudes and satisfaction levels, and the debates about the viability and meaning of tenure. However, the most substantial change from the 1970s to the 1990s has been the increasing proportion of faculty members, both full and part-time, who are non-tenure eligible.

- From 1970 to 1995, the proportion of part-time faculty doubled from 22% to 42% (Huber, 1998, Finkelstein, Seal & Schuster, 1998). In absolute numbers, however, part-timers increased 266% from 104,000 to 381,000 while full-time positions rose only 49% (Chait, 1998; U.S. Department of Education, 1998).
- In 1975, 29% of full-time faculty members were in tenure-track status; by 1995, this had dropped to 20%. In the same period, the percentage of non-tenure track full-time faculty members increased from 19% to 28% (Chronister & Baldwin, 1999).
- The proportion of full-time faculty with tenure has remained at about 54% between 1975 and 1997. But when part-timers are added in, only about 36% of the total faculty are tenured (Chait, 1998).

(The extent of change in tenure appointments is discussed more thoroughly in the next section on current faculty demographics.)

While scholars' opinions about these trends may vary, prospective faculty members can no longer assume that an academic career will follow the traditional route through a probationary period ending with tenure. And, while the migration away from tenure eligible appointments may be more rapid in certain types of institutions, such as two year colleges (60% part-time), or disciplines (over 40% part-time in the fine arts and education), virtually all institutional types and academic disciplines are experiencing an increase in the numbers of full and part-time faculty who are not eligible for tenure (Kirschstein, Mattheson & Jing, 1997).

Generational Differences in Faculty Perceptions of the Academic Career

At the height of the period of expansion and affluence in American higher education, roughly the mid 1950s to the mid 1970s, a period sometimes referred to as the "golden era", higher education gained in public esteem and prospered financially. The academic profession became an attractive magnet for capable and ambitious prospective faculty (Bowen & Schuster, 1986). The number of Ph. Ds granted tripled, and there were jobs for the increasing numbers of Ph.D recipients.

In these heady times of what appeared to be limitless growth and opportunity, a consensus emerged among faculty nationwide about what it meant to be an academic professional (Rice, 1996):

- research is the central professional endeavor and focus of academic life and knowledge is pursued for its own sake,
- the pursuit of knowledge is best organized by discipline-based departments,
- quality in the professions is maintained by peer review and professional autonomy,
- reputations are established in national and international disciplined-based associations.

Today's senior faculty members who head departments and influence tenure and promotion decisions were in graduate school and entering the career during the late 1950s and 1960s. They continue to pass down this enduring professional vision, despite the different context in which new faculty members find themselves. In this vision, a new faculty member begins with a Ph.D and a tenure-track appointment, achieves tenure in a prescribed time, and is promoted through the ranks based upon research performance. Rice (1996) found this prevailing view of the faculty career narrow and limited, and endorsed the challenges to it that began in the late 1980s and 1990s. The move to reexamine the faculty role and career accelerated with the publication of Boyer's *Scholarship Reconsidered* (1990) which called for expanding the definition of scholarly work beyond the narrow confines of specialized research and publication. According to Rice (1996), this enlarged vision of scholarly work has only begun to gain acceptance from a professoriate trained in earlier times, but it now provides the potential to offer faculty members a richer variety of choices and institutions greater options for faculty careers.

By telling their own stories, Carlson and Kimball (1994) illustrated some of the generational differences affecting faculty views of academic careers. In a conversation for a Lilly Endowment sponsored faculty development workshop, they explored whether their attitudes about the academic life were a reflection of individual personality or of the context of the times.

At the time their article (Carlson & Kimball, 1994) was published, Elof Carlson, sixty-three, was a distinguished teaching professor at the State University of New York in Stony Brook. He had begun his career as a traditional scientist at UCLA, where his research was funded by the National Science Foundation, and he loved his profession. He did not plan to retire until he was seventy years old. He had lived in his own home located two miles from the campus with his wife, a clinical embryologist, for the past 25 years. The Carlsons had five children and eight grandchildren.

In tracing his career, Carlson described his first seven years as a traditional scientist teaching graduate and advanced undergraduate courses and publishing articles, and his subsequent continuous growth as a teacher, scholar and mentor in a variety of positions. Though he and his wife did not have a two-career marriage until later in his career, he had made accommodations to meet his family's needs throughout his career. He depicted his career as fortuitously evolving in new and satisfying directions. "Academic life has been what I dreamed it would be, an opportunity to explore my scholarly capacities, to do research, to write, to have my summers free to do creative work, to keep on learning, and to wake up each day with enthusiasm for meeting students, teaching, writing, thinking and talking" (Carlson & Kimball, 1994, p. 13).

Bruce Kimball, forty-two, was professor and department chair in the Graduate School of Education at the University of Rochester (New York). Married to a physician at the New England Medical Center of Tufts University in Boston, he commuted to his work by plane or car. The Kimballs had two children, ages six and three. At the time of his conversation with Carlson, Kimball was twelve years out of graduate school and "one-third of the way through my career" (Carlson & Kimball, 1994, p.6). He saw himself as having a number of personal and professional choices and dilemmas that had caused him much anxiety and turmoil. After eight years of graduate training at Harvard University, he spent five years looking for a full-time tenure-track position and moving among short-term positions at three different universities. "The risk that one takes in preparing for an academic job is tremendous. . . . The odds of finding the kind of position for which one was trained are generally slim. As I struggled through those early years, I became somewhat resentful about the tightening academic marketplace and the response of academic institutions to that changing marketplace" (p.7). Concerns about fairness in compensation, inability to find housing within the budget of a faculty salary, and his obligation to support his wife in her career added to the ambivalence with which Kimball viewed the academic career. "The result has been a commuter marriage that has endured for nine of the past thirteen years. . . . the strain of commuting and holding together a marriage in which both partners are fully committed to their careers is complicated" (p.8). Kimball's view of the academic career, in contrast to Carlson's, was ambivalent and conflicted.

Kennedy (1997) attributed differences in the career histories of faculty nearing retirement and faculty earlier in their careers to a cohort effect. Carlson and Kimball illustrate his concept that "demography is destiny" (p. 37ff). Carlson had entered his career at a time when the job market was wide open, federal funds were plentiful, and optimism prevailed. Kimball, on the other hand, entered his career at a time when jobs were not plentiful and competition was keen. Federal support for institutions had declined and the view of higher education's future was less optimistic. Kimball's story also illustrates the increased conflict and stress of a dual-career commuting marriage.

Generational differences in faculty were a major source of anger and frustration for junior faculty interviewed by this author for "Heeding the New Voices", a study conducted for the New Pathways Project at the American Association for Higher Education (Austin & Rice, 1998; Rice, Sorcinelli & Austin, 2000). As a participant in that study, this author interviewed probationary faculty members in engineering, and their department heads. The junior faculty who were interviewed expressed great concern over a tenure process that was not clear to them, the ability of the senior faculty to understand the competitiveness of securing financial support for research and publishing articles, and the pressures for achievement in a very short period of time. Regardless of their personal circumstances, they all were having difficulty managing their time and balancing their personal and professional lives. Their department heads, on the other hand, were generally unsympathetic regarding time pressures, stating that the environment was competitive and those who made the extended commitment (60-80 hours a week) got the rewards. Their major concern with the tenure process was to make sure they did not grant tenure to mediocre people. They felt occasional failures to tenure people who subsequently became "superstars" were a reasonable price to pay for a conservative attitude about tenure. In part, their views reflected their inability to understand the complex lives of the junior faculty as they struggled with the spiraling pressures of the tenure decisions and family life (personal communication to R. Eugene Rice, 1995).

Generational Changes in Faculty Attitudes and Satisfaction with the Career

Have faculty attitudes and satisfaction with the career changed over a generation? One would expect they would. Certainly, faculty members themselves and their careers have changed. The change in the sheer numbers of faculty members — which has altered the supply-demand equation of several decades earlier — would indicate a change in attitudes over a generation. In 1970-1971 there were 474,000 faculty member, of whom 369,000 (78%) were full-time and 104, 000 (22%) were part-time (Bowen & Schuster, 1986). By 1992, there were 904,935 faculty members in 3,000 institutions of higher education, of whom 528,260 (58 %) were full-time and 376,675 (42%) were part-time (Kirshstein, Mattheson & Jing, 1997).

Beginning with the mid 1970s, higher education entered a period of prolonged financial stringency that affected faculty compensation and working conditions. Since then, according to Bowen and Schuster (1986), the attractiveness of the academic profession to those in or contemplating it has diminished noticeably. In an era of declining resources, shifting enrollment patterns and retrenchment, real faculty earnings fell and the work environment became less satisfactory. Reaction to the changed circumstances led to growth in faculty unions and increasing numbers of part-time faculty. But, by and large, faculty members did not defect. Faculty members who entered the academic career embracing certain values associated with academic life have opted to stay with what their colleges and universities had to offer.

But, Bowen and Schuster (1986) suggested that there was serious risk that academic careers would become less attractive, and wondered if colleges and universities would be able to attract their share of "the inevitably tiny pool of exceptionally gifted and creative scientists, intellectuals and artists who are important far beyond their numbers . . . (or) make progress towards diversifying their faculties" (p. 8). There is ample evidence that attitudes and beliefs of current employees across similar professions have changed dramatically. Research by Bailyn (1993) indicates that workers are no longer simply employees, they are people leading complicated lives for whom employment is a critical but not the only activity. The work force is now heterogeneous, forcing employers to give up uniform and monolithic expectations for reaching their goals. Today's workers are more autonomous and anti-hierarchical, less competitive and more cooperative than their predecessors. They want to work, but they want to work differently.

Organizations must find ways for employees to contribute to increased demands for productivity without neglecting their personal lives (p. 10).

Actual evidence of changes in faculty attitudes and satisfaction with the academic career over a generation is scarce because of a lack of comparable data. Until the 1987 and 1992 National Studies of Postsecondary Faculty by the U.S. Department of Education, there were no routinely administered and published data regarding faculty attitudes about the academic career. Early surveys from the Higher Education Research Institute are not available and later surveys are proprietary (Linda Sax, personal communication, January 4, 2000.) The Carnegie Foundation for the Advancement of Teaching sponsored surveys of a random sample of faculty six times (1969, 1975, 1984, 1989, 1992 and 1997), seeking opinions on a variety of issues important to students, scholars, administrators and public policy makers. A few questions aimed at assessing faculty attitudes and satisfaction levels have been routinely included. But, regrettably for researchers trying to analyze trends, most survey questions changed over the years as the interests of the Carnegie Foundation changed; and the survey results were published in a variety of formats, some of which are difficult to find or unavailable. With the assistance of Alex McCormick at the Carnegie Foundation for the Advancement of Teaching, earlier surveys were examined to determine if they contained the same or similar questions to those in the 1997 questionnaire about faculty attitudes and satisfaction levels (Alex McCormick, personal communication, February 29, 2000). His review of all the survey questionnaires showed that a few indicators of attitudes about the career had been replicated between 1969 and 1997.

Using the published results of these surveys, **Table 1** (p. 436) summarizes the responses to questions that were repeated in the surveys from 1969 or 1975 to 1997 (Bayer, 1970; Bayer, 1973; Clark, 1987; Carnegie Foundation for the Advancement of Teaching, 1989; Boyer, 1990; Huber, 1998). They give a broad overview of faculty attitudes. For the most part, responses to these questions from 1969-1997 show that faculty members' attitudes have not changed much.

Faculty members remain generally satisfied with their career choices and their institutions. Very few indicated they would change their profession if they had it to do over again. They retained these attitudes even though they expressed dissatisfaction with escalating workloads and with salaries that did not keep pace with inflation through most of the decade.

Why are faculty members so satisfied with their careers? Clark (1987) suggested that faculty receive their "compensation" through the strength of their intrinsic motivation and rewards for doing academic work for its own sake, and through their strong belief in education. The extensive differentiation among institutions of higher education also played an important role. Using self-

Table 1: Faculty attitudes: Generational similarities and differences (Percentage agreeing strongly, or with reservations, at all institutions)

Statement	Year				
	1969	1975	1984	1989	1997
In general, my institution is a very good place	49	51	42	49	47
My salary is excellent or good	54	44	40	48	46
Intellectual environment at my institution is fair or poor	47	52	54	56	46
If I had to do it over again, I'd not become a college teacher	14*	N/A	21	15	10
My interests lie primarily in or leaning toward teaching	76	73	69	71	73
Teaching effectiveness, not publications, should be the primary criterion for promotion of faculty	78	74	64	62	57
I tend to subordinate all aspects of my life to my work	44	36	38	40	46**
I hardly ever get the time to give a piece of work the attention it deserves	46	41	45	43	63
My job is the source of considerable personal strain	43	36	40	44	39

* *If I had a chance to retrace my steps, I would not choose an academic life.*
** *I feel I have less control of my time than I had five years ago.*
(Data taken from Carnegie Foundation for the Advancement of Teaching Surveys of the Faculty)

selection, faculty could seek careers in teaching or research settings, urban or rural settings, or settings emphasizing bright undergraduates or open access. Clark (1987) acknowledged that in the mid-1980s there had never been so many American academics who were so well off and they knew it (p. 225). But Clark also drew attention to the fault lines within the faculty. He recognized that much of the satisfaction expressed came from the firmness of the academic job, the chance to be a member of the regular faculty with security of employment and dependable movement up the ranks. He understood that satisfaction came at a price, a price that would became higher and higher in the 1990s. "The growth of a peripheral work force is a staggering phenomenon, a massive lump an integrated profession would find hard to swallow" (p. 232).

Generational Debates over the Pros and Cons of Tenure

The 1940 Statement of Principles on Academic Freedom and Tenure promulgated by the American Association of University Professors (AAUP) and the Association of American Colleges (AAC) states:

> Tenure is a means to certain ends; specifically: (1) freedom of teaching and research and of extramural activities, and (2) a sufficient degree of economic security to make the profession attractive to men and women of ability. Freedom and economic security, hence, tenure, are indispensable to the success of an institution in fulfilling its obligations to its students and to society (AAUP, 1990, p. 3).

No definition has generated more debate over its meaning, intentions and relevance than this statement of purpose. Chait and Ford (1982) point out that the AAUP statement is more a partisan characterization than a definition. "Tenure is no more freedom and economic security than marriage is bliss" (p. 3). They endorsed a later, more precise definition. "Tenure is an arrangement under which faculty appointments in an institution of higher education are continued until retirement for age or physical disability, subject to dismissal for adequate cause or unavoidable termination on account of financial exigency or change in institutional program" (AAUP/AAC Commission on Academic Tenure, 1973, p.256).

Professors and administrators have praised or vilified tenure since its inception. The pros and cons of tenure fill volumes, but the arguments are remarkably similar generation to generation. Attacks on tenure are routine; major assaults occur when the external public speaks out about faculty behavior or institutional responsiveness to societal needs. In the late 1960s and early 1970s, state legislators and others became disenchanted with campus activists and student demonstrations and questioned faculty accountability to their institutions (Chait, 1995). The tenure debates began anew. The reasons and rhetoric from a generation ago are surprisingly similar to the current debates:

> A number of factors have stimulated this reexamination during the past few years: an increased politicization of elements within academic institutions; diminished public confidence in the performance of colleges and universities, especially the quality of teaching within them; a nationwide debate about the purposes and direction of higher education; and severe financial constraints. These and other factors have prompted reconsideration of tenure, as many began to argue that tenure, though created to safeguard academic freedom and promote job security, has actually contributed to featherbedding, protection from responsible critique, and financial insolvency." (Smith, 1973, p.ix),

and had the same passion:

> Higher education has run the full gamut, from public accolade to public wrath, and that wrath has a focus. No longer do citizens aim their weapons at institutions of higher education — nor even at administrators or students within these institutions. Instead, the principal target is now the academic man. And tenure is the bull's eye" (Blackburn, 1972, p.1).

Others participated in the debate either by extolling the benefits of tenure or citing the dominance of research over teaching, the perpetuation of established departments and disciplinary specialties, and the autonomy and power of the tenured faculty as criticisms of tenure (AAUP/AAC Commission on Academic Tenure, 1973; Jencks & Riesman, 1968; O'Toole, Van Alstyne & Chait, 1979).

The same pro and con debates about the value and meaning of tenure have proliferated during the 1990s with the same general underlying reasons for the debate: public criticism of higher education, tuition increases, shrinking federal and state support, elimination of the mandatory retirement age for faculty, the need for flexibility in an era of rapid change, and the predominance of research over undergraduate teaching (Massy & Wilger, 1992; Heydinger & Simsek, 1992; Kennedy, 1997; Plater, 1998; Levine, 1997). And, again, as it did a generation ago, tenure has proven to be a durable institution, resilient against attack and valued by most faculty and administrators (Bowen & Schuster, 1986). No other system has demonstrated that it is any better than tenure nor is there compelling evidence that institutions have been ill-served by tenure or that tenured faculty as a group are any less productive than non-tenured faculty (Chait, 1995). Tierney and Bensimon (1996) concluded that changes in the tenure system will come only when structures or systems that protect academic freedom, the ideal of the faculty community, replace it. In other words, reforms of tenure, where and when they occur, will not spring from a national movement; instead they will come from institutional responses to their varied circumstances.

Conclusions

Academics value tenure. Despite external pressures and internal pro and con debates, the tenure system as a whole has changed little over the last generation, though changes are being made within some institutions, and newly adopted post-tenure review processes hold the prospect of more change even among those with traditional tenure. And, by and large, faculty members remain satisfied with their careers. The real change has occurred in faculty demographics and careers. The numbers of faculty members have roughly doubled since 1970, but, proportionally, fewer and fewer of them are in tenure track or tenured appointments. Slowly, but inexorably, institutions have migrated away from tenure eligible to non-tenure eligible appointments, which do not have the academic freedom or job security associated with tenure. This change has enormous implications for the academic workplace, and the future of faculty and of higher education. The rest of this chapter explores these shifts and their effects, and looks at possible modifications and alternatives to tenure to make the career attractive to current and potential faculty members.

CURRENT FACULTY DEMOGRAPHICS AND ATTITUDES

According to the National Study of Postsecondary Faculty and other sources, in 1992 the total number of faculty members was 904,935, of whom 528,260 were full-time and 376,675 were part-time (Kirststein, Mattheson & Jing, 1997). Aside from overall growth in the numbers of faculty members, up from 769,825 in 1987, the major change was in the distribution of faculty members between full- and part-time. **Table 2** shows that in every type of institution the percentage of full-time faculty has declined while the percentage of part-timers has increased.

While the numbers of part-timers have increased, their status within higher education has not. **Table 3** shows that, for the most part, full-timers occupy the tenure and tenure eligible ranks; part-timers occupy the non-tenure eligible positions.

Table 2.* Percentage of higher education instructional faculty and staff, by employment status and type and control of institution: Fall 1987 and Fall 1992

Institution Type by Year	Full-time		Part-time	
	1987	1992	1987	1992
All institutions	67	58	33	42
Public research	86	81	14	19
Private research	78	65	22	35
Public doctoral	83	72	17	28
Private doctoral	63	61	37	39
Public comprehensive	75	67	26	33
Private comprehensive	61	51	39	49
Private liberal arts	69	65	31	36
Public 2-year	48	40	52	60

**Tables 2-8 were prepared by Chun-Hui Sophie Ho, Research Assistant, using National Study of Postsecondary Faculty, NSOPF:88/93: Public Access Data Analysis System (DAS). National Center for Education Statistics, Office of Educational Research and Improvement, U.S. Department of Education, 1997.*

Table 3. Percentage of higher education instructional faculty and staff, by tenure status, part- and full-time status, and type and control of institution: Fall 1992

Institution Type	Faculty Rank & Status									
	Tenured		On tenure track		Not on tenure track		No tenure system for faculty status		No tenure system at institutions	
	FT	PT	FT	PT	FT	PT	FT	PT	FT	PT
All	54	3	22	2	11	47	5	44	8	5
Public Res.	63	10	20	3	12	55	5	32	<1	<1
Private Res.	50	2	23	1	18	52	9	41	1	4
Public Doct.	54	6	27	2	16	55	4	38	<1	<1
Private Doct.	46	4	27	2	14	49	8	41	6	4
Public Comp.	61	3	25	2	11	51	3	44	<1	1
Private Comp.	53	2	26	1	12	46	4	46	5	5
Private Lib Arts	46	4	25	2	13	51	5	38	11	5
Public 2-year	53	2	15	1	6	43	4	48	22	6

The distribution of part- and full-time faculty and tenure status holds true for program area or discipline as well. **Table 4** shows that across disciplines full-time faculty are most likely to occupy tenured and tenure track positions while part-timers do not.

Table 4. Percentage of higher education instructional faculty and staff in 4-year institutions, by tenure status, part-and full-time status, and discipline: Fall 1992

Institution Type	Faculty Rank & Status									
	Tenured		On tenure track		Not on tenure track		No tenure system for faculty status		No tenure system at Institutions	
	FT	PT	FT	PT	FT	PT	FT	PT	FT	PT
All	54	3	22	2	11	47	5	44	8	5
All four-year	55	4	24	1	12	50	5	41	4	4
Ag./Home econ.	72	17	19	—	4	59	4	24	<1	—
Business	52	2	30	2	10	49	4	41	5	5
Education	55	3	24	1	14	49	5	45	3	2
Engineering	62	7	28	4	6	53	1	33	3	3
Fine arts	53	6	22	2	10	48	3	36	12	8
Humanities	60	2	19	<1	12	47	6	48	4	3
Natural sciences	64	5	21	1	9	42	3	47	3	5
Social sciences	63	3	23	4	9	54	3	35	3	5
All other fields	49	3	26	2	14	51	7	43	5	3

Table 5 shows the similarities and differences among full- and part-timers in their levels of satisfaction with their jobs. Full- and part-time faculty members are almost identical in their overall satisfaction with their jobs, and similar

Table 5: Summary of job satisfaction analysis, National Study of Postsecondary Faculty, Fall 1992

Area of analysis	Rating Choices	Full-time faculty (%)	Part-time faculty (%)
A. Satisfaction with job overall	Very dissatisfied	4	4
	Somewhat dissatisfied	12	11
	Somewhat satisfied	48	46
	Very satisfied	36	39
B. Satisfaction with workload	Dissatisfied	32	17
	Somewhat satisfied	40	37
	Very satisfied	28	46
C. Perception of pressure to increase workload in recent years	Worsened	51	29
	Stayed the same	34	31
	Improved	8	6
	Don't know	6	34
D. Satisfaction with salary	Dissatisfied	45	46
	Satisfied	55	55
E. Satisfaction with benefits	Very dissatisfied	7	33
	Somewhat dissatisfied	18	24
	Somewhat satisfied	45	28
	Very satisfied	30	15
F. Satisfaction with opportunity for advancement	Very dissatisfied	13	28
	Somewhat dissatisfied	19	28
	Somewhat satisfied	35	27
	Very satisfied	34	17
G. Satisfaction with job security	Very dissatisfied	8	25
	Somewhat dissatisfied	11	20
	Somewhat satisfied	31	29
	Very satisfied	50	26

in their satisfaction with salaries. Part-timers' satisfaction with salary may be due to the fact that the majority of them have their primary employment outside academe. However, there are important distinctions between full- and part-timers in their satisfaction with workload, benefits, opportunities for advancement, and job security.

The attitudes of full-time faculty members about their careers have been more extensively surveyed by the Higher Education Research Institute (Sax, Astin, Korn & Gilmartin, 1998) and TIAA-CREF (Sanderson, Phua, & Herda,

2000). (Part-time faculty members were not included.) Their results agree with and amplify those of the National Study of Postsecondary Faculty. Full-time faculty members of all ranks have become increasingly supportive of tenure, with the strongest advocates being the tenured faculty (Sax, Astin, Korn, & Gilmartin, 1998). Almost nine out of ten full-timers (87%), *regardless of tenure status*, said that if they could begin their professional career anew, they would definitely or probably pursue an academic career; 55% favored retaining tenure as it now is, and 41% favored some modifications to tenure (Sanderson, Phua & Herda, 2000). Full-time faculty also reported increased satisfaction with their jobs (75%) and working conditions (72%) (Sax, Astin, Korn & Gilmartin, 1998).

However, survey results indicate this improved satisfaction with their jobs has been accompanied by increasing pressures in their personal lives. A higher percentage of the full-time faculty over the decade (1989-1998) reported stress due to household responsibilities (71%), their own physical health (48%), and caring for elderly parents (34%). Time pressures (86%) and lack of personal time (80%) were the most frequent causes of stress. Women faculty perceptions of the academic climate remain less favorable than men's, particularly with respect to the review and promotions process, job security, and demands on their personal time (Astin, Korn & Dey, 1991; Sax, Astin, Korn & Gilmartin, 1998).

The satisfaction versus stress dichotomy may be partially explained by the results of the TIAA/CREF survey (Sanderson, Phua & Herda, 2000). It asked faculty members to rate seventeen factors for how important they were to them and for how satisfied they were. A key finding of the survey was the extent of the disconnection between these two faculty views. For example, 76% of faculty members rate time for family as very important but only 30 % said they were very satisfied with the time they had. Similarly, 52% rated attractive salaries and benefits as very important, but only 13% were very satisfied with what they had.

This brief overview of current faculty demographics, attitudes and satisfaction levels introduces the sections that follow. They explore in more detail what makes academic careers attractive or unattractive to new faculty on tenure-track and to full- and part-time faculty in non-tenure eligible appointments.

TENURE-TRACK FACULTY: THE PROBATIONARY PERIOD

In *The New Academic Generation*, Finkelstein, Seal and Schuster (1998) developed a profile of full-time faculty members with seven years or less full-time experience. The authors' inter-cohort comparisons illustrate differences between junior and senior faculty:

- Junior faculty members are diverse, with more women, people of color and foreign nationals than the senior cohort. White, U.S. born males (43.2%) are no longer the majority of full-time faculty.

- New faculty members have a richer variety of experiences and a more diverse educational background then their senior colleagues.
- The two cohorts hold similar attitudes about their work and satisfactions with their careers. They use similar pedagogical approaches to teaching and express the same preference for doing less teaching and more research. Thus, new faculty members appear to have been well socialized by their mentors into the "old ways" (p. 103).

However, the satisfaction levels of new faculty members are all lower than their senior colleagues for job security, advancement opportunities, keeping current in their disciplines, and spousal employment. These satisfaction levels may reflect their experiences with the tenure-track probationary period and conflicts between their personal and professional lives. Probationers' dissatisfaction with the academic career is focused on the lack of a comprehensive, clear and rational tenure process, a lack of community, and inability to manage their time, their workload and their personal and professional lives (Rice, Sorcinelli & Austin, 2000; Austin & Rice, 1998; Tierney & Bensimon, 1996; Boice, 1992; Olsen, 1993; Olsen & Near, 1994; Barnes, Agago & Coombs, 1998).

The Tenure Process and Time Line

New tenure-track faculty members arrive optimistic, enthusiastic and idealistic. They enter the academic career because they believe faculty work involves freedom to pursue academic interests, autonomy, flexibility, and opportunities to serve society through education. Unfortunately, what early career faculty members hope for and what they actually experience does not fully match (Rice, 1996; Rice, Sorcinelli & Austin, 2000). The "Heeding New Voices" study showed that what new faculty find is stressful work.

All faculty members, but especially new faculty, face multiple demands for their time and high expectations for their accomplishments in teaching, research and service. Their time at work is fragmented among diverse and conflicting priorities. Students expect excellent faculty performance in the classroom; senior colleagues expect participation in departmental, campus and professional service. Simultaneously they must produce research and scholarly work (Gappa & MacDermid, 1997). Bailyn (1993) describes this paradox:

> The academic career therefore is paradoxical. Despite its advantages of independence and flexibility, it is psychologically difficult. The lack of ability to

> limit work, the tendency to compare oneself primarily to the exceptional giants in one's field, and the high incidence of overload make it particularly difficult for academics to find a satisfactory integration of work with private life. . . . It is the unbounded nature of the academic career that is the heart of the problem. Time is critical for professors, because there is not enough of it to do all the things their job requires: teaching, research, and institutional and professional service. It is therefore impossible for faculty members to protect other aspects of their lives, and work tends to dominate (p.51f).

Early career faculty interviewed for the "Heeding the New Voices" study (Austin & Rice, 1998; Rice, Sorcinelli & Austin, 2000) did not want to eliminate tenure, but found the tenure process mystifying. They were troubled by vague, unclear, shifting and conflicting expectations for performance. Over and over again, they made comments like "Everything is so vague, ambiguous, and elusive" or "There is no steady, reliable feedback" or "I cannot get a good read on what it takes to get tenure." (Rice, Sorcinelli & Austin, 2000, p. 10). One new faculty member referred to the tenure process as "archery in the dark" (Rice, 1997, p.31). Grogono (1994) refers to it as hazing.

Participants in the "Heeding the New Voices" study also found the tenure process problematic and stress producing (Rice, Sorcinelli &Austin, 2000). Insufficient, unfocused and unclear feedback on their performance only served to exacerbate the lack of clarity around expectations and their progress towards meeting them. Furthermore, early career faculty worried that senior colleagues, responsible for providing feedback and evaluation, were constantly changing or raising their expectations or their messages were often in conflict. Even when the expectations were clear, participants perceived the "tenure bar" being raised far above the achievements required for the senior colleagues who would decide their fate. They were also concerned about frequently rotating department chairs, turnover in membership of personnel committees, and closed committee meetings. These flaws were seen as contributing to the instability of the process. One participant commented, "The chair has a tremendous impact on the tenure decision. We changed chairs after my hire and I am bitter, upset, and frightened by the way the current chair controls and dominates the process" (Rice, Sorcinelli, & Austin, 2000, p. 11). As Chait (1998) points out, faculty do not learn until the end of the probationary period whether good was indeed good enough (p.5). Or, Sawsilak (1999) would add, based on her experiences at Stanford University, whether the decision was at all fair.

For Tierney and Bensimon (1996), the end result is that "people stagger to the end of the tenure review" (p. 73). If they attain tenure, they feel relieved rather than elated. One respondent, the first to be tenured in his school in ten years, said, "It's been dehumanizing. There's been tremendous soul searching that goes on, but it's not productive because you always end up thinking you're not good enough. I'm disheartened by the whole thing" (p.73). Another commented, "I've got it. I will never give it up, because I would never put my family through that again. Never" (p.73). Hogan (1998) would agree. He characterized the process of denying someone tenure as one of systematic cruelty even under the best of circumstances; and points out that it is a process not only of taking away someone's job, but of taking away his/her self respect.

For most probationers, the tenure timeline is the most critical aspect of the tenure process (Austin & Rice, 1998). While performance expectations are high, funding opportunities are decreasing, causing greater competition for grants to support research. Journal publication review processes and schedules often result in long delays before accepted manuscripts appear in print. Infrastructure problems can compound these difficulties. Early career faculty in the natural and physical sciences and engineering frequently discussed how delays in getting laboratory space and equipment or funding for graduate assistants or post-docs delayed their ability to start their research. The inflexible tenure timeline can put probationary faculty in serious binds.

It also puts unnecessary stress on women and men with family responsibilities. The seven year probationary period is difficult for women who have postponed childbearing through their graduate school years and now face age constraints. Choices between waiting to have a family until after tenure is achieved or caring for children during the pre-tenure years are difficult (Austin & Rice, 1998).

Membership in a Community

Early career faculty members want to pursue their careers in a community where collaboration is respected and encouraged, and where interaction and talk about one's ideas, work, and the institution are common. They experience, however, isolation, separation, fragmentation, loneliness, competition and, occasionally, incivility (Tierney & Bensimon, 1996; Boice, 1992; Austin & Rice, 1998; Rice, Sorcinelli & Austin, 2000).

> When they recruited me, they couldn't be complimentary enough. They courted me. Now that I'm on campus, I feel ignored. They not only don't care about my lab and my research, they've actually undermined my efforts to set it up. If I had known what things would be like here, I wouldn't have come" (Boice, 1992, p. 23).

Participants in the "Heeding the New Voices" study frequently mentioned problems and misunderstandings with senior faculty (Austin & Rice, 1998).

They felt that senior faculty members had limited understanding of the time pressures or obstacles they faced and could not appreciate the stress involved in the conflicting demands of dual career couples because they had not experienced them. Participants questioned whether or not senior faculty members were sufficiently productive as scholars to be able to adequately judge their work; or they worried that they must mold their work to the interests of senior faculty who would ultimately evaluate it for tenure. They also worried about the little things in departmental life such as feeling uncomfortable with declining requests from senior colleagues who wanted them to serve on departmental committees or engage in other time-consuming activities that would not contribute to their tenure dossier. In their study, Barnes, Agago and Coombs (1998) found that the two most important predictors of faculty intent to leave academia were a sense of frustration over time commitments and a lack of sense of community at their institution.

Issues of community and collegiality are particularly keen for non-majority faculty (Austin & Rice, 1998; Rice, Sorcinelli & Austin, 2000; Tierney & Bensimon, 1996; Johnsrud & Des Jarlais, 1994; University of Wisconsin System, 1990; Tack & Patitu, 1992.) Women respondents to the "Heeding New Voices" study reported difficulty finding advisors or mentors among senior faculty, and environments where subtle discrimination caused them to struggle to be taken seriously. Tierney and Bensimon (1996) suggested that the particular experiences of women junior professors are shaped not only by individual behaviors but by gender and power relations within a department or institution that produce behavioral patterns they labeled as "smile work" and "mom work" (p. 101). Minority probationary faculty members are frequently the "only one" in their department or institution. As one of few representatives of their group, they feel obligated to show good citizenship by serving on committees or demonstrating their knowledge and commitment to a cultural group. Tierney and Bensimon (1996) labeled this "cultural taxation" and "hidden workload", and found it can cause substantial extra workloads (p. 115f). Alone or with limited peer support, one African American woman characterized the predominately white environment with this comment: "I still feel myself a stranger. That is, I am comfortable but not at home" (p.122).

A Balanced Life

New faculty members envisioned the career as offering flexible time that they could shape and control, and sufficient time for thinking, focusing and creativity. What they reported was inability to manage their time and imbalances with their work and family lives (Rice, Sorcinelli & Austin, 2000).

While long working hours and lack of balance between personal and professional lives are problems for most of the professoriate, new career faculty interviewed for the "Heeding the New Voices" study said finding enough time to do their work and fragmentation of their time were major sources of stress. Participants felt strongly that their time and attention were spread too thin across too many conflicting duties. "Life before tenure is a juggling act that involves long hours and keeping all the balls in the air long enough to get through it" (Rice, Sorcinelli, & Austin, 2000, p.17). Faculty interviewed by Tierney and Bensimon (1996) said they worked all the time. "I take Friday afternoons off — they're for myself, and I get Sunday mornings for my family. Other than that I work every day." Another commented, "I get up by five so I can write, and then I get to work by eight and stay here until about seven" (p.60).

Efforts to balance the demands of professional work and personal life compound faculty stress (Bailyn, 1993; Olsen & Near, 1994; Gappa & MacDermid, 1997). Very few probationers in the "Heeding New Voices" study who were making choices about how to spend their precious time were satisfied with their choices. Erring on the side of work, one commented, "I have two kids, ages 9 and 11. I don't have time to even look at their homework. I'm up at 6 AM and gone, back at 11 PM. All I have time to do is sleep" (Gappa & MacDermid, 1997, p. 8). Other probationary faculty members are concerned that finding time for families would jeopardize their careers. "What this means is you are making compromises when not everyone is making them. You are in a horse race with others, and it is very, very costly to start making those compromises" (Wilson, 1995, p. A24).

The majority of applicants for faculty positions now have partners who have careers and expect to continue in them (Norrell & Norrell, 1996). Strains on both partners accelerate when faculty members are simultaneously members of dual-career couples and in commuting situations (Tack & Patitu, 1992). A preliminary study of institutions who are members of the American Association of Colleges and Universities indicated that institutions were helping by offering the spouse or partner a tenure-ineligible position, a tenure-track position, a shared position, or by creating a suitable job. However these efforts are usually informal, and there is no national study of how effective they have been (Wolf-Wendel, Twombly, & Rice, 2000).

The problems of balancing work and family affect most probationary faculty, but women are more heavily disadvantaged by their dual roles. According to Tack and Patitu (1992) women faculty are likely to work eighty or more hours per week, with thirty-five of those hours focused on housework and children.

When the family includes small children under the age of three, women average ninety hours per week (p. 43). The effects on women who strive to balance the demands of a faculty career with family life are shown in the choices women make. While women represent 40% of all assistant professors, they are only 15% of professors at universities. Overall 73% of men have tenure as compared with 45% of women (Finkel & Olswang, 1996, p. 123.) Women are more heavily represented in non-tenure eligible positions, particularly part-time (Lomperis, 1990). Finkel and Olswang (1996) found in their study that over 44% of women assistant professors have no children, 30% reported that they had decided never to have children, and 49% said they had postponed having a child. Because the probationary period conflicts with the prime child bearing years, this decision can mean that women never have children. For those women assistant professors who had children, 59% reported that the time required by children was a serious threat to tenure. One respondent reported, "My colleagues are quite empathetic and understanding; however, although the chairman may understand my commitment to my family he is not willing to acknowledge that this may affect my ability to obtain tenure on the designated time schedule" (Finkel & Olswang, 1996, p. 132). However, 99% of the women assistant professors studied reported they would like to remain in academe.

In conclusion, studies of probationary faculty have found that commitment to the academic career is accompanied by deep concerns about some of its fundamental aspects: an incomprehensible tenure system, lack of community, and the inability to achieve an integrated professional and personal life (Rice, Sorcinelli & Austin, 2000; Tierney & Bensimon, 1996; Gappa & MacDermid, 1997). Women and minority faculty members experience additional problems as they try to assimilate themselves into a traditionally white male career. They achieve tenure and are promoted more slowly than their white male counterparts, have qualitatively different experiences, and are more likely to leave an institution before gaining tenure (Johnsrud & Des Jarlais, 1994). Austin and Rice (1998) sum up the views of early career faculty:

> The tenure system, as it is currently structured and carried out, is central both symbolically and practically to how early career faculty think about their work and workplaces. They welcome the academic freedom they assume it promises, the security it offers, and the rigor represented by the tenure system. Yet, they worry about its role in maintaining a culture that leaves new faculty uncertain, stressed, and often alone in figuring out how to go about their work in ways that are rewarding for them as individuals and for the institution. The tenure system in its current form is undermining collegial cultures whose hallmarks have been community, mutual understanding and respect, and shared communication. In its present form, the tenure system is leading early career

> faculty to replace their idealism, energy, and willingness to address the various missions of the academy — including teaching and public service — with tension, anxiety, and limited views of the kind of work and contributions they can make. Academic freedom is compromised by the very system established to protect it (p.748).

Possible Modifications to the Current Tenure System

Researchers studying the tenure system and probationary period are motivated by their desire to improve satisfaction with the faculty career and the ability of colleges and universities to hire potential faculty of high ability. They do not advocate doing away with tenure; but they do recommend "mending, not ending" the tenure system By and large, faculty researchers in the 1990s share Bowen and Schuster's (1986) opinion that "the present rules and practices relating to tenure, because of their rigidity, threaten to undermine the whole tenure system and are therefore endangering academic freedom, collegiality, and legitimate job security" (p.244).

The Unbounded Nature of the Work. Early career faculty desire and need clear, positive and regularly communicated information about what they are expected to do. Austin and Rice (1998) recommended extensive orientation programs that provide information about institutional expectations and resources. Department chairpersons and deans play pivotal roles in communicating what is expected and what constitutes success. Rice, Sorcinelli & Austin (2000) recommended department heads update detailed expectations annually, and help pre-tenure faculty members learn to set realistic goals and priorities and keep detailed records of their accomplishments. Department heads and senior faculty should also assist each pre-tenure individual to find the right path towards tenure and helped to stay on that path. This presumes that the criteria and expectations for tenure remain the same throughout the probationary period, and that the department head or mentor is monitoring and brokering potential requests for time consuming activities from senior faculty that new faculty find difficult to turn down.

Boice (1992), writing from a faculty development perspective, approached the unbounded nature of faculty work through his IRSS theory. He advocated helping new faculty gain Involvement, Regimen, Self-management and Social network (IRSS) skills that would allow them to manage the probationary period. Boice's theory encouraged mentoring through faculty development programs outside the department to help new faculty stay focused on their goals and expectations.

Bailyn (1993) pointed out that scholarly research creates a great deal of mental overload. Research is a long-range activity and needs constant attention; successful books and articles cannot be written in small and scattered fragments. Thus, during the academic career, there is much input for long-delayed output. But faculty members are also expected to prepare and teach classes and serve their institutions and professions. This multiplicity of demands hits hardest the new faculty, who are juggling these demands for the first time. She recommends that probationary faculty have clear expectations that take into account multiple demands, and time to experience and recover from mistakes.

Clear expectations for tenure should include a balanced perspective on research and scholarly accomplishments. The predominance of research and scholarly output for the tenure decision, regardless of type of institution, has been challenged by many (Clark, 1987, 1997; Bowen & Schuster, 1986; Damrosch, 1995; Boyer, 1990; Glassick, Huber & Maeroff, 1997). Tierney and Bensimon (1996) used examples to illustrate the skewed reward system and the need to change the academic culture: "I have over 20 articles in refereed journals," said one person, "but people keep telling me I need a book. The dean wants a book" (p.65). Austin and Rice (1998) recommended evaluation for tenure be based upon the "person as a package"; all aspects of the person's work should count towards the tenure decision. Glassick, Huber and Maerooff (1997) suggested evaluations of teaching performance be comparable to those of research performance, with multiple sources and types of information used.

In sum, researchers are stressing the importance of clear expectations that are related to institutional mission and individual strengths, criteria for excellence that take into account the full range of faculty work, consistency in evaluating performance, and faculty development activities to help alleviate the unbounded nature of the profession for inexperienced new faculty.

The Tenure Process. Researchers have a variety of opinions about how to "fix" the tenure process. Rice, Sorcinelli and Austin (2000) and Tierney and Bensimon (1996) stressed two critical reforms: making the process clear, and having it provide useful feedback. What is familiar to senior faculty is unknown to new career faculty. Department heads should review the steps in the tenure process with new faculty including the schedule of the review, the participants in the evaluation, the procedures under which it is conducted, and the proper format and types of information needed for the review. From the very beginning of the probationary period, new faculty also need regular, systematic, comprehensive and informative feedback about their work and their progress towards tenure. The feedback should provide the probationer with useful and specific ways to improve his or her work. Taking the mystery out of the tenure process and decision would be a major step forward in ensuring a fair and consistent decision for the institution and the individual.

Another important step would be fixed membership on the tenure review committee to ensure consistent feedback and guidance throughout the probationary period (Chait, 1998).

Hogan (1998) claimed that tenured faculty are making ethical decisions when they decide whether or not a junior colleague should be awarded tenure. Using ethical principles, he recommended senior faculty base their tenure determinations on a genuine and thorough presumption of tenurability.

> Thus, we should reject narrow, arbitrary criteria of evaluation, including those that go by the name of 'high academic standards'; we should apply our non-arbitrary criteria consistently across candidates and we should apply them to any given candidate consistently from hiring to the final probationary evaluation; we should broadly assume the trustworthiness of the candidate's apparent accomplishments unless we have positive reason ('probable cause') to doubt them; and we should refuse to cooperate with the cruelty which so easily and so frequently becomes a part of tenure determinations. Significant pieces of evidence in favor of the candidate should be taken to nullify arguments against tenurability. In order to be successful, those who wish to argue against tenurability need to establish their case 'beyond a reasonable doubt' (p.38).

Hogan's "ethical" decision-making process, which requires fairness and consistency and emphasizes the importance of the decision to an individual's total academic career, would go a long way towards alleviating the concerns of probationary faculty about unclear and secretive tenure processes.

Others have proposed more radical reforms of the tenure process aimed at remedying some of the most criticized aspects of the tenure process. Trower (1996) chronicled the types and extent of tenure reforms underway at 280 institutions. They ranged from no change in the traditional tenure system (31%) to no tenure system (15%).

Chait (1998) has suggested tenure by objectives (TBO). TBO ties down the expectations and criteria for evaluation at the beginning of the process and eliminates the "up or out" decision at the end of a fixed length probationary period. In TBO, the department chair, candidate and a mentor committee develop a "performance contract" at the beginning of the probationary period. This "contract" proscribes the precise mix of teaching, research and service suitable for that candidate's interests, the department's needs and the institution's priorities. It also defines what constitutes appropriate and ample evidence of proficiency in each area. Under TBO, the candidate submits a portfolio annually of pertinent documentation to substantiate proficiency and goal attainment as outlined in the performance contract. If the department chair and/or tenure committee judges the evidence to be persuasive, the candidate's proficiency in that area is established or "certified". Once "certified", this aspect of the candidate's qualifications is no longer at issue for the purposes of a positive tenure recommendation. Each candidate continues this process at an individual pace as long as the department observes satisfactory progress toward tenure. (Substantial evidence of inadequate progress towards tenure would lead to non-reappointment with due notice.) Chait (1998) suggested that some departments might want an upper limit (e.g. ten years) for the tenure decision to be made.

In keeping with Chait's idea of eliminating the "up or out" system, some medical schools have integrated tenure-eligible and non-tenure eligible tracks so that they have similar review processes and criteria. For example, the University of Nebraska Medical Center appoints all new faculty members to a Health Professions Appointment (HPA). HPAs are contract appointments for up to five years, renewable indefinitely. Faculty members may apply for tenure at any time, but they do not need to do so to remain employed. If they are denied tenure, they may continue in contract appointments (Wigton & Waldman, 1993).

Tenure timeline. The American Association of University Professor's "Statement of Principles on Academic Freedom and Tenure" (1990), with its fixed probationary period of seven years, no longer seems so necessary. Researchers have recommended flexibility in the probationary period to accommodate a diverse faculty with varied lifestyles, and to help resolve the difficulty of meeting tenure criteria in that time period for some disciplines. The most common solution has been "stop-the-tenure-clock" provisions which allow individual faculty members to extend the probationary period for legitimate reasons for one or two years (Austin & Rice, 1998; Gappa & MacDermid, 1997).

Some institutions, particularly medical and other professional schools, have created flexibility in the probationary period by extending it to give probationary faculty more time across the board. Others allow faculty members to transfer from tenure-track status to contract status for several years and then return to the tenure-track; or to serve in non-tenure track appointments for several years before beginning probation (Trower, 1996; Jones & Sanderson, 1994). Other institutions allow tenure in part-time positions or flexibility in time base during the tenure track period (Bickel, 1991). These reforms broaden the potential pool of new faculty to those, who, for whatever reasons, seek less than full-time academic careers.

Collegiality and Community. Researchers have also recommended formal and informal actions by senior faculty and administrators to help new faculty find collegiality and community within and across departments (Tierney & Bensimon, 1996; Austin & Rice, 1998; Boice, 1992). Formal mentoring by the department head and senior faculty throughout the probationary period is essential to communicate basic knowledge about the institution and the tenure processes and expectations. Informal mentoring fosters inclusion in departmental "inside circles" that facilitate publishing, conference presentations and a better understanding of the professorial role. Informal mentoring also helps new faculty members feel comfortable and included in social events in their departments and beyond. Faculty development programs outside the department offer probationers alternative sites for gaining assistance with their work and for conversation about their work that is not part of an evaluative process (Boice 1992). Cross disciplinary associations and activities can provide important alternative opportunities for socializing and information exchanges. For example, Tierney and Bensimon (1996) found that women and minority groups tend to bring together people with similar interests who may feel excluded from informal mentoring within their departments.

Achieving Balance. Because their work is inherently ambiguous and unstructured, new faculty must understand and accept the fact that they are responsible for organizing and structuring their time in order to achieve balance. When faculty members understand that they control their time, they are empowered to change how they manage time (Boice, 1992).

However, the pressing issues of achieving balance in personal and faculty lives supercede time management. Bailyn (1993) has pointed out that true flexibility of time flows from a basic belief by the employing institution in the legitimacy of a balance of commitments between the private and public spheres. Thus, institutions must commit themselves to changing old assumptions and cultural beliefs about work design. Modifications to the current tenure system such as "stop the tenure clock" policies, extensions of probationary periods, or tenure for less-than-full-time effort must be supported by the campus culture. Olsen and Near (1994) found that faculty productivity is linked to individuals' satisfaction with non-work life. Thus, recognition of non-work life enhances productivity, while denial of the demands of life outside work inhibits productivity. Therefore, Olsen and Near (1994) and Olsen (1993) suggest that colleges and universities provide services and programs that can help reduce the conflicts between the demands of work and non-work life.

Making specific policies, programs or services available to faculty does not necessarily mean they will be used. The attitudes and behaviors of department chairs and senior faculty will determine which faculty members take advantage of family-friendly policies that are available in their institutions. In part, the level of use of work-family programs such as "stop-the-tenure-clock" is dependent upon potential career penalties. If faculty members perceive that the policy or program may have a potential negative impact, they will be less likely to use it even though it is available (Gappa & MacDermid, 1997). Gappa and MacDermid (1997) recommended colleges and universities train and encourage department chairs to be adaptable and responsible, give them resources and programs to work with, and hold them accountable. Successful work life programs require the support of the president, academic and administrative leaders and faculty.

Traditionally, equity has been defined as treating all employees in a given position the same. But equity is not the same as uniformity. In a diverse society, equal treatment may have very unequal consequences (Bailyn, 1993). Inequity is particularly likely when employers fail to respond to the differences in the external constraints their employees face. The fact that women and minority faculty members tend to be promoted and tenured more slowly than their white male counterparts is one possible example (Johnsrud & Des Jarlais, 1994).

If equity means having the opportunity to be effective, then each employee must be treated as an individual. Different strategies can accomplish the same result. In this concept of equity, career development is individualized but standards and criteria do not change (Bailyn, 1993). The flexibility and options already discussed for the probationary period would go a long way towards allowing individualized approaches to meeting tenure standards and criteria, as would a variety of services and programs. Gappa and MacDermid (1997) provided a "smorgasbord" of established work-family programs in industry and academe to illustrate the wide range of assistance currently available.

In sum, the prevalent view among scholars today is that tenure-track faculty members are, by and large an unhappy group. The proposed solutions "mend" but do not "end" the tenure system. The primary starting points for reform recommended by researchers are the tenure processes, timelines, lack of community, and work-life balance. An equally important starting point for reform is the status and employment arrangements for the non-tenure eligible faculty, the new faculty majority, to which this chapter now turns.

NON-TENURE ELIGIBLE FACULTY: EMPLOYMENT ARRANGEMENTS AND STATUS

The majority of faculty members teaching in American colleges and universities today are non-tenure eligible. Their appointments either explicitly state tenure is not an option, or they teach in institutions that do not grant tenure. This new faculty majority may be employed either part or full-time. Forty-two percent of all faculty members are employed part-time, and 96% of them are ineligible for tenure (Gappa & Leslie, 1997). In addition, 28% to 31% of all full-time faculty members now occupy non-tenure eligible positions (Leatherman, 1999; Schuster, 2000). Perhaps of even greater importance is the rate of increase of the non-tenure eligible faculty. The percentage of part-timers jumped from 22% of the total faculty in the early 1970s to 35% in 1987, and to 42% by 1993 (Schuster 2000). Charfauros and Tierney (1999) and Schuster (2000) project that they represented 45% to 50% of the total faculty by the late 1990s. Full-time non-tenure eligible faculty climbed from 19% to over 24% of the total full-time faculty workforce by 1993, and, according to Schuster's (2000) projections, they have reached 31% (Leslie, 1998; Baldwin & Chronister, 2001). In raw numbers, part-timers increased from 254,687 to 376,675 (47.8%), while all full-timers increased from 515,138 to 528,260 (2.5%).

For purposes of discussing non-tenure-eligible faculty employment conditions and careers, this chapter makes a distinction between part- and full-time faculty members because the reasons for their use and the nature of their appointments are different. While part-timers are hired primarily to teach on short-term appointments, full-timers have more varied roles, types of appointments and responsibilities as teachers, researchers, clinicians and administrators (Gappa, 1996; NEA, 1996; Gappa, 2000; Baldwin & Chronister, 2001).

This section begins with a brief overview of career models from other professions. The overview provides examples of careers outside higher education that have possible relevance for faculty employment. The section then examines employment conditions and satisfaction levels for part-timers, followed by full-timers who are not tenure-eligible. It concludes with researchers' recommendations for employment arrangements for both part-time and full-time non-tenure eligible faculty.

Overview of Employment Concepts from Outside Academe

The rise of non-tenure eligible faculty members to majority status and the creation of more flexibility within the tenure system echo changes occurring in corporate and other sectors of employment. Throughout history, American higher education and industry have traded employment practices back and forth (Heydinger & Simsek, 1992). Innovations such as sabbaticals for retooling, flexible working hours, greater job autonomy, on-site day care and substance abuse counseling, now common attributes of colleges and universities, had their origins in the corporate work place. Trower (1998) found that, the legal and medical professions, historically similar to higher education, have restructured themselves due to external pressures to contain costs and to increased competition. Alternative career models in many law firms have replaced the traditional counterpart to tenure in the legal profession, the up-or-out decision after six to ten years as an associate lawyer. Gappa (1996) found clinical and basic sciences faculties in medical schools have developed different tracks and made tenure one of several options.

Heydinger and Simsek (1992) examined other professions to see what they might suggest regarding relationships between faculty employment arrangements and productivity. They found a direct correlation between: individual productivity and income levels in the medical, legal and sales professions; strict standards for behavior, licensing and maintaining skill levels coupled with flexibility in assignment for airlines pilots; and the importance of clarifying and linking customer expectations directly to performance for police officers. They concluded that linking productivity directly to a large portion of income, and performance to continuation in a position, are powerful individual incentives; that productivity problems are often rooted in confusion about the ultimate objective and lack of clarity about the ultimate customer for police officers; and that airline pilots demonstrate that there can be significant individual flexibility within work assignments while adhering to very strict standards of performance. Their conclusions provide an enriched perspective for examining the faculty career.

Waterman, Waterman and Collard (1994) argued for a new covenant between employer and employee: "... most people — and most companies — now hardened by downsizings, delayerings, right-sizings, layoffs, and restructurings, have concluded that the old covenant is null" (p.87). In exchange for lifetime employment, they suggested that: " ...we should forget about clinging desperately to one job, one company, or one career path. What matters now is having the competitive skills required to find work when we need it, wherever we can find it" (p.87). They recommended that the employer and employee share responsibility for maintaining and enhancing the employee's employability inside and outside the company. Under this new covenant, employers would give individuals the opportunity to develop enhanced employability in exchange for better productivity and some level of commitment for as long as the employee works there. The employee's job security would reside in his or her new skills. The result, according to Waterman, Waterman and Collard (1994), would be a "win-win" for both parties. In their view, a workforce that is constantly updating its skills not only responds to change, but anticipates it; it is a "career-resilient" workforce. And companies are also healthier if employees have multiple skills, can move easily across functional boundaries, and are comfortable switching back and forth between regular duties and special projects, or moving on when the right fit with one company can no longer be found. This new career-resilient workforce understands that the purpose of the organization is to provide goods and services that customers value, and if the organization does not do that, no one will have a job (Waterman, Waterman and Collard, 1994).

Handy, as cited in Edgerton (1993), suggested that three very different workforces are associated with an organization. The first is the full-time professional core. The second is contractual organizations or sub-contractors, who are members of their own organization but perform services that are outsourced by others. The third work force comprises the independents who are either temporary, part-time, and semi-skilled workers helping out at peak times, or who are independent professionals hired to do specific pieces of work (Edgerton, 1993). Handy called the life of the independent the "portfolio worklife" where the independent professional builds a career around a portfolio of clients and different types of work. Handy's view is similar in many ways to Waterman, Waterman and Collard's (1994) career-resilient worker. Handy argued that the efficient company is cutting its core people, and pushing as much of its work as possible to subcontractors and independents outside the organization.

Handy's concepts can be applied to the relationship between the tenure-track and non-tenure eligible faculty. The professional core is the equivalent of the tenured and tenure-track faculty. Non-tenure eligible faculty members now perform much of the academic work previously accomplished by tenure-track faculty members, including much of the undergraduate teaching (Kennedy, 1997; Plater 1998). They can be viewed as either subcontractors or independents, depending upon the circumstances; and they are in academic career paths that, in some cases, are similar to the career-resiliency advocated by Waterman, Waterman and Collard (1994).

These new employment concepts from outside academe such as flexibility, work-life, career resiliency, continuous improvement, and linking productivity to rewards appeal to many new faculty, both on and off the tenure-track. They have already been considered in some of the recommendations for reform of the probationary period. This chapter has explored their relevance to tenure-track faculty; it now turns to their application to non-tenure eligible faculty.

Part-time Faculty

Hired primarily to teach, part-time faculty members are employed in substantial numbers in all types of institutions (See Tables 2 and 3). Research and doctoral universities use proportionately fewer part-timers (23% and 32% respectively) because they rely on graduate teaching assistants. Similarly, individual disciplines also use part-timers in different proportions. (See Table 4). Part-timers are roughly half or more of the faculty in: law (61%), fine arts (51%), English and literature (50%) computer science (49.5%) and mathematics and statistics (49%) (Leslie, 1998a). The heavy reliance on part-time faculty in fields such as business (47%), health sciences (36%) and law (61%) is due to the value of practitioners in professional fields. The reliance on part-time faculty in English and mathematics is different. In these disciplines they are employed in large numbers to replace full-time teachers in core academic subjects (Benjamin, 1998).

Who They Are, What They Do. Most part-timers (77%) have other jobs outside academe, and for 64% of the part-timers, these jobs are full-time (Gappa & Leslie, 1997). Mean household income for all part-timers is $67,637 compared to $81,248 for full-time faculty (Leslie, 1998b). Individual part-time faculty members are the principal income producers in their households, averaging $48,761 in total individual income from all sources compared to $60,613 for full-time faculty. **Table 6** compares the mean income of part- and full-time faculty by type of institution and source of income. Overall, part-timers earn about 20-25% of their total income through college teaching.

Despite their part-time affiliation, part-timers are committed to their colleges and universities and want to be part of an academic environment. They have occupied their present teaching position for an average of 6.3 years versus 11.2 years for full-timers (Leslie, 1998b.) While only 15% of part-timers hold the doctoral degree with an additional 11% holding a professional degree, most part-timers (52%) have one or more master's degrees (Leslie, 1998a). **Tables 7 and 8**

Table 6. Mean income of part-and full-time faculty and staff by source of income and type and control of institution, Fall 1992

Institution Type	Total earned income		Source of income			
			Income from institution		Outside income	
	FT	PT	FT	PT	FT	PT
All	60,613	48,761	52,738	11,342	7,874	37,419
Pub research	73,928	55,121	64,543	16,321	9,385	38,801
Priv research	86,504	61,765	72,671	10,771	13,834	50,994
Pub doc	64,845	47,973	57,486	13,294	7,358	34,679
Private doc	74,527	92,699	62,686	16,977	11,841	75,722
Pub comp	54,429	42,417	47,323	13,727	7,106	28,690
Private comp	55,499	49,974	47,570	8,151	7,930	41,822
Priv lib arts	44,979	47,775	39,978	12,695	5,001	35,081
Public 2-year	48,982	41,148	43,154	9,147	5,827	32,002

Table 7: Percentage of part-time faculty responding yes: Have doctoral or first professional degree, by type and control of institution, Fall 1992

Institution Type	"Yes" Response — Have doctoral or first professional degree
All	26
Public research	48
Private research	50
Public doctoral	46
Private doctoral	60
Public comprehensive	24
Private comprehensive	32
Private liberal arts	25
Public 2-year	13

show the breakdown of degrees held by part-time faculty by type of institution and by discipline respectively.

To summarize, most part-time faculty members work full-time or nearly full-time when all their employment is combined. They are reasonably well off in economic terms and professionally qualified for the work they do. The differences among part- and full-timers are not as great as most think and an outsider would assume they constitute a community of peers (Gappa & Leslie, 1997). The most striking difference between part- and full-time faculty is gender, since women are much more likely to be employed as part-timers (49% of all part-timers) than as full-timers (33% of all full-timers). Responses to the National Study of Postsecondary Faculty suggest, however, that women do not prefer part-time work arrangements any more than men do (Leslie, 1998b).

Table 8: Percentage of part-time faculty responding yes: Have doctoral or first professional degree by program area, Fall 1992

Institution Type	"Yes" Response — Have doctoral or first professional degree
All 4-year	38
Agriculture/Home Economics	13
Business	23
Education	32
Engineering	41
Fine arts	8
Humanities	28
Natural sciences	39
Social sciences	49
All other fields	44

Part-timers teach for a variety of reasons. Gappa and Leslie (1993) described them as belonging to one of four general categories. Most part-timers are employed elsewhere in their primary careers as "professionals, specialists or experts". These part-timers are motivated to teach because of their intrinsic satisfaction with the work itself and their dedication to the constituencies they serve. Most have an altruistic desire to help others, particularly those who come from similar backgrounds. Other part-timers, the "career enders", are in life transitions to retirement or are retired. Some part-timers, "the freelancers", prefer working simultaneously in a variety of positions, one of which is part-time teaching.

Only 16% of all part-timers, the "aspiring academics", want full-time, tenure-track faculty positions. However, there are significant differences by discipline. Over 36% of the part-timers in the humanities, versus 1.5% in the health sciences, seek tenure track positions. Sixty five percent of part-timers in the fine arts and 61% of those in the humanities reported they were teaching part-time because full-time jobs were not available either in academe or elsewhere. (Leslie, 1998a). These aspiring academics generally teach for economic reasons, sometimes at several campuses simultaneously, hoping that they will achieve a tenure-track position eventually (Gappa & Leslie 1993).

Colleges and universities seek part-time faculty for many reasons (Leslie, 1998b; Haeger, 1998; Wyles, 1998). The expansion of community colleges and the leveling off of state support for higher education in the early 1990s are the most compelling. From 1970 to 1995 the number of faculty members at two-year institutions grew by 210%, compared to 69% growth in four-year institutions, and the proportion of part-timers in community colleges rose from 50% to 60%. Employment of part-timers is part of the wider pattern outside academe of downsizing, subcontracting, and outsourcing. Increasing enrollment, financial hard times, the loss of control over mandatory retirement, and the need for flexibility have all made institutions more wary about long-term commitments to tenure. In addition, the preference of some individuals for part-time work, and the lack of evidence that part-timers teach any less effectively have contributed to the use of part-timers.

Thus, both colleges and universities and part-timers benefit from part-time employment. Eighty-five percent of part-time faculty report they are somewhat or very satisfied with their jobs. However, while they express satisfaction with their teaching assignments, they are dissatisfied with various aspects of their employment (See Table 5).

Employment Policies. Part-timers are heterogeneous, with highly varied life circumstances and motivations for teaching, but their employment conditions are not. Regardless of the quality of performance, length of employment, qualifications for their positions, or the needs of their institutions, part-timers in most colleges and universities are employed under uniform and exploitative practices. Part-time faculty employment tends to be a casual affair based on informal practices and commitments within departments rather than on centrally promulgated and monitored institutional policies that provide fair and consistent treatment. In good circumstances, part-timers become valued and established colleagues despite the informality and insecurity of their employment. In the worst circumstances, part-timers remain marginal and are subject to capricious and arbitrary treatment (Gappa & Leslie, 1997, 1993; Rhoades, 1998). Some examples of employment practices that cause the most distress and dissatisfaction among part-timers and that can hamper their ability to perform well are described in the paragraphs that follow (Gappa, 2000; Gappa & Leslie, 1993).

In contrast to the rigorous national recruitment of tenure-track faculty, recruitment of part-timers is usually informal and handled by department heads. Some vacancies are advertised regionally or locally, but most recruiting is by word of mouth. "Bottom fishing" for the least expensive and most vulnerable (but not necessarily best-qualified) can occur when department chairs are not accountable for their hiring practices.

Most part-timers are appointed term by term, and notification of an appointment or renewal (regardless of the numbers of semesters previously employed) often comes very late. Thus, part-timers are left with little time to prepare, which can have a deleterious effect on the quality of their teaching performance. Failure to be notified in a timely fashion can have a seriously disrupting effect on the lives of those part-timers who are dependent upon the income. Term by term appointments, policies limiting the numbers of continuous appointments possible, and arbitrary limits on the amount of work part-timers can be assigned contribute to the insecurity part-timers feel about their employment and may disqualify them for benefits. These policies are unfortunate responses to institutional desires for flexibility and unnecessary institutional worries that continuous employment without interruption could lead to de facto tenure.

Resources for support services, supplies, equipment and office space are scarce, and part-timers usually receive the lowest priority. Frequently, offices that supply services require part-timers to turn in requests far in advance, and are closed during evenings and weekends when many part-timers teach. Unavailability of adequate support services or office space can hamper part-timers' teaching and make meeting with their students difficult. Other perks, such as funds for professional travel or sabbaticals, are virtually non-existent for part-timers.

Salary policies for part-timers vary greatly depending on institutional culture and ability to pay. Part-timers' views about their salaries also vary. Those employed full-time elsewhere are generally less concerned; others dependent on their salaries as an important source of income want a fair wage and merit increases. One part-timer remarked: "We get the low-level, non-glamorous courses and take low pay to teach them. I can't afford to teach part-time much longer. I'm netting the same amount of money teaching part-time that I made typesetting full-time. I can't rely on getting any summer support, either" (Gappa & Leslie, 1993, p.162). The vast majority of institutions use either a flat rate for all part-timers or an established range, frequently defined on the basis of qualifications and/or seniority. However, some institutions are inconsistent in their salary policies. In rare circumstances part-timers negotiate their salaries individually with high-level administrators, thus leading to complete erosion of salary policies.

Very few institutions provide benefits for part-timers. Lack of benefits was the issue receiving the highest response of dissatisfaction (57%) by part-timers. (See Table 5). Subsidized medical insurance (available to 17% of part-timers versus 97% of full-timers), retirement plans (available to 20% of part-timers versus 93% of full-timers) and tuition grants or waivers (available to 9% of part-timers versus 48% of full-timers) are the most important to part-timers. One part-timer recounted her story: "I don't have health insurance here. I panicked. I started working at a financial planning service to get the benefits. I work there one-half time. I work one-third time at an art gallery. I work two-thirds time at this institution. That is my schedule for this fall. My daughter just turned two. I got laid off from my arts curator job. I don't know what the future is for me" (Gappa & Leslie, 1993, p. 163). Because institutions formulate benefits policies according to the time base of an individual's appointment rather than years of service, part-time faculty with ten to fifteen years of continuous teaching experience are usually treated the same as part-timers hired to teach for one semester (Gappa, 2000).

Many part-timers have enjoyed long and mutually productive associations with their colleges and universities, but these stable employment histories resulted from institutional goodwill, not from any right part-timers have to job security. One department head said: "We are being cut by eleven sections next year because we are anticipating a smaller freshman class, and we lost several more sections because of the budget. . . I sent a note last fall to alert the part-time faculty early. I said things look bad for next year. Start planning" (Gappa & Leslie, 1993, p. 173f). Part-timers believe that a system in which long service and distinguished performance do not ensure continuing employment is unfair.

Part-timers also express anger and frustration about their second-class status and the lack of appreciation for their efforts. Instead of feeling "connected to" or "integrated into" campus life, they often feel alienated, powerless and invisible. One part-timer commented: "In my department they have a reception for new teachers. I'm teaching for the first time and I was invited. But as a part-timer I was not mentioned. No one thought of introducing me as a new person. I'm a non-person. I'm teaching the course better than it's ever been taught, but I'm a non-person" (Gappa & Leslie, 1993, p. 192). This "invisibility" is often due to departmental culture and the leadership (or lack thereof) of department chairs. Many part-timers expressed annoyance about the lack of consultation and involvement in campus or departmental decisions affecting them, an annoyance that is exacerbated by the knowledge that protesting could jeopardize their continued employment (Gappa & Leslie, 1993).

In summary, part-timers responding to the 1993 National Study of Postsecondary Faculty said they experienced intrinsic satisfaction from teaching, but they were dissatisfied with many aspects of their employment. While 85% of part-timers and full-timers expressed overall satisfaction with their jobs, their satisfaction with various aspects of their jobs varied considerably. (See Table 5.) Using the 1993 National Study of Postsecondary Faculty, Benjamin looked at the satisfaction and dissatisfaction of part-timers in four-year institutions according to whether they taught in a vocationally oriented (VOC) or liberal arts oriented (LAC) discipline. His analysis indicated that the VOC part-timers were substantially higher than the LAC part-timers in their overall satisfaction, as well as in their satisfaction with benefits, salary, job security and time to keep current in the field. He found that the LAC faculty members had substantial reasons for their greater discontent. They were more dependent on their part-time employment because their household income was lower on average than the VOC part-timers, and job security and health and other benefits did not come as frequently from another employer (Benjamin, 1998). Ultimately, the satisfaction levels of part-timers with their academic employment can have a direct bearing on the quality of their teaching. Leslie (1998a), Benjamin (1998), and Clark (1987, 1997) have recommended more research into the differences among disciplines and types of institutions in the use of part-timers and the relationships of those differences to satisfaction levels.

Full-Time Non-Tenure Eligible Faculty

In response to concerns about excessive use of part-timers, colleges and universities are employing more full-time non-tenure eligible faculty (Baldwin & Chronister, 2001). For example, in 1999, Georgia State University's College of Arts and Sciences reduced the number of courses taught by part-timers from 900 to 227 and added 65 new full-time tenure-ineligible faculty members (Wilson, 1999). According to Chronister and Baldwin (1999), non-tenure eligible faculty represented 28.3% of all full-time faculty in 1995, a 92% increase since 1975. They see this trend as a permanent shift in faculty staffing.

Full-time, tenure-ineligible or non-tenure track faculty members (FTNTT) are employed to achieve more continuity in academic programs, staff entire areas of the curriculum, focus on one particular area of faculty responsibility such as teaching, research or clinical practice, or add significant experience and expertise available only outside academe (Gappa, 1996). The heaviest concentration of FTNTT faculty members is in the research universities (39.5%), followed by doctoral granting universities (18.5%), comprehensive universities (16.9%), community colleges (12.3%) and private liberal arts colleges (7.8%). The health sciences employ the largest percentage (28%), followed by the natural sciences (15.7%) and the humanities (12.5%) (NEA Update, 1996.) (See also Tables 3 and 4). While FTNTT faculty members are hired primarily in teaching appointments, they are also employed as research professors, professors of practice, and distinguished senior lecturers. The medical schools have used full-time non-tenure eligible faculty appointments for years, primarily in clinical positions. By 1981, 72% of the 112 U.S. medical schools had non-tenure eligible tracks. From 1983-1993, the total number of clinical faculty in medical schools nearly doubled while the percentage in tenure-track or tenured positions declined (Jones & Sanderson, 1994).

When institutions consolidate part-time faculty positions into full-time appointments for the purposes of teaching undergraduates or specialized areas of the curriculum, the full-timers generally are treated better than the part-timers they replace. Their appointments typically are for one year or longer, either renewable without limit or of fixed-duration with limited renewals. Compensation, which includes benefits, is better than that of part-timers. Most receive funding for professional development. However, these faculty members frequently experience some status differentials, such as rights to participation in governance or to receive sabbatical leaves. For some teaching faculty, job security is a critical issue, depending on the nature of their contract (Gappa, 1996; NEA, 1996).

When FTNTT faculty are hired as clinical or research faculty or as distinguished senior lecturers, they typically enjoy the perquisites of the tenure-track faculty, with the possible exception of full voting rights, and are fully integrated into their departments. As one tenured faculty commented: "Everyone contributes to the teaching enterprise. We recognize the contribution. It is a team effort. There is no resistance to the clinical faculty, no problem with attitudes with the tenure-track faculty. We need clinical faculty" (Gappa, 1996, p. 25). But, some FTNTT faculty members expressed concern about the lack of job security inherent in renewable appointments; others commented occasionally about status differentials. One research faculty member commented: "Basically, the research professor is a slave. A university franchise. 'We'll give you a lab, space. You bring in the money. If you don't, you're history'. . . . People have to have something. What about the person who brings in grants for 20 years? Then he reaches 50 and the grants drop off. What do you do, fire him?" (Gappa, 1996, p. 27,29).

By and large, however, FTNTT faculty members have equivalent credentials to their tenure-track colleagues, have chosen this type of employment, are respected and valued by their colleagues for their expertise, and have similar employment conditions to the tenure-track faculty. They tend not to be interested in tenure-track positions because they are fully employable in their professions, or have lifestyle concerns that preclude tenure-track appointments. One full-time non-tenure track professor commented: "I was a tenured professor. . . I was well-situated. My wife was an academic, we had young kids. My wife got an offer. I gave [tenure] up. I came here. I renovated the laboratory and got three NIH grants. I served as a member of committees. Then I got a three-year appointment as a professor without tenure. My wife was tenured. They said 'What do we do with him?' They gave me an endowed chair!" (Gappa, 1996, p. 26).

Baldwin and Chronister (2001) developed three different employment models to describe FTNTT teaching faculty, based on their research at 12 four-year institutions. The "marginalized model" uses full-time non-tenure eligible appointments for staffing flexibility and cost saving. These faculty members are hired on annual contracts, renewable for a fixed period. They carry heavy teaching loads, receive lower salaries than their tenure-track peers, and have little if any support for professional development and limited voting rights. These faculty members most closely resemble part-timers in their employment conditions, but they do have better salaries, benefits and longer-term appointments.

The "integrated model" is used for hiring individuals with distinctive skills and interests that enhance program offerings and compliment tenure-track faculty qualifications. They have greater status and respect than those in the "marginalized model". They are employed on annual contracts for a "probationary period" followed by renewable multi-year contracts, and have ranks and titles similar to the tenure-track faculty, voting privileges, and support for professional development.

The "alternative career track" model is similar to the integrated model but is designed to be a viable alternative to tenure. In addition to having the attributes of the integrated model, the alternative career model has teaching loads and faculty roles comparable to the tenure-track faculty, a clear career progression system and extensive support for professional development. These faculty members are eligible for sabbatical leaves and have salaries that are comparable to or higher than the tenure track faculty. They function as full-fledged members of the academic community. Faculty members in the alternative career model are most similar to the clinical and research faculty or distinguished senior faculty in the professions as described by Gappa (1996). As one FTNTT professor remarked: "My whole career has been in academe and off the track; it's been an idea-driven career. I've paid no attention to what one needs to succeed, and I've had an extraordinarily rich career" (p. 18).

Regardless of model, Baldwin and Chronister (2001) did not find an ideal package of personnel policies for FTNTT faculty. Though the full-timers were clearly better off, for the most part, than their part-time colleagues, their employment conditions were not as carefully developed as those for the tenure-track faculty. Baldwin and Chronister (2001) outlined nine policy areas that they recommended institutions address: defined probationary periods, multiyear appointments following probation, defined dates for contract renewal or termination, equitable salary and benefits systems, career progression systems, supports for professional development, involvement in governance, protection of academic freedom, and access to recognition and rewards. However, Gappa (1996) described several models of integrated tracks in professional schools that do address all of these policy areas. Among all disciplines and types, the medical schools have made the greatest progress in developing integrated, equitable employment policies for FTNTT faculty that strive to eliminate status differentials (Jones & Sanderson, 1994; Bickel, 1991; Froom & Bickel, 1996; Lovejoy & Clark (1995); Bland & Holloway, 1995; Kelley & Randolph, 1994.)

Campus climates, cultures, histories and current situations underlie the faculty employment systems that colleges and universities have. Baldwin and Chronister (2001) found that status differentials and distinctions among types of faculty occur at varying levels in different institutions because of explicit actions or institutional policies, or because of implicit or inferred differences in faculty quality. As one dean remarked, "The practical reality is that they (tenured faculty) do not view (non-tenure-track faculty) the same." (p.129). Baldwin and Chronister (2001) attribute some of the tenure-track faculty attitudes to fears over the future of tenure.

By and large, however, senior non-tenure eligible faculty members who have credentials equivalent to or better than the tenured faculty experience few status distinctions. Concerns about status differentials and career development opportunities are felt more strongly by FTNTT faculty members who are building their academic careers and by women (Gappa, 1996). One senior professor of practice commented that for persons like him who had had successful careers outside academe, career development was moot. But for those developing careers, the career path is important. He recommended money, status and image as important incentives, and sabbatical eligibility, full voting rights, and a clear progression system through the ranks as important tangible indicators of respect and a proactive attitude about non-tenure eligible faculty (Gappa, 1996, p. 33).

The different roles and career paths among the FTNTT faculty make it difficult to interpret data on levels of satisfaction. Of those responding to the 1993 National Survey of Postsecondary Faculty, most were somewhat or very satisfied with their authority to make decisions about the courses they teach and the non-instructional aspects of their jobs. Three-quarters of the respondents were satisfied with their workload. However, there was less satisfaction with long-term career prospects and ability to keep current in their academic fields. Forty-three percent expressed dissatisfaction with job security, 47% with salaries, and 54% with opportunities for advancement in rank (NEA, 1996). Others expressed resentment about being seen as "second-class citizens" who are denied full opportunities for professional development and participation in governance. Given the wide range of personal circumstances involved, one would expect a wide range of reactions from great satisfaction to anger and resentment (Breneman, 1997).

Researchers' Suggestions for Non-Tenure Eligible Appointments

The idea that tenure is the only way to promote quality is unrealistic when the majority of today's faculty members are not eligible for it. As colleges and universities redefine faculty appointments and as increasing numbers of people with more diverse interests, motives and qualifications enter the academy, it is time to rethink who "the faculty" are. Members of the new faculty majority who are not eligible for tenure include people with high-level professional experience, cutting-edge clinical and research skills, broad and unusual life experiences, distinguished records of community leadership, perspectives from different cultural points of view, creative and original artistic ideas, experience in politics and government leadership and a deep and genuine humanity that may not be measurable in conventional terms. Many of these faculty, or prospective faculty, do not seek or want a tenure-track appointment (Gappa & Leslie 1997). Thus, researchers are searching for how to make non-tenure-track appointments more attractive.

First, researchers have investigated what factors influence job choice for academic positions, including those without tenure. Trower (2000) surveyed doctoral students and faculty members in their first or second year of employment, who had completed doctoral degrees in one of the top 25 doctoral programs as ranked by *U.S. News and World Report*. While the respondents said they preferred tenure-track appointments generally, when they were asked to weigh specific job offers they gave top consideration to geographical location and the balance between teaching and research in the job, whatever the employment arrangements. Salary and institutional prestige were the lowest ranked variables (Trower, 2000; Magner, 2000). Chait and Trower (1998) studied characteristics of faculty hires at Florida Gulf Coast University, a new institution that did not plan to offer tenure. In its first year, Gulf Coast University hired 92 faculty members. About 40% of those hired left their tenured or tenure-track positions to work under term contracts; many came from research universities. What attracted them was the opportunity to launch a new university focused on undergraduate instruction. After several years, however, concerns about job security had risen, and 22% of the new faculty cohort had left. Gulf Coast University is now considering rolling contracts to improve job security (Wilson, 2000).

Second, researchers are looking at what employment arrangements provide sufficient academic freedom and economic security. Colleges without tenure are rare. They are mostly found among private four-year colleges (9%). Chait and Trower (1997) found that features of their employment arrangements merit consideration by any institution considering eliminating tenure or offering attractive alternatives to it. These institutions offered sufficient academic freedom and economic security under term contracts to satisfy the vast majority of faculty. They also found that, at institutions offering both tenure track and non-tenure track appointments, most junior faculty preferred the non-tenure track option when it had incentives; and the preponderance of faculty on contracts found academic life agreeable (Chait & Trower, 1997). Contract faculty objected to tenure because they saw it as debilitating junior faculty, imposing rigidity, and creating unhealthy competition.

Third, researchers have examined other professions that are similar to academe: for example, law, business, medicine, engineering and research science for ideas about how they attract diverse and high-quality employees, both full- and part-time, and retain flexibility (Trower, 1998). Within the academy, researchers are finding that some faculty and prospective faculty are disenchanted with the rigidities of traditional tenure systems and pleased with the wider array of career tracks available now to non-tenure eligible faculty, particularly in professional schools. This availability of career tracks outside the tenure system can lead to far less emphasis upon an individual's "track" and far more consideration of the individual's contribution to the institution (Gappa 1996). New career tracks, and the opening up of governance to include tenure-ineligible faculty members, can have the added benefit of helping to eliminate status differentials that persist in the current system.

Fourth, some researchers have suggested institutions experiment with incentives for faculty to forego tenure. Breneman (1997) and Chait (1994, 1995) have recommended offering higher salaries to compensate for the additional risk of lack of job security. Breneman sees higher salaries as a powerful signal to other faculty that "such appointments are not second-class" (1997, p.10). Chait (1994) suggested providing choices related to compensation and to more frequent leaves with pay. When Webster University offered more frequent faculty development leaves as an alternative to tenure, the majority of faculty (86%) chose that alternative (Chait, 1995).

Fifth, alternatives to tenure can provide job security and career resiliency. For example, Gappa (1996) found that junior lecturers in the Harvard Graduate School of Education were often Harvard graduates who were not willing to leave the Boston area. They opted for annual appointments, renewable without limit. They worked on various projects, moving laterally as they built their portfolios while also engaged in teaching, service and research. Often the positions were combined with administrative assignments or external positions that gave them some stability. They saw their affiliation with Harvard as enabling them to maintain an academic identity and build their portfolios without the pressure of tenure-track reviews. One remarked: "Our security is in our portfolios, and having Harvard helps. Harvard opens lost of doors for us; it provides us with opportunity" (Gappa, 1996, p. 17).

But, researchers also found a troubling problem persisted for faculty in non-tenure eligible appointments — the existence of status differentials. Gappa (1996) found that professional schools were more likely to eliminate status differentials in new career tracks when all faculty members fully participated in the change process and understood the need for flexibility and collegiality. Tenured faculty members' attitudes were influenced by their valuing of professional practice, recognition that faculty in non-tenure eligible appointments had qualifications equivalent to or better than theirs, and the integration of non-tenure eligible faculty through employment policies and practices, participation in governance, and physical location. Tying faculty rewards and recognition directly to exemplary performance, regardless of time base or career track, went a long way toward achieving integration and improving quality.

Responding to the challenge of changing faculty roles and rewards or going bankrupt (Bland & Holloway, 1995), the University of Virginia's School of Medicine took a proactive, school-wide approach in its new promotion and tenure policy which combined six faculty career tracks, half tenure-eligible and half not. The choice between a tenure bearing or non-tenure bearing appointment became a choice of career emphasis, thus creating an environment that helped eliminate status differentials. To assist faculty in adjusting to the new system, the School organized an extensive career development system with comprehensive orientation and mentoring programs (Gappa, 1996). The School exemplifies the "role of the company" in Waterman, Waterman and Collard's (1994) career resiliency model.

To achieve attractive employment options for part-time non-tenure eligible faculty will require the most reform (Gappa, 2000), because they are at the bottom of the stratified faculty hierarchy (Rhoades, 1998). Gappa and Leslie (1993) made four overarching recommendations for improving the status of part-timers. First, the use of part-time faculty should be based on educational, not fiscal, reasons. Institutions with a clear sense of mission should develop faculty staffing plans that define the kinds of faculty they need and select the members of that faculty on the basis of their ability to perform, not because of their full- or part-time status. Second, colleges and universities must develop employment policies and practices that ensure all part-timers are treated fairly and consistently, and given the tools they need to do their jobs. Fair and consistent does not mean equivalent to the tenure-track faculty; but it does mean carefully thought out employment policies and practices that are consistent with the institution's overall employment philosophy. These employment policies and practices should be disseminated to all faculty members and reviewed and updated regularly. Third, employment policies and practices should provide for differences among part-time employment, from temporary, contingency appointments for a specific time period only, to continuing, extended appointment periods with a specific academic purpose. Finally, part-timers must be oriented and integrated into their departments and institutions as fully participating members of the faculty who are eligible to participate in faculty-development programs and opportunities (Gappa & Leslie, 1993, 1997; AASCU, 1999).

CONCLUSIONS

A report from AAUP's Committee A on Academic Freedom and Tenure captures the prevailing beliefs that have led to the current bifurcated faculty employment system.

> . . . . Ultimately, however, the general development of a more or less permanent two tier system brings with it a class consciousness that affects the faculty's perception of itself, the students' perception of the faculty, and the outside world's perception of academe. . . . We believe, however, that the reasons which have been advanced for the use of tenure-ineligible full-time faculty appointments are without merit and that, for the sake of higher education, of academic freedom, and of the professional security and future of coming generations of scholars and their students, the abuse of these appointments should be stopped (AAUP, 1990, p. 47).

The AAUP had the right view of the problem but the wrong solution. As a work force, the faculty is being restructured and is increasingly stratified (Rhoades, 1998; Bowen & Schuster, 1986; Clark, 1987). However, the issue, as this chapter has demonstrated, is no longer how to maintain the tenure system as the predominant mode of faculty employment. Now that non-tenure eligible faculty members are a majority, the question has become how to restructure faculty employment so the best and the brightest potential faculty members are attracted and retained, regardless of tenure status.

The answers to this question are coming from researchers whose work has been explored in this chapter. They include reforming the tenure probationary period and offering attractive employment options outside the tenure system. These concerns have become more pronounced during the last decades of the twentieth century. Review of generational similarities and differences among faculty members showed that faculty attitudes about tenure and the desirability of an academic career have not changed much since the 1970s, but levels of satisfaction with the career have. Meanwhile, the greatest change for faculty members' careers has been the rapid rise to majority status of full- and part-time faculty off the tenure track. Studies of probationary faculty have documented the need for tenure reform, and research on non-tenure eligible faculty has shown the need to improve employment practices to make the career attractive.

Tenure has been the driving force behind most college and university employment systems since the early twentieth century. The award of tenure has been a means for exercising quality control, making the academic career attractive, and protecting academic freedom. As the number of faculty members has grown and diversified, as higher education has experienced shifts in financial support, and as the public has become more outspoken about its expectations, the need to examine current faculty employment systems has intensified. Faculty researchers have studied faculty careers and made thoughtful recommendations for reforms. The advent of the National Study of Postsecondary Faculty holds promise for continuous, consistent collection of data about faculty members and their work, status, attitudes and satisfaction levels. There is no lack of scholarly interest in continuing research or thoughtful ideas for colleges and universities to put into practice.

This chapter has attempted to describe faculty employment today, focusing on what are the greatest stresses and strains in the faculty employment system. The chapter concludes with some ideas about future faculty employment policies and practices for those interested in changing their current faculty employment systems. These ideas are based upon the author's premise that tenure will continue to exist, but not in its present form and only as one among a series of career paths available to faculty members. It is now time to expand the goals of tenure — exercising quality control, making the career attractive, and protecting academic freedom — to *all* members of the faculty.

Change within individual institutions. Change will occur within individual colleges and universities rather than by national movements or consensus. The higher education enterprise is too large and diverse to adhere to any one set of principles and guidelines for faculty employment. Each institution will make its own decisions about changing its faculty employment policies and practices to serve its needs. These changes in policies and practices will be formulated with the participation of those affected by them. The current tenure probationary period and process and employment practices for part-timers are prime targets for overhaul.

Multiple career tracks. Non-tenure eligible faculty members are now the majority. Thus, it is time to move away from the emphasis upon what "track" faculty members are in, and towards an emphasis upon each individual's contribution to the institution, regardless of tenured or non-tenured, or part- or full-time, status. "Opening up" the academic career with multiple respected and valued career paths has the potential to improve collegial relationships among all faculty members, provide fairer and more thoughtful attention to individual faculty careers, and enhance productivity.

Along with the tenure system, attractive career paths for continuing faculty, regardless of role or time base, are being used more frequently. These continuing appointments should be clearly separated from employment practices aimed directly at contingency or temporary appointments of limited duration. Placement of faculty members, both full- and part-time, in any one of the three employment types — tenure-eligible, tenure-ineligible, or temporary — needs to be based upon institutional needs and prospective faculty choices. Currently, in too many institutions, practices put in place for contingency faculty hires have been retained for all part-time and full-time non-tenure eligible faculty members, regardless of their length of employment or contribution.

Integration. Successful faculty employment systems will depend upon their ability to attract and retain the most talented people and to draw all faculty together around a clear set of values that promote a collegial environment, high-quality teaching and professional responsibility (Gappa & Leslie, 1997). Reconceptualizing the work force as *one faculty* that sets high standards for all faculty members, shares work equitably, and allocates rewards in line with real productivity is a starting point. The current polarized system with its emphasis upon separate and unequal employment treatment and status differentials needs to be rethought and replaced.

Fairness and consistency. As new employment tracks are designed, exploitative and arbitrary practices that have characterized the employment of part-timers should disappear. All faculty members, regardless of the "track" they are in, should be guaranteed the tools they need to do their jobs, opportunities to progress in their careers, and freedom from arbitrary and capricious treatment.

Flexibility and choice. Potential faculty members want choices that best meet their career and personal needs. They seek more balance in their lifestyles. Options and flexibility serve both the institution's efforts to attract and retain talented faculty, and individuals' personal and professional needs. Institutions need to put in place work-life policies and programs that allow faculty members to achieve success in both their careers and personal lives. These programs can promote balanced life styles and increase retention, and are cost efficient.

The role of the department head. The department head is key to the success of faculty members and their satisfaction with their careers and institutions, yet department heads vary a great deal in their knowledge and interest in faculty employment and career development. In an employment system characterized by flexibility and choice, department heads will increasingly be called upon to use understanding and knowledge in the exercise of their administrative responsibilities. They need support, time, resources, incentives and rewards for their efforts to hire and retain the best faculty.

All faculty members represent a major capital investment by colleges and universities. Just as buildings and equipment need maintaining and renovating, faculty members need support and opportunities to learn, grow, develop and renew. With an adequate and fair investment of resources, all faculty, part- and full-time, tenure-eligible and non-tenure eligible, can work together to enhance the overall quality of their colleges and universities.

REFERENCES

American Association of State Colleges and Universities. (1999). *Facing change, building the faculty of the future.* Washington, DC: American Association of State Colleges and Universities.

AAUP/AAU Commission on Academic Tenure. (1973). *Faculty tenure: A report and recommendations by the commission on academic tenure in higher education.* San Francisco, CA: Jossey-Bass Publishers, Inc.

American Association of University Professors. (1990). *Policy documents and reports.* Washington, DC: American Association of University Professors.

Astin, A.W., Korn, W. S., Dey, E. L. (1991). *The American college teacher: National norms for the 1989-1990 HERI faculty survey.* University of California, Los Angeles, CA: Higher Education Research Institute.

Austin, A. and Rice, R.E.. (1998, February). Making tenure viable: listening to early career faculty. *American Behavioral Scientist.* 41 (5): 736-54.

Bailyn, L. (1993). *Breaking the mold: Women, men and time in the new corporate world.* NY: The Free Press.

Baldwin, R. G. and Chronister, J. L. (2001). *Teaching without tenure: Policies and practices for a new era.* Baltimore, MD. John Hopkins University Press.

Barnes, L. B., Agago, M. O. and Coombs, W. T. (1998). Effects of job-related stress on faculty intention to leave academia. *Research in Higher Education* 39 (4): 457-469.

Bayer, A. E. (1970) "College and university faculty: A statistical description" Washington, DC: American Council on Education. Research Reports 5 (5).

Bayer, Alan E. (1973) *Teaching faculty in academe: 1972-73.* Research Reports 8 (2). Washington, DC: American Council on Education.

Benjamin, E. (1998). Variations in the characteristics of part-time faculty by general fields of instruction and research. *The growing use of part-time faculty: Understanding causes and effects.* New Directions for Higher Education. 104. 45-61. San Francisco, CA: Jossey-Bass Publishers, Inc.

Bickel, J. (1991, May). The changing face of promotion and tenure at U.S. medical schools. *Academic Medicine* 66 (5). 249-256.

Blackburn, R. T. (1972). *Tenure: Aspects of job security on the changing campus.* Atlanta, GA: Southern Regional Education Board.

Bland, C. J. and Holloway, R. L. (1995, September/October). A crisis of mission: Faculty roles and rewards in an era of health care reform. *Change* 27 (5).30-36.

Boice, R. (1992). *The new faculty member.* San Francisco, CA: Jossey-Bass, Inc.

Bowen, H.R. and Schuster, J.H. (1986). *American professors: A national resource imperiled.* NY: Oxford University Press.

Boyer, E.L. (1989). *The conditions of the professoriate: Attitudes and trends, 1989.* Princeton, NJ: Carnegie Foundation for the Advancement of Teaching.

Boyer, E. L. (1990). *Scholarship reconsidered: Priorities of the professoriate.* Princeton, NJ: Carnegie Foundation for the Advancement of Teaching.

Breneman, D.W. (1997). *Alternatives to tenure for the next generation of academics.* New Pathways Working Paper Series # 14. Washington, DC: American Association for Higher Education.

Carlson, E. and Kimball, B. (1994 fall). Two views of the academic life. *Liberal Education.* 80 (4). 4-15.

Carnegie Foundation for the Advancement of Teaching. (1989). *Condition of the professoriate: Attitudes and trends, 1989.* Princeton, NJ: Carnegie Foundation for the Advancement of Teaching.

Chait, R. P. (1994, January/February). Make us an offer: Creating incentives for faculty to forsake tenure. *Trusteeship* 2(1). 28-34.

Chait, R. P. (1995, Spring). The future of academic tenure. *AGB Priorities* 3. 1-11.

Chait, R. P. (1998). *Ideas in incubation: Three possible modifications to traditional tenure policies.* New Pathways Working Paper Series # 9. Washington, DC: American Association for Higher Education.

Chait, R.P., and Ford, A.T. (1982). *Beyond traditional tenure.* San Francisco, CA: Jossey-Bass, Inc.

Chait, R. P., and Trower, C. A. (1997). *Where tenure does not reign: Colleges with contract systems.* New Pathways Project Working Paper Series # 3. Washington, DC: American Association for Higher Education.

Chait, R.P., and Trower, C. A.. (1998, September/October). Build it and who will come? *Change* 30 (5). 20-29.

Charfauros, K. H., and Tierney, W.G. (1999). Part-time faculty in colleges and universities:Trends and challenges in a turbulent environment. *Journal of Personnel Evaluation in Education* 13 (2). 141-151. Boston, MA: Kluwer Academic Publishers.

Chronister, J. L. and Baldwin, R.G. (1999, fall) "Marginal or mainstream? Full-time faculty off the tenure track. *Liberal Education* 85(4). 16-23.

Clark, B. R. (1987). *The academic life: Small worlds, different worlds.* Princeton, NJ: The Carnegie Foundation for the Advancement of Teaching.

Clark, B.R. (1997). Small worlds, different worlds: The uniquenesses and troubles of American academic professionals. *Daedalus* 126 (4): 21-43.

Damrosch, D. (1995). *We scholars: Changing the culture of the university.* Cambridge, MA. Harvard University Press.

Edgerton, R. (1993, September). Upside-down thinking: An interview with Charles Handy. *AAHE Bulletin* 46 (1). Washington, DC. The American Association for Higher Education.

Finkel, S. K., and Olswang, S. G. (1996, winter). Child rearing as a career impediment to women assistant professors. *Review of Higher Education* 19 (12). 123-139.

Finkelstein, M. J., Seal, R.K. and Schuster, J. H. (1998). *The new academic generation: A profession in transformation.* Baltimore, MD. John Hopkins University Press.

Froom, J. D. and Bickel, J. (1996, January). Medical school policies for part-time faculty committed to full professional effort. *Academic Medicine* 71(1). 92-96.

Gappa, J. M. (1996). *Off the tenure track: Six models for full-time nontenurable appointments.* New Pathways Working Paper Series # 10. Washington, DC: American Association for Higher Education.

Gappa, J. M. (2000, Spring). The new faculty majority: Somewhat satisfied but not eligible for tenure. *Understanding What Contributes to Job Satisfaction Among Faculty and Staff.* Hagedorn, L.S. ed. New Directions for Institutional Research # 105. San Francisco, CA. Jossey-Bass Publishers, Inc.

Gappa, J.M. and Leslie, D. W. (1993). *The Invisible Faculty.* San Francisco, CA: Jossey-Bass Publishers, Inc.

Gappa, J. M. and Leslie, D. W. (1997).*Two faculties or One? The conundrum of part-timers in a bifurcated work force.* New Pathways Working Paper Series # 6. Washington, DC. American Association for Higher Education.

Gappa, J. M., and MacDermid, S.M. (1997). *Work, family, and the faculty career.* New Pathways Working Paper Series # 8. Washington, DC. American Association for Higher Education.

Glassick, C. E., Huber, M. T., and Maeroff, G.L. (1997). *Scholarship assessed: Evaluation of the professoriate.* San Francisco, CA: Jossey-Bass Publishers, Inc.

Grogono, A. (1994, Winter). Tenure the teacher; let research be its own reward. *Educational Record:* 75 (1). 37-41.

Haeger, J.D. (1998, Winter). Part-time faculty, quality programs, and economic realities. *The growing use of part-time faculty: Understanding causes and effects.* Leslie, D.W. ed. New Directions for Higher Education, # 104. San Francisco, CA: Jossey-Bass Publishers, Inc.

Heydinger, R. P. and Simsek, H.(1992). An agenda for reshaping faculty productivity. Denver, CO. State Higher Education Executive Officers.

Hogan, P. C. (1998). The ethics of tenure decisions. *Higher Education Review* . 30 (3): 23-41.

Huber, M. T. (1998). *Community college faculty: Attitudes and trends, 1997.* Stanford, CA: Carnegie Foundation for the Advancement of Teaching.

Jencks, C. and Riesman, D. (1968). *The academic revolution.* Garden City, NY: Doubleday and Co., Inc.

Johnsrud, L.K. and Des Jarlais, C.D. (1994). Barriers to tenure for women and minorities. *Review of Higher Education* 17 (4). 335-353.

Jones, R. F. and Sanderson, S. C. (1994, September). Tenure policies in U.S. and Canadian medical schools. *Academic Medicine* 69 (9). 772-778.

Kelley, W. N. and Randolph, M. A., eds.. (1994). *Careers in clinical research.* Washington, DC. National Academy Press.

Kennedy, D. (1997). *Academic duty.* Cambridge, MA: Harvard University Press.

Kirshstein, R. J., Mattheson, N. and Jing, Z. (1997). *Instructional faculty and staff in higher education institutions: Fall 1987 and fall 1992.* Washington, DC. U. S. Department of Education.

Leatherman, C. (1999, April 9). Growth in positions off the tenure track is a trend that's here to stay, study finds. *The Chronicle of Higher Education.* A 14-16.

Leslie, D.W. (1998a, May). *Part-time, adjunct, and temporary faculty: the new majority?* Report of the Sloan Conference on Part-time and Adjunct Faculty. Williamsburg, VA: The College of William and Mary.

Leslie, D.W. (ed.). (1998b, Winter). *The growing use of part-time faculty: Understanding causes and effects.* New Directions for Higher Education #104. San Francisco, CA: Jossey-Bass Publishers, Inc.

Levine, A. (1997). How the academic profession is changing. *Daedalus* 126 (4): 1-21.

Lomperis, A. M. T. (1990, November/December). Are women changing the nature of the academic profession?. *Journal of Higher Education* 61 (6): 643-677.

Lovejoy, F. H. and Clark, M. B. (1995, December). A promotion ladder for teachers at Harvard medical school: Experience and challenges. *Academic Medicine* 70 (12): 1079-1086.

Magner, D. K. (2000, April 7). The right conditions may lure scholars to jobs off the tenure track, study finds. *Chronicle of Higher Education* p. A20.

Massy, W. F. and Wilger, A. K. (1992, Winter). Productivity in postsecondary education: A new approach. *Educational Evaluation and Policy Analysis* 14(4): 361-376.

NEA Higher Education Research Center. (1996, September). Full-time non-tenure track faculty. *Update* 2(5): 1-4. Washington, DC: National Education Association.

Norrell, J. E.and Norrell, T. H. (1996, March). Faculty and family policies in higher education. *Journal of Family Issues* 17 (2):204-226.

Olsen, D. (1993). Work satisfaction and stress in the first and third year of academic appointment. *Journal of Higher Education.* 64 (4): 453-71).

Olsen, D. and Near, J. P. (1994). Role conflict and faculty life satisfaction. *The Review of Higher Education.* 17 (2): 179-93).

O'Toole, J.O., Van Alstyne, W.W. and Chait, R. (1979). *Tenure: Three views.* Washington, DC: Change Magazine Press.

Plater, W. (1998, February). "Using tenure: citizenship within the new academic workforce. *American Behavioral Scientist.* 41 (5): 680-715.

Rhoades, G. (1998) *Managed Professionals.* Albany, NY: State University of New York Press.

Rice, R. E. (1996). *Making a place for the new American scholar.* New Pathways Working Paper Series # 1. Washington, DC: American Association for Higher Education.

Rice, R. E., Sorcinelli, M. D. and Austin, A. E. (2000). *Heeding new voices: Academic careers for a new gen-*

eration. New Pathways Working Paper Series # 7. Washington, DC: American Association for Higher Education.

Sanderson, A., Phua, V. C. and Herda, D. (2000). *The American faculty poll.* NY, NY: TIAA-CREF.

Sawislak, K. (1999, September 17). Denying tenure: Who said anything about fairness? *Chronicle of Higher Education.* B4-6.

Sax, L. J., Astin, A. W., Korn, W. S. and Gilmartin S. K. (1999). *The American college teacher: National norms for the 1998-1999 HERI faculty survey.* University of California, Los Angeles: Higher Education Research Institute.

Schuster, J. (2000, November 16). Windows and mirrors: Vantage points on a profession in metamorphosis. Sacramento, CA. Presentation at the Association for the Study of Higher Education Conference.

Smith, B. L. and associates. (1973). *The tenure debate.* San Francisco, CA: Jossey-Bass Publishers, Inc.

Sorcinelli, M. D.and Gregory, M. W. (1987). Faculty stress: The tension between career demands and "having it all". *Coping with faculty stress.* New Directions for Teaching and Learning #29. San Francisco, CA: Jossey-Bass Publishers, Inc.

Tack, M. W.and Patitu, C. J. (1992). *Faculty job satisfaction: Women and minorities in peril.* ASHE-ERIC Higher Education Report # 4. Washington, DC: The George Washington University Clearinghouse on Higher Education.

Tierney, W. G.and Bensimon, E. M. (1996). *Promotion and tenure: Community and socialization in academe.* Albany, NY: State University of New York Press.

Trower, C. A. (1996). *Tenure snapshot.* New Pathways Working Paper Series #2. Washington, DC: American Association for Higher Education.

Trower, C. A. (1998). *Employment practices in the professions: Fresh ideas from inside and outside the academy.* New Pathways Working Paper Series #13. Washington, DC: American Association for Higher Education.

Trower, C. A. (2000, February 5). Illuminating archery in the dark. New Orleans, LA. Presentation at the AAHE Conference on Faculty Roles and Rewards.

U.S. Department of Education, National Center for Education Statistics (1998). *Fall staff in postsecondary institutions, 1995.* Washington, DC: U. S. Department of Education,

University of Wisconsin System. (1990). *Retaining and promoting women and minority faculty members: problems and possibilities.* Madison, WI: Board of Regents of the University of Wisconsin System.

Waterman, R. H., Waterman, J. A., and Collard, B. A. (1994, July/August). Toward a career-resilient workforce. *Harvard Business Review* 72 (4): 87-95.

Wigton, R. S. and Waldman, R.S. (1993, March). An innovative faculty appointment system at the University of Nebraska. *Academic Medicine* 68 (3): 190-191.

Wilson, R. (1995, November 17). Colleges help professors balance work and family. *Chronicle of Higher Education.* p. A24.

Wilson, R. (1999, June 11).Georgia State U. cuts some part-time positions to add 65 full-time faculty jobs. *The Chronicle of Higher Education.* A18.

Wilson, R (2000, May 12) A new campus without tenure considers what it's missing. *Chronicle of Higher Education* A 18.

Wolf-Wendel, L. E., Twombly, S., and Rice, S. (2000, May/June). Dual-career couples: Keeping them together. *Journal of Higher Education* 71 (3): 291-322.

Wyles, B. A. (1998, Winter). Adjunct faculty in the community colleges: Realities and challenges. *The growing use of part-time faculty: Understanding causes and effects.* Leslie, D.W. ed. New Directions for Higher Education # 104. San Francisco, CA: Jossey-Bass Publishers, Inc.

Subject Index

Author Index

Contents of Previous Volumes

Affirmative-Action Employment Discrimination Monique W. Clague, *University of Maryland*

Evaluation Research and Educational Decision-Making Jonathan Z. Shapiro, *Louisiana State University*

Rates of Return to Higher Education: An Intensive Examination Larry L. Leslie, *University of Arizona* and Paul T. Brinkman, *National Center for Higher Education Management Systems*

Research on Academic Programs: An Inquiry into an Emerging Field Clifton F. Conrad, *University of Arizona* and Anne M. Pratt, *College of William and Mary*

Trends and Issues in Curricular Development Cameron Fincher, *University of Georgia*

Social Control in the Academic Profession John M. Braxton, *Loyola University of Chicago*

Theories of Student Departure Revisited Vincent Tinto, *Syracuse University*

Emerging Perspectives on Continuing Professional Education Wayne D. Smutz, Mary Beth Crowe, and Carl A. Lindsay, *Pennsylvania State University*

Author and Subject Indexes

1986: 462 pages ISBN: 0-87586-078-8

VOLUME III

Qualitative Research Methods in Higher Education Robert L. Crowson, *University of Illinois at Chicago*

Bricks and Mortar: Architecture and the Study of Higher Education John R. Thelin and James Yankovich, *College of William and Mary*

Enrollment Demands and Their Policy Uses in Institutional Decision Making William C. Weiler, *University of Minnesota*

State Regulation and Campus Autonomy J. Fredericks Volkvein, *SUNY at Albany*

Administrative Leadership in Higher Education Cameron Fincher, *University of Georgia*

Department Reviews for Product Improvement in Higher Education Everett K. Wilson, *University of North Carolina at Chapel Hill*

Diversity in University Governance: Attitudes, Structure, and Satisfaction David A. Whetten and Kenneth Bettenhausen, *University of Illinois*

The Influence of College on Moral Development Larry Nucci and Ernest T. Pascarella, *University of Illinois at Chicago*

An Analysis of Student Academic Rights D. Parker Young and Martha C. Braswell, *University of Georgia*

The Expansion of Higher Education Enrollments in Agrarian and Developing Areas of the Third World William Edgar Maxwell, *University of Southern California*

The Organization and Provision of Continuing Professional Education: A *Critical Review and Synthesis* *Ronald M. Cevero and William H. Young, Northern Illinois University*

Author and Subject Indexes

1987: 462 pages ISBN: 0-87586-080-X

VOLUME IV

The College Environment Revisited: A Review of Research and Theory Leonard L. Baird, *University of Kentucky*

Outcomes, Assessment, and Academic Improvement: In Search of Usable Knowledge Peter T. Ewell, *National Center for Higher Education Management Systems*

Higher Education and Work in Europe Ulrich Teichler, *Gesamthochschule Kassel, FRG, and Northwestern University*

Master's Degree Programs in American Higher Education Clifton F. Conrad and David J. Eagan, *University of Wisconsin-Madison*

Doctoral Study in the Field of Higher Education Barbara K. Townsend, *Loyola University of Chicago*

The American College History: A Survey of Its Historiographic Schools and Analytic Approaches from the Mid-Nineteenth Century to the Present Lester F. Goodchild, *University of Denver*, and Irene Pancner Huk, *University of Chicago*

A Survey of Academic Advising as an Area of Inquiry Richard A. Voorhees, *Black Hills State University*

Thanks for the Memories: The Fusion of Quantitative and Qualitative Research in the Study of the College Student and the College Experience Roger G. Baldwin and John R. Thelin, *The College of William and Mary*

The Melancholy of Anatomy: The Personal and Professional Development of Graduate and Professional School Students Leonard L. Baird, *University of Kentucky*

Putting Power into University Governance Cynthia Hardy, *McGill University*

LISREL: An Introduction and Applications in Higher Education Research Frances K. Stage, *Indiana University*

An Analysis of State Formula Budgeting in Higher Education Martin M. Ahumada, *University of Arizona*

Author and Subject Indexes

1990: 536 pages ISBN: 0-87586-094-X

VOLUME VII

Perceived Control in College Students: Implications for Instruction in Higher Education Raymond P. Perry, *University of Manitoba*

The Changing Locus of Control Over Faculty Research: From Self-Regulation to Dispersed Influence Melissa S. Anderson and Karen Seashore Louis, *University of Minnesota*

The Federal Role in American Graduate Education Patricia J. Gumport, *Stanford Institute for Higher Education Research*

Effective Teaching Behaviors in the College Classroom Harry G. Murray, *University of Western Ontario*

Differential Progress of Women Faculty: Status 1980–1990 Mary M. Dwyer, Arlene A. Flynn, and Patricia S. Inman, *University of Illinois at Chicago*

Measuring, Understanding, and Doing Something About the Rise in Doctorate Completion Time Howard P. Tuckman, *Memphis State University*

Faculty Mobility in an Organizational Context Dolores L. Burke, *Duke University*

Instructional Interventions: A Review of the Literature on Efforts to Improve Instruction Maryellen Weimer and Lisa Firing Lenze, *Penn State University*

Professional Education: Stratifying Curricula and Perpetuating Privilege in Higher Education Gary Rhoades, *University of Arizona*

Leadership in Community Colleges: Looking Toward the Second Century Susan B. Twombly and Marilyn J. Amey, *University of Kansas*

Religious Higher Education in America: An Historiographic Survey F. Michael Perko, *Loyola University of Chicago*

Author and Subject Indexes

1991: 492 pages ISBN 0-87586-097-4

VOLUME X

Student Learning at Metropolitan Universities George D. Kuh, Nick Vesper, and Lee E. Krehbiel, *Indiana University—Bloomington*

Applications of Generalizability Theory in Higher Education Assessment Research Gary R. Pike, *University of Missouri—Columbia*

Policy Models and Policy Instruments in Higher Education: The Effects of Governmental Policy-Making on the Innovative Behavior of Higher Education Institutions Frans A. van Vught, *University of Twente, The Netherlands*

Reframing Policy Research: A Critical Examination of Research on Federal Student Aid Programs Edward P. St. John and Richard J. Elliott, *University of New Orleans*

Educational Paradigms in the Professional Literature of the Community College John H. Frye, *Triton College*

Logistic Regression Analysis in Higher Education: An Applied Perspective Alberto F. Cabrera, *SUNY—Albany*

Integrating General Education, Wellness, and Athletics: A Conceptual, Historical, and Reform Agenda Lester F. Goodchild, Sheila M. Arredondo, and Robin B. Glaser, *University of Denver*

The Matrix Representation System: Orientation, Research, Theory and Application Kenneth A. Kiewra, *University of Nebraska—Lincoln*

New Faculty Socialization in the Academic Workplace Dana Dunn and Linda Rouse, *The University of Texas*, and Monica A. Seff, *Bowling Green State University*

Author and Subject Indexes

1994: 454 pages ISBN 0-87586-111-3

VOLUME XI

Variation Among Academic Disciplines: Analytical Frameworks and Research John M. Braxton, *Vanderbilt University*, and Lowell L. Hargens, *The Ohio State University*

Public Policy and Public Trust: The Use and Misuse of Performance Indicators in Higher Education Brian P. Nedwek, *St. Louis University*

Integrated Qualitative and Quantitative Research: Epistemology, History, and Designs John W. Creswell, *University of Nebraska-Lincoln*, Lester F. Goodchild, *University of Denver*, and Paul P. Turner, *University of Nebraska-Lincoln*

Developments in State Funding for Higher Education Daniel T. Layzell, *The University of Wisconsin System*

Gender and Academic Publishing Kathryn B. Ward, *Southern Illinois University*, and Linda Grant, *University of Georgia*

The Dimensionality of Student Ratings of Instruction: What We Know and What We Do Not Philip C. Abrami, Sylvia d'Apollonia, and Steven Rosenfield, *Concordia University*

Organizational Effectiveness and Quality: The Second Generation Kim S. Cameron and David Whetten, *Brigham Young University*

Theory and Research in Administrative Leadership Cameron Fincher, *University of Georgia*

Governments, Governance, and Canadian Universities Glen A. Jones, *Ontario Institute for Studies in Education*

Doctoral Programs in American Higher Education Jennifer Grant Haworth, *Loyola University Chicago*

VOLUME XII

VOLUME XIII

VOLUME XIV

Teaching, Learning, and Thinking About Teaching and Learning W. J. McKeachie, *University of Michigan*

Costs and Productivity in Higher Education: Theory, Evidence and Policy Implications Darrell R. Lewis and Halil Dunbar, *University of Minnesota*

Institutional Adaptation: Demands for Management Reform and University Administration Patricia J. Gumport, *Stanford University*, and Barbara Sporn, *Vienna University of Economics and Business Administration*

University Restructuring: The Role of Economic and Political Contexts Patricia J. Gumport and Brian Pusser, *Stanford University*

Understanding Strategy: An Assessment of Theory and Practice Jennifer B. Presley, *WestEd*, and David W. Leslie, *College of William and Mary*

New Colleges for a New Century: Organizational Change and Development in Community Colleges Richard L. Alfred and Patricia Carter, *University of Michigan*

Rasch Measurement in Higher Education Rita K. Bode, *Rehabilitation Institute of Chicago*, and Benjamin Wright, *University of Chicago*

Greek-letter Social Organizations in Higher Education: A Review of Research David H.Wilder and Hugh F. McKeegan, *Bucknell University*

Cultural Capital as an Interpretive Framework for Faculty Life Jeffery P. Bieber, *University of Kentucky*

Cruel Environments: Sexual Abuse and Harassment in the Academy Linda Serra Hagedorn, *University of Southern California*

The Global Emergence of a Field: Content, Form, and Promise in Women's Studies Nelly P. Stromquist, *University of Southern California*

Author and Subject Indexes

1999: 510 pages Paper ISBN 0-87586-125-3 Cloth: ISBN 0-87586-126-1

VOLUME XV

Developing a Career in the Study of Higher Education Burton R. Clark, *University of California, Los Angeles*

Economic Perspectives on Rising College Tuition: A Theoretical and Empirical Exploration Michael B. Paulsen, *University of New Orleans*

The Governance of Higher Education Edward R. Hines, *Illinois State University*

Approaches to Studying and Levels of Understanding: The Influences of Teaching and Assessment Noel Entwistle, *University of Edinburgh*

Analytic Framework of Institutional Support for Student Assessment Marvin W. Peterson and Marne K. Einarson, *University of Michigan*

Organizational Behavior in Higher Education and Student Outcomes Joseph B. Berger, *University of Massachusetts Amherst*, and Jeffrey F. Milem, *University of Maryland*

Value Congruence and Organizational Climates for Undergraduate Persistence Marguerite Bonous-Hammarth *University of California, Los Angeles*

Field of Dreams: Organization Field Approaches to Understanding the Transformation of College Access, 1965-1995 Patricia M. McDonough, *University of California, Los Angeles*, Marc J. Ventresca, *Northwestern University*, and Charles Outcalt, *University of California, Los Angeles*

Contesting Values in American Higher Education: The Playing Field of Intercollegiate Athletics J. Douglas Toma, *University of Missouri-Kansas City, and* Michael E. Cross, *Princeton University*